A REVOLUTION IN LANGUAGE

A Revolution in Language

The Problem of Signs in Late Eighteenth-Century France

Sophia Rosenfeld

STANFORD UNIVERSITY PRESS
STANFORD, CALIFORNIA

Stanford University Press
Stanford, California
© 2001 by the Board of Trustees of the
Leland Stanford Junior University
Printed in the United States of America

Library of Congress Cataloging-in-Publication Data

Rosenfeld, Sophia A
    A revolution in language : the problem of signs in late eighteenth-century
France / Sophia Rosenfeld.
        p.   cm.
    Includes bibliographical references and index.
    ISBN 0-8047-3314-7 (alk. paper)
    ISBN 0-8047-4931-0 (pbk.: alk. paper)
    1. Semiotics—France—History—18th century.   I. Title.

P99.37.F8 R67   2001
302.2—dc21   2001020688

This book is printed on acid-free, archival-quality paper.

Original printing 2001

Last figure below indicates year of this printing:
10   09   08   07   06   05   04

Typeset by John Feneron in 9.5/12 Trump Mediaeval

Acknowledgments

I would like first to thank the many institutions that supported my research and writing of this work from its first incarnation as a dissertation to its present form as a book. I have benefited greatly from grants from the Frederick Sheldon Fellowship and the Center for European Studies at Harvard University, the Krupp Foundation, the Josephine DeKármán Foundation, the Spencer Foundation, and, especially, the Mellon Foundation. The College of Arts and Sciences at the University of Virginia funded additional research at an opportune moment, and the Remarque Institute at New York University proved an ideal place in which to complete the book. Thank you too to the Society for French Historical Studies, the Western Society for French History, the Northeast American Society for Eighteenth-Century Studies, the Western Society for Eighteenth-Century Studies, the ISECS/East-West Seminar, and the organizers of various seminars or conferences at the University of Virginia, the University of Washington, Columbia University, and the University of London for the opportunity to present parts of this work and to receive so many thoughtful responses to it as I was writing and revising.

My most fundamental debts are, however, to the many individuals who generously aided me with aspects of this project along the way. Simon Schama enthusiastically supported my interest in pursuing this topic and saw it through the dissertation stage. A number of other historians in the United States and France—including Andrew Aisenberg, Caroline Ford, Jacques Guilhaumou, Patrice Higonnet, Alexis Karacostas, Jacques Revel, and Philippe Roger—kindly offered their guidance or reactions. Then, at various moments, the whole manuscript was read by an extraordinarily knowledgeable and thoughtful group of scholars: David Bell, Lenard Berlanstein, Roger Chartier, Dena Goodman, Daniel Gordon, Lynn Hunt, Stephen Innes, Daniel Rosenberg, Jerrold Seigel, and Downing Thomas. I am deeply grateful to all for their comments, suggestions, and interest. I would also like to thank my many colleagues in the History Department at the University of Virginia, who have provided me with a much-appreciated combination of intellectual inspiration and friendship over the last five years. Three different department chairs—Mel Leffler, Peter Onuf, and Michael Holt—supported this project in multiple ways. At Stanford University Press, Norris Pope and John Feneron have been of immeasurable help, and I am grateful to them as well. Finally, like many authors, my greatest debts and sense of gratitude are reserved for my family, immediate and extended. Lucy Rosenfeld and Charles Affron deserve special thanks in this large category for their invaluable technical help. Matthew Affron deserves far and away the most. This book is dedicated to Matthew and Isaiah for reasons both obvious and difficult to express fully in ordinary words.

Contents

Introduction   1

1. The Gestural Origins of Semiosis and Society:
   An Enlightenment Solution, 1745–60   13

2. Pantomime as Theater, 1760–89   57

3. Pantomime as Pedagogy, 1760–89   86

4. Revolutionary Regeneration and the Politics of
   Signs, 1789–94   123

5. Ending the Logomachy, 1795–99   181

   Conclusion: The Savage, the Citizen, and the
   Language of the Law after 1800   227

   Notes   249
   Bibliography   345
   Index   399

Illustrations

1. Frontispiece of Bulwer's *Chirologia* (1644)   30

2. "Jason et Medée, ballet tragique" (1781)   70

3. Iroquois Dances from Lafitau's *Moeurs des sauvages
    amériquains* (1724)   77

4. Hieroglyphic alphabets from Court de Gébelin's
    Histoire naturelle de la parole (1776)   114

5. "Orphée, ou Les Effets du Discours" from Court de
    Gébelin's *Le Monde primitif* (1774)   115

6. Table showing the sources of grammar, rhetoric, and other
    fields of knowledge from Talleyrand's *Rapport sur
    l'instruction publique* (1791)   124

7. Caricature from Desmoulins's *Révolutions de France et
    de Brabant* (early 1790)   135

8. Telegraphic signals from Edelcrantz's *Traité des télégraphes*
    (1801)   201

9. Advertisement for De Maimieux's pasigraphy (c. 1798)   206

A REVOLUTION IN LANGUAGE

Introduction

The history of the Revolution of France is a collection
of prophecies.
            —Rabaut Saint-Etienne, 1792

Two years before the French Revolution began, the Protestant
pastor Jean-Paul Rabaut Saint-Etienne published a scholarly
tome entitled *Lettres sur l'histoire primitive de la Grèce*. The purpose of
this late Enlightenment text was primarily antiquarian: to uncover an
ancient form of picture writing and use it to reveal an archaic mental
world. But embedded in this study was also a theory of historical causa-
tion and change, a hypothesis that critical breakthroughs in the realm of
communication inevitably produce corresponding "revolution[s] of the
mind."[1] And this idea led Rabaut, like many eighteenth-century chroniclers of the vicissitudes of *l'esprit humain*, to tie his history of the distant past to that of the present and future. In a lengthy aside in his historical *Lettres*, Rabaut insisted that it was now only a matter of time before the form of modern languages, and, therefore, thinking were transformed again. What Rabaut prophesied in 1787, based on current advances in science and metaphysics, was nothing less than the emergence of a thoroughly philosophical system of notation "in which the
signs, being themselves definitions, will produce exact and complete
meanings ... [and] he who says *sign* will say *truth*."[2]

Rabaut Saint-Etienne ceased studying and writing about antiquity
once the Revolution of 1789 was underway. Much like Jean-Sylvain
Bailly, the celebrated historian of ancient astronomy to whom Rabaut
dedicated his musings on the primitive history of Greece, the scholarly
pastor plunged instead into the present-day concerns of national politics. Rabaut found his calling as an important revolutionary polemicist
and a deputy to the National Assembly and then Convention. Yet Rabaut never abandoned either his theory of historical change, with its
characteristic semiotic determinism, or his utopian vision of a coming
moment in which truth would be known with certainty and error would
be a thing of the past. Rather, as the *Précis de l'histoire de la Révolution
française* that he wrote in late 1791 makes clear, Rabaut simply assimi-

lated his earlier ideas about a future semiotic and epistemological transformation into the story of the Revolution that was unfolding all around
him. In the same manner as a whole generation of Enlightenment-inspired revolutionary intellectuals, Rabaut imagined a rationalized, democratized, and distinctly revolutionary sign system as a fundamental
instrument—as well as goal—of political change and moral regeneration.

But the Revolution of 1789 was not to turn out, either politically or
intellectually, in the way that Rabaut Saint-Etienne had hoped. Indeed,
already in his *Précis* of contemporary events, Rabaut could point to certain ominous developments that seemed to be causing the revolutionary trajectory to veer off its expected course. Borrowing again from sensationalist histories of the human mind, he explained many of these de-
viations and missteps in a way that was rapidly gaining appeal in the
early 1790s. He attributed the errors of the Revolution to the inadequacies of the current language of politics, an idiom whose meanings and
uses were increasingly exceeding the control of enlightened revolutionaries like himself. While the French people had initially rallied together
around "two words, *equality* and *liberty*," these same abstract terms
now appeared, much to Rabaut's dismay, to be turning into sources of
misunderstanding and, consequently, disagreement, factionalism, and
even violent confrontation.[3] Writing about the French colony of Saint-
Domingue, for example, Rabaut reported that "the word *liberty*, so little
known in those climates, introduced there confusion and dissension."[4]
Similarly, he claimed that the terms of the civic oath required of the
clergy beginning in 1791 had created "one of those great quarrels that
are termed a *schism* and in which men separate from each other and
then fight for the sake of abstractions that they do not understand."[5] It
seemed to Rabaut that the current means for representing and conveying complex political concepts could, in other words, be held responsible
for many of the evident disappointments and failures of the Revolution.

Our exemplary revolutionary historian, Rabaut Saint-Etienne, did
not live to see which of his predictions—that of a triumphal philosophic
idiom creating a world of perfect understanding or that of a flawed and
equivocal political language undermining the promise of the revolutionary order—was to prove correct. The Girondin sympathizer faced
the guillotine in December 1793. But after the conclusion of the Terror
in the summer of 1794, many discussions of both the immediate past
and the near future continued to revolve around questions of language
and, especially, signs. From Rabaut's fellow republican Conventionnel
Michel-Edme Petit, who tried to explain the causes of the Terror with
only several months hindsight, to the learned and increasingly royalist
journalist Charles de Lacretelle, who took it upon himself in the late
1790s to extend the scope of Rabaut's *Précis* up to the present, commen-

tators on recent history repeatedly looked to the nature, form, and effects of contemporary language practices to understand what had just transpired. Collectively, the Thermidorean intellectual elite insisted that the dictatorship of Robespierre had succeeded in good measure not simply because the Montagnards had spoken an exaggerated idiom that was (in Lacretelle's terms) "empty of sense." The Jacobin leadership had also, by "making orators into sovereigns," given this novel language an extraordinary power over "the property, liberty, [and] life of so many millions of men."[6] Or, as Petit concluded in front of the National Convention in September 1794 before laying out a new language-planning strategy of his own, the Jacobins had effectively "seduced" the public with words.[7]

In certain ways, this late eighteenth-century fixation on the role of language and signs within the dynamic of the French Revolution now seems odd and even rather alien, especially since it was frequently coupled with a vision of semiotic transformation as a solution to social and political ills. During the nineteenth century, such explanations for the Revolution's successes and failures were largely rendered obsolete by arguments stressing class conflict, political machinations, ideological warfare, and other factors that pepper the writings of historians from Michelet to Marx. Yet in other ways, the comments of Petit and Lacretelle, like those of Rabaut before them, can also strike the modern reader as surprisingly contemporary in nature. One hundred and eighty-four years and many thousands of histories of the Revolution later than Michel-Edme Petit's attempt at exegesis, the French historian François Furet's very similar claim about the failures of Jacobin language to reflect a clear material reality became one of the cornerstones of a new reading of the Revolution's course. In a highly influential book entitled *Interpreting the French Revolution*, Furet credited competition among political discourses, rather than social conflict, with creating the conditions of the Terror. The peculiarity of the Revolution, he stated succinctly, owed to the fact that, in the hands of the Jacobins, "language was substituted for power."[8]

Furet's conception of the French Revolution as primarily a linguistic event—a revolution in and by the signs of power—has, by now, had a profound impact on several decades of historiography on both sides of the Atlantic. In part, this has been a result of the confluence of this model with a more general (and largely separate) intellectual trend commonly referred to as the "linguistic turn." Over the last quarter-century, along with the demise of many of the traditional explanatory models of social history, historians in all fields have become increasingly willing to view language as a force that helps to shape and to constitute meaning or experience rather than simply to reflect it. And in the

case of the historiography of the French Revolution, such efforts to consider language as a historical dynamic in its own right have led both to
an explosion of interest in the study of revolutionary modes of expression and to a spate of influential books on the ways in which particular
terms, images, and symbols—from the word *révolution* to a real severed
head on a pike—were deployed within late eighteenth-century political
culture.[9]

Despite all this attention to discourse, surprisingly little energy has,
however, ever been devoted to historicizing this semiotic approach to
revolutionary culture. What remains little appreciated today is not simply that Furet's remarks on the linguistic dimension of the revolutionary struggle themselves constituted a deliberate intervention in the political debates of his own moment (in this case, Paris in the 1970s).[10] It is
also that the precedent for this kind of commentary was established by
men like Petit and Rabaut in the Paris of the 1790s. When eighteenth-
century participants and observers of the Revolution chose to understand and to explain the events of 1789–94 in terms of the profound
connections between semiotic change and sociopolitical development,
they too did so for explicitly polemical and partisan reasons. In fact, discussions of the uses, power, and consequences of revolutionary language were a constituent element of both the ideology and the practice
of revolutionary—and counterrevolutionary—politics from the start.

Perhaps then Furet's interpretive model can be used to open up a different line of historical inquiry. Specifically, Furet's attention to the
dramatic effects of language on the revolutionary moment leads one to
question why contemporary commentators so frequently understood
and reacted to their situation as if it were above all a problem of representation and communication. How did Rabaut Saint-Etienne, Petit,
Lacretelle, and so many others come to see themselves as engaged in a
high-stakes linguistic power struggle? Why did they frequently respond
to political problems with extensive and partisan language-planning
strategies, from introducing laws prohibiting obsolete terms to constructing new dictionaries, instruction manuals, and even sign systems?
And what did they hope to accomplish by treating the Revolution as a
fight for authority over words? The first goal of this book is to describe
the sources, development, and eventual decline of this distinctive semiotic conception of and approach to the revolutionary experience. For
while we now have many studies of the creation of a revolutionary vocabulary prior to 1789 and the uses made of it after, we still know little
about the emergence of revolutionary attitudes toward language or their
subsequent fate. This study represents an effort to reconstruct the extended historical process by which language became a major site of political controversy and experimentation, and politics became a key locus

of linguistic controversy and experimentation, from the middle of the eighteenth century to the opening of the nineteenth.

Of course, the late Enlightenment was not the first moment in French history when language and politics became intertwined. As the first chapter will show in greater detail, French national identity had already been tenuously connected to the French language for several centuries (despite the fact that France has always been a multilingual country). The power to determine and to control this language had also long been sought by the absolutist state and contested by various other corporate bodies in France, including the parlements and the Catholic church. Indeed, many historians, beginning with Ferdinand Brunot, the author of a monumental and triumphalist early twentieth-century study of the fortunes of the French language, have placed the revolutionary era into a long-standing history of state concern with linguistic standardization and *dirigisme*.[11]

In this book, however, I argue that during the Enlightenment, a moment of exceptional attention to linguistic questions, there developed an acute and singular sense of the power of language to shape human destiny. In advancing a "natural" explanation for the origin of sign-making or semiosis, the *philosophes* effectively linked intellectual and social progress to linguistic advance; they identified improved communication as one of the keys to the realization of their utopian ambitions and failure in communication as one of the chief sources of society's ills. Moreover, this conception of signs—and the various semiotic experiments that it encouraged in the last decades of the Old Regime—shaped the worldview of educated French people in such a way that they were predisposed to see the revolutionary struggle as fundamentally a problem of language and to respond accordingly: by rendering language both a subject and a tool of their plans. Yet, that said, I do not consider revolutionaries' claims about language politics as evidence that words did, indeed, assume a "unique, magical quality" in the revolutionary period, as Lynn Hunt has notably argued.[12] Nor do I present participants as victims in a war of words that they could neither comprehend nor control. The present work is not, despite its subject, intended to prove a philosophical point about the role that language actually played in the late eighteenth century or any other historical moment. Instead, based on the premise that historians and their subjects must rarely think identically about how language functions and with what effects, this book constitutes an effort to understand the revolutionaries' own conceptions of the linguistic dimension of their own activities. By considering a range of late eighteenth-century Frenchmen's language about language, I trace the advent and development, from the 1740s to the end of the Consulate, of a very particular form of linguistic-political consciousness. This consciousness was rooted in both fear of the effects of faulty communication and faith in semiotic reform as a means to transform perceptions of the world and thus intellectual and social relations within it. What I seek to explain is precisely why many key participants in the revolutionary struggle continually attempted to fashion high Enlightenment epistemological principles into deliberate, partisan, political strategies—while simultaneously denouncing the power of words and the dangers that they represented.

But what becomes evident in telling this story is not simply that late eighteenth-century men and women were unusually attentive to the relationship between language and political power, even in the midst of physical violence. I argue that the leading revolutionaries' particular way of thinking about the nature and functioning of words and other signs—or what we might call the metasemiotic of elite, late eighteenth-century culture—also had an enormous impact on these revolutionaries' efforts to imagine and then to institute a radically new vision of the French nation.[13] From recent scholarship, we know that certain key epistemological problems of the Enlightenment—for example, questions about the ownership of ideas or the nature of representation—became explicit political issues during the 1790s.[14] We are also aware that critical revolutionary actors, such as the Marquis de Condorcet, held specific conceptions of the nature of knowledge and truth that played decisive roles in shaping and determining their political as well as scientific philosophies.[15] And certainly historians of festivals, schools, and other revolutionary educational projects have noted the centrality of aspects of Enlightenment psychological and communicative theory in the formulation of these undertakings.[16] But I am interested in a broader problem: understanding the relationship between the evolution of this metasemiotic and the development during the late eighteenth century of a very distinctive conception of how an ideal polity might be realized. The second, and ultimate, aim of this book is to demonstrate the effects of late Enlightenment epistemology and linguistic theory on the emergence, form, and development of French revolutionary political culture.

This intention remains, despite the so-called linguistic turn, a relatively unusual one, especially in the Anglo-American context. As the political theorist Melvin Richter has pointed out, even those Anglophone scholars of politics most interested in languages and discourse (such as J. G. A. Pocock and Quentin Skinner) have generally paid little attention to "philosophical and political controversies in the past about language," leaving such issues to specialists in the history of linguistic thought.[17] Indeed, relying reflexively upon late twentieth-century (and thus potentially anachronistic) conceptions of the uses and function of words, scholars of political theory have rarely thought it worthwhile to consider the impact of "the history of semantics, that is theories of meaning and signs self-consciously held or contested at the time of inquiry" on contemporaneous political thought.[18]

But in the non-Anglophone study of the French Revolution this situation has been changing since the mid-1980s. As Richter has also noted, German practitioners of the history of concepts, or *Begriffsgeschichte*, have tried in recent years not only to analyze the political discourse of the Revolution but also, to a limited degree, to show how, in the 1790s, "metatheories of language became indispensable to political controversy."[19] Similarly, and more extensively, the French scholar Jacques Guilhaumou, building on the work of the research group at the Ecole Normale Supérieure of Saint-Cloud devoted to political *lexicométrie*—the quantitative analysis of political discourse—has also turned his attention to the theory and politics behind revolutionary language. The purpose of his bicentennial book entitled *La Langue politique et la Révolution française* is, Guilhaumou stated, "to demonstrate the decisive impact of reflection on political language on the revolutionary process" as a whole.[20] However, Guilhaumou sees this "revolutionary process" as coterminous with the creation, through Jacobin intermediaries, of a concrete, rational, and popular political discourse that ultimately gave the French people the chance to become sovereign citizens. In the end, the authors of the *Handbuch politisch-sozialer Grundbegriffe in Frankreich, 1680–1820*, as well as the members of the Saint-Cloud group, have shown interest in the language politics of the Revolution primarily as it affected the formation and nature of political language(s), which are taken to be the Revolution's chief achievement.

I believe, however, that we can actually see the impact of late eighteenth-century linguistic speculation and experimentation in a broader realm: the socio-political imaginary or culture of the revolutionaries. The complex assumptions about signs held by certain significant revolutionary participants impacted not only the languages that they developed but also, I argue, the very ideals that they set out to realize and the way that they thought about their purpose and goals in this struggle. More specifically, I propose that understanding these values as they manifested themselves in both key texts and deliberate actions or events helps to elucidate the distinctive fixation in late eighteenth-century France on the achievement of ideological, moral, and social consensus within the context of popular sovereignty. In this regard, the present book may be said to engage not only with the body of historical writing stemming from the work of Furet but also with an argument most closely associated in recent years with the writing of the historian Keith Michael Baker.

In an important collection of essays entitled *Inventing the French*

Revolution (1990), Baker argued that revolutionary political culture was created out of the multiple political languages of the Old Regime, even as the revolutionaries proclaimed its end. More precisely, Baker proposed that the antiliberal tendencies in revolutionary thought—including the revolutionary notion that a single, sovereign nation, despite being made up of multiple citizens, must speak with a single authoritative voice—expressed the legacy of France's foremost political tradition, royal absolutism, transformed into an oppositional "discourse of will" in the middle years of the eighteenth century.[21] This argument remains extremely persuasive. Yet it also seems clear (as Baker himself has noted in other of his works) that the rhetoric of politics always stems from a wider variety of sources and is supported by a wider set of beliefs than simply the political theories or political languages of the past. In the present study, I explore the ways in which a central tenet of Enlightenment epistemology—specifically, the idea of language as both the prime source of factional conflict and the key to any potential solution—found expression in prerevolutionary social and cultural practices, as well as philosophical treatises. And I propose that this particular conception of language profoundly shaped and limited the very possibilities available to revolutionary participants as they tried to construct an effective and just means of governing a heterogeneous society profoundly divided along both ideological and economic lines.

On the one hand, the persistence of the Enlightenment assumption that disputes generally stem from faulty communication helps account for revolutionary intellectuals' basic refusal to accept the idea that a healthy political system could be built on debate and contestation. On the other hand, an Enlightenment conviction about the restorative effects of a perfect language, crystal clear and impervious to misuse, encouraged many of the leaders of the French Revolution to believe that deliberate language-planning efforts, in keeping with the principles of "nature," would eventually make possible the creation of a thoroughly consensual and harmonious revolutionary state. It is the chief contention of this book that late Old Regime linguistic theory, as formulated by the *philosophes* and modified by practical reformers, contained the seeds of both revolutionary intolerance for pluralism of opinion and revolutionary faith that competition of interests was something that could be overcome, even in a republic. Finally, I argue that it was only with the rise of challenges to these enlightened sociolinguistic ideals and initiatives resulting from the disappointments of the revolutionary decade that the emergence of a contestatory quasi-democratic political culture became imaginable (in a positive sense) and thus possible in the nineteenth century.

This is, certainly, an inherently problematic argument for a historian to make. For how can one uncover the history of epistemological assumptions when they are only rarely explicitly articulated as such? And how can their causal relationship to actions, events, or even other ideas be demonstrated? As a solution, this book focuses only partly on debates about political language. It takes as its central subject a very particular intellectual and cultural phenomenon of the second half of the eighteenth century: a widespread fascination with gestures and pantomime as means of communication and expression. On the surface, this may well appear a surprising or even perverse choice for a book that is ultimately centered on language, politics, and collective psychological theory. Yet thinking about gestures has often been a way of thinking about words. Furthermore, interest in gesture has, historically, been strongest at moments and places characterized either by great skepticism about the capacity of vernacular language (as in the fin-de-siècle Vienna of Karl Krauss) or great faith in the potential of an ideal sign system (as in the circles of the Royal Academy in seventeenth-century England).[22] In the case of the revolutionary era, both tendencies were clearly operative. Here we would do well to recall Rabaut Saint-Etienne's vision of an archaic picture writing with which this introduction began. In eighteenth-century France, the idea of a primordial language of visual signs became the basis—first literally, then metaphorically—for a range of projects and semiotic experiments aimed at transcending the problems and limitations associated with vernacular words. And it is in the traces of these iconic and often ideographic languages and the discussion around them that we are best able to find clear evidence of two larger cultural trends. The first is the dissatisfaction that many late eighteenth-century thinkers experienced with conventional, modern means of communication. The second is the utopian hope that these same individuals pinned on language reform as a way of instituting new sorts of intellectual and emotional exchange, sociability, and, ultimately, governance rooted in popular consensus.

Of course, my approach is not intended to reveal the mentality of "average" Frenchmen; the people who figure prominently in this book were, with certain notable exceptions, well educated, well connected, relatively well off, urban, and male. But for these same reasons, they were well situated to impose their visions of the society of the future. I start from the assumption that though my subjects' ideas were structured and even constrained by the range of ideas and ways of expressing them available at their moment, they maintained a significant degree of agency in deciding how and when to use these options. And because of their privileged status, including access to the written and often printed word (and in some cases, the backing of the state), their choices substantially impacted the subsequent decisions of others. Indeed, although I am interested in outlining the shared assumptions and suppositions about language that were common to the revolutionary and even counterrevolutionary *mentalité*, I am also concerned with documenting the various claims and strategies used by different individuals or groups, with different motives, at distinct moments, and in response to changing pressures. In this book I seek, therefore, to tell a dual story: of how a small set of believers in the power of a natural gestural language tried to establish models for a new communicative order, and of how their efforts to impose this vision shaped the political world of late eighteenth-century France. In conclusion, I take up the question of whether this distinctive vision left any lasting mark. For in the end, this book is intended to be a twenty-first century variant on the eighteenth century's *histoire de l'esprit humain*: a study of the connections between certain early modern epistemological developments and the rise of modern French political culture.

The first chapter, entitled "The Gestural Origins of Society and Semiosis: An Enlightenment Solution, 1745–1760," examines the appeal of the idea of an original *langage d'action*, or universal language of natural, bodily signs, in the context of a broad cultural anxiety about the intellectual and social consequences of the "abuse" of words. This chapter proposes that the notion of a primordial pantomimic idiom not only offered some of the key *philosophes*—Condillac, Diderot, and Rousseau, among others—a way to illustrate the symbiotic development of language, knowledge, and society from their common genesis; it also established an ideal and set of natural guidelines for the construction of a communicative utopia. The next two chapters, "Pantomime as Theater, 1760–1789" and "Pantomime as Pedagogy, 1760–1789," explore two self-contained realms within late absolutist France in which the supposedly primitive language of gesture was recovered and put to new, experimental uses in an effort to transform the way that ideas and sentiments were represented and transmitted in the modern world. The first concerns the *ballet d'action* and the debates occasioned by the revival of a pure pantomimic language on the French stage. The second takes up the new analytical or "methodical" sign language of the deaf as it developed in the classroom and was bolstered by members of various learned *sociétés* eager to use its example for their own purposes.

The fourth and fifth chapters then deal directly with the decade of the Revolution, exploring the impact of these varied ideas and practices on key groups and actors from Rivarol to Robespierre. For in the 1790s these earlier projects became models for a series of prescriptive and partisan language-planning initiatives designed to render politics a science based on self-evident and, hence, consensual truths and to restore social harmony by eliminating the possibility of the *abus des mots*. Chapter

Four, "Revolutionary Regeneration and the Politics of Signs, 1789–1794," looks at the ways in which the sign language paradigm, in particular, was employed in the service of the Revolution and at the consequences thereof. The fifth chapter, "Ending the Logomachy, 1795–1799," focuses on a new set of linguistic inventions—this time ideographic systems of notation, from telegraphs to pasigraphies, modeled on *la langue des signes*—which were encouraged after Thermidor with the hope that they would halt the Revolution and reverse the disastrous course of the Terror. However, as will be made clear by this chapter in conjunction with the concluding one, "The Savage, the Citizen, and the Language of the Law after 1800," by the last years of the 1790s, many French intellectuals were no longer convinced of either the efficacy or the desirability of state-sponsored linguistic remedies for political dissension. The dream of a perfect social scientific language as a political panacea finally came crashing down in ruins as Napoleon rose to power at the century's close. The final objective of this book is to demonstrate the connection, in the first years of the nineteenth century, between the eventual, grudging acceptance of the instability of the abstract linguistic terms that are central to modern conceptions of the state and society, and the emergence of a new, hierarchical political vision in which citizens are valued in direct relation to their ability to use this political idiom without "abuse."

1

The Gestural Origins of Semiosis and Society: An Enlightenment Solution, 1745–60

"LA TERRE DES PERROQUETS"

The semiotic preoccupations of prerevolutionary France reverberated first in the domain of the fantastic. We begin, therefore, by turning our sights to a work of fiction. In 1750, Pierre-Charles Fabiot Aunillon, the elderly canon and vicar-general of Evreux, published a strange tale that he claimed to have heard from an English savant named Popinjay. Like many other eighteenth-century accounts of extraordinary voyages, *Azor, ou le Prince enchanté, histoire nouvelle, pour servir de chronique à celle de la terre des Perroquets* concerns the arrival of shipwrecked Europeans on an unknown island in a remote region of the globe. What distinguishes this particular locale is that it is populated elusively by mutes, men and women who communicate solely by means of gestures, bodily signs, and, on ceremonial occasions, dance. And in this silent realm, a bizarre story about language and communication unfolds.

The narrative of *Azor* commences with the appearance on the island of two unlikely outsiders: an English merchant and a magus. The merchant, upon becoming king of the local mutes, decides to make it his mission to bring speech to his subjects. He is, however, astonished to learn that the people of his new land do not regret their lack of access to this strange European faculty that Aunillon calls *parole*. Indeed, in Aunillon's telling, the islanders' dependency upon an elemental physical means of expression hardly appears to be a liability. As the wise, polyglot magus explains to the Englishman: "In their country a sign of the head, a gesture of the hand, the movement of a single finger, the contraction or expansion of various parts of the face creates an entire speech."[1] Moreover, the magus insists, these bodily practices are "so intelligible that these same signs sometimes make us conscious of the falsity of our own words."[2] Words, he notes, often have ambiguous significations or mask the true intentions of their users. In contrast, the instinctive gestures of the mutes serve as infallible and unequivocal signs of their makers' thoughts, emotions, desires, and needs; for all their obvious limitations in terms of range, these bodily signs pose none of the communicative problems endemic to words. Therefore, the wise man declares to the incredulous merchant, "far from being jealous of this type of advantage [speech] that we believe that we have over them, they [the island's natives] pity us for having lost an advantage that they enjoy."[3]

But it is not only at the level of epistemology that Aunillon's magus makes his case for the superiority of gesture. The principal assumption underlying this tale of a nonverbal utopia is that signs constitute more than simply a means of expressing or even conceptualizing ideas; language also functions as a type of social contract, binding individuals together and to the ruling power. Furthermore, the magus implies, the nature of the language that a society employs plays an active role—for better or for worse—in defining and structuring its social, political, and ethical life. To make this point, he draws another startling series of contrasts. The civilized realm of the West, the prophet announces, is overrun by those who speak without anything of consequence to say, "tiresome chatterboxes [who] seem to have received the use of speech only to become the scourges of society."[4] The spoken language has been thoroughly debased, rendered "an art that courtesans, women, especially flirts . . . and people in high office immerse themselves in acquiring every day."[5] Real reasoning has practically disappeared. And superficiality, deception, and meaningless disputes have become the hallmarks of social and intellectual experience. But the situation is completely different on Aunillon's distant isle. For the silent existence of the residents of the Terre des Muets has never been troubled by argument. In this imaginary state, which Aunillon depicts in terms that can only be characterized as prelapsarian, the unvarying and unequivocal idiom of the natives has worked to prevent moral corruption and intellectual factionalism and to preserve the unity of the social order. Here, in Aunillon's text, two common features of early modern literary utopias—a universal language that creates perfect communication among all peoples and the perpetual reign of peace—are rendered a single, symbiotic entity.[6]

During the century preceding the publication of *Azor*, authors of similar tales of fantastic voyages had often incorporated hints of ideal, imaginary languages into their work. Such details about unknown tongues had served an important function in these accounts, allowing fiction writers both to borrow a critical feature from serious travel literature and to suggest the possibility of heightened communication in distant lands.[7] Moreover, in several cases, the perfect languages that these writers had pictured depended less upon words than upon the natural expressivity of the body. Traditionally, in imitation of classic tales of exploration, such as Columbus's depiction of his voyage to the New World or, later, the reports of Jesuit missionaries in New France, chroniclers of fantastic voyages had paid particular attention to the gestures and universal "signs" used by various protagonists to establish contact with uncomprehending natives upon arrival in some remote location.[8] Certain seventeenth- and eighteenth-century authors had also imagined countries where a gestural language was the quotidian idiom of at least part of the population. In Savinien Cyrano de Bergerac's *Histoire comique, ou Voyage dans la lune* (1650), common people converse by agitating different parts of the body, while the upper classes speak in a musical language. Likewise, in Gabriel de Foigny's *Les Avantures de Jacques Sadeur dans la découverte et le voiage de la Terre Australe* (1692), gestures constitute the ordinary language for everyday conversation, while words are reserved for reasoning and abstract discourse. And in another *voyage imaginaire merveilleux*, also of 1750, the Chevalier de Béthune's *Relation du monde de Mercure*, nature is responsible for having given the residents of Mercury "a mute language composed of expressions, actions, and different postures which are hardly less intelligible than speech" in order to bridge the gap in comprehension between animals and humans.[9] The author of this fiction points out that, of course, "conversation with a nightingale does not turn on ethics or political matters," but for Béthune this ultimately proves to be an advantage. On Mercury, metaphysical conversations about abstract ideas are forsaken in exchange for direct, unmediated, and unambiguous communication about sentiments and the natural world.[10]

In contrast to these other tales, however, the gestural language in Aunillon's story transcends the level of textual embellishment. Much like Mme de Graffigny's better-known novel *Lettres d'une Péruvienne* (1747), in which the heroine graduates from Peruvian *quipos* (or writing by colored knots) to written French, the central subject of *Azor, ou le Prince enchanté* is the transition from an obscure, primitive sign system to a contemporary, Western mode of communication.[11] Indeed, this book is, finally, a parable about the consequences of speech.

The second part of Aunillon's narrative centers upon the arrival, approximately forty years after the original Englishman, of other shipwrecked Westerners, this time two siblings who come with a parrot in tow. Fulfilling the magus's prophecy that speech would inevitably one day reach the island, the parrot—a former prince who has been punished for his mindless facility with words by being forced to assume the form of a talking bird—succeeds in teaching the native people to speak. Immediately, the Terre des Muets is transformed in profound ways. The demise of the natives' gestural idiom marks a decisive step toward civilization and enlightenment. However, the institution of *parole* also brings a sudden end to years of peace both within the ruling family of the aptly named Roi Babil and across the land as a whole. And despite the fact that tranquillity is ultimately restored and the parrot is eventually returned to his original status as a prince, the land he rules over becomes a society of talking birds, or a "Parrotocopolous." After all, the gift of speech has been brought to the island by a being who has been schooled to repeat the expressions of others mechanically, servilely, and without regard for their effects. Throughout this tale, reason—the judgment of the merit of facts—is associated with silence or limited speech, while the garrulous parrot becomes a metaphor for the many people in the modern world, from society types to savants, who constantly use empty or borrowed terms to signify nothing. Ultimately, Aunillon evokes an imaginary, transparent sign system as a way both to attack the verbal gymnastics made possible by the sophisticated languages of civilized Europe and to question the consequences of linguistic "progress" in general.

Azor, with its strange moral, prompts an obvious question: why might Aunillon have written a fanciful story (the truth of which he insists upon throughout the text, though he claims to have heard it from a "popinjay") in which he suggests that most men and women in the contemporary world are mere parrots? Aunillon was himself a professional, if unremarkable, orator and *homme de lettres*. In his official role as the head of the church in Evreux, Aunillon had, in 1715, undertaken a rhetorical exercise of considerable importance in Old Regime France: the funeral oration for Louis XIV in the cathedral of that city. He had then gone on to publish several comic plays and novels, as well as some light verse, and, in the 1740s, to work as a government spy in Bonn—all activities that depended upon having the polished literary and verbal skills that he seems, in *Azor*, to scorn. But Aunillon's particular career path and interests can probably tell us little about the reasons why, in 1750, at the age of sixty-five, this worldly cleric might have chosen to write a story like *Azor*. To answer this question we need to look beyond both this isolated text and Aunillon's professional concerns. The primary interest of this far-fetched tale lies in how it echoes certain sentiments frequently heard in "enlightened" French intellectual milieus in the middle decades of the eighteenth century. Most obviously this story suggests a fascination with the possibility of an entirely gestural idiom. But it also conveys a widespread sense of dissatisfaction with the superficiality and contentiousness of contemporary social and intellectual exchange and a suspicion that a language which lent itself to abuse was at the root of the problem.

The idea that many negative consequences stemmed from the insincere, inaccurate, and ambiguous use of words—or the *abus des mots*, as it was commonly called in eighteenth-century France—had a long prior history.[12] Francis Bacon's famous warning about the "Idols of the Market Place," the danger of naming things that are either ill defined or nonexistent, was well known in Enlightenment Europe. Early in the seventeenth century, Bacon had claimed that many of the terms most commonly employed in contemporary metaphysics either failed to correspond to any external reality or had no clear, distinct referent. And, he had concluded, endless attention to this terminology, rather than actual things, had clouded men's minds and "rendered philosophy and the sciences sophistical and inactive."[13] Mid-eighteenth-century writers were also well aware of the arguments about the misuse of language developed first by Thomas Hobbes in a short passage of his *Leviathan* (1651)[14] and then by John Locke in his long discussions of the "Imperfection of Words" and the "Abuse of Words" in his *Essay concerning Human Understanding* (1690). In theory, according to Locke, language functions primarily as an aid to thought; it is a tool for ascertaining truths. But in practice it had often proved to be a barrier, "so much insignificant Noise" disconnected from knowledge of, or reference to, any set of distinct ideas or things. The problem turned out to be twofold. To begin with, Locke argued, words, or linguistic representations, have an inherent epistemological limitation; it is impossible ever to bridge the gap between language and things or ideas of things completely, especially in the case of abstract or general terms. This constitutes a shortcoming of language itself. But to compound the difficulty, Locke also pointed to the "abuses" or "faults and neglects" concerning language for which humans are themselves responsible or "guilty"; the inevitable poor fit between language and the world makes possible a further disjunction between expression and intentions. The combined effect, whether a result of ignorance or malice, has been overwhelmingly deleterious, especially in the realm of morality and metaphysics. Using the same image that Aunillon would depend upon sixty years later, Locke warned that frequent use of empty abstract terms, disengaged from clear conceptions or given a reality that they could never have, had resulted in the common spectacle of philosophers who had a greater resemblance to parrots than to men:

> [It] often happens that Men, even when they would apply themselves to an attentive Consideration, do set their Thoughts more on Words than Things. Nay, because Words are many of them learn'd, before the Ideas are known for which they stand: Therefore some, not only Children, but Men, speak several Words, no otherwise than Parrots do, only because they have learn'd them, and have been accustomed to those Sounds.[15]

When French writers borrowed such images and made similar claims in the next century, their most obvious target was what they commonly called "old philosophy," the intellectual tradition rooted in scholasticism. Following in the footsteps of Locke and Descartes, as well as the humanists before them, Enlightenment thinkers frequently invoked the idea of the *abus des mots* to attack what they saw as the prime remnants of scholastic culture in the modern world: the obscure technical terminology of theologians, with their universals, categories, and other metaphysical abstractions left over from the teachings of medieval universities, and the practice of engaging in formal disputations based on these terms.[16] More specifically, in taking a nominalist position on general ideas, sensationalist philosophers regularly attempted to expose some of the most cherished principles of Christian thought as mere linguistic constructs or chimeras. The Baron d'Holbach, for example, liked to point out that even the word *Dieu*, "exciting in all hearts respect and fear, is only a vague word that men have continually in their mouths, without being able to attach to it ideas or qualities that are not contradicted by facts or evidently inconsistent with one another."[17] Such empty rhetoric, he went on to note, should perhaps be a subject of indifference. But he claimed that these meaningless terms, learned at a young age and repeated constantly throughout life, became the primary producers and conveyers of false ideas and prejudices in the modern world. And these misconceptions, in turn, led to endless technical disputes, or what the great *Encyclopédie* of Diderot and D'Alembert termed "logomachies," vain arguments about words in which neither party understands the other because their subject is ill defined or, by its very nature, inexplicable.[18] In other words, from the vantage point of eighteenth-century empiricism, a good number of the abstractions essential to past philosophy appeared to function as sources of mystification, confusion, and, ultimately, disagreement, rather than as paths to true knowledge and accord. Following Locke, many of the principal *philosophes* concluded that the practice of metaphysics had become largely a linguistic game based upon the misuse of complex words.

Yet Enlightenment critics found in Locke's discussion of the *abus des mots* more than just a guide to the origins of philosophical obscurantism or the impediments to scientific progress. In an important passage of the *Essay*, Locke pointed to the fact that the effects of the schism in normal parlance between signs and signifiers, or words and ideas of things, had not stopped in "logical Niceties, or curious empty Speculations" but had extended as far as the "great Concernments of Humane Life and Society." Most worrisomely, and most important for his French disciples, Locke argued in the wake of the English Civil War that the use of false, ambiguous, and deceptive terms, in law as in religion, had "brought Confusion, Disorder and Uncertainty into the Affairs of Mankind."[19] According to Locke, language is, ideally, not only a tool of cognition but also "the great instrument and common tie of society," the source of the bonds that guarantee peaceful coexistence within various kinds of communities.[20] But just as language has the capacity to hinder as well as to aid in the expression of truth, so, Locke believed, it has the potential, in the hands of the powerful, to become an instrument of "domination" and a way to "unsettle Peoples Rights" as well as to realize their mutual interests.[21] In the tradition of Thucydides, Locke thus also offered his readers a dire, if brief, warning about the connections between linguistic and political factionalism and disorder.[22]

In the France of the late Old Regime, this argument provided a small circle of *Lumières* with a very particular lens for viewing their own society and its political culture. Armed with ideas derived from Montesquieu as well as Locke, many came to believe that the most vital abstractions of contemporary economic and political life—from *justice* to *patriot* to, most especially, *liberté*—were just as ill defined and variable in meaning as the key terms of scholastic debate.[23] Furthermore, enlightened thinkers increasingly held inflated rhetoric and linguistic sleight of hand based upon the misuse of such mutable terms responsible for many of the most serious social, political, and moral "abuses" in the modern world. When, in the mid-1750s, the philosopher Claude Adrien Helvétius took stock of the horrors that marked the society in which he lived, he concluded that the fault lay primarily in the realm of language. As he put it in a chapter of his highly controversial *De l'Esprit* specifically labeled "De l'abus des mots": "One sees what an eternal seed of disputes and disasters is ignorance of the true signification of words. Without speaking of the blood spilt by theological hatreds and disputes, controversies almost always founded on *un abus des mots*, what other misfortunes, moreover, has not this ignorance produced, and in what errors has it not thrown Nations?" And, like a good Lockean, he warned that "these errors are more common than one thinks."[24]

Yet the *philosophes'* desire to explain the workings of the world in linguistic terms—and, consequently, to fight some of their most important battles in the realm of language criticism and reform—cannot be linked exclusively to their passion for Locke or to their professional interest, as *gens de lettres*, in the meaning and use of words. Neither can it be attributed solely to existing restrictions on more direct forms of political commentary or action. Despite the later claims of revolutionaries and counterrevolutionaries alike that the Revolution had politicized the existing idiom, the potency of words as both a source of social and political might and a potential threat to established power was continually made manifest in Old Regime France.[25] Indeed, in the culture of absolutism, language and politics were already profoundly linked.

Language was, of course, one of the key realms in which the French monarchy sought to extend its power in the early modern period. As the great seventeenth-century political theorist Bishop Bossuet explained, a king's strength necessarily resides in the absolutism of his word as the expression of his will, while his subjects' obedience depends on the impossibility of their contesting his speech with their own, especially "since murmuring implies an indication to sedition." Indeed, Bossuet illustrated this theory with a quotation from Ecclesiastes 8:25, "Observe the commandments that issue from the king's mouth. . . . [H]is word is full of power. Neither can any man say to him: why dost thou so?"[26]

During the Old Regime, the crown crafted its policies to reinforce this principle. Beginning in the early seventeenth century, the French monarchy took considerable pains to ensure that comments injurious to the king and his authority, whether published or uttered aloud, would be policed and punished. Through a policy of regulative censorship that actually increased in the following century, the state attempted to determine the limits of acceptable speech, as well as to ensure that only the single voice, or will, of the king could make itself heard in France.[27] Then, with the establishment of the Académie Française under monarchical charter in 1635, the royal state found another way to expand its control over the language of the nation's subjects. As a result of the founding of this institution, the monarchy not only gained an opportunity to associate itself with a perfected national tongue but also itself seized the authority to determine the "proper" meaning of words.[28] In an effectively tautological fashion, the Académie Française, following the purism of Malherbe, took the conversational practices of the men and the women of the court to constitute the standard of *bon usage*—and the power and status of both the court nobility and king were reinforced by the fact that they spoke in an officially approved and royally sanctioned tongue, the exclusive language of French political discourse and administration.[29] The Bourbon kings established a tradition of linguistic *dirigisme* rooted in customary elite usage as a way, simultaneously, to solidify the existing sociopolitical hierarchy and to expand the power of the state.

But to understand the significance of accusations of the *abus des mots* in the middle of the eighteenth century, it is essential to keep in mind that France during the last five decades of the Old Regime remained an extremely linguistically diverse nation. Not only did many languages other than French—including German, Italian, Flemish, Catalan, Basque, Breton, and variants of Occitan—still flourish within its boundaries, but many different regional and popular dialects, jargons, and *patois*, each with its own forms, expressions, and meanings, continued to exist right alongside the Académie Française and its official dictionaries.[30] On the eve of the Revolution, two-thirds of French subjects routinely spoke a language other than French; there was no assumption that the king's authority required all French people to conduct their daily lives in the same idiom as their ruler.[31] Moreover, at the same time as the principles of royal absolutism were consistently being rearticulated, the king's ability to control what was said, how it was said, and what it meant was subject to repeated challenges both in practice and in principle.

From the moment of its founding, the Académie Française was a site of internal struggles, especially over the question of how exactly to define the public whose usage would be normative and dictionary-sanctioned. Increasingly in the eighteenth century, certain members of the Académie asked just how "tyrannical" and "capricious" (to use their politicized metaphors) laws of speech should be allowed to become, or how much space might be set aside for neology and linguistic innovation, especially on the part of writers. Furthermore, as the historian Hélène Merlin argues, there was always some ambiguity in the platform of the Académie about whether *la langue*, with its close associations with *la coutume*, or customary law, should not be subject to the king's protection rather than his direct and absolute control.[32]

The limits of royal authority over the French language became an explicit subject of contention during the first half of the eighteenth century, especially in the context of the long fight over Unigenitus, the papal Constitution of 1713 condemning Jansenism. The issue was complicated by the fact that in the area of religion, the Catholic church saw itself, in the words of the bishop of Soissons, as not simply the guardian of the truth but also "the mistress of the language used to enunciate the Truth, putting that language in the scales, weighing expressions, introducing new words, proscribing others as need be . . . in the interests of the faith."[33] Yet the boundaries between spiritual and temporal truths— or language—were certainly never entirely clear. And in the course of this struggle over the survival of Jansenism, another group within the corporate kingdom, the pro-Jansenist magistrates of France's parlements, asserted its own customary right to determine and to regulate linguistic meaning for the nation—in direct opposition to both the mainstream clergy and the crown.[34] Already, in the late seventeenth century, the Jansenist grammarians associated with the Port-Royal cloister had indirectly challenged the Académie Française by insisting on reason, rather than *bon usage*, as the primary guideline in determining linguistic standards. Now Jansenist sympathizers accused both the king and French bishops of distorting the "proper" senses of key terms (such as *constitution française*) in this struggle and insisted on their own definitions as the correct ones. The result, argues the historian Jeffrey Merrick, was nothing less than a new pattern in judicial or constitutional struggles in France; beginning with the political-religious conflicts of the early 1730s and continuing into the 1750s and 1760s, domestic crises in

France repeatedly took the form of "disputes over words."[35] Thus one could argue that the rise in the middle decades of the eighteenth century of what Keith Baker has called the "politics of contestation" was actually marked as much by a crisis in the politics of language as by a crisis in the language of politics.[36] As the participants in these constitutional disputes themselves pointed out, the principal parties were actually arguing over more than questions of interpretation. While still insisting on their loyalty to the monarch, they were also challenging the state's power over words and their values and meanings. Or, as Pierre-Guérin de Tencin, the bishop of Embrun, put it in the 1730s, the key participants were engaged in a struggle over which body, or *corps,* in the French kingdom had "the prerogative of fixing the language of the faith" and according to what principles and traditions.[37] The net effect was a vivid illustration of the enormous difficulties "unfixed" words could cause—and the power that could come from having the authority to "fix" them.

Not surprisingly, in this political context, a certain small group of French intellectuals, beginning in the 1740s and continuing into the second half of the century, found new applications for an old argument about the dangers of ill-defined and ambiguous terms. Indeed, once the connection between controlling ideas and controlling or "fixing" words had been made apparent, the concept of the *abus des mots* became increasingly useful to Enlightenment types not only as a hermeneutic tool or way to understand the world (in the fashion of Locke) but also as a potential political weapon of their own. At the most basic level, drawing public attention to the multiple or faulty meanings assigned to a specific word in official discourse functioned as a way to challenge the dominant understanding of that concept. For example, the physiocrat Jean-François Melon, in an effort to rebut traditional economic theory, took pains to demonstrate that the term *luxe* was still often used in law and commerce in a way that was "vague, confused, and false" and, consequently, had the potential to "stop industry itself at its source."[38] But like many other Enlightenment cries of "abuse," such accusations could also serve as ways to challenge larger social or political forces: in this case, the normative ethical standards and comportment of the ruling classes. By emphasizing how current language practices preserved prejudicial ideas and hypocritical behavior within the culture of the court as well as the church, the *philosophes* effectively joined the pro-Jansenist magistrates in the elite linguistic-political struggles of the mid-eighteenth century.

On the one hand, Enlightenment authors such as D'Alembert followed a long critical tradition in attacking the "tortured, error-ridden, barbarous language" of high society as a way to call into question its prevailing values (and distinguish them from those of true *gens de let-*

tres).[39] From Fénelon to Boileau, seventeenth-century moralists had not only decried the highly artificial way of speaking associated with those learned society women known as *précieuses*; they had indirectly blamed these women for fostering an elite cultural norm that rewarded affect, style, and appearance over content and that encouraged deception and seduction rather than (masculine) simplicity and directness.[40] And in the era of Louis XV and then Louis XVI, the highly stylized and often frivolous banter of *la bonne compagnie* continued to be taken as both a symptom and a source of the overly feminized and unnatural culture that had come to dominate the French court.[41]

On the other hand, mid-eighteenth-century writers also took pains to expose the "doublespeak" common to the language of men of state. Indeed, it was widely assumed that cunning rulers, in domestic as in diplomatic affairs, routinely used words in misleading ways so as to trick their subjects and cover up self-interest or demagoguery. The result, according to certain of the more radical writers of this moment, was a political culture marked by social division and conflict, as well as by dishonesty. In *Le Livre jaune*, an anonymous work of 1748 subtitled "some conversations on logomachies, which is to say, on disputes of words, abuses of terms, contradictions, *double entente* [and] false senses that get used in speech and writing," the author offered multiple concrete historical examples of deceptive linguistic practices on the part of princes and kings that had resulted in nothing less than civil and international wars, including the endless struggles over religion of the previous century. Then this champion of absolute monarchy declared dismissively, "Politics is nothing other than the Science of knowing how to usefully employ the great art of Logomachies."[42] Because it was widely believed that language, whether handed down from on high or developed out of a people's daily needs, was the glue that held society together, exposés of the prevalence of the *abus de mots* often functioned, as in Aunillon's odd tale, as ways for eighteenth-century polemicists to illustrate the corruption and disorder at the heart of modern society as a whole.

Yet it is essential to realize that embedded in this discourse was not only a critique of the status quo. The constant use of the word *abus* in describing current social and political practices suggests that these same men believed that the national language should have—and had once had—a kind of fixity and clarity that had been violated through specific actions but that could, in the right hands, be rectified. For the other side of the argument about the dangers of the misuse of words was a conviction that, first, it was essential to work toward correcting the instability of words and restoring their "proper" meanings, and, second, that this activity would have enormous benefits both for knowledge and for society. If the truth were always evident, Voltaire argued in his famous essay on "sects," all parties and all factions and splinter groups would simply disappear because all people would be forced to agree.[43] And just as the *philosophes* blamed an ill-defined, ambiguous language for obscuring truths and causing much of contemporary discord, they argued (again in the spirit of Locke) that a language of ethics and metaphysics which was well defined and made truth apparent could ideally be a recipe for peace.[44] What is more, it is clear that these same *philosophes*, as men of reason and professional *gens de lettres*, saw it as their responsibility not only to explain the liabilities of language and to point out examples of abuse to an ignorant public but also to help remedy the situation. *Gens de lettres*, explained D'Alembert, were "made for studying, for knowing, and for fixing *la langue*."[45] André Morellet concurred: "The greatest service that philosophers can render to reason is to determine the meaning of terms."[46] Ultimately, D'Alembert, Morellet, and their associates dreamed of taking charge of the French language themselves, free of royal interference (though not royal governance) and unaffected by the language of the *bas* or the *précieux*, so as collectively to stamp out manipulation, *tromperie*, deceit, and dispute and pave the way for an enlightened, consensual sociolinguistic order.

But what kind of remedies did they really consider feasible? How did they think that they could make language more representative and more effective as both an epistemological and a social tool? Here the question becomes complicated. Like many of his contemporaries, Helvétius believed that, hypothetically, a language created entirely by philosophers would indeed serve as a useful instrument in combating oppression and disorder and in establishing shared principles and truths.[47] On a smaller scale, he also suggested in *De l'Esprit* that there were enormous benefits to be gained from simply encouraging interlocutors to define or to verify their terms before arguments could develop. And in a characteristically eighteenth-century manner, he mused about the extraordinary impact that a new dictionary constructed solely by men of reason and translated into many languages would surely have on achieving this goal. By "fixing" the precise signification of every word, such a volume would, Helvétius argued in his later *De l'Homme*, "dissipate the mysterious obscurity that still envelops ethics, politics, metaphysics and theology . . . terminate so many disputes that are perpetuated by the *abus des mots* . . . [and finally] reduce the science of men to what they really know."[48]

At mid-century, Helvétius was not alone in holding these beliefs. From the *Encyclopédie, ou Dictionnaire raisonné des sciences, des arts et des métiers* (1751–65) edited by Diderot and D'Alembert to the *Dictionnaire philosophique* (1764) of Voltaire, high Enlightenment thought can, in fact, be interpreted as a series of efforts on the part of philosophers to fight against faulty, variable usage ("national caprice" in the words of D'Alembert) and then to re-establish the meaning of words as they saw fit.[49] Even the *philosophes'* general eagerness to abandon their quasi-oppositional political stance in the last decades of the Old Regime and to join that official court organ for controlling the nation's language, the Académie Française, makes enormous sense when seen in this light.[50] In their campaign against established norms of speech, they saw themselves fighting against one of their chief enemies—usage or custom—and all its negative associations with errors, prejudices, and superstitions. And in their work as rational, empirical grammarians and lexicographers, they saw their best chance to reshape human consciousness and, ultimately, to establish a true "science" of society that would transform the world in which they lived.

Ironically, however, French Enlightenment thought was also marked by a strong strand of skepticism about the potential representativeness of words. In the tradition of Locke, Helvétius invoked the ideal of a true philosophical language, an immutable idiom without artifice, arbitrariness, or the potential to generate multiple interpretations, only to dismiss the possibility of its realization in the foreseeable future. Explaining his pessimism, he stated, "It is not to philosophers, it is to need that one owes the invention of Languages."[51] And most of his contemporaries agreed that the invention of an ideal language—just as much as the rediscovery of a lost Adamic one—was destined to remain a pipe dream. In his recent account of the decline of interest in universal languages after the seventeenth century, the semiotician Umberto Eco points out that high Enlightenment theoreticians were generally critical of all a priori language systems and suggested only minor reforms in existing vernaculars precisely because they tended to believe (contrary to the Cartesians) that language does not reflect a preconstituted mental universe but collaborates in its growth.[52] And even the authors of the many alternative dictionary projects of the eighteenth century seem to have been acutely aware of their limitations. The collaborators on that vast semantic enterprise, the *Encyclopédie*, were no exception. In the formulation of the author of the article on "logomachies," the dictionary's lexicographers always ran the risk of trying to cure a sporadic migraine with a habitual headache; "for in multiplying the words in definitions, one necessarily also multiplies disputes."[53] Indeed, the many volumes of the *Encyclopédie* are full of commentary on the indeterminacy and temporal variability of language as a critical obstacle to the enterprise. The Encyclopedists may have been Cratylists, convinced that language should ideally be mimetic and mirror the elements of reality exactly; but most of them believed that the goal of perfect representation and true transparency remained, regrettably, impossible to achieve.[54] No language system, they argued, could ever completely reproduce either the external world or individual experience. No language system could avoid the flux endemic to all social institutions. And as Aunillon's tale suggests, mid-century French writers were especially hard pressed to envision the words of any modern vernacular—generally believed to be arbitrary sounds attached to ideas solely by means of convention and dictated by a changing set of public needs—as ever satisfying their desire for a sign system that would remain immune to distortions, falsehoods, multiple interpretations, and other misuses and misunderstandings.

Thus, right alongside their efforts to change the subject of language and, under the badge of reason, to replace Adam, the king, and even the court elite as givers of names and meanings, enlightened French *gens de lettres* frequently looked for ways to transcend the realm of ordinary words. Sometimes, in their desire to avoid the cognitive or perceptual problems seemingly endemic to modernity, they chose to celebrate purely sensual experiences, such as sexual relations or certain kinds of empirical science, which seemed not to require mediating signs of any kind. But more often, they tried to envision alternative sign systems, novel means of communication that could work actively to draw people together in common sentiments and opinions because every object or sensation had been accorded a perfectly legible and, hence, transparent corresponding sign. And in the middle of the eighteenth century, the raw material of this hypothetical ideal language often took the form not of vocal articulations but, rather, of silent and visually accessible gestures much like the ones used in the fictional paradise that Aunillon called the Terre des Muets.

Certainly, few people at mid-century suggested that this alternative semiotic mode, *le langage des gestes*, could actually function as a practical substitute for verbal interaction. No one (to my knowledge) argued that writers should permanently put down their pens. Instead, like all utopian projects, evocations of a transparent gestural idiom functioned as foils, as means of highlighting the limitations of existing idioms and of illustrating the effects that new, improved ways of perceiving, communicating, and understanding could have on the intellectual or socio-political order. Accordingly, in the mid-eighteenth century, a complex set of opposing strengths and weaknesses was called into play whenever the topic was broached. Where words were thought to be arbitrary signs of ideas that varied according to region, background, and individual temperament, certain gestures and movements of the body (such as a shrug or a cascade of tears) were considered natural and universal, equally intelligible to all, regardless of education, heritage, *état*, or locale. Where words were seen to be thoroughly implicated in history, corporeal signs were thought to be ahistorical and immune to change over time. Furthermore, advocates of sensationalism argued that these two distinct systems of communication had divergent affective mechanisms and specialized areas of signification: words, the language of the mind, were indeed helpful for conveying moral and philosophical abstractions; but the visual language of gestures, which issued directly from the heart and required no reflection or interpretation on the part of interlocutors, was uniquely suited to the expression of passions and sentiments and the representation of concrete things. Indeed, it had, as Diderot put it, an "energy" and warmth, as well as a simple, laconic beauty, that abstract or intellectualized discourse simply could not match.[55] Most significantly, gestural and verbal languages were believed to operate in conjunction with very different social worlds. In contrast to various European tongues, which were blamed for many of the ills as well as achievements of modern civilization, bodily sign language became emblematic of a timeless linguistic golden age, a Cratylian or mimologic moment during which there had been universal agreement about the meanings of things and the *abus des mots* or even discord was still impossible to imagine.

The ultimate goal of this first chapter is to demonstrate how the idea of a primordial gestural idiom helped a small group of French *philosophes* to reconceptualize the relations among linguistic, cognitive, and social progress and to imagine a way of reforming their world through the medium of perfected signs. But before we can make this leap, we must first trace how this vision came to be. The next section will explore the eclectic historical background for the utopian notion of gestures as universally intelligible signs of the passions and sources of harmonious and transparent interpersonal communication. The following sections of the chapter will then detail the prominent and novel role assigned to this natural means of expression in mid-eighteenth-century accounts of the origin and development of human language, knowledge, and society.

GESTURES AS LANGUAGE:

A HISTORY OF SPECULATION

"Very eloquent hands, speaking fingers, touching silence": writing in 1751, the historian Claude-François-Félix Boulenger de Rivery claimed that he could not help but be struck by the prevalence of linguistic metaphors running through ancient descriptions of pantomime.[56] For the notion of physical gestures constituting an effective means of communication was not by any means an Enlightenment invention. Rather, eighteenth-century writers found precedents for their claims across a vast range of sources that began with the great texts of antiquity. So great was the historical evidence for the expressivity of gestural signs that Boulenger de Rivery despaired: "If we wanted to collect all the passages in which the Ancients spoke of the language of the hands, to use their term, we would have a volume instead of an essay."[57]

As early as the fourth century B.C., Plato had argued in his *Cratylus* that if humans did not possess voices, they would certainly resort to using their faces, hands, and body to indicate ideas or emotions mimetically.[58] Following in this tradition, both Greek and Roman historians told marvelous tales of the efficacy of various forms of gestural communication and pantomime. Eighteenth-century writers regularly repeated Anthenaeus's account of how the philosopher Memphis was able to explain the teachings of Pythagoras solely through mime, or Macrobius's story of how Cicero and the comedian Roscius would vie with one another to see whether sentiments could be better expressed through words or gestures. In particular, Lucian of Samosata's second-century essay *Peri orcheseos (De Saltatione)*, an imaginary argument between an advocate and an opponent of the artform of pantomime, became a frequent source for later writers. Lucian's telling of how, after seeing an astonishing pantomimed performance, a barbarian chief from Pontus asked Nero for the gift of a mime who might serve as an interpreter with the polyglot notables of neighboring lands, suggested to many eighteenth-century authors the limitless potential of pantomime as a language in its own right.[59]

It was in Roman texts on oration, however, that Enlightenment writers found the most fully theorized antique discussions of the *sermo corporis* (language of the body) and the *eloquentia corporis* (eloquence of the body).[60] As was widely known to all recipients of a humanist education, *actio*, the fifth part of classical rhetoric, consisted of two parts, *vox* and *gestus*, the latter being divided into gesture and posture. True gestures, as Cicero explained in *De Oratore*, mirrored the passions or inner movements of the soul: "Every motion of the soul has its natural appearance, voice and gesture, and the entire body of man, all his facial and vocal expressions, like the strings of a harp, sound just as the soul's motion strikes them."[61] Since the passions of the soul were thought to be the same in all humans, Roman theorists of oration concluded that, accompanied by speech, certain gestures representative of particular sentiments would move and excite the same emotions in each member of an audience. According to Quintilian, who developed the most extensive antique rules for *actio* in the eleventh book of the *Institutio oratoria*, these expressive gestures constituted a "common language" for all mankind.[62]

The writings of Cicero, Quintilian, and other ancient authorities on these questions were known to eighteenth-century French writers not only in their original form but also through the glosses of seventeenth-century manuals on sacred oration, texts in French or Latin that often drew heavily on Roman as well as Christian sources. For in the seventeenth century, a revival of interest in ancient rhetoric drew new attention to *actio* and, more generally, to the possibility of gestural communication.[63] The rebirth of theories of gestural eloquence began with the publication of the Jesuit Louis de Cressolles's *Vacationes autumnales sive de perfecta oratoris actione et pronunciatione* in Paris in 1620. Other manuals dedicated to refining the ancient rules for sacred purposes followed. Expanding upon the dictates of Quintilian, Valentin Conrart, the first secretary of the Académie Française, published a *Traité de l'action de l'orateur* in 1657 in which he laid out guidelines for the art of gesture, while further developing a theory of the effects of expressive bodily signs. Central to this work was the old idea that the face betrays interior truths that transcend both national and linguistic boundaries; raised eyelids and an extended lower lip could, for example, be read— and felt—as an expression of anger by the deaf and the hearing alike.[64] As the author (actually Michel Le Faucheur) explained, seemingly oblivious to the fact that acceptance of this principle would logically obviate the need for guidebooks on gestural eloquence:

> Gesture even has this advantage over speech, that while through speech we become accustomed to understanding only those of our own Nation, through Gesture we make known our thoughts and passions to all Nations indiscriminately. It is like a common language of Humanity, which does not affect the eyes any less than speech affects the ears.[65]

But in the first half of the seventeenth century, this ancient notion of expressive gestures as "a common language of humanity" served an additional purpose, one that was also to prove important to language theorists in the following century. The concept of a natural body language provided a source of inspiration, and, in several instances, what appeared to be the raw material for a concrete solution to another of the key intellectual preoccupations of the seventeenth century: the post-Babel confusion of tongues.[66] The search for the original language of Adam, or, more often, a manmade philosophical language that would possess all the perfections of the lost Edenic tongue, drew the attention of many of the most important thinkers of the era, including Bacon, Descartes, John Wilkins, Cave Beck, John Amos Comenius, Gottfried Wilhelm von Leibniz, and Marin Mersenne.[67] This international, polyglot community of scientists interested itself especially in the creation of ideographic (rather than phonetic) written symbols—"real characters" or, in the words of Bacon, "notes of things"—that were intended to yield nothing less than immediate, true, and unequivocal knowledge of nature.[68] Later

FIG. I. Frontispiece from John Bulwer, *Chirologia* (1644). At the top, God is communicating with humans in the universal, natural language of gesture. The large hand at the center, "the fountain of eloquence," is situated between "Natura loquens," on the left side, and "Polihymnia," the Greek muse who taught the art of mime along with grammar and literature, on the right side. Photograph courtesy of the Rare Books Division, the New York Public Library, Astor, Lenox and Tilden Foundations.

in the century, several scientists, including Descartes and Leibniz, emphasized that universal characters had to be coupled with plans for the reclassification of natural phenomena, that the structure of a language had to match isomorphically with that of reality in order for that language to convey the connections between natural things. But most seventeenth-century grammarians assumed that the relationship between language and reality was based primarily in the physical parts of writing and speech, namely characters and sounds, and drawing on such varied sources of inspiration as Egyptian hieroglyphics, Indian pictographs, and Chinese characters, as well as common gestures, many sought to make that relationship visible to sight.[69] Indeed, in this vein, a few seventeenth-century writers, such as Giovanni Bonifacio, the author of *L'Arte de'Cenni con la quale formandosi favella visibile, si tratta della muta eloquenza, che non è altro che un facondo silentio* (1616), went so far as to suggest that, logically, the solution to the problem of the linguistic fragmentation of the world could be found not in the creation of an artificial idiom but in the recovery of the original language of natural gestures or visual "signs." Similarly, in two volumes of 1644 entitled *Chirologia: or the Naturall Language of the Hand* and *Chironomia: or the Art of Manuall Rhetoricke*, the English physician John Bulwer also laid out a plan for restoring the sacred language of hand and finger gestures which, he declared, was nothing less than the initial language of men, animals, and Adam himself [see Fig. 1]. As he noted in regard to this gestural idiom, "Being the only speech that is natural to man, it may well be called the tongue and general language of human nature, which, without teaching, men in all regions of the habitable world do at the first sight most easily understand . . . as it had the happiness to escape the curse at the confusion of Babel."[70] Citing Cicero, Quintilian, and Cressolles, Bulwer thus proceeded to amplify their claims and to argue for the superiority of gesture and pantomime over speech in terms of speed, efficiency, international intelligibility, and successful communication between God and man.

Nevertheless, most seventeenth-century arguments for the effectiveness of gestural communication were more modest in scope. The efficacy of bodily or manual sign languages as a practical means of communication within certain distinct communities—among silent monks or members of particular "savage" tribes, for example—had been noticed for centuries. In the late sixteenth century, Michel de Montaigne had tried to demonstrate that the capacity to speak with the hands is the common property of all humans prior to their acquisition of *parole*; his evidence came from the hand gestures made by children, lovers, and, especially, mutes, who "dispute, argue, and tell stories by signs."[71] The literature of voyages of exploration had gradually added new examples.

Generations of travelers to the Orient had reported that the Ottoman mutes had recourse to an elaborate system of expressive gestures to communicate with one another.[72] Likewise, explorers in the New World, from Cabeza de Vaca to Jacques Cartier, had described the complex manual "signs" used by various Indian peoples for trading with their neighbors.[73] The result of such observations was that numerous other early modern Europeans began to experiment with the establishment of normative hand signals for specialized purposes such as communication with the deaf, commerce across national boundaries, or the transmission of secrets—usually with the justification that such signs were indeed natural in character.[74] Alongside plans for universal gestural languages, a whole literature thus emerged in the seventeenth and early eighteenth centuries devoted to such obscure areas of study as bodily *semaeologia* and *chirosophy*.

Yet the explosion of interest in Enlightenment circles of the 1740s and 1750s in the potential of gestural communication cannot be explained as a direct development of several centuries of odd experiments and investigations, despite the dazzlingly heterogeneous sources and historical authorities upon which eighteenth-century claims for an original, universal gestural language relied. Between the late seventeenth and the early eighteenth centuries, the growth of Cartesianism effectively recast linguistic thought in France. Not only did the rationalist philosophy of Descartes greatly influence the study of grammar. It also produced a philosophical shift in emphasis away from the problem of the correspondence between language and external reality and toward the problem of the relationship of speech (or the material series of sounds used to convey ideas) to the operations of the mind. As a consequence, attitudes toward bodily communication, and especially gestural signs, were greatly altered as well.

To explain the differences among the various languages humans had at their disposal, the Jansenist grammarians associated with Port-Royal categorized languages in terms of the nature of their "signs."[75] According to the Oratorian Bernard Lamy, the author of one of the most important and comprehensive late seventeenth-century rhetorics in the rationalist or Cartesian tradition, a sign is "a thing which, in addition to the idea that it conveys when one sees it, conveys a second."[76] In other words, a sign has a dual function, conveying an idea of itself and an idea of a thing represented. But signs could work in two different ways. In Lamy's taxonomy, signs could be "natural," meaning that "they signify by themselves, just as smoke is a natural sign that there is a fire there where one sees the smoke," or they could be artificial and "institutional," meaning that the relationship between sign and idea is conventional and established solely by agreement or habit, as in the case of the vocabularies of all vernacular tongues.[77]

Lamy placed gestures in the first category, thereby endowing them with all the advantages and disadvantages that rationalist grammarians associated with natural signs.[78] This bodily "language of Nature," he argued in the spirit of seventeenth-century physiognomy, effectively and instinctively conveyed the inner sentiments and passions of both humans and animals.[79] Changes in the emotional state of an individual became visible in outward, corporeal movements that could be read as signs of the soul; the body functioned, in other words, as a kind of natural index. But Lamy also insisted that the sum of such physical signs did not and could not ever constitute a true human *langue*. For according to his Cartesian conception of language, it is precisely the capacity to speak which manifests the universality of reason and thus distinguishes humans from animals. Only words can ever effectively represent the mind's contents, since the laws of thought correspond to those of a grammar of words. Echoing a common notion, Lamy wrote of gestural signs: "This manner of explaining thoughts is very imperfect; it is, furthermore, incommodious; for one can not, without tiring oneself, convey with eyes and fingers all the different things that come into one's mind."[80] In the French classical tradition, the natural language of gesture was thus established as the antithesis of French. The French language, with its trademark clarity and closeness to the reasoning process itself, epitomized a successful conventional sign system for thinkers such as Lamy. It was not only pleasing to the ear and appropriate for polite conversation but it was especially suited to science and philosophy; indeed, one of its most vaunted attributes was that it required little auxiliary gesticulation on the part of its users for its meanings to be clear.[81] In contrast, rationalist language theorists relegated communication by means of the face or hands to the lowest rung of the linguistic ladder in terms of both elegance and efficacy. In effect, in an era of increasing emphasis on bodily restraint in daily life, the distinction between natural and artificial signs served not only to separate men from animals but also to distinguish levels of civilization, politeness, and reason within humankind itself.[82]

The essential outlines of this semiotic hierarchy remained in place during the first half of the eighteenth century, even with the rise of a sensationalist philosophy. In an important sense, certainly, the advent of comparative treatments of the arts rooted in Lockean epistemology, beginning with the Abbé Jean-Baptiste Dubos's oft-quoted *Réflexions critiques sur la poésie et sur la peinture* (1719), accorded new stature to natural signs, including gestures, as sources of signification. In an influential passage of this ground-breaking work, Dubos allowed that "the sign which receives part of its force and signification from nature is more potent and operates more effectively upon us than one which owes all its energy to chance, or to the caprice of the institutor."[83] In addition, he proposed that those arts built out of visual signs, such as painting and pantomime, were mimetically superior to poetry; because ideas were essentially images in the mind, the eyes, unlike the ears, provided a direct path to knowledge.[84] Nevertheless, Dubos also insisted that natural, gestural signs were necessarily imprecise and equivocal as an independent means of communication, except when conveying the strongest of passions in moments of great emotion. In other words, he continued to maintain that bodily signs could never constitute the material basis of an autonomous language.

It was not until the mid-1740s that Dubos's mixed verdict on the function of gestural signs was effectively challenged. During that decade, a small group of *philosophes* began to ask anew the potentially radical question once posed by the Epicureans: could one give a "natural" explanation for the origin of language? The standard answer to the question of how language came into being had long been provided by the Book of Genesis, where the divine origin of language was explained in detail by the story of Adam naming the animals. In contrast, the empiricist *philosophes*—including the Abbé de Condillac, Denis Diderot, and Jean-Jacques Rousseau—who tackled the question of the origin of language in the middle of the eighteenth century, attempted to explain how spoken language, with its seemingly arbitrary relationships between words and things, could have emerged though human agency alone. These thinkers did not reject the Adamic story outright. Rather, following elaborate disclaimers, they sketched alternative hypotheses, fictional tales that borrowed many structural elements from the standard biblical account, as well as from traditional *voyages imaginaires*. And in the process, they found a new use for the old idea of gestures as the natural, universal means of communication among all humans; they substituted the instinctive language of gestures and cries for the original divine idiom as the foundation for the entire story. Circa 1750, the most common solution to this philosophical puzzle was to posit that the natural language of gestures was not only the initial, primordial means of communication among humans but also the source and model out of which all peoples were able to "discover" their innate language-making capacity and, eventually, to form distinct, conventional linguistic systems by themselves.[85]

The epistemological underpinnings of this response to the question of the origin of language have been extensively analyzed in recent decades by philosophers and literary critics, as well as by a small number of intellectual historians concerned with the history of linguistic thought.[86] These scholars have tended to explain both the attention lavished on this problem and the form of the answers given in many Enlightenment texts as the product of a shift in conceptions of knowledge instigated primarily by Locke's *Essay*. In order to advance the argument that even complex ideas are not innate or a priori but, rather, the product of reflection upon sense experience, sensationalist *philosophes* realized that they had to address the one issue that Locke had largely neglected: namely, they needed to reconceptualize the relationship between language and thought beginning with their common genesis. Language, like ideas, had to be re-established as a human, rather than sacred, construct. Enlightenment accounts of the function of gestures in this process are thus generally explained by historians as one of several clever tactics used by mid-eighteenth-century philosophers to root sensationalist accounts of the origin of ideas firmly in the developmental psychology of men and women.

However, the purpose of this chapter is to propose that these mid-eighteenth-century texts on the origin of language need also to be understood as innovative and influential exercises in social theory.[87] In claiming this, I do not want to suggest that we should ignore the epistemological and psychological dimension of these tales. On the contrary, I am arguing for looking at the ways in which these stories bring the semiotic and the social together—at the moment of their foundation and throughout their history. The central interest of these essentially literary projects for historians of eighteenth-century France lies in the way that their authors posited a symbiotic and organic relationship between the ethical, political, and intellectual growth of a given society and the evolution of its signs. For these sketches of the origin and development of signs indirectly suggested not only a new way to think about the history of language but also a new way to conceptualize language as an instrument for shaping history. In these texts (just as in the better-known lexicographic projects of the Enlightenment), linguistic-social determinism effectively lays the groundwork for a form of semiotic utopianism and, ultimately, activism that would prove to have extraordinary implications for late eighteenth-century French culture.

It is this claim that brings us back to the question of the function of the original gestural idiom within these complex stories of linguistic, intellectual, and social progress that Enlightenment thinkers told themselves. Clearly, the concept of an initial, instinctive body language served as an important tool for these sensationalist philosophers in formulating the "natural" connection between the advent of semiosis and the advent of society in the distant past. But more to the point, this same concept also provided late Old Regime theorists of language with a basis

for analyzing the strengths and weaknesses of their own vernacular
tongues and alphabetic system of notion and, finally, with a theoretical
model for reforming them. On the one hand, the notion of a primordial
gestural idiom offered readers a way to measure the current distance between eighteenth-century Frenchmen and an ideal point of origins. On
the other hand, this formulation suggested a set of natural guidelines for
restoring these effectively prelapsarian epistemological and social conditions in the future.

IN THE BEGINNING:

THE "LANGAGE D'ACTION"

The problem of the natural origins and development of language
emerged in the middle years of the eighteenth century as an important
question for consideration within an informal circle of writers living in
Paris. The Abbé Etienne Bonnot de Condillac, a young provincial nobleman and former student of theology, completed the manuscript of his
first work, the *Essai sur l'origine des connaissances humaines*, in 1744.
The following year, the philosophically inclined *abbé* entered into
friendship with two fellow writers and budding *philosophes*: Denis
Diderot, the author of a recent book entitled *Pensées philosophiques*,
and Jean-Jacques Rousseau, an emerging opera composer whom Condillac had initially met in Lyon. According to Rousseau's *Confessions*, the
three men dined together regularly in the mid-1740s, and Rousseau and
Diderot tried to engage Condillac in their project of publishing a journal
called *Le Persifleur* (the "banterer" or the "tattler" in the English tradition), while helping Condillac to find a publisher for his first work.[88] Little came of these journalistic plans, but so began an extensive and enduring conversation among the three men on the issues at the heart of
Condillac's *Essai*, including the question of the role of gestures in the establishment of both language and society. Over the next decade, following the publication of this work in 1746, Diderot responded to Condillac's hypotheses about the nature of gestural signs in his *Lettre sur les
sourds et muets, à l'usage de ceux qui entendent et qui parlent* (1751),
and Rousseau challenged the place that Condillac had accorded to this
pantomimic idiom in both his *Discours sur l'origine de l'inégalité parmi
les hommes* (1755) and his *Essai sur l'origine des langues* (composed in
the mid-1750s but not published until 1781). Condillac himself returned
to the theme in his treatise on animals and his late writings on logic and
mathematics, while Diderot and Rousseau continued to address the
topic of visual and iconic signs in essays on painting, music, drama, and
dance. Indeed, during the middle years of the eighteenth century, speculation about the power and function of gestural communication, espe-

cially in the early stages of human society, rapidly spread well beyond Condillac's dinner table and became a common feature of intellectual gatherings in many European cities.

However, the fact that this semiotic debate was initially born out of friendship and casual discussion is significant in two respects. First, it suggests that for these young *philosophes*, the links among social interaction, the pursuit of knowledge, and oral and written communication were not only of theoretical interest. They were also a subject of practical concern that grew directly out of their personal experiences as mid-eighteenth-century participants in the Republic of Letters. Condillac, Diderot, and Rousseau, like others of their extended circle, found themselves engaged during these years in a wide range of collaborative linguistic practices, from private conversation and correspondence to very public literary production. And in all, the close connections among language, sociability, and intellectual progress were continually made manifest. Moreover, as the historian Dena Goodman has recently suggested, many of the mid-century French *philosophes* saw themselves, in conjunction with a small number of *salonnières*, providing examples for the transformation of the larger world in conformity with their own distinctive epistemological and social values.[89] One can, therefore, profitably read these essays by Condillac, Diderot, and Rousseau on the problem of the origins of semiosis and society as commentary on their authors' particular situation as members of a community with a special responsibility for perfecting the related arts of sociability and communication, as well as for generating theoretical discussions of the distant past.

But there is an additional reason why it can be useful to understand the social conditions out of which these "high" Enlightenment texts emerged. Awareness of their context of production also encourages us to interpret the foundational *Essai* of Condillac and the responses of Diderot and Rousseau, with their generally digressive, conversational tone and obvious citations, corrections, and clarifications of one another, as themselves the constituent parts in a lengthy, extended dialogue. Furthermore, this knowledge pushes the modern reader to uncover the larger intellectual and scholarly frame of reference in which (and against which) all three men were writing.

After all, the Abbé Bonnot de Condillac, the initial framer of this mid-century discussion, did not derive the outlines of his description of the original gestural idiom or even the idea of providing a genealogical account of the advent of language out of thin air. As he openly acknowledged in his own *Essai*, Condillac borrowed heavily from an explanation of the development of language that he had found in an unlikely place: an English book on Egyptian hieroglyphics first appearing in French in

1744. The author of this work on ancient visual signs was the Anglican bishop of Gloucester, a latitudinarian named William Warburton. Several years earlier, in one section of the massive tomes that he published under the title *The Divine Legation of Moses Demonstrated on the Principles of a Religious Deist* (1738–41), Warburton had challenged the hermetic interpretation of ancient hieroglyphics in order to make a historical argument about the antiquity of Egyptian civilization. But extracted from its context and translated into French by a high-ranking Parisian magistrate named Marc-Antoine Léonard des Malpeines, this so-called *Essai sur les hiéroglyphes des Egyptiens* appeared to the bishop's contemporaries across the Channel to constitute a radical, philosophical history of writing and language itself.[90]

Warburton's text began with a rebuttal of two common assumptions. Egyptian hieroglyphics, he claimed, were initially neither a secret invention of an ancient priestly class, as was widely believed in the middle of the eighteenth century, nor a source of enormous hidden wisdom. Rather, he proposed that these characters had once constituted a simple form of picture-writing, or *écriture en peinture*, invented for the easy promulgation of laws, customs, and other matters of public record.[91] According to Warburton, nature was everywhere the same. Thus, he argued, in all early civilizations, ideas were first conserved in the form of pictographs, or graphic images of natural things. But as humans' mental capacities and social needs developed and their ideas accordingly grew in number and complexity, this kind of literal picture-writing came to seem too cumbersome and limiting; hence, pictographs were gradually replaced by hieroglyphs, shorthand abridgments based on the principles of metonymy, metaphor, or analogy, and then by more abstract ideographs better suited to conveying qualities and passions as well as things. Finally, written signs lost even their metaphorical connection to the original, mimetic form of picture-writing, and the phonetic sign— the alphabetic character—triumphed over and replaced the graphic sign entirely. This global evolution owed nothing to art or choice, in Warburton's conception, but, rather, was the inevitable result of the progress of civilization.

Indeed, for Warburton, comprehending this natural process by which writing slowly ceased to be mimetic also provided the key to understanding the development of spoken languages. For just as the natural history of writing could be explained by the gradual but progressive rejection of iconic signs, so could the history of speech. Warburton insisted that the many tongues of the world had, in early history, deviated from an original language that was itself firmly rooted in images. He demonstrated this idea by arguing that hieroglyphics were themselves condensed representations, or translations, of the world's oldest language: the figurative *langage d'action*. Almost a century and a half earlier, in the Second Book of the *Advancement of Learning*, Francis Bacon had suggested that bodily gestures were corporeal and "transitory hieroglyphics," which bore a real resemblance to, or "affinity with," the object or idea they denoted.[92] For Warburton, however, this relationship between gestures and hieroglyphics was not simply analogic but the product of historical necessity. Drawing on both the Old Testament and secular histories, the Anglican bishop argued that at the dawn of human society, people were "simple, crude, and immersed in their senses," incapable of easily explaining their imperfect conceptions of abstract ideas or the operations of their minds.[93] To compensate for their limitations, these people, like the biblical prophets, had to rely heavily on "actions" and "signs" as means of communication: "[T]he *langage d'action* was therefore, and especially in the case of the Jews, a common and familiar means of conversing."[94] But the gradual development of human society meant that gestural communication eventually met the same fate as did the pictorial or hieroglyphic rendition of natural images. The *langage d'action*, with its mixture of expressive sounds and iconic gestures, gave way to figurative speech—apologues and fables, then similes and metaphors—and, finally, to the largely abstract and no longer universally intelligible idioms rooted in reason that are characteristic of modern civilization. Then, and only then, Warburton argued, did hieroglyphics become a mysterious and obscure symbolic language and a powerful tool of oppression in the hands of a priestly class.

In the context of mid-century intellectual life in Paris, Warburton's thesis, despite its antiquarian focus and its grounding in an alien English religious tradition, had considerable appeal.[95] In a general sense, the essay introduced several fundamental and related concepts that would prove to be very important for subsequent French language theorists: the idea of a universal, figurative *langage d'action* as the foundation for all later forms of language; the reciprocal influence of speech and writing in their formation and development; and the natural evolution of any language toward abstraction in terms of both concepts and signs for them. Most important, Warburton's text could also be read as an elaborate and novel assessment of the benefits of linguistic progress. For Warburton put forth the idea that the history of language, dependent as it was upon necessity, inevitably involved certain tradeoffs. Naturally, the growth of abstraction in language produced an accompanying expansion of complex reasoning; he did not challenge the commonplace eighteenth-century assumption that the number of general words in a given language was an excellent indicator of the relative intellectual development of the people who relied upon it.[96] But Warburton argued that this advance came at a certain price. According to his rule: "The conduct of

man, as we see, has always been, whether in speeches or writing or
whether in clothing and lodging, to change necessities into spectacles
and ornaments."[97] In terms of writing, society's gradual adoption of abstract marks, rather than iconic characters, had greatly diminished the
attention that individuals paid to signs themselves; as a result, the original marks had become thoroughly enigmatic. Similarly, as words grew
in quantity and sophistication, the original figurative language, which
had once been the result of a necessarily concise vocabulary, had
evolved into the ornamental debris of a poetic imagination. It was first
and foremost this argument—that humans' natural progression away
from the simplistic golden age of the *langage d'action* and toward the
realm of abstract reason involved both gains and losses for society—
which drew writers to the work of Warburton during a ten-year period in
the middle of the eighteenth century. The fundamental French Enlightenment texts on the origin of language and the nature of gestural communication must be read, therefore, first, as elaborations of Warburton's
model and second, as refinements of one another.

Léonard des Malpeines's translation of Warburton's essay found its
way into Parisian literary circles just as Condillac was engaged in writing
his *Essai sur l'origine des connaissances humaines*. The influence of
Warburton's treatise on Condillac's conception of the development of
speech can be measured by the liberal quotation from and extended
commentary on the earlier work buried within Condillac's text. Yet the
Abbé Bonnot de Condillac took up the problem of the origins of language from a philosophical perspective that would have been entirely
foreign to Warburton.[98] Condillac's initial goal in his *Essai* was to challenge the concept of innate ideas by offering new insights into the workings of the human mind. Thus he did not address the problem of the collective and temporal development of language until the second half of
his treatise, well after he had demonstrated that individuals' initial ideas
came exclusively from sense perceptions and that all operations of the
individual mind were rooted in the connection of ideas made possible by
"the habit of [using] signs." And then, at the most basic level, his account was again intended to buttress Lockean epistemology by demonstrating the importance of language in giving form to and shaping human understanding. As Condillac put it himself, he aimed to show that
"the use of signs is the principle which unfolds all our ideas as they lie in
the bud."[99] But, in fact, Condillac's ambitions for his story of the origin of
language did not stop there. In Condillac's hands, Warburton's *langage
d'action*—a mixture of expressive gestures and natural cries—ceased to
be simply the first means of communication among humans. It also became the site of the vital transition from natural to arbitrary signs, or
from nature to culture. In other words, it provided the basis for an expla-

nation of the formation of society and all its subsequent institutions, from families to legal codes. And as Condillac himself pointed out, the shape of this hypothetical history had serious implications for the advancement of knowledge and communication and the prevention of "error" in the modern world.

Condillac's discussion of the origin of language within the *Essai sur l'origine des connaissances humaines* began with a philosophical proposition: What if humans' ability to communicate ideas and emotions linguistically had not been a gift of God but instead an organic development? How might a philosopher ostensibly explain this process "according to the ordinary course of nature"?[100] Without ever explicitly challenging orthodox religious answers to this question, Condillac put forth a new hypothesis, a theory of how the primordial couple, isolated from human society, could have created the arts, languages, and institutions of civilized life based only on human potentiality. As a mental experiment, Condillac wrote a fable in the fashion of a *voyage imaginaire* in which he stranded two children, one male and one female, alone in the wilderness sometime after the Flood. He then posited that this young couple would have instinctively, and out of necessity, invented some means of conveying ideas and sentiments to one another. The system of signification created by these initial community-builders would, in turn, he proposed, have set in motion all the mental or intellectual developments that gradually became the hallmarks of advanced human societies.

In the *Essai*, the successive steps in this process are explained in careful detail. According to Condillac's speculative anthropology, the original couple's cries and gesticulations were at first only symptoms, inadvertent responses to various painful or pleasant sensations. Soon, however, the boy's inevitable interaction with his female companion led him to identify these instinctive or "accidental" gestures and vocal sounds as the effects of various sense experiences and to attach them to the specific but universal perceptions and emotions that they naturally signified. Condillac explained this process of association with an example: "He who suffered by being deprived of an object which his wants had rendered necessary to him . . . moved his head, his arms, and every part of his body. The other, struck with this sight, fixed her eye on the same object, and perceiving some inward emotions for which she was not yet able to account, suffered in seeing her companion suffer."[101] At this crucial point, the raw materials of reflexive and immediate bodily responses became the first "natural" signs.[102] But then, gradually, as a result of their continual "mutual converse," the two children reached another milestone. They learned to use these "natural" gestural and vocal signs to represent ideas at will. Their growing capacity to remember and to reflect, coupled with simple repetition and habit, made it possible for the young couple to recall and to deploy their previously instinctual expressions of their sentiments as what Condillac called "arbitrary" signs.[103] As the *abbé* illustrated with another example: "[He] who saw a place in which he had been frightened, mimicked those cries and movements which were the signs of fear in order to warn the other not to expose herself to the same danger."[104] In this way, the first intentional human language was born.

Condillac too referred to this initial means of communication, the universal idiom formed of these natural cries, bodily contortions, and "violent agitations," as the *langage d'action*. And, like Warburton, to support his thesis, Condillac drew on evidence from a wide range of sources both temporally and geographically distant, from the ancient Jews to modern "savages," such as "the Negroes, the Cannibals, and the Iroquois," all of whom, Condillac assumed, lived in closer proximity to the original and natural human state than did modern men and women.[105] Condillac even repeated the well-worn stories that he had read in the Abbé Dubos's treatise on the sister arts in order to show that traces of the original *langage d'action* continued for centuries to make themselves known in the declamatory and mimic practices of ancient Rome, even after the eventual triumph of the vocal component of language. But what really distinguished Condillac's account of this primordial sign system was that his interest in it was neither purely nostalgic nor antiquarian. The *abbé* had many compliments for this obsolete "primitive" sign system—for its energy, its extraordinary effects on the imagination, its efficacy and force in conveying the truths of religion or state. Yet for Condillac, the real reason that the advent of this arbitrary sign system out of natural sense reactions constituted the pivotal event in human history was that it effectively "produced every art proper to express our thoughts," including speech, and thus set in motion all other forms of progress.[106] In the genetic explanation of the origin of language that emerged in the pages of Condillac's first work, the opposition between gestural and verbal languages, as well as between natural and arbitrary signs, was replaced by a temporal, historic filiation. And signs themselves were accorded a dynamic function as agents of intellectual, moral, and social transformation, shaping as well as recounting lived experience and ideas.

According to Condillac's story, the development of conventional language, the expansion of knowledge, and the advancement of society continued hand in hand from the moment of the discovery of arbitrary signs. Just as the advent of the *langage d'action* allowed its early users to expand their intellectual and social capabilities and to begin to develop the judgment, reason, and memory necessary both to understand the world around them and to lay the foundations for a community, so these subsequent achievements necessarily stimulated a demand for new ways to fix and to communicate ideas. And as the ideas in circulation grew ever more copious and complex and social needs continued to increase, the initial community builders began gradually to outgrow their primitive idiom and to replace their pantomimic and essentially metaphoric *langage* with ever more abstract and less mimetic signs—until the last vestiges of the original language were thoroughly obscured. It was, finally, this inevitable semiotic shift that paved the way for the emergence of all the social, scientific, economic, judicial, and political institutions and conventions of the modern world.

Yet Condillac, like Warburton, refused to view linguistic progress as an entirely one-way street. At the level of epistemology, Condillac insisted that while representational practices were more essential to the development of thought than previously realized, they were also more dangerous to understanding than generally acknowledged, since signs always had the potential to distort the original idea.[107] And just as the proliferation of ever more arbitrary and abstract signs could be held responsible for the greatest of human achievements, it could also legitimately be considered the principal source of intellectual and hence social corruption, the root cause of the modern propensity for superficiality, delusion, and especially error.

Condillac spread the blame for this development widely. Ordinary people, as a result of the imprecise and unempirical way in which they acquired vocabulary as children, had for centuries used specific words habitually, without clear conceptions of their significance, assuming that names alone were adequate explanations of the essence of things. Thus, over the years, the imprecise and often empty expressions of the unschooled had become the source of intractable webs of prejudices and faulty opinions. With similarly negative effects, literary figures, in their desire to establish an original style, had introduced "the reign of subtle and strained conceits, of affective antitheses, of specious paradoxes, of frivolous and far-fetched expressions, of new-fangled words, and in short of the jargon of persons whose understandings have been debauched by bad metaphysics."[108] Other artists, Condillac claimed, had followed suit. Poets, musicians, and choreographers had, for a long time, been the only people in society to continue to make profitable use of the original, energetic sign system; but now they too had stripped gestures and sounds of their power as signs by using them to create purely ornamental art without any communicative significance. Condillac reserved his greatest scorn, however, for contemporary metaphysicians, who, rather than directing their attention to the development of precise terminology, tended either to speak an "unphilosophic language of obscure and con-

fused ideas" or to reason about that which did not exist at all.[109] The
work of these men, Condillac maintained, was the chief impediment to
real intellectual advancement. In their desire to create abstractions, they
had formed a language almost entirely unmoored from its original basis
in sensible ideas.

It was for this disaster that the *Essai* offered a solution. The Abbé
Bonnot de Condillac both opened and concluded his book with the declaration that he intended his work to be read not only as a treatise on
metaphysics but also as a guide to method, a key to avoiding errors in
thought stemming from the misuse or "abuses" of language. As he put it
early in this text: "This history of language will disclose the circumstances in which the signs were invented, will show the true meaning of
them, [and] will help to prevent the abuse they may be turned to." And
he continued, "[N]othing but the simplicity of language can prevent the
abuses of it. This whole work shall be a proof of it."[110] The final chapters
of the *Essai* he thus gave over to a lengthy discussion of ways to prevent
faulty reasoning based on the *abus des mots*. The basis of his argument
was not that advanced societies must rush to return to the original language of gesture—though his nostalgia for its energy and effectiveness
made its mark throughout his book and, as will become clear in the next
chapter, provided a solid foundation for a sensationalist aesthetics. More
centrally, he argued that modern men and women needed to look to this
primordial idiom and the method of its invention and expansion as a
model for their own cognitive and communicative actions, especially in
the realm of philosophy. Unlike Locke, Condillac did not denounce
figurative language as the chief culprit in perpetuating the modern propensity for linguistic abuse. Instead, he praised true poetic language for
not obscuring the sensible basis of ideas or the genealogy of thought, and
he proposed that all subsequent linguistic reforms be conducted in keeping with the values that he imagined as the original, lost properties of
that first, gestural language, the *langage d'action*.

On the one hand, Condillac argued that the principles of analogy and
necessity, so essential to the development of the original language,
needed to govern the construction of all new terms.[111] On the other hand,
he insisted that existing metaphysical and moral terms needed to be redefined and given precise significations according to nature's own
method for preventing error and ascertaining truth. This method was
what he called *analyse*, or analysis, the process of linguistic decomposition and then recomposition designed to uncover the buried metaphors
and sense perceptions at the heart of abstract concepts and then to reconstitute them in the same, analogic manner as they had initially been
generated.[112] Only in this way, he insisted, only by continually replaying
the whole history of language and thought on a miniature scale, could

one arrive at clear, distinct, and "true" notions, the type of imagistic ideas that Descartes had posited as the key to reasoning and clear communication, especially in the moral realm. It was, after all, this very method—stripping abstract ideas back to their sensible, concrete origins and reconstituting their formation—that Condillac had himself employed both in constructing his *Essai* on ideas and in conjuring up his vision of the original language. In effect, Condillac used the opportunity of this treatise to establish a set of ideal communicative principles that he then attempted to associate with the first (and thus most natural) human societies. What he imagined was a world where all conversation produced direct and spontaneous communication, where signs and meanings corresponded perfectly, and where the *abus des mots* was unknown. In Condillac's plan, the key to the restoration of this linguistic Eden lay in the form and structure of the *langage d'action* itself.

Five years passed before Diderot offered the public his response to Condillac's conception of an original language of gesture as the basis of all human achievements, a theory that Condillac continued to recast during those same years. Then in 1751, the same year that the notorious "Affaire de Prades" threatened to link sensationalism with a forbidden materialist philosophy and just months before the *Encyclopédie* was itself condemned for its employment of "obscure and equivocal terminology" that opened the way to unbelief, Diderot published his daring *Lettre sur les sourds et muets, à l'usage de ceux qui entendent et qui parlent.*[113] Ostensibly, Diderot wrote this *Lettre* in order to make a contribution to an ongoing grammatical debate about whether Latin or French syntax corresponded more closely to the canonical or "natural" word order in which human thought occurs.[114] But Diderot's insistence on approaching the problem of syntactical "inversions" from the perspective of the genealogy of language, coupled with his equation of a gestural language with the original and natural one, allowed his readers to understand his text largely as a response to Condillac's earlier theses on the invention and development of signs. In fact, in the *Lettre sur les sourds et muets*, Diderot not only successfully undermined the very terms of the debate on inversions in Latin and French. By questioning whether the words of any conventional, verbal language, regardless of their order, could ever adequately represent thought, he ultimately answered a considerably more radical question than the one that he had initially posed. And in the process, Diderot both expanded upon and challenged certain fundamental propositions in Condillac's earlier text.[115]

In his "Lettre sur la phrase françoise comparée avec la phrase latine," the Abbé Charles Batteux, an important rhetorician of the mid-century, had already argued that the order of gestures one would use to convey any complex idea would necessarily correspond to the natural and, hence, original order of words.[116] Diderot, by suggesting early in the *Lettre sur les sourds et muets* that the solution to the problem of determining the natural order of words should rest upon recovering the natural, gestural idiom and comparing its syntax with that of French, thus initially led his readers to believe that he was situating himself as an ally of Batteux in this debate. Diderot furthered this association by purporting to devise two practical experiments for arriving at the natural order of words. One plan was to employ an experimental mute subject, "who would forgo the use of articulate sounds and try to make himself understood by gesture alone" in the manner of the first language; the other was to find a *philosophe* to translate into French the gestures of a real mute who was ignorant, uncorrupted by the conventions of *parole*, and thus closer to truth than prejudice, much like all humans in their infancy.[117] But almost immediately after introducing these ideas for rendering French sentences in the "natural" language of gesture, Diderot pointed to their impossibility and inadequacy as solutions to Batteux's puzzle. As it turns out, Diderot had proposed this comparison with a very different purpose in mind: to challenge the established notion that a syntactical translation between the two forms of language—gestural and verbal—could be done at all. Indeed, it was the impossibility of the second of his two scenarios that set up the central problem of this complex, winding text.

The chief function of Diderot's failed experiments was, therefore, not to demonstrate that gestures make inadequate signs of thoughts. On the contrary, what he aimed to prove was that certain gestures successfully convey particular ideas that no verbal language can ever effectively represent or reproduce. As evidence, Diderot referred to two moments in the dramas of Corneille and to the celebrated sleepwalking scene in Shakespeare's *Macbeth*. Such moments of intense energy and powerful emotion, he argued, simply cannot be captured by words as we know them and thus fall into a category that he labeled the gestural "sublime." In effect, Diderot used his deliberate experimental failures in translation to point to the essential shortcomings inherent in conventional, verbal forms of communication. By setting up these negative examples, Diderot attempted to demonstrate that in all modern languages there is always, already, a fundamental discontinuity between verbal signs and thought or between language and sensation.

Here a comparison with Condillac becomes instructive. While Condillac had postulated the smooth transition from instinctive bodily motions to gestural signs to words, each stage based on the model of the one before, Diderot indirectly challenged this account of the history of language based on the impossibility of establishing correspondences between different types of signs. And while the author of the *Lettre sur les sourds et muets* accepted the reciprocal relationship between the development of signs and the advancement of thought as central to the Condillacian model, he also illuminated a profound gap in signification—between words and ideas—at which Condillac's *Essai* had only hinted. For Diderot insisted that the mind naturally functions as a "moving tableau" of simultaneous thoughts, while conventional language is, by necessity, a linear succession of distinct ideas expressed syntactically over time. This had not, however, always been the case. At the beginning of human history, Diderot claimed, the first signs had necessarily been synthetic and metaphoric, conveying diverse ideas and sensations simultaneously to multiple senses. In these early years, natural gestural signs had faithfully approximated the way humans thought. But gradually, the poetic, energetic language of gestures had been replaced by a more rational and extensive vocal sign system replete with vast numbers of combined and abstract terms. This newer idiom, Diderot proposed, had functioned as a spur to, as well as a product of, the growth of reason. But this was precisely because the newer idiom had ceased to reflect mimetically the natural functioning of the mind and had distanced its users from their initial, bodily sensations. "Ah, how our understanding is modified by words, and how cold a copy of reality is the vigorous utterance!" he exclaimed in dismay at one point in his text.[118]

Diderot's central argument was that the human capacity for rational analysis—for thinking in a linear and genetic fashion—had actually come at a very high price indeed. Like Condillac, Diderot praised the French language if not as the embodiment of innate rationality (as the Cartesians had before him) then as the apex of the historical development of reason. From the vantage point of the mid-eighteenth century, it was axiomatic that French, among national tongues, best corresponded to the principal object of language: the clear and precise communication of ever more complex and scientific ideas. But Diderot also insisted that the French language, with its plethora of inversions and abundant vocabulary, suffered as well as benefited as a result of its great distance from the prerational, primitive language of gesture. Its gains in cognitive value were matched by a loss of vigor, warmth, affective value, and, especially, *énergie*, as the inherent limitations of verbal language were exacerbated by historical achievements. Condillac had accused the French language of falling short in philosophical terms, of becoming a language of deceitful and obscure abstractions, as well as a product and source of muddled thought. But for Diderot the complaint was different; in his opinion, the overrefined idiom of the French nation had become the least effective medium to date for the forceful communication of passions and emotions. Speakers and writers in the French language now had to strain to touch their interlocutors' hearts and, consequently, to unite them in a sympathetic community because these speakers and writers were forced to utilize a cold, sterile, and overly intellectualized means of communication.

Diderot too offered a solution of sorts that depended upon the original state of language as a lost ideal. After throwing up certain roadblocks regarding Condillac's argument, Diderot ultimately endorsed the idea that a cure for the problem of the *abus des mots* depended upon the resuscitation of the values or principles embodied in the communicative practices of the first societies. Indeed, both men sought to discover a way for a univocal, immediately intelligible, and truly representative language to play a new role in cognition and interpersonal communication. But where Condillac had emphasized the simplification of philosophical language as a panacea, Diderot turned to the realm of poetry and the aesthetic. And where Condillac had advocated analysis, or the systematic unpacking of composite ideas, in an effort to compensate for the instability and polysemy of conventional language and to prevent the emergence of logomachies, Diderot urged artists and writers to approach language differently. He suggested that they seek a way to "paint" thought, or bring ideas together through metaphor, metonymy, and synecdoche, and thereby to re-create (at least in spirit) the gestural sublime that he associated with the actor and his audience, a community of deaf-mute individuals, or the original human couple. Diderot hoped that by experimenting with a literary version of "hieroglyphics"—synthetic, visual, and ostensibly "primitive" signs that could be woven into a *tissu* reflective of the multiplicity of the soul and senses—poets might once again be able to convey meaningful sentiments and passions and, hence, to make socially integrative art.[119] Moreover, he posited that this kind of theoretical blending of word and image, by potentially "hasten[ing] in advance of" the mind, could work not simply to reflect the present state of knowledge but actually to spur it on to greater advances.[120] In the context of the chaotic and experimental labyrinth of the *Lettre*, Diderot thus went well beyond Condillac in terms of both his critique of the state of modern languages and the radicality of his epistemology—even as he essentially continued to forward the idea of harnessing the power of the original *langage d'action* toward a broad social and intellectual goal.

Several years went by following the publication of Diderot's *Lettre sur les sourds et muets* before Rousseau too chose to address the subject of the origins and development of signs. Then, Rousseau turned his attention to one aspect of this discussion that both Condillac and Diderot had largely ignored: the political implications of the failure of modern language as a means of reflecting and conveying moral or emotional truths. This question was at the heart of two of Rousseau's chief essays of the 1750s, the *Discours sur l'origine de l'inégalité parmi les hommes*

(1755), written in response to an essay contest sponsored by the Académie de Dijon in 1753, and the *Essai sur l'origine des langues*, composed in the middle of the 1750s but not published until 1781.[121] Many commentators have pointed to the ways in which these elaborate logical "conjectures" (in Rousseau's words) about the development of society and language appear to contradict one another in certain details, not least in the sections devoted to the origin of language and the specific role of gestures in paving the way for speech. But the two works in question also display surprising unity at the level of their intent. In both, the inevitable turn away from the original, poetic language is important precisely because it produces and then continues to sanctify the oppressive social and political conditions characteristic of modern European societies and, especially, of France.[122]

Rousseau explicitly challenged Condillac's language theory on two fronts: first, he questioned Condillac's seamless presentation of the role of gestures and natural cries in the development of language, thought, and society; and, second, he rebutted Condillac's generally positive account of the results to be derived from the triumph of the conventional language of reason over the initial language of passion. In the so-called *Second Discours*, Rousseau introduced his comments on the origin of language with a tribute to Condillac: "I could be satisfied to cite or repeat here the researches that the Abbé de Condillac has made on this matter, which all fully confirm my sentiment, and which perhaps gave me the first idea of it."[123] But then Rousseau quickly drew his readers' attention to the essential flaws in Condillac's reasoning. The most fundamental of these was the assumption that man is a naturally social being who was already eager to convey his ideas and perceptions to his neighbors in the state of nature. In contrast, Rousseau suggested that in their original state—here theorized as a real historical period covering the centuries prior to commerce, property, and conscious morality—humans had had little need for either society or any kind of communication beyond basic gestures and cries in order to survive and prosper. Therefore, it was almost impossible to imagine what requirements or what events could have led them initially to invent either languages or communities. Similarly, assuming the eventual emergence of a need for a real language, he questioned how humans could ever have managed to transcend their initial instinctive idiom and to construct a conventional method of oral communication: "For if men needed speech in order to learn to think, they had even greater need of knowing how to think in order to discover the art of speech."[124] In other words, each of Condillac's chief concepts—language, thought, and social development—seemed to Rousseau to presuppose the pre-existence of the others.

It was only in the later *Essai sur l'origine des langues* that Rousseau developed an elaborate explanation for how speech and society might have come into being in tandem. In this text too Rousseau argued that the original language of gestures, inarticulate cries, and imitative noises had been satisfactory to meet most essential needs in the earliest centuries of human development, when humans "had no society other than that of the family, no laws other than those of nature."[125] Long before their tenets were ever explicitly articulated, the laws of nature manifested themselves in the natural language of instinctive gestures. In fact, the early chapters of the *Essai* open with a catalogue of the many advantages of natural gestural communication in relation to conventional, verbal languages: the close resemblance of the sign to what it represents; the extraordinary impact of visual forms on the senses; the unsurpassed eloquence of the isolated dramatic gesture employed to convey a virtue or strong emotion; the economy of means associated with synchronic physical expression. By the mid-1750s, assigning such qualities to an imagined gestural idiom was not unusual, though it certainly would have seemed odd to one schooled exclusively in the rationalist linguistic tradition of Port-Royal. But then Rousseau's argument took an unexpected turn. Conventional speech, Rousseau insisted, had developed not as a result of hunger, thirst, and practical humans needs, as Condillac had suggested before him, but, rather, out of "the moral needs [and] the passions . . . love, hatred, pity, anger."[126] Furthermore, he proposed (in contradistinction to Condillac) that verbal signs were more appropriate than gestural ones for expressing passions; for while "visible signs make for more accurate imitation . . . interest is aroused more effectively by sounds."[127]

Rousseau did not dismiss the possibility that gestural signs could constitute a proper language in their own right; drawing on such wide-ranging evidence as Jacob Rodrigue Péreire's recent efforts to learn the language of mutes in order to teach them spoken French and the Chevalier Chardin's reports on the manual signs used for transacting business in Persia, Rousseau went so far as to claim that, hypothetically, gestural signs would be adequate to satisfy all of humans' physical needs, from the establishment of laws to the creation of mechanical arts. However, in the *Essai*, Rousseau insisted that the emotional cries resulting from the interaction of men with women—the vocal expression of the passions born of nascent family life—first propelled all humans toward the creation of both conventional forms of language and complex, advanced societies. Here the *Essai* appears to contradict the *Second Discours* too, since in the earlier work the raw materials of language—sounds and gestures—are given overlapping functions as signifiers. But this distinction is ultimately less important than the larger argument that informed both of Rousseau's essays. In these works, he proposed that the historical demise of the natural language and the rise of a conventional one (thanks in good measure to women, who play the negative role of civilizing agents in this discourse) has fostered and now continues to preserve artificial and inequitable social arrangements that are detrimental to human happiness.[128]

The vast collective genealogy laid out in the *Second Discours* and the historical geography bluntly sketched in the *Essai* are both tales of humans' gradual estrangement from their original, instinctual language and the negative consequences that followed. Ultimately, Rousseau, unlike Condillac, identified no communal benefits from this history of linguistic and social progress away from the state of nature, only the advent of steadily more oppressive social and political institutions increasingly founded on artifice and lies. In the *Second Discours*, Rousseau claimed that property was first established as an act of speech; the articulation of the words "this is mine" paved the way for the production of all of the most harmful of civilized values: social inequality, dishonestly, jealousy, competition, excessive concern with appearances rather than substance, and constant social strife. Then, as people's mental capacities expanded, language became an increasingly effective tool of deception and, in the hands of the ruling class, a useful way to mask self-interest and to perpetuate unjust social divisions. Indeed, language gradually replaced physical violence as a means of domination. Now, in the final corrupted state of the present, Rousseau insisted that humans routinely "abuse" the very faculties, including language, that honor them as beings: "for the vices that make social institutions necessary are the same ones that make their abuse inevitable."[129]

The picture in the *Essai* is hardly any prettier. The languages of Northern Europe—at once the most abstract and methodical and the furthest from any passionate roots—have, over time, become unmusical, sterile, cold, and enervated. The spirit of alphabetic writing, in its remove from its utterer, has, in particular, rendered all Northern tongues, including French, inexpressive and "servile." In fact, the national tongue of contemporary France, Rousseau argued in the final chapter, has become especially inhospitable to expressions of liberty, which (he suggested in the tradition of many classical authors) depend upon opportunities for eloquence rooted in the accents and gestures of public oration rather than print. Modern French political speech is instead without inflection and empty of content, more often a source of mystification than illumination. He despaired: "Societies have assumed their final forms: nothing can be changed in them anymore except by arms and cash, and since there is nothing left to say to the people but *give money*, it is said with posters on street corners or with soldiers in private homes; for this there is no need to assemble anyone. . . . Some languages are conducive to liberty; namely, the sonorous, rhythmic, harmonious languages in which speech can be made out from far away. Ours are made for the buzz in the Sultan's Council Chamber."[130] In other words, the decline of the political liberty and sense of community associated with direct, participatory democracy and the decline in the communicative value of words have gone hand in hand. In Rousseau's version, Condillac's equivocal history of the turn away from natural signs became a blunt critique of the devastating political and social effects of the development of linguistically advanced "civilizations" and a description of profound loss.[131]

Compared with Condillac and Diderot, Rousseau offered little by way of concrete recipes for addressing the inadequacies of contemporary communication. But he hinted at the desirability of a profound transformation. In effect, Rousseau suggested that because the nature of a language and the nature of a society and government are always thoroughly implicated in one another, it is incumbent upon modern individuals to restore not only a lost language of primal eloquence that would transform political culture but also a lost social and political world devoid of radical disjunctures between actions and speech that would make such a language possible. In both texts, Rousseau insisted that the return of freedom—both freedom from a restrictive, overly feminized, inequitable social order and freedom to speak publicly about political concerns—must accompany the revival of a language with the expressive power of the original *langage d'action*. And this truly free, eloquent speech could be the precondition as well as the result of political liberty. It could bring about the end of the reign of servitude that the current language continued to sanctify.

In effect, Diderot and then Rousseau progressively radicalized Condillac's epistemological and genealogical claims of the 1740s. Neither Diderot nor Rousseau challenged Condillac's central equation of instinctive gestures with an original state of nature and, by extension, with all "primitive" or precivilized peoples, from infants to wild children to American Indians. All attributed certain moral and political power to this language, for in its closeness to sensations, the language of gesture was generally assumed to have indisputable cognitive clarity and energy. Yet what began in Condillac's *Essai* as a new way of conceptualizing linguistic and social evolution ended in Rousseau's *Essai* as a striking means by which to condemn the role of an increasingly abstract language in the creation of a morally bankrupt and thoroughly debauched modern society. And what began in Condillac as a way to defend the method of analysis ended in Rousseau as a nostalgic plea for linguistic and political freedom. The cumulative implication of the arguments of Condillac, Diderot, and Rousseau was that just as the disso-

lution of the bonds holding the earliest societies together was dependent
upon the growing abstraction of language, so contemporary intellectual,
social, and political redemption needed to be linked to radical linguistic
and epistemological transformations.

THE BIRTH OF AN EPISTEMOLOGICAL MODEL

Rousseau and Diderot were not alone in taking up Condillac's hypotheses and creating variants in the decade after the publication of the *Essai
sur l'origine des connaissances humaines*. From the 1740s through the
1750s, numerous stories with only subtle differences from that of Condillac were proposed as solutions to the problem of the "natural" origin
of language. Furthermore, many of these authors continued to emphasize the invention of the first *langage d'action* as a decisive moment in
human evolution, making the idea of an original language of gestures
and cries a standard feature of universal or conjectural histories and a
common element of mid-century enlightened European intellectual
discourse, from the pages of the major literary journals to the debates of
the Royal Academy in Berlin.[132]

Assessments of the viability of such "philosophical histories" were,
however, always mixed, and the very enterprise of writing a speculative
account of the natural origins and development of human language had
its vocal detractors from the start. Even within such thoroughly Enlightenment institutions as the Prussian Academy, of which Condillac
himself soon became a corresponding member, the sensationalist version of the history of language was attacked on both epistemological and
methodological grounds. The academician Jean-Henri-Samuel Formey,
a firm believer in the theory of innate ideas and the divine foundations of
language, publicly ridiculed both the concept of a preverbal human
"state of nature" and the notion that the empirical study of humans—
whether isolated, deaf, savage, "old, young, sick, or healthy"—could
ever yield information useful to the study of language origins.[133] Members who were more receptive to the philosophical orientation of Condillac's ideas, such as Pierre-Louis Moreau de Maupertuis, the president
of the Prussian Academy and the author of several works on the history
of language, also questioned the scientific accuracy of Condillac's findings. Stressing the importance of the study of language origins as a way
both to clarify the source of ideas and to avoid errors in reasoning, he
called for further empirical evidence and experimentation to bolster
what he saw as largely unsubstantiated speculations on the part of contemporary theorists.[134]

Nineteenth- and twentieth-century commentators have tended to
agree with these eighteenth-century critics. With a nod to the promi-

nent place accorded to arguments regarding gestural language in numerous articles in the *Encyclopédie*, from *déclamation* to *hiéroglyphe*,
historians have, until relatively recently, tended to dismiss this quarrel
as a minor byproduct of sensationalist psychology, one of many short-
lived and misguided philosophical exercises conducted by a disparate
group of *philosophes* eager to challenge church orthodoxy on all fronts.
Furthermore, it has often been pointed out that the eighteenth-century
debate on the origin of language had little lasting impact on either historical theory or the nascent field of comparative linguistics.[135] It is universal grammar, growing out of Cartesianism, that Michel Foucault, for
example, takes as representative of the ahistorical and premodern
"classical episteme" of the seventeenth and eighteenth centuries.[136] And
the very fact that discussion of this problem of origins, as formulated and
approached by Condillac, ceased soon after the middle decades of the
eighteenth century has suggested to many historians of the Enlightenment that its public interest or impact was seriously limited even at the
time.

I maintain, however, that historians have by and large looked for the
repercussions of this discussion about the invention of signs and the social and epistemological consequences of their development in the
wrong places. This is primarily because they have misconstrued the *philosophes'* objectives. These speculative essays by Condillac, Diderot,
and Rousseau were clearly never intended to be read as statements
about a "real" past. But neither were they meant to be treated as works
of pure philosophy. Rather, the "origins" project, with its firm foundations in the idea of language as a social contract and society as a linguistic invention, ultimately had a decidedly presentist and pragmatic goal.

What then was its purpose? In a sense, it was dual. Much like the ra-
tionalists before them, sensationalist theorists of language desired nothing more than to discover a realm of perfectly unambiguous and universal communication. The authors of these mid-eighteenth-century texts
on the origin of language never fully abandoned the Cratylist aspiration
of correcting the current instability of words so as to pave the way for a
language that was truly univocal and immutable, a perfect reflection of a
universal mental order and, consequently, the objective, external world.
In a certain sense, therefore, one can argue that the *philosophes* elaborated a vision of an ideal primordial language and Edenic origin with the
hope that the story of human progress would eventually come full circle
and a way would be found to make mediating signs essentially disappear. Yet there was always another side to the semiotic ambitions of
these sensationalist theorists of language origins. After all, their evocations of the hypothetical *langage d'action* were not designed to make a
case for this obsolete sign system as the source of original truths or a to-

tal lost knowledge that might be recovered whole. Rather, the *philoso-phes'* descriptions of the construction and evolution of the initial hu-man language were also scripted to elevate the status of signs and to ad-vance the concept of signs as active instruments, tools to shape (as well as reflect) thought or knowledge and, consequently, to alter or transform social realities.[137] By insisting on the temporality of all language systems and by reversing the Cartesian hierarchy between idea and sign, Condil-lac, Diderot, Rousseau, and their disciples effectively established the idea of language reform or experimentation according to natural guide-lines and principles (as embodied by the *langage d'action*) as a precondi-tion for improved communication among individuals in society and, po-tentially, between society and representatives of the state. In every as-pect of life, arbitrary signs made errors possible; illustrations of the *abus des mots* provided ample demonstration of this fact. But the very muta-bility and variability of these same signs—indeed, their undeniable epis-temological and social shortcomings—also made possible the truly op-timistic notion that improvement in the representativeness of signs could bring about new, more successful ways of understanding and con-veying the world and thus pave the way for more harmonious relations among peoples. And the *philosophes*, with their special interest in these questions, proposed themselves as the obvious group to guide the proc-ess. The Enlightenment story of the formation and expansion of the *lan-gage d'action*, for all its failings as a way of explaining the past, offered contemporaries an intriguing model for the crafting of a new politics of language based upon very different premises from that already well es-tablished by the French crown.

In order to understand the wider implications of this conversation on language origins that began among a private circle of friends in Paris in the 1740s, we need, therefore, to explore the ways in which the "histories" postulated by Condillac and a few of his close associates permeated additional realms of inquiry and sociocultural experience, beyond speculative philosophy or linguistic theory, during the last years of the Old Regime. More precisely, we must examine how the *philoso-phes'* ideas on language origins and development were understood, ap-propriated, and put to use in ensuing decades by thinkers and practitio-ners working in other, seemingly disparate domains. The primary essays considered in this chapter were hybrid affairs, complete with textual ref-erences to everything from the sign systems of Ottoman mutes to the si-lent nature of American Indian family life. They were also marked by frequent explicit discussions of their own significance, of the potential conclusions that one might draw from their findings for a wide variety of pursuits, from poetry to sexual relations. Accordingly, we can find evi-dence of the impact of these linguistic-social theories in an extraordinary range of fields during the second half of the eighteenth century, including biology, chemistry, medicine, anthropology, music, the visual arts, rhetoric, and economics. The next two chapters focus on two distinct realms—the theater and the classroom—where, following the directives of the *philosophes*, the *langage d'action* was recovered not just as an inspiration but also as an actual form of modern communicative practice. For it was in the overlapping arenas of aesthetics and pedagogy that the social, ethical, and political implications of the epistemological challenges of Diderot, Rousseau, and Condillac were first and most thoroughly investigated and debated.

2

Pantomime as Theater, 1760–89

The idea of a primordial gestural language entered European
consciousness in the middle of the eighteenth century as
nothing more than a hypothesis, an educated guess about the nature of
human psychology and the origins of human society. But in the context
of the Enlightenment, pure speculation had little long-term appeal as a
goal unto itself. The picture of this primitive sign system drawn first by
Condillac seems to have been sufficiently seductive to have almost immediately generated practical plans for its recovery and revival. Soon after the publication of the essential sensationalist treatments of the origin and development of semiosis, the idea of a natural body language,
sundered from its narrative context, came to represent a transhistorical
epistemological ideal. And by the end of the 1750s, proponents of the
theory of an original *langage d'action* had begun to argue for the restoration of this language as a means not only to re-create the transparent
semiotic practices of a distant, idealized past but also ultimately to
transform the nature of modern intellectual and social relations.

But how could this desire be fulfilled? Surely, this long-forgotten, gestural idiom could not suddenly be reconstituted on a global scale. First,
scores of individuals would have to be convinced to give up well-en-
trenched habits of communication and become skilled anew in the obsolete art of conveying and reading ideas through bodily actions. More
broadly, France's firmly entrenched linguistic hierarchy, not to mention
the established course of human progress, would have to be turned on its
head. Accordingly, the reintroduction of the natural language of pantomime seemed to many mid-eighteenth-century French commentators
to necessitate the construction of a specially constituted and clearly de-
limited space for experimentation. What this endeavor required was a
protected arena in which new semiotic practices could be tried out and
cultivated at some remove from society as a whole and without directly
challenging the structure and customs of the state (especially since all
such projects still required the permission, if not direct patronage, of the
crown).

Thus, the first of these experiments with the revival of gestural expression were conducted within the rarefied realm that eighteenth-

century aestheticians referred to as the "arts."[1] According to Condillac's *Essai*, the methods of communication presently associated exclusively with the fine and performing arts had once been coterminous with daily life. In early societies, poetry and ordinary conversation—just like painting and basic notation—had been indistinguishable enterprises. But in modern Europe, the philosopher pointed out, the canvas, the theater, and even the pages of a work of literature had, both in theory and in practice, become distinctive and ultimately utopian sites with rules that distinguished them from other ordinary social settings. Indeed, the contemporary Marxist literary critic Terry Eagleton has argued that such Enlightenment efforts to define the distinctive realm of the aesthetic were themselves complicit in the establishment of this crucial feature of modernity: the sequestering of art from all other social practices until it became an isolated enclave in which the dominant social order could find an idealized refuge from its own actual values.[2] By the middle of the eighteenth century, those specific settings deemed to be art had come to seem one of the rare places where individuals could attempt to transcend the deceptive and often opaque discursive practices of contemporary life. Here alone they could temporarily experience anew the effects of older forms of communication—from picture-writing to gesticulation—now largely obsolete in the culture at large. Above all, the hypothesis of the original *langage d'action* suggested the possibility of creating a new kind of drama, a visual spectacle rooted in pantomime and designed to evoke what Eagleton calls the chief moral aim of eighteenth-century art: "the utopian image of reconciliation between men and women at present divided from one another."[3]

For Eagleton, looking back over two hundred years, these aesthetic experiments of the late eighteenth century appear primarily to have been a form of escapism, a way of retreating from trying to change the real world and thus of thwarting true political movement. But he also acknowledges that late Enlightenment theorists viewed these projects as having the potential to encourage or, at the very least, to prefigure social transformations to come. And I argue that in their efforts to reactivate humans' most archaic mechanisms of communication in the space of the theater, Enlightenment aestheticians and theatrical reformers—following the guidelines of Condillac, Rousseau, and especially Diderot—sought to accomplish nothing less than to renew the culture of the present in anticipation of the ideal society of the future. In other words, they hoped that, through pantomimed performance, it would ultimately be possible to re-create the kind of unified, intersubjective moral community devoid of misunderstanding and strife that the *langage d'action* had supposedly once, long before, ensured. It was an idea that proved highly enticing and continually controversial in the last decades of the

Old Regime. For just as its chief admirers and opponents expected, its application—both within and apart from explicitly royal institutions—turned out in the long run to have profound consequences for efforts to reimagine the social and political order in France.

FROM THE LANGAGE D'ACTION TO
THE BALLET D'ACTION

Jean-Georges Noverre, a celebrated dancer and choreographer, formally introduced his plan for the restoration of the neglected language of pantomime in 1760. In that year he issued a sustained polemic in favor of the development of a new form of dance based in natural, gestural expression. His argument opened with a virulent critique of ballet as it was then practiced at the official Royal Academy of Music in Paris and at the opera houses of most other European capitals. Contemporary ballet *divertissements*, he complained in his *Lettres sur la danse et sur les ballets*, functioned primarily as decorative interludes within operas; characterized by technical feats, they served little purpose except to please the eyes and divert the audience's attention from the opera's narrative.[4] In place of this abstract and "soulless" spectacle, Noverre proposed that dance should—like poetry or painting—be an imitative art, a means of representing and conveying human sentiments. To accomplish this goal, the ballet master of Lyon argued, choreographers and dancers alike needed to rediscover the universal art of painting the soul's passions through gestures and actions, or what the ancients called pantomime. At its purest, Noverre claimed, dance was simply a form of communication, a method of "transferring our [dancers'] sentiments . . . to the souls of the spectators by means of the true expression of our movements, gestures and features."[5] The purpose of a choreographer was to give collections of movements an order or syntax so that they, indeed, "spoke" clearly and eloquently to their intended audience and elicited an emotional response. "Dancing is possessed of all the advantages of a beautiful language," he explained, ". . . [and] when a man of genius arranges the letters to form words and connects the words to form sentences, it will cease to be dumb; it will share with the best plays the merit of affecting and moving, and of making tears flow."[6] The name that Noverre gave this spectacle was a *ballet d'action*. In his *Lettres*, Noverre imagined a form of theater that would allow dancers and audience members alike to experience the passionate, direct exchange of sentiments that had characterized the world of the first, instinctive human language.

As a result of these propositions, Noverre has often been credited as an extraordinary innovator in the history of dance. The idea of Noverre as a theatrical "revolutionary" is, in fact, as old as the choreographer himself, who proved to be a relentless publicist throughout his career for both his ideas and his own genius. However, the immediate renown and impact of the *Lettres sur la danse* across eighteenth-century Europe should indicate that Noverre's battle cry did not actually mark a dramatic break with prevailing aesthetic trends. Rather, it constituted the culmination and meeting point of several older intellectual currents. Many of his ideas—about the function of art, the effectiveness of gesture and pantomime, and especially the need for dance to speak—had already become widely accepted in preceding years.

The notion that mimesis, or the imitation of nature, constituted the original purpose of all of the arts—dance, as well as painting, sculpture, music, and poetry—hardly amounted to a shocking claim in 1760. The Enlightenment inherited this idea from seventeenth-century neoclassicism, and, before that, from Aristotle. And as a result of the rise of comparative sensationalist aesthetics in the wake of the writings of the Abbé Dubos, it was generally agreed by the mid-eighteenth century that different arts simply made use of different means or "languages," themselves directed toward different senses, to attain their common goal. Furthermore, a significant change in the hierarchizing of those means was already underway. As the Abbé Charles Batteux pointed out in his oft-quoted treatise *Les Beaux-arts réduits à un même principe*, which appeared in 1745, the same year as Condillac's *Essai*, speech, for all its importance in modern life, could be considered in many ways the least advantageous of the media available to those with something to say. Those arts that relied upon natural signs—musical tones or physical gestures—not only represented or denoted natural emotions more accurately, but they also affected their audience more quickly, more directly, and more powerfully than did those arts that depended upon conventional signs, such as words. For Batteux, a professor of rhetoric in Reims and then Navarre, this distinction was simply a product of human psychology. As he explained:

> Speech instructs us, convinces us, it is the organ of reason; but tone and gesture are the organs of the heart: they move us, win us over, persuade us. Speech explains the passions only by way of the ideas to which sentiments are tied, and by reflection. Tone and gesture reach the heart directly and without any detour. In a word, speech is a language of institution that men have made in order to communicate their ideas more distinctly among themselves; gestures and tones are like a dictionary of simple nature; they contain a language that we all know from birth and which we use to announce all that relates to our needs and to our conservation and our death: it is also lively, brief, energetic. What better foundation for the arts whose object is to stir the soul than a language in

which all the expressions are those of humanity itself rather than those of individual men![7]

Moreover, Batteux insisted, like Dubos, that visual signs, with their generally composite rather than successive nature, had certain significant advantages over verbal ones. Batteux thus concluded (just as Noverre would after him) that an art form directed to the eyes and rooted in natural gestures would indeed be able to bypass the mind and speak directly to the heart, which "has an intelligence independent of words and when it is touched, it understands everything."[8]

But this idea of gesture providing the basis for dance to become a communicative art was not simply motivated by recent developments in psychology and epistemology. Prior to 1760, curiosity about the potential of pantomime as a means of theatrical communication was also stimulated by the ongoing vogue for the antique. A century's worth of historical research, from the Latin tomes of Isaac Vossius in the late seventeenth century to the antiquarian studies of Charles Pineau Duclos and Jean Racine of the Academy of Inscriptions in the 1740s, had succeeded in drawing renewed attention to the wondrous achievements of antiquity in the realm of dance and declamation.[9] This knowledge had, in turn, stimulated in fashionable aristocratic circles of the early eighteenth century several experiments billed as entertainments in the style of the ancients. By the 1750s, these performances had already taken on the quality of modern legends. The most celebrated of them had been planned by the Duchess of Maine, the granddaughter of Louis XIV, in 1712. On the fourteenth of the "grandes Nuits de Sceaux," she had arranged for two dancers from the Opéra ballet to perform a pantomime of a scene from the fourth act of Corneille's *Horace* in which Horace kills his sister Camilla.[10] According to Dubos, the duchess had wished to see "an attempt at the Art of the Ancient Pantomimes, which would give her a clearer idea of their performances than she had visualized when reading about them in the Classics."[11]

As a result of these various arguments and experiments, the notion that contemporary ballet had fallen into a state of decadence already had considerable currency in the decades prior to Noverre's composition of his *Lettres*. Certainly ballet was enormously popular among elite audiences at the mid-century; its most brilliant and virtuosic dancers, male and female, had become celebrities with international reputations. But there was a growing sense among theatrical critics as well as *philosophes* that ballet had lost touch with its original purpose and had ceased to have any real communicative value. In their early writings on the origin of language, Condillac and Rousseau had already used the example of pantomime not only to develop an argument about the poetic nature of the first human sign system but to point out, by contrast, the expressive limitations inherent in conventional, civilized forms of art, including ballet. Opera critics of the mid-eighteenth century, such as Toussaint Rémond de Saint-Mard, had frequently concurred, complaining that danced interludes were often little more than distractions from an opera's plot.[12] And in the 1750s, under the pens of the Encyclopedists, including Louis de Cahusac, the Baron Grimm, the Chevalier de Jaucourt, and Diderot himself, such criticisms had come to serve as arguments for the immediate reform of contemporary French ballet by means of the revival of pantomime. In entries in the *Encyclopédie* for *ballet, chant, danse, déclamation*, and *geste*, the librettist and choreographer Cahusac drew on both the speculative history of sign-making, beginning with the universal language of gestures, and the scholarly history of dance, from the *hiéroglyphs d'action* of ancient Egypt to the pantomimes of Greece and Rome and after, to argue for a much-needed transformation of opera ballet into a mimetic and affective experience rooted in "gesture . . . the language of all nations."[13] Similarly, during the same years, Diderot relied upon the principles of sensationalist aesthetics and contemporary sign theory, not to mention a few references to antique declamation, to justify his own call for the restoration of pantomime as an integral part of all theatrical forms.[14] Already in his *Lettre sur les sourds et muets*, Diderot had outlined his notion of a gestural sublime and explained his perverse pleasure in attending the theater with his fingers stuffed in his ears. In the essays that accompanied his major *drames* of the late 1750s, he returned to this theme, stressing the greater effectiveness of action over speech, from the dramas of Euripides to the novels of Richardson, and arguing for the importance of pantomime, or live *tableaux*, as a potent means of conveying great emotions in drama, ballet, and even, metaphorically, poetry. In fact, Noverre's *Lettres* of 1760 have often been read as a response to Diderot's call in his *Entretiens sur le Fils naturel* of 1757 for a man of genius to realize that, ultimately, all dance must be "a genre of imitation . . . a restrained pantomime."[15]

What made Noverre's text so powerful was thus not the fact that he alone imagined pantomime as the key to the transformation of contemporary theater. Rather, it was the way that he succeeded in uniting the epistemological and semiotic ideals prevalent in these high Enlightenment texts with practical ideas for reform drawn from his own extensive experience, prior to the writing of his *Lettres*, as a dancer, choreographer, and observer in the theatrical worlds of Potsdam, Marseilles, Lyon, London, and Paris. In fact, one might argue that Noverre's principal intellectual achievement was simply to accelerate and to cement this combination. Noverre clearly acknowledged the inspirational powers of Diderot's ideas. He sprinkled his own writing with classical citations as well as references to the comparative aesthetic principles advanced by Dubos, the recent scholarly literature on pantomime summarized by Cahusac, and even the experiments of the Duchess of Maine. But, equally important, Noverre, unlike most other scholars and critics of the moment, had absorbed many of the formal and narrative innovations in recent European performance practice during the decade before the publication of his *Lettres*. Most significantly, he had participated directly in the ingenious efforts of the unofficial fair theaters in Paris to substitute gestures for words as a primary method of communication.

At the moment that Noverre was engaged in writing his *Lettres*, pantomime was already a well-established, if lowly, French theatrical genre. In fact, since the beginning of the century, gesture had become an increasingly vital part of popular entertainment in Paris. The monopolies on speech, music, and dance that the crown had accorded to the official Parisian theaters (the Opéra and the Comédie-Française) at the end of the previous century had left the entrepreneurs at the St. Germain and St. Laurent fairs scrambling throughout the ensuing decades for ways to circumvent the onerous and evolving restrictions that had been placed on their activities.[16] In particular, state actions to prevent the unofficial fair theaters from using spoken dialogue in French had spurred the invention of a range of new and often hybrid theatrical forms in the early eighteenth century. Many entertainers began then to incorporate pantomime, based initially on the characters and gestures of the *commedia dell'arte*, into their spectacles.[17] Alongside tightrope acts, acrobatics, animal and freak shows, parades, child acts, and marionette displays, the fairs also saw, in the course of the century, the development of short narrated pantomimes, *pièces à la muette* (in which actors spoke only nonsense syllables while miming), parodic English pantomimes, *pièces à écriteaux* (in which scrolls or placards with dialogue were unfurled to accompany the action), *opéras-comiques* combining speech, pantomime, and programmatic music, and pantomimes accompanied by *vaudevilles*. Some of these theatrical entrepreneurs referred to the ancient precedents for their efforts.[18] But generally these early experiments were motivated by prohibitions on traditional theatrical forms rather than explicit aesthetic goals. As Jacques Bonnet explained in 1723, "Those [performers] of our day, not having the liberty to speak during their plays, imitated for a while the art of the Pantomimes, who explained themselves through gestures and then by song and *tableaux*."[19] Yet, by the 1740s, silent pantomime had become a popular component of theater in its own right, as exemplified by the appearance of Jean-Nicolas Servandoni's pantomimic "Spectacles d'Optique" at the Salle des Machines in the Tuileries and François Riccoboni's *ballets-panto-*

mimes at the Théâtre Italien, as well as other activities at the fairs. Furthermore, in the 1740s and 1750s, mimed scenes were increasingly performed to instrumental music alone, without accompanying songs, speeches, signboards, or other linguistic props, though often with explanatory *livrets*. It was, finally, in this nonofficial milieu, outside of the Royal Academy of Music and squarely in the world of Jean Monnet's Opéra-Comique at the St. Laurent fair, that Noverre's own career as a dancer began in the early 1740s.

By the time Noverre was called to England in the mid-1750s at the behest of the actor David Garrick, the French dancer had already made several attempts to adapt fair theater styles to ballets of his own creation in Marseilles, in Lyon, and at the Opéra-Comique in Paris, where the spectacular *tableaux* and pantomimic interludes in his compositions drew notice. But it was only after he had witnessed the theatrical effects of Garrick himself, Noverre claimed, that he was able to conceive of a form of full-length pantomimed dance drama such as that which he would later outline in his *Lettres* of 1760.[20] Noverre wrote his treatise on composition immediately after an unsuccessful stint as Garrick's guest performer in London, a visit that had to be aborted due to anti-French sentiment on the other side of the Channel. Despite this setback, Noverre insisted in his *Lettres* that he remained indebted to the Englishman's example. Above all, Noverre celebrated Garrick's mimic technique and the effect that it had on spectators: "He [Garrick] was so natural, his expression was so lifelike, his gestures, features, and glances were so eloquent and so convincing. . . . [In] tragedy he terrified with the successive movements with which he represented the most violent passions. And, if I may so express myself, he lacerated the spectator's feelings, tore his heart, pierced his soul, and made him shed tears of blood."[21] Most likely, Noverre had also witnessed recent efforts on the part of the great thespians of the Comédie Française, LeKain and Mlle. Clairon, to incorporate elements of a supposedly antique pantomime style in their portrayal of tragic roles. Surely, he had seen Franz Hilverding's innovations in Vienna, where this choreographer had attempted to stage the dramas of Racine, Crébillon, and Voltaire as ballets. But these displays did not come close to that of Garrick in terms of the use of the body as a whole. What particularly struck Noverre was that the physical movements of Garrick, or the "English Roscius," were so expressive that Garrick's dramatic performances were entirely comprehensible to the visiting Frenchman (or so he claimed) even though he understood not a word of English.[22]

Out of these disparate performances and aesthetic dictates, Noverre thus successfully fashioned both a sensationalist theory of dance and a call for concrete changes in theatrical practice. He encouraged efforts to develop bodily expressivity, to break down distinctions between pure dance and pantomime, and to make ballets into visual dramas. He called for new attention to the arms and the face (rather than legs), since he considered the upper body to be the dancer's chief vehicle for conveying the multiple, conflicting, and fleeting sentiments in his or her heart. He argued too that dancers needed to do away with cumbersome costumes and, especially, facial masks, which disguised expressive nuance. In sum, the choreographer continually emphasized the potential for gestures to function as signs and for dance to be accorded equal status with its sister arts as a means to depict human passions. Ultimately, he imagined the mimic ballet, like other forms of theater, as a viable way to "execrate vice and reward virtue" in fictional characters.[23]

Yet it is important to note that Noverre never sought simply to recreate established theatrical forms by substituting gestures for words. Rather, he hoped to institute a novel type of aesthetic experience, one that transcended not only the viewing of a painting, with its frozen images, but also the audition of poetry and drama, with their dependence upon successive but highly intellectualized words. In the tragic *ballet d'action*, he prophesied, "words will become useless, everything will speak, each movement will be expressive, each attitude will depict a particular situation, each gesture will reveal a thought, each glance will convey a new sentiment."[24] The dancer's actions will be more animated and direct than the "most impassioned harangue," he continued in the same vein.[25] In other words, Noverre promised the advent, within the theater, of a new kind of communication, a means of conveying ideas and sentiments that recalled the techniques of antiquity and even prehistory insofar as this method faced none of the expressive limitations currently associated with words and could be effectively used to forward moral precepts in the present and future.

However, despite their forceful written articulation, Noverre's ideas about dance as a potentially expressive and didactic language were not immediately adopted in French theaters. Certainly, his treatise was celebrated in enlightened circles. Voltaire corresponded with Noverre on several occasions in ensuing years to praise his "work of genius." Calling the dancer alternately a Prometheus and a modern Pylades, the elderly philosopher expressed his astonishment that France had not made more of an effort to secure the services of the choreographer in an official capacity.[26] Likewise, the Abbé Claude-Henri de Fusée de Voisenon of the Académie Française wrote to Noverre to agree that ballet should be "a genuine poem and so made that the deaf could imagine they were spectators of a comedy or a tragedy."[27] And the Baron Grimm produced a long review in his *Correspondance littéraire* in which he claimed to be eager to see a "danced poem" taken from one of the finest tragedies.[28] Commentators even noted that interest in enacting such spectacles quickly took hold in private, upper-class settings, where Garrick's "scenes" were fashionable evening entertainments.[29] Yet the officials of the Paris Opéra, France's most important setting for musical theater, remained unconvinced. Following the publication of his *Lettres*, Noverre spent the next fifteen years abroad attempting to realize his prescriptions in compositions for the stages of Stuttgart, Vienna, and Milan under the patronage of various enlightened nobles and monarchs. Only gradually did a wider French public become convinced that pantomime constituted a potentially desirable path to progress, both within the theater and outside it.

GESTURES ON THE STAGE: A FIRST DEBATE

Louis-Sébastien Mercier was among those easily persuaded in the 1760s that the revival of the language of gesture was both highly desirable and inevitable. In his futuristic, utopian novel published in 1770 and entitled *L'An 2440*, Mercier predicted that by the twenty-fifth century the French theater would once again be a school of morals, virtues, and sentiments. One of the chief reasons for this happy turn of events, he prophesied, was that society would certainly have "resuscitated the art of pantomime, so dear to the ancients" by then.[30]

Pantomime actually returned to France in considerably fewer years than Mercier foresaw. In the two decades following the publication of Mercier's book, many of Noverre's suggested reforms were finally realized, and gestural expression became a central element of Parisian theatrical practice from the new boulevard theaters of Nicolet and Audinot to, finally, the stage of the royal Opéra. Indeed, the silent rhetoric of pantomime made its mark on many aspects of French urban culture at the close of the Old Regime. Choreographers were not the only people to experiment with new modes of bodily communication. Painters, following the lead of Jean-Baptiste Greuze and then Jacques-Louis David, increasingly relied upon dramatic gestures to depict domestic or historical scenes in the style of tragic pantomimes.[31] Rhetoricians encouraged public speakers to apply the lessons of recent writings on the gestural origin of language and the birth of pantomime to judicial and ecclesiastical oration.[32] Playwrights influenced by Diderot's *drames* called upon actors and actresses, in moments of great passion or distress, to give up speech in favor of silent displays of emotion.[33] Novelists offered detailed written descriptions of physical responses, especially on the part of their female characters, as a means of both depicting and conveying a *sensibilité* that ostensibly exceeded the capacity of words.[34] And following the dictates of Johann Caspar Lavater, who stressed the untrustworthiness and falsity of ordinary spoken language, even physiognomy, the ancient art of reading bodily and facial expressions as indices of moral character, found new practitioners.[35]

In fact, the vogue for gestural communication was so great by the middle of the decade after the publication of Mercier's novel that the hack dramatist Pierre Jean Baptiste Nougaret facetiously claimed it would only be a matter of time before speech became obsolete in many aspects of modern life—and with exceptionally positive results. Nougaret proposed in his *Traité du geste* of 1775 that by turning the contemporary mania for gestural communication to good use, society might well see shorter court trials, a reduction in poor writing and badly performed plays, an increase in the number of self-styled *savants*, and a general quieting of domestic disputes. Calling himself an *acteur pantomimiste*, Nougaret purported to desire nothing more than "to have in this genre all the inhabitants of the world for colleagues."[36]

The outposts of the fair theaters that sprang up along Paris's Boulevard du Temple in the 1760s and 1770s were the first places to try to put Noverre's precepts into practice. As before, these attempts to create nonverbal dramas had their origins primarily in economic and political necessity rather than aesthetic polemics. The official union in 1762 of the French actors of the Opéra-Comique with the Italian players of the Comédie-Italienne brought with it a series of new royal initiatives designed to restrict even further the acceptable theatrical practices of the minor stages of Paris. When, in 1769, the combined comic troupes finally won the exclusive rights to the *opéra-comique* and preliminary review and censorship of all dramatic productions of the lesser theaters, the ground was set for the newly established boulevard theaters, like the fair theaters before them, to expand once again their capabilities in the silent art of pantomime.[37]

Two men led the way in the development of this genre of entertainment in the 1770s and 1780s: Jean-Baptiste Nicolet, the proprietor of Les Grands-Danseurs du Roi (originally called the Théâtre de Nicolet when it was established in 1759), and Nicolas-Médard Audinot, the proprietor of a *spectacle* founded in 1769 and named the Ambigu-Comique in 1774. Audinot, in particular, sought out new ways to make the theater "speak first to the eyes, and to reach the heart or the mind only with the assistance of this organ," as he explained it in the advertisement preceding one of his librettos.[38] Under a banner reading *Sicut infantes audi nos* (meaning "Hear us speak as children" or "Hear us speak as those who possess no words speak"),[39] Audinot designed elaborate pantomimes—sentimental dramas, as well as fables, allegories, historical tales, and farces—underscored by expressive programmatic music and elaborate sets and performed by a cast of child actors and dancers.

Certainly, part of the appeal of such wordless productions was derived, as it was throughout the century, from their success in eluding the censors, whose mandate was to screen written expression alone.[40] But the attraction of Audinot's and Nicolet's performances for audiences from multiple social strata cannot simply be explained by reference to their subversive aspect. As Jean Charles Levacher de Charnois's *Journal des théâtres, ou le Nouveau spectateur* noted in 1777, "Audinot, Nicolet, without Actors, without Music, with some mediocre decorations, have discovered how to make all of Paris run to see their Pantomimes."[41] Boulevard pantomime theater even garnered praise in court circles during this period; by 1772, Audinot's troupe was so widely respected that Madame du Barry brought his players to Choisy-le-Roi to perform for the king, and the prince of Soubise invited them to Saint-Ouen.[42]

What, then, made Audinot's pantomimes so appealing to his broad audiences? For the radical journalist Simon-Nicolas Linguet, they represented the realization of the "revolution" in theater begun by "the celebrated Noverre." He explained:

> A small theater, almost unknown outside of Paris and worthy perhaps of more encouragement than it has received, the Ambigu-Comique has contributed more than one generally believes to make us feel the value of Pantomime. Le Sieur Audinot, a man full of talent and enthusiasm, has been the first to walk in the steps of Noverre. . . . He [Audinot] has realized with young Actors . . . some of the unbelievable things that the ancients tell us about the Mimes.[43]

Based on the *livrets* for the pantomimes that met with the greatest response from Audinot's and Nicolet's spectators, it is clear that gestures and miming were employed in successful productions both as a means to advance a story and as a vehicle for eliciting emotional responses. In Pierre-Germain Panseau's very popular pantomime *Sophie de Brabant* (Théâtre des Grands Danseurs du Roi, 1781), for example, specific indicative gestural signs constituted the building blocks of the narrative; one character, in a typical scene, by "applying two fingers to the mouth," conveys the need to keep quiet to another. But at other moments, expressive and mimic gestures were used to depict characters' mental states and passions in a vivid fashion; in the final scene of *Sophie de Brabant*, according to the *livret*, "trouble and dread are painted on his [the villain's] face. He wanders across the theater with faltering steps, like a man led by despair. He stops, absorbed in somber thoughts" and then proceeds to mime poisoning himself.[44] For audiences, this mixture of different kinds of gestural scenes proved to be highly effective. The ultimate pleasure one found in watching a spectacle at the Ambigu-Comique, Linguet continued, stemmed from the fact that Audinot, with his pantomimes, "has extracted tears, excited terror [and] admiration [in his spectators]; he has produced all the effects that are often missing on the great stages and in the best plays."[45]

Some critics of contemporary theater and dance were, however, unwilling to view Audinot's spectacle as a fully satisfactory answer to Noverre's *Lettres*. Louis de Laus de Boissy, a minor writer and comic playwright, pointed out in a letter to the editor of the *Spectateur français* in 1771 that one might get some vague idea of the nature of these proposed reforms by attending an evening's performance at the Ambigu-Comique. Yet he complained of his continual frustration while watching the opera ballet, and he begged Noverre to return to Paris in person "[to] give the Nation a new and interesting spectacle . . . [to] resuscitate the *jeux* of Rome and Athens."[46] For in the early 1770s, Noverre was at the height of his fame, creating multi-act dramatic and tragic ballets rooted in pantomime for the opera houses of Vienna and many other European capitals, with the exception of Paris.

Gradually, following the appointment in 1770 of a new ballet master, the celebrated dancer Gaetan Vestris, the climate at the Paris Opéra began to grow more hospitable to Noverre's ideas. Vestris had himself danced in Noverre's ballets in Stuttgart in the preceding decade, and first in 1770 and again in early 1776, Vestris introduced the *ballet d'action* to the Paris Opéra by restaging Noverre's *ballet tragique* entitled *Jason et Medée* [see Fig. 2] and giving himself the maskless title role.[47] Soon Vestris gained some influential aesthetic allies. During 1775, the assistant ballet master at the Opéra, Maximilien Gardel, wrote a lengthy introduction to his own "allegorical ballet on the subject of the coronation of the King [Louis XVI]" in which he lamented that the "restorer" of the *ballet d'action* was forced to make his reputation at foreign courts, "where his genius did not find itself constrained in perpetual shackles."[48] Finally, in late 1776, as a result of the intervention of the Empress Maria Theresa, who had recommended Noverre to her daughter, Marie-Antoinette, the itinerant ballet master returned to Paris.

The fall of 1776 marked Noverre's debut as a choreographer at that key royal institution, the Paris Opéra. He began with two uncontroversial ballets, *Apelles et Campaspe* and *Les Caprices de Galathée*. Then, in January 1777, with much fanfare, Noverre presented an epic, full-length *ballet d'action*, *Les Horaces et les Curiaces*, in the presence of the queen.[49] A five-act, mimed version of Corneille's well-known tragedy, this work, set to the music of Josef Starzer, marked Noverre's most ambitious essay to date in this new wordless genre. It was also clearly meant to be a significant advance beyond the tentative experiments of the Duchess of Maine with the same subject. Over the next four years, Noverre preceded to choreograph and restage many other ballets in both this novel style and more traditional ones.[50]

JASON ET MEDEE   BALLET TRAGIQUE.

FIG. 2. "Jason et Medée, ballet tragique," caricature by Francesco Barto-
lozzi (London, 1781). Etching and aquatint, 41.5 x 47 cm. Depicted, left to
right, in Noverre's famous *ballet d'action* are Giovanna Baccelli as
Creusa, Gaetano Vestris as a heroic Jason, and Mme Simonet as Medea
armed with a knife. Cia Fornaroli Collection, Dance Division, the New
York Public Library for the Performing Arts, Astor, Lenox and Tilden
Foundations.

In many regards, however, Noverre's years in Paris were not the success that one might have expected. The alliance between Noverre and
the other members of the company was quickly fraught with tensions,
and many of his compositions were poorly received by audiences and
critics alike. Finally, in 1781, he was forced out of Paris, leaving Maximilien Gardel to fill his shoes as ballet master. As Noverre himself
commented hyperbolically in the introduction to the second edition of
his *Lettres* in 1783, "They shouted anathemas; they treated me as an in-

novator; and they regarded me as a man that much more dangerous insofar as I attacked the ancient rubrics of the Theater."[51] Nevertheless, his
reforms were imitated and respected by subsequent choreographers
across Europe, and Noverre boasted that as a result of his efforts, the
Paris Opéra "finally emerged from its childhood; it spoke the language of
the passions that it had not previously even stammered. Pantomime,
this art that was once the delight of Athens and Rome, left its tomb, became associated with dance, and, in lending [dance] its eloquence, acquired itself a charm that it did not have either among the Greeks or the
Romans."[52]

One significant result of both the pantomimes of the Parisian boulevards and the *ballets d'action* of the Opéra was, in fact, the advent of an
extensive public argument for and against the form, effects, and content
of these gestural spectacles. During the last two decades of the Old Regime, a second generation of *philosophes* and an assortment of writers of
all types engaged in numerous debates over contemporary cultural phenomena. The Republic of Letters seems to have thrived on these kinds
of extended disputes. Indeed, the war of the Gluckistes and Piccinistes
over the future of French opera and the fight between the physiocrats
and their opponents over the regulation of the grain trade are only two of
the better known examples. Beginning around 1770, the new gestural
practices of the French theater, from the *drame* to the *ballet d'action*,
generated the same type of enthusiasms in articles, pamphlets, reviews,
and even a new literary form, the polemical prefaces to *livrets*. The very
partisan *Mercure de France* described the "public" in 1781 as "split . . .
into two factions" on the subject, depending in part on where one stood
on that "monstrous old Horace" of Noverre.[53] And in the course of the
reign of Louis XVI, these arguments spilled over from the boulevards all
the way to the court at Versailles. For at stake in this disagreement was
not only the issue of whether or not pantomime could stand alone as a
form of entertainment, as Noverre had proposed. Neither was it simply a
matter of the validity of the hierarchy of genres traditionally enforced
(along with standards of language usage) by the Académie Française.
Rather, just like the seemingly minor subjects of some of the better
documented controversies of late Old Regime, the new gestural practices of the French theater served as a springboard for a broader conversation about the goals and aspirations appropriate to an enlightened society.[54] What makes these debates about pantomime especially interesting is that, at their core, they revolved around the question of how the
development of new modes of communication in the theater might
permanently alter the nature of public discussion itself. While one side
saw in pantomime the potential to transform the exchange of ideas and
sentiments and, in this manner, to ameliorate modern social relations,

the other saw in this ancient sign system a dangerous precedent for the future of both morality and sociability.

Let us, therefore, consider the arguments of the most vocal advocates of a silent theater before we approach the negative reactions that such experiments (and the polemics around them) provoked. Not surprisingly, a certain number of the proponents of these new spectacles, such as the Abbé Arnaud and the Marquis de Chastellux, were members of official academies or frequent participants in other high Enlightenment institutions and activities during the last decades of the Old Regime. Others, like Diderot, hovered at the margins of these circles. Still others formed part of the Grub Street of hack writers, journalists, and *frondeurs littéraires* that included men like Restif de la Bretonne, Mercier, Nougaret, and Linguet.[55] Such a diverse group necessarily entered this debate with a variety of aims and motivations ranging from concern with the ethical content of contemporary theater to a more general antiestablishment impulse. To some degree, then, their arguments necessarily betrayed their social and political heterogeneity. Yet the aesthetic philosophies of these individuals stemmed from many common suppositions, foremost among them those that they borrowed from the linguistic and anthropological literature of the previous few decades. Where Condillac had used aesthetic history and theory to bolster his epistemological and social claims, pantomime's supporters now relied upon recent explanations of language origins and human psychology to argue for broad changes in the social function of the arts. Increasingly, the question of the moral role of the theater became bound up in metaphysical debates about the representation and transmission of ideas.

In the first place, proponents of the revival of pantomime endlessly repeated that the purpose of all dance was, as the poet Claude-Joseph Dorat put it, "to speak without words, and to paint without brushes."[56] Dance at its most effective, concurred a poet named Duplain, was a form of "mute eloquence," a "too rare language" used as "a true form of declamation."[57] Such linguistic analogies were, of course, common to late eighteenth-century discussions of all the various arts since it was widely assumed that, at their origins, dance, poetry, music, and even architecture were but complementary methods of communication, outgrowths of a single, original language.[58] But reformers hoped that this emphasis on the initial and, hence, natural semiotic function of dance would help to justify the development of a new form of physical theater, one in which movements, gestures, and facial expression would serve, once again, as "signs" of the passions, weaknesses, vices, and virtues of human life.

That said, the desire to see pantomime as the basis of a new form of dance was, however, never simply a question of making dance into a

form of communication comparable to speech. Advocates of the introduction of pantomime into ballet also eagerly attacked certain kinds of
representational dance, including the allegorical ballets that had long
been composed to illustrate abstract concepts in both Jesuit education
and absolutist political culture. In his often-quoted essay on dance, Dorat, for example, ridiculed the old court ballets that required performers'
bodies to be used as conventional signs for unrelated and often complex
ideas:

> If one wanted to personify the world, one gave the dancer Mount Olym-
> pus for a coiffure and a geographic map for clothing: one wrote France in
> capital letters on the stomach; Germany on the abdomen; Italy on the
> arm; and on the backside, *Terre australe* or *Terre inconnue*. That is, ap-
> proximately, the idea which one should have of these cold allegories
> which usurped for so long the title of *grands Ballets*.[59]

The major problem with these "imitations of imitations," as Rousseau
explained it in his entry on ballet in the *Supplément à l'Encyclopédie*
published in 1776, was that they required spectators to decipher and to
interpret characters and events in both a literal and a parallel, symbolic
sense. This, in turn, created the potential for both enigmatic exchanges
and estrangement: "All the art in these sorts of Dramas consists of presenting purely intellectual relationships in the form of sensible images,
and of making the Spectator think something entirely different from
what he sees, as if, far from binding him to the Stage, there was merit in
distancing him from it."[60] Supporters of the new silent theater stressed
instead the importance of creating gestural spectacles that built on the
distinctive capacity of the body to produce naturally expressive signs,
signs that resisted transposition or interpretation into words precisely
because they did not follow the representational operations of conventional language. As the Marquis de Chastellux noted, dialogue and pantomime could happily coexist within an opera because "their means of
painting the same thing are very different."[61] Ultimately, late eighteenth-century literature on the reform of dance was structured as much
by the distinctions between these two forms of communication—one
the language of words, the other the language of gestures—as by the
similarities.

But what were these differences? Here the *Journal des théâtres, ou le
Nouveau spectateur* provides some guidelines. Speech, or the "artificial
language of the mind," explained a journalist in this paper in 1777, was
best suited to cold logic and abstract matters, was entirely variable according to social class and standards of *bon usage*, and lent itself to myr-
iad forms of "abuse."[62] In contrast, natural gestural and facial signs were
the special province of the sentiments and the imagination; they gave

energy to ideas; and they belonged to all people around the world, regardless of social station or character, from the *philosophe* to the ignoramus, from the nobleman to the artisan.[63] Most important, at this moment of doubt about the trustworthiness of linguistic statements, this journal proposed that pantomimic gestures were never subject to either misuse or misinterpretation because they constituted the language of the soul or truth. As Noverre himself explained in an essay of 1774, "a man who studies his counterpart will often be deceived by his speeches." But one who reads his fellow man's gestures and expressions "will find in his external signs either confirmation of his sentiments or the exact opposite of his argument."[64] As such, this potent form of silent communication was increasingly presented as a semiotic ideal: an invariable, mimological form of expression. Mercier summarized this position in his *Mon Bonnet de nuit*:

> Gesture, which is the voice of the body, has an expressivity that vocal tones do not. Gesture speaks with a precipitation and an energy that sometimes makes [verbal] language a weak and useless method. . . . [W]hat a spoken word has never known how to do, a gesture executes in the twinkling of an eye. . . . A gesture is clear, never equivocal; it does not lie. . . . Pantomime actors, if one lets them do it, will succeed in Paris, as in Rome, by chasing all the speaking and declaiming actors from the theater.[65]

But according to its chief supporters, the real benefit of the new pantomime theater had less to with representational efficacy than with the way all this staged gesticulation impacted its audience. It followed from these epistemological principles, they believed, that an idea or sentiment conveyed through naturally expressive bodily signs acted with extraordinary force on an interlocutor or audience member, producing an immediate reaction that it was impossible for dialogue (which required mental processing and interpretation) to emulate. At its most effective, therefore, pantomime served to re-create the communicative utopia of the original, hypothetical "society" in the space of the theater and to cast spectators and performers alike back into the role of the first signing couple. In Condillac's fiction, natural signs of distress had initially generated both the need for and the tools of communication. In the theater, similarly natural, universal expressions of transient passions, from tears to flailing limbs, were believed to be capable of producing sincere and profound emotional reactions, themselves often physically manifested in involuntary tears, sighs, and other corporeal demonstrations on the part of the audience.[66] According to one recent historian of the bourgeois *drame*, in the theater of this period the bodies of actors and spectators alike became "sign-producing instruments," making visible and legible the moral values that the particular composition was designed to circulate.[67] Thus, for contemporary commentators, the audience's physical reactions—their immediacy, intensity, and authenticity—constituted an indicator of the effectiveness of the spectacle on the stage. And on this scale, according to its defenders, pantomime scored exceedingly well. Based on Cahusac's testimony, Laus de Boissy claimed that, in antiquity, spectators watching "the dance of Ajax" were prone to "become imbued with the same furors that animated the Greek Hero, to strip off their clothes like him, to stir up a fight, and often, to come to blows."[68] More recently, trumpeted a contemporary guidebook to Paris, the responses of Audinot's audiences demonstrated that the master of silent spectacles had discovered "the secret of interesting and moving [the public] to the point of exciting its laughter and provoking its tears at his will."[69] Such was the role of pantomime in the culture of sensibility that flourished at the end of the Old Regime.

There was, of course, a certain irony in literate, upper-class Parisian male writers advocating the essentially base language of the body as the basis for a new kind of communicative experience. First, emphatic gesticulation had long been associated with the unschooled and the provincial rather than the elite and urban; earlier eighteenth-century aestheticians, from Dubos to Watelet, had, in fact, despaired of painters ever locating models of natural expressivity in upper-class settings, where the outward and physical expression of emotion had gradually become undesirable.[70] Second, an emotionally expressive body, and, especially, blushes and tears, were commonly thought to be the special province of women and children (though, in the case of women, such physical reactions were often assumed to be strategic and feigned rather than instinctive). Indeed, polite sociability increasingly demanded that men refrain from excessive displays of passion or sentiment, something excitable and irrational women were considered less capable of doing.[71] But now, the new gestural theater could be presented as a means of erasing these distinctions, at least temporarily, in a way that class-bound and even gender-specific words could not. And for its male literary champions, the fact that pantomime could be used both to depict and to speak in similar terms to people from all walks of life gave it much of its force. The new gestural theater seemed to promise the restoration of a timeless, natural utopia, where men and women alike could experience a common bond based on their shared human natures. As the engraver Charles-Nicolas Cochin explained in defense of his proposal for a new genre of operatic spectacle entitled a *pantomime dramatique*: "It is an almost strict imitation of nature that can fail to strike you the first time but incite tears the second; in the end, nature is always the strongest."[72] For Cochin maintained that pantomime evoked in its audience a long-forgotten but universally affecting sound, "the cry of nature."

It was precisely the possibility of generating this kind of collective emotional experience that lent gestural communication the potential to become a form of public moral instruction. Theatrical reformers, such as Nicolas Edme Restif de la Bretonne, argued that what he called *le mimisme*, or "the noble as well as useful Art of explaining with energy the diverse passions of men," could be used not only to animate edifying dramas and to help convey moral messages in narrative form but also to generate a new kind of integrated sociability or community based on the audience's shared investment in apprehending emotional truths through a set of naturally expressive and transparent signs.[73] Both Restif de la Bretonne and Mercier hoped to find ways to use the emotions incited in individual audience members by means of such devices as *tableaux vivants* to dissolve differences of opinion, to strengthen social bonds, and, finally, to unite a heterogeneous public, through identification, in pity and compassion.[74] In this manner, they believed that they might truly be able to use the theater to transform moral attitudes. Noverre, of course, claimed to have found a way to realize exactly these effects with his historical and mythological works such as *Les Horaces*. Nicolet too, various journalists insisted, had finally turned his pantomime theater into a school for morals by presenting such hybrid dramatic works as Mayeur de Saint Paul's *L'Elève de la nature*, a lesson in the relationship between natural language and natural morality delivered in bodily actions as well as words.[75] But critics continued to condemn the majority of contemporary theaters for offering spectacular and morally bankrupt fare—and to insist that the full potential for pantomime theater to serve as a means of changing the world had yet to be appreciated in Europe.

To find true illustrations of the power and utility of pantomime, champions of the new art form turned instead to other parts of the globe, exotic places where it was assumed that people were living closer to the state of nature and farther away from the corrupting powers of abstract modern languages. The last decades of the Old Regime saw a growing number of travel reports testifying to the prevalence of pantomime in distant non-Western or "primitive" cultures. George Forster noted the "pantomime drama[s]" of Tahiti;[76] Claude Etienne Savary described the eloquent "ballet-pantomimes, by which they [the natives] represent the actions of communal life" in modern Egypt;[77] the Abbé Raynal referred to the seductive "pantomimes of love" common to the West Indies;[78] Pierre-Augustin Guys pointed out the "mobile tableaux" used by dancers "to explain interesting situations and facts" in modern Greece.[79] Furthermore, following Lafitau, numerous authors from Jean-Bernard Bossu to Jacques Grasset de Saint-Sauveur commented on the predilection of American Indians for pantomimes, hieroglyphics, and all types of

Pl. 18. Tom. 1. pag. 522.

FIG. 3. Iroquois Dances, plate from Lafitau's *Moeurs des sauvages amériquains* (1724). Lafitau's detailed descriptions and depictions of Native American rituals were an important source for later eighteenth-century French writers on dance and gestural communication. Photograph courtesy of the General Research Division, the New York Public Library, Astor, Lenox and Tilden Foundations.

pictorial and gestural sign-making [see Fig. 3].[80] Even southern Europeans were objects of study in this regard. In his 1777 study of Sicily, the
Comte de Borch noted the "national penchant for gestures" and remarked that normal conversation among Sicilians constituted "the
most sublime pantomime that I have ever seen in my life."[81] In fact, in
most of these cases, authors drew attention to the exotic gestural practices that they had witnessed in order to contrast the physical means of
expression common to less evolved cultures with the communicative
norms of eighteenth-century France. When, that same decade, Louis
Antoine Bougainville brought a Tahitian named Aotourou back to Paris,
the celebrated around-the-world explorer reported that he was surprised
to discover that amidst all the spectacles of life in the French capital,
only the opera appealed to the "savage"; though cultural differences
made it impossible for Aotourou to learn the French language, he
understood the opera "because he passionately loved dance."[82] In the
purportedly over-civilized world of eighteenth-century, upper-class, urban sociability, the refined physicality of the pre-Noverre opera ballet
had, ironically, almost come to seem like the last bastion of natural
expressivity.

But for advocates of the new gestural theater, the real failure of most
European dance was that it rarely found itself directed toward either
morally or socially useful ends. When the pantomimes of foreign cultures and the primitive taste for bodily expression found their way into
contemporary French writing about dance, such examples served not
simply as a way to reproach Europeans for their loss of contact with the
original, universal language but also as a means to illustrate the important public function that pantomime had played in different settings—
and could perhaps play again in France. Specifically, illustrations of
other national practices showed that bodily movement had the potential to serve as the basis of a potent public rhetoric that could draw individuals together around a common cause. For the Abbé François Arnaud, whose "Mémoire sur les danses chinoises" appeared in the first
volume of his *Variétés littéraires* of 1768, the example of ancient Chinese dance made evident "how much the signs, and if one can explain it
thus, the hieroglyphics of this art, have lost their nobility and importance. Dance . . . once explained not only actions, but predilections, habits, manners; it illustrated the greatest events."[83] Similarly, the minor
romancier Charles Compan included much information about the battle pantomimes and funeral dances of the American Indians in his extensive *Dictionnaire de danse* in order to demonstrate the utility of imitative dance as a means of political oration—a function not evident in
the modern West where, he claimed, a stubbornly inexpressive written
idiom made it difficult even to describe the primitive rites in question.[84]

Even Moreau de Saint-Méry, whose brief essay on the dances of the Cre-
oles rested on the already outdated premise that the art of dance was initially born of spontaneous joy rather than a desire to communicate, explained the relative restraint of European dances by the fact that people
in northern climes, such as the French, were obliged "to live practically
without communicating among themselves."[85] The implication of all of
these statements was not just that every culture got the kind of dance
that it deserved but that pantomime had the potential to affect the world
beyond the confines of the theater.

Indeed, by the eve of the Revolution, descriptions of the "natural"
pantomime performances of exotic places had become useful to late
eighteenth-century French moral reformers as indicators of the need for
regeneration in the modern, Western world and, ultimately, blueprints
for how a more virtuous and harmonious order might be constructed.
Witness the case of Jacques-Henri Bernardin de Saint-Pierre's best-
selling novel *Paul et Virginie* of 1788. Unlike many of his Enlightenment contemporaries, Bernardin de Saint-Pierre made explicit the biblical precedent for his vision of a natural and atemporal paradise.[86] However, the qualities of this golden age (here a product of modern colonial-
ism) have everything in common with those of Condillac's picture of the
first society, down to the original, youthful, gesticulating lovers. In a
crucial passage in this book, the author reminds the reader that pantomime "is the first language of man and is known in all nations; it is so
natural and expressive that the children of the white settlers lose no
time in learning it themselves once they have seen it practiced by the
black children."[87] Bernardin de Saint-Pierre uses the two children's pantomime performance to demonstrate not only the pleasures to be derived from living entirely in accord with nature but also the connection
between natural expression and virtue. By the close of the 1780s, pantomime represented nothing less than one potential means of recovering the values and social practices associated with an earlier, more innocent world, a now-forgotten state of peace and social harmony that had
preceded the "fall" toward opaque, conventional signs. And in this fictional context, such scenes offered a hint of what might still be possible
in a spatially and socially controlled environment such as that created
(in the case of Bernardin de Saint-Pierre's novel) by Christian values, imperial politics, and the luck of island geography.

Yet for all the success of such images, not all commentators believed
that this critical celebration of a lost pantomimic language represented a
promising development within contemporary French culture. Two very
different kinds of argument against the new gestural theater emerged in
the late eighteenth century right alongside the principal statements in
its favor. One line of reasoning outlined the epistemological limitations

and shortcomings of gestural communication. The other addressed that which natural bodily signs seemed to do only too well.

First and foremost, numerous critics complained that gestures simply did not work (and never would) as successful means of communication in the modern world. Hostile pamphlets attacking Noverre's innovations as ineffective made their first appearance in the early 1770s in the context of the choreographer's efforts to stage his works in various Italian cities. Initially, these diatribes were the weapons of a territorial war that Noverre waged with his chief rival, the Italian choreographer Gasparo Angiolini, who had also spent the last decade crisscrossing Europe in order to stage danced dramas rooted in the mimic practices of antiquity.[88] In a series of pamphlets, Angiolini and various acolytes attacked Noverre for his many failures, including his misguided efforts to explain complex and even metaphysical concepts—ideas that depended upon a literary program—through movement and dance.[89] Soon they were joined by foes of the *ballet d'action* in general, writers in various European capitals who insisted that gestures could never function as the equivalent of words and that it was absurd to try to develop such projects either in theory or practice. The most prolific of these critics was a writer and friend of the adventurer Casanova named Ange Goudar, an itinerant commentator on questions of music and theater who often wrote under the name of his wife, Sara. Earlier, in 1759, Goudar had penned a savage satire of the *ballets-pantomimes* then prevalent on Parisian stages; in this pamphlet, he had argued that even if certain concepts were difficult to convey verbally, gestures could hardly be expected to compensate for the shortcomings of speech, and he had insisted that the proof of the impossibility of this new, silent genre lay in its obligatory reliance on printed librettos.[90] Now in Italy in the mid-1770s, Goudar took up many of the same themes—the difficulty of following a pantomimed drama (as evidenced by the need for programs); the impossibility of conveying moral messages, correcting popular prejudices, or presenting historical events through gestural means; and the silliness of all the recent philosophical speculation about the uses of the legs and feet—in a new series of essays concerning the *ballets d'action* currently popular in Italy.[91] In all of these texts, Goudar emphasized once again the false equation of dance and language:

> Do we need the ancients in order to follow the laws of nature? Must we consult the Romans in order to know that we have *la langue* to explain our passions and feet to transport us from one place to another; that one is the mirror of our soul and the other only an active faculty? . . . It is much easier for a man or a woman to say I love you than to go search for this expression in *tours de jambes*, which, not being designed to explain love, cannot convey it.[92]

Meanwhile, as Goudar's essays made their way from Venice to Northern Europe, similar complaints greeted the Parisian pantomime productions of both the boulevards and the Opéra during the same years. Opponents of these *jeux muets* formed as heterogeneous a group of literary figures as did pantomime's partisan supporters. Yet these critics found themselves united in opposition to what they took to be the ludicrousness of pitting gesture against speech, especially given the prevailing Aristotelian belief that the ability to form and to use words was the key source of humans' potential for perfection. And these critics tended, like Goudar, to gravitate toward satire and a dismissive irony as strategies for making this point. It shocked common sense, claimed one typical opponent calling himself only the Baron ***, to think dance could explain anything as well as even mediocre oration; otherwise, why had Cicero not simply become a "mute Orator?"[93] Furthermore, he asked after facetiously "testifying . . . how completely mortified I am not to have the secret of making myself understood without speaking," why did he, as the author of this pamphlet, find himself requiring words to articulate this argument?[94] Such comments, designed to defend the pleasure of pure dance *divertissements* by exposing the idea of a gestural "language" as a ridiculous folly or chimera, only increased after Noverre arrived in the French capital to display his pantomimed dramas. Many reviewers—even those who had greeted the prospect of his residence in Paris with pleasure—found Noverre's *Les Horaces* to be, at best, slightly silly, and, at worst, a pure "logogriphe," or completely unintelligible language.[95] To take one example, the chronicler Jean-François de La Harpe, who had tried to excuse Noverre's initial failures by blaming the conservative culture of the Opéra, now attacked the weaknesses of the *ballet-pantomime* as a genre of communication by paraphrasing Dubos: "As someone once said very well, there are things that no pantomime can render, such as the famous *qu'il mourût* [of Horace]: how can this word be danced?"[96] Or, as the Chevalier de Meude-Monpas put it in an effort to denounce the recent turn in opera ballet, it was impossible to take any interest in "a man who jumps to explain his sadness."[97]

The argument against pantomime as an effective form of language did, however, also find several serious exponents in the 1780s, critics who developed their case by re-examining the status of gestures as communicative signs. Among the most important of these critiques was elaborated in 1785 by an author of *drames moraux*, professor of philosophy and rhetoric, and member of the Academy of Berlin named Johann Jacob Engel. Translated into French three years later as *Idées sur le geste et l'action théâtrale*, these polemical letters constituted a massive effort to systematize and to codify (through both illustration and written description) the precise gestures that an actor should make in order to convey specific emotions.[98] Yet Engel was adamantly opposed to Noverre's notion that pantomime or the actor's *jeu* could form the basis of non-verbal dramas; indeed, he refused to accept the idea of pantomime as a *langage* or compensatory alternative to discursive speech. Why? According to both the French translator of this work and the original German author, pantomime was based on a false premise. Spectators were fooled into believing that "this would-be language of gesture" could produce an "aesthetic" or intuitively affecting experience only because their minds were working overtime to recall past associations that they might attach to these ultimately indeterminate, equivocal, and uncertain signs.[99] Similarly, in a series of learned treatises, the French aesthetic theorist Michel Paul Guy de Chabanon proposed that Noverre's efforts to "imitate" nature, like those of programmatic composers, necessarily failed because of an epistemological deceit:

> Just as modulated sounds do not themselves have a precise and distinct signification, movements, [and] the gestures that result from them, do not either. Music and Dance say nothing positive to the mind. Their effect is a sensation and, as a result, remains somehow sketchy. Mental labor is required to attach a situation or analogous words to this sensation; and it is this operation which makes Dance and Music both imitative arts.[100]

Together, Chabanon and Engel, with their mutual focus on the necessity of subjective interpretation on the part of spectators, attempted to dash the late Enlightenment dream of naturally signifying gestures as the key to true, unmediated, and thoroughly transparent exchange.

Yet not all criticisms of pantomime theater were rooted in the dismissal of the equation of pantomime with the original and most potent of semiotic systems. Certain important Enlightenment figures—most notably, Jean-François Marmontel—attacked all plans for the expanded use of theatrical pantomime precisely because they feared just how powerful a means of expression gestural and mimic signs could be. Throughout the Old Regime, Catholic moralists had, of course, continued to rail against the dangers inherent not only in partaking of but also in watching all forms of dance—a hedonistic exercise that inflamed the spectator's passions through the eyes and threatened to harm the soul.[101] What worried a new group of secular critics was that pantomime appeared to be that much more potent as a means of conveying emotions and sentiments than any previously known form of entertainment. Dismissing recent arguments that the stages of the boulevards had become infected with a new moral spirit, various minor literary figures, such as Charles Desprez de Boissy, denounced the pantomime theaters precisely because of their success in awakening dangerous desires and temptations. The primary threat of these novel spectacles, according to Desprez de Boissy, came not from the ideas conveyed (as he was quite sanguine about the reading of plays based on similar subjects), but from the manner of their live depiction or "declamation." Much like pantomime's advocates, he touted the affective power of an actor's gestures: "[T]hrough them, hearts can speak to each other immediately, without help from words; and a single gesture can convey with great force a passionate sentiment that a Poet could only weakly explain."[102] But from this assumption, he deduced that pantomimed theater and, especially, dance ("an imitative art whose object is to incline hearts toward vice by painting the most lively passions, such as those that M. Dorat traced in his didactic Poem on Declamation") could only be a pernicious source of moral corruption.[103]

The most visible writer to take this stance was Marmontel, an author of moral tales and opera librettist, as well as the *historiographe de France*. Marmontel articulated his position in a prominent article entitled "Pantomime" in the *Supplément à l'Encyclopédie*, which appeared in print in the middle of Noverre's controversial tenure at the Opéra. Despite the fact that the Chevalier de Jaucourt had already produced a lengthy article under the same heading in the original *Encyclopédie*, Marmontel decided that the *Supplément* of 1776–77 required another, and he elected to write it himself, most likely because the new theater was a subject about which he held strong opinions. In earlier entries on both *pantomime* and *langage*, Jaucourt had followed Diderot, Cahusac, and others in taking the position that the *langage d'action* had been the first language of the world and continued to be the most expressive.[104] Marmontel did not dispute these claims in his new article. He too stressed the connections between the original *langage* and pantomime, and he emphasized the latter's enduring warmth and force as a means of communication. In fact, like Desprez, Marmontel seems to have been convinced that an actor's gestures were often more potent than an actor's words. This distinction in terms of impact stemmed from a divergence both in the way an actor approached and an audience member mentally processed the two different types of signs:

> [P]antomime speaks to the eyes a more passionate *langage* than that of words; it is even more vehement than eloquence, and no *langue* is in a position to equal it in terms of force or warmth. In pantomime all is in action, nothing languishes; one's attention is not exhausted; while surrendering to the pleasure of being moved, one can almost spare oneself the pain of thinking, or, if ideas are present, they are vague like dreams. Speech slows down and chills action, it preoccupies the actor and makes his art more difficult. Pantomime owes everything to gestural expression; his [the pantomime's] movements are not planned; passion alone is

his guide. . . . [O]ne [the actor] is enslaved to the sentiments and to the thought of other people, the other [the pantomime] surrenders and abandons himself to the movements of his own soul.[105]

In effect, within this paragraph lauding the effectiveness of pantomime, Marmontel disclosed the essence of his fears. If acting demanded a kind of slavery to the text, pantomime, he claimed, constituted an extreme form of liberty, a freedom to represent one's own subjective emotions and sensations without any checks. Moreover, the pantomime performer's expressive gesticulation functioned as a form of seduction, rendering viewers passive victims of their own imaginations. Instead of developing spectators' capacity for clear, rational judgments about fixed notions, it cast them back into the realm of indistinct emotions and bodily sensations that Marmontel associated with the natural state. Rather than moderating the passions, this figurative language simply inflamed them. Hence, Marmontel continued, it was no accident that the reign of pantomime theater in Rome had corresponded with the most dissolute and decadent period of its history. Pantomime, an effeminate and base form of entertainment, could have no value as a form of moral instruction.[106] If the government did not currently take steps to discourage the flourishing of *ballets-pantomimes* and other forms of gestural theater, he warned, French culture could soon meet the same fate.

In a certain sense, Marmontel's aesthetics appear to owe more to the classicism of the seventeenth century than to the late Enlightenment culture of sensibility. His antipathy to the expression of obscure sentiments and temptations, and his desire for masculine order and reason in face of primitive and messy passions, betray a strong debt to an earlier age.[107] Yet, in another way, Marmontel, the Encyclopedist, simply articulated the growing and widespread fears of many of the *philosophes* who found themselves confronted by an outpouring of sentimental "free" expression beginning in the 1770s.[108] This attitude ultimately made itself manifest in the realm of language theory as well. In an essay that he read before the Académie Française in 1785, Marmontel, a member of that body's new "enlightened" cohort, denounced in strong terms the static and abuse-ridden notion of *bon usage* established by the court and *le monde*, "whose language turns on a small number of words, most vague and confused, with equivocal or half-veiled senses, as is suitable to politeness, dissimulation, extreme reserve, light jesting, refined malice, or skillful flattery."[109] But this opponent of purism and advocate of "a more masculine vigor and a more naive truthfulness" in literary language also rejected the idea that academicians might accept the unchecked flourishing of the expressions of the unschooled, or *le peuple*, which he associated with the restoration of the irrational language of the passions and the dissolution of the standard written idiom. On both the aesthetic and the linguistic front, what Marmontel, like many of his contemporaries, sought at the close of the Old Regime was an enriched and even gradually democratized idiom that lent itself to rational, philosophical controls. And even in its heyday, Noverre's revival of pantomime seemed, in practice, to disappoint as many people as it encouraged.

Yet Marmontel's critique of the new theater left unanswered certain vital questions. Could gestural communication, with all its directness and force, ever be harnessed to rational ends? Might it be possible to attach natural, universal signs to referents other than the passions? And could a class of *philosophes* or men of reason maintain control of the process? These were issues that demanded responses outside the realm of dance or drama.

Within the hierarchical, corporate culture of the late Old Regime, the aesthetic arena initially offered one important site for experimentation with new forms of communication. Noverre's writings marked the first major attempt to resuscitate Condillac's model of a *langage d'action* for modern, didactic ends. And after 1770, the enlightened ballet master's ideas found a temporary home both in the official center of French opera and in the often oppositional, non-elite realm of Parisian boulevard theater, where these projects generated considerable public debate. However, once the problems inherent in Noverre's example as a model for a broader form of cultural regeneration became fully evident, enlightened attention increasingly turned toward another site of semiotic experimentation, the classroom, and toward a different plan for how to make use of the original pantomimic idiom, namely, as a pedagogic tool. What distinguished these new efforts is that their inventors tried to make up for the shortcomings of the *ballet d'action*—its inability to convey complex moral abstractions, on the one hand, and its potentially irrational seductiveness, on the other—by applying to the original bodily idiom the method of thinking and language-construction that Condillac had referred to as *analyse*. Here, in "methodical" sign language, a new vision of a representational and communicative ideal was worked out just in time to play an important role in the shaping of the Revolution.

3

Pantomime as Pedagogy, 1760–89

Only a few years after the appearance of Noverre's treatise calling for the creation of a dance theater rooted in the natural language of gesture, France witnessed a second surge of interest in the potential uses of pantomime. Now it was theorists of pedagogy who were inspired by the idea of a primordial, universal *langage d'action*. In the course of the 1760s, a small number of educators and philosophers, including Jean-Jacques Rousseau, began to suggest that recent speculation about the origins and progress of language could be instrumental in reforming how children were taught to think and to communicate. What these educators proposed was that a pedagogy which, in the rarefied space of the classroom, retraced the natural development of language from the first gestural *langage* all the way to advanced written *langues*, could help mold individual beings (and, eventually, whole communities) capable of avoiding common and deleterious mistakes about the meaning of words. Soon others sought to make the language of gesture into a full-fledged *langue* in its own right. The success of this plan was such that by the late 1780s, the original language of signs, expanded according to the principles of the analytic method to cover an extraordinary range of human sentiments and ideas, finally came to seem like a solution to one of the key epistemological problems of modern life. After two decades of experimentation, this revamped gestural idiom promised to provide nothing less than a method for overcoming the present-day variability of opinions and for achieving certainty in thought and communication once again. As such, pedagogical innovation can be said to have provided the foundation for the development of both a new social and moral vision and a new style of political intervention in the last years of the Old Regime.

A NEW KIND OF TEACHING

Of course, in any discussion of pedagogical reform in Old Regime France, one has to keep in mind that few French men and even fewer French women received much by way of formal education, even at elementary levels, before the very last years of the century. It is also important to remember that those who did were generally educated within the confines of the Catholic church, which retained extraordinary control over the practice of teaching. Girls who left their familial homes for further training often attended convent schools attached to religious sisterhoods. Boys from prosperous families were typically schooled first in *petites écoles* and then at institutions called *collèges* run by members of one of the various Catholic orders. The final step, should a young man choose to continue, was likely to be attendance at one of the old universities to study theology, law, or medicine.

The majority of the *philosophes* followed exactly this path. Rousseau was a notable exception, being self-taught except for a few years spent in a private pension with a Protestant minister outside Geneva. But the educations of Condillac and Diderot, despite their divergent social backgrounds, conformed to this model. Condillac was schooled at a Jesuit *collège* in Lyon, followed by the seminary of Saint-Sulpice and, finally, the Sorbonne; Diderot was educated at a Jesuit *collège* in Langres and the Jansenist Collège d'Harcourt in Paris, before going on to the University of Paris for a masters of arts.

This common intellectual debt did not, however, prevent criticism of the educational practices followed by Catholic institutions from becoming a recurrent feature of Enlightenment discourse in the second half of the eighteenth century. The *philosophes* directed their critiques largely at a pedagogy that was rooted in what Helvétius referred to in *De l'Esprit* as "the insipid study of words" and D'Alembert, in the *Encyclopédie* article "Collège," called learning "how to speak without saying anything."[1] For in the Jesuit system, in particular, the whole curriculum emphasized the study of Latin to the extent that reading and writing were taught only secondarily in French. Relying on Latin alphabets and *syllabaires* for guidance, young students were required to devote most of their energy to the sounding out (*épellation*) and then rote recitation of Latin terms. The result of this system, complained many adherents of sensationalist psychology, was legions of students who were largely ignorant of the precise ideas and things signified by the various terms that they had learned to recognize and to pronounce.

The closing of the Jesuit *collèges*, ordered in 1761 before the entire Jesuit community was expelled from France, only inflamed a pre-existing desire among Enlightenment figures and *parlementaires* alike for an entirely new system of "national education" in France. Adherents of the new *philosophie* saw better schooling as central to their project of liberating the literate classes (and in a few cases, *le peuple*) from inherited superstitions and prejudices. At the same time, many anti-Jesuitical Catholics, not least those sympathetic to Jansenism (a group whose ranks included many magistrates associated with the parlements, as well as members of other teaching orders, such as the Oratorians and Doctrinaires), sought to provide more people with access to the religious truths contained in the Scriptures. They also hoped to use schooling to help those same people develop the judgment and reason that might increase their chances of salvation. And in both philosophic and Jansenist quarters, a new kind of language education, rooted in sensations and designed to compensate for the prevalence of the *abus des mots*, came to seem vital to these ambitions.[2]

Consequently, the early years of the 1760s saw an outpouring not only of critiques of the perceived shortcomings of the traditional Latin-centered, humanist curriculum and teaching methods employed in most of the nation's schools but also of plans for reform.[3] Isolated writers, following the tradition of Locke, began with new vigor during this decade to promote an alternative model of teaching, one that focused initially on observation and experience, or the reality of things rather than words, with the goal of making learning both more pleasurable and more sure. As Louis-René de Caradeuc de La Chalotais, the Breton author of the important *Essai d'éducation nationale, ou Plan d'études pour la jeunesse*, argued in 1763: "All that one must know is not contained in books. . . . Almost all our philosophy and our education revolve only around words, but it is things themselves that it is necessary to know. Let us return to the true and the real."[4] Influenced by Condillac as well as Locke, La Chalotais, like many of his fellow Jansenist *parlementaires*, maintained that the education of children should follow the path of "nature," commencing with sensible impressions rather than abstract, general ideas, and proceeding gradually from the known to the unknown.

During the first half of the eighteenth century, a small number of pedagogues had already attempted to devise methods for changing the way that children learned to read and to write so that their knowledge of words would ultimately be more securely rooted in reality.[5] Some had encouraged the teaching of the language of the state and elite society (French) before the language of the church (Latin) on the grounds that it would be easier for young people to learn to read a language that they already understood in its spoken form. Using the argument that the path of the eyes was especially effective for fixing ideas in children's minds, other reformers, following in the Port-Royal tradition, had also experimented with the production of new teaching aids based on the association of letters and sounds with visible impressions.[6] A form of *pédagogie par le jeu*, these initiatives included the production of hieroglyphic or symbolic alphabets and illustrated *abcdaires*; the display of actual objects corresponding to various words; and the use of visual *tableaux* to render groups of ideas simultaneously. The *Journal d'éducation* even went so far as to suggest that instead of relying on a "dreary *syllabaire*," teachers might help students learn to read by establishing a small theater in which various letters of the alphabet could be assigned different roles.[7] But the use of these tools never became widespread outside of a few private Parisian contexts, and as critics, including Rousseau, were to point out, these tricks ultimately did little to shift the focus of language pedagogy away from letters and syllables and toward the meaning of words themselves.

In fact, these educational toys and devices were only one among many aspects of contemporary pedagogy that Rousseau roundly denounced in *Emile*, his seminal educational treatise of 1762.[8] In this work, Rousseau sketched a radically innovative plan for the ideal education of a single boy outside of an institutional (and hence royal or clerical) setting. Much of the force of Rousseau's proposals came, however, from his thorough condemnation of the form and substance of contemporary instruction, which he saw as a hindrance to the individual's natural development. Drawing on the speculative history of language that he had recently laid out in his *Second Discours* and his *Essai sur l'origine des langues*, Rousseau insisted that all young children instinctively utilized the language of nature—an idiom made up of gestures, facial expressions, and, especially, cries—well before they learned to speak the conventional languages of adults. The qualities of this natural idiom corresponded to those innate in children (like all primitive peoples) in the early stages of their development: honesty, directness, and responsiveness to sensations rather than abstract thought. Unfortunately, these juvenile traits, Rousseau argued, were prematurely destroyed by the prattle of nurses, who showered each youth with "a multitude of useless words of which he understands nothing other than the tone she gives them," and then by the verbiage of contemporary teachers.[9] In the standard curriculum, children were bombarded from their earliest years with nothing but "words, more words, always words," Rousseau complained.[10] As a result of this habit, he continued, "the unfortunate facility we have for dazzling people with words we do not understand begins earlier than is thought."[11] Excessive attention to book learning, foreign languages, rhetoric, and sciences dependent on terminology rather than empirical investigation had cumulatively worked to produce, in Rousseau's formulation, a nation of *babillards* or chatterboxes: superficial people who used words as a source of competition rather than as a method for establishing meaningful and unmediated social bonds.

As a remedy, Rousseau proposed a radically ascetic linguistic diet for young people, male or female. While he accepted the fact that membership in society required knowledge of certain abstract terms, he admonished teachers in reference to his model, Emile: "Let us set aside an effort

of attention too great for his brain and not rush to fix his mind on conventional signs."[12] Similar ideas emerge in his plan for Sophie, Emile's
female counterpart, despite the otherwise marked gender differences in
the form and purpose of their educations. In both cases, in an effort to
keep children's attention focused on concrete things (*les choses*) rather
than signs for them (*les mots*), Rousseau urged instructors to restrict
their pupils' vocabulary and to spare them endless definitions, or word-
based explanations of other words. Whenever possible, he encouraged
lessons through actions, examples, objects, and experiments. Most important, Rousseau prodded teachers in their role as prophets of immediacy to pay greater attention to what he called the "language of signs."[13]
In a key section of *Emile*, the author juxtaposed the state of the art of
persuasion in ancient Rome with that of modern France. Roman orators,
he argued, were never more effective than when they spoke the least:
"What was said most vividly was expressed not by words but by signs.
One did not say it, one showed it. . . . Alexander placing his seal on his favorite's mouth, Diogenes walking before Zeno—did they not speak better than if they had made long speeches? What series of words would
have rendered the same ideas so well?"[14] Rousseau despaired that only
brute force could have this kind of impact in the corrupt world of the
present, where self-interest and violence had replaced real eloquence;
but he urged instructors of youth to try to apply the lessons of Roman
orators to the tutoring of their charges. "Clothe reason in a body if you
want to make youth able to grasp it," Rousseau implored. "Make the
language of the mind pass through the heart, so that it may make itself
understood. . . . I shall put in my eyes, my accent, and my gestures the
enthusiasm and the ardor that I want to inspire in him [Emile]."[15]

   Rousseau had already tried a decade earlier to incorporate didactic
pantomime into an opera that he had called *Le Devin du village*, and he
was soon to set to work on a "monodrama" entitled *Pygmalion* that
would depend upon pantomime as well. In between these two events, in
the context of his *Emile*, Rousseau called for the expanded use of this
same natural, bodily "language of signs" outside the theater: to make
moral concepts immediately visible and to give them a potency and energy that conventional language simply could not. For Rousseau believed that instead of seeking to destroy the idiom natural to the unschooled, teachers ought to do all within their power to preserve it and
make it a reinvigorated tool of an honest and eloquent community.
What Rousseau seems to have had in mind is not only a temporary solution to the problem of modern education—in the form of the limited relationship between a tutor and subject—but also a model for a new kind
of society redolent of a distant, idealized past before signs came to represent obstacles to true communication. With *Emile*, Rousseau hoped to

foster nothing less than a way of training the natural individual so that he and his counterparts could eventually make civilized society and all of its institutions better.

The Parlement of Paris's official condemnation of Rousseau's iconoclastic and, ultimately, deeply antimodern text did not prevent others from adopting and then adapting these ideas for new purposes over the next few decades. In the later 1760s, a slew of fictional stories picked up on Rousseau's concern with the ethical consequences of language acquisition by describing the initiation of imaginary "wild children," previously isolated in their natural states, into the realm of collective life and conventional signs.[16] Innovative instruction manuals for parents and teachers outside the established *collège* system grew in number as well. And a few theorists, influenced by Condillac too, took seriously Rousseau's emphasis on the pedagogical uses of the *langue des signes* in the creation of alternative habits of thought and communication among the young.

One such individual was Claude François Lyzarde de Radonvilliers, the *sous-précepteur* of the four sons of the dauphin (including the future Louis XVI) and, consequently, an esteemed member of the Académie Française when he published his treatise *De la Manière d'apprendre les langues* in 1768. Radonvilliers had himself been educated at the University of Paris and the Jesuit Collège Louis-le-Grand, where allegorical ballet had long served as a visual means of conveying moral precepts.[17] But Radonvilliers's novel ideas for teaching language were inspired less by his own formation than by the experiments of the distant past—including those of an early sixteenth-century monk named Nicolas Clenard who had taught Latin by staging plays in which the sense of unknown words became intelligible through the interpretation of the actors' gestures—and the tales of language origins published in recent years.[18] In short, Radonvilliers believed that students should learn to speak and to read Latin not by memorizing abstract rules and dictionary definitions but in the same fashion that they had once, naturally, learned their mother tongue: through natural bodily signs. For each new word a student learned, Radonvilliers proposed that "a term taken from the natural Language, corresponding to one taken from the articulate Language, must impose itself, interpret the unknown word, and unite it with the idea."[19] That way, he reasoned, students would ultimately garner a secure knowledge not just of pronunciation but also of the precise meaning of their utterances.

Radonvilliers justified this plan by way of a long introduction to his treatise in which he retold the conjectural story of the human invention of language sometime after the Flood, from gestures and cries to imitative sounds and then words, from signs for objects to metaphors and, finally, abstractions. He emphasized the universality and transnational quality of the original idiom: "Is there anyone who does not know that ... the hand advances in order to threaten someone and that the arms extend themselves in order to ask for grace?"[20] He repeated the standard claim that the connection between thought and gesture is natural and necessary, while the link between thought and words is conventional and often equivocal, and he analyzed the relative advantages and disadvantages that stemmed from both systems of signification. He even made the obligatory references to pantomimes and mutes. The only novelty in Radonvilliers's account was that, in keeping with his educational mission, he turned the initial linguistic innovators into two individual men. In this way, he offered a plan for making the (all-male) community of the private classroom into a microcosm of the first society, complete with an inherently truthful and natural means of communication, stripped of its association with the passions, through which to learn about the world.

Radonvilliers's teaching method was probably never put into practice. In fact, with the exception of a few minor educators, the novel pedagogy described in his treatise garnered little public response.[21] It was, finally, another man—the Abbé Charles Michel de l'Epée—who succeeded in bringing the idea of a pedagogical sign language to the attention of intellectuals all over France and, eventually, Europe. This cleric, whose Jansenist beliefs prevented him ever becoming an active priest, spent most of the 1760s working out a method for instructing a set of deaf female twins in the tenets of religion and civics, as well as the French language.[22] Reluctant to imitate Jacob Rodrigue Péreire's celebrated "art of making mutes speak" through lip-reading and other such tricks,[23] Epée began to develop an alternative approach to the problem of educating those individuals who were incapable of learning the meaning of the terms of their national language through ordinary means. As he would later declare, the key to his method lay in appropriating the form and principles of an ancient and universally familiar idiom: "[It] is a natural language, it is that of signs."[24] But instead of simply relying on a crude form of pantomime, he subjected the "natural language" to a logic that he hoped would make up for all of the epistemological limitations associated with Noverre's *ballet d'action*. And rather than simply announcing this solution in print in the manner of Rousseau or Radonvilliers, Epée tried, beginning in 1771, to prove the efficacy of his language of manual signs in frequent public demonstrations of his pupils' abilities at his newly established Parisian school. Combining grammatical theory with pantomime, pedagogical experimentation with spectacle, the *abbé*'s methods soon came to the forefront of intellectual debate in France.

"METHODICAL" SIGNS

During 1777, the year of Noverre's biggest successes and failures at the Opéra, the major journals of the Republic of Letters also paid close attention to a different form of Parisian silent theater: the open sessions at the Abbé de l'Epée's school for the deaf. Side by side with articles on *ballets d'action* and *ballets-pantomimes*, Bachaumont, Grimm, Linguet, La Harpe, Pidansat de Mairobert, and other such chroniclers reported on the parade of notable events that transpired at the *abbé's* establishment over a period of some eighteen months. In May, just a year after Epée's *Institution des sourds et muets, par la voie des signes méthodiques* appeared to glowing reviews, the Holy Roman Emperor, Joseph II, who was traveling under the thin disguise of the Comte de Falckenstein, brought enormous attention to Epée's school by visiting and declaring his amazement at what he witnessed there.[25] Then, later in the summer, Epée took up the cause of a poor, abandoned deaf boy who, the *abbé* announced, had been discovered in the course of one of his public sessions to be the presumed dead son of the Count of Solar. The tale of the boy's misfortunes, combined with the novel legal proceedings that ensued, quickly turned the case into a cause célèbre.[26] Only one year later, finally, the Jansenist priest was elected to the Academy of Châlons-sur-Marne, which took a special interest in both pedagogy and social policy in the 1770s, and Epée's school (which Joseph II had called shamefully neglected during his visit the previous year) gained official recognition when Louis XVI granted it his protection in a formal decree.[27]

As a result of all of this publicity, observers could not help but draw connections between the gestural practices prevalent on the Parisian stage and those that flourished at Epée's institution. Actors, dramatists, and theatrical entrepreneurs, in particular, capitalized upon the new cachet of the gesticulating deaf. Pantomimes appeared as products of deaf authors, and mute characters grew in popularity on the stage.[28] The *Mercure de France* even reported that a M. Alexis Bacquoy Guédon, a former member of the Théâtre Français, had taken it upon himself to use "certain signs to teach the deaf and mute to dance."[29] Conversely, following the emperor's visit, Epée's public sessions became a highly fashionable form of entertainment for well-heeled Parisians and tourists alike.[30] Guests soon included members of the French court, foreign heads of state, noted academicians, and even the papal nuncio and the queen. Not surprisingly, these visitors often described the communicative exercises that they witnessed among Epée's young pupils of both sexes as a form of pantomime performance.

Throughout the 1770s, in fact, Epée did much to encourage this association, despite his declarations to the contrary. After all, the foundation of Epée's pedagogical theory was the notion that bodily signs formed the essential and instinctive basis of communication among people everywhere.[31] As he put it in the program for one of his public demonstrations, "The history of all centuries furnishes us with no example of a man who died of hunger, thirst, or cold as a result of not being able to find the signs to explain his needs and his misery."[32] For Epée imagined these signs, born of necessity, as a form of universally intelligible pantomime. In his major treatise of 1776, Epée offered a long description of how, if he were ever a parish priest near a battleground, he might use a combination of mimed actions and natural signs of compassion to communicate with the wounded of all nations and tongues. His pedagogy rested on the hypothesis that a community of deaf people, rescued from their isolated existences and determined to find a means to convey ideas to one another, would, in a similar fashion, naturally develop a way to use gestures and other forms of bodily expression to satisfy their communicative needs. The resulting sign system, Epée concluded, should be regarded as the "maternal language" of the deaf.

However, rather than focusing his efforts on trying to wean the hearing-impaired from their reliance on this elemental idiom, Epée insisted that the first job required of an instructor of the deaf was to learn the natural language of signs himself. Only after the instructor had mastered this skill could he begin the long process of teaching his pupils how to "translate" from their natural mother tongue—a series of iconic signs, or representations of things, completely independent of speech—into the written and, lastly, oral forms of a "foreign" (conventional) language. Following in the Port-Royal tradition of his own education, Epée assumed that this second language could just as well be German or Italian as French or Latin, since he believed that all languages conveyed a finite number of universal ideas according to certain common or "general" grammatical principles, and that the connection between particular sounds and ideas was essentially arbitrary. However, his teaching method also owed much to the sensationalism and nominalism of Condillac, with its emphasis on the expressivity of natural, visual signs and its explanatory model called the *langage d'action*. Epée's lesson plans corresponded to a series of *jeux*, or pantomimed dramas, in which, beginning with physical actions indicating basic verbs, his deaf pupils were gradually and simultaneously exposed to new relationships and new ideas along with both written and gestural signs for them. Bypassing alphabets and *syllabaires*, Epée claimed that his students' language education simply followed the path established by nature. When the public came to witness and to participate in Epée's long, biweekly open sessions, what they experienced was this whole generative process in reverse. Translation back and forth between verbal and written signs, on the one hand, and gestural signs, on the other, became a form of performance for a cosmopolitan, multilingual audience eager to witness the direct and unequivocal exchange of ideas associated with the earliest of human societies.[33]

Yet, much as Epée stressed the roots of his project in a natural *langage* of imitative and expressive signs, he also took great pains to demonstrate that his gestural idiom could succeed where pure pantomime could not. The *abbé* insisted that his "methodical signs," as he called them, were an effective medium for representing not only sensations, passions, and material objects but also the abstract and metaphysical concepts of religious and civic life—the very concepts that Noverre's critics and even some of his defenders claimed that gestures could never successfully convey. Epée argued that with the help of the scientific method of *analyse*, all abstract terms, no matter how complex or metaphysical, could be broken down into their simplest, sensible constituent elements and attached to their natural signs. Then, when these basic signs were recombined in the order of the generation of ideas, even the most immaterial religious notions would become clear and comprehensible. The verb *croire* (to believe), for example, could be decomposed into its parts: *connaître* (to be acquainted with), *sentir* (to feel), *dire* (to tell), and *ne pas voir* (to not see). Each part of this abstract concept could then be given a natural, self-evident sign referring to the physical reality at its core, along with a sign for the grammatical part of speech (in this case, a verb) that the whole word represented. The resulting conglomeration of signs—"the ones joined with the others in a single instant in order to convey a whole word which, containing complicated ideas, cannot be explained by a single sign"—would accurately communicate both the precise meaning of the term in question and its syntactical relationship to the other signs around it.[34] Epée often boasted that he had convinced a skeptical journalist, Simon-Nicolas Linguet, that methodical signs made it possible for the deaf to understand not only isolated abstractions, such as the word "intellect," but the differences among its many variants, including intellectual, intelligent, intelligence, intelligibility, intelligible, unintelligible, intelligibly, unintelligibly, and unintelligibility.[35] The secret, Epée proposed, was not simply "natural" signs but signs "rendered natural by analysis."[36]

In fact, Epée argued, what he called the *langue* of methodical signs was so great an analytic tool that its applications went well beyond teaching the deaf to think logically or to communicate complex ideas. Ultimately, these gestural signs marked the solution to a very old problem that Enlightenment thinkers had recently begun to address with new enthusiasm. This was the possibility of discovering a universal philosophical language.[37]

For almost a century after Locke, the seventeenth-century effort to create a perfect artificial or a priori idiom that would render the world fully intelligible to all had, as we have seen, been looked upon as a desirable but ultimately impossible quest. Learned attention had turned instead to the question of which vernacular was most suited to become the international language of science and philosophy or to the question of why French had already attained that status.[38] But recent developments in general grammar, etymology, and other fashionable linguistic sciences, not to mention the posthumous publication in the 1760s of the works of Leibniz in French, led to a late eighteenth-century revival of interest in this older pursuit of a single, perfect universal idiom or form of notation. Indeed, it is here that we see the merging of several supposedly distinct trends in early modern linguistics, including the sensationalist account of the origin of language with the rationalist search for a more perfect sign system better able to represent the things of the world or to make knowledge a product of logical calculation. After Condillac, it was increasingly felt that if a philosophical language were ever to succeed, it would have to have a natural idiom as its basis.

The writings of Epée, at once the rationalist, Jansenist grammarian and the sensationalist *philosophe*, epitomize this emergent synthesis. For the advantage of "methodical" signs as a global idiom, Epée pointed out, stemmed from the fact that the raw elements—in the form of iconic gestures that represent things directly—had been given by nature. All that was missing, he explained, was for this bodily language to be perfected or, more precisely, expanded by analogy to represent abstract concepts, subjected to the rules of general grammar, and, finally, codified. For years, the *abbé*, who called himself a "living dictionary" of this new idiom, claimed to be at work on a written dictionary and grammar of methodical sign language, a project that he intended to bequeath to posterity as a key to the solution of this long-standing philosophical problem.[39] According to a fantasy that Epée spelled out in his treatise of 1776, with its subtitle "a work that includes the plans for a universal language established by means of natural signs and subjected to a method," this nomenclature of methodical signs could serve as a prototype for a global idiom to be taught around the world, regardless of differences in local tongues. Not only would the citizens of many nations be brought together in this fashion; they would also learn to communicate among themselves in new ways. Epée believed that he had found a way to restore the traditional social values associated with the natural *langage d'action* and its primitive speakers: honesty, simplicity, and direct expressivity. But at the same time, Epée also insisted that he had managed to discover a means of representing precisely, permanently, and unprejudicially the enormous range of ideas common to all cultures, including those ideas most abstracted from basic sensations.

Of course, some of Epée's contemporaries, such as Pierre-Nicolas Changeux, the author commissioned to write the article on *réalité* in the *Encyclopédie* and an enemy of a metaphysics that he believed to be dominated by the "reign of words," claimed that the very appeal of the idea of a visual sign language stemmed from its inability to represent ideas that were neither concrete nor pictorial. In a treatise published in 1773, the nominalist thinker explained the desired effect of the institution of a universal form of notation "intelligible even to mutes" in terms of this limitation:

> It is true that a philosophical Language composed of signs that are images of natural things would also be sterile and inappropriate for depicting arbitrary things and would be commodious and exact [only] when it was a question of depicting nature; but it is perhaps primarily for this reason that it merits the name "philosophical." All that is arbitrary passes and is of little importance in the eyes of wise men; only real things are immutable and have some value. . . . [T]his difficulty or weakness in painting abstractions should be regarded as a great advantage by those who are familiar with the immense riches of Nature and the frightful limitations of human reasoning and systems.[40]

It was the epistemological modesty enforced by natural sign languages, Changeux believed, that would ultimately allow for the return of intellectual certainty.

Yet the Abbé de l'Epée had no intention of eliminating all metaphysical concepts or invisible abstractions from his course of instruction simply because of the chronic errors, falsehoods, and misunderstandings produced by ordinary language. The whole point of his method, after all, was to develop students' intelligence to the point that they could gain access to the word of God. Thus where Changeux took pains to differentiate a *langage* (natural signs of sentiments, passions, and natural things) from a *langue* (conventional signs of ideas), Epée claimed to have put them back together. He insisted that he had found a way to convey essential spiritual notions to all humans without running the risk of constructing vain systems, on the one hand, or resorting to materialism, on the other.

Epée realized, however, that the general public was not so easily convinced by his rather extravagant claims. Indeed, Epée continually rearticulated his positions in response to an evolving collection of very vocal critics. In 1772, he noted that both theologians and *philosophes* doubted the efficacy of his method: followers of Augustine dismissed the idea that religious truths could be learned apart from hearing them; and unnamed philosophers who rejected the concept of innate ideas insisted that abstract ideas were inaccessible to those deprived of the critical sense of audition. Exponents of the oral education of the deaf, including the celebrated Péreire and his premier deaf student, Saboureux de Fontenay, also publicly challenged Epée's claims for his "methodical signs" and continued to argue for the greater efficacy of *dactylologie* (finger spelling) in teaching pupils, ultimately, to articulate French words.[41] Epée took on all of these critiques in various texts of the 1770s, exaggerating the differences between the two feuding camps and warning that reliance on alphabetic finger spelling left "a man endowed with a rational mind in the class of parrots."[42] Similar arguments broke out in ensuing years with opponents in German lands, including Samuel Heinicke of Leipzig and the Berlin academician Christoph Nicolai. Following a series of angry letters on both sides, the academies of Lyon, Zurich, and finally Berlin were called in to adjudicate in the early 1780s.[43] Meanwhile, the public nature of the Solar case, which was built on a series of sign language revelations and exchanges, produced new critiques of Epée's undying faith in his own method; in both the press and published *plaidoyers*, some of France's most prominent lawyers, including Elie de Beaumont, Prunget des Boissières, and Tronson de Coudray, insisted that the use of sign language to convey legal abstractions constituted a danger to the judicial process itself.[44] As one barrister concluded in response to Epée's grandiose claims: "[Epée] comforts [his pupils], but he does not create them. . . . Nihil ist in intellectu, quod non prius fuerit in sensu."[45]

At stake in these disagreements was not a clear ideological or political contest between a group of *philosophes* and an unenlightened public. Neither was it simply a question of religious difference, since sensationalist epistemology had, from the mid-century, frequently been used to bolster Christian doctrine, and participants on both sides in this controversy included Jews and Protestants as well as Catholics of varying orientations. And as in the concurrent debates on theatrical pantomime, variations in class or *état* were not decisive factors in determining individual stances. In fact, few simple oppositions can be identified in sorting out the range of responses provoked by Epée's experiments. Rather, as illustrated by the example of the Abbé Claude François Deschamps— a chaplain of the church of Orléans and a private teacher of the deaf who relied upon pedagogical methods similar to those of Péreire—this debate seems to have revolved primarily around a difference in understandings of the historical function of signs. The argument between Deschamps and Epée turned specifically on their divergent answers to the question of the degree to which linguistic instrumentalism, rooted in the example of an analytic sign language, might produce cognitive or social benefits in the future.

What strikes the reader immediately upon comparing Deschamps's and Epée's writings of the same years is how much the two abbots shared in terms of their intellectual positions. Like Epée, Deschamps announced his intentions in educating the deaf as twofold: to rescue the deaf from their purely physical, animalistic existence, and to make them into "Citizens" and "Christians."[46] Furthermore, the Abbé Deschamps agreed that the eyes could be as effective a path to knowledge as the ears, since "sight is the first and most precious of the senses," and he insisted that all humans compensate for weaknesses in one sense by developing superior strengths in others.[47] The cleric from Orléans even posited that the deaf, like all humans, have a natural penchant for making their physical needs known through bodily signs.

But the Abbé Deschamps was also convinced that too great a reliance on gestural signs in the education of the deaf would have negative consequences for this unfortunate sector of the population, as well as for the greater society in which the two abbots lived. Why? The most basic of Deschamps's objections bore many similarities to those of critics of theatrical pantomime, a mode of communication that Deschamps did not distinguish from methodical sign language. Indeed, Deschamps himself referred to the example of the stage to explain why gestures, for all their energy and passion, could never approach words in terms of their precision or accuracy:

> Suppose a person deaf and mute from birth was taken to one of our Plays at the Théâtre Français. . . . In those parts where sentiment and passion are painted with so much truth, what will my deaf and mute person remember of this spectacle? Some emotion of the soul, some sensation of tenderness and pleasure, sometimes sadness, but without knowing exactly what could have caused it or what its object was. Will he feel the beauty of the dream of Athalie, the force and truth of the last scene of Mérope. . . . No, the sublimity of these bits . . . is lost for him.[48]

For Diderot, the failure of comprehension on the part of the viewer that Deschamps imagines would have signaled the ineptitude of either the actors or the playwright in question. This idea was central to all of the *philosophe's* polemics of the 1750s and 1760s.[49] But for Deschamps, this hypothetical example simply illustrated the inherent weakness of physical signs as means of communication, especially when it came to ideas that were not themselves inherently visual. The real danger, Deschamps claimed, was that with gestural signs, one could never really guarantee that a deaf person had not taken a purely physical notion to be a spiritual idea:

> Let us take, for an example, an abstract word for which knowledge of the thing that it designates is essential. *God*: with words, we can easily ex-

plain that He is the pre-eminent Being, who has made all things and brings together all perfections. With signs, we show the Sky, the place where the Almighty lives. We describe how all that we see comes from His hands. Who can be sure that the Deaf and Mute do not take the firmament for God himself and that they do not address their prayers to the sky ... ?[50]

In Deschamps's estimation, the real possibility of encouraging confusion and error about religious truths, the most fundamental aspect of education, negated Epée's entire project.

Yet these criticisms were not merely pedagogical, a question of skepticism in face of Epée's supposedly wondrous "methodical" sign method. The Abbé Deschamps also strenuously objected that a fundamental human value was being compromised by Epée's approach. According to the teacher from Orléans, it was *parole*, not gestures or any other means of communication, that separated men from animals and ultimately made humans alone capable of perfection and moral life. Knowledge, reason, and the rights and responsibilities of society all depended upon speech, he maintained in good Aristotelian fashion, and without the capacity to make their ideas known in spoken terms, the deaf would be forced to remain "strangers among men," a community left apart and behind.[51] In sum, Deschamps believed that the advancement of sign language marked an antienlightenment turn. If gestures were capable of "enlightening minds, softening manners, and destroying prejudices," he asked, then why were they only prevalent in those primitive cultures marked by ignorance, lawlessness, and lack of material comfort?[52] Why was Epée determined to alter the natural course of both intellectual and social progress?

It was this issue that Epée's most prominent defenders took up on the *abbé*'s behalf. In the 1770s and 1780s, Epée welcomed to his public spectacles an array of distinguished *philosophes* and scientists, as well as philanthropists and statesmen, much as Péreire had done before him.[53] Among these visitors were some of the most important language theorists of both Europe and the New World, including Lord Monboddo, John Adams, Dugald Stewart, Sir William Jones, Father Bohusz, and Condillac himself.[54] And in the course of their visits, many of these guests found not only evidence to back up their own theories about the natural history of language and the surest path to knowledge. They also discovered an inspirational model for how prescriptive language planning rooted in both natural signs and the analytic method might be used to prevent the faulty use of words and, ultimately, to inculcate new ways of thinking and communicating in society at large.

The Abbé de Condillac prominently set the stage for these broad claims on behalf of sign language in his *Cours d'études pour l'instruc-*

tion du Prince de Parme. Upon returning to Paris in 1767 after nine years in exile in Parma as the tutor to Prince Ferdinand, Condillac's reputation as a philosopher and an educator continued to grow in both intellectual and court circles. Finally, after several additional years of delay, his magnum opus, a sixteen-volume guide to the pedagogical system and method that he had put into practice in educating Prince Ferdinand, the grandson of Louis XV, appeared in print in both Parma and Paris. Not surprisingly, the first volume of this work, published in 1775, focused on grammar.

Two purposes overlapped in this initial tome. In the course of the book, Condillac laid out a fresh account of the origin and development of language. Simultaneously, he proposed a sequence of lessons detailing the order in which a teacher ought to expose his pupil to the principles of grammar. And since he believed that every child should essentially retrace the natural, step-by-step process through which the initial humans had learned about their world, he made the common starting point for these dual narratives the original language of gestures.

Yet Condillac's account of natural signs in his *Grammaire* of 1775 deviated in certain noteworthy ways from that of the *Essai* he had published thirty years before. Originally, Condillac had argued that signs ceased to be "natural" as soon as they were used deliberately and consciously, even if the signs themselves remained iconic, pictorial, and spontaneous in origin. In the *Grammaire*, however, he reformulated his categories, replacing the old dichotomy between natural and "arbitrary" signs with a new distinction between natural and "artificial" signs.[55] This shift then led him to differentiate between two kinds of *langages d'action*: "one natural, whose signs are created by the structure of our organs; the other artificial, whose signs are created by analogy."[56] One example of the latter type of *langage d'action* was Roman pantomime, in which gestures gained meaning by analogy to one another, and all bodily signs, while remaining rooted in sense experience, could be decomposed in a linear fashion.[57] His most extraordinary example, however, was the pedagogy of the Abbé de l'Epée, who "made out of the *langage d'action* a methodical art as simple as it is easy with which he can teach his students every kind of idea." This idiom was so astonishing, Condillac continued, that it yielded, "I dare say, more exact and precise ideas than those that one commonly acquires with the aid of our sense of hearing."[58]

It is not clear whether Condillac's admiration for Epée's invention led Condillac to reformulate his theory of the development of language, or whether the sign language of the deaf simply offered an excellent illustration of the philosopher's latest theories. But it is evident that Condillac saw in Epée's methodical signs the possibility of a language that

could explain even the most abstract areas of human knowledge without becoming "arbitrary." As such it promised to yield a solution to the
dissociation of ideas and signs common in contemporary education.
Condillac explained the potential effects of Epée's method as follows:

> Since in childhood we are reduced to judging the meaning of words by the
> circumstances in which we hear them pronounced, we often grasp them
> only approximately, and we content ourselves with these approxima-
> tions our whole lives. It is not the same for the deaf and mute people that
> M. l'Abbé de l'Epée instructs. He has only one method for giving them
> ideas which do not fall under the senses; it is to analyze and make them
> analyze with him. He thus leads them from sensible ideas to abstract
> ideas by simple and methodical analyses; and one can judge the advan-
> tages of his *langage d'action* over the articulate sounds of our govern-
> esses and preceptors.[59]

In the opinion of the elderly philosopher, Epée's artificial *langage
d'action* appeared, like algebra, to be one of the rare modern languages
that constituted a true method of analysis in its own right, a way finally
(in contradistinction to Lockean nominalism) of making abstract philosophical principles demonstrable and clear.[60]

Condillac left it to others, however, to address the broad social consequences that might result from the advent of such new ways of teaching
people to think and to communicate. In the early 1770s, a few younger
language theorists, including the Abbé Alexis Copineau, began to take
up the task. For Copineau, whose *Essai synthétique sur l'origine et la
formation des langues* was published just a year before Condillac's new
grammar, "methodical signs" only secondarily served to buttress historical research on the origin of language or psychological claims. Primarily, they demonstrated the possibility that the deliberate recuperation of certain lost linguistic values could indeed be used to transform
the nature of modern society itself.

Copineau, an amateur scientist, a friend of Epée's, and the Jansenist
deacon and canon of the church of St. Louis du Louvre in Paris, wrote his
Essai synthétique in response to a prize contest announced by the Berlin
Academy's speculative philosophy class in late 1769. The academy's
question, which elicited responses from all over Europe (including a
celebrated winning essay by Johann Gottfried von Herder), concerned
the origin of language: "Imagining humans left to their natural faculties,
are they in a position to invent language? And by what means would
they arrive, on their own, at this invention?"[61] Copineau's anonymously
published answer—a "hypothesis" derived from a fictional scientific
experiment involving a young boy and girl on a deserted island who are
left to invent a means of communication based upon nothing but human nature—did not meet with much critical success.[62] By the 1770s,

such speculative and literary "science" was already largely out of fashion in France. However, within this text, Copineau introduced an idea that he would soon go on to develop in a much more striking and novel way: that the original "mimic language," a concrete and exact gestural idiom, could, with Epée's help, be expanded into "a sort of simplified and perfected Hieroglyphic Language, which embraces everything" and that this universal metalanguage could change forever the nature of cognition, allowing humans to "feel in a palpable manner the connections and relationships among [analogous] ideas."[63]

But what consequences might this development have for social relations? Copineau only hinted at an answer in his *Essai synthétique* of 1774. It was Copineau's next project, a highly unusual publishing venture that he embarked upon five years later in conjunction with the Jansenist bookseller Benoît Morin, that directly addressed this question.[64] In 1779, with this *abbé*'s and, perhaps, Morin's editorial guidance, a thirty-two-year-old deaf bookbinder and paper hanger named Pierre Desloges wrote and published what was touted at the time as the first book ever composed by a deaf person.[65] The author was not a student of Epée's or even, apparently, fully familiar with Epée's system. However, Desloges took it upon himself to demonstrate that sign language was not only a highly effective means of communication within deaf communities but also an idiom in many ways preferable to spoken French. Furthermore, he allowed Copineau to use the notes to this volume to draw out the implications that the use of this novel language might have for society as a whole.

Desloges's book, entitled *Observations d'un sourd et muet sur 'Un Cours élémentaire d'éducation des sourds et muets,' publié en 1779 par M. l'abbé Deschamps*, was, in equal parts, an autobiography, a treatise on metaphysics, and a refutation of the Abbé Deschamps's recent attack on sign language. In fact, all of these themes came together in a written defense of what Desloges referred to as "my own language." Deaf from the age of seven and lacking any formal schooling (though apparently capable of reading), Desloges claimed that he had spent most of his life unaware of the existence of any developed visual or physical method of communicating with others. He had always relied on unconnected, isolated gestures to convey basic ideas, he explained; but hc had formulated no conception of "the art of combining them to form distinct pictures with which one can represent various ideas, transmit them to one's peers, and converse in logical discourse."[66] Then, finally, at age twenty-seven, thanks to the deaf servant of an actor at the Comédie-Italienne, Desloges was initiated into the silent language that the Parisian community of deaf laborers had established through "common sense and the company of their own kind."[67] This gestural sign language was not,

Desloges insisted, limited to the expression of physical things and bodily needs, as Deschamps had wrongly claimed, but could convey such subtle matters as differences between levels of the nobility or even the idea of God. In fact, Desloges noted that, contrary to Deschamps's assertions, it would be quite impossible in the deaf idiom to mistake the sign for "God" with that for "firmament," since the gestural expression of God contains "no ambiguity or circumlocution." As he explained: "[W]hen I want to designate the Supreme Being by indicating the sky, which is His dwelling place or rather His stepping-stone, I accompany my gesture with an air of adoration and respect that makes my intention quite evident."[68] The genius of Epée, Desloges suggested, stemmed from the *abbé*'s recognition of the fact that deaf people had a language of their own, a natural idiom that needed only the addition of "methodical rules" and a bit of repair in order to serve as the basis for a thorough educational system.

But Desloges did not stop there. For the bookbinder was not only concerned to convey what a rich means of expression sign language could be. He also argued that the silent language of the deaf actually possessed certain extraordinary advantages over conventional discursive speech:

> Our ideas concentrated in ourselves, so to speak, necessarily incline us toward reflectiveness and meditation. The language we use among ourselves, being a faithful image of the object expressed, is singularly appropriate for making our ideas accurate and for extending our comprehension by getting us to form the habit of constant observation and analysis. This language is lively; it portrays sentiment, and develops the imagination. No other language is more appropriate for conveying great and strong emotions. . . . I cannot understand how a language like sign language—the richest in expressions, the most energetic, the most incalculably advantageous in its universal intelligibility—is still so neglected and that only the deaf speak it (as it were).[69]

Ultimately, by suggesting that it was the hearing population rather than the deaf who were truly deprived of an effective means of communication, Desloges sought to do nothing less than to turn the established linguistic hierarchy on its head.

In the extensive notes to this volume, Copineau made this same point even more explicit, calling on his ordinary hearing and literate readers to stop wasting time in pursuit of an inadequate knowledge of dead and foreign tongues and to devote themselves instead to learning Epée's simple sign system, "which could become a supplement for all other languages."[70] Desloges's collaborator expressed little faith in the state of contemporary communication. The sloppy linguistic habits of children remained prevalent among adults. Everywhere people claimed to understand one another without any assurance that they were not attaching different ideas to the same words. Indeed, most spent their lives as mindless "parrots," Copineau declared, borrowing from Locke's famous description of the manner in which most humans formulated their phrases. The Jansenist cleric insisted, however, that these problems were not insoluble. Were these same individuals to choose to explain themselves in a "mimic" sign language rather than with arbitrary sounds and characters, the barriers to true communication would fall away. For "the excellence of sign language" stemmed from its great advantages in two important regards: "my certainty that the gesturer has a clear conception of the object he is representing, because of the impossibility of depicting, with either pencil or gesture, what is not conceived in this way; my certainty that this manner of depicting my ideas will communicate them just as I conceive them, for he can see only the way I represent them and I can represent them only as I conceive them."[71]

And what would be the final result for contemporary society were this precise and unambiguous system of communication to become generalized? Copineau foresaw extraordinary changes. Methodical signs would help individuals to overcome problems of miscommunication or the *abus des mots*. Moreover, such a language would allow people to reach general agreement about questions that had long seemed to be open to varied interpretations. In this semiotic utopia, Copineau explained, "We would at least understand each other, and there would be no issues that we could call *arguments about words*." Because sign language ensures that "we see in each expression—as through a transparent mirror—the precise idea he [an individual] has of objects," it would become "an invaluable aid in the pursuit of [accepted] truth."[72] In Copineau's conception, Epée's sign language seemed a recipe for the creation of enlightened social harmony and perpetual intellectual accord built, as in the very first human societies, around a set of indisputable moral certainties.

With such claims, Copineau thus helped establish Desloges not only as an intellectual curiosity—a poor deaf laborer capable of writing a book in French—but also, amazingly, as a model for a new kind of *savant*, the natural thinker of the future. Much to the annoyance of the Abbé Deschamps, who commented soon after its publication that Desloges's brochure had been announced with "the greatest speed and the greatest tributes," the Republic of Letters quickly welcomed the young deaf man into its ranks.[73] Shortly after the appearance of his *Observations*, Desloges found himself visiting with the Marquis de Condorcet, the celebrated secretary of the Academy of Sciences, to discuss this dispute; publishing new essays on sign language and related questions in such notable journals as the *Mercure de France*, the *Journal encyclopédique*, and the *Affiches de Paris*; and even appearing at Claude-Mammès Pahin de La Blancherie's "regular meeting for savants and artists" in order to demonstrate and defend his linguistic claims.[74] The editor of the *Journal encyclopédique*, who claimed to have met with Desloges in the presence of Epée, praised the quality of Desloges's thinking: "It would be desirable if all who listened, spoke and even wrote had as much intelligence and judgment, precision and sharpness in their ideas as our deaf and mute." This writer then went on to emphasize the importance not only of Desloges's ideas about language but also of his way of expressing himself for "a philosophical reader."[75] Pahin de La Blancherie, who edited the *Nouvelles de la République des lettres et des arts*, did not disagree. Following Desloges's attendance at one of Pahin's "salons de la correspondance" designed to facilitate communication among artists, scientists, and intellectuals of all types, the journalist and entrepreneur commented: "We know that it is hardly permitted to be enthusiastic about the public good during a century where everyone is crazy for frivolity; but we have had the pleasure of knowing certain worthy men concerned with protecting the good of others, and some of them still exist. It is to them that M. Desloges should be recommended. He does not speak, he does not hear, but he *feels*."[76] In the deaf bookbinder, the Republic of Letters found not just a strange object of scrutiny, like the Tahitian Aotourou or the fantasy savages of contemporary pantomimes, but an actual embodiment of the idealized epistemological values that many *philosophes* saw as the key to the creation of a truly enlightened society.

What, then, were these values? One of them was certainly a propensity for analysis; many commentators remarked that Desloges's reliance on sign language had given an admirable rigor and logic to his manner of thinking that carried over into his written expression. But just as prized was Desloges's particular kind of "savage" ignorance. The real reason for his clarity of expression, mused the editor of the *Mercure de France*, was that Desloges's ideas were derived exclusively from empirical observation and serious books and were thus unsullied by the prejudice-laden gibberish and ambiguous terminology of ordinary conversation.[77] At the same time as signing deaf people were assumed to have extremely clear, uncluttered conceptions of the limited body of ideas to which they had been introduced, these same individuals were also thought to remain blissfully unaffected by the wealth of variable and often contradictory or mistaken notions circulating verbally in late Old Regime France. And in the last decade before the Revolution, it was this combination of intellectual values that led thinkers as ideologically and stylistically divergent as Condorcet and Mme de Genlis to suggest that the model of the analytic language of signs developed for the deaf had the potential to alter the very nature of social and moral life in modern France. Condorcet saw science as the source of methods for bettering social relations, while Mme de Genlis believed in the importance of returning to religion. Yet they both reasoned that if an insufficiently rigorous and corrupted language were responsible for many of the problems plaguing contemporary society, then an improved system of representation and communication that limited the scope and effects of mindless or misleading chatter might become part of the solution.

Condorcet first made explicit his desire to reform the nature of contemporary moral debate at a noteworthy moment: in the course of his reception speech at the Académie Française in 1782. He began this important address by celebrating what he took to be the distinguishing feature of this century of progress, namely, the development of remarkably sure methods for discovering scientific truths. As a result of close observation of natural phenomena and techniques of decomposition and recomposition, scientists had been able to create precise, analytical languages of description for almost all of the natural and physical sciences. These specialized languages had proven essential to recent advances in knowledge in these fields. But in the context of his first speech as a member of the academy charged with delimiting and securing the national language according to the principle of "usage," the mathematician also insisted that an important task remained unfulfilled. The analytic methods associated with the natural and physical sciences had yet to be successfully applied to problems of human behavior. A comparably rigorous and methodical language for addressing questions of ethics and politics and social relations did not exist.

Condorcet conceded that the establishment of a "science" of society with its own specialized idiom would be a difficult and slow task; after all, at least two "classes" of people had an active interest in combating any such development: current authority figures (meaning the state) and priests (meaning the church). But, according to this scientist, certain recent experiments undertaken by the philosophic party pointed to the very real possibility that analysis, applied to language, could indeed eventually become a tool of social and moral progress. Among his examples was the construction of a specialized, methodical sign system rooted in sense experience and designed for the explicit purpose of making deaf youths into productive citizens. Only two years after having taken an interest in the case of Pierre Desloges, Condorcet referred to Epée's undertaking (though not by name) as a monument to the philosophic spirit: "These unfortunate beings, who have been condemned to imbecility and sorrowful solitude as a result of their loss of the sense that links man to his fellow beings, have found an unexpected resource in the happy application of metaphysical analysis to the art of language."[78]

The key to the creation of a rational and sure social order, the mathematician insisted, lay in the application of analysis to the terminology of the moral and political sciences—or the advent of "an equally exact and precise language" for ethics as that which existed for the physical sciences or the education of the deaf.[79] Condorcet proposed that if such a language, determined by philosophers, were to be substituted for ordinary, historically determined patterns of usage in discussions of moral issues, then endless differences in opinion might well give way to rational, enlightened consensus. Just as the ambiguous language of daily conversation had made fights about the meaning of terms a common feature of modern society, so, Condorcet hoped, a rarefied, "scientific" language for analyzing social questions represented France's greatest chance for moral certainty and, ultimately, peaceful accord and widespread happiness.

Yet the appeal of sign language as a model for the future was not restricted circa 1780 to the scientific circles around Condorcet, where analysis was already seen as a key path to progress. Here the example of the Comtesse de Genlis is also instructive. Genlis was certainly no intellectual ally of Condorcet's at the beginning of the 1780s. And surely, with her belief in the importance of the Christian moral tradition as the means to salvation, she had little interest in the development of a self-consciously secular "science" of morality. Yet, in her writings of this same period, we find, albeit in very different terms, the same opposition between an idealized sign language and ordinary usage of the vernacular. For the Comtesse de Genlis, the distinguished so-called *gouverner* of the sons of the Duc de Chartes and the author of many volumes on education, chose to praise the ethical possibilities inherent in sign language precisely because, in its remove from speech, it blinded its users to the irrational, mean-spirited, and immoral sides of life in contemporary society.

In her celebrated epistolary novel, *Adèle et Théodore, ou Lettres sur l'éducation* (1782), Mme de Genlis recounted a story concerning the effects of sign language that she claimed might interest a young *philosophe*. One day, the narrator receives a letter from Paris from a young deaf man of tender heart, a certain Hippolyte, whom the narrator had nursed through a terrible illness eighteen months earlier. Thanks to the extraordinary instruction of the Abbé de l'Epée, writes the deaf adolescent, he is finally able to explain his gratitude to God for saving his life "in your language" (French).[80] Yet Hippolyte, whose recent education has occurred in the silent world of methodical sign language, can not and does not suddenly see things with "our" eyes. In learning about the world through the pages of the Bible and the lessons of Epée rather than in conversation with those around him, Hippolyte has discovered only perfection, joy, virtue, and comradeship among people. As the narrator points out, Hippolyte remains, in his isolation from speech, as if in a bubble: "[I]ndiscretion, slander, libel are all vices of which he has no idea; he judges humans only by their deceptive demonstrations [of their sentiments]; . . . he takes falsity for tenderness, politeness for sensibility." As a result, "he believes that he inhabits a terrestrial Paradise; [and] he looks upon all men as his friends, his brothers!"[81] What, then, was Genlis's point in including this anecdote? Clearly, it was not to illustrate the dangers of self-deception; Genlis, like Rousseau, routinely stated that young people needed to be taught to protect themselves from a corrupted world. Rather, she aimed to illuminate the connection between widely accepted contemporary speech practices—from mindless *bavardage* to slander—and the perversion of modern social relations.[82] Only by entirely bypassing instruction in accepted *usage* (verbal or written) can Epée mold citizens who inhabit a utopian sphere where they see solely virtue in the world. As the narrator asks rhetorically in the last line of this letter, "To have a good opinion of mankind, must one be deaf and mute from birth," unable to hear humans' nastiness and falsity?[83] Or, some of Genlis's contemporaries might have inquired, would the adoption of a truly rational, analytical idiom such as the language of signs be enough to ensure the restoration of virtue and harmony to modern society? It was a question that educated French people seem to have found increasingly provocative in the course of the 1780s. And it was a question whose answer became especially important to the intellectually inclined participants in the nation's burgeoning *musées* and other small societies in the last decade before the Revolution.

MODEL SOCIETIES

During the 1770s and 1780s, proponents of gestural communication continually emphasized the potential for bodily signs to become a universal language, an idiom that fostered social and intellectual harmony and transcended the boundaries of nation, race, or *état*. Yet despite this universalist rhetoric, the sign language experiments of the last decades of the Old Regime were conducted almost entirely in the context of finite and specialized communities established by a small, urban elite. As we have seen, the two principal test sites for these endeavors—the theater and the classroom—were public but physically and socially restricted spaces. Furthermore, the values that these projects were designed to encourage corresponded less to those of the world at large than to those operative in a growing array of small-scale voluntary *sociétés*, relatively independent centers of intellectual and egalitarian sociability within the absolutist, Catholic, and resolutely hierarchical culture of late eighteenth-century France. For the private persons who increasingly assembled in these rarefied enclaves within the larger *société civile* saw themselves, much like Epée or Noverre or the audiences at their respective spectacles, as builders of model communities: temporary associations of individuals constituted and held together primarily through communication.

Accordingly, during the last decade before the Revolution, formally constituted learned societies replaced the informal café and salon culture of the 1740s and 1750s as the primary locus of interest in and support for recent semiotic experimentation. The most important of these newer institutions from the vantage point of language questions were a type of privately supported "society" called variously a *musée* or a *lycée*. The earliest were created under the auspices of the celebrated Loge des Neuf Soeurs in Paris. This iconoclastic Masonic lodge, founded in 1776 according to a plan conceived by the late Helvétius and the astronomer Joseph-Jérôme Lefrançois Lalande, flourished as a center of enlightenment thought and sociability in the late 1770s, despite its rocky relationship with the more conservative Grand Orient of Paris.[84] Then, in 1780, perhaps inspired by the temporary success of Pahin de La Blancherie's "salon de correspondance," several members of the Loge des Neuf Soeurs, led by the Protestant *savant* Antoine Court de Gébelin (who had attended Pahin's salon in its earliest months), decided to form a subsidiary organization with a more decidedly pedagogical and utilitarian mission. That year, Court de Gébelin became the president of the Société Apollonienne, a literary society that soon changed its name to the Musée de Paris.[85] The following year, another member of the Neuf Soeurs, Jean-François Pilâtre de Rozier, founded a scientific society called the Musée de Monsieur after its august patron, the king's brother, and this organization eventually became the Lycée de Paris in 1785. By the end of the decade, similar institutions were thriving in many French cities, including Toulouse, Metz, Lyon, Amiens, and Bordeaux, where they provided the public with an attractive alternative to *collèges*, academies, and other more entrenched scholarly or educational establishments.[86]

Historians have generally been rather dismissive of the intellectual significance of these *musées* of the 1780s, viewing them as poor relations of the official provincial academies peopled, with the notable exception of the Lycée de Paris, by a socially ambitious and intellectually marginal bourgeoisie.[87] As a result, relatively little effort has been dedicated to investigating the form or, especially, the substance of the debates conducted in the public assemblies and courses of these institutions.[88] Yet it is clear that their founders sought to do more than simply ape the academic customs of their more prestigious peers. As contemporary commentators frequently pointed out, the intellectual and social functions of these *musées* were intended to complement one another in a distinctive way.[89] Philosophically, these organizations were constituted with the express purpose of breaking down what were seen to be false academic distinctions between the sciences, on the one hand, and arts and letters, on the other; the very name of these societies, after all, suggested that members wished to worship all nine sister goddesses or muses under one roof. In the same spirit, within their own ranks members of the *musées* of the 1780s attempted to dissolve social distinctions—among people of different regions, ages, education levels, religious affiliations, financial status, professional accomplishments, and, to a limited degree, even sexes[90]—to a greater extent than was customary in either salons or official academies. And, in comparison to the participants in France's many provincial academies, the founders of these *musées* also tried to make the boundaries between members and the general public more fluid, frequently inviting in a certain prosperous segment of the public for lectures, concerts, readings, and free courses and reaching out to a different, less privileged element through philanthropic work.

These intentions translated into a special interest in the production and smooth transmission of ideas and, more specifically, questions of language and signs. One of the chief ways the men and occasional women of the *musées* tried to realize their combined social, philosophical, and utilitarian ambitions was by looking for ways to improve "reciprocal commerce" both within their own small society of "friends and scholars" and across the intellectual and social divisions of elite eighteenth-century culture.[91] And in this connection, the members of these newly constituted *musées* in Paris and other French cities seem to have taken a particular interest in language planning and semiotic innovation, including the novel experiments in reviving the *langage d'action* as a means of cultural change that had been occurring over the last two decades. To understand the reasons for their concern with these developments, we must begin by looking at the specific sources of their sociolinguistic values, especially those that they shared with that distinctive Parisian institution of the 1770s: the Loge des Neuf Soeurs.

First, it is important to note that the members of these new *musées*, like the members of the Neuf Soeurs, were steeped in the culture of Freemasonry, which had long been dedicated to devising novel ways to ensure friendship, unity, and accord among its initiates. Like most other institutions of sociability in the early modern Republic of Letters, lodges deliberately prohibited mention of divisive issues (including questions of religion, politics, and morality) and maintained elaborate rules for conducting discussions.[92] This policy was effected so as to avoid stirring up the hatreds and disagreements of the external world, as well as to preclude inciting the ire of the royal government or the church. But the Freemasons, in particular, seem to have believed that one of the primary ways to cement fraternal bonds and to prevent disagreements within their own ranks was through specialized linguistic mechanisms. Not only did they promote the ritual use of certain words, sometimes with the claim that they represented clues to a lost language or lost knowledge of a golden age. Among late eighteenth-century Masons, symbolic and often secret codes—languages of hieroglyphics, gestures, and other visual signs—also functioned as vital tools in the establishment of a cosmopolitan but socially exclusive, homosocial sensibility.[93] Certainly, members of advanced learned societies, including the Neuf Soeurs and the various *musées*, distanced themselves considerably in the last decades of the century from the most byzantine or mystical of these customs. The connection to traditional Freemasonry was always extremely tenuous in all of these newer institutions. Yet, in a general sense, the Masonic linguistic tradition endured. Specialized signs were used both as keys to recover an idealized past and as means to ensure community among men who made it their business "to cultivate the arts, without forming parties, without quarrels" (in the words of a member of the Loge des Neuf Soeurs and then the Musée de Paris).[94]

But Freemasonry was only one of several sources for the linguistic self-consciousness of the members of the Loge des Neuf Soeurs and the *musées*. Participants in these institutions were also heavily indebted to the liberal Enlightenment notion that private individuals had a responsibility to work to improve the world through philanthropy, advocacy for just causes, and sponsorship of projects of public utility. Moreover, in this capacity, they continued to believe in the importance of promoting the enlightened values of their own small "society"—concern with the advancement of useful knowledge, as well as consensus born of egalitarian and rational discourse—on a larger scale. As Bricaire de la Dixmerie put it circa 1780, "We [in the Loge des Neuf Soeurs] join to the very praiseworthy project of enlightening ourselves that of aiding and helping our fellow brethren."[95] And well into the decade of the Revolution, participants looked to recent exercises in applied sensationalist epistemology as means to achieve these goals. Of course, the members of the Neuf Soeurs were not unique in agitating on behalf of new methods for educating the deaf, novel forms of gestural theater, or the possibility of establishing a philosophical or universal language. The *questione della lingua* still occupied the attention of most of the significant European institutions of elite sociability in the eighteenth century, just as it had since the founding of the Italian academies several centuries earlier;[96] and certain vocal participants in these debates, including Marmontel and Condorcet, appear to have been members of both the Académie Française and this unusual lodge. But the Académie Française continued in the 1780s, despite the growing presence and power of the *philosophes* within its ranks, to define itself as an institution dedicated to the safeguarding of the French language of a circumscribed literary and cultural elite. In contrast, many of the initial members of the Loge des Neuf Soeurs—from Pierre-Nicolas Changeux to Benjamin Franklin—manifested a profound interest in prescriptive language planning and semiotic experimentation, moving away from "usage" or "custom" toward an ahistoric notion of "nature" or "reason" as a guideline.[97] Furthermore, the members of this latter group tended to see their plans for improved communication as efforts on behalf of the good of the public as a whole. Indeed, some even argued that rational language reform would ultimately be instrumental in bringing about cognitive and, consequently, social and moral transformations in the future.

Especially important in this regard was the work of Antoine Court de Gébelin, whose home had become the meeting place for the lodge beginning in 1778. Throughout the decade of the 1770s, in a series of massive volumes entitled *Le Monde primitif, analysé et comparé avec le monde moderne*, Court de Gébelin had set about trying to rediscover and to catalogue the original, universal mother tongue, the collection of radical sounds and images that he took to be given by and representative of nature—or, in Genette's terms, "mimological"—rather than arbitrary.[98] How did he hope to recover this primal language? Court de Gébelin assumed that the best course was to attempt to decipher all the traces or debris of this primeval idiom still extant in the modern world. Emblems, myths, ancient words, coats of arms, coins, hieroglyphs, Indian languages—all these "mute monuments" became grist for his etymological and analytical mill. Even Epée's "methodical signs" promised clues, Court de Gébelin claimed, as to the original universal grammar, the invariable principles by which all languages had developed, and the "universal writing that has been sought after with so much care and which can succeed only if it is drawn from nature and not from arbitrary projects."[99] But it is important to note that what drove Court de Gébelin in this quest was not simply antiquarianism or a fascination with the burgeoning field of comparative linguistics. The physiocratic philosopher believed that the discovery and reconstruction of this original idiom, or protolanguage, would allow modern men nothing less than a chance to uncover the timeless, natural laws governing human happiness, and thereby to restore peace and prosperity on earth. For Court de Gébelin insisted that this lost knowledge, both visual and aural, would provide the key to the construction of a superior modern language, one

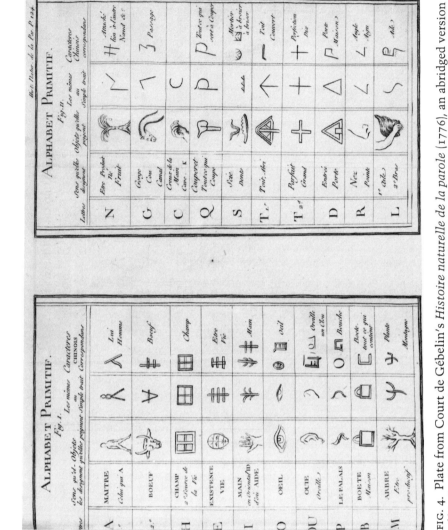

FIG. 4. Plate from Court de Gébelin's *Histoire naturelle de la parole* (1776), an abridged version of his *Le Monde primitif*, designed to show that all written languages have their roots in basic pictographs and hieroglyphs of natural things. Photograph courtesy of the General Research Division, the New York Public Library, Astor, Lenox and Tilden Foundations.

FIG. 5. "Orphée, ou les Effets du Discours," frontispiece engraved by
Antoine-Louis Romanet, from volume two of Court de Gébelin's *Le Monde
primitif, analysé et comparé avec le monde moderne* (1774). In this alle-
gory about imagistic or allegorical communication, Orpheus's poetic
speech reveals the eternal truths of primitive religion and produces
perfect harmony in the world. It is this kind of language that Court de
Gébelin hoped to recover and to employ to similar effect in the future.
Photograph courtesy of the General Research Division, the New York
Public Library, Astor, Lenox and Tilden Foundations.

which would aid in restoring the purity and perfection of an earlier golden age in which people communicated without impediment and easily realized their common bonds [see Figs. 4 and 5].

Not all savants greeted with pleasure either Court de Gébelin's extraordinary conclusions or his strange blend of sensationalist and rationalist epistemology, physiocracy, Freemasonry, philology, Protestant theology, and faith in the redemptive potential of language reform. His conviction that the original language had once made nature utterly transparent remained a minority position in the late eighteenth century.[100] But Court de Gébelin's project garnered considerable public attention and acclaim, not least in Parisian philosophical circles of the early 1780s.[101] Under the brief leadership of Court de Gébelin, the members and associates of the Musée de Paris (many of whom also had prior ties to the Loge des Neuf Soeurs) tried to build on this heterogeneous group of sources, hoping to use rational language reform to accomplish external good works, on the one hand, and to enhance group solidarity and internal "concord," on the other.[102] And the mission of this organization, however vague, remained fundamentally unchanged after Court de Gébelin's premature death as a proponent and then victim of Mesmerism in 1784. The legacy of Court de Gébelin's life work, his former student Rabaut Saint-Etienne explained in 1784 to his fellow members of the Musée, was an appreciation of the historical connection between the form of language and the nature of society; changes in the nature or means of communication had made possible all of the major transformations in the mental capacities of humans.[103] Moreover, the discovery of this relationship, commented another of Court de Gébelin's eulogizers, the Comte d'Albon, now paved the way for a new "revolution in ideas."[104] Indeed, it was the influence of Court de Gébelin's teachings that led Rabaut Saint-Etienne to postulate a short while after Court de Gébelin's death that another graphic "revolution," capable of producing an impact comparable to the invention of the alphabet, was on the immediate horizon.[105]

Rabaut offered few practical guidelines for how this transformation in representation and, consequently, cognition could be accomplished or even affected by current strivings. But in this intellectual climate, other members of the Musée de Paris came to the unsurprising conclusion that deliberate, rational language planning aimed at improving the nature of communication in the present should constitute one of this learned society's principal concerns. Antoine Tournon, a grammarian and teacher of French, announced this idea in a paper entitled "De la nécessité de créer des mots," which he first read at the Musée in 1786 before publishing it in the *Journal de la langue française* of Lyon (a periodical closely connected with the *musée* of that city, as well as the

Musée de Paris).[106] In this essay, the author insisted, contrary to the traditional purist wing of the Académie Française and even the more moderate stance exemplified by Marmontel, that the evolution of language should no longer be left up to the whims of usage, either on the part of nobles at court or esteemed writers. Only by curtailing an anarchic system of coinage and circulation would the public ever be freed from "enslavement" to words or learn to avoid the dangerous errors in thought that led directly to social strife. As Tournon explained in another essay in the *Journal de la langue française* of the same date, the *abus des mots* could be held responsible for many of the world's most serious ills:

> How many vague words there are in our language! How many words signify everything and signify nothing! From this, these interminable disputes, these ruinous lawsuits, these dangerous errors, these disguised vices that accompany an absurd charlatanism. No one gets along any longer; as a result, disorder, inconsistency, and, sometimes, loss of judgment. . . . Do you ever see two men argue about the form of an object that they have right under their eyes? What is, therefore, the source of errors? The *abus des mots*, their triviality, the different ideas that everyone attaches to them. . . . How many legal proceedings have been prompted, how many families ruined, how many incredible reversals have been caused by the misuse of a single word![107]

But Tournon also argued that philosophically minded individuals could play a vital role in repairing this kind of linguistically inspired social turmoil. By clarifying and "fixing" the meaning of unstable terms, by establishing rules for the creation of new ones, and by encouraging the public to follow prescribed and rational rules for language use, Tournon concluded that men like himself could effectively combat the *abus des mots*. The result, declared the grammarian, would be just what Rabaut Saint-Etienne had prophesied: the end of error or controversy in all of the sciences, including that of morality. For Tournon believed that the establishment of a mathematically precise political and ethical language would finally make the true meaning of even the most contested terms—from *bien* to *vertu* to *liberté*—self-evident and indisputable. Indeed, he insisted that just as a faulty language could be held responsible for many of France's most entrenched problems, so language reform could ensure the future happiness of the nation.

To this end, the members of the Musée de Paris made various attempts both to establish model systems of communication and to reach out to an amorphous public in need of better linguistic knowledge and examples. They offered free classes in modern European languages, including French.[108] They subscribed and contributed to the *Journal de la langue française*, the first French journal to attempt to establish rational or "positive" laws for the perfection (and hence enrichment) of the national tongue.[109] They established ties with far-flung centers of learning, including Franklin's American Philosophical Society in Philadelphia, a body that also took the study of language to be one of its chief concerns.[110] They made honorary members out of men such as Peter Pallas, the great German linguist hired by Catherine the Great to compile the vocabularies of all the languages of the world. They even briefly published a journal, the *Mémoires du Musée de Paris*, containing articles on related subjects such as a new method of musical notation. Yet the Musée de Paris seems to have been constantly riven by petty fights and internal discord.[111] In the final analysis, its members never found a way to establish a coherent agenda that united their philosophical, pedagogical, and philanthropic, as well as social, interests.

Instead, it was the Musée de Bordeaux that led the way toward this goal during the last years of the 1780s. The Abbé Dupont des Jumeaux, a mathematician, a Freemason, and the prior of Eymet in Périgord, founded the Musée de Bordeaux in 1783.[112] Building on the Bordelais tradition of Masonic *bienfaisance* as well as his own experience as a member of the Musée de Paris, Dupont des Jumeaux attempted to fashion a voluntary association that would be dedicated, in contrast to the official local academy, to the broad dissemination of useful ideas as both a principle and a practice.[113] Dupont des Jumeaux found support for this project in the person of the Archbishop of Bordeaux, Jérôme Marie Champion de Cicé. In the early 1780s, Champion de Cicé was also involved in sponsoring a local priest and Freemason named Roch-Ambroise-Cucurron Sicard in his studies of the pedagogical methods of the Abbé de l'Epée, a fellow member of the Société Philanthropique, in Paris.[114] Eventually, the archbishop's two interests came together. When the Abbé Sicard returned from Paris with the intention of establishing a school for the deaf in Bordeaux, the members of the local *musée* immediately seized upon his project as the perfect charitable and pedagogical commitment for a new learned society.

From its founding in early 1786, Sicard's Institution des Sourds et Muets de Bordeaux was intimately linked with the Musée de Bordeaux.[115] Financially, the members of the Musée de Bordeaux supported the functioning of the school. Intellectually, Sicard's deaf students provided the members of the Musée with a subject of scientific scrutiny, as well as a model for the association of social activism with Enlightenment epistemological theory. Sicard lectured frequently at the Musée on problems of language and pedagogy (citing Court de Gébelin, among others, as an inspiration).[116] Moreover, the instructor of the deaf, himself a prominent member of the Musée, used this institution as a setting for the public display of his pupils' learning and patriotism, a practice clearly modeled after that of Epée in Paris.[117]

News of the joint civic project undertaken by these two institutions reached Paris almost immediately, as Parisian associates of the Musée de Bordeaux, many of whom were also members of the Musée de Paris and the Société Philanthropique, were kept abreast of simultaneous developments in both Bordelais establishments.[118] Furthermore, the *Journal de Paris*, which was founded in 1777 by three philanthropically inclined members of the Loge des Neuf Soeurs, drew national attention to Sicard's achievements at the close of the 1780s. According to a poem by a member of the Musée de Bordeaux that appeared on the first page of the *Journal de Paris* in 1787, Sicard was using sign language to "create" new beings for the benefit of both the church and the state.[119] By associating themselves with such activities, the members of the *musées* of Paris and Bordeaux thus encouraged the public to view the propagation of a rational, philosophic idiom rooted in natural signs as an act of spiritual and civic duty, as well as enlightened charity.

Not surprisingly, when the Parisian Academy of Inscriptions and Belles-Lettres held a contest in 1787 and again in 1789 on the "origin, progress, and effects of pantomime on the Ancients," the winner was a member of both the Musée de Paris and the Musée de Monsieur named François-Henri-Stanislas de L'Aulnaye, the same *avocat au Parlement* and *bibliothécaire* who had recently presented the Musée de Paris with his plan to right the imperfections in the sign system used for musical notation.[120] L'Aulnaye's response was the only one that this academy received which was thoroughly rooted in both sensationalist language theory and contemporary ethnography.[121] The barrister used these sources to evoke a distant, primitive society in which pantomime had functioned simultaneously as a powerful political language, a "Catechism of Morality, more efficient than all of our pedagogical institutions because of the attraction that it had for these Peoples," and as an irresistible incentive to "join together with our fellow men."[122] L'Aulnaye lamented the historical demise of this socially integrative sign system just as he despaired about the state of contemporary mores. However, he refused to give up hope for the restoration of this older form of communication. L'Aulnaye believed that certain signs, such as a red flag, which he called "a thousand times more eloquent than all the proclamations in the world," continued to suggest what this preverbal force must have been like.[123] Moreover, L'Aulnaye proposed that the propagation of such energetic and iconic signs could actually help bring back the natural values and "fixed" moral notions of an earlier age.

L'Aulnaye did not, however, provide his readers with much detail about what his vision of the future really entailed. As a result, by the time that L'Aulnaye was awarded the Academy of Inscriptions's essay prize in the middle of the excitement of the summer of 1789, his ideas about signs and morality had, in one sense, already come to seem the product of an earlier way of thought. But as the language debates surrounding the semiotic innovations of recent decades rapidly spilled out of self-contained social spaces such as classrooms, theaters, or private meeting rooms, the latent political and even revolutionary content of responses such as that of L'Aulnaye was also increasingly apparent. After all, L'Aulnaye's dream of a modern equivalent to the *langage d'action*, cultivated within the confines of two Parisian *musées* in the late 1780s, was already that fateful summer well on its way to becoming both a tactical reference point in partisan interventions in contemporary events and an essential aspect of a burgeoning revolutionary political imagination.

The question of the relationship between the activities of learned societies as places of voluntary association within Old Regime civil society, on the one hand, and revolutionary political culture and theory, on the other, has attracted considerable scholarly attention in recent decades. The problem is complicated by the fact that despite obvious points of continuity, the members of these relatively elite establishments of the 1770s and 1780s never explicitly sought either to undermine existing authority or to reconstitute the current regime on the basis of popular sovereignty or will prior to 1789.[124] Indeed, as we have seen, regardless of their individual predilections, members of these organizations were always restricted to discussing that which did not threaten the state's monopoly on political judgments or political language. Thus most historians have concluded, following either Furet or the contemporary German philosopher Jürgen Habermas, that it was the particular kind of sociability, rather than the set of ideas that these voluntary associations cultivated, which prefigured and paved the way for revolutionary political culture. Furet proposed that the intellectual sociability of eighteenth-century *sociétés de pensée* was governed by a democratic ethos that would eventually make itself manifest in Jacobinism. Habermas described these same institutions as providing a new public space from which public opinion based on rational, critical judgment could emerge.[125]

But can we so easily separate the social practices from the specific ideas propagated in these small *sociétés* in the years before the Revolution? Indeed, the desire to create harmony and unanimity—and the faith that this could come about through the development of better means of intellectual exchange—seems to have governed not only the internal policies of the *musées* and similar kinds of institutions but also their intellectual preoccupations. And, I propose, it is this interest in communication, as practice *and* theory, that ultimately gave such institutions their nascent political salience. Neither the idea of the *abus des mots* as a problem of modern life nor the concept of a new idiom based on the model of the *langage d'action* as a solution can be said to have constituted a direct challenge to authority of any kind prior to 1789. However, both these notions gave late Old Regime intellectuals, clustered in small, idealized *sociétés*, a reason to think about and then to try out—as both a tool for establishing internal cohesion and as a broad civic gesture—a set of obsolete communicative practices belonging, ostensibly, to a pre-Christian, premonarchical, prenational, and socially unified past. And as the judicial Revolution of 1789 became a reality, earlier experiments in recovering the *langage d'action* as a form of modern cultural practice suggested one potential means of reviving this mythic paradise in the present.

In fact, already in the last year or so before the meeting of the Estates-General, while social and ideological tensions were steadily mounting in all quarters, the approach to language that had been developed and nurtured within such restricted contexts as the Musée de Paris began to be utilized to new ends. Specifically, denunciations of certain individuals or social groups for deliberately misusing ambiguous terms, as well as calls for a freshly purified language to form the basis of a universal moral code, became viable rhetorical strategies among oppositional political figures. Precedent for such actions could be found in the writings of earlier radicals, such as Jean-Paul Marat, who, in the course of the Revolution, was to find novel uses for his scathing 1774 attack on tyrannical politicians for "denaturing the names of things."[126] One might even trace this strategy back farther to such anonymous mid-century texts as that anti-English exposé of the *abus des mots* entitled *Le Livre jaune*.[127] But the tactical use of the new epistemology, with all its references to (linguistic) laws and police and jurisdictions and truth,[128] became increasingly prevalent in the late 1780s in the context of the radical political propaganda of men such as the amateur scientist and member of the Musée de Paris, Jean-Louis Carra. In the hands of this very minor and angry *savant*, the controller-general Charles-Alexandre de Calonne could, in 1788, be denounced for indulging in exactly those habits—of "evad[ing] the positive meaning of words," of giving sentences "vague and uncertain nuance[s]," of employing "contradictory and improper expressions of indulgence and pity" in discussions of virtue and justice—that had quite recently been treated as broad social and epistemological problems in the context of the Musée de Paris. Moreover, the solution to recent troubles, such as that posed by the duplicitous royal finance minister, could be said to lie in unmasking and exposing his hypocritical language and then introducing in its place a purified, exact "language of truth" whose external signs would make "the true nature of good and evil, of justice and injustice" totally clear and indisputable.[129]

In other words, while circumventing royal laws controlling language (not to mention royal censors), the *libellistes* of the late 1780s began to create out of several decades of linguistic experimentation and speculation a new kind of language politics. A broad epistemological problem—the lack of an exact correlation between words and things—was now transformed into a moral problem to the extent that people could be accused of deliberately failing to make the two correspond. Similarly, an epistemological ideal—of a perfectly transparent, representative language—was now made into a political ideal to the extent that fostering this language became associated with virtue. And at the same time as the champions of the Third Estate began to claim that the ideal state of free and perfect communication long imagined by the *philosophes* was imminently realizable on a larger scale than anyone had previously envisioned, political agitators from Carra to Condorcet had also already begun to draw upon that other central Enlightenment idea: that power was rooted in finding new means to control the words and meanings of others. The result of this confluence of epistemological principles was not to be what anyone in the late 1780s could have expected.

4

Revolutionary Regeneration and the Politics of Signs, 1789–94

I n September of 1791, as the National Assembly debated the future form of the new French constitution, Charles-Maurice de Talleyrand attempted to draw his fellow deputies' attention to a related problem: the future form of the French language. This revolutionary assembly, Talleyrand pointed out in the context of his plan for a comprehensive system of national education, was certainly aware "how much power or, rather, impact signs have on ideas and, as a result, on the customs that it wants to generate or strengthen" [see Fig. 6]. After all, he noted, the deep connection between thought and communication had become "particularly evident" as of late.[1] This celebrated deputy thus argued that the nation's representatives had an obligation to craft a new language policy distinct from that of the Old Regime. Not only should the Assembly concern itself with refining and democratizing "the language of the Constitution and laws." He also proposed that the time had arrived to renew Leibniz's century-old quest to discover a truly philosophical and universal sign system in which there was perfect accord between signs and their referents, like gold for wealth. And to illustrate how close a solution lay, Talleyrand pointed to the one existing sign system that seemed to him to be "the living image of thought, in which all the elements apparent to the eye show nothing arbitrary, through which even the most abstract ideas become almost visible and which, in its simple and learned decomposition, introduces the true grammar not of words but of ideas."[2] That language was the gestural and "methodical" sign system developed in the preceding decades for the education of the deaf. In Talleyrand's estimation, what he called *la langue des signes* had the potential to become "perhaps the first method for making the mind perfectly analytical and for putting it on guard against the multitude of errors that we owe to the imperfection of our [ordinary] signs."[3] In the midst of the ideological, political, and linguistic discord that followed the king's flight to Varennes earlier that summer, Talleyrand used this example to advance the idea that the time when language would finally cease to be a source of variable and mistaken opinions was now at hand.

TABLEAU DES SCIENCES PHILOSOPHIQUES,

DES BELLES-LETTRES ET DES BEAUX-ARTS.

N° I.er

L'HOMME sent, il pense, il juge, il raisonne, il invente, il communique ses idées par des gestes, par des sons, par des discours écrits ou prononcés; il communique ses affections par l'harmonie des vers, des sons, des formes et des couleurs; il les consacre par des monumens; il recherche quelle est la nature des êtres, ce qu'il doit, ce qu'on lui doit, ce qu'il peut et ce qu'il fut.

(Insc.tut National.)

Sent . . . . Ses sensations sont . . . Sensations directes. / Sensations réfléchies.

Pense . . . Ses idées sont . . . Positives. / Abstraites.

Juge . . . Ses propositions . . . { Sont . . . Simples. / Complexes. } { Servent à . . . Énoncer. / Comparer. / Diviser. / Définir. }

Raisonne . . . Ses raisonnemens se disposent en . . . Syllogisme. / Enthymème. / Dilemme. / Induction.

Invente . . . Ses méthodes sont . . . L'analyse. / La synthèse.

Ses idées par des signes.

Des idées . . . . Logique.

Des propositions . . . SCIENCE.

Du raisonnement.

Des gestes . . . La Pantomime { Logiqr., enin- cement des beaux. (en Marts.) }

Le Vocabulaire . . . La Grammaire.
La Syntaxe.

Contenus. / Disposés pour former des propositions.

Écrits avec des caractères . . . Hiéroglyphiques (dans l'enfance du monde.) idéaux. (chez les Chinois.) / Élémentaires ou lettres, avec accens. et quantité. / Colonne proposition les En relief, qu'on distingue par le toucher; (enseigne- ment des aveugles.)

Des sons ou mots . . . .

Invention . . . Plan.
Disposition . . . Exorde. / Division. / Narration. / Confirmation. / Péroraison.
Élocution . . . Diction. / Style.

Arrangés pour composer un discours.

Exprimés . . . Articulation. / Déclamation. . . . La Rhétorique.

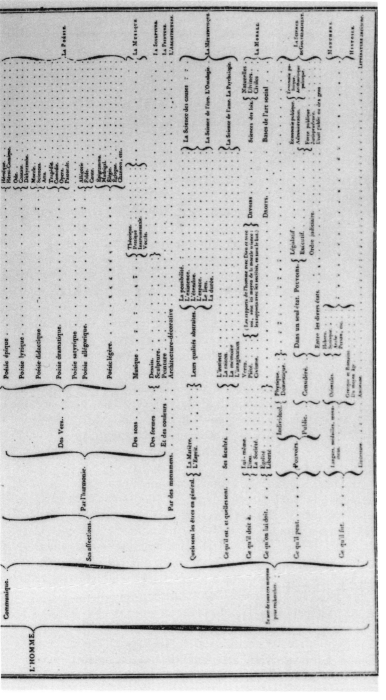

FIG. 6. "Tableau des Sciences philosophiques, des belles-lettres et des beaux-arts," a table published by the National Assembly in Talleyrand's *Rapport sur l'instruction publique* (1791) to illustrate which branches of knowledge stem from which aspects of *l'homme moral*. Note the centrality within the whole schema of man's ability to represent ideas with signs and, more specifically, the importance of gestural sign language to the development of grammar.

What he sought above all was a language that could become a "vigorous instrument" for making the enlightened moral ideals of the early Revolution universally accepted on rational grounds.[4]

Of course, sign language never came into wide use during the French Revolution (despite the satirical prediction of the royalist writer Jean-Claude Gorjy that the revolutionaries, in their pursuit of extreme novelty and uniformity, would soon be banning French in favor of a silent *système pantomimique*).[5] But Talleyrand was neither the first nor the last revolutionary leader to hold up this recent invention as a combination of goal and potential weapon in the effort to secure the principles of 1789. For the celebration of sign language during the first years of the Revolution was symptomatic of the endurance of a distinctive semiotic vision, inherited from the last decades of the Old Regime, that both helped to make the idea of a comprehensive "revolutionary" transformation of social and political life conceivable at this historical juncture and played a substantial role in determining the form that this protracted struggle would take. Revolutionary political culture, with its emphasis on consensus and harmony and its antipathy to factionalism or even contestation (at least in theory) must be seen not only as an outgrowth of earlier political practices or beliefs, including the tradition of royal absolutism and Rousseau's concept of a general will. Additionally, and more fundamentally, it should be viewed as a direct result of its framers' historically specific epistemological suppositions and assumptions. The first of these was the idea that the *abus des mots*, rather than legitimate differences of opinion, constituted the root cause of most dissension and strife. The second was that a perfected language, modeled after the "methodical" language of signs, could be a panacea, a means to achieve certainty and consensus about the true nature of things, including the abstractions of a brand new political theory, and consequently a vehicle of peace in the social sphere.

To make this claim about the significance to the Revolution of a particular enlightened understanding of signs is certainly not to deny that the revolutionary *querelle des mots* was, in large part, imposed by educated participants upon an underlying social, economic, and ideological struggle. The key purpose of this chapter is, however, to explain why the Revolution appeared to work the other way around. To many of its chief architects as well as critics, it seemed to be a battle over language and definition that promised, for better or for worse, to produce extraordinary social, political, and moral consequences. What is ultimately surprising about the language politics of the Revolution is not simply that the model of sign language encouraged "enlightened" revolutionary leaders (such as Talleyrand) in their faith that the right signs would make it possible for the nation to speak with one authoritative, rational

voice. Much less self-evident is how this inherited linguistic vision ultimately aggravated the struggle to actualize the principles laid down in
the great revolutionary texts. It caused what appeared to be a contest
over leadership in language as well as governance and an extended fight
over who, on behalf of the now-sovereign people, held the authority to
name the real world according to what conception of it. For one of the
aspects of the revolutionary struggle that participants on all sides found
most perplexing was that the more deputies like Talleyrand insisted on
the importance of making the national language perfectly reflective and
"fixed," the more it seemed that these same men were using words and
other communicative signs as tools to constitute and to encourage new
and competing realities.

REGENERATION: METHODS
AND MODELS, 1789–91

The French Revolution began in mid-1789 with a series of dramatic political gestures and a groundswell of popular violence. No less significantly, the same crucial months brought forth an extraordinary and un-
anticipated outpouring of words. From street corners to private societies
to the newly constituted National Assembly, individual subjects seized
the opportunity to make public declarations of their ideas and thoughts.
New journals, pamphlets, and other political tracts proliferated, many of
them employing titles with terms such as *bouche* and *voix* and *cri* to
suggest their connection to this eruption of speech. And in all of these
novel forums, new spokesmen using new combinations of words before
unfamiliar audiences found that an ability with language could suddenly be a ticket to unprecedented influence or power.[6]

At least, that is how the events of this pivotal year figure within early
revolutionary discourse. For the public *prise de parole* of 1789 quickly
became a key subject of the speeches and texts that it generated. In the
early days of this conflict, the seeming explosion of language provided
patriots with two essential things: evidence to support the idea of the
present as a historical rupture, and proof of the importance of signs to
the process of revolutionary regeneration. Changes in language usage
and function quickly became a central element in a burgeoning revolutionary mythology.

Almost immediately, the idea that 1789 marked a full-scale and in-
stantaneous break with the nation's past infused contemporary explanations of recent events.[7] France, it was widely postulated that first revolutionary year, had suddenly been released from the weight of its traditions and the tyranny of the past; the nation was ready to enter a brand
new phase in its history and, indeed, in the history of the world. For evi-

dence of this rupture, this argument continued, one had only to look at the new conditions governing speech. Whereas France's political system had long been characterized by secrecy and deception, conversations about the future health of the nation had suddenly become open to all. In opposition to the official restrictions and informal limitations on public communication common in the past, the authors of the Declaration of the Rights of Man and of the Citizen agreed that "the free expression of thought and opinions is one of the most precious rights of man."[8] And the idea of an expanded and open sphere for the exchange of ideas had quickly developed into one of the hallmarks of this transformation. The real indicator of the advent of "the new world," according to a pamphlet of that same year, was that people suddenly spoke to one another "with passion, [and] especially with liberty."[9]

Yet it is important to note that the members and allies of the Third Estate who produced the countless political pamphlets, journals, and speeches that appeared in the months immediately following the meeting of the Estates-General clearly did not believe that everything around them had changed overnight or that a revolutionary society could be forged without any points of reference. Simply announcing a break with past customs or practices was not enough to create an ideal state. Thus they repeatedly insisted that the establishment of a new model of governance based on popular sovereignty and natural rights required the recuperation of a moral ideal that they conceptualized as the property of a distant golden age, a primordial time and place characterized less by what people were than by what they had not yet become. More precisely, what many champions of the Revolution advocated in 1789 was the regeneration of the French people in accordance with the basic principles—freedom, equality, sociability, honesty, vitality, virtue—that, they believed, had characterized the first societies to emerge from the state of nature. Enlightenment teachings had, of course, long stressed the malleable, perfectible character of humans. But through the use of the word *régénération*, one of the central terms of 1789, the Christian ideals of *nouvelle création* or *seconde naissance* were effectively linked with both Enlightenment epistemology and the utopian goals of the early Revolution.[10] In the near future, many speeches and texts suggested prophetically, the Revolution would provide the political and social conditions for a rediscovery of the moral purity that corrupt governing had sapped. For some, this meant that paradise on earth would be realized anew; for others, it simply indicated that the French people were on the road toward unmitigated progress. But in either case, it was assumed that the French language could function not simply as a sign that a transformation had already occurred but as a tool in the construction of this new world. Such efforts as the writing of a Declaration of the

Rights of Man in the late summer of 1789 can also be seen as evidence of the faith revolutionaries held in regeneration through language, in the spelling out of basic laws or truths as a means to their realization. The same might be said of early efforts to translate such foundational texts into foreign and regional tongues, to read them aloud, and to disseminate them as widely as possible until they were universally known. Just as language provided an indicator of changes from the past to the present, it also seemed to offer a means to an ideal future.

However, the anticipated partnership between language and regeneration soon proved to be rife with problems as well. As the authors of the Declaration realized (much to their frustration) in the course of composing this document the first summer of the Revolution, they were hampered in their task by the limitations of the suddenly outmoded and often polysemous political lexicon that they had at their disposal. Or, to put it another way, they quickly became convinced that before they could effectively set out the rights of all citizens, they needed first to discover a way for reason to speak "a purer language" (in the words of one delegate) than had the American Declaration of Independence. They required an idiom that allowed "all men to feel, without needing to think about it, that the truths announced were always in their hearts" (according to another), and a means to explain a set of principles so that, in their lucidity, veracity, and directness, they might become a "children's alphabet taught in schools" (as stated by a third).[11]

Of course, the revolutionaries of 1789 may well have derived some practical advantages from the unfixedness of the existing idiom. François Furet and Ran Halévi have, for example, argued that the very imprecision and flexibility of such inherited terms as "constitution" made possible almost universal acclaim for the idea of instituting one during the first years of the Revolution.[12] And it is indeed probable that the ambiguity of many such critical concepts initially facilitated their use as rallying points. However, contemporary discourse suggests that even while enormous hopes were placed on language as a path to regeneration, this kind of instability of meaning, the fact that the vocabulary of politics had not been precisely "defined," "determined," or "fixed" and was still contaminated by the values of the past, was a constant source of worry. For many early revolutionaries, both within the Assembly and outside it, also insisted that in order to ensure the recuperation of the ideal moral state that they imagined, they would have to replace the elaborate and often empty language through which the king and his coterie had traditionally manipulated the mass of French people. What they would require instead was a simple, natural public idiom, a corollary of natural law that was precise, laconic, unembellished, devoid of "metaphor or abstraction," and thus impossible to misunderstand or even contest.[13] In other words, it was increasingly argued during the early months of the Revolution that in order to become an effective tool in destroying the hold of the recent past and in bringing about the moral transformation of the French people, the French language needed already to have been "regenerated" itself.

Initially, some revolutionaries believed that this idiom would gradually develop of its own accord. The emergence of new concepts and new issues would, it was assumed, surely alter the vocabulary, form, and delivery of the French language, making some words obsolete and giving others new or strengthened meanings. After all, the Abbé Emmanuel Sieyès had already famously declared in the winter of 1789 that it was only a matter of time before terms that had long signified "nothing" (such as the critical "third estate") came to mean "something," or before the lost harmony between *les mots* and *les choses* was restored as an inevitable result of political developments.[14] But during the months after the meeting of the Estates-General, it also became clear that the invention of names could lead to the spontaneous creation of new entities with new, revolutionary identities—for institutions like the self-declared National Assembly, for places like the newly created *départements*, and even for individuals with such self-imposed monikers as Anacharsis Cloots or Olympe de Gouges. And increasingly, it appeared that strategic modifications and improvements in the teaching and form of the French language could produce beneficial changes in the judgments, opinions, and even actions of those who relied upon this idiom to think and to communicate with people around them. The author of an anonymous tract sent to the National Assembly in 1789 imagined the effects of a perfected, uniform national tongue, one that was simple, clear, with "no more dissidence, no more frivolous distinctions, no more equivocal terms, no more disputes about words because they were all defined." The result, he claimed, would be nothing less than the emergence of "uniform sentiments," which would, in turn, lead to "the purification of morals" until it was finally evident exactly what virtue really was.[15] By the end of the first year of the Revolution, deliberate steps to purify and to rationalize the national language in accordance with the rules ostensibly provided by nature (rather than tradition or usage) were considered by many "enlightened" patriots to be essential to the larger project of revolutionary regeneration.

Nevertheless, despite years of prior discussion regarding hypothetical modifications intended to enhance the efficacy of the French language, few ideas were put forth in 1789 for ways to institute these changes. Furthermore, few concrete examples of such practices existed upon which reformers could draw in their planning. Then, in early 1790, there emerged a striking model of an already regenerated language—a language constituted not out of haphazard customs but, rather, deliberately out of analysis, reason, and naturally iconic signs—aiding directly in the larger process of social and moral renewal. This was the "natural" and "methodical" sign language that had been developed for use in the education of the deaf over the last two decades.

Ironically, it was the untimely death of the Abbé de l'Epée in December of 1789, half a year after the storming of the Bastille, that brought his work firmly into the public eye and made it more than just a philosophical curiosity. His funeral two months later effectively introduced a larger and broader audience than ever before to the extraordinary spectacle of young students communicating complex ideas through gestural signs. Moreover, following the upheavals of the summer months, this memorial service provided a group of prominent Parisian patriots with a platform for recasting Epée's success in instructing the deaf and mute as a revolutionary triumph.

The Commune of Paris, remarking on the history of governmental indifference and even hostility to Epée's work, now took the lead in efforts to protect the future of the *abbé*'s school and to honor his memory.[16] According to the report that a lieutenant mayor named Jean-Louis Brousse-Desfaucherets read to the Commune in early February 1790, the city had a responsibility to recognize and to perpetuate Epée's methods, "which give an existence to these Unfortunates whom Nature seemed to have condemned to eternal ignorance . . . and to endow them with thought and life."[17] Ten days later, when the members of the Commune appealed to the National Assembly for help in honoring the Abbé de L'Epée, they utilized this same logic. The Commune's address depicted the *abbé* as a father who had bestowed upon Nature's orphans, his adopted children, the gift of "intelligent life." Epée, a representative of the Commune noted, had elevated his students to a level where social interaction was not only possible but where "the most abstract ideas of physics" might be explained "with all the plenitude and even elegance to which they were susceptible."[18] By inventing a new language, Epée had created a means of fashioning intellects, raising up individuals to the point where they were no longer slaves to their senses but were capable of understanding the abstract ideas and immutable laws of a civilized society. In light of this accomplishment, explained Marc-Etienne Quatremère fils, another representative of the Commune, Epée's funeral tribute was to be a great patriotic occasion appropriate to the honor of a "true citizen" and "a glorious example to imitate."[19]

The National Assembly reacted in a similar fashion. Talleyrand, then president of this body, responded to the Commune's request by pledging the Assembly's support and the attendance of a deputation at Epée's funeral to be held the following day at the parish church of Saint-Etienne-

du-Mont in Paris.[20] Finally, on February 23, 1790, in front of an audience
that included the mayor of Paris, the Commune, representatives of the
National Assembly, and groups of both deaf and blind students, the
Abbé Claude Fauchet delivered a funeral oration which, the press reported, moved all present to tears.[21]

What Epée might have been surprised to hear on this sad occasion
was that the Abbé Fauchet's fifty-page printed funeral oration explicitly
linked Epée's religious and pedagogical goals with the promises of the
early phase of the Revolution.[22] For Fauchet, a priest and founding member of a radical new political club called the Cercle Social, the Revolution was a moment of liberation for both the church and the monarchy,
a time when the Gospel, or true Christianity, could be reconciled with
the Rights of Man.[23] And as both a priest and an enlightened pedagogue,
Epée typified for Fauchet the ideals that the orator hoped to promote in
the future. Not only did Epée represent a new order of clerics eager to use
religion to promulgate "the communal and popular virtues that constitute the soul of Society"; Epée's creation of a new class of citizens
through his "science of signs" was in itself a "miracle of patriotism."[24]

Fauchet did not, however, limit his enthusiasm for sign language to
its function as a tool for initiating the hearing-impaired into the world of
abstract ideas. Instead, in hyperbolic terms that would foreshadow Talleyrand's later comments to the National Assembly, Fauchet presented
the sign language of the deaf as a model for a new system of human
communication through which ideas could be transferred and compre-
hended with a speed, purity, and accuracy never previously thought
possible. Epée, this revolutionary priest announced, had succeeded in
making the deaf into "pure minds who seize ideas more exactly than we
do and transmit them more rapidly." As he explained:

> He [Epée] teaches them the universal language of intelligence with
> which one can get along and communicate in all the idioms of the Uni-
> verse. . . . One sees (with extreme astonishment and infinite admiration)
> men who have only half of our senses extend our intellectual faculties
> beyond their known limits. The precision is incredible, the rapidity
> seems supernatural. We proceed tentatively with our words; they soar
> with their signs. Our minds crawl and drag on in long articulations;
> theirs have wings and fly without abatement in the immensity of
> thought. Time no longer seems the measure of ideas, which are not suc-
> cessive, but simultaneous. A sudden collection of signs chains together
> twenty diverse conceptions. . . . [M]en of genius find themselves as if re-
> duced to idiotism in front of these demi-humans who seem elevated by
> the rapidity of their intellectual communications to the sphere of celes-
> tial spirits. And it is, in effect, Messieurs, the language of the Angels
> that the Disciples of M. de l'Epée speak.[25]

From the Abbé Fauchet's universalist Christian perspective, language was of vital importance as a means of both spreading a religiously inspired revolutionary message and fostering fraternal bonds. In subsequent years, Fauchet's primary political organization, the Cercle Social, was to build upon the legacy of this vision, working to encourage networks of communication among ordinary citizens and advocating such means of eradicating linguistic boundaries as the publication and diffusion of polyglot versions of the constitution of 1791.[26] It is thus not surprising that on the occasion of Epée's funeral, Fauchet took the opportunity to celebrate what appeared to him to be a means of overcoming the limitations of existing spoken and written vernaculars. For Epée, his eulogizer believed, had found in *le langage des signes* the human counterpart to the immediate, unmediated, and universal language of divine truths that characterized the Christian vision of paradise. The discovery of such a language on earth, Fauchet promised his audience, was certain to be instrumental in helping to "consummate the regeneration of the social order" in revolutionary France.[27]

The Abbé Sicard, Epée's successor as director of the Institution des Sourds-Muets de Paris after its founder's death, never ceased to rely upon this modified religious language when defending the social and political value of his own pedagogical project. After being named to his new position in April 1790, Sicard worked tirelessly to promote the idea of himself as a "creator" and the education of the deaf as a model of revolutionary "regeneration." In fact, his efforts in this regard had commenced months earlier with his campaign to assume Epée's mantle.

Sicard had, of course, begun his career as a student of Epée in Paris, and the younger man had already, as we have seen, achieved national attention as director of France's second school for the deaf in Bordeaux. Nevertheless, in early 1790, Sicard was not the most likely choice for the post in the capital city.[28] Sicard's success in assuming control of the Paris school for the deaf stemmed largely from his own publicity efforts, beginning shortly after Epée's death, when the Commune established a committee to consider the appointment of a successor to Epée. To his long-time advocate Champion de Cicé (now the Keeper of the Seals of Louis XVI), Sicard proposed that the representatives of the city determine their choice for a new director of Epée's institution by means of a contest. Champion de Cicé, in turn, suggested to Jean Sylvain Bailly, the new mayor of Paris, that the Commune ask each candidate to summarize his pedagogical method and to display the accomplishments of one of his students.[29] The effect of Sicard's presentation—two memoirs on the education of the deaf and the exhibition of his most remarkable student, a young man of eighteen named Jean Massieu—convinced the mayor that Sicard was not only an intelligent disciple of Epée but that the younger man had added his own improvements to the "methodical" sign method.[30]

It is not surprising that Bailly and the other members of the prize committee, a distinguished group of academicians and leaders of the new Parisian political establishment, took an immediate interest in Sicard's work.[31] A majority of them were steeped in the culture of the *musées, loges,* and *sociétés de bienfaisance* of the 1780s, and many, including Bailly, Brousse-Desfaucherets, Condorcet, La Rochefoucauld-Liancourt, and La Fayette, as well as Talleyrand, had recently become members of a new Parisian voluntary association in this same tradition called the Société de 1789. Furthermore, not only did Sicard present himself as a serious student of sensationalist epistemology; he astutely chose a subject for his essay of 1790 that was currently of great concern to intellectuals of widely varied political orientations, including the prominent moderate liberals who now gathered at the Société de 1789. That issue was how, in the midst of this proliferation of "free" speech and print, to prevent the growing threat of the *abus des mots*.

In elite, educated circles in 1790, advocates as well as opponents of the revolution-in-progress worried incessantly that the gap between signs and the things that they signified was being exacerbated by current trends in usage. By the beginning of the last decade of the eighteenth century, it was, as we have seen, widely accepted that words, by their nature artificial and usually arbitrary signifiers, made errors in word-choice and confusions about meaning possible. But as new vocabulary was being invented for new ideas, and as old terms took on altered meanings in 1789 and 1790 in the hands of an ever-expanding number of public spokesmen, the sense that the significations of words were becoming dangerously unstable and malleable increased as well.[32] And in this context, accusations of the misuse and deliberate *abus des mots* on the part of one's political adversaries grew on all sides. According to the counter-revolutionary press, which followed in the rhetorical tradition of royal and ecclesiastical censors, the leaders of the Third Estate were deliberately distorting the "true," historically sanctioned meanings of French words and employing empty expressions like *citoyen* without real referents. As a consequence, ordinary French people were being seduced into supporting preposterous and fictional claims. Conversely, the Revolution's proponents routinely insisted that they were only attempting to correct old abuses (which used falsely to be called "rights"), and the more radical among them faulted their political enemies either for actively encouraging a credulous public to attach varied and often mistaken meanings to new revolutionary terms or for speaking a hypocritical jargon [see Fig. 7]. All that could be agreed upon was that the Revolution had taken an unexpected turn; it had increasingly become a strug-

Portraits des Impartiaux, des Moderés, des Moderateurs, autre fois dits, les Aristocrates.

FIG. 7. Caricature with caption reading "Portrait des Impartiaux, des Moderés, des Moderateurs, autre fois dits, les Aristocrates" from Camille Desmoulins's radical *Révolutions de France et de Brabant* 1, no. 9 (early 1790). The target of this caricature, which plays on the relationship between double-facedness and double speak, is the Monarchiens and, especially, Louis de Fontanes. The caricature is intended to expose the verbal deception or *abus des mots* characteristic of those who call themselves moderates or impartials while actually thinking and acting like aristocrats. Photograph courtesy of the General Research Division, the New York Public Library, Astor, Lenox and Tilden Foundations.

gle over who had the authority to determine good or even conventional standards of usage, an extended *querelle de mots*. And, in the process, the power of deceptive words over opinions and actions continued to grow. For how else, commentators wondered, could the success of one's adversaries be explained? Thus in multiple camps it was quickly accepted that the problem of the *abus des mots* on the part of the opposition could be checked only through new politico-linguistic strategies.

In 1790, staunch defenders of royalist tradition were particularly fond of constructing satirical dictionary definitions as a way to inveigh against not only the people and ideas of the Revolution but its linguistic inventions as well.[33] As can be discerned from the titles of many of these dictionaries—*Dictionnaire raisonné de plusieurs mots qui sont dans la bouche de tout le monde, et ne présentent pas des idées bien nettes;* or *Avis à mes chers concitoyens sur les querelles d'Allemand, ou Dissertation sur les noms de parti qu'on se donne réciproquement sans vouloir s'entendre;* or *Extrait d'un dictionnaire inutile, composé par une société en commandite, et rédigé par un homme seul* (in which Jean-Pierre Gallais claimed to write "without aim, without motive, and often without even understanding myself")—their authors were anxious to suggest that the Revolution was itself the product of misunderstandings, a social disorder created largely by the obfuscation of meanings and the proliferation of ill-defined abstractions.[34] Most of these dictionary writers accepted that some semantic evolution was an inevitable result of the progress of time, especially since political and social terms remained among the most debated of concepts.[35] But many of these counterrevolutionary authors saw the struggle over language as a class issue as well. The right to judge good usage or to determine the terms of reality appeared to have been usurped by a second-rate group of men whom Antoine Rivarol, in his *Petit dictionnaire des grands hommes et des grandes choses qui ont rapport à la Révolution*, called "the enemies of language [who] have suddenly become the defenders of the nation": lawyers, deputies, journalists, pamphlet writers, and others whose very profession involved the manipulation of language.[36] By employing words in their "contrary" rather than customary senses and by rejecting, as Gallais put it, "the very tedious clarity of our language," these prorevolutionary insurgents and parvenus were deliberately using language to turn the established world upside down in an effort to further their own, particular social interests.[37] The authors of counterrevolutionary dictionaries thus claimed that merely by pointing out these abuses they were actively helping restore linguistic—and hence, political and social—order. But, in fact, the model of the dictionary served largely as an excuse; under the cover of an impartial form in which one was ostensibly "forced to call things by their proper names ... [and] sacrifice politeness for truth,"[38] opponents of the Revolution, with their unabashedly partisan definitions of royalist and Catholic institutions and their virulent attacks on revolutionary ideas, took their place early in the Revolution in a highly polemical battle of words.[39]

The self-proclaimed patriots, following in the Enlightenment tradition of philosophy as lexicography, also began, in 1790, to produce dictionaries of the new political terminology, as well as lists of key words, from *bourgeois* to *privilège* to *torture*, sure to "go out of use" as a result of recent events.[40] These texts were generally filled with earnest rather than satirical definitions of revolutionary institutions and terminology, as the chief polemical function of these dictionaries was to distinguish the old from the new. However, prorevolutionary journals took up the problem of the misunderstandings and false conceptions of common words and expressions at the same moment and from the same epistemological premises as did the opposition.[41] Not only the notion that political success was dependent upon having the power to dictate the meaning of words, but even the terms that were thought to require "accurate" or "exact" definitions—liberty, patriotism, aristocracy, despotism, regeneration, sovereignty, constitution, people, nation, and law, to name a few—became the common property of revolutionaries and their opponents alike in 1790. Meanwhile, the rhetoric on all sides grew increasingly heated.

However, in no sector was the problem of controlling or "fixing" the meaning of revolutionary terms taken up with as much seriousness as among those with ties to late Enlightenment model *sociétés*, where an interest in the work of Epée and Sicard and other innovators in the realm of language planning had already taken hold over the last two decades. A majority of the remaining *philosophes* and their supporters endorsed the principles of the Revolution in its early months. But some—such as Louis de Fontanes, Jean-François de La Harpe, and André Morellet (who began referring to himself as "Le Définisseur" as of 1790)—became worried almost immediately about the consequences of the democratization of the French language.[42] In their collective opinion, the national idiom was changing too fast and too unsystematically, causing the kind of conceptual errors that inevitably led to social conflict. Furthermore, as La Harpe liked to point out, the frequent use of such novel rhetorical strategies as the pairing of favorable adjectives with negative nouns (think *crime héroïque*) was paving the way for linguistic demagoguery.[43] These men of letters thus insisted that their status as experts in words gave them a particular obligation—and right—to supply their fellow citizens with the correct definition of moral and political terms. And while some of these individuals worked alone or in small teams to defend what they alternately called the *propriété* or the *justesse* of words, the Old Regime tradition of small *sociétés* also sparked the creation of a wealth of voluntary associations, many with provincial affiliates, that took the prevention of semantic subversion and the definition of the language of politics to be a fundamental part of their purpose. The stated mission of these new revolutionary societies and clubs, beginning in 1789 with the Société des Amis de la Révolution de Paris (renamed the Société des Amis de la Constitution in 1790 and often referred to as the original Jacobin Club), was, as with the older societies, to serve as places where patriotic citizens' varied points of view could be molded into a single, common opinion synonymous with the general interest and then disseminated as inviolable principle in articles and public speeches.[44] But after 1789, the focus of discussions in most of these spaces shifted from some vague idea of utility to explicit concern with contemporary events and affairs of state. Furthermore, many members of these organizations were themselves, for the first time, participants in the real world of political decision-making, including the National Assembly, where personal contacts, models of intellectual sociability, and even topics of discussion stemming from the culture of learned *sociétés* were to prove enormously important.[45]

Indeed, not surprisingly, these new associations proved to be central to the establishment of a distinctly revolutionary version of Enlightenment language politics. The Abbé Fauchet's and Nicolas de Bonneville's Cercle Social, whose official organ, *La Bouche de fer*, frequently offered guidelines for political discussions and admonitions to define all terms based on the principles of analysis, constituted one of the most important settings for the framing of early revolutionary linguistic values.[46] The Société de 1789, an offshoot of the Société des Amis de la Constitution which functioned as a cross between a literary society and an informal political party, was another.[47] Under the leadership of the Marquis de Condorcet and the Abbé Sieyès, this organization brought together well-known liberal intellectuals and deputies to the National Assembly, such as Rabaut Saint-Etienne and the chemist Lavoisier, with "enlightened" businessmen, Freemasons, and unaffiliated savants such as the Abbé Copineau. The particular significance of this society from the perspective of the language politics of 1790 is that it took the development of a well-defined language to be a central factor in the realization of its primary goal: the cultivation of *l'art social* or a set of public policies based upon reason and the study of human nature. The wealthy and prominent members of the Société de 1789, many of whom had already been involved in the reform of the monarchy, imagined using the rational analysis of the terminology of contemporary politics to do nothing less than dissolve differences of opinion rooted in misunderstanding and, consequently, end partisan strife on a national scale.

Early in 1790, Joseph-Antoine-Joachim Cérutti, an important participant in this society, published a satirical *Prospectus d'un dictionnaire
d'exagération* in which he denounced the passionate rhetoric of current
political oration—"the language of effects"—by pretending to celebrate
its success in replacing exact definitions and causing each word to become "a subject of dispute."[48] In a more serious fashion, the dangers of
the irresponsible and misleading use of political terms—whether in the
satirical writings of the right or in the heated diatribes of the left—assumed prominence in many of the articles printed in the *Journal de la
Société de 1789* during the summer of 1790. Everywhere, one writer
pointed out, a small number of expressions (such as "civil power" and
"military power") determined the fate of nations. The problem was that
ignorant people and "superficial minds" heard the often deceptive
speeches of revolutionary spokesmen and repeated their words without
having a clear conception of what they meant. This author thus believed
that it was the responsibility of an enlightened elite, such as the members of the Société de 1789, to rectify the situation. As he explained it: "It
is up to men who are on the lookout for *liberty* to denounce the intentional misuse of these words by those who are trying to slip them into
laws where their meaning will mislead the government and will be
prejudicial to the well-understood interests of the nation."[49]

But it was not enough in the opinion of many members of the Société
de 1789 simply to follow Locke in showing how words "form the opinions of many men and, as a consequence, the destiny of many others," as
the Chevalier de Pange put it in one of his articles in this journal, or to
expose specific examples of faulty usage.[50] Solving the problem of the
abus des mots required enlightened legislators to work to correct overly
"general" terms, such as the neologism *lèze-nation* (high treason),
which, in their inexactitude, were especially susceptible to abusive ex-
tensions in meaning and arbitrary interpretations. In another article,
Philippe-Antoine Grouville, a former member of the Loge des Neuf
Soeurs and the secretary of the Société de 1789, concurred. If current debates in the Assembly were indeed primarily "quarrels about words . . .
which obscure real things and disturb the impartiality of our best
minds," his colleagues needed to demonstrate the importance of applying a rational, philosophical method to the discussion of political dilemmas. For how, he asked, do philosophers deal with complex issues?
"They begin by defining their words, then carefully, they draw together
all their positive conceptions of the given subject in order to compare
them with the nature of things, and, finally, they reduce the question to
its simple elements only after having considered it in respect to both inviolable principles and necessary proprieties."[51] From the first year of the
Revolution, the men of the Société de 1789 thus attempted to bring En-

lightenment language theories and methods to bear on the rapidly changing, socially heterogeneous, and often seemingly irrational political situations that were unfolding before them. They realized early on that language was to have extraordinary power in determining the political stakes of the months to come. And they believed that the proliferation of ill-defined and misunderstood terms in contemporary discourse posed a significant threat to the realization and eventual closure of the Revolution itself, which would depend upon arriving at a rational, enlightened consensus.

In the two memoirs that he submitted to the contest for a new director of the Paris school for the deaf in early 1790, the Abbé Sicard indirectly took up this very problem. More important, he seemed to offer a solution to it that fit squarely with the desires of the members of the Société de 1789 and its sympathizers. Sicard's first *Mémoire sur l'art d'instruire les sourds et muets de naissance* was originally composed and published under the auspices of the Musée de Bordeaux in 1787. Reprinted in 1789, this initial essay laid out the basic and constant tenets of Sicard's linguistic and pedagogical philosophy and showed him to be Epée's disciple in his enthusiasm for an analytic or "methodical" sign language as a means of instilling ethical principles in his pupils.[52] However, in his *Second Mémoire sur l'art d'instruire les sourds et muets de naissance*, Sicard identified what he saw as the major pitfall in Epée's method of educating the deaf. Written expressly for the competition designed to produce Epée's successor and published in Paris in 1790, the *Second Mémoire* centered upon a worry that resonated strongly in contemporary Parisian intellectual circles: How was it possible to verify that a deaf person—or, by extension, any person speaking any conventional language—had a precise and accurate sense of the words or signs that he or she was using?

The possibility that Epée's pupils were performing purely mechanical routines, employing signs without any notion of their significance, had been raised before, most noticeably in the exchange of letters between Epée and Christoph Nicolai that had been published in the *Journal de Paris* in 1785.[53] Now, Sicard enforced this anxiety by evoking the mimetic behavior of the animal kingdom: "Animals, trained through hard work to be curiosities, haven't they sometimes displayed, for the admiration of spectators, equally astonishing phenomena?" What if, similarly, the performing deaf only appeared to comprehend "the nuanced ideas that nature has not furnished and which are only the happy and laborious effect of Metaphysics," but actually had only vague or mistaken conceptions of the words in question?[54] What if the signs themselves were poorly chosen, ambiguous, unrelated one to the next, or riddled with exceptions to their original meanings? Was there not a danger,

then, that the education of the deaf would simply encourage the proliferation of misunderstanding and the *abus des mots?*

Sicard credited Epée with the creation of a nomenclature, a dictionary
of manual signs corresponding to each physical or moral notion in the
French language. But he criticized his predecessor for failing to teach his
pupils the foundation of grammar, or syntax, and thus preventing them
from learning to compose or to decompose a sentence in the purely conventional word order of French. Syntax was for Sicard, as for many of his
contemporaries, itself a guide to the relative sophistication of the ideas
of a given culture.[55] Like Diderot, the Abbé Batteux, and other participants in the earlier debate about inversions in French and Latin, Sicard
assumed that the "natural" language of signs corresponded to the
"natural" order of words. But in this case Sicard was not about to identify the natural with the ideal. Armed with only the limited syntactical
structure supplied by nature, the deaf, Sicard believed, were restricted to
thinking in a primitive and confused manner: "[O]ne is familiar with the
sentences of Negroes; one can thus judge the form of sentences made by
the deaf and mute, who are even closer to nature."[56] However, Sicard
claimed that by introducing the deaf to words and signs in their grammatical contexts, he had found a way not only to give his pupils clear
and unwavering conceptions of the essential abstractions of the civilized world. He had discovered how, simultaneously, to make these pupils into logical thinkers who understood the connections between
ideas and could begin to express them to others.

Sicard's discourse about the problems of miscommunication and the
importance of universal grammatical principles as a foundation for
knowledge thus functioned as a response to a widespread fear of the
early years of the Revolution. In a climate rife with suspicion about the
articulation of specific words indicating precise, well-determined ideas
on the part of speakers or writers, Sicard warned that Epée's much-
touted "talking" deaf might be but another manifestation of the meaningless manipulation of language, whether gestural or verbal, in an as-
yet unregenerated France. And in a culture eager to find a means to
combat the problem of the incapacity of the French language to support
clear and unchanging meanings, Sicard used the opportunity of his *Second Mémoire* to suggest that the general adoption of his method of instruction, rooted in the sensible basis of ideas and the principles of general grammar, could be helpful in the task of "fixing" any language or
firmly attaching dissociated signs and ideas in the minds of all citizens.
Through his approach, he implied, all French people could acquire the
unwavering knowledge of complex French ideas and the disregard for
the vagaries of conventional usage that was characteristic of his pupils.
What he offered was not only a possible means of fulfilling the Enlight-

enment desire to eradicate ignorance and superstition but also an opportunity to alter permanently the cognitive foundations of society. This
point was not lost on Sicard's contemporaries. Noted the Abbé Tessier,
whose review of the two memoirs appeared in the *Journal des sçavans*:
"It would be desirable to see a plan this well bound together [and] this
well organized used in the education of children who are not deprived of
any sense." For based on his reading of Sicard's two essays, Tessier believed that such a method might well result in students who "knew the
[national] language more perfectly than people endowed with a sense of
hearing and instructed according to the ordinary method."[57]

The new head of the Paris school for the deaf wasted little time before
attempting to capitalize on such praise for his two *Mémoires*. In fact, he
immediately set about in the late spring of 1790 trying to interest the
National Assembly in both the financial and intellectual promotion of
his new school.[58] And to advance his purposes, Sicard developed a timely
strategy that was deliberately distinct from that of his predecessor, the
Abbé de l'Epée. First, Sicard sought to present the uneducated deaf as the
most lowly and pitiable of humans. Second, he tried to display his own
students, the products of his distinctive pedagogical method with its basis in an analytic sign language and the principles of general grammar, as
ideal revolutionary citizens. The deaf pupils of the Paris school for the
deaf were potentially, for Sicard, walking advertisements for the benefits
of his system of simultaneous linguistic and moral regeneration.[59]

Sicard sent the first of many petitions on behalf of his students to the
National Assembly's Committee on Mendicity in May 1790.[60] By August of that year, he had secured an appearance with four of his pupils before the Duc de la Rochefoucauld-Liancourt and the other members of
this committee. Then, at the Committee on Mendicity's behest, Sicard
was given the opportunity to present a group of his disciples, including
Jean Massieu, in front of the entire National Assembly. On this occasion, Massieu, using the methodical sign language in which he had been
instructed, called upon the state to adopt him and his fellow students
and to participate in the process of molding them into valuable members
of the new society that was unfolding around them. Epée, he claimed,
drawing once again on the quasi-religious metaphor of creation, had
pulled the deaf "from the state of worthlessness to which nature had
condemned them."[61] Now the deputies of the National Assembly had a
responsibility to continue Epée's work, "to repair the errors of Nature
and to make useful citizens out of those who would otherwise be a bur-
den to society."

In response to this plea, several members of the Assembly became eager to help the institution by placing the school immediately under the
government's protection.[62] Soon afterward, the welfare and education of

Massieu and his fellow pupils became an important philanthropic and intellectual cause in revolutionary Paris. Massieu, in particular, from the beginning of Sicard's tenure, was made into a popular performer of linguistic feats, appearing in numerous and frequent public demonstrations before official governmental bodies, clubs, learned societies, and the crowds of men and women who attended the weekly open sessions at the Institution des Sourds-Muets de Paris. At these events, Massieu displayed himself as a paragon of virtue, simple and honest but profoundly knowledgeable about the key concepts of metaphysics, religion, politics, and morality. Never were his "natural" or innate qualities and his newly acquired values allowed to clash with one another. For unlike the savages of eighteenth-century fiction, such as Lahontan's Adario, who arrived in France and learned the national idiom only to critique the corrupt, civilized ways that he witnessed, Massieu appeared anything but critical of the "new world" of revolutionary France.

We know little, of course, about Massieu's own sentiments. Generally, Sicard spoke for or through his pupil, holding himself, as instructor, responsible for Massieu's rebirth and giving increasingly dire reports on Massieu's natural, prelinguistic condition prior to Sicard's intervention.[63] In fact, Massieu's symbolic status as a creation of revolutionary pedagogy, utterly dependent on his teacher for endowing him with a moral or social life, seems to have made speaking on behalf of Massieu an appealing way for others to illustrate the possibility of using signs as a path to religious or ethical rebirth. After Massieu appeared before a group of Freemasons in Bordeaux, a M. François Ferlus took it upon himself to publish in the *Journal encyclopédique* of September 1790 a first-person rendition of Massieu's sentiments. According to Ferlus's poem, Massieu had once found himself worse off than even the animals around him: "But me! nothing lightened the excess of my misery. The sweet names of son and mother were nothing to my heart, nothing, not even a vain sound, and the torch of reason hid me forever from the flash of its light." Only when his benefactors occupied themselves with his cause did Massieu, in his "own" words, believe himself to be a man: "You have made me born again to the happiest fate. Yes, if my soul opens itself to the light of thought, if I adore the laws of religion, if with your guidance words traced in the air both interrogate and respond without ears and without a voice, if the court [and] the city, eager to see me, witness a marvel once impossible, if I am, finally, a man, it is to you alone that I am indebted."[64]

But it was not only a coincidence of timing that made the educated deaf well-positioned to become symbols of the "new men" of revolutionary France. It was also a question of the particular qualities that they were thought to embody. At one level, Sicard's students appeared to remain *hommes de la nature*: naive, innocent, and completely free of the handed-down prejudices, discredited opinions, and superstitious beliefs that other people acquired in daily commerce with those around them. The deaf alone, it seemed, had the capacity to enter the linguistic and conceptual world of the Revolution devoid of historical memory, or indeed of any prior ideas except an innate sense of the laws of nature and an aptitude for the original, universal means of communication. Explaining Massieu's sense of the principles of the constitution, the deputy Pierre-Louis Prieur (called Prieur de la Marne) declared in a speech before the National Assembly in July 1791 on the occasion of the nationalization of Sicard's school: "[H]is [Massieu's] soul has grasped [these constitutional ideals] with a special avidity because it has never been sullied by any of our past prejudices."[65] Or as a letter-writer put it in the *Feuille villageoise*, a journal founded by Cérutti and other former members of the Société de 1789 to enlighten a rural population about the principles of the Revolution: "When my [deaf] son raises his adoring and imploring hands to the sky, his soul embraces and imagines the Supreme Being more clearly and with more dignity than so many millions of men who have been affected by vulgar superstitions that are worse than ignorance."[66]

For at the same time that deafness became a symbol of moral purity, the educated deaf were also widely believed to have, in the words of the *Journal de Paris*, "much better formed and more exact ideas than the majority of men do."[67] As Sicard explained it, his "methodical" signs, invented and introduced in the order of the generation of ideas, not only protected his pupils from contact with a variable and often arbitrary spoken idiom but also managed "to convey the precise value of each word in the minds of the deaf and mute."[68] And this formation, according to the Abbé Sernin, the new director of Sicard's former school in Bordeaux, permanently distinguished deaf students from ordinary children in terms of their relationship to language: "But, one might ask, children often learn words without any meaning for them; don't you risk turning your deaf-mutes into parrots as well? But this [form of] abuse does not threaten the education of the deaf and mute, whose teachers do not let a single word that does not convey a known idea, not a single word that does not follow the [natural] rules of language enter the heads [of their pupils]."[69]

Sicard's pupils were, as a result, often called upon to apply their much-touted cognitive skills to the abstract language of revolutionary politics. The desire among patriots for "true" definitions, theoretically unencumbered either by ancient biases or by the vagaries of common usage, produced numerous requests for the recently educated deaf to offer their own written explanations of the complex and much-debated terms of revolutionary civic life. In the summer of 1791, for example, in a brief piece in Urbain Domergue's resuscitated and now explicitly pro-revolutionary *Journal de la langue française*, a deaf person was asked to give a definition of the word *patriotisme*. Much like *La Feuille village-oise*, though aimed at a different audience, this periodical, which first appeared in Paris in January of that year, took as one of its key purposes "defining the new words that new ideas have made it necessary to adopt" and "making the language of liberty intelligible to everybody."[70] And in this particular neological note, the editor of the *Journal de la langue française* announced that the deaf person's manner of decompos-ing a word into its composite parts not only allowed him to grasp the concept of "patriotism" in a highly logical and accurate fashion; it also led him to coin a neologism for the enemies of France—*les impatrio-tes*—for which "a thousand applauses have foretold the future impor-tance."[71] On another occasion, Massieu was asked in a public presenta-tion attended by members of the Committee on Mendicity to write a definition of the word *aristocrate*. His reductive but politically astute re-sponse, which survives in his own hand, reads, "An Aristocrat is some-one who is unhappy with Good laws, and who wishes to be a sovereign Master and to be very rich."[72] Clearly, it was the childlike simplicity, combined with the frank revolutionary bias of such definitions, that made them so attractive as examples of revolutionary expression.

In a certain sense, Massieu's pat answers sound to us much like the responses traditionally drilled into students of religion. It is evident that the aphoristic model of the catechism, with its standard question and answer form, played a large role in Sicard's, as well as Epée's, system for educating the deaf.[73] But at the time of the Revolution, what made these definitions striking was their predictability and their distance from common parlance. In effect, Massieu and his fellow pupils offered a model for a new kind of ordinary citizen. These deaf students may have learned to grasp, in some absolute sense, the meaning of complex politi-cal terms and the "natural" rules of the language. But they remained un-able either to reinterpret these meanings so as to influence perceptions of reality or to use these skills to their own advantage; in essence, lan-guage controlled them rather than the other way around. Sicard's educa-tional system seemed to promise that certain peoples could indeed be made into devotees of revolutionary principles while simultaneously remaining excluded from the linguistic power struggle that revolution-ary politics appeared to be. After all, regeneration was always ultimately intended to lead to enlightened consensus rather than more informed or empassioned debate.

Indeed, in 1791, right alongside the emphasis in revolutionary dis-course on "correct" definitions derived from analysis, we can also find a return to the idea that the establishment of a universal and natural language system could help to foster the creation of a truly harmonious and unified social and intellectual community. And here the *langue des signes*, with its roots in the original *langage d'action*, also continued to serve as a model. In Prieur's speech nationalizing Sicard's institution, one finds not only an emphasis on how well his pupils have learned such advanced subjects as metaphysics, calculus, and law and how thoroughly they have mastered the most sophisticated communications technology of the age, the printing press.[74] Prieur also makes reference to the enduring dream, which was to figure prominently in Talleyrand's educational plan the following fall, that a truly universal, philosophical language, one which would lead to social as well as intellectual unity, would finally emerge hand in hand with the revolutionary triumph.[75] As Prieur put it: "It [sign language] is not only made up of cold and purely conventional signs; it depicts the most secret affections of the soul. . . . If the long desired project of a universal language could be realized, this would, perhaps, be the one that would merit preference; at least it can boast of being the oldest of all."[76]

Prieur's speech was greeted with much enthusiasm by the rest of the National Assembly. At the suggestion of one deputy, a clause was added to the decree reading, "The name of the Abbé de l'Epée, the original founder of this institution, will be placed among the ranks of those citizens who have done the most for humanity and for the nation."[77] In his obsequious response which followed the reading of the new law, Sicard noted: "All families afflicted with the curse that ruptures all communication between the mother and her child will give thanks forever to the wise legislators who, at this moment, are repairing the great, deplorable error of nature. The tongues of a thousand unfortunate people, condemned to remain quiet forever, are finally going to come loose in order to form a concert of benedictions and commendations of which you will be the object."[78]

But, in fact, the nationalization of Sicard's school for the deaf was only a first step toward making the deaf into exemplary revolutionary citizens and deaf schools into model communities. One provision of the new law that Prieur did not discuss on the occasion of his speech was the reconfiguration of this institution's current home, a former Celestine monastery, so that two distinct populations—the deaf and often mute pupils of the Abbé Sicard and the blind students under the tutelage of Valentin Haüy—could be educated in the same space and by the same means. The appeal of this plan was not primarily practical, though the two instructors were both disciples of Epée, and the blind and the deaf were generally believed to have parallel afflictions of the senses.[79] Rather, subsequent discussions indicate that revolutionary leaders sought to create the novel spectacle of unfettered communication between the two populations believed to be most naturally restricted in their ability to learn and to convey ideas. The point was to demonstrate that the last and most rigid barriers dividing peoples could be abolished in revolutionary France now that a semiotic system existed which could create a common bond among all.

Sicard, though unwilling to swear his allegiance to the revolutionary state as required by the controversial Civil Constitution of the Clergy and increasingly hostile to the course of the Revolution in general, never neglected to capitalize on many revolutionaries' desire to witness such miracles of regeneration and reunion. Thus, in 1791, he set about constructing a means of communication for these two groups of handicapped people and, consequently, a model for an all-inclusive revolutionary social system. Once again, he first nurtured and presented his ideas in the context of a small learned *société*: in this case, the Société Nationale des Neuf Soeurs, a new incarnation of the celebrated and now defunct Loge des Neuf Soeurs and Musée de Paris.

Much like its ancestors, the revolutionary Société Nationale des Neuf Soeurs continued to uphold bylaws against overtly partisan political debate, a stance that, in 1790, immediately caused this so-called literary society to be tarred by *L'Observateur* and the *Révolutions de Paris* as an association of aristocrats.[80] Yet the members of this organization had no intention of turning back the clock; these self-declared "patriots," whose ranks now included participants in the National Guard, as well as delegates to the National Assembly and the Commune, also insisted on their dedication to the revolutionary cause, ostentatiously swearing the civic oath and announcing their purpose to be "the regeneration of the nation" through the arts, sciences, and education. The Société Nationale des Neuf Soeurs thus provided Sicard with an ideal platform from which to launch an experiment intended not to stir up further social or political divisions but to help the nation overcome them.

On the same day as the Prieur report was being read in the National Assembly, the new Neuf Soeurs witnessed a highly unusual demonstration. The performance began with a deaf boy writing verses dictated to him in manual signs. Then a blind person conversed in writing with the same deaf boy, and a delegation of deaf and blind children publicly printed some verses of Roman history. Finally, a young person without hands wrote some verse with a pen in his mouth in order to show that he too could express his ideas to the other handicapped people present. According to the report in the Société's printed memoirs, "[T]his meeting, so extraordinary and so touching, has proved that nature can no longer pose any obstacle to the communication of men among themselves, nor can it have any secret that cannot be stolen from it."[81] But for Sicard, clearly this display was not sufficient. Two months later, in September 1791, Sicard read a talk in the same setting in which he announced that he had finally succeeded in breaking down the last obstacle to meaningful exchange between the deaf and the blind by inventing a new, tactile sign system, again with roots in the manual signs of "the first inhabitants of the world." And as contemporary Paris was the only place in the world where one might have a chance to witness such a phenomenon, Sicard declared that "it is here that the crowd of travelers will come to envy this consoling triumph over nature."[82]

Jean Baptiste Massieu, a member of the Committee on Mendicity (and no relation to Sicard's pupil, Jean Massieu), clearly had this image in mind when he confirmed the permanent educational union of the deaf and blind before the National Assembly that same September. Returning to the well-worn Enlightenment narrative trope of the isolated locale, J. B. Massieu asked his fellow deputies to conjure up "a deserted island suddenly inhabited by settlers, some of whom cannot see and some of whom cannot hear and none of whom have received any instruction since birth; it is easy to imagine that communication will never be established between the two groups because they will never be able to understand each other."[83] Endowed with reason, but unable to use it due to the failure of their most vital senses for the transmission of ideas—vision and hearing—the deaf and the blind, in J. B. Massieu's imagination, would be reduced to a condition worse than that of animals. But through the application and the redirection of this sensationalist philosophy, this deputy claimed that he could also foresee a strikingly different scenario. By tracing palpable signs of ideas in the hand, why couldn't a blind person and a deaf person have a reasoned and consistent conversation? And why couldn't this kind of exchange form the basis of a new type of community? As he envisioned it:

> Assembled in the same location, brought together in the same workshops, the blind person and the deaf person will form a society every bit as perfect as that composed of a man who sees and one who hears. One will be able to see the blind person print the pages composed by the deaf-mute person; the deaf-mute individual weave the thread spun by the blind person; one polish the glass, the other turn the spinning wheel; one design, paint, engrave, enliven canvas, stone, and marble; the other celebrate the Supreme Being and virtue in song.[84]

Merged together, in other words, the two schools could form a microcosm of a productive society, isolated from the corruption of the external world and its ideas or language and unified by a common sign system and purpose. Sicard's institution would become not only a place for shaping model citizens but a blueprint for the harmonious society to come.[85] For this utopian image also reinforced the notion of the present as a historic chasm: "What a picture this lively meeting of talents and arts makes in a place where one saw, just a few years ago, only silence, shadows, misery, and desolation!"[86]

By the third fall of the Revolution, the same season that Talleyrand issued the report with which this chapter began, the history of the education of the deaf had thus become firmly attached to the rhetoric of both rupture and regeneration. While the deaf in their previously silent, unsociable, and amoral condition had been made into a metaphor in revolutionary discourse for the neglect of an earlier, corrupted French state, the educated, signing deaf had come to represent the dawning of a new era rooted in an idealized vision of a natural society and a natural language. That December, when the administrators of the department of the Gironde attempted to encourage the newly formed Legislative Assembly to extend national protection to a second school for the deaf, Sicard's former institution in Bordeaux, departmental officials once again drew upon this contrast: "Once, under the reign of arbitrary power, when one spoke to the despots of justice and humanity, one was sure to provoke their boredom and obtain only their indifference. Their ears were deaf, their hearts insensitive. Friends of humanity seemed to speak a Language that was foreign to them."[87] But in the new era, two traditional forms of deafness—one deliberate, callous, and institutionalized, the other the fault of nature—could be simultaneously overcome through recourse to the new language of natural rights:

> It is not the same with the representatives of a Free People entrusted with making Laws after the sacred principles of a constitution founded on the rights of man and specially consecrated to his happiness. To speak to them of humanity, to present for their consideration objects that could give them the opportunity to diminish humanity's ills and augment the happiness which humanity has the right to expect from wise legislation, is, for them, the most active incentive to be heard religiously; it is to speak to them in the language most sure to interest their minds and hearts and to capture their attention.

In other words, these provincial bureaucrats believed that the Revolution had made possible the triumph of a new form of language and that this language had, in turn, become an agent of social and moral transformation in its own right. By the end of 1791, the fate of the nation and the fate of its language had, in the minds of many people, become effectively indistinguishable. The utopianism of the early Revolution was, just like that of the fictional isle of Azor, heavily linguistic in character. The epistemological ambitions of the Enlightenment had become a driving force in shaping France's political and social future.

Nevertheless, France's political difficulties—and, consequently, its linguistic difficulties—only seemed to grow as the National Assembly dissolved in September of 1791 and the Legislative Assembly came into
power. A limited number of key terms, from *aristocrate* to *nation* to *peuple*, still dominated political discussion. Moreover, articles, pamphlets,
and even government debates continued to turn on contested definitions of these words. But the gradual fragmenting of the political and intellectual alliances of 1789 and 1790 following the events of the summer
of 1791 meant that, by fall, the same concepts no longer functioned as
rallying points for the same people or meant the same things to them.
Even more ominously, the power of the most important of these buzzwords in determining allegiances and actions outside the halls of the
Legislative Assembly seemed to be constantly growing. Talk of a specific word (such as *roi* or *fanatisme*) having a "magic force" or "producing astonishing effects" became increasingly common—as if writers
hoped that simply by pointing out the "cabalistic" or "talismatic" force
of a term they could help to break its spell.[88]

As before, commentators tended to agree that the main cause of the
problem was the prevalence of the *abus des mots* among unscrupulous
revolutionary spokesmen. At both ends of the political spectrum, various individuals began to demand government action, such as the establishment of a legislative committee to cement the meaning of political
terms, as a corrective to the situation.[89] But in the opinion of many
"enlightened" revolutionaries, political discord or factionalism could
not be attributed solely to the intentional misuse of words by powerful
individuals. It was also the result of high rates of popular misunderstanding and incomprehension. Liberal intellectuals, including Talleyrand,
Condorcet, and the Abbé Sieyès, all of whom deserted the withering Société de 1789 to return to the Jacobin Club following the schism between the moderate Feuillants and the followers of Brissot and Robespierre in mid-1791, took the lead in making this point. For all three men
believed that not only did ignorance of the true meaning of revolutionary terms make the public more susceptible to the dangerous and
wrong-headed ideas of priests, aristocrats, and other enemies of the
Revolution; it also left the public incapable of understanding its own
rights or responsibilities. And if devotion to representative government
and civic participation depended upon a commitment to obey the language of the law, then the inability of many individuals to use accurately
or even to make sense of this complex and often abstract language nec-

essarily threatened the stability of revolutionary principles and, as a result, the functioning of the revolutionary state. As the Abbé Grégoire warned his fellow deputies, "this inevitable poverty of language, which confuses the mind, will mutilate all your addresses and decrees."[90] In a political system built upon a series of mental abstractions, popular linguistic confusion, according to this reasoning, was and would continue to be one of the principal sources of political and civil discord.

How did these well-placed intellectuals know that many ordinary people failed to comprehend the language of the Revolution? For the Abbé Grégoire, it was a matter of common sense. Like the savages of late eighteenth-century travel literature, peasants—the often illiterate speakers of foreign idioms, dialects, and ungrammatical French—were widely thought to have great difficulty generalizing their ideas or forming clear conceptions of abstract, nonmaterial terms. Indeed, Voltaire's conclusion that "more than half the habitable world is still populated by two-footed animals who live in a horrible condition approximating the state of nature . . . barely enjoying the gift of speech" retained its force.[91] Consequently, even when the population in question was the vast rural citizenry of France, its ability to understand the key debates and decrees of the Revolution was assumed to be extremely limited. As the Abbé Sernin bluntly stated before the Convention, "Artisans and people in the countryside, although elevated by the Law to a new level of Liberty and destined to fill the most important positions in the State, these men are, for the most part, still deaf and mute" when it came to any public functions that they might be called upon to play.[92]

Such suspicions were only exacerbated by letters to the Committees of Public Instruction of the Legislative Assembly and the Convention, reports that often contained ominous tales of public incomprehension of the formal language of France's laws and constitution. A correspondent from the department of Seine-et-Oise, for example, wrote to express his fear that the young children he regularly heard reciting the Declaration of the Rights of Man from memory did not actually understand what they were saying: "I am sadly convinced by questions which I have posed to the oldest among them that they understand the significance of none of the words used in it. I have reproached their fathers in a fraternal way for not bothering to explain these words to their children. They have replied that they do not understand any more than their children and that they themselves need someone to explain these words to them as well."[93] Similarly, a schoolmaster from Fourny wrote to *La Feuille villageoise* to say that every Sunday he read this journal aloud to the local peasants and answered, to the best of his abilities, their frequent questions about vocabulary that they did not comprehend. But, he complained, he was afraid that he was spoiling the journal's lessons and deceiving his disciples, because "I often encounter words that I know only a little or badly."[94] Unfortunately, the words that the schoolmaster failed to grasp ranged from "democracy" and "coalition" to "analysis" and "metaphor."

Revolutionary leaders easily identified what they took to be the sources of this confusion. One was the prevalence of foreign idioms and *patois*, "that collection of corrupted dialects, the last vestiges of feudalism," which, according to Talleyrand, continued to bolster rural, Catholic values, while keeping much of the population ignorant of a revolutionary message that depended upon French.[95] Another was the fact that when people were actually familiar with the French language, their knowledge was usually based on the unphilosophical vagaries of daily parlance, with its residue of traditional and religious prejudices. Furthermore, this knowledge tended to be extremely limited in scope. Widespread illiteracy, the result of the inaccessibility of primary education in reading and writing, meant that many people possessed no appropriate tools for making sense of the more complex language of the constitution or Declaration of the Rights of Man. And in the minds of many intellectuals, who echoed the complaints of educational reformers of the 1760s and 1770s, the instruction that did exist in revolutionary France left most citizens with only a superficial understanding of moral and political principles. Attacking both the traditional curriculum and the prevailing educational methodology, Condorcet accused contemporary teachers of using the everyday terminology of the moral and political sciences imprecisely and arbitrarily so that students were allowed to attach a variety of meanings to single terms. Moreover, Condorcet argued, many students were subjected to moral indoctrination, forced to memorize incomprehensible abstract definitions where "the sense [of moral ideas] is determined neither by rigorous analysis nor by the natural qualities of a real object."[96] In numerous locales, after all, the terms of the national language were still learned after the example of Latin. Finally, certain spokesmen, including Talleyrand, identified the endurance of irrational grammatical forms, nonstandardized orthography, and equivocation and redundancy in the definition of linguistic signs themselves as prime culprits.

Of course, none of these problems were new to French life in the early 1790s. Literacy rates were actually on the rise in the second half of the eighteenth century. But prior to this moment, Enlightenment-inspired intellectuals had paid scant attention to questions of popular education. Only now that the fate of the Revolution seemed to depend on questions of language and comprehension, on the one hand, and popular sentiment, on the other, did national political leaders turn their sights toward the fact that many French men and women were forced to accept or to reject a set of propositions that they hardly understood, except in terms supplied by local priests or other opponents of the Revolution.

In the late months of 1791, after Talleyrand's plan for national instruction was dismissed by an impatient National Assembly and ignored by a recently opened Legislative Assembly, prorevolutionary forces both within and outside the government thus became increasingly convinced that they needed to take the initiative in rectifying this situation. Simply removing the legal barriers to free communication or offering the public an occasional well-reasoned definition had proved insufficient. The nation demanded a new pedagogy, aimed at both children and adults, which worked to inculcate and secure the principles of the Revolution through instruction in the French language. The formation in the fall of 1791 of a linguistic *société délibérante*, the Société des Amateurs de la Langue Française, marked the revolutionary left's first major effort in this direction. The members of this organization saw efforts to "fix" or standardize the meanings attached to the new political terminology as a public service insofar as they took the French language to be the foundation of revolutionary engagement and consensus. Similar pedagogical projects and strategies for combating ignorance of the "true" meaning of key political abstractions followed in 1792 and the first half of 1793. These included the development of a collectively edited periodical called the *Journal d'instruction sociale* and a comprehensive plan for a new system of language education that would extend from public festivals to classrooms.

In all of these pedagogical initiatives, Sicard's epistemology and language theory continued to play an important conceptual role, much as it had earlier in the plans of Talleyrand. What the instructor of the deaf offered with his sign language was no longer a potential substitute for the French language but, rather, a model for how to teach and reform the national idiom so as to make it a means to what enlightened revolutionary leaders considered to be clear, unquestionable conceptions of revolutionary values. Yet, at the same time, as new cleavages and factions emerged among prorevolutionary forces, Sicard's now well-known opinions and teachings met with a series of challenges. Between late 1791 and early 1793, radical republicans within the Jacobin movement became increasingly skeptical of this elite, philosophical approach to the problems of contemporary politics. Concurrently, many former *philosophes*, such as Morellet, turned against the Revolution as they came to see the attack on the language of the Académie Française as symptomatic of a general disregard for the sanctity of culture among revolutionary leaders.[97] Thus, gradually, the "methodical signs" model that Sicard had long advocated became the exclusive intellectual domain of the political circle around Condorcet, Daunou, and other Girondin-sympathizers who remained sure that the metaphysical considerations first broached in late Enlightenment institutions of sociability provided a solution to the political dilemmas of a nation engaged in what was increasingly becoming a trans-European as well as a civil war.[98] It is in this development, after the easy successes of 1789 and 1790, that we can identify the beginning of a schism in the language politics of the Revolution. By the time of the founding of the republic, the Enlightenment ideal of consensus and harmony through language, while never abandoned, had become a thoroughly divisive subject by itself.

Initially, however, in 1791 and early 1792, it appeared to many Parisian Jacobins, both moderate and radical, that Sicard's purported methods for securing the precise meaning of signs could indeed be successfully adapted to their political needs. Sicard, in turn, encouraged this association by making himself instrumental in the establishment of an association dedicated specifically to the founding of a revolutionary language politics. In November of 1791, Urbain Domergue, the so-called Jacobin "grammarian patriot," succeeded in expanding his *Journal de la langue française* into a society of savants, writers, political leaders, and others interested in what the society's prospectus called "the regeneration of the language."[99] Domergue saw the notion of a "well-made" political language, where political terminology was used only in its proper sense, as essential to the protection of the principles of natural rights and law embodied in the constitution. As he explained in late October 1791 in his opening address at the first meeting of the Société des Amateurs de la Langue Française held at the old "Musée Gébelin" on the rue Dauphine: "[Of] the different errors that contribute to the unhappiness of men, the most disastrous is perhaps the abuse of words [*mots*], which deceives us about things [*choses*]."[100] By encouraging a collective consensus regarding the signification of words and by providing the public with models of good writing and rational rules for the establishment of neologisms, Domergue felt that he and his circle could wage a major battle in support of the Revolution. The importance of the Société's undertaking, he continued, stemmed from his belief "that without a well-made language, there are no clear ideas, and without clear ideas, there is no happiness."[101]

Sicard was not the only well-known figure whose help Domergue enlisted in his project of furthering the revolutionary cause through the reform of the French language. In addition to such prominent veterans of the linguistic debates of the late Old Regime as the grammarian Antoine Tournon and the etymologist Charles Pougens, the Société soon boasted many important participants in Jacobin clubs among its members, including Condorcet, Carra, Brissot, Rabaut Saint-Etienne, Fabre d'Eglantine, Boissy d'Anglas, Mercier, Ducos, François de Neufchâteau, Lanthenas, Anacharsis Cloots, Marie-Joseph Chénier, and even Robespierre.[102] Many of these individuals had earlier participated in either the Musée de Paris or the Loge des Neuf Soeurs.[103] And after founding his Société, Domergue immediately established close ties between it and two other revolutionary intellectual institutions with these common roots: the Société des Neuf Soeurs and the Lycée de Paris, where Domergue concurrently offered a course in French grammar.

In effect, Domergue believed that he was establishing a revolutionary alternative to the Académie Française. Like this older institution, the Société des Amateurs de la Langue Française made construction of a dictionary its ultimate goal. But Domergue, following in the distinctive tradition of the *musée*, insisted on including a wider range of people in this process than the national academy ever had: ordinary writers as well as academicians, foreigners and provincials as well as Parisians, women (including Mme de Condorcet and Fanny de Beauharnais) as well as men. Moreover, Domergue argued that the goal of his society was not simply to establish standards and definitions based on elite patterns of usage (like those of the Académie Française) but to use reason, as defined by the society's philosophically inclined and public-spirited members, to establish the rules of language. Indeed, the parliamentary structure of the Société des Amateurs de la Langue Française, with its "legislative assembly of language," suggests that Domergue envisioned his organization as a sort of national body for the governance of French, taking that power away from aristocrats, priests, and especially the monarchical state in favor of an impartial and enlightened intellectual elite. To this end, Domergue divided the members of his organization into various subcommittees, each dedicated to fixing the principles of a complementary but distinct linguistic science that would aid in the composition of "a truly philosophical dictionary" appropriate to the needs of the revolutionary nation.

Not surprisingly, Sicard was assigned to the committee on grammatical theory. Domergue, in his capacity as editor of the *Journal de la langue française*, had consistently drawn attention to the importance of Sicard's work with the deaf for understanding the general principles of this discipline. When Sicard wrote to the editor early in 1791 to encourage curious readers to attend his public lessons and to read his two memoirs, Domergue responded in print that all of the *Journal*'s readers should interest themselves in the relation of "metaphysical grammar" to "the language of the deaf and mute," through which Sicard was able to create not just "odd machines," as his predecessor had, but "men."[104] Then, throughout the summer of 1791, Domergue, a fellow product of the training of the Doctrinaires, paid repeated attention to Sicard's methods of teaching about the world through grammar, reviewing and reprinting parts of Sicard's first memoir, as well as the speech he delivered at the National Assembly on the occasion of the nationalization of his school.[105] Indeed, as we have seen, the journal even made use of the language skills of Sicard's pupils. For in sign language, Domergue saw proof of the validity of the progressive grammatical foundations upon which he hoped to regenerate the French language:

> Here is true metaphysics. Mallebranche, who saw everything in God, who believed the fiction of innate ideas, would never have been able to achieve the miracle that we have witnessed. The Abbé Sicard, embracing the only reasonable system and believing that nothing passes into the mind except by way of the senses, derives from this principle of the ancient philosophers a new method . . . and because of him, the mute speaks to the deaf person who is enchanted to hear him.[106]

Yet, despite Domergue's history of public praise, Sicard's grammatical positions quickly put him in conflict with the other members of the committee, including a French teacher and disciple of the grammarian Beauzée named Julien Duhamel and Domergue himself.[107] In one of the first meetings of the committee, Sicard repeated his familiar argument, namely that the study of grammar required one to begin at the beginning and to return to the time of man's first impressions before retracing the way in which modern languages developed from the common *langage d'action*. In defense of this system, the method of analysis, Sicard asked rhetorically: "In effect, Sirs, is there not a sort of pleasure in crossing the immensity of the centuries to look back at the first epoch of the world, at the first childhood of human beings and to repeat in some sense their steps: here is the first step of the first man, here is the second, here is the third."[108] For in Sicard's opinion, the study of grammar constituted nothing less than a means to reconstruct the history of knowledge.

Sicard's propositions did not, however, convince all of the assembled company. According to a report published in the *Journal de la langue française*, each stage in Sicard's developmental tableau provoked disagreement and further sets of questions. Domergue himself complained that the field of grammar should be restricted to the "motives for grammatical things," or how humans explain their thoughts and sentiments by the voice or on paper. Neither how they feel and think nor how they might express themselves with gestures or hieroglyphics should be the grammarian's concern. "The first belongs to the domain of anthropology and the art of pantomime; the second, to ancient history," Domergue argued.[109] Taking Domergue's position one step further, Julien Duhamel then demanded that the role of the committee be limited to the examination of the French language in its modern state. Duhamel, whom the Société's *Journal* called "a contradictor full of merit," wanted

the committee to restrict its work to the analysis of linguistic propositions, especially those concerning current moral and political ideas, and
he therefore objected strenuously to Sicard's references to the functioning of the human mind in the state of nature. By following Sicard, Duhamel warned, the committee would itself soon enter "the obscure ways
of error and prejudice."[110]

Ultimately, the committee accepted the more moderate position of
Domergue, agreeing to the single compact proposition that "Man feels,
thinks, compares, judges; the expression of his judgment is called a
proposition" as the starting point for its grammatical inquiries.[111] As
such, the Société eliminated from its program all reference to primitive
linguistic forms—hieroglyphic or gestural—as well as all discussion of
the history and evolution of language or signs. But the real significance
of this fight was that it illustrated the emergence of varied strategies for
participating in revolutionary language politics. Over the previous hundred years, France had already witnessed a long, drawn-out contest between those who took usage and those who took reason to be the most
appropriate source of rules when it came to the national tongue. But as
early as February 1791, Domergue had begun identifying these two established camps with specific contemporary political positions, distinguishing between so-called "aristocrats" (backward-looking advocates
of traditional usage) and so-called "demagogues" (revolutionaries eager
to pay tribute to abstract reason without regard for individuals).[112] Now,
almost a year later, he found the members of his own Société embodying
these contrary stances. Domergue chastised Duhamel for being overly
petulant, "electrified by love and by revolution, impatient of preliminar-
ies," and eager to reform every aspect of the French language at the expense of traditional standards or established patterns of usage. But he reserved his more serious criticism for the position of Sicard. Both men,
claimed Domergue, were eager to "marry" grammar; Sicard, however,
was bogged down in history and ceremony. In Domergue's clever formulation, "The former [Sicard], a lover of etiquette, has wanted to comb
through the parchments of the future; he is seriously concerned about
titles of nobility. . . . [He] has let the spirit of the *ancien régime* break
through."[113] Sicard's own explanations for his pedagogical project, which
had been so celebrated in the previous few years as a means of political
and social regeneration, were thus denounced as relics of the past, products of the backward thinking of the corrupted Old Regime. The pragmatic linguistic ideology of the Jacobin theorists clustered around
Domergue, as articulated in December 1791, was to be concerned only
with the present and the promises of the language of the future.

For Sicard, however, this was only the first of a series of setbacks.
Temporarily, he continued to exert considerable influence over French

language politics. His school for the deaf remained a popular charity after 1791, and despite his own personal hostility to the course of the
Revolution, Sicard conspicuously continued to teach his pupils to answer sympathetically all questions about revolutionary principles. During 1792, he lectured on the education of the deaf at the Lycée and presented his Parisian students before the Legislative Assembly in a recitation of the Declaration of the Rights of Man.[114] Moreover, in the widely
reprinted speech that he gave supporting Jean Massieu's testimony
against an individual who had tried to steal the young deaf man's wallet
during that same year, Sicard again drew attention to the compatibility
of his teachings with revolutionary goals. In reference to Massieu's testimony, Sicard insisted that his pupil had, at once, learned to exercise
"the rights of man" and maintained "this native candor, this truthful
exterior that civilization has not yet made disappear. . . . [His gestures]
recall the first language of the Universe, still young, still just, still
good."[115] In effect, Sicard continued to promulgate the idea that the natural methods by which his students learned the abstract terms of contemporary politics afforded them a special ability to grasp the essential
harmony between the laws of the state of nature and the principles of
revolutionary France.

But the political situation in Paris changed around Sicard at a pace
that he could not or was unwilling to match. A refractory priest, Sicard
just narrowly escaped death in the September Massacres of 1792, leaving
him for the duration of the Revolution in the precarious position of both
celebrated citizen ("the worthy successor of the Abbé de l'Epée, the rival
of Locke and of Condillac," in the words of the watchmaker who saved
him from execution), and counterrevolutionary Catholic zealot.[116] In
August 1793, before Sicard was arrested for a second time, the Committee of Public Safety wrote to the Committee of General Security to
say that it was unable to decide on Sicard's fate, since, "in this man
[Sicard], one can see two: one very dangerous and the other very useful
for the services that he has rendered and that he continues to render."[117]
And as the relationship between Sicard's own political and religious positions and those of the revolutionary government became increasingly
strained, so did the match between his language theory, with its emphasis on origins and metaphysical speculation, and that of the dominant
culture of a now republican France.

In the early months of 1793, following the execution of Louis XVI, Sicard was, however, still prized in certain intellectual circles for the potential social and political benefits to be derived from his methodology.
Especially in Girondin and in what increasingly seemed to be "moderate" republican contexts (including the new clubs and salons that provided an alternative to the Robespierrist-dominated Jacobin club), the

idea of "fixing" the language—making ideas and words firmly attached in the minds of the public—came to be intimately connected to the idea of stabilizing and, finally, halting the Revolution. But the preferred strategy was no longer the construction of alphabetical dictionaries with their constant juxtaposition of unrelated ideas and their often synthetic or axiomatic definitions. In a wide range of forms of publicity, the revolutionary opponents of the Robespierrist Jacobins tried instead to encourage the use of analysis and general grammar in understanding and thus solving the political problems of the moment, namely, civil discord and resistance. Already in 1792, Charles-Philippe-Toussaint Guiraudet, a former member of the Société de 1789 and an ally of Condorcet, had published a pamphlet entitled *Explication de quelques mots importants de notre langue politique, pour servir à la théorie de nos loix et d'abord: de la loi* in which he had called on the nation to rid itself of undetermined and borrowed political terms and to use analysis "to secure the language of the constitution just as it [the constitution] has secured forever what it has put into words."[118] In *La Chronique du mois*, the main Girondin journal for educated readers, Brissot and Nicolas de Bonneville, one of the original founders of the Cercle Social, continually hammered home the same point in late 1792 and early 1793, stressing the ongoing political problems caused by ill-defined and imprecise terms such as *peuple* and arguing for the continued utility of the analytic method in the pursuit of truths, especially in the midst of a Revolution.[119] Even the faculty of the old Lycée, where Condorcet continued to teach, now took as its purpose the study of government, society, and ethics as demonstrable sciences and repeatedly emphasized the importance of tracing the generation of ideas from initial sense perceptions in this project.

How this concern with method translated into a new politico-linguistic strategy can best be seen in a text by Sicard's former colleague in the Société des Amateurs de la Langue Française, Julien (also known as Jules-Michel) Duhamel. At the end of 1792, Duhamel, now identifying himself as an assistant instructor of the deaf and as Sicard's student rather than his detractor, published a long pamphlet in which he too argued for new attention to the problem of the malleability of current political terminology. "Language is the first means of communication among men," Duhamel warned in his *Essai analytique sur cette question: quelle est l'instruction nécessaire au citoyen français?*, "and if this means is imperfect, they will never be able to agree among themselves, nor extend the narrow sphere of their knowledge."[120] For Duhamel believed that dangerous consequences stemmed not only from the intentional abuse of words by demagogic leaders. He also declared that conversation among ignorant citizens, who routinely repeated words without fully understanding their precise value or signification, opened the way for "waves of opinion" and the arbitrariness and discord that led, ultimately, to the creation of political factions. Disagreements, like crimes, according to Duhamel, were always only the product of faulty judgments, the result of false notions derived from ignorance of the true signification of words. As he asked rhetorically: "Have you not seen that men have always been governed by words? Do you not see today that most Citizens are, as a result of their ignorance of their language, overgrown children that the troublemaker leads at will?"[121]

Duhamel thus argued that if the government wanted to defend itself against both fanaticism and factionalism, a general education in the moral and political language of the Revolution was essential for all citizens. Questions of morality and politics, he insisted, should be subject to solutions, much like geometric proofs. And if the best-made method or language for arriving at demonstrable truths were to be thoroughly explained to the public, the nature of French politics would be transformed. Indeed, Duhamel firmly believed that in this process lay the solution to the establishment of a peaceful and consensual republican order.

Yet Duhamel, like many of his contemporaries, saw no hope in the construction of alphabetical dictionaries or the promulgation of endless new definitions of unrelated terms. Instead, as a critical step toward rectifying the inadequacy of current political discussion, Duhamel proposed the creation of a journal dedicated to "social education" or the exposition for a popular audience of the principles and terms of the four fields of knowledge that he viewed as essential for making and sanctioning laws: natural law, civic law, political economy, and the national language itself. Then, later during the winter of 1792–93, Duhamel laid the foundations for the realization of this plan by joining forces with two better-known revolutionary intellectuals, the Abbé Sieyès and Condorcet.[122] Sieyès had long been interested in both abstract questions of epistemology and precise problems of political language; evidence to this effect can be traced from his metaphysical essays of the 1770s on the possibility of constructing a philosophical idiom impervious to abuse through his commentary on *l'art social* composed under the auspices of the Société de 1789 and then the Lycée.[123] Similarly, Condorcet had continued, in pamphlets, journals, and speeches, to critique the unscientific vocabulary of the political sciences, where the same commonplace words were routinely used in multiple senses in the course of any day. And he had repeatedly warned against the dangers of exaggeration, irrationality, old prejudices, or personal passions entering revolutionary discourse. What the three men shared on the eve of the fall of the Girondins was, in fact, an assurance that the basis of sound governing and social order had to be a clear and fixed language of the political and moral sciences, a language that was well determined and well understood by all.

Sicard was initially designated to be the fourth participant, in charge of the sections of the journal dedicated to "the development of intellectual faculties and methods of instruction," according to Condorcet's notes.[124] And despite the differences in opinion between the two men regarding both political and religious matters, Sicard was not a surprising choice for a collaborator in this project. Sicard and Condorcet had come into contact with one another in numerous settings, including the Société des Amateurs de la Langue Française, over the previous three years. They had also often expressed complementary ideas about language education, including a distrust of usage and a belief in the importance of analysis as a pedagogical tool.[125] Duhamel had become Sicard's pupil and colleague, and Condorcet had recently chosen, in April of 1793, to use Sicard's press, the Imprimerie des Sourds-Muets, for the printing of his pamphlet *Ce que les citoyens ont droit d'attendre de leurs représentans*. However, Sicard was ultimately excluded from participation in the establishment of this new journal. In a conclusion that was reminiscent of Sicard's thwarted attempts to collaborate with Domergue in the grammatical work of the Société des Amateurs de la Langue Française, Condorcet rejected Sicard's plan as "much too extensive." In addition to political differences between the two men, Sicard's tendency toward metaphysical speculation and his constant attention to hypothetical and distant "origins" in the state of nature seem again to have appeared problematic to his potential collaborators.

However, the model of methodical sign language instruction proved to be central to the *Journal d'instruction sociale, par les citoyens Condorcet, Sieyès et Duhamel*, which finally appeared, after much delay, on June 1, 1793. The editors drew attention to this connection in several ways. The *Journal* was conspicuously described as printed at the Imprimerie des Sourds-Muets, with proceeds generated by the publication to be directed to the Institution Nationale des Sourds-Muets.[126] More significantly, Duhamel dedicated himself to bringing the pedagogical method used at this school to bear on the discussion of the moral and political sciences, prompting the *Chronique de Paris* to note about his involvement in this enterprise: "One could not have chosen better for this type of work than a man accustomed to demonstrating the metaphysics of language to the deaf. . . . [W]ords do not serve as currency for the deaf, one speaks to them with [manual] signs, and in order to make oneself understood among them, these signs must absolutely be explained to them."[127] Ultimately, Condorcet and Duhamel agreed that "the pressing need of the moment," when representative government appeared to be threatened by the ignorance of the mob, was "to attach clear, distinct, and precise ideas to the words of the Constitution, which are always being so grievously abused."[128] And this depended on teaching, through examples, a broad, poorly educated public how to decompose and trace the key terms of contemporary politics back to their roots. After all, as a sympathetic *Chronique de Paris* continued, "One can be sure that the earth has been drenched in the blood of more than one hundred million men only as a result of disputes over words; the less they were explained, the crueler were their hatreds."[129]

But despite Duhamel's ambitious plans, his analysis of the language of the constitution did not long succeed in preserving either its values or the principles of its defenders. Due to the very sort of politics that the journal aimed to combat, the publication of the *Journal d'instruction sociale* ceased during the first week of July after only six issues. Faced with imminent arrest, Condorcet fled into hiding several days after the last copies of his periodical were printed.

That same month, Pierre Claude François Daunou, a deputy to the Convention, the *grand vicaire* of the Constitutional Church of the Pas-de-Calais, and a former member of the Oratorian teaching order, made one final attempt to argue for the adoption and generalization of Sicard's pedagogical method as a tool for forging a consensual revolutionary political culture. A few weeks earlier, in late June, a former Doctrinaire named Joseph Lakanal had presented the Convention, on behalf of the Committee of Public Instruction, with an education plan developed primarily by Daunou and Sieyès.[130] Central to the first version of this proposal was an emphasis on making the public recognize the function and significance of language by dramatizing its evolution in a series of thematic festivals. Cantonal *fêtes* were to be devoted to "the perfection of language" and "the invention of writing," while departmental festivals were to include ones dedicated to the celebration of printing, along with numerous abstract revolutionary principles. Yet the project had been instantly met with much hostility from other deputies. According to Joseph-Marie Lequinio, festivals celebrating these concepts were liable to produce only false ideas and new superstitions.[131]

Daunou refused, however, to abandon this broad-based effort to use both innovative pedagogical methods and instruction in the history of communication as means to create a stable, enlightened republic. Since the beginning of the Revolution, the Oratorian teacher had made the development of public education a special concern.[132] And Daunou remained convinced in 1793 that the most effective of instructional methodologies had the potential to transform not only the business of forming young republicans but also the process of thinking in general, especially in the new realm of public politics. The failure of the original

Declaration of the Rights of Man, Daunou argued in an essay on the new constitution in the spring of 1793, stemmed not just from the principles it contained. Above all, it was the result of the faulty method employed to craft it. Certain terms (including "constitution") were never attached to precise ideas; others were explained only by disjointed and didactic definitions unrelated one to the next. "All these ambiguities, all these uncertainties," Daunou declared, "I attribute to a sole cause: the synthetic method used by the committee," a method which, in Daunou's mind, was linked with despotism and tyranny because it, like usage, "masters those whom it instructs."[133] The only way to right this situation, this deputy concluded, was to draft a new document informed by and dedicated to promoting the distinctive method of nature and of republics. That method was analysis, "the unique secret of teaching as well as discoveries"; for according to Daunou, it was the slow, austere, careful work of retracing human ideas back to the first sensations that had to inform all efforts to arrive at secure truths. But unlike many earlier eighteenth-century French philosophers, Daunou also made it clear that the starting point in this process should not be the sensations of a lone, primordial man in the state of nature. Rather, it should be those that resulted from the first social relations among humans. By this date, Daunou, like many liberals, believed that the universal laws governing civil society—not natural rights—should provide the foundation for all subsequent reform efforts. And in the spring and into the summer of 1793, teaching naturally social humans this method of self-instruction continued to strike Daunou as vital to securing the future of the new republic.

Thus, in July 1793, one month after taking the fateful step of publicly registering his opposition to the arrest of the leaders of the Girondin faction, Daunou went ahead and published an impassioned defense and explanation of the principles of the pedagogical plan that he had crafted in collaboration with Sieyès. Closely echoing the ideas of Condorcet, Daunou argued once again that the development of "moral" knowledge and the eventual perfecting of *l'art social* depended upon instructing the young in "the analysis of sensations, ideas, and signs."[134] Unfortunately, he pointed out, it was the process of learning the irregularities of alphabetic spelling—the endeavor "which first introduces bad habits of thought, transports the mind far from the path of analysis, and creates the habit of believing instead of reasoning"—that set the tone for most contemporary primary instruction.[135] As a corrective, Daunou called for reforms in orthography and grammar. But more important, he proposed that France institute special schools for teaching "the art of teaching." And how should France's teachers be taught? Daunou replied that the method and principles of each such school should be derived from those of an associated school for the deaf. Like many of his contemporaries, Daunou believed that Sicard's pedagogy provided a rare opportunity to see the methods of Condillac and, consequently, those of nature, put into practice in a visible form.[136] Only with this example before them, Daunou argued, could teachers of the young make language education into a means of instilling reasoned thought rather than credulous acceptance of a stream of confused letters, words, and isolated ideas. For Daunou, the results promised to be beneficial not only to pedagogy but also to the political process itself.

Yet following the fall of the Girondins and Condorcet's exit from public life, Daunou's arguments were largely ignored. In a sense, his plan came both too late and too early in the revolutionary decade to have any impact. Beginning in the summer of 1793, the Jacobins close to Robespierre were finally able to begin to develop and to implement their own language policies relatively unimpeded. Rapidly, they became much less sure that Condillac's or Sicard's epistemology could provide the way to a unified and truly revolutionary society.

JACOBIN LANGUAGE TROUBLES,
SUMMER 1793–SUMMER 1794

"We have revolutionized government, laws, usages, manners, customs, commerce, and even thoughts; let us therefore revolutionize the language which is their daily instrument," wrote Bertrand Barère in January 1794.[137] That same winter, François Louis Michel Deforgues told the Convention, "Everything, even the language, must be regenerated according to the republican system."[138] And an anonymous author echoed: "What indeed! The old laws are destroyed, the aristocracy brought down, fanaticism fulminated! Will the Convention thus allow a language to remain that equals them in imperfections and which served as their interpreter? New laws, new mores; new language as a result. One can not advance without the other."[139] The idea of "revolutionizing" the French language—of making it not only the single language of France but an effective, modern, rational revolutionary instrument—was central to the pedagogical ambitions of the Jacobins. An abiding faith in the power of language to alter reality, or what Grégoire described as "the reciprocal influence of manners on language and language on manners," only underlined the importance of this task in a new republic eager to discover a means to moral and social harmony.[140]

Twentieth-century historians of the French language, from Ferdinand Brunot to, most recently, Brigitte Schlieben-Lange, have thus tended to view the language planning initiatives of the First Republic as marking an acceleration of and deepening commitment to an estab-

lished revolutionary course. The Jacobins of the Year II, from this perspective, were not the first revolutionary faction either to argue for the
possibility of isomorphism between speech and action or to encourage
state-sponsored efforts to regulate the national tongue—from the elimination of obsolete terms and grammatical anomalies to the introduction
of new, egalitarian forms of address—so as to advance the revolutionary
cause. The Convention's Committee of Public Instruction simply became more active in trying to realize these utopian goals during 1793–
94.

Yet it is essential to remember that for many of the Conventionnels
of the Year II the power of words, whether uttered in private settings or
disseminated through printed matter, was perceived to cut two ways. As
Grégoire warned, a language could just as well encourage error and factionalism as patriotism and virtue: "Every century of history provides
evidence that, on the one hand, people quarrel and butcher each other
over certain words, and, on the other, that some words produce heroic
actions."[141] And for the radical revolutionaries of the First Republic, the
very rhetorical practices in which they were actively engaged turned
into the source of some of their greatest fears. Indeed, the other and perhaps more important impulse of Jacobin language policy was an overrid-
ing nervousness that the language of the Revolution would exceed the
control of its leaders and subtly but insistently work to subvert the
Revolution from its proper course. This fear went well beyond earlier
anxieties about the "abuse" of specific political terms. The most basic
elements of republican and, indeed, enlightened life—public speaking,
publication, discussion, and debate—seemed to pose extraordinary
threats to the actualization of the Revolution. It was this perception that
helped engender the Terror as a critical component of the Jacobin Revolution, even as its pedagogical mission remained in place.

Certainly, from club meetings to the floor of the Convention, revolutionaries continued to depend on oration and speech-making to convey
their ideas. But at a moment when one writer could declare, despite all
the physical violence around him, that "the celestial gift of speech and
the faculty of making it sensible through the organ of the tongue have
more strength than a canon and bayonets," Jacobin leaders also saw oral
discourse as posing a potentially enormous threat to the kind of revolutionary society that they were trying to construct.[142] In particular, they
feared the existence of disjunctions between words spoken and true intentions, between stated plans and real actions or deeds. No longer could
legitimacy as a revolutionary simply be a question of uttering the right
buzzwords or outwardly complying with current standards of speech; in
this climate, ability as a rhetorician or a special facility with words was
increasingly taken as a sign that one had something to hide.[143] Of course,

criticism of verbal pyrotechnics predated the Revolution. However, by late 1793 and into 1794, the sophisticated mastery of political discourse became, in Jacobin terms, a sign of counterrevolutionary intentions, a dangerous mark of overcivilization, insincerity, attachment to aristo-cratic mores, and above all, "feminine" wiles—at the same time that it was deemed essential to the functioning of a republic.[144] Indeed, though the early years of the Revolution had given French women, with their designation as *citoyennes*, a new power to speak and even to assert their rights over the shape of the language of the future, the Jacobins eventu-ally reversed this process, tarring both rhetoric and women through the equation of one with the other.[145] Both constructs became associated with seduction, confusion, emotionalism, decadence, and other threats to the new expressive ideal of masculine severity and "laconism" or verbal restraint. For the other side of Jacobin attempts to create a dis-tinctly republican political language was an overwhelming suspicion of the dangers inherent in the very rhetoric that revolutionary leaders were so invested in promoting.

Similar fears surrounded writing and the printed word, even as they too remained essential to Jacobin political culture. Since well before the Revolution, the printing press had been celebrated as a means of both fixing elusive ideas and circulating them in ever-widening patterns, and these tributes continued into the Year II alongside government sponsor-ship for numerous revolutionary publications. But the Jacobins were in-creasingly worried about the distancing effects of print culture, the po-tential discrepancies not only between true emotions and the written word but also between the notated and the spoken, between orthogra-phy and pronunciation, between the single meanings of solitary writers and the heterogeneous interpretations of varied readers.[146] Indeed, one of the things that most scared the revolutionaries of the Year II was the pro-liferation of multiple languages dependent upon various forms of media-tion or translation: literary languages unintelligible to ordinary people; old idioms that had not yet fully disappeared; minority languages that belonged exclusively to members of a particular class, region, religion, or ethnicity. All of the above threatened to exacerbate the gap between dif-ferent peoples' conceptions of the same ideas and thus to distance even further *les mots* from the reality of *les choses*.

Thus at the same time as the republican state chose to promote the creation of a truly "revolutionary" tongue, it also took it upon itself to try to censor or prevent other idioms from flourishing. During the Ter-ror, fear of language as a source of excess, uncontrollable meaning and hence deception governed legislation just as much as faith in its regen-erative and reformist powers. Examples abound. During the summer of 1793, the guarantee of freedom of the press established by the Declaration of the Rights of Man was increasingly curtailed amidst arguments about the dangers of the written circulation of faulty, misleading, or seditious ideas.[147] That summer and fall, many clubs and *sociétés* centered around discussion were dissolved as well. This measure included all existing women's clubs, which were frequently attacked as places that thrived upon women's deleterious verbal habits, including their tendency toward loquacity, dissimulation, and senseless babbling.[148] And that same fall, when the Law of Suspects warned the public of the "distinguishing characteristics of suspected persons," almost all of these traits also turned out to be a matter of speech practices. Enemies of the Revolution, it was announced, were not only those who declared counterrevolutionary ideas but also any of a number of types who engaged in hypocrisy when it came to their words. According to this law, the public needed to be protected from those who arrest the energy of public assemblies through "crafty discourses, turbulent cries and threats"; those who "speak mysteriously of the misfortunes of the republic, are full of pity for the lot of the people and are always ready to spread bad news with an affected grief"; those who "have changed their conduct and language in line with events"; and those who "have the words *liberté, république,* and *patrie* constantly on their lips, but . . . consort with former nobles, counterrevolutionary priests, aristocrats, feuillants, [and] moderates, and show concern for their fate."[149]

The following winter and spring, the Convention then attempted to pass legislation declaring obsolete the daily languages of many ordinary French people as well. Historians have tended to view Jacobin language policy—in particular, state-sponsored efforts to encourage the use of standardized French in all corners of France—as evidence of the intensely nationalist and centralist impulses of the Terror.[150] And certainly Jacobin language reformers took pains to argue that the smooth functioning of a republic in which all French men were called upon to exercise their rights and responsibilities as citizens demanded that all be familiar with a uniform national language. But a growing fear—of supposedly prejudice-ridden dialects and *patois*, of foreign tongues that communicated the secret plots of counterrevolutionaries, of the concept of linguistic pluralism itself—played an equally central role in the efforts of certain prominent Jacobins to impose the French language upon the entire nation. In fact, the mania in the Year II for eradicating *patois* and other minority languages stemmed from the same insecurities that prompted parallel efforts to do away with "expressions that still recall the debris of the monarchy," in the words of Deforgues, and names that evoked the institutions and privileges of the Old Regime or the Catholic church.[151] As Bertrand Barère memorably explained this impulse: "Federalism and superstition speak Bas-Breton; emigration and hatred of the Republic speak German; the counterrevolution speaks Italian, and fanaticism speaks Basque. Let us break these instruments of shame and error."[152] For Barère, even the idea of reproducing French laws in other tongues appeared dangerous.

Several years earlier, in 1790, the National Assembly had declared that its decrees would henceforth be translated into the multiple dialects and languages of France so as to disseminate its decisions as widely as possible.[153] This idea had, at the time, been widely embraced by local authorities and provincial Jacobin clubs. But now, in 1793–94, translation seemed risky because it required an intermediary, a person with the power to interpret the meaning of words as he or she saw fit. The assumption underlining this policy was that a republic necessitated uniformity of thought rather than diversity of opinion and that this uniformity was predicated on the establishment of a single, unchanging national idiom, a conveyor of universal values, that could be immediately and invariably understood, both in print and in speech, by each and every citizen. Urbain Domergue made this requirement explicit in a speech of February 1794: "It is very difficult to be united in opinion when we are separated by language. . . . All children of the same family, we must all have the same thoughts [and] be moved by the same sentiments."[154] Barère concurred, arguing that this was what distinguished monarchies from republics. A monarchy had to resemble a Tower of Babel, dividing and conquering, in order to survive: "The despot needed to isolate peoples, separate countries, divide interests, hinder communication, stop the simultaneity of thoughts."[155] In contrast, by the summer of 1794, freedom of thought and expression in a republic had come to mean the freedom to think and speak as one—or to accept punitive measures.

But it is not only to policy that one should look to see the impact of this linguistic paranoia on the Revolution of the Year II. In fact, the same epistemological assumptions behind these concrete efforts to control the revolutionary flood of words strongly colored Jacobin ideology—or political language—as a whole. Furet rightly points to Robespierre's obsession with unmasking and denouncing hidden conspirators who ostensibly disguised themselves as friends of the Revolution the better to subvert it.[156] One can go further and link Robespierre's desire to expose his enemies' hidden intentions to his profound sense of the untrustworthiness of words as indicators of virtue. In fact, such ideas run throughout Jacobin, and especially Robespierre's, rhetoric, right alongside declarations about the need to create a revolutionary tongue. During the course of the Revolution, Robespierre grew increasingly fearful of what he called "the *empire* [power] that words have over the minds of men," especially of the popular classes.[157] More and more, this veteran of numerous late Enlightenment institutions of intellectual sociability (including the Amateurs de la Langue Française) saw fancy words and empty pieties not only as successful means of deception on the part of those surrounding him, from aristocrats to Girondins, but also as the key to the persistence throughout France of widespread opposition to the Jacobin Revolution. Robespierre filled his speeches of 1793 and 1794 with warnings about "enemies of the people" who disguise themselves as "the people" and then use manipulative expressions to convince the true people of what is not in their best interest.[158] And he tried to call attention to the stylistic techniques such dangerous individuals used, including emotional appeals, "vain metaphysical abstractions," and ostentatious or "difficult" forms of speech, to win the undeserved support of an honest but uneducated and credulous public.[159] Journalists, as well as orators, came under especial censure in this capacity.[160] In a typical speech of February 1794, Robespierre railed before the Convention against false revolutionaries of all types who duped the public with their rhetoric, "full of fire for great resolutions that signify nothing, more than indifferent about those that could honor the cause of the people and save *la patrie*." He then called on ordinary but virtuous citizens to begin to see through and resist their deceptive charms. Instead of these "solemn oaths and bombastic speeches," he exhorted his audience, "ask them [moderates or supposed revolutionaries] for real services," the mark of truly sincere republicans.[161] Similar demands can be found in numerous contemporaneous speeches by Saint-Just.[162] In the case of both men, the calculated use of political rhetoric to call for a return to a literal "language of actions" and a simple, unembellished, and unmistakable verbal code underscores a central tension in Jacobin thinking: an ongoing fear of, as well as belief in, the redemptive power of language.

Borrowing from Jean Starobinski's influential study of Rousseau, historians have in recent years often identified "transparency," the abolition of all distancing or mediating mechanisms, as the principal goal of Jacobin ideology and, especially, Jacobin linguistic initiatives.[163] But the semiotic ambitions of the Jacobins were at once more complex and more confused than this term suggests.[164] Clearly, Robespierre and his closest associates sought to make signs invisible to the greatest degree possible; they decried linguistic virtuosity, mistrusted most forms of representation, and did all they could to promote a kind of intuition that could operate independent of words. But the Jacobins of the Year II also continued to encourage and to propagate an instrumentalist conception of signs, treating them as a means to reshape reality in their own terms and, hence, as tools of power. At the heart of these Conventionnels' efforts was a desire to create a new national political language that would work actively in theaters, assembly halls, and private homes to instill an orthodox revolutionary worldview in the minds of those who used it, while also ensuring that variant opinions could find no means of expression. As such, it was not easy for the Jacobins to imagine either the form their language ought to take or, more broadly, how far their pedagogical impulse ought to extend.

Certainly, some elite revolutionary language reformers continued, in the spirit of Condorcet and, before then, Condillac, to promote regulation at the expense of traditional patterns of usage. The authors of the numerous linguistic initiatives of the Year II, many of which were put forth in textbooks written for a contest sponsored by the Committee of Public Instruction in 1794, tended to emphasize the multiple ways in which the national idiom (rather than a global one) could be made more rational, more stable, simpler to learn, and less subject either to misunderstandings or subjective interpretations.[165] These efforts at improvement included the eradication of grammatical irregularities or anomalies, the standardization of pronunciation, and the reform of spelling so as to reduce the ever-widening lacuna between spoken sounds and written words.[166] Many also suggested reforms in French vocabulary, including the addition of systematic neologisms established through analogy and analysis, the restoration of various handy terms that had fallen into disuse, and the elimination of redundant, equivocal, or obsolete ones. And for models for this standardization process, revolutionary theorists continued to look both to the hard sciences, including Lavoisier's new nomenclature of chemistry, and to recent successes in educating the deaf.[167]

Other Jacobins, however, remained suspicious of abstract reason or even words as instruments of social change and called instead for a return to a pure *langage d'action*, an eloquent and "energetic" language of natural signs and symbols that might speak directly to the heart through the senses, much as Rousseau had described in *Emile* or Diderot had imagined in his writings on the *drame*. Michel-Edme Petit, the editor of a short-lived journal of the spring of 1794 called *Entendons-nous* (literally, "Let's Understand One Another" or "Let's Agree") and a self-conscious disciple of Rousseau, was not alone in advocating this path.[168] Like many of his contemporaries, Petit argued that words remained responsible for almost all of the republic's problems. But as a solution, he stressed not simply the development of a more spare or precise public idiom. He insisted that the government had a special obligation to cultivate "all that can speak to the eyes, all that, affecting the senses, can inspire republican morals." In other words, he urged the revolutionary state to pay renewed attention to what he referred to as the *langages* of "actions" and "exterior signs" in addition to speech.[169]

Such ideas translated into a wide range of image-based pedagogical practices during the months of the Terror. This was not only a question of using ordinary objects, from hats to playing cards, as deliberate signs of political allegiances or as substitutes for alphabetic writing. Mona Ozouf has brilliantly shown the educational significance of the new, visual "language of forms"—from liberty trees to statuary—that accompanied the verbal inscriptions, banners, songs, and speeches of revolutionary festivals.[170] Bronislaw Baczko has done the same for revolutionary architecture and urban planning.[171] And in recent years, Lynn Hunt and Antoine de Baecque have both paid considerable attention to the ways in which revolutionaries used allegories to make corporeal or embodied versions of linguistic abstractions immediately comprehensible to a semiliterate population.[172] Of course, many of these undertakings hark back to long popular, Catholic, and even royal traditions of French visual pedagogy. But many also had close links with the sensationalist epistemology of the recent past. Indeed, a good number of the specialized visual *langages* of the body developed in classrooms or on stages at the end of the Old Regime were employed toward new ends in republican France. Not the least of these was the *langage* of pantomime, whose traditionally lowly status had recently been elevated by Noverre's efforts to make it the basis of serious tragedies. In outdoor festivals, theaters, and even the new Lycée des Arts established by the Société Philomathique in 1792, pantomime and *tableaux vivants* were frequently used during the First Republic to make moral or revolutionary values visible and material.[173] The Théâtre de la Cîté in Paris, for example, in an effort at efficacious public education, regularly staged pantomimes of revolutionary events, including major festivals that had themselves involved pantomime restagings of other recent events.[174] Even the Opéra, which turned to political topics later than many other theaters, found ways, beginning in the fall of 1792, to insert topical danced or pantomimed interludes into productions such as Gossec's *La Triomphe de la République*.[175] For these visual displays were thought to reproduce even more clearly than the laconic speeches of revolutionary leaders the kind of unmediated, unintellectualized, profoundly sensual communication made possible by the original, universal language of gesture and thus to engender true community.

Of course, historians should be wary of establishing any clear dichotomy or obvious conflict between these two contemporaneous approaches—what the enlightened intellectual Pierre-Louis Roederer considered the equally essential language of analysis (for which "Condillac has so clearly made us see the necessity and Epée and Sicard have so well prepared us") and the physical *langage d'action*.[176] The new calendar of the Year II, for example, was ultimately constructed out of a heterodox mixture of the decimal language of mathematics and a series of names that the poet Fabre d'Eglantine hoped would recall both the sights and

sounds of a pastoral nature.[177] Since no mode of conveying political concepts was deemed entirely trustworthy or sure to prevent multivocal interpretations, the Jacobins often attempted to combine the scientific and
the poetic or to reinforce their more austere verbal messages with color-
ful figures of speech or images. Revolutionary culture can be said to be
distinctive precisely in its reliance on these kinds of hybrids and amal-
gams: images with inscriptions, pantomimes with dialogue, printed versions of oral discourses, public readings of printed texts. This dual sensationalist impulse also helps to explain what Roland Barthes took to be
the peculiar nature of Jacobin rhetoric, its tendency to be both inflated
and exact, metaphoric and spare.[178] When trying to justify efforts to bring
together the energy of natural signs and the precision and clarity of
analysis, the Abbé Grégoire, the Jacobin's chief theorist on these matters, had only to say that they all owed their debt to the dictates of an
ahistoric "Nature."

But even Grégoire, the author during the Year II of important tracts on
the eradication of *patois*, the renaming of cities and streets, and the proper
language for inscriptions on public monuments, could not long disguise
his growing doubts about whether the much sought-after perfect idiom
that would, once and for all, resolve disparity of opinion, could ever be
achieved. Well before the Revolution, he had argued that the eradication
of dialects and *patois* was essential to the spread of enlightenment in
France.[179] And from the Revolution's earliest days, the constitutional
bishop of Blois had suggested that the present moment offered the chance
not only to realize this long-standing ambition but also to restore to the
national idiom "its antique naïveté" and energy and "this spirit of truth
and laconic pride that is the rightful possession of republicans."[180] Therefore, despite his uncertain relation to the Jacobins during the Terror, Grégoire became their main spokesperson for state-sponsored efforts to help
make the national language a rational, effective, and exclusive political
tool that no individual or faction could use to its own subjective advantage. But this Jansenist, republican *abbé*'s conviction about whether a
language could ever be made so accurate as to eliminate entirely political
argument or contest seems to have waned. Perhaps, he conceded in his
June 1794 report on the destruction of *patois*, Condillac had insisted on
too much; it was impossible either to create a number of expressions equal
to the changing number of sentiments or ideas in a culture or "to restore a
language to the plan of nature and liberate it entirely from the caprices of
usage."[181] Pragmatically, Grégoire announced in this text that he was
skeptical that a perfect, unchanging language—rooted in natural signs
but developed through reason and analysis—would ever be within the
realm of possibility. Not that he was suddenly willing to embrace the inherent ambiguity of language. Much like Robespierre, Grégoire contin-

ued to desire nothing more than to find a way for *vérité* to be evident within signs themselves. But after five years of the revolutionary struggle, Grégoire's faith in the "classical episteme," or the idea that words and things should—and would one day again—correspond isomorphically so as to produce intellectual certainty, seems to have been severely tested.

Not surprisingly, growing doubts about the potential perfectibility of language eventually threw into question the whole revolutionary pedagogical enterprise and, especially, the idea of using a regenerated sign system as a means to instill a set of clear and unchanging principles in the minds of all citizens. And once again, these insecurities made themselves especially evident in discussions about the sign language education of the deaf, which had become a model for this process. Sicard had advanced his career by insisting on the special qualities that constituted the core of his "methodical" *langue des signes*—the combination of a sensible link to the original language of the state of nature and an analogic relationship to the precise, rational, static language of the Revolution—and by showing why these qualities made his sign system such an effective tool for molding a citizenry and a political culture impervious to the *abus des mots*. Similarly, as late as the summer of 1794, Grégoire could refer to the deaf as model logicians insofar as they had learned to think following exclusively "the path of nature."[182] But when, in the course of the Terror, the question emerged of whether or not to disseminate Sicard's methods more widely across France, some of the contradictions inherent in the enlightened language theory out of which revolutionary politics had emerged were laid bare. In the end, the example of the sign language education of the deaf became a focal point for the expression of anxieties within the Jacobin-dominated Convention about the extent to which the abstract idiom upon which the new nation depended could ever be used to make French society more just, more virtuous, and more harmonious.

Even in late 1793, the now politically suspect Abbé Sicard still harbored grand plans for himself, his ideas, and his institution. After two years of strained relations with Valentin Haüy, Sicard decided to seek the support of the Convention not only in legally separating the Paris school of the deaf from that of the blind[183] but also in establishing a series of new educational institutions, including a central school for training teachers, with himself at the head. Finally, the Committee of Public Assistance came to his aid. According to a deputy and committee member named Etienne-Christophe Maignet, Sicard's elaborate plan to oversee additional facilities for the deaf across the nation was justified by the results that he had already produced. "Visit the institution which houses these unfortunate peoples," Maignet urged the Convention in December 1793; "it is there that you will find real republicans."[184] Indeed, Maignet insisted a month later that his visit to Sicard's school in the company of other members of the Committee of Public Assistance had convinced him that Sicard had found the best way to instill sure moral principles, without regard for the sense "usage" has given to them, in the children of the future.[185]

Yet the Convention's Committee of Public Instruction was not so easily convinced during that winter of Terror. For the last half year, this committee had been bitterly divided over the LePeletier-Robespierre, Romme, and Bouquier plans for national public instruction.[186] The future of the education of the deaf proved no easier a case. André Jeanbon Saint-André was the first to object to Maignet's proposal, finding it excessive largely on practical grounds, much as he had many of the earlier educational plans debated by his committee.[187] Days later, after members of the Committee of Public Instruction had also paid a visit to Sicard's school,[188] the elderly Jacobin Nicholas Raffron presented the Convention with another set of objections to Maignet's report, this time on epistemological and ethical grounds. At the heart of Raffron's complaint was what he saw as a confusion; it appeared to him that the centerpiece of Sicard's pedagogy, the sign language that the Abbé de l'Epée had ostensibly "created," was not really an invention at all. For though "before the Abbé de l'Epée, deaf-mutes were not such learned theologians perhaps," Raffron noted, "they communicated their thoughts fairly easily among themselves, as well as to those with whom they lived. . . . They have a language of their own; it is the first that ever existed among men, the language of signs."[189] Based on this assumption, Raffron concluded that the deaf did not need a more extensive education than others in order to become active members of society. In fact, Raffron argued the opposite, namely, that the uneducated deaf represented a natural ideal that education should not be allowed to spoil. In this deputy's opinion, it made more sense for mainstream society, already too in thrall to an untrustworthy language, to look instead to prelinguistic communities, such as that of the uneducated deaf, for models.

In adopting this position, Raffron too demonstrated the consistency of his educational philosophy. In opposition to the LePeletier plan for communal boarding schools, which Robespierre had presented to the Convention in the preceding July, Raffron had already argued for the family's "natural" role in the moral instruction of children. Evoking Rousseau, Raffron had insisted on the superfluity of paid instructors taking it upon themselves to educate young citizens: "The facial features of the father and the mother are engraved in children's imagination and make a great impression on it: their [parents'] countenance, their nature, stature, tone of voice, their gestures, all, in fact, induce ideas of respect, recognition, and subordination. . . . [It] is through the senses that virtues enter the heart."[190] In the case of the deaf, Raffron simply affirmed this same conviction that sensory experience had to be the basis of morality and that innate, natural goodness was best represented by and cultivated through truly natural signs. Where the signs of civilized language might make artifice and manipulation possible, those of the original, physical language of nature, employed outside an institutional setting, seemed to preclude the possibility of dishonesty or insincerity as a result of their very form.

With this argument, Raffron not only challenged the position adopted by the Committee of Public Assistance and other supporters of Sicard. He also shifted the terms of the Convention's discussion from one centered on language and method to one about language and morality. Furthermore, he made explicit an important undercurrent in Jacobin ideology that rejected the seemingly elitist idea of rational philosophers fixing and disseminating an abstract political vocabulary for and on behalf of the nation. Instead, he evoked the equally "enlightened" myth of the preverbal *homme de la nature*, happy in his familial context, unencumbered by the weight of history and tradition, inherently industrious and virtuous, and yet blissfully free of worry about (or the ability to manipulate) the meaning of concepts that were not immediately visible to him.

This particular kind of linguistic populism reared its head in numerous places in the culture of the Year II, effectively undermining, at least temporarily, the philosophy of rational linguistic or semiotic *planification* that could be traced to the earlier initiatives of the revolutionary *philosophes* of the Société de 1789 or even the Société des Amateurs de la Langue Française. Not only did this antielitist vision bolster arguments against the introduction of comprehensive systems of national education; it also led, on occasion, to the valorization of unschooled or even faulty forms of communication—that which Domergue, for example, had been so anxious to work against—as signs of authenticity. When Pierre Desloges (who now referred to himself as "the republican Esope-Desloges, deaf and mute, inhabitant of Bicêtre") published an *Almanach de la raison* in late 1793 dedicated to the Jacobins "who are waging a courageous war against prejudices and superstition," he noted that he had neglected to correct several errors in the text. But he justified his results as a way of giving youths "an idea of the natural religion of the honest man" who owed his education entirely to "nature."[191]

This tendency to celebrate the connection between natural language and a timeless moral code—in contrast to the corrupted language of politics and the hypocritical morality of civilization—was also at the heart of one of the most important dramas to be performed in the Year II. That was Sylvain Maréchal's one-act "prophecy," *Le Jugement dernier des rois*, in which the *sans-culottes* of the world finally overthrow the monarchs. In this drama, a trans-European group of *sans-culottes* arrives on a distant volcanic island with their monarchs in tow only to discover an old man, an exiled victim of the corruption of the Old Regime, who has, over the years, befriended the local savages and rediscovered the primitive language of gestures common to these wise and virtuous people. As the old man tells the *sans-culottes*, it does not matter that he is ignorant of the savages' native tongue: "[T]he heart is the same in all countries; we keep up with each other through gestures, and we understand each other perfectly."[192] But there was more to the language politics of Maréchal's drama than just a rehashing of the semiotic utopianism of the best-selling novelist Bernardin de Saint-Pierre. The pure and honest savages of *Le Jugement dernier des rois* are also shocked by the hypocritical and unnatural speech of the dethroned monarchs. The last scene of this play draws an explicit contrast between the natural pantomime of the noble savages and the endless verbal warfare of the selfish, individualistic monarchs; as the kings and queens try pathetically to justify their former, tyrannical actions, the old man translates their speeches into *le langage des signes* and "the savages make, by turn, signs of astonishment and indignation."[193] And what of the language of the global *sans-culottes*? In Maréchal's telling, the *sans-culottes* are still forced to employ the corrupt language of European politics while dealing with the debased monarchs in the present, provisional moment. But once they eventually regain their natural rights and freedom, these honest, simple men will have no trouble communicating and fraternizing with their "older brothers in liberty," the savages. For Maréchal, the author of a polemical prorevolutionary dictionary just several years earlier, the final triumph of the Revolution would be marked by a return to a linguistic equivalent of the simple, concrete, gestural language of nature, an idiom that would, in turn, signal the end of all political or social discord.[194] Like many other radicals of the Year II, Maréchal's interest in the role of language in shaping reality appears to have been motivated not simply by the idea of recuperating a lost ideal that he associated with the state of nature but also by his enduring fears of the moral effects of a world increasingly structured and characterized by the proliferation of abstract signs.

The fight over the desirability of expanding Sicard's influence did not, however, end with Raffron's moral challenge. While spokesmen for the Committee of Public Instruction, such as the deputy Antoine-Clair Thibaudeau, continued to advance Raffron's (and by extension, Maréchal's) position that Sicard's method could only be a source of anxiety from the perspective of the nation's ethical health,[195] a contrary moral argument, also rooted in egalitarian sentiments, developed within the Committee of Public Assistance. The deputy Pierre Roger-Ducos explained this position as follows: "[E]very thinking being, no matter what his structure or color, should enjoy the benefits of the French government . . . which has an obligation to facilitate the means" by supplying a sufficient education in the abstract language of the French political system to all.[196] The key to this argument was the idea that neither civic laws nor even the principles of natural law could be internalized by individuals unless they had recourse to a set of names and a grammar to explain the relationships among them. And in support of this claim, Sicard's defenders held up the obvious moral deprivation and debasement of the uneducated deaf person, the individual limited to the manipulation of purely natural signs, as an illustration. In a *Réponse aux Observations du citoyen Raffron* sent to the Committee of Public Instruction during this debate, Citizen Périer, a former professor of rhetoric at a *collège* in Périgueux and a teacher-in-training at the Institution des Sourds-Muets, did not hesitate to argue that without the "regenerative hands" of Epée, most deaf people were reduced to a deplorable state, deprived of both the charms of sociability and the ability to reason.[197] Moreover, in response to Raffron's declaration that the deaf might just as well stay in the comfort of their families, Périer insisted that citizenship required more than an instinctual sense of one's basic rights; the true republican was not someone who submitted to no authority other than his own will but, rather, someone who learned and obeyed the laws and moral values of civilization, a process that depended upon learning conventional signs for these concepts. In fact, taking this position one step further, Périer argued that the existence of citizens uneducated in the language of society actually posed a danger to society's laws and moral values. As he put it:

> The [uneducated] Deaf-Mute is a savage always on the brink of ferocity, always on the verge of becoming a monster. While he is equipped with the faculty of thought, it remains inactive and unexercised as long as one neglects to make him a man. Until that point, he knows no other laws than those of nature, no other duties than those of procuring his own pleasure. He knows no consideration for conventions that he has not helped establish. He is thus always coming close to committing crimes, and no law can justly reach him when he indulges in this way.[198]

From the perspective of the Committee of Public Assistance, the formation of an *école centrale* for teaching instructors Sicard's method presented itself neither as a favor to the impoverished deaf nor as a potential source of their corruption. It was an indispensable prerequisite for securing the principles of a revolutionary civilization.

How can we explain this divergence in approach among those concerned with planning a national education system for the deaf in the Year II? Surely, it cannot simply be reduced to a conflict of opinion or personalities between the two committees. Similar tensions emerged within the Convention's Committee of Public Instruction each time this single committee was required to tackle a new plan for nationally sponsored schools, a situation that has been plausibly explained as representing either a contest between rational "instruction" and moral "education" or a conflict over different conceptions of regeneration.[199] This particular case points, however, to a different but equally fundamental dilemma within Jacobin ideology: a disagreement about how a republic can best cope with the problems associated with the language upon which it is founded.

One way to read this debate, then, would be to see in it one enlightened linguistic value (instrumentalism) pitted against another, seemingly incompatible one (transparency). After all, Sicard's supporters, operating on the assumption that instruction in linguistic abstractions was essential to understanding the rights and responsibilities of citizenship in a republic founded upon texts, sought to find a way to control individuals' grasp of these terms to the greatest degree possible. Indeed, they continued to seek a way to take charge of the national language and to use it to advance the revolutionary cause. Sicard's detractors, however, worried that even the highly touted "methodical sign" method involved too many potential risks; it was better to shelter ordinary people from the language of national politics to the extent that it was possible and to keep them focused on purely natural and necessarily transparent signs instead.

But what is also striking is how much the two sides in this debate shared during the winter of 1793–94. That included an enduring desire to find a way to make linguistic (and hence, social and ideological) struggle a thing of the past. It also included a mutual and increasing suspicion that the uncontrolled democratization of the language of the Revolution was actually exacerbating the very conditions that had made the Terror necessary: pluralism of understanding, interpretation, and opinion. And never did any of the leading French revolutionaries suggest this as a goal.

In this regard, Jacobin language planning initiatives bear comparing with contemporaneous reform efforts in late eighteenth-century America. Both Atlantic republican experiments frequently found participants and observers interpreting current events in linguistic terms. Both produced heated debates about the variable meaning of critical words. And in each of these contexts, concern with establishing a new, national language of "truth" figured heavily as well.[200] Thomas Jefferson's close friend William Thornton, for example, dedicated considerable energy in

the early 1790s to the construction of a phonetic alphabet that he promised would be impervious to falsehood, and he even sent it off to
Robespierre in June 1794 with the hopes that it might be of use in perfecting "the language of the regenerated French."[201] But in the American
case, another linguistic discourse emerged in the 1780s and 1790s
alongside that of Antifederalists like Thornton, a discourse that demonstrated a very different way of thinking about the function of language.
The best evidence for this alternative conception can be found in the
Federalist of 1787–88. In response to similar arguments about the use
and misuse of words in the debate surrounding the ratification of the
American constitution, Madison tried out in no. 37 a novel argument
concerning the ambiguity of words. Rather than insisting on the importance of "fixing" his terms definitively, Madison self-consciously argued
that, in fact, no set of words can ever point unambiguously to a set of
things and that ambiguity, which "forces readers to look beyond the letter to the spirit," is built into politics because it is built into human nature.[202] Then, based on this notion—that politics can not depend upon
the establishment of an idiom which is immune to the effects of variable
usage in determining definitions or meanings—Madison insisted that
the constitution could not rise or fall on problems of language. In this
manner, he managed to turn the inherent unfixedness of the national
language into a political advantage.

But such a conclusion was never an option in revolutionary France.
Statements of Jacobin epistemology, in contrast to their American
equivalents, repeatedly betrayed the greatest fear of their creators: that
their own universalist, republican language might provide the seeds for a
truly contestatory political system. And this possibility kept progressive
French revolutionary intellectuals, into the middle and late 1790s, looking for a way to use language reform not just to improve communication
but also to transcend faction and eliminate political conflict and dissent
once and for all.

Ultimately, after Thermidor, the position on deaf education put forth
by Raffron and Thibaudeau triumphed, and the initial plan of the Committee of Public Assistance was abandoned as excessive. But in the report of February 1795 that settled this particular matter, the deputy
charged with presenting the final resolution found himself arguing both
sides of the question over again. Thomas François Ambroise Jouenne-
Longchamp, a medical doctor before the Revolution, emphasized that
the deaf needed to replace their naturally impoverished grammar with
the philosophical grammar of French in order to be in a position to understand their civil and political rights. Otherwise, he proclaimed, their
silence reduced them to a cruel dependence and a "sort of servitude,"
making them victims of the first tyrant interested in oppressing them or

taking their possessions. Yet in rhetoric that recalled that of Epée several decades earlier, the deputy from Calvados described Massieu's own declarations as evocative of "the noble candor of innocence and the ingenuity of a savage firmly imbued with the ideas of the sacred rights of nature, as if nature itself had entrusted them to his memory." And he concluded, "What could be more sublime, citizens, than the simplicity of the accounts of this man of nature[?] ... What a subject of reflection for a philosophical man!"[203] In the Year III, this topic remained important for a "philosophical man" because the Revolution had as yet established no consensus about what kind of signs could best be made to serve what set of political values or goals.

5

Ending the Logomachy, 1795-99

Immediately following the fall of Robespierre on 9 Thermidor Year II, the Convention took up the vital question of how to explain why the Revolution had gone so wrong. What had happened to the principles of 1789? How had the dictatorship of Robespierre and his small circle of Jacobin associates become possible? Many Conventionnels believed that they needed to find answers to these difficult questions before they could either dismantle the institutions of the Terror or distance themselves from the principles that it had represented.

The explanations offered in the Convention during the early months of the Thermidorean Reaction took a variety of forms.[1] Some Thermidoreans saw the failures of the Revolution as the result of an accident and as a temporary, unfortunate turn of events. Others pointed to deep structural problems inherent in the creed of 1789. Still others blamed the warped personality of Robespierre. There was, in fact, little consensus in the months after Thermidor about history that was still too recent to comprehend. However, across the various revolutionary plot lines put forth in the second half of 1794, one phenomenon was consistently identified as a prime factor in making the Terror possible: the political rhetoric of the Jacobins.

Among the first in the Convention to formulate an argument about the advent and success of the Terror, along with a strategy for engendering postrevolutionary stability, was the deputy Michel-Edme Petit. In early September 1794, Petit appeared before the Convention to argue that the Jacobins' deliberate denaturalization and "abuse" of words had produced the Terror. Seductive phrases had been used to disguise crimes as virtuous acts; old words—liberty, patriotism, republic, even revolution—had been given self-serving meanings contrary to their true senses; new words had been coined to mislead public opinion. The Jacobins' efforts to "revolutionize" the language or, more accurately, to exploit the inevitable gap between *les mots* and *les choses*, had resulted in just what they had promised to avoid: contestatory politics and social anarchy. "[T]he French language, disfigured by new words invented as passwords for crimes; lies, false principles spread in speeches delivered in the name of the government; such were the causes of 9 Thermidor," he declared.[2] And now, Petit argued, the resulting disfigurement of the French language was impeding efforts to draw the Terror to a close and to restore peace both in the Convention and at large. Even among good men, he insisted, linguistic instability continued to produce insecurity about where absolute moral truths lay. Hoping to end the revolutionary logomachy and to encourage moderate republican values, Petit thus proposed that the Thermidorean Convention develop a linguistic strategy of its own—a means of controlling the vagaries of usage—by outlawing the use of terms such as *jacobin* or *montagne*, which had served only factional interests, and by publishing an official periodical that would give back to French words their "true senses."[3]

Petit's rhetoric was not, of course, especially novel in late 1794. Just months earlier, Robespierre had similarly accused counterrevolutionaries of using a corrupted language to advance their own private interests. Robespierre's allies had, in turn, proposed parallel linguistic initiatives designed to discourage political debate and ensure consensus, from Grégoire's plans to eradicate regional idioms and rename offending structures to Domergue's attempts to standardize the coinage of revolutionary neologisms. However, once Robespierre's days were over, Petit, like many Thermidoreans, showed himself to be fully prepared to turn formerly Jacobin political strategies, as well as modes of denunciation, against the Jacobins themselves. Indeed, the idea that the former head of the Committee of Public Safety and his Jacobin associates had used words in terribly misleading ways soon became a common, unifying theme among former Jacobins who now forswore their earlier allegiances, moderates, and royalists alike.

In August 1794, Daunou condemned Robespierre's misappropriation of the word *peuple* to refer to himself, as well as his many other attempts to seize power by playing on the instability of linguistic signs. "In the end, he [Robespierre] spoke nothing but the mystical jargon of a sham missionary," Daunou declared.[4] That same month, the deputy Jean-Lambert Tallien read a speech written largely by Pierre-Louis Roederer in which he explained the perverse way that tyranny had taken hold in recent years: "[O]ne could ensure . . . morality only by disguising all crimes as virtues and all virtues as crimes, rationality only by overturning all principles and prostituting their remains, by which I mean the words that are used to speak the language of principles and to conserve their memory!"[5] The *Mercure de France* followed with a series of articles entitled "Sur l'abus et les différentes variations des idées dans une révolution," which purported to show how "a handful of scoundrels . . . without any other talent than to impress people by a simulated patriotism and some artificial word games that influenced the masses all the more when their understanding of words was poor" had thrown the whole Revolution off its initial enlightened course.[6] Then in December, in a speech marking the annual opening of the renamed Lycée Républicain, La Harpe too denounced the brutal and obscene language that the Jacobin "barbarians" had deemed republican. Like Petit and Tallien, La Harpe argued that tyranny had been made possible by a strategy in which all words were made to evoke their inverse sense and any attempts to challenge this strange and monstrous language were met with physical violence. And to make matters worse, La Harpe decried the impossibility of describing these horrors without further tainting the national tongue: "[T]here are men of whom one cannot speak without soiling words as they have soiled nature."[7]

This linguistic conception of the Terror—the belief that it had been rendered possible by deception and division stemming from the abuse of words—had a profound impact on the political culture of the Thermidorean period and the Directory. In one sense, this reading of recent history encouraged continuity, as it underlined the importance of language as a political force, capable of producing consensus or disunion depending on its nature. But at the same time, it prompted a serious change in state policy. For after 1794, little interest remained in using language to "revolutionize" the world. What the moderate republican intellectuals who dominated the major public institutions of the middle and late 1790s sought was a way to use signs to counteract and to reverse the conditions that had produced the excesses of the Terror and to draw the revolutionary struggle to a close. This chapter concerns the efforts of these individuals to develop new semiotic initiatives that would help to secure the liberal values enshrined in the governments of the Thermidorean Reaction and the Directory while preventing at all cost a return of the barbarism and anarchy that had, in their opinion, characterized the last few years.

THE ENLIGHTENMENT AFTER THERMIDOR

The power struggles of the summer of 1794 produced a profound shift in the nature of intellectual life in France's capital city. Several of the most important thinkers of the late Enlightenment, including Condorcet and Lavoisier, had fallen victim to the Terror. Their places at the summit of the philosophical establishment were assumed by a group of generally moderate republicans who had themselves been strongly affected, both intellectually and politically, by their experiences between 1789 and 1794. Many of these men, including Daunou, Roederer, Pierre Louis Ginguené, Antoine-Louis-Claude Destutt de Tracy, the Comte de Volney, and Pierre-Jean-Georges Cabanis, had spent months of the Terror in prison or in hiding; others, such as Dominique-Joseph Garat and the

Abbé Grégoire, had continued to hold positions as leaders in the national government throughout the Year II and had only denounced the revolutionary dictatorship after the demise of Robespierre. The Thermidoreans cannot thus be said to have constituted a single political school, despite their continued support for most of the primary principles of 1789 and, in many cases, the positions of the Girondins before the summer of 1793.[8] As a group, their sense of union stemmed mainly from their opposition to Jacobin "vandals," on the one hand, and insurgent royalists, on the other. What they shared after 9 Thermidor was, primarily, a common desire to halt the Revolution and to stabilize the republic so as to prevent the return of the dominant values of either the distant or the recent past.

To this end, the members of the Thermidorean intellectual elite dedicated themselves to reversing what they took to be the anti-intellectual values of Jacobinism—fanaticism, dogmatism, superstitiousness, and obscurantism—and to encouraging reason and progress in their place. And with this goal in mind, many of these men argued that they would need to succeed where the original members of the Société de 1789 and their allies had not: in creating new institutions for the broad diffusion of knowledge and then in refashioning the language of politics. Moderates and conservatives alike now agreed that Jacobin discourse had disguised its true object through flowery and emotionally hyperbolic rhetoric that catered exclusively to the passions. But most liberals were hesitant about regulating either the content or form of the French language by enacting strict, punitive censorship laws. What the Thermidorean republic required, its intellectual leaders believed, was a rational idiom that would make such abuse impossible, a truly pedagogical national language that would reveal only fixed and certain notions and would itself work to make hypocrisy and deception things of the past.

For some Thermidoreans, a first, essential step toward putting the principles of the Revolution of 1789 on secure footing was to link the rights of citizenship to knowledge of written French. Public oration, with its abstract and often metaphoric terminology, was understood to be an essential component of republican political life. Yet in its fluidity and seductiveness, verbal eloquence was widely thought to promote both the accidental and the deliberate abuse of words, with negative effects for all of society. In contrast, communication through the written word seemed to generate stability and reason. The slogan of the Société Libre d'Institution in the Year III made the implications of this position explicit through reference to a major counterrevolutionary insurrection: "If all French people had known how to read, the Vendée would never have happened."[9] Based on such logic, certain Conventionnels argued vehemently that the new constitution of the Year III should include a proposition stating, among other requirements, that: "Young people can be inscribed on the civic register only if they prove that they know how to read and to write."[10] The idea met with resistance as soon as it was announced, and some deputies immediately opposed the article as not only impractical but also liable to create a new "aristocracy of the sciences."[11] Others, however, including Daunou and Boissy d'Anglas, insisted that such measures to encourage literacy and reliance upon the written word were vital to the process of reversing the conditions, both social and intellectual, that had produced the Jacobin revolution. As Daunou persuasively put it: "We have all been witnesses to the danger that exists in admitting men who know neither how to read nor how to write into primary assemblies," and with this argument, his side succeeded in making the measure an element of the law (though it was never put into effect).[12] Simply establishing this rule was, in the minds of the framers of the new constitution, an important move toward healing the rifts caused by the contestatory, divisive politics of the Terror and preventing their return.

Yet within the same circles, a good number of Thermidoreans insisted that encouraging the use and comprehension of written French throughout the nation was only a first step. The written language also needed to be reformed along specific lines so that it not simply mitigated the possibility of vocal opposition, factionalism, and dissent but made them henceforth impossible. In short, these men argued that the time had come once again to revive the search for a perfectly clear, incontestable sign system, a *langage philosophique* for daily concerns. They found the guidelines for their quest by turning back to some of the pillars of Enlightenment language theory.

It was Condillac (and decidedly not Rousseau, now tainted by association with Jacobinism) who provided the central principles for mainstream Thermidorean epistemology. In particular, Condillac's last work, his *La Logique* of 1780, indicated to some of the most prominent intellectuals of the middle and late 1790s that if a language were "well-made"—simple, clear, concise, structured by analogies, and resistant to changes stemming from variations in usage—it could become a tool of analysis and a path to sure knowledge in its own right.[13] Certainly, Condillac had made it clear that different sciences required different sign systems. However, he had also proposed that by following his "natural" guidelines for perfecting languages, all sciences could achieve the level of clarity and precision associated with algebraic demonstration (his favorite example). Because a "well-made science" and a "well-made language" were essentially equivalent, "all sciences would be exact if we only knew how to speak the language of each," he had explained in an oft-quoted passage.[14] Thus, by extension, Condillac's last writings suggested to many Thermidorean intellectuals that the construction of a stable, analytic language of politics and ethics, distinct from vulgar or everyday parlance, might well be used to make the art of governing into an accurate and sure science of its own.

But Condillac had not set his late ideas in a temporal or collective framework. The other major source for Thermidorean language reform efforts was the last, sweeping work of Condorcet, which did. The posthumous publication in early 1795 of Condorcet's *Esquisse d'un tableau historique des progrès de l'esprit humain* introduced Thermidoreans to an extremely promising theory of the symbiotic development of language, thought, and social organization. Written by Condorcet while in hiding during 1793-94, the *Esquisse* explained progress in human affairs in terms of a series of revolutions in communication, beginning with the invention of an articulate language (which initially allowed humans to distinguish themselves from animals) and continuing through the subsequent discovery of writing. Humans' capacity to perfect their own situation, according to Condorcet, depended upon their increasing ability to order the world through signs of their own invention. Advances in technology and increased chances for communication could speed up the process of man's gradual (linguistic) dominance of the natural and physical world, but it was the discovery of writing which was the basic precondition of history itself.

From this essential principle of human development, Condorcet offered post-Jacobin France a theory of applied social science and a prescription for continued progress. In an upcoming epoch of history, Condorcet suggested, the perfection of the sciences and the safeguarding of human knowledge against barbarous anti-intellectualism and manipulative rhetoric would depend on one thus-far unattainable dream: the invention of a universal written language impervious to the effects of common usage. Such a sign system, Condorcet rhapsodized, "would serve to bring to all objects embraced by human intelligence a rigor and precision that would render knowledge of the truth easy and error almost impossible. Then each science would advance as surely as mathematics, and the system of propositions comprising it would have the same certainty, which is to say all the certainty that the nature of their subject and their methods would permit."[15] With this discovery, not only would the language of each science reproduce the logical structure of that discipline but reasoning about its principles would become a form of calculus for arriving at demonstrable and thus incontestable truths.

The 1795 version of the *Esquisse* left open-ended the question of whether or not such a project could be extended to comprise the so-called moral and political sciences. In an unpublished fragment regarding the future of human history, Condorcet warned that the project would remain impossible as long as so few ethical notions were precise and well determined as ideas.[16] In the latter years of his career, however, Condorcet had continually argued for the necessity of establishing a social science in which abstract moral truths were both subjected to analysis and identified by a precise system of signs with which certain and reasoned calculations could be made. Furthermore, he had repeatedly pointed out that revolutions in communication always had profound social and political implications. In the immediate aftermath of the Terror, Condorcet's ideas could thus be understood to mean that social harmony, rooted in a science of governing, would be the inevitable result of the invention of a universal and perfectly analytical written language. As in many earlier eighteenth-century utopian visions or prophesies, it was perfect communication that would eventually ensure perpetual peace.

Such arguments appealed especially to moderate republicans within the Thermidorean bureaucracy, and the Thermidorean Convention's Committee of Public Instruction ordered numerous copies of Condorcet's *Esquisse*, as well as Condillac's *La Logique*, to be distributed to the nation's new schools.[17] But the government which replaced that of the Terror had larger intentions than simply turning these philosophical treatises into important textbooks. It also aimed to use the epistemological principles contained in these works to more general effect, making them the basis of a broad effort to reform the nation's political climate.

In the Year III, it was Joseph-Dominique Garat, the head of the Executive Commission on Public Instruction, who took the greatest steps to institutionalize the ideas on language put forth earlier by Condorcet and Condillac. Garat, like Condorcet, had initially established himself in enlightened Parisian philosophical circles in the 1780s, participating in the Loge des Neuf Soeurs, teaching at the Lycée, writing for the *Journal de Paris*, and finally joining in the attempts of the Société de 1789 to elaborate a *science sociale* during the first years of the Revolution. After an unsuccessful stint as Minister of the Interior during 1793, Garat had, unlike Condorcet, managed to remain on favorable terms with both Girondin sympathizers and the Jacobin inner circle. Nevertheless, it was only after Thermidor that Garat began to hold the kind of intellectual and political power that allowed him to impose his own educational vision on France. By November 1794, the Convention's Committee of Public Instruction was filled with Garat's friends, including Petit, Thibaudeau, Grégoire, J. B. Massieu, Boissy d'Anglas, and, most important, Lakanal. And with this committee's support, Garat was able to use his position on the affiliated Executive Commission to exert considerable influence over both the shape and content of Thermidorean intellectual life.

From the fall of 1794 to the spring of 1795, Garat channeled most of his energy into the establishment of a model Ecole Normale in Paris. The idea of a special school for the training of France's teachers had been debated in revolutionary assemblies since 1792 and remained under consideration in the Convention throughout the Terror. Amidst all the discussion of a new system of national primary instruction, the Committee of Public Instruction was continually confronted with the question of how best to mold the people who would themselves be given the formidable task of forming revolutionary citizens. Yet, as a result of the earlier Convention's inability to settle on a single educational plan, it was not until September 1794 that the development of a school devoted specifically to pedagogy was voted into law.

A speech of October 1794, read before the Convention by Lakanal and almost certainly written by Garat, outlined the theory of education that was to guide the establishment of the Ecole Normale.[18] Despite continual Jacobin support for the project prior to Thermidor, Garat opened his discourse with the now-obligatory denunciation of the anti-intellectualism of the tyrants and brigands who had tried over the last several years to obfuscate knowledge and to "cover it in shadows." Against this image, he then offered a contrasting view of a new government eager to halt the political revolution and to encourage a nascent revolution in the *esprit humain* instead. Universal enlightenment, Garat explained, depended upon public instruction in the inviolable and basic principles of the constitution. But this goal required a new pedagogical method: "When, in the middle of so many crises and so many novel moral experiences, new truths are broadcast every day, how can education be used to establish immutable principles?" he asked.[19] Garat thus insisted that the Ecole Normale should take as its purpose the training of teachers in what he saw as the vital *langage* or methodology for all the sciences, not only physical but social and political as well: *analyse*. In the Ecole Normale, Garat promised in the spirit of Condorcet, "the moral sciences, so necessary to people who govern themselves by their own virtues, are going to be subjected to proofs as rigorous as those in the exact and physical sciences."[20]

As Garat envisioned it, the four-month course at the Ecole would provide elementary teachers from every region in France with an education not in particular subjects but in scientific methodology and pedagogy itself. This emphasis upon approaches to teaching was underscored by the fact that the distinguished scholars picked at the beginning of November 1794 to become professors at the Ecole Normale were drawn primarily from the list of those who, just several days earlier, had been chosen to compose new elementary textbooks for use throughout France.[21] As Garat wrote about this prestigious group of scholars: "Several are known for having created or perfected the *methods* that have helped the sciences to make new progress, or that have made learning them easier."[22] What many of these scholars, with several notable exceptions, seemed to share was, in fact, a series of convictions: that Condillac had been correct in insisting that sensations were the basis of all ideas; that analysis was the most trustworthy path to all types of knowledge; and that well-made languages were essential to the process of ascertaining proof in all sciences. Claude Louis Berthollet, the newly named professor of chemistry who had been instrumental in the late 1780s in the establishment of a new nomenclature for this field, exemplified the approach to the physical and natural sciences that Garat sought to generalize.[23] On the side of the human sciences, it was the pedagogical-linguistic system of Sicard, the methodology that had previously so impressed Condorcet, Grégoire, Roederer, and Daunou, among others, that Garat hoped to popularize as a model for the education of ordinary children as well.[24]

The Ecole Normale of Paris finally opened on January 20, 1795. A heterogeneous group of adult pupils, many already teachers, had been convened from all over France in order to spend four months listening to an array of lectures and participating in structured *débats* with some of the great thinkers of the day. Based on the preliminary program (written by each of the professors in conjunction with Garat and Lakanal), as well as the stenographic journal that was established to provide an immediate, verbatim transcription of all sessions at the school, we know a considerable amount about both the content of these lectures and the discussions that they provoked.[25]

Written language was a central concern from the beginning. Garat, a noted orator, immediately insisted on the significance of public lectures in a republican culture where "speech exerts great influence and even has an authority [of its own]."[26] Yet, at the same time, he made sure that each and every word uttered at the Ecole would be duly recorded and made public in periodical form, and he emphasized the importance of disseminating ideas through proper written French.[27] Indeed, Garat claimed that accurate notation was essential as a corrective to the slipperiness of oral argument and as a means to ensure that "exact precision without which there is no truth."[28] This same desire to control the meaning and effect of verbal display through the medium of permanent, written signs manifested itself in the curriculum of the Ecole as well. Instruction in rhetoric was conspicuously absent from the school's program. But reform of the written language figured prominently in many areas within the new Ecole Normale, including Sicard's course on general grammar or "the art of speech," Volney's lectures on history, and, finally, Garat's own ambitious teachings on "human understanding,"

the course that was intended to link together the multiple subjects offered at his school.[29]

All three men advised their students to study the languages of primitive peoples, including those of savages and the deaf, in order to learn to
value the purity and clarity of an uncorrupted, analogic idiom and to
understand the generation of ideas. But these pedagogues also agreed
that ethnographic study was not enough to counteract the inexactitude
and errors that had taken seed in civilized *parole*. Stressing both the
theoretical importance of writing in giving permanent fixity and authority to fugitive ideas and the political advantages of a clear, rational mode
of notation, Sicard and Volney used the opportunity to propose practical
changes in the alphabet itself. The current system of letters needed to be
reformed, they agreed, so that no sign could ever represent more than
one sound and, conversely, no sound could ever be signified by two, distinct signs. Moreover, the alphabet had to be expanded to include all the
basic sounds of human speech.

What Volney hoped to construct was a universal phonetic alphabet,
or what he had recently described in a letter to the Abbé Grégoire as a
uniform and international "canon of signs."[30] In his lectures at the Ecole
Normale, Volney emphasized the untrustworthiness of information
that had been passed down orally and the importance of regular alphabets in encouraging people around the world to keep accurate written
records that could be consulted and compared by subsequent generations.[31] Furthermore, he stressed the ways in which an international notation system could become a conduit for revolutionary values. Not
only would a universal alphabet make the learning of foreign tongues
easier for Europeans. It would also (as Volney went on to explain in his
Simplification des langues orientales, a book that he composed simultaneously with his lectures at the Ecole Normale) encourage the substi-
tution of reason for political and religious fanaticism in distant parts of
the globe and help to establish a much-needed "moral affinity, an exchange of practices, needs, opinions, mores and, finally, laws" between
Europe and the Orient.[32] For the historian was convinced that it was the
graphic nature of the characters of exotic languages—"these exterior
forms, these forbidding and bizarre figures"—that constituted the greatest obstacle to the universal acceptance of progressive Western ideas.
And in Volney's opinion, it was the responsibility of Western intellectuals, including himself and his allies, to help correct the problem.

Sicard took up the same argument, but in a domestic context, drawing similar comparisons between the irregular form of the modern Latin
alphabet and the disordered moral and linguistic state of contemporary
France.[33] One solution, he proposed, was to limit young children's expo-
sure to this irrational system of notation, beginning their education with

pictures, gestures, and whole words, but not individual letters. Another was to turn instead to the reform of vernacular grammar based on the universal principles of general grammar, which was itself a form of immutable logic. But Sicard, like Volney, also used his lectures to advocate new efforts to construct "signs that are certain, well-determined, and everywhere the same."[34] Pronunciation and penmanship would only become uniform throughout the nation, Sicard declared, when France had developed a republican system of orthography based on a canon of signs. And only with this kind of uniformity could enlightened principles be accurately communicated throughout France. Writing in the *Ami des citoyens*, a journalist enthused: "Citizen Sicard was made to carry out this revolution [in the alphabet], and we, therefore, must believe that he will know how to save us from the anarchy that several scheming letters could use in order to hinder its progress."[35] Such comments effectively spread the idea that there was, in fact, a rational connection between the graphic or visual form of linguistic signs and the prevailing political order.

Neither Sicard's nor Volney's actual plans for reform received much public support in the Year III. But the principles behind their teachings were prominently reinforced in the concurrent lectures of Garat himself, who prophesied that the moment had finally arrived not just for alphabetic reform but also for a true universal written language. Like Sicard and Volney, Garat also warned his students about the dangers of oral eloquence, its potential to serve as a cover for lies, injustices, and false religions: "[It] is this [eloquence] which lent the flood of deceptive acts that inundated the land this brilliant and violent language which, after having led astray or silenced reason, subsumed or carried away people's willpower."[36] His proposed solution was, however, even more ambitious. The way to combat the dangers of passionate political rhetoric and demagoguery, he declared, was to model a written language for the social sciences on the example of mathematics or chemistry, where signs were iconic and analogic rather than purely arbitrary in their construction.[37] Overlooking Condorcet's hesitations about the current state of moral principles themselves, Garat pointed out the reasons why such a development was no longer impossible to imagine:

> Is it a dream, or is it one of those great ideas that many centuries entertain as a beautiful chimera and that the most lucky centuries execute? And I will note that today a very great number of ideas in the moral sciences and in the physical sciences have, across all of Europe, the same language, which can very easily be recognized despite the minor changes to which each people has subjected the words of its own tongue. I will note that today, when the entire machinery of languages and all the artifice of their construction are well known, the formation of a new lan-

guage for all types of ideas is not, by far, the project that presents the most difficulties to sound philosophy.[38]

In other words, for Garat, as for Volney and Sicard, the path to universalizing the moral truths established by the Revolution, as well as to preventing their distortion, lay in the construction of a new system of characters that would, literally, impose order on thought.

However, despite Garat's great (and probably unrealistic) expectations for his larger educational project, the Ecole Normale was a failure. The school closed after only four months on May 19, 1795, the day before the insurrection of 1 Prairial. The purpose of the school had been confused from the start, as the distinction between teaching particular sciences and teaching pedagogical methods had been left uncertain. To compound this lack of clear direction, rivalries had developed between professors, notably between La Harpe and Garat, on a combination of political, ideological, and personal grounds. Hostile students had posed challenges of their own; Louis-Claude de Saint-Martin, for example, had loudly attacked the sensationalism at the root of Garat's teachings.[39] Other dissatisfied pupils had exposed the school to public ridicule. A satire printed with the ironic title *La Tour de Babel au Jardin des Plantes, ou Lettre de Mathurin Bonace, sur l'école normale* and with purported origins in "Babylone, De l'Imprimerie Polyglotte, an 4878 après le déluge" made the serious point that the babble of different pedagogic languages to which students had been subjected had resulted not in a single cross-disciplinary methodology but in vast linguistic confusion, the very type of intellectual anarchy that the school had been established to combat.

Because of its brief duration and the harsh criticism that it received, the original Ecole Normale has generally been dismissed by historians as a misguided experiment. Indeed, it was many years before another Ecole Normale was established in France. But, as we will see, this initial, short-lived attempt at higher education for teachers had a vital impact on the political culture and, specifically, the language politics of the Directory. First, the lectures and debates of the Ecole Normale contributed to an intellectual vogue for Condillac's epistemology; not only were his complete works, including the posthumous *La Langue des calculs*, published with much fanfare in 1798, but Condillac's later conceptions of ideas and signs also became a key source for deriving principles of legislation, education, and social policy after 1795.[40] Second, the teachers at the Ecole Normale, in their search for rhetorical safeguards, effectively reoriented the focus of public discussion of language reform by constantly valorizing written signs and suggesting the possibility of their rationalization and even universalization (at the expense of customary and variable speech) as a panacea for political and social woes. As Jean Delormel told the Convention in the Year III while presenting his own plan for a universal revolutionary idiom, the time had finally arrived for the government to destroy the "tyranny" of usage, to abandon "this servile and routine imitation that still draws us close to barbarism, and to create an absolutely new language."[41] Finally, and perhaps most important, the Ecole Normale played an essential role in establishing a new, state-sponsored intellectual elite. This group would continue to forge certain common notions regarding the importance of understanding and controlling linguistic signs in many of the Directory's major institutions, including various branches of the government, the new *écoles centrales* spread across the departments, the many independent Parisian learned societies and *lycées* that came to life after Thermidor, and the primary intellectual body of the period, the official Institut National des Sciences et des Arts.

THE INSTITUT AND THE PROBLEM OF SIGNS

The old Enlightenment question of how language reform might function as both a tool and a goal of social science—an issue that had only been hinted at in the curriculum of the Ecole Normale—provided the impetus for the first public essay contest announced by the Second Class of the Institut National des Sciences et des Arts in the summer of 1796. The Institut, which had been founded by a constitutional act the previous August, was intended to fulfill many of the same functions formerly undertaken by the Academies of Science and of Inscriptions.[42] One of these was the prerevolutionary practice of holding open essay contests to encourage research in particular fields. In response to perceived Jacobin obscurantism, the founders of the Institut insisted on the importance of public discussions dedicated to the advancement of knowledge and the promotion of a new intellectual elite. However, the Institut's essay contests, like many of the other projects upon which this institution was soon to embark, had an explicit political purpose as well. To an unprecedented degree, the members of the Institut viewed their public competitions as a means to help the new government establish fundamental principles and policies for the betterment of postrevolutionary society.

This practical orientation was especially evident in the Institut's Second Class, or Class of Political and Moral Sciences, the innovative section of the Institut that was established both to develop the science of man and to derive basic tenets for the smooth, rational functioning of the republic.[43] Here many of the subjects that had briefly been debated at the Ecole Normale were revived. Indeed, the Second Class became the primary home of the so-called Ideologues, a loosely constituted group of philosophers who believed in a sensationalist and genetic epistemology stemming from the late theories of Condillac, as well as the potential of *science sociale* to generate peace and order in a moderate republican state.[44] For the inner core, these convictions were also frequently coupled with associations with the salon of Mme Helvétius at Auteuil and the periodical *La Décade philosophique, littéraire et politique*.[45] But it was the Ideologues' ties to the government-sponsored Institut and, especially, to the Second Class that gave them their primary opportunity to influence public policy.

The Second Class was itself divided into six sections: ethics, history, geography, social science and legislation, political economy, and the "analysis of sensations and ideas." The Ideologues and other prominent former associates of Condorcet figured prominently across all of them. Of course, the Ideologues never had a monopoly on these positions; the Second Class also contained many former members of the Academy of Inscriptions and several notable figures, including Bernardin de Saint-Pierre and Louis-Sébastien Mercier, who were staunchly opposed to the new thinking. But the newer disciplines, in particular, attracted a group of relatively like-minded men, including Daunou (in the section on social science), Lakanal and Grégoire (in the section on ethics), and Sieyès, Roederer, and Talleyrand (in the section on political economy), who soon came to constitute a loosely defined but influential school of thought.[46] In fact, it was the section devoted specifically to analysis, the most unusual addition to the intellectual profile of the Institut, that rapidly became the center of Ideologue activity.[47] Volney and Garat, acting as the "electing third" of this section, were responsible for bringing into their midst four other members from Paris—Ginguené, Cabanis, Joachim Lebreton, and Alexandre Deleyre—and six nonresident members, including Pierre Laromiguière of Toulouse and Destutt de Tracy of Auteuil. And while an interest in language, and particularly in signs, was common to almost the entire Second Class, the section devoted to the analysis of sensations and ideas was especially concerned with investigating the role of signs in the construction and understanding of social relations. Indeed, all three founders of the Institut, Antoine-François Fourcroy, Lakanal, and Daunou, agreed that the "scientific" principles of ethics, economics, and legislation had to be deduced from the essential facts of human nature, notably the ability of humans to experience sensations and to name them as ideas.

Thus the Second Class's choice of topic for its first essay contest must have come as no surprise to those who had been following its activities. By the time the Class took it upon itself to ask the public to clarify the exact nature of the relationship between signs and thought, the question had already been taken up in two highly influential memoirs that were read aloud by members of the section on analysis during the Year IV. Cabanis, a physician and philosopher who had once been a member of the Société de 1789, began to deliver the first section of his multipart memoir, "Considérations générales sur l'étude de l'homme, et sur les rapports de son organisation physique avec ses facultés intellectuelles et morales" in February 1796, just several months after the opening of the Institut.[48] A little over two months later, beginning in April, Destutt de Tracy, a nobleman and *philosophe* of similar intellectual orientation who had served in the Estates-General and the National Assembly before being imprisoned during the Terror, expanded on Cabanis's ideas. More precisely, Destutt de Tracy read an extensive essay entitled "Mémoire sur la faculté de penser" in which he proposed that a science of "idéologie" (his coinage), or the analysis of ideas, was a necessary foundation for a science of society.[49] Both men drew heavily on theories that they found in the later works of Condillac in order to argue for the centrality of signs in their respective intellectual enterprises. Despite their differences of opinion on such questions as whether humans' first ideas required signs to be established, the papers of the two men, taken together, testify to the singular emphasis placed at this moment on the idea that progress in knowledge and the promotion of happiness at the level of society depended upon channeling human nature toward greater enlightenment through the medium of improved communicative signs.[50]

It was early July of 1796, only months after Destutt de Tracy and Cabanis had presented their memoirs, when the Second Class made public the program for its first essay contest.[51] Building on established concerns, the Class elaborated five interrelated questions for respondents to consider in the course of the coming year:

> 1. Is it really true that sensations can only be transformed into ideas by means of signs? Or, what comes to the same thing, do our earliest ideas depend on the help of signs? 2. Would the art of thinking be perfect if the art of signs were brought to its highest degree of perfection? 3. In those sciences where the truth is received without contest, is this the result of the perfection of the signs used in them? 4. In those branches of knowledge which are a constant source of disputes, is this division of opinions the necessary result of the inexactitude of the signs employed? 5. Is there any means of correcting signs that are badly made and of rendering all sciences equally susceptible to proof?[52]

Members of the public were thus invited to ponder simultaneously both an abstract problem about human understanding and a practical matter of importance to contemporary governance and social life. The first of the Second Class's questions, which was formulated based on the assumption of the sensual basis of all ideas, asked whether or not signs were necessary for all human thoughts. The next three questions then built upon this first one in order to get at a fundamental problem for post-revolutionary society: how to ensure the degree of certainty characteristic of reasoning in the physical and natural sciences in the realm of the moral and political ones. The Second Class's chief mission in this contest was to ascertain, first, whether vague and uncertain terms could be held responsible for discord in contemporary social and political life and, second, whether specific measures for fixing these signs might result in secure truths—and hence, consensus—in moral and political spheres. Finally, in the section of the program that clearly distinguished the new direction of the Institut, the Second Class, assuming an affirmative answer to the preceding question regarding the possibility of a social "science," asked the public to consider what the nature of these linguistic reforms ought to be. How, in other words, could the language of quotidian affairs ever be entirely freed from the dangers associated with rhetoric?

Between July 1796 and July 1797, the Institut received thirteen responses from all corners of France.[53] It is possible to determine the professions of only two of these authors: a teacher at an *école centrale* in Strasbourg and a naval engineer. As for their names, the majority of the respondents remain as anonymous today as they were on the day that they submitted their essays. What is most striking about these individuals as a group is their common moderation, regardless of their social, regional, and professional differences, in matters of both politics and philosophy.

Almost all of the respondents accepted the basic premises upon which the contest had been constructed. Words—generally referred to interchangeably with signs in these essays—were assumed to be human inventions, signifiers that evolved out of a limited but expressive, primordial *langage d'action*. Following Destutt de Tracy's recent memoir, most of the essayists denied that signs were necessary for determining an individual's very first ideas based on simple sensations; but they all agreed that ideas could not be fixed, judged, or combined without the use of signs. And just as they viewed the development of artificial signs as vital to the evolution of abstract thought and the advancement of civilization, so these writers were also convinced of the growing danger posed by the proliferation of equivocal signs for complex concepts in all domains.

In particular, the contest respondents writing in the Years IV and V were, like many of their contemporaries in the press and in the government, very ready to place much of the blame for contemporary discord and for the instability of public opinion on the vague and uncertain signs that formed the principal support of current political discourse. Indeed, these essays are filled with commentary on the role of the French language in producing the Terror and the disorder that continued after its demise. P. F. Lancelin, for example, argued that disputes about morality and legislation—the sources of factional politics—stemmed directly from the prevalence of ill-defined and, hence, divisive terms in the French language: "How many people in a revolution are victims of these denominations: aristocrats, royalists, demagogues, Whigs, Tories, anarchists, heretics, and so many others that parties, factions, and sects use as so many deadly weapons to destroy each other?" he asked.[54] An anonymous writer from the Ardèche similarly faulted the French language for its dangerous "scholastic jargon" and the "superabundance" of meanings often attached to single terms.[55] "This fatal inexactitude produced almost all the misfortunes of the revolution," he announced, claiming, in opposition to earlier Jacobin attempts to destroy regional idioms, that even the impoverished *patois* of his home region was preferable to official French. And various essayists blamed other persistent social ills— from the susceptibility of the general population to deception at the hands of manipulative priests and politicians to the meaningless chatter characteristic of recent public discussions—on a malleable and arbitrary ethical language that lent itself to distortion and misunderstanding.

Almost none of the respondents to the Institut's prize contest were prepared to admit that language reform alone could be counted on to establish secure truths or to ensure consensus in the political sphere. They were also skeptical that the existence of truths in any science could be attributed solely to the quality of the signs employed to represent them. They overwhelmingly agreed, however, that the inexactitude of contemporary terms for moral and political concepts had severely curtailed the likelihood that a rational approach to politics and ethics would develop any time soon in France. The growth of social science as a discipline with secure laws applicable to republican public policy remained impossible without precise terminology with which to reason. As the first respondent insisted in an entry forwarded on his behalf by a member of the Directory's Council of Five Hundred, in every science "imperfect and equivocal signs check and slow down the activity of the mind, throw obscurity, confusion, and uncertainty into our thoughts, explain poorly our ideas, as well as their relations, give us false conceptions, and lead us into errors."[56] Many of the people who submitted essays to the Institut's first contest concurred that official measures were needed to help counteract the nefarious effects of manipulative, extremist political rhetoric and to make the French language a "tool" (in the words of Lancelin) of stable, moderate republicanism.

Most of the respondents could not, however, define what form these measures ought to take. Suggestions included the introduction of grammatical reforms, the construction of new dictionaries dedicated to upholding the purity of the French language or uncovering the roots of words through etymology, and the pruning of synonyms, revolutionary terms, and rude expressions from the national idiom. One writer promised that if legislators simply relied upon analysis in all their decision-making, they would easily solve all the "errors that pollute the social state" and "like a lever, lift up the moral world and secure the destiny of the human species."[57] But the authors of the first set of responses to the Second Class's prize contest had few fresh ideas on this score, and most respondents simply delineated the qualities—simplicity, precision, and stability—that they hoped the national language would one day possess.

In fact, a majority of writers stressed the futility of official efforts to correct the language of the social sciences. Trying to remake any sign system by artificial means only results in confusion, argued one essayist. Several pointed out that a "perfect" language was an impossibility, as truths were arrived at in distinct ways in different disciplines. Most devastatingly, one respondent insisted that diversity of opinion and disagreement about moral matters were inherent in human nature:

> Even with the greatest exactitude in signs, we will always be divided about abstractions, metaphysics, and all subjects that require hypotheses for proofs. Our minds will always be too limited, our eyes too weak, our passions too active, our lives too short, [and] our methods insufficient to succeed in obtaining all the knowledge that we will ever covet.[58]

The committee designated to judge the contest was dissatisfied with these responses and, following the conclusion of the essay contest in the summer of 1797, the same *concours* was officially reopened the following spring. Lancelin's study, the most optimistic of the first group, was awarded an honorable mention in January of 1798; but it was not found worthy of an actual prize. We can not know the exact reasons for the committee's disappointment, as Garat's report on behalf of the examining committee has been lost. Either he and the committee rejected the philosophical moderation characteristic of most of the responses received or, equally likely, they felt that the answers to the vital last question about an appropriate language politics for the Directory were too weak to merit a prize. For as it turned out, in the year between the announcement and the conclusion of the contest, the members of the Institut had witnessed an explosion of potentially radical solutions to the very problem posed by the final question of the Second Class's first essay contest.

THE PASIGRAPHIC SOLUTION

By the Year V, many French intellectuals had developed a singular interest in the planning and construction of nonverbal systems of communication, including telegraphic and marine signals, stenographies, shorthands, and *pasigraphies*, as universal written languages were then known. Indeed, some commentators took these linguistic projects to be not only solutions to the Institut's ongoing contest but the hallmark of the new age ushered in following the demise of Robespierre. In 1797, the political economist Roederer characterized the contemporary moment as one

> where all minds are turned towards the perfecting of means of communication among men; where stenography, pasigraphy, and telegraphy share the attention of grammarians, logicians, and physicists; where men vie with one another in order to form a universal language or mode of writing; where the language of action invented for the deaf-mute is not only another language to add to the two society already enjoys [writing and speech] but has even become a very important instrument of the analytic method... a moment, finally, when the Institut National has asked the public to bring to light the influence of signs on ideas and where the signs of writing have, as a consequence, become a special object of zealous interest for the sciences.[59]

Two years later, an anonymous writer in the journal *Magasin encyclopédique* asked rhetorically what Cicero would have said if he had lived to witness such developments as "the blind and the deaf-mute restored to society, to the sciences and arts... our telegraphy at the point where it is a perfected pasigraphy, [and] finally the new stenography, which must take its place among these admirable inventions of the human mind."[60]

Certainly, the origins of this fascination with new, silent modes of communication and notation predated the Directory. In the last years of the Old Regime, the Academy of Sciences had taken a certain interest both in Dom Gauthey's nascent plans for a telegraphic machine, which the Academy examined in 1782,[61] and in Jean Félicité Coulon de Thévenot's abbreviated alphabetic system for writing "as quickly as one speaks," which was examined in 1776 and again in 1787.[62] However, it was only after 1789, in the course of the Revolution, that real opportunities emerged for such projects to be put into practice. The international war sparked by the national conflict, on the one hand, and the emergence of domestic political assemblies structured around oral debate, on the other, led inventors to believe that interest in new communication technologies with practical applications would surely increase.

In May 1789, Coulon opened a course in his shorthand *tachygraphie* between meetings of the Estates-General at Versailles; other proponents of other shorthand methods, including Théodore Pierre Bertin and Jean-Jérôme Roussel, quickly established classes of their own.[63] All of these teachers argued that instruction in abbreviated notation systems was essential if the public were to be provided with literal renditions of speeches and oral debates, as had long been the tradition in England. With this purpose in mind, Roussel also established a Société Logographique in June 1790 to record the proceedings of the National Assembly verbatim.[64] Several short-lived journals based on stenographic reporting of other public assemblies soon followed; François Elie Guirault of Bordeaux, for example, briefly, in 1792, published a periodical entitled the *Journal logotachigraphique de la Société des Amis de la Constitution, séante aux Jacobins* in order to make word-by-word transcriptions of conversations in this club available through what he promised was the most accurate medium of notation to date.[65]

At the same time, in the spring of 1792, the Committee of Public Instruction in the Legislative Assembly was given responsibility for examining a new procedure created by Claude Chappe "in order to communicate, over extended distances and with great speed, news of pressing interest."[66] Chappe's plan called for the construction of a series of stations, each outfitted with a tall machine topped by wooden arms, whose various positions could signify not only numbers and letters but also specific names and phrases that could be decoded with the aid of a special "vocabulary" at the last station [see Fig. 8]. Chappe initially referred to this invention, whose characters he based on "the figure and the position of the body," as a *tachygraphe* or *sténographie numérique*, since his goal was to represent a series of words quickly, with the smallest number of signs possible.[67] However, the following spring, at the suggestion of Miot de Mélito, an official in the Ministry of War, Chappe's invention was renamed a *télégraphe* in order to emphasize that his system—now endowed with an expanded number of signals—also allowed one to communicate over great distances.[68] When Chappe was finally able to demonstrate his telegraph in the summer of 1793, the success of the trial prompted Lakanal, a member of the committee set up to examine the invention, to comment: "For several years, Citizen Chappe has been working to perfect the language of signals, convinced that carried to the degree of perfection of which it is capable, it would perhaps have a great utility in a multitude of circumstances. . . . [T]he results permit no equivocation in the literal transmission of different characters belonging to the language of signs."[69] Yet neither Daunou nor Argobast, the other members of the committee, shared Lakanal's enthusiasm. In fact, the telegraph, like most of the new stenographies, was met largely with indifference on the part of both the government and the press throughout the early 1790s.

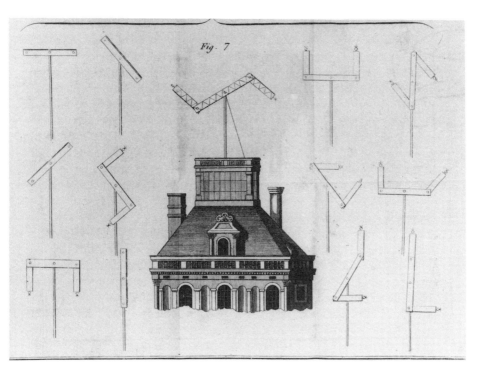

FIG. 8. Plate from Edelcrantz's *Traité des télégraphes* (1801) illustrating some of the almost two hundred possible positions or "signs" for words or phrases that could be formed by manipulating the arms of Chappe's telegraph and decoded with the aid of a special vocabulary. The post is here shown installed atop a pavilion of the Louvre in the 1790s. Photograph courtesy of the Science, Industry and Business Library, the New York Public Library, Astor, Lenox and Tilden Foundations.

This situation began to change only in late 1794. Immediately after Thermidor, the telegraph was finally put to effective use as a means of announcing military victories between Paris and Lille.[70] Deputies then started to tout the telegraph as one of the great inventions of the revolutionary era. Fourcroy, who had been active in reforming the language of chemistry, called the device "this new revolutionary courier, whose discovery has closely followed the foundation of the Republic," while Lakanal, in another report, compared Chappe's invention with the fire signals that the Swiss had used to overthrow despotism, and Jacques-Antoine Rabaut-Pommier prophesied that the telegraph's usefulness would one day be extended to commerce, physics, agriculture, and even politics.[71] Stenography too grew in stature after Thermidor, as it was increasingly used for the verbatim transcription of political speeches, court proceedings, and public lectures, most prominently at the Ecole Normale, where several of Bertin's former students were hired to record for posterity the ostensibly spontaneous utterances of France's great savants.[72] Suddenly, a growing contingent of competitors began working to develop easier and more successful systems of notation and asked representatives of the government to consider their efficacy. During the Year III, numerous projects for new signal systems and specialized types of telegraphs were sent to both the Convention's Committee of Public Instruction and the Temporary Commission on the Arts.[73] A former major in the German infantry announced in the fall of 1795 his collaboration with the Abbé Sicard in the invention of a universal written script called a *pasigraphie*.[74] That same year, the editors of the *Magasin encyclopédique* published a lengthy article entitled "On a universal language, the new pasigraphy; and by extension, on the art of stenography and telegraphy, writing with numerals and the art of deciphering this writing," in which these recent inventions were situated within a long intellectual genealogy including Bacon, Leibniz, and the Bishop Wilkins.[75] Such articles marked the beginning of a trend that only accelerated after the coup d'état of Fructidor Year V (September 4, 1797) temporarily strengthened the nation's moderate republican leadership.[76] By the late 1790s, the historical significance of these projects was routinely acknowledged by grammarians and journalists alike.[77] Moreover, new systems for writing and transmitting ideas were presented and lauded in many of the key institutions of the era, from the two legislative chambers of the government to the numerous learned societies that flourished in Paris during the "Fructidorean" Directory and Consulate, including the two Lycées, the Société Philomathique, the Société Philotechnique, and the Société Libre d'Institution.[78]

From late 1797 onward, it was, however, the Institut that constituted the central locus for the examination, discussion, and encouragement of these plans. In fact, each Class of the Institut made a point of producing reports on a series of new projects of this sort. Telegraphic systems were analyzed by the First Class (the Class of Mathematical and Physical Sciences), many of whose members had been instrumental in developing the new language of chemistry; stenographies and shorthands were received by the Third Class (the Class of Literature and the Beaux-Arts), whose ranks included both Domergue and, briefly, Sicard; and plans for universal written languages, or pasigraphies, were taken under consideration by the Second Class.[79] During the last years of the century, many of these projects actually made their way into the hands of the Institut's members with the backing of the Ministry of the Interior, where Nicolas-Louis François de Neufchâteau, the chief minister and himself a member of the Third Class, harbored a personal interest in these new writing systems.[80] But inventors also took it upon themselves to send their proposals directly to one or another Class, relying on the Institut's concern with the development of the technical arts and practical "inventions," on the one hand, and the advancement of signs, on the other, to generate enthusiasm for their projects.[81] Auguste-Savinien Leblond, a professor of mathematics at the Lycée des Arts and the author of numerous plans for new systems of notation, even decided that the significant technical and semiotic issues at the heart of his decimal telegraphic language justified sending his proposal to all three Classes of the Institut simultaneously.[82]

It is difficult to know the real motives of the various men who asked the Institut to consider their semiotic experiments at the close of the eighteenth century. Their ranks included individuals as varied as Charles-Claude Montigny, a former *avocat au Parlement* in Rouen and collaborator on the supplement to the *Encyclopédie*, and Zalkind Hourwitz, a polylingual Polish-Jewish immigrant, journalist, and interpreter, and the author of numerous plans for public improvement through signs.[83] Not only did these inventors belong to diverse social classes. They had also exhibited very different degrees of engagement in revolutionary politics, seemingly choosing sides in certain cases more as a result of opportunism than ideology.

However, in the process of promoting their novel sign systems at the close of the eighteenth century, all of these theorists and inventors made use of a vocabulary and set of claims that clearly reflected the change in political and intellectual climate that took place after Thermidor. Following their Enlightenment predecessors, these thinkers still tended to emphasize the didactic function of well-made signs in vanquishing prejudice and in encouraging scientific progress. In the same vein, they also continued to stress the importance of new technologies for improving the speed, accuracy, and uniformity of communication and for breaking down barriers between peoples. But this group of late eighteenth-century inventors deliberately capitalized on the distinctive mood of linguistic caution and even fear that followed the end of the Terror. From La Harpe to Mme de Staël, most prominent intellectuals of the Directory despaired that ordinary French, whether written or spoken, would ever free itself from the distortions, exaggerations, and false sentiments of the Jacobin Revolution. In a wide variety of articles and books composed in the late 1790s, La Harpe, for example, repeatedly made the case for the lasting impact of revolutionary language in deforming reality.[84] Thus the need for verbal restraint and silence ("the reign of things" rather than the "reign of words," as La Harpe put it) constituted a constant theme in writing of this period, especially among linguistic and grammatical theorists such as Volney and François de Neufchâteau. As the latter insisted in an instruction manual for children published in the Year VI, "Man, in order to avoid discord and trouble, must listen a lot and speak very little."[85] And it is against this backdrop of linguistic anxiety and self-consciousness that the inventors of these new, nonverbal sign systems also developed a hyperbolic rhetoric for defending their own enterprise. They claimed to have discovered a concrete means of freeing the French nation from the thrall of a corrupt vernacular and of encouraging carefulness, stability, and (linguistic) peace instead.

The authors of the numerous stenographies and similarly named forms of rapid transcription developed during the late 1790s emphasized above all the way that their sign systems helped to hold vocal language (and its speakers) accountable. The major claim of these men was that they had isolated a form of writing which prevented any ambiguity or opacity from creeping into renderings of oral discourse, a "faithful mirror," in the words of an inventor named Honoré Blanc, to be applied to fugitive comments and expressions.[86] Indeed, their proponents insisted that these novel systems of notation could serve as an assurance to the reader that the truth behind verbal eloquence had been captured and fixed. The stenographers responsible for rendering numerous important judicial proceedings in the last years of the century explained this promise in the introduction to one of their reports as follows: "[O]ne will find in this work the faithful representation, the physiognomy, so to speak, of an interesting legal process. . . . Nothing has been added, nothing has been omitted. In reading it one can say with assurance: here is the truth. Stenography imparts to its productions a cachet that one cannot fake."[87] On what basis could they make this claim? Stenographers argued that the use of abbreviated characters made that much more immediate the connections among thoughts, sounds, and notation. As Montigny put it, "Speech is the audible sign of ideas; letters are the visible signs of speech, and the briefer the intermediary between thought and sounds, the quicker the imagination to explain them."[88] The stenographer, according to Clément, was essentially "penetrated" by truths rather than "weakly struck by fugitive sounds."[89] All of these inventors claimed, in keeping with the suggestions of both Volney and Sicard several years earlier at the Ecole Normale, that only the rationalization of the alphabet—its systematic expansion or contraction—could replace the chaos of subjective interpretation with orderly, precise, and accurate thought.

However, in the opinion of other inventors, these purely alphabetic reform projects did not go far enough. Why couldn't the relationship between thoughts and visual signs become truly immediate, they asked? Why did characters have to refer to sounds rather than to ideas themselves? After all, as Leblond explained, "[It] is only fictitiously that letters belong to the eye. . . . Nothing in writing is calculated on the analogy between thoughts and things; all is relative to sounds which themselves almost never have any real relationship with what they announce."[90] Thus, Leblond, like many of his contemporaries with an interest in problems of language and communication, attempted during the late 1790s to create an international sign system or form of notation in which characters might represent concepts directly.

It is, in fact, this widespread resurgence of interest in the invention of ideographic (though not generally iconographic) characters that constitutes the hallmark of French language politics in the wake of Thermidor. Some linguistic theorists of the late 1790s imagined new kinds of visual signs. Others recycled existing pasigraphies. But they all stressed the connection between their projects and various nonverbal and transnational sign systems devised in the past. Joseph De Maimieux compared the twelve oddly shaped, figurative characters of his pasigraphy to chemical signs and musical notes, both of which he believed to be universally intelligible, regardless of regional linguistic differences, "from Petersburg to Malta."[91] Likewise, certain inventors drew analogies between their new nonalphabetic signs and Egyptian hieroglyphics or Chinese characters.[92] For those eager to establish a French precedent for the use of ideographic characters or "steganography," the etymologist Charles Pougens offered examples in his study of the runes of the north.[93] Finally, Arabic numerals provided both inspiration and a model to several creators of universal written languages, including Zalkind Hourwitz, the Abbé Montmignon, and Leblond, who was so taken with the philosophical perfection of the "methodical" language of numbers that he argued for its application to many different realms of human life.[94] He placed his decimal telegraphic language at the point of culmination of a long history of visual sign systems, beginning with "the language of signs," which had brought people together in the state of nature, and continuing via the Oriental language of flowers, Masonic symbols, and ancient fire signals to what he saw as the most perfect ideographic language of all.[95]

Leblond was not alone in emphasizing the initial basis of his project in the original "language of signs." Following Condillac, who had insisted in both *La Logique* and *La Langue des calculs* that the logical, analytic structure of mathematics stemmed from its roots in the primordial language of finger calculations, the pasigraphic inventors of the next generation routinely pointed to various natural, bodily languages or pantomime as the basis for their own work.[96] In this way, they hoped to demonstrate their projects' continuing connection to the immediacy, energy, and "primitive vivacity" of the visual sign systems of the first, preliterate societies, as well as their ability to make signs and referents isomorphic once again.[97]

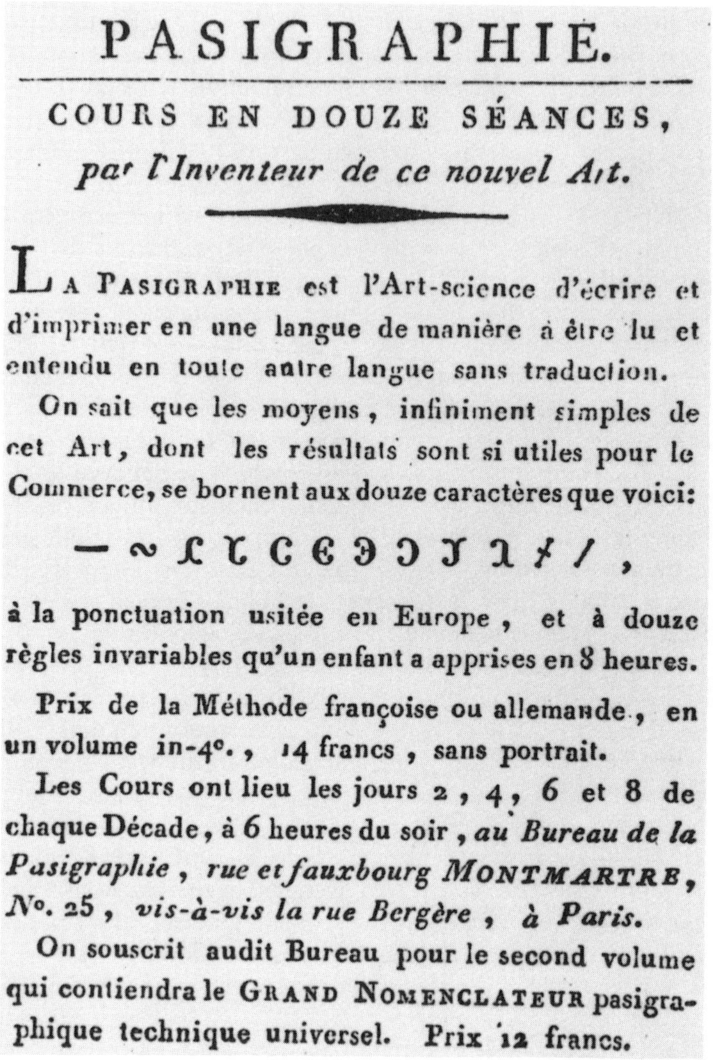

PASIGRAPHIE.

COURS EN DOUZE SÉANCES,

par l'Inventeur de ce nouvel Art.

LA PASIGRAPHIE est l'Art-science d'écrire et d'imprimer en une langue de manière à être lu et entendu en toute autre langue sans traduction.

On sait que les moyens, infiniment simples de cet Art, dont les résultats sont si utiles pour le Commerce, se bornent aux douze caractères que voici:

$$- \sim \int \mathcal{L} \, \mathcal{C} \, \mathcal{C} \, \mathcal{D} \, \mathcal{C} \, \mathcal{J} \, \mathcal{L} \, \not \! \! / \, / \, ,$$

à la ponctuation usitée en Europe, et à douze règles invariables qu'un enfant a apprises en 8 heures.

Prix de la Méthode françoise ou allemande, en un volume in-4°., 14 francs, sans portrait.

Les Cours ont lieu les jours 2, 4, 6 et 8 de chaque Décade, à 6 heures du soir, *au Bureau de la Pasigraphie, rue et fauxbourg MONTMARTRE, No. 25, vis-à-vis la rue Bergère, à Paris.*

On souscrit audit Bureau pour le second volume qui contiendra le GRAND NOMENCLATEUR pasigraphique technique universel. Prix 12 francs.

FIG. 9. Advertisement for a course in De Maimieux's *pasigraphie* held at the Bureau de la Pasigraphie in Paris (c. 1798). The advertisement shows the twelve ideographic characters that formed the basic components of this notational system. Archives de l'Institut de France.

But the authors of plans for ideographic sign systems were clearly not anxious to conjure up older, Rousseauist images of either a figurative language of the passions or a gestural sublime that transcended the intellect and spoke only to the heart. In keeping with the later work of Condillac, these same men also never failed to mention the advanced "methodical" or "analytic" structure of their new languages and the way that they made evident both the genealogy of ideas and the relations among them. Here the systematic sign language created by the Abbé de l'Epée and the Abbé Sicard served as a common reference point and model,[98] much as it did in the general grammar curriculums of many of the new *écoles centrales*.[99] Indeed, some of these inventors of new sign systems even tried to market their respective plans by pointing out their usefulness as conceptual aids in perfecting the language of the deaf.[100] Sicard reinforced this connection by arranging for his deaf pupils to give public demonstrations of the stenography of Bertin at the Société Philotechnique, the telegraphy of Leblond at both the Lycée Républicain and the Lycée des Arts, and the "lexicology" of Butet de la Sarthe at the Institution des Sourds-Muets.[101] Such displays were intended to illustrate that individuals with both a natural aptitude for using simple, visual signs to communicate their ideas and a special capacity for systematic, analytic thought found the workings of these recent semiotic inventions, including telegraphy and stenography, to be self-evident. The real appeal of these new, ideographic sign systems rested on the notion that with them not only could written signs once again become "the image of thought"; knowledge itself, including moral and metaphysical abstractions, could be redefined, reclassified, and permanently "fixed."[102]

How might this be possible? De Maimieux's pasigraphy, to take one example, depended upon only twelve characters [see Fig. 9].[103] A written word could be constructed of three to five characters, each of which would, in turn, refer to a particular notion in a series of classificatory tables in which ideas had been categorized according to both their generation and their analogies to each other. From this nomenclature— which Sicard described as "tending to form a clear, simple, and easy-to-remember system out of the universality of ideas"[104]—the precise and invariable meaning of that word, in any language, as well as the relation of that word to other, similar terms, would ostensibly become apparent. This point was often illustrated by the trope of a map of human intelligence, where each particular idea and its sign had been given a longitudinal and latitudinal position.[105] For instead of the prevailing "alphabetic chaos," De Maimieux promised to substitute "a natural order, where the place of a word fixes the signification of it and works towards determining that of neighboring words, where the order of characters leads one towards the idea, while the gradation of ideas draws one equally surely back to the characters."[106] The ultimate goal of all of his semiotic experimentation, De Maimieux explained in reference to an auxiliary project, was to make it possible "to apply our understanding to the universe and speech to our understanding with none of the equivocations [and] none of the prejudices that are born of the obscurity that one poorly understood word introduces into the meaning of many others."[107]

But what did such experiments have to do with the power struggle that continued after Thermidor both within government assemblies and in French culture at large? In theory, there was to be very little connection. What the creators of these new sign systems promised was, in fact, an antidote to the partisan bickering and strife characteristic of contemporary political debate. In the wake of the Terror, these inventors routinely hinted that their new sign systems, by separating *la langue* from *la parole*, could provide a needed corrective both to the fanciful, corrupt stylization associated with aristocratic political discourse and to the divisive, fiery rhetoric of Jacobin speech. Hourwitz called his written idiom or "polygraphie" a solution to all kinds of "verbiage," and De Maimieux boasted about his own pasigraphy: "Let it irritate those whose language, odious instrument of tricks and shame, robs and kills us while treating us as friends, those impudent and maliciously shallow rhetoricians, who, with stylets and daggers, sharpen their words."[108]

Instead, De Maimieux, like his competitors, made much use of the terms of science in describing his pasigraphic project. Universe, nature, classification, mapping, method, and truth are words that recur in the discourse of all of these inventors, and comparisons with other natural or quantitative branches of knowledge abound. Pierre-Roland-François Butet de la Sarthe, for example, called for the philosophy of signs, even for quotidian subjects, to be treated like a natural science, comparable to the "botanical philosophy" of Linnaeus or the "chemical philosophy" of Fourcroy.[109] Lancelin and Laromiguière similarly insisted that a new, universal language of ethics should be developed with the model of algebra as its basis.[110] Others sought ways to make grammar or even poetry "an art-science as certain in its principles and as rigorous in its demonstrations as the physical-mathematical arts-sciences."[111] In all of these cases, the advantage of such references stemmed from their association with science's much-vaunted objectivity and factual basis. The semiotic experiments of the era of the Directory were often presented as conscious efforts to remove communication from the passionate and variable realm of daily life, where choice always plays such a central role, and to make it a matter of incontestable reason.

It was, certainly, this idea of a creating a truly "fixed" language, a language impervious to the *abus des mots* and designed to convey

only "fixed" ideas, that made the projects of De Maimieux and his contemporaries so attractive to the many learned societies of the fin-de-
siècle that were self-consciously dedicated to the advancement of concrete, objective knowledge rather than partisan causes.[112] And it was
largely this pretense of scientism that made the inventors of these new
systems of communication so eager to associate themselves with the
flourishing postrevolutionary equivalents of the Old Regime's *lycées*
and *musées*. At the end of the century, members of the Société Philomathique, France's most important scientific association after the Institut's First Class, looked to telegraphy, lexicology, and even sign language for guidelines in the reform of the natural and physical sciences.[113] Like many of their contemporaries, these men thought scientific progress depended largely on the simplification of principles and
the gradual elimination of the obstacles dividing the world from its
representation—in other words, problems connected to language.[114]
Conversely, learned societies in the tradition of the *musées*, such as
the two Parisian Lycées and the Société Philotechnique, also believed
they had much to learn from these semiotic innovations. The members of these small *sociétés*, which took the study of the *sciences de
l'homme* and the arts to be among their purposes, hoped that these
new linguistic projects could help to bring a much-needed scientific
rigor, precision, and objectivity to underdeveloped realms of human
inquiry, from literature to legislation.[115]

The appeal of a "science" of signs at a moment of great unhappiness
about the public uses and misuses of ordinary language should not,
however, be taken to mean that either the creators of these new systems
of communication or the grammarians and engineers who endorsed
them actually sought to escape the realm of the political, in theory or in
practice. Nor is it plausible to conclude that ideological neutrality or de-
tachment was their primary motive. Indeed, the intellectual climate of
the late 1790s makes this claim highly unlikely, if not impossible. After
Thermidor, science itself had increasingly come to be looked upon as
the basis for a very particular kind of sociopolitical utopia, one distinct
from that envisioned by Jacobin leaders, popular insurgents, or royalist,
Catholic elites. Furthermore, at a moment when the question of
whether or not to penalize individuals for writing or uttering the word
monsieur (instead of the revolutionary *citoyen*) was still a live issue for
representative assemblies to debate, all language choices were necessarily politicized; signs of all kinds remained important tokens in an ongoing struggle over ideology and power.[116]

Rather, for the "enlightened" republican establishment, experiments with pasigraphy, telegraphy, vigigraphy, and the like actually
suggested a radical new way of using signs instrumentally. Certainly,

each inventor swore that his semiotic system was that much more accurate, simple, and sure, that much more likely to preclude faulty word
choices or obscure readings, and that much more resistant to transformation, variation, or degeneration than those of his predecessors. Yet
the real attraction of these plans was that they seemed to offer their
supporters the extraordinary power that came with the ability to determine and then to control the content of the ideas that their signs
would be used to transmit. As inheritors of the philosophy of 1789,
most of the advocates of these plans were reluctant to attack civil lib-
erties directly or to suggest the restoration of overt government censorship in an effort to prevent dissension.[117] But especially after the coup of
Fructidor in 1797, they also remained convinced of the importance of
preventing the return of either the dishonesties of the Old Regime or
the horrors of the Terror. And most of them continued to espouse a
kind of linguistic determinism—that a poorly made language could
"hinder the perfection of society" while a well-made one could help
"increase its pleasures and its daily happiness"[118]—since, as Cabanis
pointed out to the Council of Five-Hundred in 1799: "One no longer
sees in this admirable creation of our intelligence [language] only a
means of communication and a means of exchanging ideas; one sees in
it an instrument that serves to produce them [ideas]."[119] The nominalist
proponents of new ideographic sign systems thus concluded that they
were well on their way toward finding a nonpunitive and rational
manner in which to delimit how ideas and concepts could be understood and expressed.[120] In these "scientific" plans for reordering knowledge and reattaching signs and ideas, some members of the new intellectual establishment saw the possibility of shaping thought according
to their own, partisan belief systems and creating that much-desired
consensus and social "happiness" on their own terms. As such, the
language reform efforts of the Directory and early Consulate promised
to function not only as antidotes to past abuses or as means of staving
off the threat of contestatory democracy but also as the basis of a new
form of power. In the claims of some of their major supporters—and,
eventually, detractors—in both the government and the public sphere,
the explicit political stakes of these extreme experiments in linguistic
dirigisme were ultimately made abundantly clear.

LANGUAGE POLITICS

In the late 1790s, two prominent members of the Institut's Second Class,
Garat and Roederer, emerged as the most vocal champions of the pasi-
graphies, polygraphies, and other linguistic experiments of the moment.
Professionally and intellectually, the paths of these men had diverged in

important ways since the Terror. Roederer, disillusioned with revolutionary politics, had retreated from government service into journalism, interesting himself in a variety of indirect economic and social mechanisms—including language—for restoring order and stability to the nation. Garat, in contrast, had never lost his taste for active participation in the world of elections and legislation, and during the last years of the century, he sought to combine a series of different official posts with the position of intellectual leadership that he had established at the Ecole Normale. In fact, his continuing desire to regulate the meanings of political and ethical terms through a new, rationally determined and universal system of signs grew directly out of his conception of the appropriate role for the *philosophe*-legislator like himself. But taken together, the positions of these two men amounted to a last-ditch argument for actualizing the utopian semiotic vision associated with mid-century French sensationalism. At the century's close, both Garat and Roederer maintained their faith in enlightened language planning as a key to intellectual, moral, and political improvement. Only now, they directed their ambitions toward increasingly conservative ends.

In the aftermath of the Revolution, both Garat and Roederer continued to see language in fundamentally political terms and politics in fundamentally linguistic terms. Indeed, in the middle and late 1790s, both men worried publicly that miscommunication, or the *abus des mots*, still pervaded French public life, producing disastrous results. In April 1797, for example, Roederer wrote angrily in the *Journal de Paris* about a controversy over the term *embauchage*: "Condillac was right to say that the art of reasoning comes down to knowing how to speak a well-made language well! Do you know that this great affair which is so essential to the Constitution, this conflict among the Supreme Court of Appeals and the Executive Directory and the Legislature that no one is supposed to notice, has arisen and sustains itself uniquely on the false interpretation of a single word?"[121] Roederer fretted too that with the disappearance of older social ties and the removal of women from the new public sphere, France had witnessed the death of many important social practices built around linguistic interaction. Conversation had been replaced by "confabulation," or the use of words without consequence, and the established, if unspoken, rules of communication had broken down.[122]

In response, both men also continued to insist on the importance of "fixing" the norms of speech and writing, especially in the realm of politics. Garat conceded in the preliminary discourse for the fifth edition of the *Dictionnaire de l'Académie française* that language, like the "spirit of the People," was always, necessarily, in flux. For this reason, he explained, it was essential to include a controversial list of neologisms, a

"Supplément contenant les mots en usage depuis la Révolution," in the 1798 edition of the *Dictionnaire* of the now-defunct national academy.[123] However, the smooth and orderly functioning of society required that strict guidelines be established for controlling the process of linguistic evolution and that each word of the national language be given "a particular stamp that marks its title and its value just like each piece of currency." For in a republic, Garat insisted, "laws of speech" were so essential that they became "more important, perhaps, than even laws of social organization."[124] In numerous articles, Roederer agreed, calling for laws of deliberation as well.[125] And both Roederer and Garat stressed the considerable potential of ideographic characters in this regard.

But what was the connection between their semiotic visions and their political ambitions at the century's close? The answer stemmed from the two Ideologues' responses to the question of who was to set the laws of language in a republic based on the sovereignty of the people—and according to what standards. In the preface to the new *Dictionnaire de l'Académie française,* Garat called upon a segment of the nation's intellectual elite—writers, thinkers, scientists, and all those who "constantly attach the same ideas to the same words"—to assume a new public function. Rather than leave the authority to control the evolution of language in the hands of a small literary caste and a group of aristocrats concerned exclusively with "le beau langage du beau monde" (as had been the case in the Old Regime) or, alternately, turn to an unenlightened public (as the populist strain of revolutionary ideology might suggest), Garat argued that enlightened representatives of the people, linguistic lawmakers with "a clear, methodical mind, exempt from prejudices and passions," were needed to make the standards of *bon usage* and the standards of reason finally coincide.[126] If men such as himself were eventually to be put in charge of a sign system that was protected in its very form from the corruption, fragmentation, or even variation associated with common usage, Garat reasoned before the Council of Ancients, society could expect no more arguments about "the language of morality and law" than about the classification of numbers or chemical elements.[127] To the Institut's earlier question about whether the proper reform of linguistic signs could, by itself, make all sciences equally susceptible to demonstration and proof, Garat provided, in effect, an unqualified affirmative response.

But a perfect, universal language functioned in Garat's thought not only as a metaphor for this legislator's hope that politics could become a science, impervious to either aristocratic whims or true democracy. Clearly, it was also a means for imagining a politics that would consistently support the interests of his own intellectual and social class and keep the interests of other sectors of the population—such as those interested in challenging the new status quo—outside of public discourse. With Roederer, this intention became explicit. For where Garat continued to stress the function of the intellectual as public servant in the realm of language, fighting against error and discord in support of what he called reason, Roederer directly emphasized the consequences of better chosen signs as a means of top-down social control. In the wake of the Revolution, Roederer imagined a truly analytic and ideographic sign system working to restrict choice of expression so that ordinary writers and speakers would have no chance either to offer opinions or to interpret the words of others except in terms that Roederer's close associates—now in the position of authorities rather than outside agitators—had already established.

Roederer himself devoted considerable time to the search for the ideal language that would fulfill this desire. Privately, he took extensive notes on types and forms of writing; he catalogued existing pasigraphies, including algebra, chemistry, music, numbers, sign language, and telegraphy; he studied novel methods for the dissemination of ideas, from sign boards to marionettes and magic lanterns; and he jotted down solutions derived from Leibniz.[128] Finally, Roederer found a prime example upon which to build a public presentation of his argument. In 1798, in a series of talks at the Institut on the foundations of stability in China, he asked why his contemporaries were always talking about the short-lived Roman or Athenian republics when it was China that had existed "powerful, peaceful, happy and always the same for 4,000 years."[129] His third and final report on the subject detailed what he took to be one of the principal reasons for that nation's conservatism: the nature of Chinese writing.[130]

The impetus and source for Roederer's claims regarding Chinese characters came largely from the 1797 French edition of Sir George Leonard Staunton's account of Lord Macartney's recent diplomatic mission to China.[131] Staunton, a doctor of both law and medicine trained in Montpellier and Oxford, challenged conventional European thinking about the difficulty and irrationality of Chinese writing. More significantly, he offered a glowing report on its efficacy and superiority to the Western alphabet. Following William Warburton and various contemporary Jesuit scholars, Staunton claimed that Chinese was a "hieroglyphic" language because the basic characters for simple ideas had been constructed according to the principle of imitation.[132] Moreover, he maintained that Chinese writing constituted a perfect system of analysis, since imitative characters standing for basic ideas formed the building blocks out of which complex characters were constructed, much like the languages of math or music or the sign system imagined by Bishop Wilkins. The result, Staunton asserted, was that none of the pitfalls endemic to Western communication figured in China at all. Problems of word order or syntax were unknown in this distant land, as groups of ideas were tied together and made simultaneous by a single character, much as they had been in the state of nature. Misconstruction of the particular sense in which a word was being used was equally impossible, since every nuance in meaning could be distinguished visually. Finally, while a Westerner could read a series of letters formed into words without having the least knowledge of their significance, such a situation would be inconceivable in the East. In China, one acquired knowledge of an idea by learning the character attached to it. As Staunton explained, "[A] dictionary of hieroglyphics is less the vocabulary of the terms of a language together with the corresponding terms of another than it is an Encyclopedia [of ideas]."[133]

Roederer repeated these claims in his talk before the Institut, complaining about a negative review of Staunton's book in the *Gazette nationale* and supporting the latter's assertion that Chinese writing had "the double advantage of being analytic like our conventional language and expeditious and simultaneous like the *langage d'action*, the most perfect means of expressing the simplest idea."[134] But Roederer's real purpose was not to argue for one or another interpretation of Chinese characters. Instead, it was to make a case for the benefits that would accrue from the institution of a similarly symbolic form of notation in postrevolutionary France. In addition to serving as a lingua franca and aiding in the study of natural phenomena, the introduction of a hieroglyphic and philosophical written language in a Western context would, Roederer believed, "preclude reasoning about subjects with which one was not sufficiently acquainted" and "prevent the many false arguments that stem from the vagueness of words."[135] Indeed, it would make imprecise metaphysical concepts—ideas that could not easily be pictured—disappear entirely. As such, Roederer concluded, it might be the very thing needed to bring about the end of revolutionary polyphony rooted in popular speech.

But was there an equivalent to Chinese characters that could effectively be applied in the French context? In the course of his exposition, Roederer mentioned stenography, pasigraphy, and telegraphy as possibilities. It was, however, the analytical sign language of Sicard, Roederer's colleague from the Institut, that particularly attracted the journalist's attention and support at the end of the 1790s. If a similar visual sign system were to become as widely used in France as it had been in China, where potential miscommunication could be avoided by tracing characters manually in the air, "it seems evident to me," Roederer commented, "that thoughts will only be better fixed and better distinguished in the mind, that it will only become easier to compare them, and finally, that one will be that much more assured in the judgments that he or she makes about their relationships to one another."[136] But what especially interested Roederer (as it had Talleyrand earlier in the decade) was the possibility of transcribing Sicard's fleeting gestural sign language into a written form, an idea that Roederer put forth not only in his essay on Chinese characters but also in a report that he read to the Institut in June 1799 entitled "Premières idées de la Pasigraphie."[137] That the project of composing a grammar and dictionary of gestural signs was indeed feasible had already been demonstrated long before by Court de Gébelin, Roederer noted. And in keeping with the antirhetorical climate of the late 1790s, he concluded: "This would be the universal writing for which people have been searching with so much care."[138]

Sicard was not unaware of the connection between his own work and a burgeoning public interest in the invention of a universal, philosophical written language at the close of the century. Between 1795 and 1797, Sicard too had attempted to reframe his project in relation to recent experiments in pasigraphy, highlighting the importance of figurative writing as a way to prevent the introduction of vague and confusing terminology in the education of small children and calling his work developing "pantomime, or the art of signs" a novel solution to the problem of "Leibnits" [sic].[139] Sicard developed these arguments in articles in the *Magasin encyclopédique* and the *Annales religieuses, politiques et littéraires*, in reports read before the Institut, and in his book-length *Manuel de l'enfance* of 1797.[140] However, after the coup of Fructidor Year V, Sicard was forced into hiding to avoid deportation to Guyana for his role as coeditor of the reactionary Catholic *Annales religieuses*, and during the next two years, the job of advancing his ideas was taken over by his many associates and friends in the Parisian intellectual establishment, including Roederer.[141] From Roederer's perspective, Sicard's political "mistakes" paled in comparison to the social and humanitarian benefits to be derived from his linguistic efforts. Roederer, an increasingly conservative republican, saw in his colleague's analytic version of the *langage d'action* not only a system for educating the deaf but also a "perfect pasigraphy" and a "philosophical and universal language" that could serve as a control mechanism in relation to society's other forms of communication and, consequently, a means to limit opportunities for dissent.[142] Fearful of rhetorical excess and distrustful of the spoken idiom in general, Roederer sought to do nothing less than encourage the development of an activist, instrumental (though self-effacing) written sign system that would help to make the political and moral ideas of an established elite appear scientific and, hence, universally valid and incontestable. In this manner, he hoped to bring the revolutionary logomachy to a permanent close.

Of course, both Roederer and Garat, along with others colleagues in the Institut, lodged numerous complaints about the limitations of particular projects that they encountered. Roederer and, privately, even Sicard, who had collaborated in the publication of *Pasigraphie*, attacked De Maimieux's nomenclature as arbitrary and contrary to the natural, universal order of the generation of ideas. Even the forms of De Maimieux's characters were deemed overly complex and illogical.[143] Moreover, members of the Institut were often pessimistic about their ability to persuade the public that the adoption and use of these new sign systems was in its best interest. Yet, contrary to many historians' findings, it is also clear that efforts to develop telegraphs, stenographies, and the like briefly garnered much support in high places during the Directory. This was precisely because they promised a small group of educated republicans both the chance to make signs and ideas more thoroughly isomorphic and the possibility of harnessing the power of signs to a decidedly postrevolutionary cause.[144]

However, with the conclusion of the Institut's contest on signs in early 1799, it soon became evident that outside of this small circle of Parisian intellectuals and its satellites, these projects—and the semiotic approach to the nation's political problems more generally—were being greeted with considerable skepticism. Of the ten respondents to the second phase of the competition (some of whom may have also participated in the first round), only two continued strongly to advance the idea that "fixing" the signs of the French language would indeed result in the perfection of all sciences, social as well as natural and physical.[145] One respondent, Butet de la Sarthe, who was concurrently developing his own theory of signs or *lexicologie* at the Ecole Polymathique, advanced the idea that society was approaching the point where "the truth will be received without contest because the perfection of signs will enable it to circulate without obstacle between discerning forces."[146] Another writer agreed that a "scientific" language, stripped of all literary qualities, would certainly introduce "the truth, totally naked and without ornament" into political life.[147] But the remaining second-round respondents, whose essays were written between January 1798 and January 1799, rejected such reasoning. Instead, they eagerly attempted to mitigate the importance of signs in determining thought and issued numerous criticisms of the notion that pasigraphies and other such experiments could serve as panaceas for social or political discord. One writer suggested that the general public would be unwilling to adopt any new sign system and that, as a result, the introduction of pasigraphies would only create new scientific elites. On more philosophical grounds, several others reasoned that the nature of certain types of ideas—such as the abstract principles debated in legislative assemblies—precluded the possibility of establishing an unequivocal language for them similar to that of mathematics. And many of the respondents proposed that imperfect thinking was not only a problem of language; political and moral uncertainties stemmed equally, if not more so, from ignorance, blind passion, excessive imagination, and fear, all of which provoked illusions and faulty associations of ideas, regardless of the type of signs in question.

The essay which finally took the first prize, that of a then-unknown young soldier and opponent of the Revolution named Joseph-Marie Degérando, elaborated and expanded upon many of these same points. In most regards, Degérando situated his essay firmly within the Ideologue tradition, from his insistence on the sensual basis of ideas to his attentions to ways of correcting the abuse of words. Even his unadorned prose style and the rigorous organization of his essay signaled the connection between his thought and the nascent field of the *science de l'homme*, with its roots in the analysis of sensations and ideas. But at another level, Degérando's claims represented the beginning of an attack on the conception of language politics that had been at the heart of the Institut's program. For Degérando not only rejected the notion that the perfection of signs could have an equal influence on all areas of knowledge; he argued as well that the Ideologues were repeatedly looking in the wrong place for a solution to contemporary ethical and political problems:

> Here is what is not widely enough understood today. Regarding knowledge of moral man, we notice that, in relation to the study of physical man, we have often fallen into a particular error. When we perceived that a remedy was very effective, we were persuaded right away that it was universal. When we saw that it would be very useful to remake our languages, we did not hesitate to conclude that that would suffice, and we repeated after Condillac: that the art of reasoning can be reduced to a well-made language. . . . [However] the absolute perfection of the art of signs is a chimera.[148]

It was Roederer who, on behalf of a new committee composed of himself, Ginguené, Volney, Jacques-André Naigeon, and Jean Philippe Garran de Coulon, was given the task of presenting the Second Class's reasons for its awards. The committee's choices—first prize to Degérando, second prize to Pierre Prévost (a former student at the Ecole Normale and translator of the work of Adam Smith), and an honorable mention to Butet de la Sarthe—indicate that it was hostile to answers that were not rooted in the sensationalist tradition or that denied any major significance to signs in the shaping of thought. Indeed, a single essay from an opposing philosophical perspective was marked "an extremely weak and superficial essay that leads to proof that signs have no influence on ideas because, he claims, they [ideas] preceded signs."[149] But the honors awarded to Degérando, Prévost, and Butet, along with the earlier recognition of Lancelin, demonstrate that the Ideologues, in the last year of the eighteenth century, were also open to a range of different responses to questions about the precise nature and impact of signs. As Roederer's public report of April 1799 made clear, the committee was eager to encourage Butet's practical efforts to diminish "equivocations" in the French language at the same time as it accepted Degérando's and Prévost's reasoning in denying the efficacy of exactly such projects.[150] While the public had been asked to develop a sign system that would ensure consensus on matters of public concern, no consensus existed in 1799, either within or outside the Institut, as to whether such a project would, in fact, ever be workable.

In his report, Roederer indicated that Degérando had dashed some of the Second Class's collective dreams, that his essay "had stricken many of the hopes that the art of signs seemed to have offered." But in the spring of 1799, Roederer could not have known how true his comment would prove to be. The prize awarded to Degérando encouraged him both to make his way into Parisian social and intellectual circles connected to the Second Class and to revise and expand his memoir for publication.[151] *Des Signes et de l'art de penser considérés dans leurs rapports mutuels*, a work in four volumes, appeared in 1800; the first two detailed "the influence of signs on the formation of ideas," and the second two explained "what precise influence perfecting the art of signs could have on the art of thinking" by applying the principles established in earlier chapters to a range of theoretical problems.[152] As a result of its prestigious origins as a prize-winning essay, as well as its perceived practical importance, this enormous book quickly garnered substantial attention.[153]

In *Des Signes*, Degérando's account of the origin of signs and the development of language did not stray far from the hypothetical tale established by Condillac half a century earlier. The problems in the story that had been pointed out by Rousseau, for example, were simply brushed aside. But Degérando seriously challenged the status of the *langage d'action* as an ideal mode of communication, arguing that Condillac had overlooked many of the weaknesses inherent in the original language in an effort to depict it as a perfect, analytic method in its own right. Natural gestures, Degérando agreed, were unrivaled in the effects that they had on the imagination; but it was this very quality that made them unsuitable for abstract reasoning, as well as a dangerous source of confused and muddle-headed thinking. In the modern world, science had to be separated from poetry. The greatest threat to sound and logical thought processes, Degérando proposed, was that one might be led to take the iconic sign, in all its visual specificity, for the thing itself.

Following these principles, Degérando then developed an extensive argument against the possible success of any philosophical or universal language that was based on ideographs, rejecting, in turn, the potential effectiveness of a range of utopian experiments, past and present, from Bishop Wilkins's and De Maimieux's real characters to Sicard's methodical signs. The great variety of our ideas, Degérando proposed, made it impossible for any sign system to satisfy both the demands of commodious usage and the desire for exactitude or fidelity of expression. For all the same reasons that the original *langage d'action* had proved insufficient—its complexity, difficulty, lack of subtlety, metaphoric tendency, and excessive effects on the imagination—any visual, ideographic sign system, whether written or communicated physically, was destined to fail.

Like his contemporaries, Degérando accepted that the limitations of the language of politics and ethics posed a problem for modern society. He agreed that in every society "a better language will make for better institutions" and "corrupt institutions protect, in turn, a language's imperfections."[154] The dynamic of revolutions, he insisted, stemmed from the tendency of those in power to take advantage of the indefinite nature of language: "We have seen, in the name of liberty, the establishment of the most absolute despotism; we have seen, in the name of equality, orders for the most iniquitous proscriptions."[155] But Degérando warned against overvaluing signs, and he rejected all grandiose linguistic solutions to political and ethical problems. Contrary to Condillac, he denied that the construction of a "well-made" language could always be counted on to produce a "well-made" science. In the case of politics, in particular, he argued, the ideas in question were so uncertain, so complex, and so far from having a sensible base that they resisted all attempts to mold them into an exact language of calculation.

Above all, Degérando claimed that the democratization of the language of politics during the Revolution represented an insurmountable obstacle to the establishment of any true "social" science in the future. In the natural and physical sciences, he noted, the right to speak in the idiom of the particular discipline belonged to experts alone. But in a nation where the laws were made for all and addressed to all alike, the language of those laws had to remain "popular," as Degérando put it. As a result, philosophers were necessarily impotent when it came to controlling the language of politics: "The Language of Politics is the only one whose definitions almost never belong to philosophers; [definitions] are, in some sense, an attribute of power or, rather, a privilege that belongs to the strongest."[156] Not only were disputes in ethics an inevitable result of the various meanings given to ideas according to one's habits, passions, and position within society, he noted, but the prerogative of determining meaning always belonged, ultimately, to the most powerful. Therefore, Degérando argued, philosophers should try to live exemplary lives rather than waste their time attempting to invent a perfect language. In fact, as Degérando made clear in a concurrent report on pasigraphies that he was invited to deliver at the Institut in April 1800, projects such as that of De Maimieux could only augment ordinary abuses of the national language by producing false associations of ideas in the minds of ordinary citizens.[157] Of this logic, Degérando became more and more convinced in subsequent years. Gradually, Degérando moved ever further from a Condillacian account of ideas and language. And as he developed into an increasingly important political appointee of the Consulate and then the Empire, Degérando only solidified his arguments against a linguistic solution to questions of ethics or politics.[158]

Degérando's dismissal of the regenerative power of ideographs in his writings of 1800 marks the beginning of a larger trend in French intellectual circles: a shift away from the particular conception of language and power that had marked the earlier work of the Ideologues. Certainly, during the Consulate, pasigraphies and other such inventions continued to find their way into print and to spark interest within various learned societies. And not all the Ideologues immediately revised their opinions on these matters.[159] But the tide was turning with the arrival of the new century. Ginguené, in a review of *Des Signes*, lauded Degérando for realizing that, after centuries of underestimating the importance of signs, the pendulum had now swung too far in the other direction; the impact of signs on the mind had, in recent years, become exaggerated.[160] And in this climate of retreat, one area of linguistic inquiry that the *philosophes* had largely ignored—the traditional Latin alphabet—began to generate new enthusiasm and interest among intellectuals, largely in contradistinction to the ideographic notation that had attracted attention in the several years preceding.

Volney, it is true, had already extolled the virtues of the phonetic Latin alphabet—its orderliness, its uniformity, its concision—in his teaching at the Ecole Normale of the Year III. But now his ideas were taken up in various other quarters. In his lectures on the natural history of man given at the Louvre between 1800 and 1802, Sicard's close associate Louis-François Jauffret finished a chronicle of the various primitive sign systems humans had used around the would with an account of the limitations of hieroglyphics, which, Jauffret claimed, always naturally degenerated into arbitrary forms and made possible the rise of multiple dialects. In contrast, he touted the efficacy of the Western alphabet.[161] Likewise, Pierre Prévost published his prize-winning essay in 1800 as *Des Signes envisagés relativement à leur influence sur la formation des idées* and included one section denouncing the dangerous potential of iconic signs to arouse the imagination by evoking only specific images and another praising the abstraction of letters for the way they facilitated the construction of the generalizations necessary for reasoning.[162] The Abbé Moussaud, the author of *L'Alphabet raisonné, ou Explication de la figure des lettres*, even went so far in celebrating the Latin alphabet as to suggest that its letters were themselves symbolic, rational, and philosophical because each had initially been the copy and image of its sound; the modern alphabet was not derived from an original pictographic one but was, instead, "a sketch of the organs of speech and even the sounds of the voice, whose appearance recalls the idea."[163] Finally, Destutt de Tracy took up the topic of the relative merits of phonetic and ideographic signs in his multivolume *Elémens d'Idéologie*. Destutt intended this work to constitute a thorough summation of the movement in which he had played a vital role, a textbook and educational plan that would lay bare the principles on which the postrevolutionary human sciences could be rebuilt. But the first two volumes of the *Elémens d'Idéologie*—tomes that contained extended discussions of both the advantages of the Latin alphabet and the impossibility of building a new political order on the reform of signs—also marked the death of the radical linguistic and pedagogical ambitions of the whole revolutionary era.

Destutt de Tracy had, from his very first public talk in his capacity as a correspondent of the Second Class, warned against the dangers of overestimating the power of signs. As a member of the Société de 1789 and an active presence in the circle around Mme Helvétius in Auteuil, Destutt de Tracy had certainly, on prior occasions, been privy to many discussions concerning the creation of a social science based on the analysis of sensations and the exact definition of terms. Yet in his "Mémoire sur la faculté de penser" of 1796–98, he had shown himself to be skeptical of many of the more extreme claims about the impact of signs that had been put forth by his close colleagues, including Garat in his course at the Ecole Normale and the framers of the Institut's program for its contest on signs and thought. In particular, Destutt de Tracy had indicated that he doubted whether what he called "that beautiful dream," a perfect philosophical language that would use signs to perfect ideas, could ever be fulfilled. Insurmountable obstacles stemming from flaws inherent in both the nature of signs and, more seriously, human nature presented themselves. Furthermore, Destutt de Tracy had rejected the idea that the creation of new signs could ever precede the formation of ideas. To create a universal philosophical language, a single man, endowed with complete scientific knowledge and no passions other than a love for the truth, would have to compose the totality of the idiom alone

and in one sitting. Otherwise, he announced in response to this deliberately preposterous notion, "a perfect language is without doubt a chimera like perfection in all other genres."[164]

Nevertheless, despite this early verdict in his first memoir, Destutt de
Tracy had gone on to become an active participant in the Second Class's
efforts to examine the numerous experiments in language construction
that it received during the Directory and early Consulate.[165] In May 1800,
he followed the example of Roederer and Degérando in presenting a public talk on pasigraphies at the Institut.[166] On that occasion, Destutt de
Tracy claimed simply to be expanding on Degérando's ideas, establishing a long list of reasons why a pasigraphic language could never work.
However, Destutt de Tracy also used this opportunity to assert the su-
premacy of the phonetic alphabet over pictographic or ideographic signs,
turning the logic of Garat and Roederer on its head by claiming that the
advantage of alphabetic writing was that it alone constituted a true form
of notation rather than an entirely separate sign system. Then, in the
first two volumes of his *Elémens d'Idéologie* (1801–3), Destutt de Tracy
developed a sociopolitical as well as philosophical rationale for his bias
in favor of the maintenance of the standard Latin alphabet.

All signs, Destutt de Tracy proposed—from paintings, telegraphic
signals, and Masonic symbols to the gestures of deaf people, mimes, or
orators—were susceptible to a certain degree of perfection. Verbal language had, however, a potential for stimulating and maintaining an enlightened culture that greatly surpassed that of other forms of communication, and, as Destutt de Tracy argued in a chapter of the second volume devoted exclusively to forms of writing, the societal benefits that
resulted from writing based on the tonal qualities of words far exceeded
those stemming from ideographic or hieroglyphic forms of notation.
These latter types of notation required what he called "a double transformation in signs" for one to move between the spoken language and
the written one. Not only did this mean that people were obliged to learn
two complete languages if they were to be fully literate (a pursuit that
required a lifetime of devotion), but it also left more room for errors, uncertainties, and "interpretation" as one switched between these two
forms of communication. To make matters worse, the metaphoric quality of hieroglyphic writing necessarily introduced the same sorts of
prejudices into writing as metaphors had always introduced into speech.
And since such ideographic languages, like all other sign systems, naturally evolved steadily away from their figurative basis, the tendency of
ideographic characters to reinforce confusions and superstitions would
only be exacerbated as the years went by.

Destutt de Tracy also turned to the example of China to illustrate the
larger consequences of a cultural dependence on a pictographic lan-

guage. But unlike Roederer, Destutt de Tracy maintained that the prevalence of ideographic signs had condemned Chinese society to intellectual parochialism, limited scientific progress, rigid social castes, and the endurance of mysteries, dangerous prejudices, and hermeticism rooted in obscure metaphors. In other words, the archaic political form of China and its hieroglyphic notation had served only to reinforce one another.

In contrast, Destutt de Tracy painted the Western alphabet as the ultimate tool of democracy: direct, economical, and easily learned by many people. The author of the *Elémens d'Idéologie* refuted the classic Enlightenment argument that the modern phonetic alphabet had evolved naturally out of the hieroglyphic writing of primitive cultures. Instead, he saw the cultural and political successes of the West as related to the early invention of a true form of notation based on sounds rather than images. For Destutt de Tracy believed that the permanent fate of each state in the world depended on whether its method of writing was initially derived from the visual or vocal dimension of the original *langage d'action*; this distinction had produced "such prodigious consequences that they alone sufficed to determine the destiny of nations and to explain social and political phenomena whose reason has never before been successfully expressed."[167]

Once again, Destutt de Tracy deemed a "perfect language" an impossible goal. That humans are simply unable to create linguistic signs with utterly determined and fixed significations marked the "root defect of men's minds" and the "sad truth" that needed to be acknowledged.[168] The complexity of our ideas, habit, faulty memory, diversity of personality, and a host of other reasons would continually force humans to fail in the pursuit of a linguistic solution to the quest for absolute, demonstrable certainties in the social and human sciences.[169] Destutt de Tracy thus argued that, given these limitations, it was a clear verbal language, unadorned with figuration and notated by regular alphabetic characters, that could do the most to destroy prejudices and to spread knowledge in the modern world.

In effect, Destutt de Tracy's conclusions signal the Ideologues' reduced expectations after the turn of the nineteenth century for the success of any radical linguistic reforms. Disappointment with the weaknesses and failures of the Directory increasingly generated disillusionment with the very idea of rational language planning. From the vantage point of many of the Ideologues, the principles of Condillac, as applied to public life, seemed to have done little to help secure the current crumbling republican regime. Moreover, the growing power of Napoleon Bonaparte, especially after the coup of 18 Brumaire in 1799, had a dramatic effect on intellectual as well as political life in France, forcing many republicans to reconsider their "enlightened" liberal values as a matter of necessity.

Initially, most of the Ideologues—including Volney, Roederer, Talleyrand, Sieyès, Daunou, Garat, Cabanis, Ginguené, and Laromiguière, as well as Degérando and Destutt de Tracy—supported the coup d'état that produced the First Consul. In the summer and fall of 1799, as the Directory foundered, Napoleon Bonaparte represented to many of the Institut's members the promise of social and political stability coupled with state support for science and advanced learning, including the "science of signs."[170] But disillusionment with Napoleon was quick in coming for most of these men (with the notable exception of Roederer), especially once the First Consul's real attitude toward the political philosophy of the Ideologues became evident. And following his deliberate efforts to thwart the Directory's educational plans, including the removal of ideology from the curriculums of the *écoles centrales* in early 1802, and then the dismantling of the Institut's Second Class in January 1803, these same individuals began to believe that even their most modest hopes for the application of "ideology" to problems of governing were liable to remain indefinitely unfulfilled.[171] Indeed, in the early years of the nineteenth century, many of the Ideologues not only felt compelled to abandon their faith in linguistic *dirigisme* as a path to political change or stability; they also increasingly decided that the introduction of alternative means of notation and communication would only bring about new political woes. In effect, writers from a wide range of viewpoints found themselves agreeing (for better or for worse) that the First Consul—through a combination of coercive public policies and force of personality—had contributed to the establishment of liberal individualism, on the one hand, and social order, on the other, in a way that a social scientific language never could. As a consequence, the earlier politico-linguistic aspirations of theorists like De Maimieux soon became an easy topic of ridicule both within Ideologue circles and without.

On the right, Catholic and counterrevolutionary, legitimist thinkers increasingly attacked not only sensationalist or Lockean principles but also the anthropological "founding myth" of the Condillacian language theory upon which Garat and Roederer, among others, had built their advocacy of the language experiments of the last years of the century. Louis de Bonald, for example, directly took on "modern *ideology*, occupied for a long time with *signs and their influence on thought*" in his *Législation primitive* of 1802, ridiculing the idea that moral truths were always dependent upon the language in which they were articulated and insisting instead on an immutable social order revealed by God through words.[172] Such claims eventually became central to early nineteenth-century anticontractual, conservative thought.[173]

Those royalist intellectuals who continued after Thermidor to view the Revolution as a war against Enlightenment ideals rather than their natural outgrowth also publicly challenged the linguistic philosophy of the Ideologues. Like certain other disillusioned *philosophes*, the Abbé Morellet now attacked the advocates of "lexicographies, lexicologies, and even ideologies" for creating a new form of scholasticism by using language instrumentally toward political ends.[174] By the early nineteenth century, Morellet and his old friend Jean-Baptiste-Antoine Suard, with the backing of the conservative press, started to call for the restoration of the Académie Française to protect the French language, and consequently French culture, against further barbarization.[175]

And in the years right around the turn of the new century, criticism of post-Thermidorean linguistic *dirigisme* began to stem from within the Institut as well. The same Louis-Sébastien Mercier who had once been a vocal supporter of the development of theatrical pantomime as a vehicle for the communication of moral sentiments and an active member of the Cercle Social and the Société des Amateurs de la Langue Française now denounced all official, centralized efforts to tinker with national or regional idioms. Mercier agreed with his colleagues in the Institut that the Revolution had ultimately become a "logomachy" or a new "tower of Babel" in which the *abus des mots* had played a terrible role.[176] But in a long list of publications and lectures after 1795, this self-declared disciple of Rousseau argued for the teaching of modern, living, mutable languages rather than a static Latin; ridiculed all efforts to depict the moral world in visual forms; and steadfastly opposed what he saw as government interference with the natural process of linguistic evolution.[177] Grammarians and "idiologues," as Mercier sometimes branded them, had solved nothing. They had, he maintained, simply replaced theologians as society's pedants, eager to direct and organize everything, even that which was better off legislating itself. Thus Mercier warned in 1802, in reference to the spate of recent linguistic experiments: "The perfection of languages is only an odd and almost chimerical hypothesis for most men. . . . If laws [of speech] are subject to the vicissitudes of politics, words will be retained by the mind no better than clothes on the body."[178] And in his contemporaneous dictionary of creative, rule-free neologisms he added, "The more ridiculous a despotic government is, the more it tries to become serious and wise. And who would not laugh at a tribunal that said to you: I am going to fix the language. Stop, imprudent one! You are going to nail it down [and] crucify it!"[179] All citizens, he declared democratically, must have the freedom to use the national language as they see fit.

Of course, a few isolated voices continued into the early Empire to insist that the development of a thoroughly analytical and fixed sign system was critical to the construction of a society rooted in scientifically determined ethical principles. Laromiguière, for example, reiterated as late as 1805 in his *Paradoxes de Condillac* that "it is not the nature of ideas which determines that, generally speaking, one reasons less well in the moral sciences than in the mathematical ones; it is the imperfections of the languages that they speak."[180] That same year, at the Académie Celtique in Britanny, the former Girondin deputy Jacques Cambry developed with the support of his colleagues a *Manuel interprète de correspondance*, an international system of communication based on the numeration of all the ideas in the world.[181] But by 1805, these texts appeared to be the residue of another time and another, outdated conception of both politics and signs. In effect, the Napoleonic era brought with it an end to the nostalgia for an earlier moment when there had been perfect accord between *les mots* and *les choses* and an end to the utopian notion of "natural" and "methodical" language planning as a political panacea. In response to the failures of the revolutionary decade, high Enlightenment language theory finally lost its pertinence and began to disappear.

Conclusion: The Savage, the Citizen, and the Language of the Law after 1800

So what can we say of the fate of this characteristic linguistic instrumentalism derived from the model of the *langage d'action*? What should we conclude about the consequences of the Ideologues' biting critique of their own sensationalist predecessors? Or, more bluntly, how does this story draw to a close?

In one sense, the turn of the eighteenth century can be said to mark the end of an era in the French political-linguistic imaginary. The new century accelerated the downfall of the long-standing Enlightenment vision of a more perfect language, constructed exclusively according to nature's rational guidelines, which would finally (or once again) make both the perception and exchange of ideas utterly unequivocal and clear. And with the decline in plans for the pursuit of this ideal came, more generally, the death of the revolutionary utopianism, characterized by a desire for social harmony and intellectual-moral consensus, that had so colored elite French political discourse at the end of the previous century. One way to conclude this book, therefore, would be to demonstrate how the rise of a self-consciously "liberal" political vision in modern or postrevolutionary France was predicated on the demise of a very particular *dirigiste* conception of language politics following the successful attacks of Degérando and Destutt de Tracy, among other fin-de-siècle thinkers.

Such a task would not be unduly difficult to accomplish. It is evident that Degérando's modified sensationalism and revisionist Condillacian language theory offered early nineteenth-century French intellectuals both a set of tools with which to challenge the model of a unanimous, consensual general will and an altered epistemological foundation upon which to build a new kind of political ideal. As we have seen, the early Napoleonic years produced, at least in the theoretical formulations of the opposition (which soon included most of the Ideologues and other inheritors of core Enlightenment principles), the growing acceptance of an alternative idea: that linguistic abstractions—the basis of all forms of constitutional governing and the foundation of modern political engagement—were always, necessarily, going to remain equivocal, unfix-able, and thus, open to varied interpretations and debate. In *Des Signes*, Degérando pointed out that the term *liberté*, to take one example, could never have meant in Sparta what it had meant in Athens, that words were always going to mean different things to different people in different contexts.[1] In the same vein, Destutt de Tracy, in his *Elémens d'Idéologie*, encouraged his readers to recognize this variability as intrinsic to the human condition. Finally, in the first years of the new century, these arguments made it possible for other theorists to imagine a world in which debate and institutionalized dissent, rooted in the inherent ambiguity of words, could be a sign of a strong and healthy political system.

This view was expressed with particular force in the numerous (and largely unpublished) political tracts written in the early nineteenth century by the Swiss Protestant thinker Benjamin Constant. Constant only became enmeshed in French political life in 1795, well after the conclusion of the Terror. But immediately after arriving in Paris that spring as a protégé of Mme de Staël, he set about integrating himself into moderate republican intellectual circles, eventually participating in many important voluntary associations from the Société Philotechnique and the Lycée (renamed the Athénée in 1802) in the French capital to the learned societies of numerous provincial and Continental cities. By virtue of his intellectual connections, as well as his enduring faith in the principles of 1789, Constant thus came directly into the orbit of the Ideologues at the turn of the century. Like them, he also soon established himself as a harsh critic of the policies of the Terror and, more specifically, of the deceitful rhetoric of the Terror, in which, he believed, idealized collective nouns (such as *peuple*) had been routinely used to paper over the oppression of individuals and the concentration of power in a few hands. For the rest of his career he remained a formidable foe of the *abus des mots* and a great proponent of clarity in definitions.[2] What made Constant's writings so unusual in comparison with his *philosophe* or even revolutionary predecessors was his insistence that a certain amount of linguistic ambiguity was not merely an inevitable feature of modern political life but a virtue. Indeed, Constant imagined permanent, unrestricted, uncensored public negotiation over the meaning of a series of unfixed (and thus potentially abusable) moral and metaphysical abstractions as the lifeblood of democratic or liberal, constitutional governance.

In his *Principes de politique applicables à tous les gouvernements* (composed between 1802 and 1806 in opposition to the trajectory of Napoleonic rule and not published until 1815), Constant directly challenged the English political theorist Jeremy Bentham's desire to submit politics to the "eternal rules of arithmetic" and to use utility to eliminate the ambiguities and equivocations stemming from the language of natural law.[3] Contrary to Bentham, Constant insisted that political terms—including Bentham's precious *utilité*—were always bound to be unstable in meaning; as Constant put it in his *Principes*, "*la parole* is infinitely plastic and obliging."[4] But he also argued that humans' best available means for solving problems was unfettered public discussion and debate, among members of the electorate and elected representatives alike, about how best to interpret the abstract language of the law—even if these activities led directly to dissension. As the scholar Stephen Holmes points out, Constant in his early work came very close to the position on the ambiguity of words adopted two decades earlier by James Madison in no. 37 of the *Federalist*.[5] And it is certainly plausible to see this vision of the free play of words open to varied interpretations—an ideal which, of course, was to become so central to the theory of modern liberalism—as impossible to imagine without the rise and fall of a particular, complex conception of language which emerged in the mid-eighteenth century and survived in France until the very end of the revolutionary decade.

To make this claim is certainly not to argue that the desire for order and peaceful accord disappeared in France after 1800. This was clearly far from the case. But by the early nineteenth century, the search for social and intellectual harmony tended no longer to be framed either in terms of the realization of a linguistic or semiotic ideal or as the result of a unified popular or general will. According to Constant's *Principes*, for example, political and social stability (though not moral unanimity) would ultimately be byproducts of the true rule of law—the "observance of forms"—rather than of the nature of the signs that constituted the law or the enhanced mental or moral capacities of citizens that such signs might make possible.[6] Most put their faith in the return of a more concrete central authority, namely, Napoleon and his army or a Bourbon king. And even in those instances in the early nineteenth century when linguistic matters remained critical to the pursuit of social and political cohesion, they tended no longer to do so for the same reasons that they had in the previous century. When, to take another example, the Académie Celtique, a learned society formed in 1805 by many former Ideologues, made recovery of the Celtic language central to its mission, it was not so much in order to rediscover a primitive idiom that could provide a blueprint for an improved modern one, as it might have been in preceding decades. Rather, the revival of Celtic was intended to provide a new source of sociopolitical unity that would become increasingly important in the nineteenth century: a shared national identity predicated on a common ethno-linguistic past.[7]

Nevertheless, even if one acknowledges the fundamental changes in ideology that came with the new century, one must also accept that the picture that I have been sketching of the decline and consequences of the *philosophes'* great linguistic vision is actually too simple to be the full story. Clearly, the legacy for modernity of the semiotic experiments and language planning initiatives of the late eighteenth century was not only a question of their repudiation or of how they paved the way for the emergence of other, more contemporary conceptions of language politics. Moreover, one can not reasonably claim that the "enlightened" politics of the early nineteenth century were affected only by the rejection, reversal, or even sublimation of the Condillacian or the Rousseauian contractual model of the joint origins of semiosis and society. For despite the gradual emergence of a liberal commitment to open debate in the writings of a small number of political theorists after the turn of the century, old fears attached to the idea of a political order based upon the abstract principles of a contract or constitution variously understood or misunderstood by all the members of a large, heterogeneous society certainly lingered in many quarters. In fact, these apprehensions only became more pronounced among enlightenment-inspired thinkers as their sensationalist convictions about the function and significance of language remained intact but their hopes of discovering a transparent, universal idiom declined. As Julien Duhamel warned in an essay of 1802: "Language is the first bond of society, and if this bond slackens, all the others lose their force. . . . If one considers men as citizens, as members of a political society, it is ignorance of their Language that explains ignorance of laws and of all social order, which is to say, the rights and responsibilities of all towards society."[8] Such worries ultimately led the remaining Ideologues and supporters, many of whom continued to congregate in various kinds of *sociétés savantes* during the Consulate and early Empire, to return one last time in the first years of the nineteenth century to a thoroughly eighteenth-century subject of study: the interdependence of linguistic, conceptual, and social development beginning in a hypothetical state of nature. Only this time the Ideologues did not simply challenge the semiotic and, hence, sociopolitical ideal that many of their predecessors had been actively cultivating over the last halfcentury. They used their inquiries into that old question of the mental and moral status of the preverbal, presocial *homme de la nature* to provide the foundation for a new political and social vision as well.

    The conclusion of this book explores how the members of one of the last truly Enlightenment-style learned societies, at the very same time as they developed their arguments against rational language planning, transformed the mid-century model of the happy, gesticulating savage with which this book began so as to carve out a new—and lasting— sociopolitical hierarchy. In the postrevolutionary order, one's role or status in society was not only to be a question of name, wealth, or sex. It was also to be based upon the closely related issue of each citizen's relative ability to understand and to use to his own advantage a series of complex, malleable and, hence, debatable linguistic abstractions which constituted the foundational principles of the new order. Gradually, the older image of an idyllic, natural, originary, and egalitarian language was relegated, once again, to the distinct world of literature, theater, and art.

THE OBSERVATION OF SAVAGES: LANGUAGE AND MORALITY

It was late in the year 1799 when Louis-François Jauffret, best known as a naturalist and children's book author, assembled a group of close colleagues and friends to found a new, quasi-official *société*. Together, these doctors, naturalists, explorers, historians, philosophers, and linguists (whose ranks included such familiar names as Cabanis, Garat, Volney, Destutt de Tracy, Sicard, Butet de la Sarthe, De Maimieux, Laromiguière, and Degérando) created the Société des Observateurs de l'Homme, an organization devoted specifically to the empirical study of the connections among the physical, cognitive, and moral aspects of humans as they developed. The chief goal of the Société, as Jauffret subsequently explained it, was to discover the sources and laws that determined man's perfectibility.[9] The key technique was to be the careful observation of various "primitive" or uncivilized peoples, at home as well as abroad.

In its mission and its personnel, this new learned society thus immediately established its links both to Ideologue circles and to the prerevolutionary intellectual world of the Musée de Paris and other, similar associations. During the 1780s, Pierre-Michel Hennin, then a member of this *musée*, had already argued for the desirability of a society of philosophically minded travelers who would collaborate in applying the analytic method to what they witnessed and heard in the course of their peregrinations.[10] The members of the Société des Observateurs picked up on this idea, among others, and stressed the importance of sensationalist principles in the pursuit of knowledge, as well as the application of new knowledge to questions of general utility. But there was a crucial, if often unstated, difference in the approach of the newer association. The members of the Société des Observateurs de l'Homme hoped that their tests would result in challenges to some of their Enlightenment predecessors' major philosophical and epistemological conjectures regarding the *science de l'homme*.

Based on a belief in the objectivity of science, as well as their own desire to avoid either falling into partisan bickering or running afoul of the

Napoleonic state, the founders of the Société des Observateurs insisted that all "political" and "religious" concerns would be strictly excluded from the society's business.[11] "Free of all passions, all prejudices, and, especially, all established systems," they promised to direct their efforts entirely toward the problem of determining what was natural or intrinsic to humans and what was the product of various external, environmental factors.[12] Indeed, they continued to believe that such deliberately nonpartisan collaborative efforts would, in the words of Leblond, ultimately help "efface even the slightest traces of political dissension" from European society.[13] Yet the members of the Société des Observateurs de l'Homme also suggested that their findings could aid in the design of state-sponsored efforts to ameliorate those conditions that had prevented all peoples from realizing their full potential for perfection and happiness. And with the claim that faulty theorizing about human nature had had detrimental effects on "public morality" in the recent past, they openly sought to establish a revised set of "scientific" or empirically derived principles to serve as the basis of postrevolutionary governing and ethics. As Jauffret put it in his summation of the organization's activities: "The Society, while searching to revive human dignity, that beautiful prerogative which was so cruelly unappreciated and so insolently insulted during the frightful regime that weighed down France for some time, will have the benefit of working, by the influence of its observations alone, toward the extinction of numerous abuses to which this odious regime gave birth and which the current government has not yet succeeded in destroying completely."[14] For the investigations of the Société des Observateurs de l'Homme were closely linked with contemporary efforts, both governmental and private, to reconceptualize the relationship between the individual citizen and the state in reaction to the perceived excesses of the Revolution.

To this end, not surprisingly, many members of the Société des Observateurs de l'Homme made signs—verbal, written, and gestural—both a vital tool and the principal subject of their work. At the time of the founding of this small society, the French Ministry of the Interior was already actively engaged in efforts to discover the significance and nature of regional dialects in the daily lives of ordinary French people; such measures promised, among other things, to reveal the extent of various peoples' intellectual sophistication and, indirectly, commitment to the nation.[15] The Société des Observateurs de l'Homme took up a closely related project, suggesting that the key to understanding the psyche of the "natural" or "primitive" man or woman, the ancestor of the modern European, lay in the study of the language of contemporary savages. First, Degérando proposed, observant travelers had to engage in a kind of detailed linguistic ethnography of each people that they encountered.[16]

Then, by comparing and compiling these samples of primitive languages, they could begin to uncover the order by which ideas and institutions had developed in all societies, or, more precisely, determine the exact role of language in shaping morals, values, and beliefs.

The members of the Société des Observateurs de l'Homme displayed their adherence to these goals in their choice of subjects for study. Volney, who maintained strong ties with the American Philosophical Society during this period, devoted considerable energy to examining the vocabulary and ideas of American Indians.[17] Sicard tried through sign language to plumb the mental world of a rare Chinese visitor to Paris.[18] Jauffret encouraged the public to pay close attention to the way that infants learned to think and to communicate.[19] The naturalist Lacépède attempted to use language as a criterion in the classification of animals, since even in beasts "different languages correspond to different degrees of industry, sensibility, and intelligence."[20] Other members hoped the bodily signs of madmen or dwarfs would also yield useful information regarding their respective intellectual and moral faculties. And, as is well known, a whole committee took it upon itself to chart the simultaneous linguistic and mental progress of Victor, the "wild child" of Aveyron, who was brought to Paris and put in Sicard's care at the Institution National des Sourds-Muets in 1800.[21] The association of the Société des Observateurs de l'Homme with the study of obscure, physical sign systems was, in fact, so ingrained that when Pierre Lemontey produced a satire of the intellectual preoccupations of this organization in 1803, he included a fake scientific lecture detailing a little-known aspect of women: their highly developed (and decidedly erotic) "language of the knees."[22]

But looking back several years later at the state of philosophy at the turn of the century, Degérando identified one subject that he considered to have been particularly revealing in efforts to understand the relationship between language acquisition (or formation) and intellectual-ethical development: the deaf and mute.[23] In fact, the observation and study of this group of disabled people was central to both the purpose and promise of the Société des Observateurs de l'Homme from the start. The appeal of this choice lay, in good measure, in the proximity of one particular individual—Jean Massieu, the best known deaf person in France—who was adopted as an active member of the Société at its inception. The other key reason had to do with the presence of the Abbé Sicard, who touted Massieu and his other pupils as ideal subjects (or "experimental machines" in the words of his colleague Louis Alhoy) for an organization eager to advance the study of ideology and the *science de l'homme*.[24] Indeed, Sicard proposed that while Degérando had recently done much to encourage the abstract study of the history of hu-

man understanding, it was the observation of real-life deaf people, cast in
the role of gesticulating savages, that would finally reveal the true nature of both humans and their society by exposing (as fellow-member Julien-Joseph Virey put it in his treatise on the wild child of Aveyron) "the
primordial state of our species" on which "the social edifice rests."[25]
More precisely, Sicard promised that the comparative study of deaf individuals in their natural and in their educated states made it possible for
philosophers to comprehend not the silent dignity of the isolated noble
savage but, rather, the extraordinary advantages that stemmed directly
from knowledge of conventional signs and grammar.

   Sicard had already laid the groundwork for the positions that he was
to develop in the context of the Société des Observateurs de l'Homme in
a series of widely noted books and essays. In his *Elémens de grammaire
générale* (1799), which was to go through many editions in the early
nineteenth century, Sicard pointed to *parole* as the basis of human superiority, the root cause of all forms of sociability and intellectual progress;
and to make this point, he insisted conversely that humans deprived of
speech were almost in the class of animals.[26] Then, in his magnum opus
of early 1800, the *Cours d'instruction d'un sourd-muet de naissance*
that he had been preparing for years, Sicard fleshed out this argument by
detailing just how impoverished and depraved the deaf were in their
natural state, prior to learning a conventional sign system. "In effect,"
he asked rhetorically in the book's introductory essay, "what is a person
who is deaf and mute from birth, considered on his own terms and before
an education has started to link him, by whatever relationship that may
be possible, to the large family to which, according to his exterior form,
he belongs?"[27] Sicard's answer, much like that put forth by his student
Périer in the educational debates in the Convention in the winter of
1793–94, was a devastating rebuke to all people who believed in the
natural goodness and inherent sociability and rationality of all humans
in all settings: "He is a nonentity in our society, a living automaton, a
statue such as that described by Charles Bonnet, and after him, Condillac. . . . Limited only to physical movements, he does not even have, before the envelope in which his ability to reason is ripped open, that sure
sense of instinct that is the sole guide of other animals."[28] Moreover, Sicard insisted that the situation of the hearing-deprived and illiterate had
become especially dire as of late. Under the current "reign of laws, when
the sacred words of *liberté* and *égalité* are written everywhere," the isolated, uneducated *homme de la nature* posed a risk not only to himself
but also to others.[29] In language that might well have shocked his predecessor, the Abbé de l'Epée, Sicard explained the problem for the benefit
of his educated, literate audience:

Relating everything to himself; obeying all his natural needs with an impetuous violence that no other considerations can reduce; satisfying all of his appetites all the time; knowing no other limits than the inability to satisfy them again . . . overturning all that stands in the way of his pleasure without being hindered by the rights of others that he does not know, by laws that he ignores, by punishments that he has not suffered: that is all the morality of this unfortunate being. . . . The moral world does not exist for him.[30]

Sicard further explored the civic consequences of this extreme ethical nominalism in the course of his participation in the trial of a young deaf man that took place in 1800 in a War Council court in northern France after a guilty verdict in a lower court.[31] In part, this case garnered public attention because of its extraordinary similarity to a contemporaneous play based on a cause célèbre of the late 1770s concerning the paternity of a deaf boy and the Count of Solar.[32] But the trial also drew notice for another reason. It coincided with an ongoing public discussion about how and when to proceed with a criminal charge against an illiterate deaf person, a debate that revolved around a critical question of postrevolutionary political theory: to what degree should the rights and responsibilities of citizenship depend upon one's familiarity with the abstract language in which those rights and responsibilities are both inscribed and embedded?[33] And in this case, Sicard and the defense lawyer offered a response that was far removed from the ethical universe of the early melodrama, with its logic of absolute good and evil. Neither made any effort to depict François Duval—an uneducated, deaf adolescent who had been found hiding under the bed in the home of a grocer following a botched burglary—as the embodiment of natural virtue or as a noble savage endowed with an innate sense of natural law. Nor did either of them try to paint the young deaf man as an imbecile, a being lacking in the capacity to reason, as a means to get him out of trouble. Instead, the adolescent's defense focused on destroying the notion that moral responsibility of any kind could exist apart from society and its conventional language. In his recent book, Sicard had made a case for expanded educational opportunities for the deaf and mute by stressing their original moral depravity and social disconnectedness. Now, under the humane guise of "protecting" the *homme de la nature*, Sicard argued that the unsocialized deaf person was incompetent to participate meaningfully in any civic activity, including his own trial and punishment, because he was necessarily incapable of understanding either the consequences of his actions within society or his abstract duties as a citizen until he could be thoroughly conversant in the conventional language that had, in effect, created these rights, responsibilities, and social relations in the first place. The defense lawyer made a point of clarifying that, in general, ignorance was not an acceptable excuse for exemption from "this convention, this social pact that we call the law."[34] But his argument was based on the decidedly postrevolutionary premise that the law depended upon a linguistic relationship between the state and the individual and, as such, was not absolutely binding but relative to an individual's ability to understand the specific linguistic abstractions that served to construct it.

The primary effect of such reasoning was to create a new and permanent social distinction, a schism at once theoretical and practical, between those educated to comprehend and to manipulate the language of the law and those unable to do so and thus outside of its purview. In such a society, it followed that one sector of the population, a broad elite, would be invested in making and following the law by using its conventional terminology and setting it in written terms. The other sector, ignorant of this language, would not only be excluded from many of the rights and responsibilities outlined by the law that it had not helped establish; this second sector would, in fact, be theorized as a threat to the stability of the laws made by others.

It was this critical, fin-de-siècle social vision that the anthropology of the Société des Observateurs de l'Homme, premised largely on repeated "interviews" with Massieu and other now-educated deaf people, was designed to bolster. Within the first months of the Société's existence, Massieu, at Jauffret's request, used both written and manual signs to present his "autobiography" to the other members of this organization. Further "interviews" and "conversations" regarding his preliterate mental and moral state quickly followed.[35] Such events were certainly not novel in 1800 either for Massieu or for other prominent deaf individuals; even before the publication of Desloges's "autobiography" in 1779, French philosophers had found the dialogue with the *sourd-muet de naissance*, who was asked to remember and to put into words his existence as an "isolated savage" before his introduction to conventional language, to be an effective way to argue for or against the Lockean conception of the origin of ideas.[36] Yet both the structure of the Société's interviews with Massieu and the nature of his responses indicate that, during the Consulate and early Empire, suddenly literate deaf people were being called upon to play new roles. No longer were they expected to set themselves up as exemplars of natural virtue or as pure thinkers untainted by the corrupted vernacular of the present world. Nor were they asked to display themselves as embodiments of revolutionary values, models for the regenerated "new men" of the future. Instead, much like the uncommunicative "wild child" who, Degérando claimed, had initially exhibited all the signs of "moral idiocy," these experimental subjects promised to illustrate the connection between social and linguistic isolation and moral depravity, on the one hand, and conventional signs and ethical development, on the other.[37] As is well known, Victor of Aveyron turned out to be a flawed example (he may well have been retarded or mentally ill), continually frustrating the chances of the experiment succeeding the way that many of the members of the Société desired. Jean Massieu, however, was very capable of explaining his own transformation in terms supplied by teachers and friends. And the deaf man complied by continually reinforcing Sicard's description of him in his original guise as a "man of the woods, still endowed with only animal habits," and contrasting that picture with his present situation as a devout, literate, rational, and civic-minded citizen.[38]

Of course, just as in the contemporaneous battle over the legal status of the deaf-mute person, Sicard's revised conception of the mental capacity of the unsocialized and illiterate individual met with a certain amount of resistance at the turn of the century. His most public challenger on this matter was Urbain René Thomas LeBouvyer-Desmortiers, a medical doctor and fellow member of the Société des Observateurs de l'Homme, who produced a long book in 1800 directly refuting many of Sicard's claims.[39] Some of LeBouvyer-Desmortiers's objections had a basis in logic. To call the deaf "automatons" and "statues" and to suggest that they had fewer instincts than animals or were insensible to maternal caresses, he argued, flew in the face of the basic premise of both Epée's and Sicard's methodologies: that the unschooled deaf had a language of their own which could, effectively, serve as the foundation for a whole educational and linguistic system. But the most important of LeBouvyer-Desmortiers's refutations were grounded in his very different view of human psychology and epistemology. Based on written interviews with both Massieu and a deaf-mute girl of the doctor's acquaintance, he insisted that the deaf could indeed develop deeply ethical notions—"ideas of order, morality, justice," as well as "the pre-existing germ of virtue and of the sweet passions that make humans so superior to brutes, pity, love of her fellow creatures, and sadness at seeing them die" and even some sense of a supreme being—without any contact with the rest of society or its language.[40] In fact, LeBouvyer-Desmortiers went so far in this text as to question whether widespread use of the natural language of signs, rather than "those [conventional] languages that often produce such fatal confusions and abuses," could have prevented the deterioration of the Revolution of 1789 into Terror.[41] As LeBouvyer-Desmortiers put it in his introduction: "I like to believe that this people [the deaf] would not have created these destructive systems which, for the last ten years, have ravaged and bloodied the four corners of the world. Happy nation! How sweet it would be to lose the ability to hear or to speak if one could be admitted into your bosom!"[42] In effect, the *Mémoire ou considérations sur les sourds-muets de naissance* represented the last serious rallying cry for two related ideas that had been articulated fifty years earlier in Aunillon's *Azor* and, more recently, in the writings of deputies like J. B. Massieu and Nicolas Raffron. One was that an ideal society would resemble a community of signing deaf-mutes. The other was that the metaphysical ideas (and language) of the civilized world could just as easily constitute an introduction to misery as a path to happiness for those still safely and peacefully ensconced in the preverbal innocence of the state of nature.

These counterreflections offered by the philosophically inclined doctor garnered a mixed response at the turn of the century. Both the major Ideologue journals, the *Magasin encyclopédique* and *La Décade philosophique*, found much to compliment in LeBouvyer-Desmortiers's *Mémoire*, including his refutation of Sicard's notion of the natural man as a pure brute.[43] Similarly, some reviewers of Sicard's contemporaneous *Cours* questioned the celebrated deaf instructor's constant equation of human perfectibility with the capacity for speech.[44] However, Sicard's argument—as opposed to that of LeBouvyer-Desmortiers—was generally greeted with words of praise, both within the Société des Observateurs and outside of it.[45] For despite LeBouvyer-Desmortiers's stated antipathy to the hypocrisies of the Revolution and numerous references to Christian ideals, his argument could not fail to strike certain of his readers as a nostalgic and undesirable form of Rousseauianism. Conversely, Sicard's depiction of Massieu's intellectual development offered the ideological allies of this pedagogue and priest a convenient way to challenge an earlier, idealized notion of a state of nature governed by a set of instinctive and humane natural laws. It also gave Sicard's supporters a means to argue for increased state-sponsored educational opportunities. To take one example, in an article of the summer of 1800 in *La Clef du cabinet des souverains*, a newspaper edited by Garat and Fontanes, among others, a disciple of the Abbé Sicard named Rey-Lacroix answered LeBouvyer-Desmortiers by accusing him of glorifying the original, desperate state of the *sourd-muet de naissance*: "This opinion, so prettily systematized by J. J. [Rousseau] and applicable to all beings, isn't it a little bit subversive of sociability and won't it soon lead us to *walk on four legs*?"[46] Rey-Lacroix then went on to thank God that his own deaf daughter had had access to an intensive sign language education modeled on the system of Sicard because otherwise, he believed, she would have remained ignorant, unsocialized, and utterly unaware of moral values until the end of her days.

It was, however, Louis-François Jauffret, the permanent secretary of the Société and a long-standing friend and admirer of Sicard, who was

most active among the Observateurs in challenging any residual glorifi-
cation of a presocial state of nature.[47] As Jauffret explained in a lecture
course on the natural history of man, attitudes about the precivilized
state of human life had traditionally divided the public into two groups:
those who believed in an earthly paradise or golden age of innocence,
equality, and happiness, and those who believed in a lawless world of
amoral humans living like wild animals.[48] Both approaches were highly
flawed, he continued; but the latter picture, which he attributed to the
Sophists and then Hobbes, appeared to be closer to the truth when one
considered savages of different corners of the world. The case of the deaf
was the same. Louis-François Jauffret, together with his brother, the
cleric Gaspard-Jean-André Jauffret, repeatedly asked Massieu to spell out
the vast difference between his earliest beliefs and those that he had
been educated, with the help of conventional signs for abstract concepts,
to hold as an adult. The purpose of such experiments, as Jauffret noted in
reference to a related endeavor, was twofold: "to enlighten us as to the
fruitlessness of a natural education" and "to teach us to cherish that
much more the benefits of the social institutions [such as language] to
which man is indebted for all that he is today."[49]

In this manner, Jauffret and his colleagues thus helped lay the
groundwork for a new and decidedly hierarchical political model, one
that emphasized the significance of French-language education to the
survival of the present logocentric order and, consequently, the exclusive value of the educated and the articulate (who tended to be coterminous with the property-owning) to the smooth functioning of the postrevolutionary polity.[50] In the hands of the Ideologues, sensationalism—
which the prerevolutionary *philosophes* had employed to destroy the
notion of innate ideas and, in many cases, challenge orthodoxies both religious and political—became useful in asserting the importance of
France's primary early nineteenth-century social institutions: the family, the church, the government, and its schools. For in the opinion of
the majority of the members of the Société des Observateurs de
l'Homme, these civilizing forces assumed the all-important task of lift-
ing men (though not necessarily women) out of their presocialized and
thus degraded situation and, with the help of the national language,
making them pious and patriotic citizens with a sure grasp of the foundational moral principles of both the church and the state. In other
words, these institutions became essential forms of protection against
the instability and open-endedness of the abstract moral notions essential to constitutional governance. And at the same time, those individuals outside of their reach were increasingly demonized as threats to the
sanctity of the nation's laws.

Subsequently, the first decades of the nineteenth century brought many attacks upon the nominalist ethics and language-based conception of citizenship indirectly promulgated by the members of this Société. Indeed, after 1804, both the political theory and the epistemology of the Ideologues rapidly declined under a variety of religious and governmental pressures until the more extreme arguments of the members of the Société des Observateurs de l'Homme, including those regarding the deaf, came to look reprehensible to individuals at both ends of the philosophical spectrum. By 1808, even Sicard felt compelled to revise his earlier claims. Regarding his *Cours* of 1800, he wrote: "One will see that perhaps I exaggerated a little regarding the sad condition of the deaf-mute in his primitive state."[51] Gradually other former colleagues followed suit. During the Restoration, Jauffret faulted Sicard with having systematically overdrawn, at the turn of the century, the "deplorable state" of the deaf person.[52] Degérando similarly referred to the novel defenses elaborated in the celebrated deaf-mute trials of that era as "a serious error . . . in the interest of humanity, philosophy, and we do not fear to say, in the interest of morality itself."[53] In fact, opinion shifted so profoundly in the ensuing years, especially as a result of the early nineteenth-century religious revival in France, that the author of an 1829 book on the intellectual capacity of the deaf believed it necessary to comment on how far the pendulum had swung in the other direction; no one would now suggest that man was an empty receptacle for knowledge, the Abbé Montaigne maintained, and no one would now dispute that some kind of natural moral sentiment was innate in everyone.[54]

However, during a crucial interval between the Revolution and the Empire, the radical argument about the nature of man that had been so forcefully articulated by various members of the Société des Observateurs de l'Homme was instrumental, much like the well-publicized deaf-mute trials and numerous publications on "ideology" of that same moment, in helping to bring about a fundamental transformation in late Enlightenment thinking. With their challenge to the concept of *régénération* rooted in the model of the *langage d'action*, the Ideologues drew to a close a half-century of linguistic speculation, debate, experimentation, and planning based on the premise that signs reformed in keeping with the invariable plan of nature could ultimately help to generate an ideal community in which all forms of contestation would become unnecessary. In other words, they helped to do away with the idealistic, populist dimension of Enlightenment thought, that which had produced both the idea of a natural golden age and the idea of an undivided general will. Yet the late Ideologues did not entirely dismiss the lessons of their *philosophe* forefathers at the conclusion of the 1790s. For as a result of their enduring commitment to both the end of customary, monarchical rule and the authority of written law, they remained convinced of the importance of conventional signs as the source of the most fundamental of social bonds and the foundation of political order. They also remained sure of their own role in explaining (if not in "fixing") this connection. Thus before the old image of a universal language capable of producing moral and political unanimity gradually gave way to the possibility of a political system built on an unfixed language, open debate, and institutionalized dissent, a new kind of division first had to emerge. Just as the Académie française's early linguistic purism had divided the French population (the urban from the provincial, the elite from the common, the ruling from the ruled) in an effort to solidify the power of the French crown, so the new constitutional and logocentric political theory of the early nineteenth century now established a different chasm in the hope of cementing a national linguistic-social contract. And this distinction—predicated on the reformulation of the old, "enlightened" model of the gesticulating savage as a threat to the general good—was to last well beyond the first years of the nineteenth century.

LES HOMMES DE LA NATURE
ET LES HOMMES POLICÉS

There was, however, one domain in which the old image of the *homme de la nature*, living according to the laws of nature and gesturing to his companions to convey his simple thoughts, remained intact after the turn of the new century. That was the popular stage. The celebration of the idea of a primitive, univocal, and unmediated language of pantomime had begun more than fifty years earlier in the realm of fiction: on the hypothetical islands conjured up by *littérateurs* such as Aunillon and speculative *philosophes* such as Condillac. Gradually, after 1800, it returned to that explicitly imaginary context and locale.

An extraordinary—and final—example can be found in a composition by J. G. A. Cuvelier de Trie, a popular playwright working in the tradition of the didactic theater of the Revolution as well as earlier boulevard pantomimes. Cuvelier got his start composing largely wordless patriotic fare in the early 1790s, and in the years following Thermidor, he continued to stage republican spectacles in which gestural communication figured frequently as both subject matter and theatrical practice.[55] At the close of the century, he was still engaged in plans to "nationalize pantomime."[56] At the same time, Cuvelier also became a close associate of many of the Ideologues in the turn-of-the-century Société Philotechnique and wrote a regular theater column for its journal *L'Ami des Arts*. Finally, in 1801, this minor figure of the postrevolutionary Parisian literary establishment composed and staged at the Ambigu-Comique a brief theatrical work, a pantomime preceded and followed by dialogue, that summarily drew together all of the commonplaces that had come to be associated with the natural language of the body over the previous fifty years.

The pretext for the action in Cuvelier's *Les Hommes de la nature, et les hommes policés* is a debate between a male and a female sylph about an old but still topical question: What role have positive laws and social institutions played in the establishment of morality? Or, to put it another way, are humans ultimately more vicious in their natural or in their civilized state? The ensuing conversation between the two sylphs touches on problems of religion, sexuality, criminal justice, beauty, and war; but their unremarkable arguments move the two protagonists no closer to a conclusion. Then the female sylph fixes on an unusual method for formulating an answer: to observe, in an unnamed colonial setting, the comparative behavior of civilized and primitive peoples and to judge their respective moral statures from this bird's eye point of view alone. She explains:

> We hover at this moment over one of the parts of the world inhabited equally by men of nature and socialized men; let us stop on one of these clouds [and] fix our gaze on this new land. A great picture is going to unfold before our eyes. We will not hear these poor humans; their language is so deceptive that even we spirits could be taken in like the others. It is by their actions alone that they must be judged, and it is in this way that we will decide the question that we have just been debating.[57]

With these lines, the play then metamorphoses into a silent spectacle, a pantomime without words that Cuvelier dedicates "to those who cannot hear."

In the end, after floating beyond the realm of speech and observing the distinctive and unambiguous *langages d'action* of the innocent "savages" and the tyrannical English soldiers, the sylphs (and the audience) become capable of reaching a clear conclusion about the philosophical dilemma at the heart of this drama. Ultimately, the female sylph, the exponent of nature, is proven correct; virtue is greater among the innocent and natural because the universe is inherently just and good. But Cuvelier's narrative pantomime was designed to do more than simply reinforce the connection between pure morality and the natural language of gestures and actions. It also proposed that the female sylph's preferred method of understanding might be useful in making a corrupted world morally transparent once again. As the subheading of the play—"Be quiet, or say something more worthwhile than silence"—indicates, the legacy of the Revolution in the theater of the early nineteenth century was a profound fear of the power of meaningless and manipulative words to disguise ostensibly self-evident ethical truths associated with humans in their original, uncorrupted state. With *Les Hommes de la nature, et les hommes policés,* Cuvelier clearly aimed to rekindle a dwindling faith in the possibility that a purified and entirely visual system of cognition and communication could effectively restore the moral certainty of a much earlier, indeed, primordial age.

Here, once again, there are two possible conclusions that can be drawn. Certainly, based on this one example, one might well claim that the story of the present book comes full circle by the early nineteenth century in terms of both context and content. After all, the image of the *langage d'action* first emerged in the fiction and philosophy of the mid-eighteenth century not only as a way to explain the natural, collaborative origins of human language but also as a key ingredient in an enticing vision of a long-lost social and moral world untarnished by the modern propensity for the *abus des mots.* Soon, reformers in a number of specialized domains—first the theater, then the classroom, and finally, the learned *société*—attempted to revive this pantomimic idiom, insisting that "natural" signs could be used as tools to liberate individuals from the thrall of deceptive, conventional signs and to (re)create perfectly harmonious communities within modern, absolutist France. Then, with the outbreak of the Revolution, the salience of these aesthetic and, especially, pedagogic experiments rapidly expanded; for such early attempts to revive the *langage d'action* almost immediately provided "enlightened" patriots with enticing models and methods for the broader transformation of French society and culture. Throughout the 1790s, these earlier projects strongly colored both revolutionary political strategies, which often took the form of exercises in prescriptive language planning, and revolutionary political aspirations, which depended upon the success of these *dirigiste* efforts in eliminating all forms of discord. Indeed, the preceding decades of semiotic speculation and innovation seem to have convinced many of the most prominent revolutionaries not only of the considerable dangers associated with the *abus des mots* but also that a linguistic solution would eventually bring the revolutionary logomachy to a close and make the principles of 1789 commonly understood and universally accepted on rational, scientific grounds. But this search for a linguistic panacea was never without its challengers. And once the idea of a natural *langage d'action* failed, first, as a model for efforts to forward the revolutionary cause, and, second, as an example for plans to halt the struggle after Thermidor, this image was finally abandoned as a key element of both contemporary epistemology and political theory, within enlightened circles as well as without. Then, it seems, this ideal language found an enduring home in the same kind of self-contained utopian and fictional space as that from which it had emerged several decades before the Revolution. In this sense, Aunillon and Cuvelier could be said to provide us with bookends for a whole era in the French semiotic and political imaginary.

Yet, at the same time, this story cannot really be said to end just where it began. For one must also pay attention to historical dissymmetry or, to put it differently, to the substantial gaps between the goals and implications of the projects of Cuvelier and Aunillon or even Cuvelier and Noverre. Two broad historical developments explain these differences.

First, *Les Hommes de la nature, et les hommes policés*, an important precursor to the melodramas with pantomiming savages that would soon flourish on numerous French stages,[58] evoked an ethical universe that now, at the conclusion of the revolutionary decade, appeared to be the residue of another era, a vision disconnected from early nineteenth-century conceptions of "progress." One can, of course, find superficial similarities between the message of this play and that of the late Ideologues in terms of attitudes, for example, toward sentiment and femininity or toward empirically discerned knowledge. But Cuvelier's core belief—that pantomime was effective in showing an inherently fraternal world where good and bad were clearly distinct and natural virtue always triumphed in the end—was a far cry from the ideology that was being propagated at the same time within such quasi-official institutions of the Consulate as the Société des Observateurs de l'Homme. In these latter settings, ethnographers were now committed to proving that the *langage d'action* was not universally intelligible, that humans in their natural state were not necessarily equal or peaceful or virtuous or sage, and that it might, in fact, be time to do away with the term *homme de la nature* once and for all.[59] In this environment, Cuvelier's conception of the connection between natural virtue and natural language could only have been seen as backward-looking, evocative of the now-repudiated discourse of the Jacobin Revolution as well as of a very distant—and unrecuperable—past.

Second, Cuvelier promulgated his message in a profoundly changed context. Certainly, many of the political values that the revolutionaries of the 1790s had sought to secure through epistemological reforms had their origins and first tests in the aesthetic experiments of the Enlightenment. So did the epistemological developments that they had hoped to secure through political change. But circa 1800, opponents of the status quo no longer looked to the theater to function in the same potentially subversive and ultimately prophetic manner as it had before 1789 or during the revolutionary decade. Thus when natural signs were used on the popular stage after the turn of the nineteenth century to bolster populist messages or to stir communitarian feeling, they ceased to have the same social or political connotations. In practice, Cuvelier's stage work, with its vision of a once harmonious world of transparent, natural communication and its dependence upon the revival of the *langage d'action* to communicate this ideal, amounted to a form of nostalgic escapism for its heterogeneous Parisian audience rather than an encouragement to regenerate contemporary society. In the wake of the Revolution, the progressive political culture of early nineteenth-century France was, despite the frequent changes in regime, premised on the exaltation of the verbally adept *homme policé*.

It is, of course, hard to speak of two distinct entities: "a Revolution" and "an Enlightenment." Historians have often warned of the pitfalls involved in treating them as concrete objects of analysis either apart or in relation to one another. Yet it is evident that the epistemology of the mid-eighteenth-century intellectual and cultural movement commonly known as the Enlightenment greatly affected the form that the political and socioeconomic crisis of the late eighteenth century would take, both making the latter's utopianism possible and limiting how that vision would play itself out. It is also clear that the failure of the Revolution to bring about either the moral renewal or the social and intellectual harmony that it initially promised led to profound challenges to and changes within this inherited epistemology and the institutions that it bolstered. Certainly, one can argue that conceptions of language and conceptions of order and strife are always linked in some fashion, and these connections are likely to become more explicit at moments of great social or political upheaval. After all, language has been an important battlefield in all the major political "revolutions" of the last two centuries. But political thought and semiotic or epistemological theory bolstered one another in a very particular way in the second half of the eighteenth century in France. It is this distinctive fusion which was in good part responsible, I have been arguing, for the singular character of the revolutionary transformation that began in that nation in 1789 and that evolved into a world-historical benchmark against which we have continued to measure both our distance and our proximity to this day.

This much was already evident to the late eighteenth-century historians of the French Revolution with whom the introduction to this book began. Those commentators, like the chief architects of the political transformation of the 1790s, steadfastly insisted that, in all languages, arbitrary signs create spaces for misunderstanding and, hence, mistaken opinion and discord. Consequently, some of the Revolution's most important *portes-parole* and analysts, from Rabaut Saint-Etienne to Michel-Edme Petit, desired nothing more of a revolution than that it would finally make signs so fixed, so self-evident, indeed, so transparent and isomorphic with their meanings that they would largely disappear except as paths to sure knowledge. But from Condillac onward, these same "enlightened" individuals were also well aware of the historicity and mutability of language, a feature, they suggested, that could be made to work to society's (and their own) benefit as well as disadvantage. For these men and, occasionally, women also insisted that not only could the social institution that they called *la langue* be reformed to better reflect the operations of the mind or the nature of external reality; it could also be used as a means to transform the reality that it was supposed to reflect and to change where authority rested. It was this dual vision of language—complicating (and complicated by) both a political theory that insisted on a univocal national voice and an actual factional struggle in which *la parole* became a tool for seizing power at the expense of others—that drew the attention of and baffled a generation of historians writing about their own time. At the end of the eighteenth century, enlightened inquiries into the evolution and function of signs had a decisive impact on how people saw the political struggle around them unfolding, how they imagined or tried to shape its conclusion, and, finally, how they wrote its history. As the disillusioned ex-*philosophe* Jean François de La Harpe explained in the late 1790s in an effort to justify his repeated attention to chronicling the Revolution's critical terms: language was "the first instrument [of the Revolution] and the most surprising of all."[60]

Reference Matter

Notes

The following abbreviations are used in the Notes.

AI-LBA Archives de l'Institut de France: Institut National, Classe de Lit-
        térature et Beaux-Arts
AI-SMP Archives de l'Institut de France: Institut National, Classe des
        Sciences Morales et Politiques
AN   Archives Nationales, Paris
BHVP   Bibliothèque Historique de la Ville de Paris
BN   Bibliothèque Nationale, Paris
INJS   Institut National des Jeunes Sourds, Paris
PVCIPC *Procès-verbaux du Comité d'instruction publique de la Conven-
        tion nationale.* Edited by James Guillaume. Paris, 1891–1907
PVCIPL *Procès-verbaux du Comité d'instruction publique de
        l'Assemblée législative.* Edited by James Guillaume. Paris, 1889

INTRODUCTION

1. Rabaut Saint-Etienne, *Lettres à Sylvain Bailly sur l'histoire primitive de la Grèce* (1787), in *Oeuvres de Rabaut-Saint-Etienne,* 1:232.

2. Ibid., 1:37. On this mode of historical writing and, especially, the importance of prophecy within it, see Dagen, *L'Histoire de l'esprit humain.*

3. Rabaut Saint-Etienne, *Précis de l'histoire de la Révolution française* (1792), in *Oeuvres de Rabaut-Saint-Etienne,* 1:293.

4. Ibid., 1:408.

5. Ibid., 1:417.

6. Lacretelle (jeune), *Précis historique de la Révolution française: Convention nationale,* 2:340–41. In 1797, the Parisian publisher Treuttel et Würtz commissioned Lacretelle to extend and bring up to the present Rabaut's earlier account of the Constituent Assembly. Lacretelle's two volumes dealing with the Convention were not, however, published until 1803.

7. Petit, *Discours prononcé à la Convention nationale, le 28 fructidor, 2e année républicain, sur les causes du 9 thermidor.*

8. Furet, *Interpreting the French Revolution,* 48.

9. On revolutionary discourse, rhetoric, or modes of expression, see, for example, Hunt, *Politics, Culture, and Class in the French Revolution* (esp. part I: "The Poetics of Power"); Blum, *Rousseau and the Republic of Virtue:*

The Language of Politics in the French Revolution; and de Baecque, *The Body Politic: Corporeal Metaphor in Revolutionary France, 1770–1810.* On the use and effects of particular terms, images, or symbols during the Revolution, see, for example, Rey, *Révolution: histoire d'un mot;* and Lüsebrink and Reichardt, *The Bastille: A History of a Symbol of Despotism and Freedom.*

10. Little attention has been paid to analyzing Furet's position on revolutionary language in terms of either its historical lineage or its postwar political significance. Critics have generally sidestepped this question and faulted Furet either for divorcing political language from its social and material origins or, conversely, for neglecting to develop a theory of his own concerning the relationship between language and power. For an especially strong critique of the former type, see Palmer, *Descent into Discourse.* For the criticism that Furet takes "the linguisticality of the Revolution as its special, temporary condition (in fact, as its motor), rather than as a status it shares with any and all events," see Hunt, review of *Interpreting the French Revolution, History and Theory.* And for an extended critique of Furet's failure to provide a "theory of language, or its relation to politics, even as he insists on its centrality to the understanding of the Revolution," see Poster, *Cultural History and Postmodernity,* esp. 88.

11. See Brunot, *Histoire de la langue française des origines à 1900,* esp. vols. 9 and 10.

12. Hunt, *Politics, Culture, and Class,* 20. In *Inventing the French Revolution,* 7–9, Keith Michael Baker, while agreeing with and developing Hunt's assessment of the weaknesses in Furet's interpretation (cited in note 10), also faults Hunt for taking the revolutionaries' comments about language literally in her own seminal work on the impact of revolutionary rhetoric.

13. In their *Sémiotique: dictionnaire raisonné de la théorie du langage,* 1:129, Greimas and Courtés define the "metasemiotic" of a culture as the attitude of a sociocultural community regarding its own signs, and they attribute this concept (which is, for them, synonymous with an "episteme," or *épistémé*) to Juri Lotman, as well as Michel Foucault. The argument that metatheories of language and signs establish guidelines for the organization of other domains or fields of knowledge is most often associated with Foucault's *The Order of Things.* However, in arguing for a "social history of language" in *The Art of Conversation,* Peter Burke makes the important—if obvious—point that every culture also has a specific and distinctive mythology or ideology surrounding language which is more sociological than philosophical, and that this too should draw the attention of historians.

14. See, for example, Hesse, "Enlightenment Epistemology and the Laws of Authorship in Revolutionary France, 1777–1793"; and Friedland, "Representation and Revolution: The Theatricality of Politics and the Politics of Theater in France, 1789–1794." Joan Scott argues in *Only Paradoxes to Offer,* 20–21, that "epistemological problems [such as the relationship between signs and referents] *were* political problems" during the French Rev-

olution. I would extend this claim to point out that political problems often became epistemological dilemmas in their own right.

15. See, for example, Richard Popkin, "Condorcet's Epistemology and His Politics," in *Knowledge and Politics: Case Studies*, ed. Dascal and Gruengard, 111–24, as well as the introduction to that volume in which the two editors discuss various ways of thinking about the connections between epistemology and political philosophy. See Roberto Unger's *Knowledge and Politics* for a more extended argument that social change is dependent upon recognition that there is "a relationship of reciprocal dependence between specific solutions to problems in the theory of knowledge and in the theory of society" (4). More often "historical epistemology" is treated as a subfield in the history of science, where it is more widely accepted that the conceptual categories by which knowledge is organized shape what knowledge exists, how this knowledge is understood, and the ways that this knowledge is used at any given historical moment.

16. See, for example, Mona Ozouf's discussion in *Festivals and the French Revolution* (esp. chap. 8) of the empiricist assumptions operative in the design of revolutionary festivals.

17. Richter, "Researching the History of Political Languages: Pocock, Skinner, and the 'Geschichtliche Grundbegriffe,' " 66–67.

18. See Richter, "Begriffsgeschichte in Theory and Practice: Reconstructing the History of Political Concepts and Languages." Under the rubric "history of semantics," Richter includes theories of language origins, of grammar, of lexicology, of synonyms, of correct usage, and of the political and social functions of language.

19. Ibid., 142. The principal text Richter discusses in this context is the *Handbuch politisch-sozialer Grundbegriffe in Frankreich, 1680–1820*, ed. Reichardt and Schmitt (1985–), esp. vol. 1. For a sustained analysis of this work along the same lines, see also Richter, "Innovation and Critique in the *Handbuch*," in *The History of Political and Social Concepts*, esp. 117–19.

20. Guilhaumou, *La Langue politique et la Révolution française*, 12. See also his recent extension of this project entitled *L'Avènement des porte-parole de la république (1789–1792)*. The lexicometric work of the Equipe "18ème et Révolution" at the Ecole Normale Supérieure de Saint-Cloud has culminated in the *Dictionnaire des usages socio-politiques (1770–1815)*.

21. Baker, *Inventing the French Revolution*, 25–26.

22. There are many possible reasons why gesture becomes a subject of interest in different cultures in different eras; however, historians of Europe have noted that the study of gesture has often been in fashion at moments when questions of social process and language have been problematic as well. On this history, see Kendon, "The Study of Gesture: Some Observations on its History"; and Schmitt, "Introduction," in "Gesture" (special issue, *History and Anthropology* [1984]): 1–18.

CHAPTER I

1. Aunillon, *Azor, ou le Prince enchanté*, in *Voyages imaginaires*, 21:277.

2. Ibid., 21:277.

3. Ibid., 21:272–73.

4. Ibid., 21:275.

5. Ibid., 21:276.

6. On common features of literary utopias, see Baczko, *Utopian Lights*, 147.

7. On ideal languages within imaginary travel literature, see Cornelius, *Languages in Seventeenth- and Early Eighteenth-Century Imaginary Voyages*; Knowlson, *Universal Language Schemes*, 112–38; Seeber, "Ideal Languages in the French and English Imaginary Voyage"; Pons, "Les Langues imaginaires dans le voyage utopique"; and Yaguello, *Les Fous du langage*. On the relationship between the linguistic discussions in "real" early modern travel literature and the depictions of ideal languages in contemporaneous imaginary travel literature, see Adams, *Travel Literature and the Evolution of the Novel*, 259–63.

8. On the assumption of the transparency of all gestural signs as a hallmark of Western tales of exploration in the New World, see Greenblatt, *Marvelous Possessions*, 86–118. For later testimony regarding Jesuits' use of gestures to communicate with and, ultimately, to convert Indians in North America, see, for example, the Relation of Frère Paul Le Jeune in Quebec (1633–34) in *The Jesuit Relations and Allied Documents*, ed. Thwaites, 5:151, 6:225, 7:87.

9. Béthune, *Relation du monde de Mercure*, in *Voyages imaginaires*, 16:203. In Jonathan Swift's *Gulliver's Travels* (1726), the main character also uses gestural signs as a means of conversing with animals. Charles Garnier, the editor of the *Voyages imaginaires*, included both Béthune's and Swift's texts, along with those of Aunillon, Cyrano, and Foigny, in the thirteen volumes of his *Voyages imaginaires* that he devoted specifically to the subcategory *voyages imaginaires merveilleux*.

10. Ibid., 16:204. In fact, Béthune's attempt to portray unmediated communication went beyond the example of gestural interaction between animals and men. In *Relation du monde de Mercure*, writing is also superseded by more direct and less material means of communication based on inner senses: "It suffices to think for the thought to be written, for the thought itself places itself on the paper. . . . A letter written carries itself to the person to whom it is addressed and lets that person know by an interior sentiment from whom it comes . . . but as soon as it is broken open, the whole text evaporates, and the paper remains white" (196). And tellingly, traitors and liars on Mercury are punished by becoming crystalline or transparent themselves.

11. On the function of the "primitive" language of *quipos,* or quipus, in Mme de Graffigny's *Lettres d'une Péruvienne*, see Miller, "The Knot, the Letter and the Book: Grafigny's Peruvian Letters," in *Subject to Change*, 125–61; and Mall, "Langues étrangères et étrangeté du langage dans les *Lettres d'une Péruvienne* de Mme de Grafigny." Though they offer very different readings of the novel, both critics claim that the effect of the heroine's transition from writing with *quipos* to writing in French is central to the development and meaning of the novel.

12. On this trope, see Ricken, "Réflexions du XVIIIe siècle sur 'l'abus des mots.'"

13. Bacon, *The New Organon*, book 1, sects. 59–60, 112–13.

14. See the paragraph entitled "Abuses of Speech," in Hobbes, *Leviathan*, part I, chap. 4, 102.

15. Locke, *An Essay concerning Human Understanding*, 407–8. The first French translation of Locke's *Essay* appeared in 1700.

16. On the linguistic dimension of antischolastic arguments, see Peter Burke, "The Jargon of the Schools," in *Languages and Jargons*, ed. Burke and Porter, 22–41.

17. Holbach, *Le Bon sens*, preface, 2. See also chap. 52 entitled "Ce qu'on appelle providence n'est qu'un mot vide de sens."

18. "Logomachie," in *Encyclopédie*, ed. Diderot and D'Alembert, 9: 642–43. See also the review and summary of this article in the *Journal encyclopédique* 7, part 1 (October 1767): 16–18. According to Raymond Naves (*Voltaire et l'Encyclopédie*), this article was among seventeen written by Antoine-Noé de Polier, the *premier pasteur* of Lausanne, who was recruited by Voltaire for this task and probably aided by him in its execution. Naves reprints (194) the expurgated first line of the article, a nasty speculation about why the word *logomachie* had been omitted from the dictionaries of Furetière and Richelet and from the *Dictionnaire de Trévoux*.

19. Locke, *Essay*, 496.

20. Ibid., 3.

21. Ibid., 495, 497.

22. Thomas Gustafson, in defense of his thesis that the American Revolution constituted a "Thucydidean moment," convincingly reads the texts of Locke and certain other seventeenth-century English philosophers as elaborations upon Thucydides' comments on the connection between linguistic and political corruption in *The Peloponnesian War* (see Gustafson, *Representative Words*). Timothy J. Reiss points out a similar use of Thucydides during the wars of religion a century earlier in France. In an essay of 1588, for example, Montaigne pointed to deceptive linguistic practices as a source of contemporary violence, writing: "[We] are experiencing what Thucydides says of the civil wars of his time, that men baptized vices with new milder names to excuse them, adulterating and softening their true titles" (see Reiss, "Montaigne and the Subject of the Polity").

23. In *De l'Esprit des lois*, Montesquieu discusses the dangerous results that stem from the vague and multiple definitions accorded to the terms *liberté* (see vol. 1, book 2, chap. 2: "Diverses significations données au mot de liberté") and *lèse-majesté* or high treason (see vol. 1, book 12, chap. 7: "Du crime de lèse-majesté" and chap. 8: "De la mauvaise application du nom de crime de sacrilège et de lèse-majesté"). In a similar vein, see François Quesnay's comments on the variability of the term *justice* in his article "Evidence," in *Encyclopédie*, ed. Diderot and D'Alembert, 6:146–57; and Charles Bonnet's remarks on the term *patriot* in his *Essai analytique sur les facultés de l'âme*, 176.

24. Helvétius, *De l'Esprit*, 48.

25. Sylvain Auroux argues that a political conception of language, rather than being a revolutionary invention, was already an intrinsic part of the classical age. See his "Le Sujet de la langue: la conception politique de la langue sous l'Ancien Régime et la Révolution," in *Les Idéologues*, ed. Busse and Trabant, 259–78; and "La Conception politique de la langue, la Révolution française et la démocratie."

26. Bishop Jean-Bénigne Bossuet, *Politique tirée des propres paroles de l'Ecriture sainte* (1709, posthum.), reproduced in translation in *The Old Regime and the French Revolution*, ed. Baker, 31–50.

27. On the development of regulative censorship policies for printed materials, see Martin, *The French Book*; and Minois, *Censure et culture sous l'Ancien Régime*. On royal efforts to protect against the informal circulation of undesirable opinions, including dangerous words, see Graham, "Crimes of Opinion: Policing the Public in Eighteenth-Century Paris," esp. 87–88.

28. On Richelieu's ambitions in establishing the Académie Française, see Fumaroli, "Les Intentions du Cardinal de Richelieu, fondateur de l'Académie Française." On the history and significance of this institution, one of whose key functions was to compile an official French dictionary, see also Fumaroli, "La Coupole."

29. The Villers-Cotterêts ordinance of 1539 established the "langage maternel françois" as the single administrative and legal language of France, and during the seventeenth century, this policy was routinely extended to annexed territories as well. On the ordinance and its subsequent history, see Peyre, *La Royauté et les langues provinciales*.

30. For a nice description of the complicated patterns of language usage in eighteenth-century France, see Roche, *France in the Enlightenment*, 239–41. For more detailed information on the multiple languages of early modern France, see Brunot, *Histoire de la langue française des origines à 1900*, esp. vols. 5, 7, and 9.

31. David Bell argues persuasively that the early modern French monarchy had little interest in making the French nation into a unified linguistic community; see his "Review Article: Recent Works on Early Modern French National Identity."

32. See Hélène Merlin, "Langue et souveraineté en France au XVIIe siècle: la production autonome d'un 'corps de langage.' "

33. Jean-Joseph Languet de Villeneuve de Gergy, *Première instruction pastorale contenant le premier avertissement de Monseigneur l'évêque de Soissons à ceux qui dans son diocèse se sont déclarés appellans de la constitution Unigenitus* (n.p., 1719), 40, quoted in Van Kley, *The Religious Origins of the French Revolution*, 82.

34. Marc Fumaroli makes the important point that the parlements had, since the Renaissance, viewed themselves as having authority over the national language, an authority that they saw the monarchy and the Académie Française steadily undermining; see his essay "La Coupole," 263, note 25.

35. See Merrick, "'Disputes over Words' and Constitutional Conflict in

France, 1730–1732," and *The Desacralization of the French Monarchy*. His argument is given further weight by the subsequent studies of Dale Van Kley (*The Religious Origins of the French Revolution*, esp. 122–28); and David Bell (*Lawyers and Citizens*, esp. 14).

36. See Baker, "Public Opinion as Political Invention," in *Inventing the French Revolution*, 167–99.

37. Merrick, *The Desacralization of the French Monarchy*, 63–64.

38. Melon, *Essai politique sur le commerce*, 129–30.

39. D'Alembert, "Essai sur la société des gens de lettres et des grands, sur la réputation, sur les mécènes, et sur les récompenses littéraires" [1753], in *Mélanges de littérature, d'histoire et de philosophie*, 1:380.

40. On the language of the *précieuses* (which was characterized by veiled allusions, ornate embellishments, artifice, and affectation), as well as the numerous critiques it generated, see Harth, *Cartesian Women*. At the same moment in England, Locke too chose to associate the beauty and deceits of "eloquence" with the "fair sex," in contrast to (and in defense of) "dry Truth and real Knowledge" (*Essay*, 508).

41. On the perceived debauchery and feminization of Louis XV's and then Louis XVI's court, see Maza, *Private Lives and Public Affairs*, chap. 4.

42. Anon. (generally attributed to either Gilles Augustin Bazin or Claude Gros de Boze), *Le Livre jaune*, 44. These "conversations sur les logomachies" were subsequently extracted and reprinted in the journal *Le Conservateur, ou Collection des morceaux rares et d'ouvrages anciens* in December 1757 and June 1760.

43. See Voltaire, "Secte" [1765], in *Dictionnaire philosophique*, in *Oeuvres complètes* 20:414–16. Conversely, for Voltaire's opinions on the danger of ill-defined words and their causal relationship to disputes, see his article "Abus des mots" [1770], in *Questions sur l'Encyclopédie*, in *Oeuvres complètes*, 17:48–50.

44. See Locke, *Essay*, 489: "But I am apt to imagine, that were the imperfections of Language, as the instrument of Knowledge, more thoroughly weighed, a great many of the Controversies that make such a noise in the World, would of themselves cease; and the way to Knowledge, and, perhaps, Peace too, lie a great deal opener than it does."

45. D'Alembert, "Essai sur la société des gens de lettres," in *Mélanges de littérature, d'histoire et de philosophie*, 1:380.

46. André Morellet, "Sur le despotisme légal et contre M. de la Rivière" (ms., 1767), cited in Gordon, *Citizens without Sovereignty*, 44.

47. Helvétius, *De l'Esprit*, 49.

48. Helvétius, *De l'Homme*, 200. In this work, Helvétius argues that the vague and uncertain signification of words such as *bon*, *intérêt*, and *vertu* is responsible for differences in opinion in ethics, politics, and metaphysics (see vol. 1, sect. 2, chaps. 16–18) and that a dictionary which fixed the meanings of these terms would finally make ethics, politics, and metaphysics into sciences as demonstrable as geometry (see vol. 1, sect. 2, chap. 19).

49. On the *Encyclopédie* as an effort to "fix" or regulate the meaning of words, see Brewer, *The Discourse of Enlightenment in Eighteenth-Century*

France, 36–55. D'Alembert himself discusses the project as an effort to combat the *abus des mots* in the "Discours préliminaire" (1:i–xlv) to this work; see page x for the quotation above.

50. On the *philosophes'* eagerness to join the Académie Française during the last decades of the Old Regime, see the following divergent explanations: Darnton, *The Literary Underground of the Old Regime*; Fumaroli, "La Coupole," 277–88; and, esp., Gordon, "Beyond the Social History of Ideas: Morellet and the Enlightenment."

51. Helvétius, *De l'Esprit*, 49.

52. Eco, *The Search for the Perfect Language*, 288.

53. "Logomachie," in *Encyclopédie*, ed. Diderot and D'Alembert, 9:643.

54. On the limited Cratylism or "secondary mimologism" of the *philosophes*, see Genette, *Mimologics*. On the skepticism that marked Enlightenment epistemology, see Russo, *Skeptical Selves*, esp. chap. 1; and Bates, "The Epistemology of Error."

55. See Diderot, *Lettre sur les sourds et muets*. On the importance of the concept of *énergie* within both classical and sensationalist language theory, see Delon, *L'Idée d'énergie au tournant des Lumières*, 58–104.

56. Boulenger de Rivery, *Recherches historiques et critiques sur quelques anciens spectacles*, 96. Boulenger de Rivery is here paraphrasing Cassiodorus, the sixth-century monk and historian who tried to preserve many aspects of Roman culture.

57. Ibid., 97.

58. Socrates comments to Hermogenes, "Answer me this question: If we had no voice or tongue, and wished to make things clear to one another, should we not try, as dumb people actually do, to make signs with our hands and head and person generally? . . . For the expression of anything, I fancy, would be accomplished by bodily imitation of that which was to be expressed." See Plato, *Cratylus*, 133 [422e–423b].

59. "Of Pantomime," in *The Works of Lucian of Samosata*, 64.

60. For a brief overview of Roman ideas about gesture, see Fritz Graf, "Gestures and Conventions: The Gestures of Roman Actors and Orators," in *A Cultural History of Gesture*, ed. Bremmer and Roodenburg, 36–58; and Schmitt, *La Raison des gestes dans l'Occident médiéval*, 33–55.

61. Cicero, *De Oratore* (3.216), quoted in Graf, "Gestures and Conventions," 40.

62. See book XII, chap. 3, in *The Institutio Oratoria of Quintilian*, 4:243–349.

63. See Angenot, "Les Traités de l'éloquence du corps"; Fumaroli, ed., "Rhétorique du geste et de la voix à l'âge classique"; and Knox, "Ideas on Gesture and Universal Languages, c. 1550–1650." Dilwyn Knox attributes the increasing attention devoted to gestures in seventeenth-century rhetorical theory to several concurrent historical developments: the standardization of manners and behavior, the increasing specialization of professions that relied on rhetoric, and, especially, the growth of the idea of "theory."

64. For a contemporaneous account of how to convey anger by "raising the eyelids horribly" and "thrusting out the lower lip," see René Bary,

Méthode pour bien prononcer un discours, et le bien animer (Paris, 1679), 104, cited in Barnett, *The Art of Gesture*, 54. Bary aimed his comments primarily at lawyers; but Barnett's compilations of the appropriate gestures for emotions ranging from terror to aversion to jealousy to grief suggest that the same facial, manual, and bodily signs for emotions were employed across fields in the seventeenth and eighteenth centuries.

65. See Conrart, *Traité de l'action de l'orateur*, 188–89.

66. See Knowlson, "The Idea of Gesture as a Universal Language in the XVIIth and XVIIIth Centuries"; and Knox, "Ideas on Gesture and Universal Language."

67. On the search for a universal language in seventeenth-century Europe, see Slaughter, *Universal Languages and Scientific Taxonomy*; Cohen, *Sensible Words*; Formigari, *Language and Experience*; Pombo, *Leibniz and the Problem of a Universal Language*; Knowlson, *Universal Language Schemes in England and France*; and Eco, *The Search for the Perfect Language*.

68. Bacon, *The Advancement of Learning*, book 2, pt. XVI, chap. 3, 63.

69. Cohen, *Sensible Words*, 7.

70. Bulwer, *Chirologia*, 16, 19. According to the preface to *Chirologia*, Bulwer originally planned to examine the natural language of the head in yet another volume.

71. Montaigne, "Apology for Raymond Sebond," in *The Complete Essays of Montaigne*, 332. This text was printed in 1580, 1582, 1588, and 1595. In this particular passage, the word *signes* replaced the word *gestes* in editions after 1588. For a discussion of the differences between various versions of this passage dealing with gestural communication, see Demonet-Launay, "Les Mains du texte, ou le dernier geste de Montaigne."

72. The grammarian Bernard Lamy was simply repeating a well-established idea when he pointed out the different ways that "mutes of the Grand-Seigneur speak to each other and understand each other even in the darkest night." See Lamy, *La Rhétorique ou l'art de parler*, 3. Seventeenth-century literature on the Ottoman empire contains many references to the mutes of the seraglio; see, for example, Sir Paul Rycaut, *Histoire de l'état présent de l'Empire ottoman*, 2d ed. (Paris, 1670); and Sir John Chardin, *Journal du voyage du chevalier Chardin en Perse et aux Indes Orientales, par la Mer Noire et par la Colchide* (London, 1686).

73. On the observations of early modern European travelers to the New World, see Mallery, *Sign Language among North American Indians*, esp. 324.

74. Important early efforts to devise finger alphabets or gestural signs for use in communicating with or educating the deaf include: Juan Pablo Bonet, *Reduction de las Letras y arte para enseñar á ablar los mudos* (Madrid, 1620); John Bulwer, *Philocophus or the Deafe and Dumbe Man's Friend by J.B., surnamed the Chirosopher* (London, 1648); and George Dalgarno, *Didascalocophus or the Deaf and Dumb Man's Tutor* (Oxford, 1680). Contemporaneous guides to secret gestural communication include: *Digiti-lingua: or, the most compendious, copious, facile, and secret way of silent converse*

ever yet discovered . . . (London, 1698); Charles de LaFin, *Sermo mirabilis: or the silent language. Whereby one may learn* . . . *how to impart his mind to his mistress, or his friend, in any language* . . . *without the least noise, word or voice*, 3d. ed. (London, 1696); and John Wilkins, *Mercury, or The Secret and Swift Messenger: shewing how a man may with privacy and speed communicate his thoughts to a friend at any distance* (London, 1641), who wrote regarding his gestural "semaeologia": "Though it be not so common in practice as either of the other [verbal or written means of communication], yet in nature perhaps it is before them both, since infants are able this way to express themselves before they have the benefit of speech" (4). See also Giovanni Battista Pacichelli's guide to liturgical hand gestures, *Chiroliturgia, sive de varia, ac multiplici manus administratione* (Cologne, 1673); Father Marquard Herrgott's record of the manual and digital signs used by Benedictines, *Vetus disciplina monastica* (Paris, 1726); and Leibniz's "Signes des Cisterciens, suivant un ms. recueilli par Leibnitz, et publié en langue latine dans ses Collectanea Etymologica [1717]," in his *Opera Omnia*, vol. 6, part 2 (Geneva, 1768). Finally, on the advantages of "chirosophy" or the "art of gestures" for merchants and missionaries engaging in commerce with those in distant lands, see, for example, Jacob Leupold, *Theatrum arithmetico-geometricum* (Leipzig, 1727), a guide to numerical hand signs based on a theory of an original connection between the shape of Roman numerals and various manual positions, as well as Bulwer's *Chirologia*, which refers to the handshake as the natural, gestural representation of a contract.

75. On the relationship between Cartesian philosophy and the language theory of Port-Royal as laid out in Claude Lancelot's and Antoine Arnauld's highly influential *Grammaire générale et raisonnée* (Paris, 1660), see Padley, *Grammatical Theory in Western Europe*, 283–324.

76. Lamy, *La Rhétorique ou l'art de parler*, 3.

77. Ibid., 4.

78. On the status of natural, gestural signs in Cartesian language theory, see Rodis-Lewis, "Langage humain et signes naturels dans le Cartésianisme."

79. It was this originally Aristotelian concept—that changes in the passions of the soul are legible in outward, bodily signs and that these signs evoke corresponding emotional responses in the beholder—that Descartes developed in *Les Passions de l'âme* (Paris, 1649). Charles LeBrun, the official painter of Louis XIV, then used this Cartesian physiology to create a semiology of gesture in his illustrated lectures of 1668 at the Royal Academy of Painting. On the significance of these developments for seventeenth-century physiognomy in general, see Courtine and Haroche, *Histoire du visage*, 87–116.

80. Lamy, *La Rhétorique ou l'art de parler*, 1.

81. The idea of French as the epitome of a clear language was not, in itself, a new idea in the late seventeenth century. See, for example, the following statement of Claude Favre de Vaugelas in *Remarques sur la langue françoise utiles à ceux qui veulent bien parler et bien escrire* (Paris, 1647): "There has never been a language in which authors have written more

purely and with greater clarity than our own, no language which is a greater enemy of ambiguity and all kinds of obscurity" (quoted in French in Padley, *Grammatical Theory*, 385). But the Cartesians offered new reasons based on logic for the presumed superiority of French, ideas that were themselves challenged in the mid-eighteenth century; see Fumaroli, "Le Génie de la langue française," 911–73. As for evidence of clarity, Fumaroli also cites (951) Louis Le Laboureur's claim in *Des Avantages de la langue françoise sur la langue latine* (Paris, 1667) that one of the indicators of the superiority of French over other languages is that it is less dependent on movements of the body, including "signs and gestures," to make ideas clear.

82. On bodily restraint and the suppression of certain physical gestures as key elements in the "civilizing process" in early modern Europe, see the classic argument of Norbert Elias in *The Civilizing Process*. For a study of the "growing cultural bipolarization expressed through the body and gestures" specifically in early modern France, see Robert Muchembled, "The Order of Gestures: A Social History of Sensibilities under the Ancien Régime in France," in *A Cultural History of Gesture*, ed. Bremmer and Roodenberg, 129–51.

83. Dubos, *Critical Reflections on Poetry, Painting and Music*, 1:253–54.

84. The presumed superiority of visually ascertained knowledge stemmed from the fact that ideas were considered by Lockeans and Cartesians alike to be "images" in the mind. The clearer and more distinct the image, the more certain the idea. On this notion of the eyes as a direct path to knowledge, see Zoberman, "Voir, savoir, parler: la rhétorique de la vision au XVIIe et au début du XVIIIe siècles."

85. Scholars have identified several isolated examples of earlier texts containing a genetic description of the origin of language based on a primordial gestural sign system, and there has been much speculation about the debt of mid-century French writers to these works. The most important of these texts is Giambattista Vico's *Scienza nuova* (Naples, 1725); however, Vico's work remained almost totally unknown outside Italy until the second quarter of the nineteenth century, rendering coincidental all superficial similarities between his account of the origin of language and that of French and British eighteenth-century writers. On this question, see the contributions of Alain Pons and René Wellek to *Giambattista Vico: An International Symposium*, ed. Tagliacozzo and White. It is more likely that French philosophers drew on the work of Bernard Mandeville, who had suggested in an important passage of the "Sixth Dialogue between Horatio and Cleomenes," in part II of *The Fable of the Bees* (London, 1729), that verbal language could have developed out of an initial gestural one. On this possible debt, see Schreyer, "Condillac, Mandeville, and the Origin of Language"; and Hundert, "The Thread of Language and the Web of Dominion: Mandeville to Rousseau and Back."

86. The early literature on this question includes: Harnois, *Les Théories du langage en France de 1660 à 1821*; Kuehner, *Theories on the Origin and Formation of Language in the Eighteenth Century in France*; and Borst, *Der Turmbau von Babel*. A whole new wave of scholarship on this question fol-

lowed the publication of Michel Foucault's *Les Mots et les choses* (1966) and Jacques Derrida's essays on the linguistic thought of Rousseau (*De la grammatologie* [1967]) and Condillac (*L'Archéologie du frivole* [1973]). Among more recent studies, see esp.: Grimsley, "Some Aspects of 'Nature' and 'Language' in the French Enlightenment"; Juliard, *Philosophies of Language in Eighteenth-Century France*; Chouillet, "Descartes et le problème de l'origine des langues au 18e siècle"; Megill, "The Enlightenment Debate on the Origin of Language and Its Historical Background"; Droixhe, *La Linguistique et l'appel de l'histoire*, 160–225; Auroux, *La Sémiotique des encyclopédistes*, 54–67; Aarsleff, *From Locke to Saussure*, 146–209; Ricken, *Linguistics, Anthropology and Philosophy in the French Enlightenment*, 63–110, 134–59; Thomas, *Music and the Origins of Language*; and Rosenberg, "Making Time."

87. Among the relatively fewer secondary works that directly address the relationship between semiotic theory and social theory in mid-eighteenth-century accounts of the origin of language, see Formigari, "Language and Society in the Late Eighteenth Century"; Ricken, "Théorie linguistique et théorie sociale en France au siècle des Lumières"; and Droixhe, *La Linguistique et l'appel de l'histoire*, 353–85.

88. Cranston, *Jean-Jacques*, 218.

89. Goodman, *The Republic of Letters*, 2–3.

90. Malpeines published his translation in 1744 with the subheading "où l'on voit l'origine et le progrès du langage et de l'écriture, l'antiquité des sciences en Egypte et l'origine du culte des animaux." His specific interest in the history of writing is evidenced by the learned essay of his own composition entitled "La Première écriture des chinois," which he added to volume two of this *Essai*.

91. Egyptian hieroglyphics, along with Chinese characters, were subjects of considerable academic interest in the first half of the eighteenth century. On the debate over their origins and interpretation and Warburton's role within it, see esp. David, *Le Débat sur les écritures et l'hiéroglyphe aux XVIIe et XVIIIe siècles*; and Iversen, *The Myth of Egypt and Its Hieroglyphs*.

92. Bacon, *The Advancement of Learning*, book 2, pt. XVI, chap. 3, 62.

93. Warburton, *Essai sur les hiéroglyphes*, 178.

94. Ibid., 122.

95. On the impact of Warburton's ideas on French thought, see Cherpack, "Warburton and Some Aspects of the Search for the Primitive in Eighteenth-Century France."

96. On the association of abstract or general terms with advanced civilizations, see Paxman, "Language and Difference"; and Pagden, *European Encounters with the New World*, 117–40.

97. Warburton, *Essai sur les hiéroglyphes*, 179.

98. On Condillac's theory of the origin of language as laid out in his *Essai sur l'origine des connaissances humaines*, see, in addition to the scholarship cited in note 86, Knight, *The Geometric Spirit*, esp. 144–75; Derrida,

The Archeology of the Frivolous; Sgard, ed., *Condillac et les problèmes du langage;* and N. Rousseau, *Connaissance et langage chez Condillac.*

99. All quotations from this text are taken from an eighteenth-century English translation entitled *Essay on the Origin of Human Knowledge.* See page 11.

100. Ibid., 171.

101. Ibid., 172. I have slightly modified the translation of this passage.

102. This language of gesture was deemed "natural" in multiple senses: it was innate to human nature; it was constituted out of natural materials as a means to refer to natural forms and expressions; it was a feature of human prehistory or the "state of nature" and thus an enduring mark of cultural primitivism; and it was "fixed," meaning not subject to modification or evolution. On the question of the signification of the term "natural" in the eighteenth century, see Lovejoy, *Essays in the History of Ideas,* esp. 14–15; Ehrard, *L'Idée de la nature en France à l'aube des Lumières;* and Charlton, *New Images of the Natural in France.*

103. In this case, Condillac uses the term "arbitrary" to mean that one can make use of these signs as one wishes or at will, not (as the Cartesians did) to mean that there is no natural link between the sign and the idea. On Condillac's conception of "arbitrary signs," see esp. Auroux, *La Sémiotique des encyclopédistes,* 26–35.

104. Condillac, *Essay,* 173. I have slightly modified the translation of this passage.

105. Ibid., 230. Condillac's sources ranged from Locke, whose *Essay* incorporated details from early accounts of American Indians in order to explain aspects of thought and language in primitive cultures, to Père Joseph-François Lafitau, whose *Moeurs des sauvages amériquains* drew attention to American Indians' predilection for military and religious pantomimes in order to make a case for the connection between Indian culture and the culture of ancient Rome. On the extraction and use of such anthropological materials in eighteenth-century French accounts of the origin of language, see Chantal Grell, "Introduction," in *Primitivisme et mythes des origines dans la France des Lumières,* ed. Grell and Michel; Schreyer, "Linguistics Meets Caliban"; and, esp., Pagden, *European Encounters with the New World,* 117–40.

106. Condillac, *Essay,* 7.

107. On the disposability or "frivolity" of signs in Condillac's conception, see Derrida, *The Archeology of the Frivolous,* esp. 118.

108. Condillac, *Essay,* 297.

109. Ibid., 25.

110. Ibid., 8, 25.

111. On attitudes toward neologisms and linguistic innovation among sensationalist thinkers, who increasingly argued during the century's course that languages had to expand along with social and intellectual needs, see Armogathe, "Néologie et idéologie dans la langue française au 18e siècle"; Mormile, *La 'Néologie' révolutionnaire;* and Rosenberg, "Making Time."

112. Condillac's faith in an analytic method, which is at the heart of all of his writings, will be discussed in greater detail in Chaps. 3, 4, and 5.

113. The *Arrest du Conseil d'Etat* of February 1752, which ordered the suppression of the first two volumes of the *Encyclopédie*, charged the editors with not only "trying to insert several maxims aimed at destroying royal authority and establishing a spirit of independence and revolt" but also, "by means of obscure and equivocal terminology, elevating the foundations of error, corruption of manners, irreligion, and unbelief." This text can be found among the papers collected in an extra proof volume of the *Encyclopédie* owned by Alderman Library, University of Virginia.

114. The Abbé Charles Batteux, the rhetorician to whom Diderot addressed his *Lettre*, had argued in an essay of 1747 that French contained more "inversions" with regard to the natural order of words than did Latin. Condillac had already made this point in his chapter on inversions in his *Essai* of 1746. Batteux's and Condillac's position was, however, subsequently refuted by DuMarsais and Beauzée, among others, who defended the supreme clarity of French in contrast to Latin. It is worth pointing out that the participants on both sides of this debate assumed that there was an order of words emanating from nature; the argument thus focused, first, on the question of what was natural, and, second, on the question of the quality of French. See Ricken, *Grammaire et philosophie au siècle des Lumières*, esp. 118–30; and Delesalle and Chevalier, *La Linguistique, la grammaire et l'école*, 37–77.

115. For different perspectives on the *Lettre sur les sourds et muets*, see, in addition to the works cited in note 86: Doolittle, "Hieroglyph and Emblem in Diderot's *Lettre sur les sourds et muets*"; Chouillet, *La Formation des idées esthétiques de Diderot*, 150–257; Hobson, "La *Lettre sur les sourds et muets* de Diderot"; Serge Baudiffier, "Diderot et Condillac," in *Condillac et les problèmes du langage*, ed. Sgard, 115–36; Thomas, "Musicology and Hieroglyphics"; and Brewer, *The Discourse of Enlightenment*, 107–31. On Diderot's attitudes about language in general, see Proust, "Diderot et les problèmes du langage."

116. See Batteux, *Cours de belles lettres*, vol. 2, part 1.

117. All quotations from Diderot's *Lettre sur les sourds et muets* are taken from an English translation entitled "Letter on the Deaf and Dumb," in *Diderot's Early Philosophical Works*. For the quotation above, see page 163.

118. Ibid., 188.

119. Ibid., 195.

120. Ibid., 184.

121. Rousseau scholars generally agree that the *Essai sur l'origine des langues où il est parlé de la mélodie et de l'imitation musicale* takes up concerns common to the *Discours sur l'origine de l'inégalité parmi les hommes* (1755) and to the *Lettre sur la musique française* (1753) and that the *Essai* was largely written concurrently with these two texts. There is also substantial evidence that Rousseau prepared the manuscript of his *Essai* for publication in the early 1760s, when he may have added or changed

sections of the text; but it was not published until three years after his death, first in a collection entitled *Traités sur la musique* (1781) and then in volume sixteen of his *Oeuvres* (1782). On the history of the dating and interpretation of this text, see Porset, "'L'Inquiétante étrangeté' de l'*Essai sur l'origine des langues*"; and Starobinski's introduction and notes to his edition of the *Essai sur l'origine des langues*.

122. Among the many commentators on the language theory of Rousseau as developed in these two texts, see, in addition to many of the works cited in note 86: Derrida, *Of Grammatology*, 165–268; Grange, "L'*Essai sur l'origine des langues* dans son rapport avec le *Discours sur l'origine de l'inégalité*"; Guetti, "The Double Voice of Nature"; Goldschmidt, *Anthropologie et politique*, 292–306; Bach, "Langue et droit politique chez Jean-Jacques Rousseau"; Baczko, "La Cité et ses langages"; Droixhe, "Rousseau et l'enfance de la parole," in *De l'Origine du langage aux langues du monde*, 13–29; and esp. Starobinski, *Jean-Jacques Rousseau*, 304–22.

123. For all quotations from this text, see Rousseau, *The First and Second Discourses*. See page 120 for the quotation above.

124. Ibid., 121–22.

125. For all quotations from this text, see Rousseau, *Essay on the Origin of Languages*. For the quotation above, see page 260.

126. Ibid., 245.

127. Ibid., 243.

128. In the writings of the seventeenth-century critics Dominique Bouhours and Jean de La Bruyère, women are depicted as embodying natural eloquence and as playing an important role in maintaining the freshness and naivete of the French language (see Fumaroli, "Le Génie de la langue française," 958, 973). One might, therefore, assume that the association of women with natural language would continue in eighteenth-century discourse, especially since women were generally thought (because of their physiological role as mothers) to be instinctive rather than reflective and to be responsive to sensations, passions, and objects in their immediate surroundings rather than reason and abstract ideas. Yet, in sensationalist writings on the origin of language in which nature is made out to be something to be cherished or a lost ideal, women are not infrequently made into agents of socialization and civilization and given responsibility for leading others—children and their male partners—ever further from the state of nature and its languages. Here we are closer to the critique of the language of the *précieuses* (see note 40). In Condillac, the sexual dimension of this role is undeveloped; a heterosexual couple establishes society and signs, but this couple's sexuality is rendered invisible both in Condillac's story and in the cultural order they found. However in Rousseau (and many writers after him), the connection becomes explicit; in his writings, women are repeatedly associated with overcivilization, artificiality, deception, and seduction, largely based on their way of speaking and their supposed effects on modern languages and culture. In other words, because women, as a result of their sexual desirability, set progress in motion, the advancement of language, civilization, and society, on the one hand, and the growing power of

women, on the other, occur in tandem. The problem is that eventually both language and society show too much feminine influence. On the idea of women as "civilizing" and ultimately corrupting agents and on the tensions in eighteenth-century French philosophy between this idea and the concept of women as natural beings, see Tomaselli, "The Enlightenment Debate on Women"; Bloch and Bloch, "Women and the Dialectics of Nature in Eighteenth-Century French Thought"; Russo, Skeptical Selves, 60–62; and Steinbrügge, The Moral Sex.

129. Rousseau, Second Discourse, 172–73.

130. Rousseau, Essay, 294. This section of the work is explicitly entitled "The Relation of Languages to Governments."

131. On this point, see Thomas, Music and the Origins of Language, 81.

132. Condillac's conception of an original gestural language figured, at least in passing, in such varied French works of the late 1740s and 1750s as La Mettrie's L'Homme machine (Leiden, 1748); Leblan's Théorie nouvelle de la parole et des langues (Paris, 1750); Pluche's La Mécanique des langues (Paris, 1751); Maupertuis's "Réflexions philosophiques sur l'origine des langues et la signification des mots," "Lettre sur le progrès des sciences," and "Dissertation sur les différents moyens dont les hommes se sont servis pour exprimer leurs idées," in Oeuvres de Maupertuis (Lyon, 1756); and Turgot's posthumous essays "Recherches sur les causes des progrès et de la décadence des sciences et des arts ou réflexions sur l'histoire des progrès de l'esprit humain" (1748), "Remarques critiques sur les réflexions philosophiques de M*** sur l'origine des langues et la signification des mots" (1750), "Plan du second discours sur le progrès de l'esprit humain" (c. 1751), and "Réflexions sur les langues" (c. 1751) (in Oeuvres de Turgot, vol. 1). See also the many articles on language theory in scholarly journals as well as collections of academic memoirs published across Europe at mid-century.

133. Formey, "Réunion des principaux moyens employés pour découvrir l'origine du langage, des idées et des connaissances des hommes," in Anti-Emile, 216. The case for the divine origin of language and against the sensationalist approach had already recently been rearticulated by Antoine-Martin Roche in his Traité de la nature de l'âme et de l'origine de ses connaissances and by the anonymous author of the article "Langue" (9:247–66) within that key Enlightenment text, the Encyclopédie of Diderot and D'Alembert.

134. Maupertuis discussed the problems involved in constructing a theoretical history of language in both his "Lettre sur le progrès des sciences" (c. 1752) and his "Dissertation sur les différents moyens dont les hommes se sont servis pour exprimer leurs idées" (1756). The principal problem, as he saw it, was that, on the one hand, children had few recollections of their first steps toward speech, and, on the other hand, no existing people were still savage enough to tell civilized men much about the original, natural language (though Maupertuis claimed that he would prefer one hour of conversation with the species closest to monkeys than with "the most beautiful mind in Europe").

135. On the impact of late twentieth-century trends in linguistics on

the historiography of eighteenth-century linguistic thought, see Aarsleff, "Introduction" and "The History of Linguistics and Professor Chomsky," in *From Locke to Saussure*, 3–41 and 101–19, respectively. Aarsleff was himself one of the first historians of linguistic thought to take seriously the French Enlightenment discussion of language origins.

136. Foucault, *The Order of Things*, 78–124.

137. Lissa Roberts, in her article "Condillac, Lavoisier, and the Instrumentalization of Science," rightly emphasizes the fact that Condillac treats language as an "instrument" that gives shape to experience. Roberts, however, concentrates on the impact of Condillac's conception of language on the sciences alone, whereas I want to argue for a more broad effect.

CHAPTER 2

1. The term *aesthetic* is, of course, itself a mid-eighteenth-century invention. The term was first used in print by Alexander Baumgarten in 1750 to mean "criticism of taste"; its first use in French dates from 1753, when it was defined as the "science of the beautiful." The word was not, however, widely used in France until the nineteenth century, despite the fact that the study of what is objectively constitutive of art took off from this moment. And only gradually did the term come to have the secondary meaning of that which concerns the artistic or the beaux-arts.

2. Eagleton, *The Ideology of the Aesthetic*, 9.

3. Ibid., 9.

4. In the first half of the eighteenth century, this was, in fact, how the purpose of ballets within operas was typically justified. According to an anonymous, early eighteenth-century set of "Règles pour faire des ballets" (MS C. 4844 in the Bibliothèque de l'Opéra), for example, "theatrical plays, poetry, and painting have instructing and moving the passions as their principal goal, while ballet has calming them and diverting its spectators."

5. For all quotations from the *Lettres sur la danse et sur les ballets*, see Noverre, *Letters on Dancing and Ballets*. For the quotation above, see Letter X, 99. On Noverre, see Charles Edwin Noverre, *The Life and Works of Chevalier Noverre*; Lynham, *The Chevalier Noverre*; Krüger, *J. G. Noverre und das 'Ballet d'action'*; and Winter, *The Pre-Romantic Ballet*, esp. 113–8.

6. Ibid., Letter II, 20.

7. Batteux, *Les Beaux-arts réduits à un même principe*, 231–32.

8. Ibid., 241.

9. The most important of these texts (following Menestrier and De Pure) include: Isaac Vossius, *De poematum cantu et viribus rythmi* (Oxford and London, 1673, with a German edition of 1759); Jean Pierre Burette, "Premier mémoire pour servir à l'histoire de la danse des anciens" and "Second mémoire pour servir à l'histoire de la danse des anciens" (both 1710), in *Histoire de l'Académie royale des inscriptions*, vol. 1 (Paris, 1717), 93–135; John Weaver, *Essay Towards an History of Dancing* (London, 1712); Niccolò Calliachi, *De ludis scenicis mimorum, et pantomimorum syntagma posthumum* (Padua, 1713); Ottavio Ferrari, *De pantomimis et mimis, dissertatio* (Wolfenbüttel, 1714); Dubos, *Réflexions critiques sur la poésie et sur la*

peinture (Paris, 1719 and expanded in 1732); Jacques Bonnet, *Histoire géné-rale de la danse sacrée et profane, ses progrès et ses révolutions, depuis son origine jusqu'à présent* (Paris, 1723); and John Weaver, *The History of Mimes and Pantomimes* (London, 1728). The historical questions raised in these works garnered renewed attention in the late 1740s and early 1750s. See Duclos, "Mémoire sur les jeux scéniques des Romains, et sur ceux qui ont précédé en France la naissance du poëme dramatique," in *Histoire de l'Académie royale des inscriptions*, vol. 17 (Paris, 1743), 206–27; and Duclos, "Mémoire sur l'art de partager l'action théâtrale, et sur celui de noter la dé-clamation, qu'on prétend avoir été en usage chez le Romains" and Jean Racine, "De la Déclamation théatrale des anciens," in *Histoire de l'Aca-démie royale des inscriptions*, vol. 21 (Paris, 1748), 191–208 and 209–24, re-spectively. On this debate, see Porset, "De l'Obscénité du geste: la théorie du partage de l'action théâtrale dans la première moitié du XVIIIe siècle." See also these subsequent works on the subject: Johann Christoph Strodt-mann, *Abhandlung von den pantomimen, historisch und critisch ausge-führt* (Hamburg, 1749); Boulenger de Rivery, *Recherches historiques et cri-tiques sur quelques anciens spectacles, et particulièrement sur les mimes et sur les pantomimes* (Paris, 1751); and Jean Lecointe, *Apologie de la danse: son antiquité, sa noblesse et ses avantages* (Paris and London, 1752).

10. On this experimental ballet, see Kirstein, *Four Centuries of Ballet: Fifty Masterworks*, 90–91.

11. Dubos, *Critical Reflections*, vol. 3, section 16. Similar experiments undertaken in other nations in the early eighteenth century include John Weaver's "The Loves of Mars and Venus," a pantomime "in Imitation of a Dancing among the Ancients" performed at London's Royal Theatre at Drury Lane in 1717, and the mimed dramas staged in later decades in Frank-furt, Stuttgart, Munich, and Vienna by Grimaldo Nicolini's touring "enfants hollandais."

12. See, for example, Rémond de Saint-Mard, *Réflexions sur l'opéra*.

13. Cahusac, "Geste," in *Encyclopédie*, ed. Diderot and D'Alembert, 7:651. Cahusac drew the material in all of these articles from his enormous and highly influential history of dance, *La Danse ancienne et moderne, ou Traité historique de la danse* (The Hague, 1754). Similar claims can be found in entries in the *Encyclopédie* ranging from "Langage" (Jaucourt) to "Poésie Dramatique" (Grimm).

14. Both the *Entretiens sur le Fils naturel*, which accompanied Diderot's *drame* entitled *Le Fils naturel* (1757), and the *Discours sur la poésie drama-tique*, which accompanied his *drame* entitled *Le Père de famille* (1758), are reprinted in Diderot, *Oeuvres esthétiques*. On the importance of panto-mime for Diderot's aesthetics, see Goodden, "'Une Peinture parlante'"; and, esp., Josephs, *Diderot's Dialogue of Language and Gesture*.

15. See Diderot, *Entretiens*, in *Oeuvres esthétiques*, 1264. On Noverre's ideas on dance in relation to those of both Cahusac and Diderot, see Virolle, "Noverre, Garrick, Diderot: pantomime et littérature"; Chazin-Bennahum, "Cahusac, Diderot and Noverre: Three Revolutionary French Writers on

the Eighteenth-Century Dance"; and Murphy, "Ballet Reform in Mid-Eighteenth-Century France: The *Philosophes* and Noverre."

16. On the monopolies granted to the major theaters and the effects that these privileges had on the *petits spectacles* of the fairs from the 1670s to the 1740s, see Isherwood, *Farce and Fantasy*, 81–97.

17. On pantomime as a component of eighteenth-century Parisian fair theater, see: Bergman, "La Grande mode des pantomimes à Paris vers 1740"; Brockett, "The Fair Theaters of Paris in the Eighteenth Century"; Christout, *Le Merveilleux et 'le théâtre du silence' en France*; Lagrave, "La Pantomime à la foire, au Théâtre-Italien et aux boulevards"; and Brown, *Theater and Revolution*, 40–64.

18. See, for example, the anonymous *Lettre écrite à un ami sur les danseurs de corde et sur les pantomimes qui ont paru autrefois chez les Grecs et chez les Romains et à Paris en 1738* (n.p., 1739) regarding the performances of an English troupe at the St. Laurent fair.

19. Bonnet, *Histoire générale de la danse sacrée et profane*, 165.

20. On Garrick's relationship with Noverre, see Hedgcock, *David Garrick et ses amis français*; and Lynham, *The Chevalier Noverre*, 25–49. Diderot's aesthetic writings of the late 1750s and 1760s display a similar fascination with the acting techniques of Garrick, who first visited France in 1751.

21. Noverre, *Letters on Dancing and Ballets*, Letter IX, 82.

22. The universal intelligibility of Garrick's physical gestures and their independence from any particular set of linguistic conventions was a recurrent theme in contemporary discussions of the actor's appeal. For example, in the late 1760s, many British newspapers reproduced the poem "On seeing Garrick act," which had ostensibly been written, despite its complex rhyming, by a deaf person: "When Britain's Roscius on the stage appears, Who charms all eyes, and (I am told) all ears, With ease the various passions I can trace, Clearly reflected from that wond'rous face; Whilst true conception, with just action join'd, Strongly impress each image on my mind: What need of sounds, when plainly I descry Th'expressive features, and the speaking eye? That eye, whose bright and penetrating ray Doth Shakespear's [sic] meaning to my soul convey: Best commentator on great Shakespear's text! When Garrick acts, no passage seems perplext." Reproduced in Green, "*Vox Oculis Subjecta*," 218–19.

23. Noverre, *Letters on Dancing and Ballets*, Letter VI, 40.

24. Ibid., Letter VII, 53.

25. Ibid., Letter IX, 78.

26. See Voltaire, *Oeuvres complètes*, vol. 43, *Correspondance XI. Années 1763–1765*, 14 (October 1763), 195 (April 1764), and 516–17 (April 1765). These letters from Voltaire to Noverre, along with Noverre's two letters to Voltaire on the subject of Garrick (March 1765 and n.d.), are all reproduced in Marignié, *La Vie de David Garrick*. Voltaire and Noverre had first become acquainted at the court in Berlin during the previous decade.

27. Letter of February 1760, reproduced in Noverre, *Lettres sur les arts imitateurs en général*, 1:13.

28. Grimm, Diderot, Raynal, and Meister, *Correspondance littéraire, philosophique et critique*, 4:451–55 (August 15, 1761).

29. On the improvisational scenes or "tragic pantomimes" that Garrick performed for private parties in the circles of Mme Helvetius, Mme Holbach, and Mme Geoffrin in 1764–65, see Hedgcock, *David Garrick et ses amis français*, 115; and Collé, *Journal historique*, 3:152–56.

30. Mercier, *L'An deux mille quatre cent quarante*, 231.

31. In 1941, Edgar Wind claimed Noverre's *Les Horaces* as the inspiration for David's work on the same subject. See Wind, "The Sources of David's Horaces." Recently, art historians have again taken up this question of the connection between late eighteenth-century theatrical style and painting in terms of the depiction of gesture, most often in relation to the work of David. See esp. Johnson, *Jacques-Louis David*, 11–69; and the treatise of David's own student, Jacques-Nicolas Paillot de Montabert, entitled *Théorie du geste dans l'art de la peinture, renfermant plusieurs préceptes applicables à l'art du théâtre* (Paris, 1813). Similarly, on late eighteenth-century French art critics' use of theatrical parallels, including the idea that painting should explain by means of pantomime, see Wrigley, *The Origins of French Art Criticism*, 247–57.

32. See, for example, Dom Gourdin's *Considérations philosophiques sur l'action de l'orateur* (Amsterdam, Paris, and Caen, 1775), in which precepts derived from Condillac, as well as Dubos, Batteux, Hume, Warburton, and Dorat, are used to argue for the importance of natural gestures to effective speaking in law courts and churches.

33. On the increased emphasis on bodily expressivity in eighteenth-century French theater, see Goodden, *Actio and Persuasion*. On the significance of expressive gestures and exclamations specifically in the bourgeois *drame*, see Bryson, *The Chastised Stage*; and Rosenfeld, "*Les Philosophes* and *le savoir*."

34. On the importance of bodily signs and "wordless" communication in eighteenth-century French novels of sensibility, see Vila, *Enlightenment and Pathology*, esp. 197–98; and Denby, *Sentimental Narrative*, esp. 24 and 82–84.

35. In his *Essai sur la physiognomonie* (The Hague, 1781–1803), the first French-language edition of his work, Lavater emphasized the differences between "natural" corporeal signs and ordinary language in terms of both their legibility and honesty, and he insisted that it is precisely because "most of our errors have their source in the imperfection of language" that physiognomy is essential (2:366). On Lavater's work and its impact in France, see Rivers, *Face Value*, 66–103.

36. Nougaret, *La Littérature renversée*, 60.

37. On pantomime as a component of late eighteenth-century boulevard theater, see Lagrave, "La Pantomime à la foire, au Théâtre-Italien et aux boulevards (1700–1789)"; Isherwood, *Farce and Fantasy*; Root-Bernstein, *Boulevard Theater and Revolution*; Holmström, *Monodrama, Attitudes, Tableaux Vivants*; and Goodden, *Actio and Persuasion*, esp. 94–111. La-

grave estimates that approximately 350 different pantomimes were performed at the boulevard theaters of Paris between 1762 and 1789.

38. Audinot, *Les Bons et les méchans* (Théâtre de l'Ambigu-Comique, January 1783), 4–5.

39. Frederick Brown, in *Theater and Revolution*, 66, points out that this slogan was also a pun on the name of the proprietor, Audinot.

40. Alexandre Jacques DuCoudray, the unnamed author of a *Lettre d'un Parisien à son ami, en province, sur le nouveau spectacle des Elèves de l'Opéra, ouvert le 7 janvier* (Paris, 1779), encouraged the public to attend this new spectacle with the following comment: "Moreover, the Public can not give too much encouragement to this effort which is going to augment its pleasures, [and] enrich the Nation with a new genre of Poem or Drama that one could call *Action muette,* if it is permitted to qualify it in this fashion: in a word, the Censors will never be able to criticize the words" (11). Even when the boulevard theaters were allowed to employ bits of dialogue or monologue, actors often produced laughter in the audience by making gestures at odds with the "official" script and thus conveying alternative or obscene meanings.

41. "Suite des Observations à MM. les Comédiens italiens: des pantomimes," *Journal des théâtres, ou le Nouveau spectateur* 2, no. 9 (August 1, 1777): 30.

42. Isherwood, *Farce and Fantasy,* 181. Robert M. Isherwood argues, contrary to Peter Burke, that popular and elite culture did not diverge but actually began to resemble one another more closely in the late eighteenth century. In the case of pantomime, his thesis is extremely convincing.

43. "Annonce scandaleuse," *Annales politiques, civiles et littéraire du dix-huitième siècle* 7 (November 1779): 240–41.

44. See Panseau, *Sophie de Brabant, pantomime en 4 actes* (Théâtre des Grands Danseurs du Roi, June 11, 1781 and Rouen, February 16, 1785).

45. "Annonce scandaleuse," 241.

46. Laus de Boissy, *Lettre critique sur les ballets de l'Opéra,* 14.

47. On the original performance of *Jason et Medée* (Stuttgart, February 1763), see Uriot, *Description des fêtes données pendant quatorze jours,* 39–45; and Kirstein, *Four Centuries of Ballet,* 122–23. On the various restagings of this work at the Paris Opéra, see the "Dossier: Jason et Medée," in the Bibliothèque de l'Opéra; and Guest, *The Ballet of the Enlightenment,* 76–77. The *livret* for this ballet is reproduced in a *Recueil de programmes de ballets de M. Noverre* (Vienna, 1778), in which, the editor claimed, one can see "the manner in which he [Noverre] puts into effect the wise precepts that he laid out in his first work [his *Lettres*]" (8).

48. Gardel, "Discours préliminaire," in *L'Avènement de Titus à l'Empire,* 35. This ballet was never actually performed.

49. *Les Horaces* ran for only nine performances in Paris, from January 21, 1777, to February 20, 1777. This tragic *ballet d'action* had already been performed during the preceding year in Milan, Naples, Vienna, and Venice, after having first been staged in Vienna in 1774. See Lynham, *The Chevalier*

Noverre, 78; and Guest, *The Ballet of the Enlightenment*, 102–9. For a description of the plot and action, see also the *Recueil de programmes de ballets de M. Noverre*.

50. Noverre's major Paris débuts, in addition to *Apelles et Campaspe* (October 1, 1776), *Les Caprices de Galathée* (November 17, 1776), and *Les Horaces* (January 21, 1777), include the following: *Les Ruses d'Amour* (March 6, 1777), *Les Petits Riens* (June 11, 1778), and *Annette et Lubin* (July 9, 1778). The last two were created specifically for the Opéra in Paris.

51. Noverre, "Avertissement," in *Lettres sur la dance et sur les ballets*, 2d ed., v.

52. Ibid., vii. Evidence of the endurance of Noverre's precepts can be seen in a note, written by the *commissaire du roi* at the Opéra in the 1780s, urging choreographers to continue following the dictates of Lucian concerning pantomime (Denis Pierre-Jean Papillon de la Ferté, ms. "sur la composition des ballets et le rôle du maître de ballet," in the Bibliothèque de l'Opéra, Res. Pièce 60 [n.d.]). And though he did not choose tragic themes for them, Gardel continued in the ensuing years to call many of his compositions either *ballets d'action* or *ballets-pantomimes*.

53. The *Mercure de France*, which was continually critical of the *ballet d'action* during these years, described the public as divided between individuals of taste, on the one hand, and those who did not mind the mixing of genres and supported anything resembling that "monstrous old Horace" of Noverre, on the other. See the issue of March 3, 1781, cited in Guest, *The Ballet of the Enlightenment*, 167–68.

54. Jeffrey Ravel has brought to light an exactly contemporaneous debate on a similarly arcane subject—the fate of the theatrical *parterre*—which also became a vehicle for discussion of a much broader Enlightenment principle (in this case, the nature of the "public"); see his "Seating the Public."

55. On these divisions within literary circles, see Darnton, "The High Enlightenment and the Low-Life of Literature," reprinted in *The Literary Underground of the Old Regime*.

56. Dorat, *La Déclamation théâtrale, poëme didactique en 4 chants, précédé d'un discours, et de notions historiques sur la danse*, 146. The fourth section was also printed separately in 1767 as *La Danse, chant quatrième du poëme de la déclamation*.

57. Duplain, *Guimard*, "Avis au Lecteur" and 21–22.

58. On the importance of sign theory and linguistic analogies to eighteenth-century French music theory, see Hobson, *The Object of Art*, 253–97; Didier, *La Musique des Lumières*, 153–71; Cannone, *Philosophies de la musique*, 42–76; and Thomas, *Music and the Origins of Language*. Both Hobson and Didier briefly discuss dance theory as well. Similarly, on the concept of signs in eighteenth-century French architectural theory, see Saisselin, "Painting, Writing and Primitive Purity"; Vidler, *The Writing of the Walls*, 7–21, 139–46; Lavin, *Quatremère de Quincy*; and Baczko, *Utopian Lights*, 250–80. On these questions more generally in the eighteenth century, see Wellbery, *Lessing's Laocoon*.

59. Dorat, *La Déclamation théâtrale*, 54.

60. Rousseau, "Ballet," in *Supplément à l'Encyclopédie*, 1:764–65. This text was originally printed with the same heading in Rousseau's *Dictionnaire de musique* of 1768. At the height of the debate on this subject, Jean-François Marmontel, the arts editor of the *Supplément*, chose to reprint a complementary article on ballet by Johann Georg Sulzer, author of the *Allgemeine Theorie der Schönen Künste* (Leipzig, 1771–74), alongside that of Rousseau (1:763–64).

61. See Algarotti, *Essai sur l'opéra*, 167. This comment is one of many on pantomime and language that the Marquis de Chastellux added to his French translation of Algarotti's *Saggio sopra l'opera in musica* (Venice, 1755 and Livorno, 1763) in response to Rousseau's comments in his *Dictionnaire de musique* on the role of pantomime in opera.

62. "Lettre d'un amateur au rédacteur de ce journal," *Journal des théâtres, ou le Nouveau spectateur* 2, no. 9 (August 1, 1777): 16–22.

63. See also "Suite des observations à MM. les comédiens italiens," *Journal des théâtres, ou le Nouveau spectateur* 2, no. 9 (August 1, 1777): 30–32, and "Observations sur l'Opéra, par un amateur abonné à l'amphithéâtre," *Journal des théâtres, ou le Nouveau spectateur* 3, no. 17 (December 1, 1777): 19–28.

64. Noverre, *Introduction au ballet des Horaces*, 6.

65. Mercier, "Geste," in *Mon Bonnet de nuit*, 2:172. Mercier expresses similar sentiments in sections entitled "Main" (2:29) and "Physionomie" (2:126–28).

66. On the cultural significance of particular physical signs of sensibility, see Vincent-Buffault, *The History of Tears*; and Courtine and Haroche, *Histoire du visage*, esp. 137–41.

67. Bryson, *The Chastised Stage*, 79.

68. Laus de Boissy, *Lettre critique*, 11.

69. Thiéry, *Guide des amateurs et des étrangers voyageurs à Paris*, 1:610.

70. Dubos, *Critical Reflections*; and Watelet, *L'Art de peindre*, 137–41.

71. Eighteenth-century assumptions about gender and bodily expression were often rooted in contemporary medical views about the differences between men's and women's nervous systems, as well as in the culture of sensibility; on this subject, see Vila, *Enlightenment and Pathology*; and Mullan, *Sentiment and Sociability*, esp. chap. 5.

72. Cochin, *Pantomime dramatique*, 7. That Cochin was inspired by Noverre can be hazarded from Cochin's praise for the choreographer in his *Lettres sur l'Opéra*, 27 and 57.

73. Restif de la Bretonne (with Nougaret), *La Mimographe*, 46.

74. On the idea of creating sympathetic solidarity among spectators, see also Mercier, *Du Théâtre*, x.

75. See Isherwood, *Farce and Fantasy*, 186–87, on the increasing concern with moral didacticism in boulevard theater. See also Mayeur de Saint Paul's *L'Elève de la nature*, a pantomime with dialogue based on a 1766 novel of the same name by Gaspard Guillard de Beaurieu. Not only does the

plot concerning the main character's simultaneous acquisition of conventional language and conventional morality necessitate the employment of
pantomime; the play also requires its characters to utter such lines as "the
most elegant language is that of nature" (35).

76. Forster, *A Voyage round the World in his Britannic Majesty's Sloop*,
412–13.

77. Savary, *Lettres sur l'Egypte*, 1:150–51.

78. Raynal, *L'Histoire philosophique et politique*, 2:31. See also the
more extensive account of the development of dance in relation to the development of language, 6:29–30.

79. Guys, *Voyage littéraire de la Grèce*, 1:176. The entire thirteenth letter (168–94) is, in fact, dedicated to a discussion of dance.

80. Jean-Bernard Bossu, a naval officer who traveled through the French
colony of Louisiana in the 1750s, reported the story in his *Nouveaux voyages
aux Indes occidentales* of a M. de Belle-Isle, who was captured by a tribe of
cannibals called the Attakapas. The Attakapas, Bossu claimed, "speak also
by signs and hold long conversations in pantomime" (140), and since their
captive was too skinny for them to eat, the cannibals spent their time
teaching the Frenchman all their customs, from hunting to "speaking in
pantomime," instead (143). Similarly, in his section on "Langues des sauvages [of Canada] et leurs signes hiéroglyphiques," in his *Histoire générale
et détaillée des peuples sauvages*, Jacques Grasset de Saint-Sauveur
claimed that "[s]avages, in general, are great pantomimes, and the air with
which they animate all their expressions often suffices for them to make
themselves understood to those who do not know their idiom" (12–13). And
in refuting Cornelius de Pauw's earlier claim that American Indians could
not count higher than three because they possessed no words to convey
large numbers, Dom Antoine Joseph Pernety argued in his *Dissertation sur
l'Amérique et les américains* that Indians relied on their fingers and toes:
"The mutes of our Continent, by showing three times the ten fingers on
their hands, communicate to us the idea that they have of the number
thirty; who doubts that the Americans can do as much?" (172). Such reports
confirmed for many of the *philosophes*, including Voltaire and Rousseau,
the essential dignity of Indian peoples. As Rousseau noted in his *Essai sur
l'origine des langues*, "The savages of America almost never speak except
when away from home; in his hut everyone remains silent and speaks to his
family by means of signs; and such signs are infrequent because a savage is
less restless, less impatient than a European, has fewer needs, and takes
care to attend to them himself" (261 [chapter 9, note to paragraph 1]).

81. Borch, *Lettres sur la Sicile*, 2:235–37. The natural aptitude of Italians
(as opposed to Northern Europeans) for gestural communication was also
noted by writers from Restif de la Bretonne to Rousseau, who made much of
this same contrast in his *Essai sur l'origine des langues*. Outside France,
however, both German and English commentators on pantomime or declamation frequently pointed out that the French, like the Italians, made
greater use of bodily signs than did their own countrymen.

82. Bougainville, *Voyage autour du monde*, 225–26. Aotourou's troubles

pronouncing French were, in fact, the subject of a study by Jacob Rodrigue Péreire, the celebrated instructor of the deaf; see, in this same volume, Péreire's essay, "Observations sur l'articulation de l'Insulaire de la mer du Sud, que M. de Bougainville a amené de l'île de Tahiti, et sur le vocabulaire qu'il a fait du langage de cet île" (403–7).

83. See Arnaud and Suard, eds., *Variétés littéraires*, 1:425–26. It is important to note that Arnaud, chief of the "Gluckistes," approached this topic as both a public supporter of the reforms of Noverre and an outspoken advocate of sensationalist epistemology and linguistic theory. See Arnaud's comments on Noverre in his *La Soirée perdue à l'opéra* (1776) and "Le Gouteux maître de danse, conte, à l'usage de plus d'un auteur" (*Journal de Paris*, July 10, 1777), both reproduced in *Querelle des Gluckistes et Piccinnistes*, ed. Lesure, 1:46–61 and 229–31, respectively, as well as his defense of the idea of an original *langage d'action* as his "Dissertation sur les accents de la langue grecque," in the *Histoire de l'Académie royale des inscriptions et belles lettres*, vol. 32 (1762).

84. With the exception of the anthropological entries in this book, most of Compan's *Dictionnaire de danse . . . le tout tiré des meilleurs auteurs qui ont écrit sur cet art* (Paris, 1787) was derived from the writings of Cahusac and Noverre.

85. Moreau de Saint-Méry, *Dance*, 11–12. This essay was composed in Paris in 1789 as part of an encyclopedia devoted to the culture of the colonies. The larger work was never published; but after the section on dance circulated in literary circles in Paris and Philadelphia in 1789, it was printed by Moreau's own publishing company in Philadelphia in 1796.

86. That no strict antithesis can be established between eighteenth-century Christian and sensationalist conceptions of a hypothetical state of nature is illustrated by such texts as Jean-Baptiste Perrin's *Essai sur l'origine et l'antiquité des langues* (London, 1767), in which the author describes Adam and Eve as communicating entirely through movements and gestures and explains speech and the use of an evolving set of artificial signs as a result of original sin. As soon as Eve ate the forbidden fruit, Perrin writes, "These signs, which were once so expressive that Eve could read the transports and movements of her husband's heart, became, from then on, equivocal" (45). In other words, the idea of an original, stable, universal, expressive *langage d'action* was not necessarily irreconcilable with the biblical account of the birth of language, despite the former's associations with materialism among certain critics.

87. Bernardin de Saint-Pierre, *Paul et Virginie*, 108. On the utopian aspects of this novel see, esp., Racault, "*Paul et Virginie* et l'utopie: de la petite société au mythe collectif"; and Francis, "Bernardin de Saint-Pierre's *Paul et Virginie* and the Failure of the Ideal State in the Eighteenth-Century French Novel."

88. In Vienna in the early 1760s, Gasparo Angiolini published several defenses of the tragic pantomime that bear many conceptual similarities to Noverre's *Lettres*. See the essay preceding his *Le Festin de Pierre, ballet-pantomime* (Vienna, 1761), which Angiolini wrote with the help of the Ital-

ian poet Ranieri Calzabigi, and Angiolini's *Dissertation sur les ballets pantomimes des anciens* (Vienna, 1765). This choreographer's continuing debt
to the same philosophical tradition as Noverre can also be demonstrated by
his later efforts to turn Condillac's metaphysics directly into a pantomime
and thereby to illuminate the theatrical conceit at the core of Condillac's
sensationalism; see Angiolini, *La Vendetta ingegnosa; o La Statua di Condillac, favola boscareccia pantomima* (Venice, Carnival of 1791). Both
Noverre and Rousseau also created pantomimes on the theme of the statue
coming to life, though there is no evidence of any direct link with either
Condillac's or Bonnet's famous statues. The importance of various retel-
lings of the Pygmalion story within Enlightenment culture remains to be
studied.

   89. In 1773, Angiolini published two letters—*Lettere di Gasparo Angiolini a M. Noverre sopra i balli pantomimi* (Milan, 1773)—in response to
Noverre's prefaces to his librettos for *Agamemnon vengé, Ifigénie en
Tauride,* and *Les Graces* (Vienna, 1771). In these letters, Angiolini accused
Noverre not only of relying on programs (which Angiolini believed to be unnecessary if a dance were well enough composed to render its subject intelligible by its own means), but also of failing to respect the Aristotelian uni-
ties of time and place in his ballets and of ignoring the importance of developing a form of notation for the *ballet d'action*. Noverre responded with the
following publications: *Introduction au ballet des Horaces* (written on the
occasion of the first performance of *Les Horaces* in Vienna in January 1774,
just before Angiolini was to arrive in that city and Noverre was to depart for
Milan); *Due lettere scritte a diversi sogetti* (Naples, 1774); and the preface
to the libretto for *Euthyme et Eucharsis* (Milan, 1775, and reprinted in *Recueil de programmes*, 1778), in which Noverre actually apologized for his
need to rely on literary programs. These texts by Noverre, in turn, elicited
several anonymous responses hostile to Noverre and another response from
Angiolini; see *Riflessioni sopra la pretesa risposta del Sig. Noverre all'Angiolini* (Milan, 1774); *Lettre d'un des petits oracles de M. Angiolini au grand
Noverre* (Milan, 1774); *Agli amatori dei balli pantomimi* (Milan, 1774); and
Angiolini's *Riflessioni sopra l'uso dei programmi nei balli pantomimi*
(London and Milan, 1775). On this pamphlet war, see Tozzi, *Il Balletto pantomimo,* chap. 5; Carones, "Noverre and Angiolini"; and Sasportes, "Noverre in Italia" and "Due nuove lettere sulla controversia tra Noverre e Angiolini."

   90. See Goudar, *Observations sur les trois derniers ballets pantomimes.*
   91. Among Goudar's many works on dance written in the 1770s in his
own name or in that of his wife, Sara, see *De Venise. Rémarques sur la musique et la danse, ou Lettres de M. G*** à Milord P[embroke]* (Venice,
1773); *Supplément au Supplément sur les Rémarques de la musique et de la
danse, ou Lettres de M. G*** à Milord Pembroke* (n.p., 1774); *Lettre de Madame Sara Goudar à Monsieur L*** au sujet du divertissement du Théâtre
del Cocomero et de la Comédie Françoise du Théâtre Sainte Marie* (n.p.,
1776); and the anonymously printed *Lettre d'un des petits oracles de M.*

Campioni au Grand Pitrot, traduit de l'Italien (n.p., n.d.). On Goudar's odd career path, see Mars, "Ange Goudar, cet inconnu (1708–1791)."

92. Goudar, *De Venise. Rémarques sur la musique et la danse*, 67, 69.

93. *Lettre de M. le Baron* *** *à une des rivales de Terpsichore*, 16.

94. Ibid., 7. In another variant of this critique, Pierre Louis Ginguené imagined a failed attempt to discuss a crisis at the Opéra in which the participants prove to be more skilled in pantomime than in French. The dancer, Mlle Heynel, explains her plight as follows: "Sirs, my art is not speech, and in my situation as a Foreigner, I can only explain to you with difficulty how I feel. . . . But if M. Noverre wanted to compose a Ballet of profane talents enslaved by a Tyrant, perhaps I would be happy to paint for your eyes, in an expressive manner, what is happening in my heart. Pray allow me this indulgence in compensating for [your] language and deign to read in mine my hope and recognition." See Ginguené, *Instruction du procès*, 36.

95. In addition to the reference to a "logogriphe" in the review in the *Annonces, affiches et avis divers*, no. 5 (January 29, 1777): 32, see the largely negative reviews of Noverre's *Les Horaces* in the following journals: *Mercure de France* (February 1777): 169–72; *Journal des théâtres, ou le Nouveau spectateur* 1, no. 3 (May 1, 1777): 126–29; Grimm et al., *Correspondance littéraire, philosophique et critique* 11 (January 1777): 411–13; and Bachaumont, *Mémoires secrets* 10 (January 22, 1777): 16–17. It is worth noting that these reviews appeared at the same moment as a spate of parodies of the tragic aspirations of the new, hybrid genre known as the *drame*; see Hobson, *The Object of Art*, 178–79.

96. La Harpe, *Correspondance littéraire*, letter 62, 2:57–59. This phrase translates as "May he die!" For La Harpe's earlier assessments of Noverre's choreography, see letters 55 and 58 in the same volume.

97. Meude-Monpas, "Réflexions sur le genre de la pantomime," *Journal encyclopédique* (September 1785): 512–13. According to the entry "ballet" in his *Dictionnaire de musique* (1787), Meude-Monpas had already used the same phrase during August 1785 in an article on the same subject in the *Journal de Paris*.

98. Like the question of gestural notation, the question of the codification of gestures was controversial in the late eighteenth century. The discussion of this issue harked back to the mid-century debate between François Riccoboni and Rémond de Sainte-Albine, among others, concerning whether or not actors should learn a method and whether or not they need to feel inspired or emotionally engaged at the time of a performance. Many French writers resisted the idea that the construction of a dictionary of gestures for dancers or actors was cither feasible or desirable. However, Engel was not alone in attempting such a project. Gotthold Ephraim Lessing also intended to compose a dictionary of *körperliche Beredsamkeit*, or body language, some time in the late eighteenth century; on his unrealized plans, see Ziolkowski, "Language and Mimetic Action in Lessing's 'Miss Sara Sampson.'"

99. See Engel, *Idées sur le geste*. Engel's position, as laid out in the

French editions of his work published in 1788 and 1795, was not very far from that of Dubos, who had, in his *Réflexions critiques*, famously described gestural signs as affecting but imperfect and equivocal as means of communication, except when used in conjunction with speech or as a means to convey a simple emotion, such as impatience. On Dubos, see Chap. 1.

100. Chabanon, *De la Musique considérée en elle-même*, 128–29. An earlier version of this text was published in 1779 as *Observations sur la musique, et principalement sur la metaphysique de l'art*.

101. See, for example, the Abbé François-Louis Gauthier's often reprinted *Traité contre les danses et les mauvaises chansons, dans lequel le danger et le mal qui y sont renfermés sont démontrés par les témoignages multipliés*.

102. Desprez de Boissy, *Lettres sur les spectacles*, 1:24.

103. Ibid., 2:450.

104. Jaucourt, "Langage" and "Pantomime," in *Encyclopédie*, ed. Diderot and D'Alembert, 9:242–43 and 11:827–29, respectively.

105. Marmontel, "Pantomime," in *Supplément au Encyclopédie*, 4:231.

106. The sexualized and especially effeminate aspects of pantomime were stressed by many writers on the subject. For example, in July 1772, the *Mercure de France*, a journal with which Marmontel was closely associated, published a detailed account of a talk on pantomime, or *saltation*, that had recently been given by Louis de Boussanelle, the director of the Academy of Bésiers. In this speech, Boussanelle had characterized Roman pantomime as "the strongest and most lively expression of the most vile passions, the faithful *tableau* of the most shameful vices, the mute recital of the follies of men," and he had blamed the popularity of this "effeminate dance" for the fall of the Empire (135–38). Similarly, the royal official Charles-Georges Fenouillot de Falbaire argued in his "Dissertation sur les ballets-pantomimes, et particulièrement sur celui du Premier Navigateur" of 1787 against the possibility of conveying moral maxims, love of glory or heroism, enthusiasm for liberty, or any precepts about virtue in a form of theater that depended exclusively upon "the grossest form of expression, that of the body" (see the *Oeuvres de M. de Falbaire de Quingey*, 1:190).

107. On Marmontel's aesthetic writings and positions, see Bardon, "L'Esthétique des passions: Marmontel et l'opéra." Marmontel, along with La Harpe, led the opposition to the position represented by Diderot, Grimm, and Arnaud, among others, in the war of the Gluckistes and the Piccinnistes.

108. See, for example, the anonymous and very positive review of Marmontel's "Pantomime" published in the *Journal encyclopédique* (September 1778): 448–56.

109. Marmontel, *De l'Autorité de l'usage sur la langue*, 19. On the politics of Marmontel's position on usage as laid out in this speech (which corresponded to that of Diderot and Beaumarchais rather than the more conservative position of Suard), see Bellot-Antony, "Marmontel grammairien et la notion de bon usage."

CHAPTER 3

1. Helvétius, *De l'Esprit,* 553; and D'Alembert, "Collège," in *Encyclopédie,* ed. Diderot and D'Alembert, 3:635–36.

2. On the pedagogical ambitions of eighteenth-century Jansenists in the realm of language, see Tsiapera and Wheeler, *The Port-Royal Grammar.* Monique Cottret, in *Jansénisme et Lumières,* points out that Jansenists shared a common interest with the *philosophes* of this period both in theories of schooling and educational method and in the idea of primordial time.

3. Harvey Chisick demonstrates that relatively little on education was published in France between 1715 and 1759 compared with the period between 1760 and 1789. During this latter period, the year with the greatest number of printed educational or pedagogical tracts was 1762, and the majority of these publications were responses to either Rousseau's *Emile* or the expulsion of the Jesuits and the need for new teachers and programs for the *collèges.* In his *Correspondance littéraire* (5:259), Grimm noted in April 1763, "Since the fall of the Jesuits and the useless book of Jean Jacques Rousseau entitled *Emile,* people have not stopped writing about education." See Chisick, *The Limits of Reform in the Enlightenment,* 42–43.

4. La Chalotais, *Essai d'éducation nationale,* 38–39.

5. On both traditional and progressive strategies for teaching reading, writing, and spelling during the Old Regime, see: Chartier et al., *L'Education en France du XVIe au XVIIIe siècle,* esp. 130–31; Julia, "L'Apprentissage de la lecture dans la France de l'Ancien Régime"; Trenard, "L'Enseignement de la langue nationale: une réforme pédagogique, 1750–1790"; Senior, "A Controversy in Eighteenth-Century France: The Teaching of Reading"; and Brunot, *Histoire de la langue française,* 7:77–182.

6. According to Irénée Carré in *Les Pédagogues de Port-Royal,* Pierre Coustel and Pierre Nicole had already, in the late seventeenth century, developed the idea that teachers should address their pupils' senses, especially sight, for two reasons: because children enjoy images and because that which enters the mind via the eyes makes an especially strong and lasting impression.

7. *Journal d'éducation* (October 1768): 28–29, cited in Py, "La Fortune d'*Emile* et l'apprentissage de la lecture," 268.

8. On language learning in *Emile* and the book's influence on the teaching of reading and writing in late eighteenth-century France, see Py, "La Fortune d'*Emile* et l'apprentissage de la lecture"; Senior, "Rousseau, la Révolution et l'enseignement de la lecture"; and, more generally, Bloch, *Rousseauism and Education in Eighteenth-Century France.*

9. Rousseau, *Emile or On Education,* 70.

10. Ibid., 108.

11. Ibid., 70.

12. Ibid., 149.

13. Jean Starobinski highlights one of the fundamental paradoxes of *Emile,* namely the fact that the tutor is called upon to be simultaneously a mediator, or an exponent of reflection and reason in relation to his sensual-

ist pupil, *and* an advocate of an immediacy, which Rousseau identified with both an early moment in human history and an early stage in the life of each individual. In this role, Starobinski claims, the tutor assumes the dual function Rousseau ascribed to himself. See *Jean-Jacques Rousseau*, 215–16.

14. Rousseau, *Emile or On Education*, 322. The importance of this brief passage on "the language of signs" to Rousseau's thought as a whole is illustrated by the fact that this section was excerpted and reprinted the following year under the heading "Signes," in *Les Pensées de J. J. Rousseau, Citoyen de Génève* (Amsterdam, 1763).

15. Ibid., 323.

16. On the popularity of the theme of the *enfant de la nature* in literature written between 1760 and 1770, see Jean-Michel Racault, "Le Motif de 'l'enfant de la nature' dans la littérature du XVIIIe siècle, ou la récréation expérimentale de l'origine," in *Primitivisme et mythes des origines dans la France des Lumières*, ed. Grell and Michel, 101–7.

17. On ballet at Louis-le-Grand and in Jesuit schools more generally, see Peyronnet, "Le Théâtre d'éducation des Jésuites."

18. On Radonvilliers's purported sources of inspiration, see the "Indication des principaux ouvrages où l'on trouve des méthodes pour apprendre les langues assez semblables à celle de M. l'Abbé de Radonvilliers," in the *Oeuvres diverses de M. l'abbé Radonvilliers*, 1:217–19. See also Hanoteau, *Notes sur M. l'Abbé de Radonvilliers*.

19. Radonvilliers, *De la Manière d'apprendre les langues*, 41.

20. Ibid., 6.

21. One of the few publications to mention Radonvillier's text was written by a *maître de pension* in Versailles named Goulier. In his *Lettre à M. L'Abbé *** sur la manière d'apprendre les langues* (Paris, 1769), Goulier too took up the fight against educating children by immediately introducing them to abstract terms that represent no fixed ideas in their minds. He also praised Radonvilliers's book: "You will see in it by what philosophical progression he le_ds the mind from knowledge of the natural language to that of articulate language, and from knowledge of the mother tongue to that of a deaf, foreign one" (67).

22. Epée's unpublished notes from his experiments of the 1760s remain in six manuscript volumes in the Bibliothèque de l'Institut Gustave Baguier in Asnières. For Epée's full biography, see Berthier, *L'Abbé de l'Epée*; and Bézagu-Deluy, *L'Abbé de l'Epée*.

23. Péreire was a Portuguese Jew who emigrated to Bordeaux in 1741 and became famous for his method of teaching the deaf to articulate French words through a combination of techniques including lip-reading, palpable speech vibrations, and a manual alphabet of *signes dactylologiques*. On his technique and achievements, see La Rochelle, *Jacob Rodrigues Pereire*; and Neher-Bernheim, "Un Pionnier dans l'art de faire parler les sourds-muets."

24. Epée, *Institution des sourds et muets, par la voie des signes méthodiques*, 137.

25. See, for example, Duval-Pyrau, *Journal et anecdotes intéressantes du voyage de M. le Comte de Falckenstein*, 48–49. The archives of the INJS

also contain requests from other foreign notables asking Epée to arrange times for their visits to this school.

26. News of the case began to appear in journals in the fall of 1777, but the most thorough account of this case, which involved accusations of mistaken identity, kidnapping, and murder, can be found in Nicolas Toussaint LeMoyne Desessart's *Causes célèbres, curieuses et intéressantes* 55 (1779): 3–240; and 69 (1780): 3–165. Additional information can be found in BHVP, Papiers Lenôtre, MS 963 (1–209): Affaire Solar, as well as such journals as the *Gazette des tribunaux*, the *Annales politiques, civiles et littéraires*, and the *Journal de Paris*.

27. See the *Arrêt du Conseil d'Etat du Roi, concernant l'éducation et l'enseignement des sourds et muets. Du 21 novembre 1778.*

28. Regarding deaf authors, see, for example, the undated manuscript in BN, n. aq. fr. 2906, fol. 182–87: "Elisca ou le Barbare indien, pantomime à grand spectacle, avec vue du temple du Soleil, par Laurent fils (sourd)." For a history of deaf characters in French theater, see Bernard, *Surdité, surdi-mutité et mutisme dans le théâtre français*.

29. "Danse," *Mercure de France* 1 (July 1777): 184–86.

30. On Epée's public sessions as a new "fashion" following the visit of Joseph II, see Mairobert, *L'Espion anglois*, 6:136–39. See also Bachaumont, *Mémoires secrets* 10 (May 19, 1777): 135, who claimed that "from this moment onwards [the emperor's visit], the curious have been coming in hordes to visit the teacher of the deaf and mute."

31. Epée's theory of education is discussed in Degérando, *De l'Education des sourds-muets de naissance*, 1:451–503; Seigel, "The Enlightenment and the Evolution of a Language of Signs in France and England"; Tridon, "L'Education des sourds-muets au XVIIIe siècle en France et en Angleterre"; Cuxac, *Le Langage des sourds*, 22–31; Lane, *When the Mind Hears*, 42–66; Markovits, "L'Enfant, le muet, le sauvage"; and Markovits, "L'Abbé de l'Epée: du verbe intérieur au langage des gestes," in *Le Pouvoir des signes*, ed. Karacostas, 34–54.

32. Epée, *Institution des sourds et muets, ou Recueil des exercices*, 50. Between 1771 and 1774, Epée wrote a letter to the public each year, and beginning in 1772, he published his annual letter together with all the letters of the preceding years and his latest program for his student demonstration. See his *Exercice des sourds et muets qui se fera le jeudi 2 juillet 1772, chez M. l'abbé de l'Epée, rue des Moulins, Butte S.-Roche, depuis trois heures jusqu'à sept* (Paris, 1772); *Exercice de sourds et muets qui se fera le mercredi 4 août 1773, chez M. l'abbé de l'Epée, rue des Moulins, Butte S. Roche, depuis trois heures de relevée jusqu'à sept* (Paris, 1773); and *Institution des sourds et muets, ou Recueil des exercices soutenus par les sourds et muets pendant les années 1771, 1772, 1773 et 1774, avec les lettres qui ont accompagné les programmes de chacun de ces exercices* (Paris, 1774). All four were reprinted once again in the *Institution des sourds et muets, par la voie des signes méthodiques* (Paris, 1776).

33. Epée's biweekly public sessions lasted four or five hours, and the audience was limited to one hundred men and women, who were asked to

accommodate others by not staying for more than two hours at a time. The questions, dictated in sign language or in writing, all revolved around religious doctrine, and the pupils responded in writing or (when possible) orally. See the programs for the public sessions of 1771–74 and Thiéry, *Guide des amateurs et des étrangers voyageurs à Paris*, 1:172–74.

34. Epée, Letter #3 (1773), in *Exercice de sourds et muets qui se fera le mercredi 4 août 1773*, 23.

35. On the ongoing dialogue between Linguet and Epée, see Linguet, "Fondation intéressante en faveur des sourds et muets de naissance," *Annales politiques, civiles et littéraires du dix-huitième siècle* 5 (1779): 95–99; and Epée's letter in response (May 31, 1785), cited in Jean-Henri-Samuel Formey's report, "Sur la meilleure manière d'instruire les sourds et muets," in *Nouveaux mémoires de l'Académie royale des sciences et belles-lettres, année 1785*, 47–52.

36. Epée, Letter #2 (1772), in *Exercice de sourds et muets qui se fera le mercredi 4 août 1773*, 19.

37. That the idea of establishing a multinational and perfectly logical language generated renewed attention and speculation beginning in the 1770s can be demonstrated by reference to the Royal Academy in Berlin, which produced lengthy reports on the new universal language schemes of both Georgius Kalmár (1772) and Christian Gottlieb Berger (1779), the latter of whom was the subject of a long article in the *Journal encyclopédique* (January 1783), tome 1, part 1: 12–20. The French grammarian Dieudonné Thiébault explained the academy's newfound interest in this topic is his "Observations générales sur la grammaire et les langues," in the *Nouveaux mémoires de l'Académie royale des sciences et belles-lettres, année 1774*: "Today, it seems that one wants to relegate it [the dream of a universal language] to the category of systems, paradoxes and other chimeras. It is, however, true that never has this aid been so necessary to us. Before printing, literature and the sciences expanded slowly and with difficulty; hardly more than one nation at a time cultivated them with success; one had then only one language to learn. Things have changed; all the languages of Europe are becoming perfected and enriched; it is becoming important to learn them all; but it would absorb the life of a man and all his mental energy; and if one consecrated all his faculties and all his time to the study of words, what would become of the more essential study of things? A universal language would, therefore, be an inappreciable treasure for all people: let's consider if it is something that we must renounce forever" (520). However, much to his dismay, Thiébault concluded that such a project was practically unrealizable.

38. The most famous responses to this question stemmed from the Berlin Academy's 1782 contest on the topic "What has made the French language the universal language of Europe?" The contest was won in 1784 by Antoine Rivarol, who was to become an important counterrevolutionary commentator on revolutionary language politics during the 1790s.

39. In the second and considerably abridged and revised version of his *Institution des sourds et muets, par la voie des signes méthodiques*, which he

retitled *La Véritable manière d'instruire les sourds et muets, confirmée par une longue expérience*, Epée insisted on the need for a dictionary of sign language in which all the definitions would be based on the principles of decomposition, just as all of his signs were based on analysis (see chap. 16 of the latter work). See also Epée's posthumous *Dictionnaire des sourds et muets, publié d'après le manuscrit original*, along with the ms. notebooks (1786) and correspondence with Necker concerning the publication of this work (also 1786) in the archives of the INJS. Some of these definitions indicate gestures or combinations of gestures (e.g., *abattre* [to demolish]: "one makes the movement of a person who breaks up nuts," or *utile* [useful]: "the sign for *bon* [good] and the sign for *pour* [for]"). Others are simply straight definitions (e.g., *abdiquer* [to abdicate]: "to leave a position") or even sentences showing how a word is used in practice. In general, the dictionary illustrates the cumbersomeness and unsystematic quality of Epée's methodical signs, despite his claims to the contrary. On this project, see also Fischer, "Abbé de l'Epée and the Living Dictionary." No manuscript of his proposed grammar has ever been located, and it is unlikely that such a text ever existed.

40. Changeux, *Bibliothèque grammaticale abrégée, ou Nouveaux mémoires sur la parole et sur l'écriture*, 111, 113, 129. Changeux's article on reality never appeared in the *Encyclopédie*; but he did publish a *Traité des extrèmes, ou des éléments de la science de la réalité* in Amsterdam in 1767. On this thinker, see Tonelli, "Pierre-Jacques [*sic*] Changeux and Scepticism in the French Enlightenment."

41. See the "Lettre de M. Saboureux-de-Fontenay, sourd et muet de naissance, à Mademoiselle * * *, datée de Versailles le 26 décembre 1764," *Suite de la Clef, ou Journal historique sur les matières du tems* 98 (October 1765): 284–98 and (November 1765): 361–72. An English version is reproduced in *The Deaf Experience: Classics in Language and Education*, ed. Lane, 17–27. See also the tribute to Péreire (May 31 and June 24, 1777) and the letter from Péreire to the editor of the *Annonces et affiches*, Abbé Aubert (July 22 and 26, 1777), reproduced in La Rochelle, *Jacob Rodrigues Pereire*, 350–56.

42. Epée, *Institution des sourds et muets, par la voie des signes méthodiques*, 151.

43. For French translations of Epée's exchange of letters with Heinicke concerning the sign language instruction offered in Vienna by Epée's pupil, the Abbé Storck, along with the response of the Academy of Zurich to this fight, see *Corpus*, no. 2 (1986): 87–115. Regarding the extensive materials sent to the Académie des Sciences, Belles-Lettres et Arts de Lyon, which then issued its own "Rapport concernant la méthode de M. l'Abbé de l'Epée" (1783), see MS 148 and MS 266 in the papers of this academy in the Bibliothèque du Palais des Arts in Lyon (I thank Allyson Dunn for kindly tracking down these manuscripts). On Epée's argument with Nicolai, see the "Lettre de l'instituteur des sourds et muets de Paris à MM. de l'Académie de Berlin, et lettre du même à M. Nicolay [*sic*], savant critique du Berlin," *Journal de Paris*, no. 147 (May 27, 1785): 604–5; and Formey, "Sur la meilleure manière." According to Epée, Nicolai had originally hoped that

Johann Jakob Engel, the expert on theatrical gestures and fellow member of the Berlin Academy who was notably hostile to the idea of a gestural language, would be called upon to resolve the dispute. Indeed, Engel's anonymous French translator added a negative reference to "methodical signs" to his critique of gestural languages in the introduction to *Idées sur le geste* (1788), an addition that may well have been inspired by this controversy.

44. In response to Epée's letter defending his pupil in the *Journal de Paris*, no. 288 (October 15, 1777) and the *Lettre de M. l'Abbé de l'Epée à M. Elie de Beaumont* in the *Mémoire à consulter, pour le Sieur Bonvalet* (Paris, 1779), see the following opposing arguments printed for public consumption: *Plaidoyers de M. Tronson du Coudray* (Paris, 1779); *Lettre de M. Moreau de Vormes et consultation pour le Sieur Cazeaux* (Paris, 1779); Elie de Beaumont, *Mémoire et réponse à M. l'Abbé de l'Epeé, pour le Sieur Cazeaux* (Paris, 1779); Elie de Beaumont, *Vue générale de l'affaire du soi-disant Comte de Solar*; and Aguesseau, *Plaidoyer prononcé en l'audience de la Tournelle du 15 avril* (Paris, 1780).

45. See the *Réponse de M. Prunget des Boissières, avocat au Parlement à M. *** au sujet de no. 38 des Annales de M. Linguet, sur l'affaire du soi-disant Comte de Solar, sourd et muet* (June 14, 1779), in Elie de Beaumont, *Vue générale de l'affaire*. Linguet's article, "Réclamation d'état en faveur d'un sourd et muet," appeared in his *Annales politiques, civiles et littéraires* 5 (1779): 353–92. In this piece, Linguet had defended Epée's actions but had denounced the judicial process that had resulted from these actions: "The pantomime scene described above is a play whose curiousness can be entertaining; [but] the Sanctuary of justice must not be a Theater, and even less should it [pantomime] be the foundation of its decisions. . . . What sure results can come from this complication of equivocal terms . . . ?" (367, 371).

46. Deschamps, *Cours élémentaire d'éducation des sourds et muets*, xxxv. This text was published with an appendix, a "Dissertation sur la parole, dans laquelle on recherche l'origine de cette faculté, et la méthode de l'exercer," originally printed in Latin in Amsterdam as *Surdus Loquens* in 1692 by the Swiss doctor Jean-Conrad Amman and translated into French by Charles-Nicolas Beauvais de Préau, a doctor in Orléans and a member of the Société Royale de Médecine. See also Deschamps's earlier essay, *Lettre à M. de S***[Sailly], capitaine de cavalerie, sur l'institution des sourds et muets*, which was also a defense of Deschamps's own method and an attack on that of Epée.

47. Deschamps, *De la Manière de suppléer aux oreilles par les yeux*, 3.

48. Deschamps, *Cours élémentaire d'éducation des sourds et muets*, 7–8.

49. See Chap. 2.

50. Deschamps, *Cours élémentaire d'éducation des sourds et muets*, 19.

51. Ibid., xlviii.

52. Ibid., 8.

53. In the middle decades of the eighteenth century, Péreire not only garnered the support of Rousseau and Diderot but he also developed friendships with such Enlightenment figures as La Condamine, de Mairan, and

Buffon; demonstrated his method at the Royal Academy of Sciences (in 1749 and 1751), as well as at the academy of Caen and at Choisy; and won recognition for his work from numerous famous observers, including Louis XV, who named Péreire "Interprète de Sa Majesté pour les langues espagnole et portugaise" in 1765. As late as 1771, Péreire was still publicly displaying a small group of his students—this time before King Gustavus III of Sweden—in what one journalist referred to as a "philosophical spectacle" (see the *Mercure de France* [April 1771]: 194–95). But Epée's demonstrations almost totally eclipsed those of his predecessor during the following decade. Péreire died in 1780 without ever systematically revealing his method, and efforts to resuscitate his flagging reputation as an exponent of oral education for the deaf did not begin until the nineteenth century.

54. Monboddo, *Of the Origin and Progress of Language*, 1:192. See also John Quincy Adams's description of his 1783 visit to Epée's school in the company of his father, John Adams (who was then actively involved in language debates in the United States), and the Scottish philosopher Dugald Stewart, in *Diary of John Quincy Adams*, 1:185. Finally, see *The Letters of Sir William Jones*, 1:540 and 2:560, in which the prominent linguist mentions that, after studying Epée's "Universal language of Signs" from Epée's book in 1780, he attended Epée's lessons "pretty constantly" in the summer of 1782 while visiting Franklin in Paris; and see the long description of a visit to Epée's school in the travel journal of Father Zsawery Bohusz, an authority on Lithuanian language and history and also a friend of Franklin, published erroneously as *Dziennik podróży ks. Stanislawa Staszica*, 245–46. I thank Izabella Zatorska for the reference and translation from Polish to French.

55. On this distinction, see esp. Auroux, *La Sémiotique des encyclopédistes*, 30.

56. Condillac, *Cours d'études pour l'instruction du Prince de Parme. La Grammaire*, in *Oeuvres de Condillac*, 5:12.

57. In the volumes of the *Cours d'études pour l'instruction du Prince de Parme* entitled *Histoire ancien*, Condillac again referred to Roman pantomime and declamation and mentioned that in antiquity both syllables and gestures were notated according to a system similar to musical notes. This fact offered readers further evidence that pantomime, rather than being an entirely natural language, could be decomposed in a linear fashion and had itself once constituted an artificial *langage d'action*.

58. Condillac, *Cours d'études pour l'instruction du Prince de Parme. La Grammaire*, in *Oeuvres de Condillac*, 5:13. Condillac's brief tribute to Epée was quoted by the educator of the deaf in his own defense in several of his writings of the early 1780s, including *La Véritable manière* (1784) and his correspondence with Heinecke (1780–83).

59. Ibid., 5:13.

60. Condillac developed this idea further in his treatise on logic written in late 1777 and posthumously published in 1780. See esp. chap. 2, "Comment le langage d'action analyse la pensée," in *La Logique/Logic*, 210–25. On this text, see also Chap. 5.

61. See the announcement of this contest in the *Mercure de France* 97 (July–December 1769): 158.

62. Both the *Journal encyclopédique* ([August 1774]: 3–17) and, to a lesser extent, the *Mercure de France* ([June 1774]: 101–8) were skeptical that there was any purpose in proposing an elaborate hypothesis in answer to this question, which the *Mercure* called "rather chimerical."

63. Copineau, *Essai synthétique sur l'origine et la formation des langues*, 22–23.

64. On Morin, a printer and bookseller (at the "ensign of the Truth" on the rue St-Jacques) with a particular interest in educational tracts and universal grammars, see the *Catalogue des livres qui se trouvent chez Benoît Morin* in the Fonds Lottin et Butard at Columbia University. Jacques Butard, a cousin of Morin and another Jansenist bookseller on the rue St-Jacques, had published Epée's *Institution des sourds et muets, ou Recueil des exercices* in 1774, and Morin himself published the *Lettre de M. l'Abbé de l'Epée à M. Elie de Beaumont* the same year as Desloges's book.

65. Copineau never identified himself in print as the editor of this book; in the text, the editor describes himself only as a friend of the Abbé de l'Epée (through whom he originally came into contact with Desloges) and an acquaintance of Saboureux de Fontenay, the prize pupil of Péreire. However, it is evident from several clues that Copineau was indeed the author of both the introduction to Desloges's text and the extensive notes attached to it. First, the same idiosyncratic phonetic spellings are used in both the *Essai synthétique* and in Desloges's *Observations*. Second, Desloges quotes Copineau's tribute to Epée from the *Essai synthétique* within the *Observations*. Third, Desloges's printer and publisher, Benoît Morin, had previously published other works by Copineau. And fourth and most conclusively, Desloges's editor is identified as "M. l'Abbé Copineau" in a "conversation" in writing that occurred between Desloges and Péreire on October 31 and November 6, 1779. See, in the INJS archives, a facsimile of this handwritten conversation; it is also reproduced without reference in La Rochelle, *Jacob Rodrigues Pereire*, 405–10.

66. Desloges's *Observations d'un sourd et muet* is translated in full in *The Deaf Experience*, ed. Lane, 29–48 and 206–12. For the above quotation, see page 32.

67. Ibid., 30.

68. Ibid., 38, 37.

69. Ibid., 37, 45–46.

70. Ibid., 212.

71. Ibid., 207.

72. Ibid., 211.

73. Deschamps, *Lettre à M. de Bellisle*, 33. In this work, Deschamps both cast doubt on Desloges's authorship and ridiculed Desloges's defense of signs with a query as to why the deaf man had chosen to write his book in words if gestural signs were, in fact, so effective as a means of communication. Deschamps also rounded up allies. Two letters by Saboureux de Fon-

tenay are included in the book: one written in defense of Deschamps and addressed to Desloges, whom Saboureux saw as a competitor, and one addressed directly to Deschamps. And the translator, Beauvais de Préau, also penned his own defense of Deschamps's claims against Desloges's accusations; this letter was published in the *Affiches, annonces et avis divers* (January 5, 1780): 3–4.

74. See the following texts by Desloges: "Lettre à M. le Marquis de Condorcet, Paris, 16 novembre 1779," *Mercure de France* (December 18, 1779): 146–50 (following an anonymous review of Desloges's *Observations* on 142–46); "Lettre à M. Bellisle . . . en réponse à celle que lui a écrite M. l'abbé Deschamps au sujet des observations de M. Desloges," *Journal encyclopédique* (August 1780): 125–32 (following a notice regarding Desloges's *Observations* on page 346 in the issue of January 1780 and a review in the issue of February 1780 on pages 446–65); and "Avis du philosophe [Benoît] Morin à tous ses généraux Concitoyens," *Annonces, affiches et avis divers* (often called the *Affiches de Paris*) (November 15, 1779): 2550. The editor of the *Affiches, annonces et avis divers* commented in the course of his review of books by both Deschamps and Desloges ([December 15, 1779]: 198–99) that the latter's letter to Condorcet had been written in Condorcet's chambers under the watchful eye of the famous scientist, and Desloges himself also mentioned, within the letter to Condorcet cited above, being interrogated by him.

75. Anon., review of Desloges's *Observations*, *Journal encyclopédique* (February 1780): 463, 451.

76. According to Pahin de La Blancherie, Desloges was one of the guests of honor at Pahin's "regular meeting of savants and artists" on both December 30, 1799, and January 19, 1780. On the first occasion, Desloges was called upon to defend his method in writing; see the *Nouvelles de la République des lettres et des arts*, no. 7 (January 4, 1780): 71. On the second occasion, Desloges introduced Saboureux de Fontenay to the assembly, and the two deaf men proceeded to debate in writing the relative merits of various approaches to the education of the deaf. In reference to this occasion the reporter noted: "If, in all our great disputes, one were obliged to explain oneself by writing only, one would fall less often into the excesses that degenerate into insults, and one would be better able to be counseled and enlightened"; see the *Nouvelles de la République des lettres et des arts*, no. 10 (January 25, 1780): 98–99. On the relationship between the *Nouvelles* and Pahin de La Blancherie's "salon de la correspondance," see Goodman, *The Republic of Letters*, 242–53; and Guénot, "La Correspondance générale pour les sciences et les arts de Pahin de La Blancherie."

77. Anon., review of Desloges's *Observations*, *Mercure de France* (December 18, 1779): 146. As explained in Chap. 1, during the eighteenth century, knowledge of abstract concepts and terms was often taken to be an indicator of the relative intellectual wealth or poverty of a given people or individual. However, sensationalist thinkers, such as Bonnet and Quesnay, also insisted that so-called "ignorant" or "primitive" men, who learned

what they knew primarily through the senses (i.e., according to nature's method) rather than through inherited words, often got closer to discovering real truths.

78. Condorcet, "Discours prononcé dans l'Académie française, le jeudi 21 février 1782, à la réception de M. le marquis de Condorcet," in *Oeuvres de Condorcet*, 1:398. This reception speech is discussed in depth in Baker, *Condorcet: From Natural Philosophy to Social Mathematics*, 85–87 and 180–83.

79. Ibid., 1:392.

80. Genlis, *Adèle et Théodore*, 3:198 (letter 35).

81. Ibid., 3:201–2.

82. On "les défauts de la parole" as a theme in the writing of Mme de Genlis, see Plagnol-Diéval, *Madame de Genlis et le théâtre d'éducation*, 138–41. Plagnol-Diéval argues that Genlis, in her educational plays, is a strong critic both of the importance accorded to speech in elite culture in general and of the uses and effects of many contemporary speech practices, from witty chatter that promotes vacuous exchanges to scandal-mongering that ruins social harmony, destroys reputations, and confuses truth and falsehood.

83. Genlis, *Adèle et Théodore*, 3:202.

84. On the Loge des Neuf Soeurs, see Amiable, *Une Loge maçonnique d'avant 1789*; Hans, "Unesco of the Eighteenth Century: La Loge des Neuf Soeurs and Its Venerable Master, Benjamin Franklin"; Moravia, *Il Tramonto dell'Illuminismo*, 55–67; and Chevallier, *Histoire de la franc-maçonnerie française*, 272–87. For a contemporary account, see Bricaire de la Dixmerie, *Mémoire pour la Loge des Neuf Soeurs*.

85. On this organization and the other *musées* and *lycées* of Paris during the 1780s, see Dejob, *L'Instruction publique en France*, 123–256 and appendices; Amiable, *Une Loge maçonnique*, chap. 5; Guénot, "Musées et lycées parisiens (1780–1830)"; Goodman, *The Republic of Letters*, 259–80; and Lynn, "Enlightenment in the Public Sphere."

86. To my knowledge, there has been no synthetic study devoted specifically to the provincial *musées* and other kinds of small learned societies that developed the 1780s. On the Société Littéraire de Lyon, also called the Musée de Lyon in the 1780s, see Société littéraire, historique et archéologique de Lyon, *Le Centenaire de la Société littéraire de Lyon, 1778–1878*; on the Musée de Toulouse, see Taillefer, "L'Echec d'une tentative de réforme académique: le musée de Toulouse (1784–1788)"; and on the Musée de Bordeaux, see note 112 in this chapter.

87. On the Parisian *musées* as "counteracademies and antisalons for the multitude of philosophes who could not get a hearing elsewhere," see Darnton, *The Literary Underground of the Old Regime*, 24. Only the lecturers at the Lycée de Paris, whose ranks at the end of the 1780s included such prestigious figures as Marmontel, Garat, Condorcet, La Harpe, and Fourcroy, have been looked upon in a different light.

88. In his extraordinary study of eighteenth-century provincial academies, *Le Siècle des Lumières en province*, Daniel Roche dedicates few

pages to such minor associations as *musées*, primarily because he believes that their chosen forms of sociability and topics of debate essentially mirrored those of the more prestigious academies in their surroundings. However, in an important article, Roche addresses the question of the social composition of these *musées*, emphasizing their openness to men in business and commerce in provincial cities; see "Négoce et culture dans la France du XVIIIe siècle" [1978], in *Les Républicains des lettres*, esp. 293–95.

89. For a contemporary statement of the goals of the Musée de Paris, see Jean-Claude Pingeron, "Précis historique de l'établissement du Musée de Paris dans lequel on démontre son utilité pour les progès des arts, des sciences et des belles lettres," [c. 1790] in BHVP, MS n. aq. 137, 222–24.

90. In *The Republic of Letters*, Dena Goodman stresses the more public but also more masculine nature of the *musées* of the 1780s in contrast to the private salons of the mid-century, where women had held considerable power. She argues, based on the example of two Parisian institutions, that women were reduced to spectators and decorative accoutrements in these newer assemblies, marking a sea-change in gender relations in the decade before the Revolution. However, she does not mention that the founders of these newer institutions almost all stress their openness to women, in contradistinction to official academies. And it is clear that in certain *musées* women were not prevented from taking an active intellectual and institutional role. Mme Deladine of the Société littéraire of Lyon, for example, not only read her poetry and prose to the other members of the group but also served as secretary of this *musée* for two brief stints in 1782 and 1783. Similarly, Pingeron (ibid.) points out that "[t]he musée [of Paris] already includes some women among its members who have made a name for themselves in the Republic of Letters"; and Pilâtre de Rozier mentions "14 dames fondatrices," as well as "63 dames abonnés," in his *Liste de toutes les personnes qui composent le premier musée* of 1785, and insists that women will share the same rights and privileges as male members. Indeed, in the late 1780s, several *musées* were also established specifically for women. Thus, in contrast to Goodman and in keeping with Janet Burke's and Margaret Jacob's findings regarding French Masonic lodges in the 1780s ("French Freemasonry, Women, and Feminist Scholarship"), I argue that women's active presence in associational life may actually have been on the rise during the last years of the Old Regime and that the advantages and disadvantages of women's participation in "intellectual sociability" remained an open question on the eve of the Revolution.

91. Pingeron, "Précis historique."

92. On the premium placed on avoiding controversial topics in the pre-Enlightenment Republic of Letters, see Goldgar, *Impolite Learning*, chaps. 4 and 5. For a demonstration of the continuity in these ideals, see Bricaire de la Dixmerie's explanation in his *Mémoire* for why the Loge des Neuf Soeurs forbade discussion of anything that could be construed as contrary to religion, the king, his ministers or other dignitaries, living authors, or morals.

93. The political content of eighteenth-century Masonic sociability has been studied in detail in recent years by historians such as Ran Halévi and

Margaret C. Jacob. Little attention has been paid, however, to examining the role of visual signs in creating this sociability, even though coded Masonic alphabets, in particular, were extremely popular among French Freemasons in the 1780s. See, for example, Jean-Baptiste Pierre Saurine's *Grille de lecture de l'alphabet maçonnique du chapitre de la Réunion des amis intimes de l'Orient de Paris* (1783), for which the *avocat au Parlement* and *garde des archives* invented two systems of coding, one based on numerals and the other based on hieroglyphics, and see the *Circulaire du Grand Chapitre Général de France* (1786) written by a barrister and "chancelier, garde des sceaux, timbres, hiéroglyphes et autres symboles du Grand Chapitre Général de France" named Oudet (included in *La Franc-maçonnerie*, 120–1 and 115, respectively). On Masonry and specialized languages more generally, see Marie Mulvey Roberts, "Masonics, Metaphor and Misogyny: A Discourse of Marginality?" in *Languages and Jargons*, ed. Burke and Porter, 133–54; and Cazzaniga, ed., *Symboles, signes, langages sacrés*.

94. For the above quotation, see the tribute to the members of the Loge des Neuf Soeurs entitled "L'Initiation d'Orphée" in Cubières, *Opuscules poétiques*, 1:137.

95. Bricaire de la Dixmerie, *Mémoire pour la Loge des Neuf Soeurs*.

96. On the importance of the *questione della lingua* or the determination of correct forms of usage first at the Florentine Academy and the Academia della Crusca in the sixteenth century and, later, in eighteenth-century French salons, see Burke, *The Art of Conversation*, 115–16.

97. On the grammarian Changeux's interest in language reform, see note 40 in this chapter. Franklin, a printer by trade and an advocate of spelling reform, also manifested an interest in the discovery of a universal, written language during the mid-1770s; see Stiles to Franklin (March 12, 1775) and Franklin to Stiles (September 1, 1775) in *The Papers of Benjamin Franklin*, 6:177 and 5:515; and Looby, "Phonetics and Politics: Franklin's Alphabet as Political Design."

98. On Court de Gébelin's project, see Manuel, *The Eighteenth Century Confronts the Gods*, 249–58; Lefèvre, "La Génétique du langage selon Antoine Court de Gébelin: une modèle linguistique de l'histoire"; Genette, *Mimologics*, 91–114; Faivre, "Antoine Court de Gébelin: du génie allégorique et symbolique des anciens"; and Faivre, "Le *Monde primitif* d'Antoine Court de Gébelin, ou le rêve d'une encyclopédie solitaire."

99. Between 1773 and 1784, Antoine Court de Gébelin produced the nine volumes that constitute *Le Monde primitif, analysé et comparé avec le monde moderne*. This quotation is taken from volume 3: *L'Histoire naturelle de la parole; ou Origine du langage et de l'écriture; avec une reponse à une critique anonyme* (1775), 106. See also the tribute to Epée's work in volume 2 of *Le Monde primitif*, entitled *L'Histoire naturelle de la parole; ou Grammaire universelle et comparative* (1774), 16. The whole project was first announced in the physiocratic journal *Ephémérides du citoyen, ou Bibliothèque raisonnée des sciences morales et politiques* 2, no. 4 (1772): 228–

40; and the parts on language were also published separately as *Histoire na-turelle de la parole, ou Précis de l'origine du langage et de la grammaire universelle. Extrait du Monde Primitif* (1776).

100. For the more common late eighteenth-century position, see the *Cours d'études pour le prince du Parme. La Grammaire,* in which Condillac insisted that it was a mistake to assume that "names in the primitive lan-guage explained the very nature of things" (24). On the contrary, Condillac suggested that such names "represented things according to appearances, opinions, prejudices, and errors, but these appearances, opinions, preju-dices, and errors were common to all those who spoke the same language and that is why they understood one another" (25).

101. For a social analysis of Court de Gébelin's admirers based on the subscription lists for *Le Monde primitif,* see Roche, *Le Siècle des Lumières,* 1:293–94, 317–18 and 2:117, 128, 508 (map); and Kirsop, "Cultural Networks in Pre-Revolutionary France." As a result of his work on *Le Monde primitif,* Court de Gébelin became a member of several provincial academies and even a royal censor in 1781. But his Protestantism made membership in any of the official Parisian academies impossible.

102. Pingeron claimed that one of the Musée de Paris's chief goals was to encourage "perfect equality and concord" among members; see his "Précis historique."

103. Rabaut Saint-Etienne, *Lettre sur la vie et les écrits de M. Court de Gébelin adressée au Musée de Paris,* in *Oeuvres de Rabaut-Saint-Etienne,* 2:355–90.

104. Albon, *Eloge de Court de Gébelin,* 13. After Court de Gébelin's death, the Comte d'Albon built a monument to the linguist on his estate in Franconville. Robert-François-Joseph Quesnay de Saint-Germain, the grand-son of the physiocrat François Quesnay and another member of the Musée de Paris, also published a eulogy to Court de Gébelin in 1784; see his *Dis-cours pour servir d'éloge à Court de Gébelin, auteur du Monde primitif* as well.

105. Rabaut Saint-Etienne, *Lettre à Sylvain Bailly sur l'histoire primi-tive de la Grèce,* in *Oeuvres de Rabaut-Saint-Etienne,* 1:37.

106. Tournon, "De la nécessité de créer des mots . . . discours, lu dans une assemblée du Musée de Paris," *Journal de la langue française* (May 15, 1786): 296–307 and (September 15, 1786): 578–85. The editor of this gram-matical journal, a French teacher in Lyon named Urbain Domergue, was a member of the Société Littéraire de Lyon (commonly referred to as the Musée de Lyon in the 1780s). Within the pages of this journal, which was es-tablished in 1784, can be found several texts stemming from the Musée de Paris (including summaries of Rabaut Saint-Etienne's address on the work of Court de Gébelin and the Chevalier de Cubières's tribute to the members of the Loge des Neuf Soeurs, as well as the essays of Tournon) and numerous discourses previously read at the Société littéraire de Lyon (including Domergue's own speech in honor of the anniversary of this "musée" or "society consecrated to friendship and to letters" in 1783). These ties did

not disappear in the next decade; when Domergue left Lyon for Paris circa 1790, he took up residence at the former home of Court de Gébelin, the previous site of Court's *musée*.

107. Tournon, "Réponse à la lettre de M. Bérenger," *Journal de la langue française* (June 11, 1785): 649–56.

108. On the growth in Paris in the 1780s of private courses in French and other modern languages, see Sokalski, "Grammars and Grottos: Language Learning and Language Teaching in Pre-Revolutionary Paris."

109. For more on this journal during the 1780s, see Chap. 4.

110. On the importance of linguistic questions to the early American members of the American Philosophical Society, including Franklin, Adams, Jefferson, and Pierre Eugène Du Simitière, see Andresen, *Linguistics in America, 1769–1924*, esp. 47–67; and *Pierre Eugène Du Simitière*. During the 1770s, Franklin and Jefferson both maintained contacts with the Loge des Neuf Soeurs (Franklin eventually became an honorary member of Court de Gébelin's Musée as well). Adams closely followed Court de Gébelin's etymological work, while Du Simitière, a collector of samples of Indian and Creole vocabularies, hieroglyphics, and calligraphies, corresponded with this savant about Indian idioms. Conversely, the nonresident members of the American Philosophical Society before the French Revolution included a number of important French language theorists—Condorcet (elected 1775), Court de Gébelin (elected 1783), and Pierre J. G. Cabanis (elected 1786)—all of whom were simultaneously active in the Loge des Neuf Soeurs and its associated societies. Moreau de Saint-Méry, the president of the Musée de Paris after the death of Court de Gébelin, also became a nonresident member of the American Philosophical Society in 1789, the same year that the French émigré and linguist Peter Stephen DuPonceau, who had served as Court de Gébelin's secretary during the period when Court de Gébelin was engaged in composing *Le Monde primitif*, gave his own collection of books to the Philadelphia institution. See also Rosengarten, "The Early French Members of the American Philosophical Society"; and Smith, "Peter Stephen DuPonceau and His Study of Languages."

111. For details on fights within the Musée de Paris and between it and other rival organizations, see Bachaumont, *Mémoires secrets* 21 (December 9, 1782): 225 and 23 (July 27, 1783): 78; (August 7, 1783): 91–92; (August 9, 1783): 96–97.

112. On Dupont des Jumeaux and the *musée* of Bordeaux, see Coutura, "Le Musée de Bordeaux"; and Céleste, *La Société philomathique de Bordeaux*. See also the *Journal de Guienne* (1784–90), edited by Dupont des Jumeaux.

113. On the goals of the founder and the relation between the *musées* of Bordeaux and Paris, see the letter of May 9, 1793, by the Intendant Dupré de Saint-Maur, the protector of Dupont des Jumeaux, requesting the approval of the royal minister, the Comte de Vergennes, for this new institution. It is reproduced, along with Vergennes's response warning the association's members not to abuse his permission, in *Archives historiques du Département de la Gironde*, 24:510–11.

114. In addition to Epée and Champion de Cicé, the membership of the Société Philanthropique during the 1780s included Franklin, Necker, Chastellux, Talleyrand, La Rochefoucauld, Lavoisier, Elie de Beaumont, Bailly, Dupont de Nemours, La Fayette, and Valentin Haüy, the founder of a school for the blind and a former student of Epée's, whose *Essai sur l'éducation des aveugles* included a long tribute to his former teacher (see 101–3). On the membership and activities of the Parisian Société Philanthropique, including its active support for Haüy's school for the blind, see Duprat, *"Pour l'amour de l'humanité,"* 65–108.

115. To understand this relationship, see the papers of the Musée de Bordeaux in the Bibliothèque Municipale de Bordeaux, esp. MS 829 (I-II), fol. 520 and fols. 531–32: Dumas to Sicard (August 1789) and Sicard to the officers of the Musée (April 1790). See also MS 829 (X): Lemsle's "Discours du 15 septembre 1786," which included a tribute to Sicard, and Sicard's "Notice pour la séance publique du jeudi 6 mars 1788." On the founding of Sicard's school, see also Cornié, *Etude sur l'Institution nationale des sourdes-muettes [sic] de Bordeaux*; and Berthier, *L'Abbé Sicard*.

116. On the relative popularity of Court de Gébelin in Bordeaux, as evidenced by the number of subscribers for his work from the city and its environs, see Faivre, "Antoine Court de Gébelin," 45.

117. See the *Recueil des ouvrages du Musée de Bordeaux, dédié à la Reine: année 1787*, to which Sicard, the secretary of the Musée in that year, contributed the closing address (344–65), as well as two essays: "Exposition de la méthode tachygraphique, ou l'art d'écrire aussi vite que la parole" (97–111) and "Essai sur l'art d'instruire les sourds et muets de naissance" (27–61), republished in 1789 as *Mémoire sur l'art d'instruire les sourds et muets de naissance, extrait du recueil du Musée*. See also Bachaumont's description of Sicard's public session of August 1788 at the Musée de Bordeaux (*Mémoires secrets* 33 [October 17, 1788]: 139), and the printed *Exercices que soutiendront les sourds et muets de naissance, les 12 et 15 septembre 1789, dans la salle du Musée de Bordeaux* in AN, F15 2584.

118. In *"Pour l'amour de l'humanité,"* Catherine Duprat emphasizes the close connection between the Musée de Paris and the Société Philanthropique of Paris (founded in 1780), both of which were outgrowths of liberal Masonic groups of the 1770s. It appears that many of the more prominent associates of the Musée de Bordeaux—including Epée, Garat, La Harpe, and Lacépède—maintained strong ties to both organizations. See, for example, La Harpe's letter of January 24, 1785 (reproduced in *Correspondance inédite de Jean-François de La Harpe*) thanking Sicard for the notice of a meeting of the Musée de Bordeaux. Furthermore, according to the *Gazette nationale, ou le Moniteur universel* (April 22, 1790), during the 1780s Sicard himself became a corresponding member of the *musées* of both Paris and Toulouse, as well as the Académie de Bordeaux and the Société Royale et Littéraire de Bayeux.

119. In addition to noting the school's opening in issues on both October 28 and December 27, 1787, the editors of the *Journal de Paris* published a long poem dedicated to Sicard on the first page of no. 328 of the newspaper

on November 24, 1787, concluding: "They [his deaf pupils] receive from their great Master, like a second Creator, a new sense, a new being. Returned to society by the efforts of his genius, they bless his virtues. And thanks to his learned magic, our Religion and the Fatherland count a few more men."

120. On this contest, see, in the Archives de l'Institut, the records of the meetings of the Académie des Inscriptions (A70–71) for June 1787, June 1789, and August 1789. L'Aulnaye's winning essay was printed as *De la Saltation théâtrale, ou Recherches sur l'origine, les progrès et les effets de la pantomime chez les anciens* in 1790. Just several years earlier, in 1785, Antoine Chrysostome Quatremère de Quincy had won the Prix Caylus for a similar essay in which he had demonstrated the relationship between the origin of language and the origin of architecture.

121. Compare L'Aulnaye's two ms. responses (preserved in the Archives de l'Institut, Académie des Inscriptions, carton D75 [responses to the Prix Caylus]: 1787, no. 2 and 1789, no. 3), with the other three received in 1787 and the other four received in 1789. Five additional people (a professor in Utrecht, another *avocat au Parlement*, a officer of the cavalry in Paris, a *conseiller* at the Cour des Comptes in Montpellier, and someone who referred to herself simply as "a woman") constituted the other respondents.

122. L'Aulnaye, *De la Saltation*, 84 and viii, respectively.

123. Ibid., xc.

124. See *Citizens without Sovereignty*, esp. 42, in which Daniel Gordon makes a strong case for the position that, in eighteenth-century France, the development of intellectual sociability was based on the privatization and depoliticization of *logos* and can not be linked to a desire to become self-governing.

125. See Habermas, *The Structural Transformation of the Public Sphere*. For a brief comparative summary of Habermas's and Furet's different approaches to this question, see Chartier, *The Cultural Origins of the French Revolution*, 16–17.

126. Marat, "Dénaturer les noms des choses," in *Les Chaînes de l'esclavage*, 183–85. Marat first published this attack on tyrannical government and, more specifically, the British regime of Lord North, in English in 1774. He then republished it in France in early September 1792. Central to his argument was the idea that despotism imposes itself by words that "denature" things and the struggle against despotism requires fighting for a language free of abuse.

127. See Chap. 1.

128. For evidence of the importance to debates about language of a vocabulary borrowed from politics and law, see, for example, the following comment in the *Journal de la langue française* penned by Antoine-Léonard Thomas: "In an empire [language] that often lacks positive laws, a vigilant police is necessary to supply them. You [the editor of the *Journal*] exercise this jurisdiction" (August 15, 1785).

129. See Carra, *De M. de Calonne tout entier*, 30–31. This passage is also quoted in translation in Crow, *Painters and Public Life in Eighteenth-*

Century Paris, 222. Robert Darnton has argued that Carra's antigovernment *libelles* were motivated almost entirely by personal venom and nihilism and "hardly contained any abstract ideas at all" (*The Literary Underground,* 34). However, in his own *Système de la raison, ou le Prophète philosophe,* first printed in London in 1773, Carra had already proposed that one of the critical steps in the story of the progress and decline of human morality had been the "confusion of all the arguments concerning human morals, good politics, and good sense in a gibberish of ordinances, rulings, and sentences [and] a maze of words through which only the rogues know the secret and the path" (76). And this quote of 1788 shows Carra engaged in a new brand of political writing in which such typical Enlightenment theories about the effects of the *abus des mots* are used toward highly partisan and personal ends. For a similar and contemporaneous attack on the Assembly of Notables for having deliberately invoked "words empty of any meaning, that each person will be able to explain according to his own interests and passions," see Jean Pierre Papon's *Histoire du gouvernement françois, depuis l'Assemblée des Notables,* 23.

CHAPTER 4

1. Talleyrand, *Rapport sur l'instruction publique,* 98, 94. Talleyrand noted that he had prepared this report on behalf of the Committee on the Constitution with the help of many of the leading scientists and thinkers of the moment, including La Harpe, Lavoisier, and Condorcet (see the *Memoirs of the Prince de Talleyrand,* 1:102–3). This was the first and only official plan for a national system of education offered during the National Assembly.

2. Ibid., 100.

3. Ibid., 100–101.

4. Ibid., 98.

5. See Gorjy, *Ann'quin Bredouille,* vol. 5.

6. On the *prise de parole* and the celebration of oration at the beginning of the Revolution, see Jean-Claude Bonnet, "La Sainte masure, sanctuaire de la parole fondatrice," in *La Carmagnole des Muses,* ed. Bonnet, 185–222. On the multiplicity of printed media (journals, pamphlets, prints, songs, etc.) through which the revolutionary message was transmitted, see Darnton and Roche, eds., *Revolution in Print.*

7. On ideas of rupture and regeneration in the pamphlet literature of 1789, see de Baecque, "L'Homme nouveau est arrivé: la 'régénération' du Français en 1789." On the historical sensibility of the revolutionaries more generally, see Baczko, *Utopian Lights,* esp. 322–24; and Diego Venturino, "La Naissance de l'Ancien Régime," in *The Political Culture of the French Revolution,* ed. Lucas, 11–40.

8. See Article 11 of the "Declaration of the Rights of Man and of the Citizen" (adopted August 26, 1789), reprinted in translation in *The Old Regime and the French Revolution,* ed. Baker, 237–39.

9. Anon., *Le Sourd du Palais-Royal,* 6.

10. On the links between Christian and revolutionary notions of regen-

eration at the beginning of the Revolution, see Mona Ozouf, "Regeneration," in *A Critical Dictionary of the French Revolution*, ed. Furet and
Ozouf, esp. 782; and de Baecque, *The Body Politic*, 131–56.

11. For the above quotations, see, respectively, the comments of Mathieu de Montmorency, *Le Courier de Provence*, no. 22 (August 1, 1789): 15,
cited in Gauchet, *La Révolution des droits de l'homme*, 50; Duc de Lévis,
Essai sur la Déclaration des droits de l'homme en société (Paris, 1789), cited
in *L'An 1 des droits de l'homme*, ed. de Baecque et al., 24; and the comments of Rabaut Saint-Etienne, in *Archives parlementaires*, ed. Mavidal
and Laurent 8:453 (August 18, 1789). Keith Baker, in *Inventing the French
Revolution*, 272, points out that similar concerns about the need to begin by
"fixing" the language emerged as soon as discussion of "fixing" the constitution began in late August and early September of 1789.

12. Furet and Halévi, *La Monarchie républicaine*, esp. 82.

13. See, for example, the comments to this effect of A. F. Pison du Gal-
land, whose *Déclaration des droits de l'homme et du citoyen* (Paris, 1789) is
cited in *L'An 1 des droits de l'homme*, ed. de Baecque et al., 24.

14. Sieyès, *Qu'est-ce que le Tiers Etat?*, 31–32. On this text as itself a
rhetorical act and the basis for much subsequent revolutionary discourse,
see Sewell, *A Rhetoric of Bourgeois Revolution*; and Baker, "Sieyès and the
Creation of the French Revolutionary Discourse."

15. Anon., *A l'Assemblée nationale. Mémoire sur l'éducation de la jeunesse par une méthode d'enseignement tout à fait nouvelle*, 27.

16. See Lacroix, ed., *Actes de la Commune de Paris pendant la Révolution*, 3:252, 312.

17. Brousse-Desfaucherets, *Compte rendu à l'Assemblée générale des
représentants de la Commune de Paris, le 8 février 1790*, 24.

18. *Adresse des représentants de la Commune de Paris à l'Assemblée
nationale, sur la formation d'un établissement national en faveur des
sourds et muets*, 1–2, 4.

19. AN, C54, no. 535: letter from Marc-Etienne Quatremère fils to the
National Assembly (February 21, 1790).

20. See Mavidal and Laurent, eds., *Archives parlementaires*, 11:664.

21. *Journal de la municipalité et des districts* (February 26, 1790), quoted
in Lacroix, ed., *Actes de la Commune de Paris*, 4:187.

22. Epée had consciously distanced himself from the political struggles
of the last year, going as far as writing to the *Journal de Paris* (no. 201 [July
20, 1789]: 906) to say that he had never, at any time, had any connection to
the deaf person (i.e., Pierre Desloges) who had recently published a letter
addressed to the deputies of the Estates-General.

23. On the Abbé Fauchet and the religious and political principles that
he advocated in the context of the Cercle Social between 1790 and May
1791, see Marcel Dorigny, "Le Cercle social ou les écrivains au cirque," in
La Carmagnole des Muses, ed. Bonnet, 49–66; and, esp., Kates, *The Cercle
Social, the Girondins and the French Revolution*.

24. Fauchet, *Oraison funèbre de Charles-Michel de l'Epée*, 30–31. On
the very positive Jansenist response to this view of Epée, see the *Nouvelles*

ecclésiastiques, ou Mémoires pour servir à l'histoire de la Constitution Unigenitus (May 15, 1790): 77–80 and (May 22, 1790): 81–84.

25. Ibid., 32–34.

26. Dorigny, "Le Cercle social," in La Carmagnole des Muses, ed. Bonnet, 58–59. See also the advertisement for the Cercle Social's Polyglotte, ou traduction de la constitution françoise, dans les langues les plus usitées de l'Europe in La Chronique du mois (February 1792): 111.

27. Fauchet, Oraison funèbre de Charles-Michel de l'Epée, 38.

28. On the other candidates for the position and the choice of Sicard, see Karacostas, "L'Institution nationale des sourds-muets de Paris de 1790 à 1800."

29. AN, AA12, pièce 12: letter from Champion de Cicé to Bailly (March 19, 1790).

30. AN, AA12, pièce 15: letter from Bailly, on behalf of the committee, to an anonymous recipient, n.d.

31. The prize committee was made up of the following members: Barthélémy and de Keralio of the Académie des Inscriptions et Belles-Lettres; La Harpe and Marmontel of the Académie Française; Condorcet and Le Roy of the Académie des Sciences; La Rochefoucauld-Liancourt, La Fayette, and Champion de Villeneuve of the Commune de Paris; and Bailly, Brousse-Desfaucherets, and Champion de Cicé (Lacroix, ed., Actes de la Commune de Paris, 5:15–16).

32. On the new coinages and neologisms of the Revolution, see Brunot, Histoire de la langue française, vol. 9, part 2; Frey, Les Transformations du vocabulaire français; and Walter, Des Mots sans-culottes.

33. In several important articles, Philippe Roger has drawn attention to the polemical dictionaries of the right during the early years of the Revolution; see "Le Débat sur la langue révolutionnaire," in La Carmagnole des Muses, ed. Bonnet, 157–84, "The French Revolution as Logomachy," and "Le Dictionnaire contre la Révolution." Some of these dictionaries are also discussed in the following: Brigitte Schlieben-Lange, "Die Wörterbucher in der Französischen Revolution (1789–1814)," in Handbuch politisch-sozialer Grundbegriffe in Frankreich, vol. 1/2:149–89; Geffroy, "Les Dictionnaires socio-politiques, 1770–1820"; Equipe "18ème et Révolution," Dictionnaire des usages socio-politiques (1770–1815), vol. 3, Dictionnaires, normes, usages, 7–46; Branca-Rosoff and Lozachmeur, "Buée: des mots contre les mots"; and Desmet et al., "What are Words Worth?"

34. Jacques Godechot, in The Counter-Revolution: Doctrine and Action, identifies hostility to the "abstract" constructions of the philosophes as a critical element of counterrevolutionary ideology, from Cazalès to Rivarol to Edmund Burke. On the Burkean argument against the use of words on paper to legislate, see also Steven Blakemore's very interesting Burke and the Fall of Language.

35. See, for example, the long philosophical discussion about why the public was, at present, more likely to misunderstand the terms of "our moral and political sciences" than those of mathematics in Dictionnaire raisonné de plusieurs mots qui sont dans la bouche de tout le monde, 10–15.

36. Rivarol, *Petit dictionnaire des grands hommes et des grandes choses qui ont rapport à la Révolution, composé par une Société d'Aristocrates . . . pour servir de suite à l'histoire du brigandage du nouveau royaume de France* (Paris, 1790), reprinted as *Petit dictionnaire des grands hommes de la Révolution*, ed. Grell, preface, 34.

37. Gallais, "Avant-Propos," in *Extrait d'un dictionnaire inutile*.

38. "Avertissement" in *Nouveau dictionnaire françois, à l'usage de toutes les municipalités, les milices nationales, et de tous les patriotes*. On this subject, see also the *Supplément au Nouveau dictionnaire françois* of 1790.

39. See, for example, the following anonymous pamphlets: *L'Abus des mots de nos seigneurs de l'assemblée des Etats généraux, restaurateur de la nation française* (1790); *Avis intéressant au peuple sur l'abus des mots aristocrate et démocrate qu'on propose de changer* (1790); *L'Abus des mots* (1790 or 1791); and *Dictionnaire laconique, véridique et impartial, ou Etrennes aux démagogues sur la Révolution française, par un citoyen inactif, ni enrôlé, ni soldé, mais ami de tout le monde pour de l'argent* (1791). The anonymous author of *Synonymes nouveaux* (late 1789 or 1790) made the same point by including such "new" definitions as "Liberty: horrible slavery for honest people" and "Patriot: in its exact sense, it is the enemy of order, of public good, of all legitimate authority."

40. See, for example, Pierre-Nicolas Chantreau, *Dictionnaire national et anecdotique, pour servir à l'intelligence des mots dont notre langue s'est enrichie depuis la Révolution* (1790); Q. V. Tennesson, *Vocabulaire des municipalités et des corps administratifs, ouvrage utile et commode à tous ceux qui voudront apprendre ce qu'ils sont aujourd'hui* (1790); and P. N. Gautier, *Dictionnaire de la constitution et du gouvernement françois, contenant la dénomination de tous les nouveaux officiers publics, la définition des nouveaux termes les plus usités* (1791). See also the many brochures aimed at defining one or two "misunderstood" terms, such as Condorcet's *Idées sur le despotisme, à l'usage de ceux qui prononcent ce mot sans l'entendre* (1789), reprinted in *Oeuvres de Condorcet*, 9:147–73; or Charles-Philippe-Toussaint Guiraudet's *Qu'est-ce que la nation et qu'est-ce que la France?* (1789).

41. Denunciations of the *abus des mots* can be found in journals ranging from *Révolutions de Paris* (November 7–14, 1789) to *L'Ami des patriotes* (December 4, 1790) to the *Mercure national et Révolutions de l'Europe* (December 14, 1790). On the question of the *abus des mots* in the linguistic debates of the revolutionary left, see Barny, "Les Mots et les choses chez les hommes de la Révolution française"; Soboul, "Equality: On the Power and Danger of Words"; Ricken, "Réflexions du XVIIIe siècle sur 'l'abus des mots'"; Rolf Reichardt, "Einleitung," in *Handbuch politisch-sozialer Grundbegriffe in Frankreich*, vol. 1/2:40–50; Guilhaumou, *La Langue politique et la Révolution française*, 51–69, 72–77; and Schlieben-Lange, *Idéologie, révolution et uniformité de la langue*, 72–87.

42. In the first days of 1790, Fontanes's *Le Modérateur*—which had already, in late 1789, pointed to the connection between crimes and inade-

quate definitions (see, for example, "Sur le mot Aristocratie" in no. 30 [October 30, 1789]: 117)—began running a regular feature with the title "Nouveau dictionnaire politique," which provoked its own backlash [see Plate 7]. La Harpe tried that same winter to offer explanations of the "proper senses" of political terms in articles such as "Diatribe sur les mots Délation, Dénonciation, Accusation," *Mercure de France* (December 19, 1789): 95–111. Morellet first referred to himself as "Le Définisseur" in an article entitled "Observations sur le mot souverain," *Mercure de France* (September 18, 1790): 235–40, which was written in response to an article by Brissot in *Le Patriot françois* (August 10, 1790): 2–4.

43. La Harpe, "Diatribe sur les mots Délation, Dénonciation, Accusation," 100.

44. On the genesis of the first revolutionary clubs and their connection to Old Regime institutions of sociability, see Kennedy, *The Jacobin Clubs in the French Revolution: The Early Years*. More generally, on the function of revolutionary *sociétés* and clubs as sources of consensus, see Singer, *Society, Theory, and the French Revolution*, 189–94, as well as Furet, *Interpreting the French Revolution*.

45. Timothy Tackett argues in *Becoming a Revolutionary* that only a very small percentage of deputies to the National Assembly can actually be said to have participated in the Republic of Letters or to have arrived in Paris with an abstract, philosophical agenda. Undoubtedly, this is true. However, it is also clear that the impact and influence of those deputies who can be characterized as having belonged to the circles of the *philosophes* or as maintaining ties to the Old Regime world of academies and literary societies was greater than their statistical presence—not just in the first assembly but in each subsequent one as well.

46. See, for example, *La Bouche de fer*, 2ème année, no. 1 (October 1790): 6–7, in which Bonneville pointed out the need to begin all political discussions by eliminating equivocations and defining terms. Bonneville fleshed out these ideas in his very successful *De l'Esprit des religions* (Imprimerie du Cercle Social, 1791 and 1792), a work with many similarities to Court de Gébelin's *Le Monde primitif* insofar as it made the decomposition of modern language and the discovery of the original, primitive idiom the key to social regeneration and harmony in the future. On Bonneville's linguistic philosophy, see Raymond Monnier, "Nicolas de Bonneville, tribun du peuple," in *Langages de la Révolution*, ed. Geffroy, 383–95.

47. On the Société de 1789, see Challamel, *Les Clubs contre-révolutionnaires*, 391–443; Baker, "Politics and Social Science in Eighteenth-Century France: The Société de 1789"; Moravia, *Il Tramonto dell'Illuminismo*, 152–57; Head, "The Origins of 'La Science Sociale' in France, 1770–1800"; Olsen, "Enlightenment and the French Revolution: The Membership and Political Language of the Société de 1789"; Olsen, "A Failure of Enlightened Politics in the French Revolution: The Société de 1789"; and Tackett, *Becoming a Revolutionary*, 279–89.

48. Cérutti, *Etrennes au public*, which included his *Prospectus d'un dictionnaire d'exagération*, 29–56. In his catalogue of the expressions that

characterized the new vogue for exaggeration, Cérutti included excessive use of ethereal terms (e.g., *nature, liberté, loix fondamentales, fluide universelle*), collective terms (e.g., *un nombre infini, le genre humain*), or contradictory terms (e.g., *bourgeois insolent* for *citoyen courageux*); associations of living men with immortal ones; disproportion between a thing and a word or a subject and a tone; learned citations and pompous illusions; metaphors; exclamations; and excessive gesticulation. On Cérutti, see de Baecque, "La Guerre des éloquences: Joseph-Antoine Cérutti et les brochures révolutionnaires."

49. M. de Shersaint, "Assemblée nationale. Observations sur le décret constitutif de l'armée de mer," *Journal de la Société de 1789*, no. 7 (July 17, 1790): 25.

50. Chevalier de Pange, "Art social. Sur le crime de lèze-nation," *Journal de la Société de 1789*, no. 3 (June 19, 1790): 18–19. The problem of the abuse of the old term, *lèse-majesté*, had already been pointed out by both Montesquieu and Voltaire.

51. Grouville, "Assemblée nationale. Sur la délégation de l'exercice du droit de la guerre et de la paix," *Journal de la Société de 1789*, no. 1 (June 5, 1790): 49.

52. Sicard, *Mémoire sur l'art d'instruire les sourds et muets de naissance, extrait du recueil du Musée*, 7.

53. See Chap. 3 on this controversy.

54. Sicard, *Second Mémoire sur l'art d'instruire les sourds et muets de naissance*, 13, 17.

55. For example, in an article entitled "Sur l'influence des mots et le pouvoir de l'usage" in the *Mercure national et Révolutions de l'Europe* (December 14, 1790), the author (probably the grammarian Antoine Tournon of the Musée de Paris) commented: "By syntax alone we can judge the virtues and vices, the liberty and slavery of nations." See Jacques Guilhaumou, "Antoine Tournon et la grammaire des sans-culottes (1794): syntaxe et acte de parole à l'époque de la révolution française," in "Langue et Révolution," ed. Guilhaumou and Schlieben-Lange (special issue, LINX [1987]): 42–76.

56. Sicard, *Second Mémoire*, 16.

57. Abbé Tessier, reviews of Sicard's two memoirs, *Journal des sçavans* (May 1790): 298, 296.

58. On the institution's dire financial situation at the beginning of the Revolution, as well as Sicard's efforts to increase funding for the school, see Karacostas, "L'Institution nationale des sourds-muets," 39; and Weiner, *The Citizen-Patient in Revolutionary and Imperial Paris*, esp. 232–39.

59. On this point, see Rosenfeld, "From Citizens to *Hommes de la Nature*."

60. For the chronology of events regarding Sicard's dealings with the Committee on Mendicity, see Bloch and Tuetey, eds., *Procès-verbaux et rapports du Comité de mendicité de la Constituante, 1789–1791*.

61. AN, F15 2584: "Adresse à l'Assemblée nationale par Jean Massieu" (August 24, 1790).

62. Mavidal and Laurent, eds., *Archives parlementaires*, 18:249.

63. On Jean Massieu's autobiography, which he wrote after the turn of the century, see Chap. 6. Based on this source, we know that he was born in 1772 in the Gironde to a family with many deaf-mute members. At age thirteen, Massieu entered Sicard's school for the deaf in Bordeaux, and four years later, at the end of 1789, he moved with Sicard to Paris, where the younger man continued to be Sicard's star pupil and eventually became a *répétiteur* for younger students at the Institution des Sourds-Muets de Paris.

64. See the "Vers de Jean Massieu, sourd et muet de naissance, à MM. les francs-maçons de la loge françoise, élue écossoise, de Bordeaux, qui le font élever, à leur frais, à l'école des sourds et muets de Paris, par M. Ferlus, Doctrinaire, interprète de J. Massieu," *Journal encyclopédique* (September 1790): 275–76. Ferlus, a professor of rhetoric at the royal college of Guyenne, as well as a member of the Musée de Bordeaux and a Freemason, had already published an "Epître à M. l'Abbé Sicard" in the *Journal encyclopédique* (February 1789): 103–9.

65. Prieur, *Rapport sur l'établissement des sourds-muets, fait à l'Assemblée nationale*, 3.

66. Reis-Lacroix, "Lettre aux rédacteurs sur les sourds-muets," *La Feuille villageoise*, seconde année, no. 2 (October 6, 1791): 46. This letter was followed by a "note from the editors" praising Sicard (47–48). On *La Feuille villageoise* and its aims and distribution, see Didier, "Feuilles citadines et villageoises," in *Ecrire la Révolution*, 89–101; and Edelstein, *La Feuille villageoise: communication et modernisation*.

67. *Journal de Paris* (May 14, 1791): 5.

68. "Prospectus," *Réglements pour l'établissement des sourds-muets et des aveugles-nés*, 1.

69. *Prospectus de l'Ecole nationale des sourds-muets de Bordeaux*, 5.

70. On the importance that the editors of *La Feuille villageoise* placed on providing definitions of the language of the constitution, see the prospectus (no. 1 [1790]: 1–15) and the "lexicons" that became a regular feature of this journal. On Domergue's goals in founding a new version of the *Journal de la langue française* in January 1791, see Dougnac, "F.-U. Domergue, le 'Journal de la langue française' et la néologie lexicale (1784–1795)," esp. 101. Before moving to Paris in 1790, Domergue had, as we have seen, published a journal under the same title in Lyon (September 1784–May 1788) with the purpose of instructing a provincial bourgeois readership in proper French.

71. "Néologie," *Journal de la langue française* 3 (July 30, 1791): 161.

72. AN, F15 2584: note signed Massieu, n.d.

73. Programs such as the *Second Exercice public qui soutiendront les sourds-muets de naissance de l'école de Bordeaux* (1791) reveal that pupils were trained to recite pat answers to questions such as "What is law and what is a citizen?"

74. In order to demonstrate his students' ability to master printing technology, Sicard had arranged for the *Journal des sçavans*, the *Journal d'agriculture*, and Prieur's report itself to be printed at his school (Prieur, *Rapport*, 4).

75. On the guidance of both Talleyrand and Sicard in the composition of this text, see AN, F15 2584: note from Talleyrand (June 18, 1791) claiming, "The report of Monsieur Prieur appears to me to be excellent," and letters from Sicard to Prieur (June 26 and 29, 1791) regarding Sicard's instructions.

76. Prieur, *Rapport*, 3–4.

77. See the *Loi relative à M. Abbé de l'Epée, et à son établissement en faveur des sourds et muets* (signed by M.-L.-F. Duport-Dutertre for the king, Paris, July 29, 1791). This celebration of the deceased educator of the deaf continued nine days later when the deaf sculptor Claude-André Deseine presented the National Assembly with a bust of Epée originally made in 1786.

78. Mavidal and Laurent, eds., *Archives parlementaires*, 28:491–92. At the end of this session the president of the National Assembly, Salomon de La Saugerie, recommended that both Sicard's speech and his own response be printed. It appears, however, that neither text was ever published in full except in the *Journal de la langue française* ("Discours prononcé à l'Assemblée nationale, relativement au décret en faveur de l'institution des sourds-muets par l'Abbé Sicard, et réponse du président" [August 1, 1791]: 211–14).

79. On Enlightenment attitudes toward the blind, see Paulson, *Enlightenment, Romanticism and the Blind in France*. On the fate of the blind during the Revolution, see Weiner, *The Citizen-Patient*.

80. On the briefly reconstituted Société Nationale des Neuf Soeurs, see Amiable, *Une Loge maçonnique d'avant 1789* (where the dates of this society are given as January 1790 to August 1792); and Lacroix, ed., *Actes de la Commune de Paris*, 2d series, 5:397–99 and 6:184,187–190 (where the given dates are March or April 1790 to December 1791). On the intellectual concerns of this society, see the monthly *Tribut de la Société nationale des neuf soeurs* (July–December 1791).

81. *Tribut de la Société nationale des neuf soeurs* (August 1791): 142. Sicard frequently displayed his students at the Société Nationale des Neuf Soeurs during 1790–91, much as he had once done at the Musée de Bordeaux, and clearly the Société saw Sicard's work as fully compatible with its goals. For example, a special celebration of October 1790 in honor of Benjamin Franklin included a group of Sicard's students writing a tribute to Franklin from sign dictation, as well as the reading of several poems, musical performances, experiments with electricity, and natural history displays (288–91).

82. Sicard, "Exposé succinct de quelques nouveaux procédés, pour faciliter la communication de la pensée entre les sourds-muets et les aveugles-nés," *Tribut de la Société nationale des neuf soeurs* (October 1791): 288.

83. Massieu, *Rapport sur l'établissement des aveugles-nés, et sur sa réunion à celui des sourds-muets*, 10.

84. Ibid., 12.

85. For a brief discussion of Sicard's school as a utopian institution or "ideal space" during the Revolution, see Karacostas, "De l'Ombre à la lumière: les sourds et la Révolution française," in *Le Pouvoir des signes*, 67.

86. Massieu, *Rapport*, 12.

87. AN, F17 1004B, dossier 485: "Adresse des administrateurs du département de la Gironde à l'Assemblée nationale" (December 13, 1791).

88. For example, the Abbé Grégoire declared in September 1792 that "this word king . . . is still a talisman whose magical force can serve to stupefy many men" (*Archives parlementaires*, 52:81, cited in Hunt, *Politics, Culture, and Class*, 89). The royalist Abbé Adrien-Quentin Buée defined the revolutionary buzzword *fanatisme* in a similar fashion: "Cabalistic term. Those who know how to remember this word produce astonishing effects. With this word, they make ignorant people, learned people, peasants and important people tremble. . . . At this word, all the furies catch fire and surpass those of fanaticism itself" (see his *Nouveau dictionnaire, pour servir à l'intelligence des termes mis en vogue par la Révolution*, 51).

89. See Barny, "Les Mots et les choses," 103, 105.

90. Grégoire, *Convention nationale. Instruction publique. Rapport sur la nécessité et les moyens d'anéantir les patois et d'universaliser l'usage de la langue française*, reprinted in de Certeau et al., *Une Politique de la langue*, 304. In August 1790, in his own survey of speakers of patois, Grégoire had inquired of his respondents whether their particular dialect or patois contained "many words for explaining nuances in ideas and intellectual subjects" (12).

91. Voltaire, "Homme" [1771], in *Oeuvres complètes*, 19:384.

92. The Abbé Jean Saint-Sernin, Sicard's successor as director of France's second school for the deaf in Bordeaux, argued with great seriousness for the validity of this analogy in front of the Convention's Committee of Public Instruction in an effort to convince its members of the importance of his practical grammar of the language of signs for all French students. See AN, F17 1004B, dossier 485: letter from Saint-Sernin to the Committee of Public Instruction (March 17, 1793) and Saint-Sernin's "Observations à faire au Comité d'instruction publique sur la démande du département de la Gironde à la Convention, concernant l'établissement de l'Ecole des Sourds-Muets de Bordeaux" (Paris, March 27, 1793).

93. AN, F17 1010C, no. 3031: letter to the Committee of Public Instruction (21 floréal an II), quoted in Sebastiano Vecchio, "Langue nationale et grammaire pendant la Révolution: la France et l'Italie," in *Les Idéologues*, ed. Busse and Trabant, 374.

94. *La Feuille villageoise*, seconde année, no. 3 (October 13, 1791): 51.

95. Talleyrand-Périgord, *Rapport sur l'instruction publique*, 95. On elite attitudes toward patois more generally, see Bell, "Lingua Populi, Lingua Dei: Language, Religion, and the Origins of French Revolutionary Nationalism."

96. Condorcet, "Second mémoire," in *Ecrits sur l'instruction publique*, vol. 1, *Cinq mémoires sur l'instruction publique*, 91. Condorcet's five memoirs were first printed between January and September of 1791 in a journal he edited called *Bibliothèque de l'homme public, ou Analyse raisonnée des principaux ouvrages français et étrangers*.

97. On Morellet's efforts in 1793 to save the manuscript of the new dictionary of the Académie Française, see the *Mémoires de l'Abbé Morellet*, 335.

98. It is notoriously difficult to paint any uniform portrait of the social, intellectual, or economic background of the Girondins or even to determine who belonged to this nebulous political group. It is clear, however, that many Girondin sympathizers (including Brissot himself) identified with a philosophical tradition that included Court de Gébelin as well as Condillac and Condorcet. Furthermore, according to Alan Forrest in *Society and Politics in Revolutionary Bordeaux*, many leaders of the Girondin faction emerged out of the milieu of the Musée de Bordeaux.

99. On the Société des Amateurs de la Langue Française, see Busse and Dougnac, *François-Urbain Domergue*. See also Dougnac, "Les Sociétés linguistiques fondées par F.-U. Domergue à Paris de 1791 à 1811," in *Les Idéologues*, ed. Busse and Trabant, 299–322; Dougnac, "F. U. Domergue"; and Guilhaumou, *La Langue politique*, 69–80. The prospectus was printed in the *Journal de la langue française* 3 (July 30, 1791): 162.

100. This text was printed in the *Journal de la langue française* 4 (November 5, 1791): 122. The location of the Musée Gébelin was not accidental, as Domergue offered the following tribute to Court de Gébelin in this same speech: "[A]nd you, who sanctifies these walls by your habitual presence and makes this place the sanctuary of the arts, where all the hieroglyphs of the primitive language are still attached, astonishing Gébelin . . . you will be the guide of your living collaborators" (127).

101. Ibid., 122.

102. For a list of members, see Dougnac, "Les Sociétés linguistiques," in *Les Idéologues*, ed. Busse and Trabant, 308–11; and Dougnac and Busse, *François-Urbain Domergue*, 203–7.

103. Rabaut Saint-Etienne, Moreau de Saint-Méry, Cubières, Cloots, Boinvilliers, Carra, and Tournon are among the members of this society who can be identified as once having been members of the Musée de Paris. Many more, including Mercier, François de Neufchâteau, and Condorcet, had been members of the Loge des Neuf Soeurs in the 1770s.

104. *Journal de la langue française* 1 (February 19, 1791): 253–58.

105. See the *Journal de la langue française* 3 (July 2, 1791): 90–96; (July 23, 1791): 125–32; and (August 1, 1791): 211–14.

106. Ibid., 96.

107. The *Journal de la langue française*, which regularly reported on the discussions that took place in the Société des Amateurs de la Langue Française, devoted numerous pages to this debate in November and December 1791. See the following issues in vol. 4: (November 26, 1791): 207–8; (December 2, 1791): 231–39; (December 10, 1791): 241–53; and (December 17, 1791): 269–72.

108. Ibid., 232.

109. Ibid., 244.

110. Ibid., 248.

111. Ibid., 244.

112. Domergue, insisting on the "middle ground" position for himself, sketched these two positions in response to an earlier letter to the *Journal*

from Duhamel on means of rectifying the "propriety of terms." Domergue explained: "If grammarians wanted to reduce everything to analogies, etymology, reason, without regard for usage, soon there would no longer be any general will; individual wills would bring about anarchy in their opposition to one another; [and] we would finish by proscribing the style of Racine and Fénélon like a grammatical aristocracy. . . . The language has its aristocrats and its demagogues: the former want everyone to obey blindly the *ancien régime*, usage; the others want immortal reason, without regard for usage, to dictate all the laws of language to mortals. But me, taking the middle ground where one always finds wisdom, I desire reform of all that is susceptible to being reformed" (vol. 1 [February 19, 1791]: 271 and [February 26, 1791]: 312).

113. *Journal de la langue française* 4 (December 10, 1791): 253.

114. See respectively Dejob, *L'Instruction publique en France*, 420; and Mavidal and Laurent, eds., *Archives parlementaires*, 43:204 (May 10, 1792).

115. Reprinted as "Discours de M. l'Abbé Sicard, instituteur des sourds-muets à Messieurs du Tribunal de police correctionnel," *Tribut de la Société nationale des neuf soeurs* (July 14, 1792): 60–64; and as "Variétés," *Gazette des tribunaux et mémorial des corps administratifs et municipaux* 5 (July 1–October 14, 1792): 155–58. The *Gazette des tribunaux*, which was founded and edited by Louis-François Jauffret, a naturalist, educator, and Sicard's colleague in both the Société Nationale des Neuf Soeurs and the Société des Amateurs de la Langue Française, also provided commentary on Massieu's testimony and Sicard's response (see vol. 5, 59–60). For further discussion of this subject, see the *Journal encyclopédique* 6, no. 22 (August 1792): 246–49.

116. On Sicard's arrest by the Commune, see "Relation authentique du Citoyen Sicard, Instituteur des Sourds et Muets, sur les dangers qu'il a courus les 2 et 3 septembre 1792, à un de ses amis," in *Extrait de différens journaux, concernant les forfaits des premiers jours de septembre 1792*, esp. 6–7. Massieu's petition to the Legislative Assembly, in which he claimed that Sicard had taught his pupils to love the Revolution and its principles and called for Sicard's release, is reproduced in Mavidal and Laurent, eds., *Archives parlementaires*, 49:150 (August 31, 1792). For the National Assembly's decrees protecting Sicard (September 4, 1792) and honoring the watchmaker Monnot who saved Sicard's life (September 2, 1792), see AN, F7 4775 18, dossier 3 on Sicard.

117. AN, F7 4775 18, dossier 3. For Sicard's version of events surrounding his interrogation by the Revolutionary Surveillance and Safety Committee of the Arsenal Section in September 1793, including his denunciation of his staunchly revolutionary colleague, Valentin Haüy, for having instigated the Abbé's second arrest, see Sicard's deposition of 27 floréal an III (BHVP, MS 1213, fol. 456).

118. Guiraudet, *Explication de quelques mots importants de notre langue politique*, viii. This text actually concerns a single term, *loi*.

119. See, among other articles in *La Chronique du mois*: Bonneville, "De

la recherche de la vérité" (August 1792): 3–15; and Brissot, "Sur le tems" (March 1793): 15–18 and "De quelques erreurs dans les idées et dans les mots relatifs à la révolution française" (March 1793): 27–39.

120. Duhamel, *Essai analytique sur cette question*, 18. For Duhamel's biography, see AN, F17 1344 3, no. 89: "Réponse du C. Duhamel, professeur à l'Ecole Centrale du Panthéon aux questions adressés à chaque professeur des écoles centrales par le circulaire du Ministre de l'Intérieur en date du 20 floréal an VII" (signed Duhamel and dated 19 prairial an VII).

121. Ibid., 19.

122. The contract for the *Journal d'instruction sociale*, signed by Condorcet, Sieyès, and Duhamel and dated February 23, 1793, is in the Papers of Sieyès (AN, 284AP 9).

123. On Sieyès's thought, see Guilhaumou, "Sieyès et la 'science politique' (1773–1789): le seuil de la langue"; Bastid, *Sieyès et sa pensée*, 299–306, 342–43; and Forsyth, *Reason and Revolution*, 31–33 and 41–48. See also Sieyès's mid-1770s notes on language in his papers in AN, 284AP 2 (2 and 3), in which his interest in the language theory of Condillac, in particular, is evident.

124. Bibliothèque de l'Institut, Papers of Condorcet, MS 872, fols. 571–72: notes on public instruction.

125. See, for example, Sicard's laudatory review of Condorcet's educational writings of 1791 in "Notice de quelques ouvrages nouveaux," *Tribut de la Société nationale des neuf soeurs* (September 1791): 205–10. In this review, Sicard noted with approval that "[t]he author [Condorcet] wants children to be presented with things that they understand instead of these unintelligible words which, because they depict abstractions, do not stay in minds that they have never entered in the first place" (7). It is worth mentioning again that Condorcet had drawn attention to the benefits of analysis in the education of the deaf as early as his first speech at the Académie Française in 1782 (see Chap. 3) and, as a member of the Commune's committee to choose a successor to Epée, had publicly defended the choice of Sicard (see Lacroix, ed., *Actes de la Commune*, 5:19 [April 5, 1790]). Furthermore, Condorcet, Sicard, and Duhamel had all worked together on the committee of the Société des Amateurs de la Langue Française concerned with lexicology.

126. *Journal d'instruction sociale*, no. 1 (1793): 12. On the foundation and purpose of this journal, see esp. Baker, *Condorcet*, 330–42.

127. *Chronique de Paris* (May 18, 1793): 2, quoted in Brunot, *Histoire de la langue française*, 10, pt. 2: 617.

128. See Duhamel, "Essai sur la langue françoise, considérée dans la morale et la politique. Discours préliminaire," *Journal d'instruction sociale*, no. 3 (June 22, 1793): 80. Not surprisingly, Duhamel's next (and final) article, published in no. 5 (June 29, 1793) and no. 6 (July 6, 1793), was entitled "Analyse et définition des mots et des expressions employés dans l'art de constituer les sociétés politiques" (129–44 and 185–92). Condorcet had emphasized in the prospectus to the *Journal d'instruction sociale* (n.d., 2–3)

that "the analysis of the ideas explained by the words of this language will be one of the main purposes of this Journal," and in the first issue (June 1, 1793), he had immediately published an article entitled "Sur le sens du mot Révolutionnaire" (1–11).

129. *Chronique de Paris* (May 18, 1793): 2.

130. Lakanal, "Projet de décret pour l'établissement de l'instruction nationale, présenté par le comité d'instruction publique" (June 26, 1793), in *PVCIPC*, 1:507–16. The plan also appeared serially in June in the *Journal d'instruction sociale* and was published in a revised edition on July 1, 1793, as *Convention nationale. Projet d'éduction du peuple français, présenté à la Convention nationale au nom du Comité d'instruction publique*.

131. *PVCIPC*, 1:529.

132. See Daunou, *Plan d'éducation, présenté à l'Assemblée nationale*.

133. Daunou, *Convention nationale. Essai sur la Constitution*, reprinted in Mavidal and Laurent, eds., *Archives parlementaires*, 66:351 (April 17, 1793). Marcel Gauchet briefly discusses this text in *La Révolution des droits de l'homme*, 279–82, as well as the similar criticisms of the Declaration of Rights put forth by Daunou's contemporaries, Rabaut Saint-Etienne and Romme (see 111). Questions of method were also central to Daunou's *Convention Nationale. Observations sur la manière de discuter la Constitution* (1793) and his "Observations sur la manière de rédiger une déclaration des droits" (probably also 1793) in BN, MS n. acq. fr. 21891.

134. Daunou, *Convention nationale. Essai sur l'instruction publique*, reprinted in Mavidal and Laurent, eds., *Archives parlementaires*, 68:171 and 173 (July 3, 1793).

135. Ibid., 68:172.

136. Ibid., 68:177. To take two other examples: Pierre-Vincent Chalvet (who identified himself as a member of both the Société des Neuf Soeurs and the Société des Amis de la République in Grenoble) suggested in his *Des Qualités et des devoirs d'un instituteur public* that one visit a school dedicated to the education of the deaf for visible proof of the effectiveness of Condillac's methods (esp. 68–69). Similarly, in his "Cours d'organisation sociale" held at the Lycée in the winter and spring of 1793, Pierre-Louis Roederer, another former member of la Société de 1789, pointed to the art of instructing the deaf as a way to illustrate the importance of recognizing the physical ideas at the root of all abstract moral notions. See the notes for these lectures in Roederer's papers (AN, 29AP 90, lesson 7 [March 1793]).

137. Barère, *Convention nationale. Rapport et projet de décret présentés, au nom du Comité de salut public, sur les idiomes étrangers et l'enseignement de la langue française*, reprinted in de Certeau et al., *Une Politique de la langue*, 295.

138. *Gazette nationale, ou le Moniteur universel* (30 frimaire an II–December 20, 1793): 364.

139. AN, F17 11648: "Nouvelle méthode pour apprendre à lire" (an II).

140. Grégoire, *Convention nationale. Instuction publique. Rapport sur la nécessité et les moyens d'anéantir les patois*, in de Certeau et al., *Une Politique de la langue*, 304.

141. Grégoire, *Convention nationale. Système de dénominations topographiques pour les places, rues, quais*, 3.

142. Fréville, *Insuffisance de nos presses pour éclairer le peuple*, 10.

143. On Jacobin ambivalence about oration and especially verbal rhetoric, see Guilhaumou, "Rhétorique et antirhétorique à l'époque de la Révolution française"; Douay, "La Langue de la Raison et de la Liberté: The Crisis of Rhetoric in the Age of Oratory, 1789–1809"; Jean-Paul Sermain, "Raison et révolution: le problème de l'éloquence politique," in *Les Idéologues*, ed. Busse and Trabant, 147–65; and Brigitte Schlieben-Lange, "Le Style laconique," in *Langages de la Révolution*, ed. Geffroy, 195–201.

144. The association of girls with excess civilization and boys with nature was frequently extended to their respective styles of speech. Warning patriots of the clever, deceptive language of girls, the anonymous author of *Principes de J.-J. Rousseau, sur l'éducation des enfans* (an II) counseled: "In order to judge the true sentiments of girls, one must study them and not trust what they say, because girls are full of flattery [and] dishonesty and know easily how to disguise themselves" (145). While the fact that girls seemingly learned to speak earlier, more easily, and more agreeably than did boys was often held against girls as a sign of their propensity for artifice, boys' relative difficulty in learning the rules of charming conversation was often touted as evidence of their sincerity and proximity to nature. On the ways in which other gendered assumptions in revolutionary language politics ultimately contributed to the exclusion of women from the revolutionary public sphere, see Dorinda Outram, "Le Langage Mâle de la Vertu: Women and the Discourse of the French Revolution," in *The Social History of Language*, ed. Burke and Porter, 120–35.

145. On the term *citoyenne* and its ambiguities, see Godineau, "Autour du mot *citoyenne*"; Annie Geffroy, "Citoyen/Citoyenne (1753–1829)," in *Dictionnaire des usages socio-politiques*, vol. 4, *Designants socio-politiques*, 63–86; and William H. Sewell, "Le citoyen/la citoyenne: Activity, Passivity, and the Revolutionary Concept of Citizenship," in *The Political Culture of the French Revolution*, ed. Lucas, 105–23. For an example of an early effort on the part of revolutionary women to use their power as *citoyennes* to demand changes in the French language—specifically that "the masculine gender [*genre*] will no longer be considered, even in grammar, to be the most noble gender [*genre*]"—see the anonymous *Requête des dames à l'Assemblée nationale* (n.p., n.d. [late 1789]), 12.

146. See Lüsebrink, "'Hommage à l'écriture' and 'Eloge de l'imprimerie.'" See also Schlieben-Lange, *Idéologie, révolution et uniformité de la langue*, 35–60, on the tensions between written and oral expression.

147. For a good overview of the gradual erosion of press freedom in France between 1789 and 1794, see Popkin, *Revolutionary News*, 169–73.

148. On stereotypes about women, and especially women's language, employed in Jacobin discourse as justifications for closing down women's political clubs, see Desan, "'Constitutional Amazons': Jacobin Women's Clubs in the French Revolution," esp. 32–33. Non-Jacobin clubs largely disappeared after June 1793 and did not reappear until after Thermidor, and

clubs and popular societies for women, even if associated with Jacobinism, were outlawed in October 1793. Not surprisingly, the silencing of these "public" women coincided with efforts to re-create the purity of the original, natural language in public speaking. By presenting world history as the story of the gradual feminization of language culminating in the effeminate and verbose culture of the French court, the revolutionaries found a way to depict the present as a long-sought-after opportunity to create a more pure philosophical idiom—without the corrupting influence of women.

149. "Extract from the Register of the Deliberations of the General Council of the Commune of Paris, 20th Day of the 1st month, Year II of the French Republic (11 Sept. 1793)," reproduced in translation in *The Old Regime and the French Revolution*, ed. Baker, 338–39.

150. For varied interpretations of the efforts of Grégoire and others, in the midst of the Terror, to make French the single, national language, see, in addition to the primary sources reproduced in Gazier, ed., *Lettres à Grégoire sur les patois de France, 1790–1794*, the following: Brunot, *Histoire de la langue française*, 9, pt. 1; Balibar and Laporte, *Le Français national*; de Certeau et al., *Une Politique de la langue*; Lartichaux, "Linguistic Politics during the French Revolution"; Higonnet, "The Politics of Linguistic Terrorism and Grammatical Hegemony in the French Revolution"; Lyons, "Politics and Patois: The Linguistic Policy of the French Revolution"; Winfried Busse, "'La Langue française est un besoin pour tous.' A propos du jacobinisme linguistique," in *Les Idéologues*, ed. Busse and Trabant, 343–71; Flaherty, "Langue nationale/langue naturelle: The Politics of Linguistic Uniformity during the French Revolution"; Achard, "Un Idéal monolingue"; Bell, "Lingua Populi, Lingua Dei"; and Rosenfeld, "Universal Languages and National Consciousness during the French Revolution."

151. *Gazette nationale, ou le Moniteur universel* (30 frimaire an II–December 20, 1793): 364.

152. Barère, *Convention nationale. Rapport et projet de décret présentés, au nom du Comité de salut publique, sur les idiomes étrangers*, in de Certeau et al., *Une politique de la langue*, 295.

153. See Schlieben-Lange, "La Politique des traductions."

154. Domergue, "Adresse aux communes et aux sociétés populaires de la République française," in AN, F17 1703, no. 1874 and reproduced in *PVCIPC*, 3:444–48. On the circumstances around this text, see Busse and Dougnac, *François-Urbain Domergue*, 119–24.

155. Barère, *Convention nationale. Rapport et projet de décret présentés, au nom du comité de salut public, sur les idiomes étrangers*, in de Certeau et al., *Une politique de la langue*, 293, 296.

156. Furet, *Interpreting the French Revolution*, 49.

157. See the "Discours de Maximilien Robespierre sur l'influence de la calomnie sur la Révolution, prononcé à la Société [des Amis de la Liberté et de l'Egalité] dans la séance du 28 octobre 1792, l'an I de la République," in *Oeuvres de Maximilien Robespierre*, vol. 9, *Discours, septembre 1792–27 juillet 1793*, 45. In this same speech, he charged the Girondins with efforts "to besmirch everything good and praiseworthy through the use of words of

opprobrium and to disguise the intrigues of the aristocracy by the most honorable of labels." See also his earlier comments on how, by "a strange abuse of words" and by "counting on the facility with which one can govern men with words," the government had established two deceptive categories (*citoyens actifs* and *citoyen passifs*) that violated the rights of man; these comments can be found in his famous speech of April 1971, "Discours de M. de Robespierre à l'Assemblée nationale sur la nécessité de révoquer les décrets qui attachent l'exercice des droits du citoyen à la contribution du marc d'argent, ou d'un nombre déterminé de journées d'ouvriers," in *Oeuvres de Maximilien Robespierre*, vol. 7, *Discours, janvier-septembre 1791*, 160–74.

158. See, for example, Robespierre's speech of February 25, 1793, at the Société des Amis de la Liberté et de l'Egalité, entitled "Sur les troubles des subsistances," reprinted, in *Oeuvres de Maximilien Robespierre*, 9:274–76.

159. On "vain metaphysical abstractions," see his speech "Sur la Constitution" (May 10, 1793) in *Oeuvres de Maximilien Robespierre*, 9:506. On the problems with "difficult language," see his speech of April 12, 1794 (23 germinal an II), at the Société des Amis de la Liberté et de l'Egalité, entitled "Sur le langage des orateurs de la Société," reprinted in *Oeuvres de Maximilien Robespierre*, vol. 10, *Discours, 27 juillet 1793–27 juillet 1794*, 433.

160. Compare the speech on orators cited in the preceding note with another speech Robespierre gave at the Société des Amis de la Liberté et de l'Egalité entitled "Sur un compte-rendu du *Moniteur* et contre les journalistes infidèles" (June 24, 1794–6 messidor an II), reprinted in *Oeuvres de Maximilien Robespierre*, 10:502–4. The latter points out why journalists too tend to falsify and dissimulate in their utterances.

161. Robespierre, "Séance du 17 pluviôse an II [February 5, 1794, but originally printed with the erroneous date of 18 pluviôse] sur les principes de morale politique qui doivent guider la Convention nationale dans l'administration intérieure de la République," in *Oeuvres de Maximilien Robespierre*, 10:360–61. For further discussion of Robespierre's fear of rhetoric and representation as untrustworthy and his faith in actions rather than words, see Huet, "Performing Arts: Theatricality and the Terror."

162. See, for example, Saint-Just's comments of March 13, 1794: "Let us not always judge men by their speech and appearance. Those who today say and act differently from the way they spoke and acted yesterday are guilty, in our eyes, of dissimulation" (Mavidal and Laurent, eds., *Archives parlementaires*, 86:436).

163. See Starobinski, *Jean-Jacques Rousseau*. For a well-known example of the application of this concept to Jacobin ideology, see Hunt, *Politics, Culture, and Class*, 44–46, 72–74. For a more recent version, see de Baecque, *The Body Politic*, 209–46. It is notable that the term *transparence* only rarely figured in contemporary discussions of the Revolution.

164. Philippe Roger makes a good case for the existence of conflicting aims and tendencies in Jacobin plans to "revolutionize" the French language in "Le Débat sur la langue révolutionnaire," in *La Carmagnole des Muses*, ed. Bonnet, esp. 176–81. In contrast, both Jacques Guilhaumou and

Brigitte Schlieben-Lange, among recent commentators, have argued that the Jacobins successfully forged a relatively coherent linguistic philosophy and platform.

165. Grégoire, *Convention nationale. Instruction publique. Rapport sur l'ouverture d'un concours pour les livres élémentaires de la première éducation*, 11–12. Two of the many categories for which textbooks were solicited dealt explicitly with language instruction: "Méthodes pour apprendre à lire et à écrire: ces deux objets traités ensemble ou séparément" and "Notions sur la grammaire française." For a detailed catalogue and analysis of submissions in both printed and manuscript form, see Harten, *Les Ecrits pédagogiques sous la Révolution*, which also notes that the two categories which dealt with language education received a disproportionately large number of submissions.

166. On the articulation of some of these goals in the context of the language textbooks sent to the Committee of Public Instruction in the Year II, see Sebastiano Vecchio, "'Les Langues sont pour les peuples.' Materiaux pour l'étude de la linguistique militante sous la Révolution française," in "Langue et Révolution," ed. Guilhaumou and Schlieben-Lange (special issue, LINX [1987]): 98–127. On spelling reform efforts more generally, see Senior, "Spelling Reform and the French Revolution"; and Schlieben-Lange, *Idéologie, révolution et uniformité de la langue*, chap. 4.

167. On the advent of the new language of chemistry in the late 1780s, see Crosland, *Historical Studies in the Language of Chemistry*. On the problematic status of this scientific nomenclature in revolutionary language politics, see esp. Riskin, "Rival Idioms for a Revolutionized Science and a Republican Citizenry."

168. *Entendons-nous*, which ran for six numbers from March to June 1794 (1 germinal–1 messidor an II), is excerpted in *PVCIPC*, 4:28–32.

169. See Petit, *Opinion sur l'éducation publique*, reprinted in *PVCIPC*, 2:561.

170. Ozouf, *Festivals and the French Revolution*, 133.

171. Baczko, *Utopian Lights*, esp. 258–60, 307.

172. Hunt, *Politics, Culture, and Class*, 87–119; and de Baecque, "The Allegorical Image of France."

173. The Lycée des Arts maintained a special theater for patriotic pantomimes beginning in 1792. The goal of this institution, according to the *Annuaire du Lycée des Arts pour l'an III*, was to develop the art of pantomime beyond the level of Audinot or the Opéra by creating pantomimes directed toward public spirit. On September 30, 1793, for example, the Lycée des Arts staged a ballet-pantomime by Gojuy entitled *Le Retour de la flotte nationale*.

174. Examples include Planterre's *La Fête de l'Egalité, mélodrame pantomime-lyrique* (November 14, 1793), Cuvelier's *La Fête de l'Etre Suprême, scènes patriotiques, mêlées de chants, pantomimes et danses* (June 8, 1794), and Cuvelier's *Les Royalistes de la Vendée, ou les Epoux républicains, pantomime en trois actes* (September 10, 1794), all of which were staged with elaborate written programs at the Théâtre de la Cité. On the first two, see

Chazin-Bennahum, *Dance in the Shadow of the Guillotine*; all three are mentioned in Lecomte, *Histoire des théâtres de Paris. Le Théâtre de la Cité, 1792–1807*. Less is known about how pantomimes were incorporated directly into the culture of festivals; but we do know that Jacques-Louis David, to take a prominent example, envisioned using pantomime as an effective way to represent the Revolution's main events at the Fête de la Réunion on August 10, 1793.

175. On ballet and pantomime at the Opéra during the Revolution, see Guest, *The Ballet of the Enlightenment*, esp. 339–40, as well as Chazin-Bennahum, *Dance in the Shadow of the Guillotine*.

176. See the unsigned document entitled "De l'Emploi de la musique dans les fêtes nationales" (2 thermidor an II–July 20, 1794), which was sent to the Committee of Public Instruction (AN, F17 1331B). This essay can be attributed to Roederer based on the ms. draft of it entitled "Lettre à Gossec sur l'emploi de la musique dans les fêtes nationales" (8 messidor an II–June 26, 1794), which is in Roederer's personal papers (AN, 29AP 111).

177. See Fabre d'Eglantine, *Convention nationale. Rapport fait à la Convention nationale, dans la séance du 3 du second mois de la IIe année de la République française, au nom de la commission chargée de la confection du calendrier*. On the debate that occurred over the naming of the divisions of the new calendar, see Baczko, "Le Calendrier républicain"; and Schlieben-Lange, *Idéologie, révolution et uniformité de la langue*, 121–23, 127–31.

178. Barthes, *Writing Degree Zero*, 22. Jacobin rhetoric might also be said to express a tension between the simplicity of pure abstractions and the figurative style of nature; see also Blum, *Rousseau and the Republic of Virtue*, esp. 188–89.

179. See, for example, Grégoire's denunciation of the "jargon" of the German Jews in his prize-winning *Essai sur la régénération physique, morale et politique des juifs* of 1788.

180. See respectively, Grégoire, *Convention nationale. Rapport sur les inscriptions des monumens publics*, 5–6; and Grégoire, *Convention nationale. Instruction publique. Rapport sur la nécessité et les moyens d'anéantir les patois*, in de Certeau et al., *Une Politique de la langue*, 316.

181. Grégoire, *Convention nationale. Instruction publique. Rapport sur la nécessité et les moyens d'anéantir les patois*, in de Certeau et al., *Une Politique de la langue*, 314.

182. Ibid., 316.

183. See the petition of the personnel of the Institution des Sourds-Muets de Paris urging the immediate separation of the two institutions for both financial and administrative reasons (*PVCIPC*, 1:382–83). A decree finally ordered the transfer of Sicard's pupils to the former seminary of Saint-Magloire in February 1794.

184. Maignet, *Convention nationale. Rapport et projet de décret sur l'organisation des établissements pour les sourds-muets indigents*, 20–21. Maignet's project was presented in December 1793 to the Convention. The report was then sent to the Committee of Public Instruction, which subsequently named Thibaudeau as its spokesperson (see *PVCIPC*, 3:265).

185. Maignet, *Convention nationale. Compte rendu à la Convention nationale de ce qui s'est passé dans l'établissement des sourds-muets dans la séance tenue en présence des membres du Comité des secours publics*, 3.

186. On the educational plans discussed by the Committee of Public Instruction in 1793–94 see, in addition to the *PVCIPC*, such synthetic treatments of the subject as: Julia, *Les Trois couleurs du tableau noir*; Palmer, *The Improvement of Humanity*, 134–90; and Vignery, *The French Revolution and the Schools*, esp. 81–93.

187. See *PVCIPC*, 3:345. Compare with Jeanbon Saint-André's earlier Rousseauist argument against the Romme plan (see his *Convention nationale. Sur l'éducation nationale*) on the grounds that children should learn from the book of nature rather than from the printed page.

188. Six delegates from the Committee of Public Instruction (Thibaudeau, Lindet, Coupé, Grégoire, Daoust, and Mathieu) attended public exercises at the Institution des Sourds-Muets de Paris on February 1, 1794, at Sicard's invitation. Other delegates had already attended several such demonstrations on different occasions in March 1793. See *PVCIPC*, 3:337 and 344–45. For Sicard's attempts to interest the Committee of Public Instruction in the plan put forth by the Committee of Public Assistance in conjunction with Sicard himself, see AN, F17 1009A, dossier 1719: letter from Sicard to the Committee of Public Instruction (n.d.).

189. Raffron, *Convention nationale. Observations sur les établissements proposés par les Comités de secours et d'instruction publique, en faveur des sourds-muets.*

190. Raffron, *Convention nationale. Troisième discours sur l'éducation nationale*, reprinted in *PVCIPC*, 2:233. Note the contrast between Raffron's utopian conception of natural, maternal gestures, as expressed in his *Troisième discours*, and his contemporaneous denunciation of the vice and corruption of society, as characterized by theaters where there are "these perverse men who make a career out of deceiving others with the craftiness of their gestures, with their sleight of hand . . . in which the art consists of making [people] see what does not exist" (*Convention nationale. Opinion du cit. Raffron . . . sur l'éducation nationale*, 92).

191. Desloges, *Almanach de la raison, pour l'an II de la République française, une et indivisible*, 1. Desloges's later biography can be pieced together from a variety of sources. In July 1789, Desloges published an anonymous *Lettre adressée à MM. les électeurs de Paris, par un citoyen français, sourd et muet* "on the patriotic conduct of the *gardes françaises* [*sic*]," which prompted a public response from Épée in the *Journal de Paris* on July 20, 1789. Then, in a letter of August 25, 1790, addressed to the Keeper of the Seals from "Desloges, sourd et muet, bon pauvre à Bicêtre" (AN, AA12, dossier 521), the author described his situation in this institution as "very cruel" and mentioned that he had just sent an address to the National Assembly soliciting a school and hospice for the deaf and the mute. As a result of his efforts on behalf of the Institution des Sourds-Muets, the Convention, based on a report by the Committee of Public Assistance, then awarded Pierre Desloges a sum of three hundred livres in July

1793 (*Procès-verbal de la Convention nationale*, 15:144 [July 4, 1793]). This is surely the same individual who published a pamphlet entitled *La Prédiction des astronomes sur la fin du monde accomplie, ou la Régénération de l'Europe en travail, dédiée à M. de La Fayette, commandant général de la garde nationale parisienne, par un citoyen français* (1790), as well as the almanac cited above, under the pseudonym "Esope-Desloges."

192. Maréchal, *Le Jugement dernier des rois, prophétie en un acte*, 15–16. Maréchal's play was enormously successful, engendering not only many different productions and imitations in both Paris and the provinces but also massive printings of the text at the instigation of the Committee of Public Safety and the Ministry of War. On this work, see Didier, "Le Jugement dernier des rois de Sylvain Maréchal," in *Ecrire la Révolution*, 171–80; and Brooks, "The Revolutionary Body."

193. Ibid., 22.

194. See Maréchal, *Dictionnaire des honnêtes gens . . . pour servir de correctif aux dictionnaires des grands hommes.*

195. Thibaudeau, *Convention nationale. Rapport sur les sourds-muets, au nom du Comité d'instruction publique*, 4. In his *Mémoires sur la Convention et le Directoire*, 1:78–79, Thibaudeau later described Sicard as a borderline fraud, "in fact, an enemy of the Revolution, but a skillful sycophant . . . He was also faulted for being motivated by self-interest, a bit of a charlatan." However, Thibaudeau also testified to the general popularity of Sicard's cause at the time of the Terror.

196. Roger-Ducos, *Convention nationale. Rapport et projet de décret sur l'organisation des établissements pour les sourds-muets*, 3.

197. Périer, *Réponse aux Observations du citoyen Raffron, sur les établissemens proposés par les Comités de secours et d'instruction publique, en faveur des sourds-muets*, 2, in AN F15 2584. Périer was originally sent to Paris by the Popular Society of Périgueux for the Fête de la Réunion in August 1793. At that time he wrote to the Committee of Public Instruction to request that he be allowed to abandon his post in Périgueux and remain in Paris in order to study with Sicard: "Two months dedicated to the study of the ingenious procedures of Sicard [and] to his new discoveries would enable me to pursue with success a difficult career in the republican education [system] that you are about to organize" (letter of August 1793, *PVCIPC*, 2:348). It appears that Périer's request was immediately approved, since several months later, in October 1793, Périer presented the Committee of Public Instruction with "a process for leading the deaf and mute to feel the influence of certain words on others." Unfortunately, this document—listed as part of carton F17 1331B in the papers of this committee in the AN—is missing.

198. Ibid., 8.

199. For these two arguments, see respectively Vignery, *The French Revolution and the Schools;* and Ozouf, "Regeneration," in *A Critical Dictionary*, ed. Furet and Ozouf.

200. On language politics in late eighteenth-century America, see Baron, *Grammar and Good Taste;* Simpson, *The Politics of American English, 1776–*

1850; Kramer, *Imagining Language in America*; Fliegelman, *Declaring Independence*; and esp. Gustafson, *Representative Words*, which also briefly considers American reactions to the language politics of the French Revolution.

201. See Thornton, *Cadmus, or, a Treatise on the Elements of Written Language* (prize dissertation honored by the Magellanic Gold Medal by the American Philosophical Society, January 1793). The dedication "to the citizens of North America" reads: ". . . You have already taught a race of men to reject the imposition of tyranny, and have set a brilliant example, which all will follow, when reason has assumed her sway. You have corrected the dangerous doctrines of European powers, correct now the languages you have imported. . . . The AMERICAN LANGUAGE will thus be as distinct as the government, free from all the follies of unphilosophical fashion, and resting upon truth as its only regulator" (vi–vii). Thornton's letter offering this work on "the regulation of our language" to "the Citizen President of France" is printed in *The Papers of William Thornton*, 1:279–80.

202. James Madison, "XXXVII: Concerning the Difficulties which the Convention Must Have," in Hamilton, Madison, and Jay, *The Federalist Papers*, 245. Among the many readings of this passage, see esp. that of Michael Kramer, who argues eloquently: "*The Federalist* reveals a world in which the philosophical ideals of truth, clarity, and virtue come up against the reality of falsehood, ambiguity, and faction, thus reflecting broadly the post-Revolutionary problem of conceiving of language as the foundation of all political process" (*Imagining Language in America*, 135).

203. Jouenne-Longchamp, *Rapport et projet de décret sur l'organisation définitive des deux établissements fondés à Paris et à Bordeaux pour les sourds et muets*, 9–10.

CHAPTER 5

1. See Baczko, *Ending the Terror*.

2. Petit, *Discours prononcé à la Convention nationale*, reproduced in the *Gazette nationale, ou le Moniteur universel*, no. 360 (30 fructidor an II–September 16, 1794): 1479–80.

3. *Montagne* was originally a term of derision used to refer to the extremist deputies of the Legislative Assembly and then the Convention who sat together during meetings up at the top and on the far left.

4. Daunou, "Extraits d'un mémoire de Daunou destiné à ses commettants, et écrit, dans la prison de Port Libre, au mois d'août 1794, pour leur faire connaître les motifs qui lui avaient fait signer la protestation contre les journées du 31 mai et du 2 juin 1793," in Taillandier, *Documents biographiques sur P. C. F. Daunou*, 349.

5. Jean-Lambert Tallien, "Discours prononcé à la Convention nationale, dans la séance du 11 fructidor an II de la République [August 28, 1794], sur les principes du gouvernement révolutionnaire," in *Oeuvres du Comte P. L. Roederer*, 7:8.

6. Anon. [probably J.-J. Lenoir-Laroche], "Sur l'abus et les différentes variations des idées dans la révolution," *Mercure de France* 12, no. 6 (October 21, 1794): 161–68; 12, no. 10 (November 10, 1794): 289–97; 13, no. 13 (No-

vember 25, 1794): 3–11; and 13, no. 16 (December 10, 1794): 97–107. The above quotation is from the first page of the first article in the series.

7. La Harpe, *Discours, prononcé à l'ouverture du Lycée*, 4. This text was originally published in 1796 as *De la Guerre déclarée par nos derniers tyrans à la raison, à la morale, aux lettres et aux arts, discours prononcé à l'ouverture du Lycée républicain, le 31 décembre 1794*, and the *Décade philosophique* (10 nivôse an III): 24, reports that the first meetings of La Harpe's course in 1794 were dedicated to explaining "l'abus des mots de la langue appelée révolutionnaire."

8. On the fate of the Girondins after Thermidor and their relationship to the liberal, intellectual elite of the Thermidorean Reaction and the Directory, see Baczko, "Les Girondins en Thermidor"; and Schlieben-Lange and Knapstein, "Les Idéologues avant et après Thermidor."

9. AN, F17 1331B: "Adresse à la Convention nationale de la Société libre d'institution, vérification et écriture" (15 fructidor an III). Formerly called the Société Académique d'Ecriture, the Société Libre d'Institution was an organization of educators and *artistes-écrivains-vérificateurs* dedicated to forwarding methods of public instruction.

10. See the *Réimpression de l'ancien Moniteur*, no. 298 (28 messidor an III–July 16, 1795): 224, for the proposed terms of title II (*état politique des citoyens*) in the new constitution of the Year III, including this article making literacy a prerequisite for citizenship. It was approved in August 1795 and established in September 1795 as article 16 in the constitution. However, from the beginning, the measure read: "This article will only go into effect in the Year IX of the republic" (224), and it was dropped from the constitution of 1799.

11. See the *Réimpression de l'ancien Moniteur*, no. 299 (29 messidor an III–July 17, 1795): 227, for the comment of Charles Lacroix cited above.

12. Ibid., 227.

13. On the impact of Condillac's ideas in the 1790s, see Staum, "The Legacy of Condillac in the Revolutionary Era"; and esp. Albury, "The Order of Ideas: Condillac's Method of Analysis as a Political Instrument in the French Revolution."

14. Condillac, *La Logique/Logic*, 303.

15. Condorcet, *Esquisse d'un tableau historique*, 280–81.

16. See, in the Bibliothèque de l'Institut, Papers of Condorcet, MS 885: "Essai d'une langue universelle" (4e fragment, Xe époque). An abridged version of this text has been reprinted by Gilles-Gaston Granger as "Langue universelle et formalisation des sciences. Un fragment inédit de Condorcet," and Keith Baker briefly discusses this fragment in *Condorcet* (127, 366–67).

17. On plans to acquire Condorcet's *Esquisse*, see Daunou, *Convention nationale. Rapport fait à la Convention nationale, dans sa séance du 13 germinal an III, au nom du Comité d'instruction publique, sur l'acquisition de 3,000 exemplaires de l'ouvrage posthume de Condorcet, Esquisse d'un tableau historique* (an III). On the Convention's purchase of fourteen hun-

dred copies of Condillac's *Logique*, ostensibly for use at the planned Ecole Normale, see *PVCIPC*, 5:491.

18. Paul Dupuy argues persuasively in *L'Ecole normale de l'an III* that Garat was responsible for writing this speech, along with several other major pronouncements on educational matters delivered during this period, and that Lakanal often functioned as Garat's spokesperson. Pierre Macherey, in "L'Idéologie avant l'idéologie: l'Ecole normale de l'an III," in *L'Institution de la raison: la révolution culturelle des Idéologues,* ed. Azouvi, 41–49, agrees that Lakanal's address was largely written by Garat but also points out that it was heavily inspired by the ideas of Daunou.

19. Lakanal, *Convention nationale. Rapport sur l'établissement des écoles normales,* 7.

20. Ibid., 9.

21. The Ecole Normale was created in conjunction with the reform of the *écoles primaires* (voted on 27 brumaire an III, following an earlier report read by Lakanal) and the organization of the *écoles centrales* (voted on 7 ventôse an III, also following an earlier report read by Lakanal).

22. "Arrêté" (24 nivôse an III) preceding the *Programme général des cours des Ecoles normales.*

23. See Guyton de Morveau, Lavoisier, Berthollet, and Fourcroy, *Méthode de nomenclature chimique* (1787), a key work in setting the stage for Lavoisier's 1789 *Traité élémentaire de chimie.* The introduction to the former work included long quotations and paraphrases from Condillac's *Logique* precisely on the connections among reasoning, analysis, and the perfecting of language.

24. Garat's enthusiasm for the methods and ideas of Sicard (with whom Garat probably first came into contact in the context of the Musée de Bordeaux in the 1780s) were not new at this moment. Dupuy claims in *L'Ecole Normale* that Jouenne's important speech on the education of the deaf (discussed at the end of Chap. 4), in which Sicard is referred to as the "unique depository of this precious method which gives us hope of one day seeing the project of a universal language . . . come to fruition," was actually written by Garat, who, as Minister of the Interior, had been actively involved in the spring of 1793 in the nationalization of the Bordeaux school for the deaf and the separation of the Paris schools for the deaf and blind. Garat's esteem for Sicard can also be measured by the fact that the former, a professor at the Lycée since the 1780s, arranged during the Year III for Sicard to offer a course on "philosophical grammar" at the Lycée, in addition to his course at the Ecole Normale (see BHVP, MS 919: Lycée Républicain. Comité d'Administration. Registre), as well as by the fact that in this same year Sicard was also appointed by the Convention's Committee of Public Instruction to write a textbook on methods of teaching reading in primary schools.

25. The program and the proceedings were published in seven volumes in 1795 and again in ten volumes in 1800 and 1808. The edition used here is *Séances des écoles normales [sic], recueillies par des sténographes, et revues par les professeurs,* published by the Imprimerie du Cercle Social in

1800. On these proceedings, see Moravia, *Il Tramonto dell'Illuminismo*, 380–409.

26. Garat, "Avertissement," in *Séances des écoles normales*.

27. It is worth noting that in 1795 almost a third of the subscribers to Domergue's revived *Journal de la langue française* (January 20–August 7, 1795) were either students or administrators connected to the Ecole Normale, including Garat, Sicard, and Ginguené, a member of the Executive Committee on Public Instruction (see the subscription list in Busse and Dougnac, *François-Urbain Domergue*, 208–12). Ginguené explained this committee's financial support of Domergue's efforts by drawing on the connection between liberty and the proper use of written French. See BN, MS n. aq. fr. 9220, fols. 736–37: Ginguené, "Rapport sur le 'Journal de la langue française' par U. Domergue (an III)."

28. Garat, "Avertissement," in *Programme général des cours*.

29. On Garat's course, see Armogathe, "L'Ecole normale de l'an III et le cours de Garat." Garat's choice of the term "human understanding," which is obviously borrowed from Locke, indicates that Garat wanted to differentiate his course in terms of both subject and method from traditional courses in metaphysics.

30. See the letter from Volney to Grégoire (dated Nice, 3 brumaire an III and reproduced in Gaulmier, *L'Idéologue Volney*, 300–301) asking for Grégoire's support for this project and telling Grégoire that Garat's support had already been obtained. As early as his *Voyage en Syrie et en Egypte* of 1787, Volney had suggested the need for such a system of transcription. On Volney's continuing interest in writing systems, see also Roussel, ed., *L'Heritage des Lumières: Volney et les Idéologues*; Deneys and Deneys-Tunney, eds., "C. F. Volney" (special issue, *Corpus* [1989]); and Volney's correspondence with William Thornton on the subject of universal alphabets in *The Papers of William Thornton*.

31. Volney's lessons were published separately in the Year VIII as *Leçons d'histoire prononcées à l'Ecole Normale en l'an III de la République française*, as well as in the *Séances des écoles normales*. See the recent annotated edition in *L'Ecole normale de l'an III*, ed. Nordman.

32. Volney, "Discours préliminaire," in *Simplification des langues orientales* [1795], in *Oeuvres de C. F. Volney*, 8:188.

33. For an overview of Sicard's course, see Désirat and Hordé, "Les Ecoles normales: une liquidation de la rhétorique? littérature et grammaire dans les programmes de l'Ecole normale de l'an III."

34. *Séances des écoles normales. Seconde partie. Débats*, 1:105.

35. *Ami des citoyens* (20 pluviôse an III), quoted in Dupuy, *L'Ecole normale*, 165.

36. *Séances des écoles normales. Première partie. Leçons*, 2:36.

37. *Programme général*, 45.

38. *Séances des écoles normales. Première partie. Leçons*, 2:37–38.

39. The argument is reproduced in the third volume of *Séances des écoles normales. Seconde partie. Débats*. On this subject, see also Nicole

Jacques-Chaquin, "Illuminisme et Idéologie. Le débat Garat/Saint-Martin aux Ecoles Normales," in *Les Idéologues*, ed. Busse and Trabant, 45–58.

40. Condillac's *La Langue des calculs* was edited for publication by Pierre Laromiguière during the Directory. However, Garat notes that the manuscript of this work (BN, MS n. aq. fr. 6344) was already in circulation among Parisian intellectuals during the Convention (see Garat, *Mémoires historiques sur le XVIIIe siècle et sur M. Suard*, 2:347).

41. Delormel, *Projet d'une langue universelle, présenté à la Convention nationale*, 10–11.

42. On the reorganization of the Institut in 1795, see Simon, *Une Académie sous le Directoire*; and Hahn, *The Anatomy of a Scientific Institution*, 286–312.

43. On the Second Class, see Staum, "The Class of Moral and Political Sciences, 1795–1803," and *Minerva's Message*. See also François Azouvi, "L'Institut national: une 'encyclopédie vivante'?" in *L'Institution de la raison*, ed. Azouvi, 51–61.

44. Over the last twenty years, the Ideologues have received much new attention from historians, who have variously attempted to define the nature of this group in social, political, and intellectual terms. See the pioneering works of Sergio Moravia: *Il Tramonto dell'Illuminismo*; *Il Pensiero degli Idéologues*; and "Les Idéologues et l'âge des Lumières." See also Gusdorf, *La Conscience révolutionnaire: les Idéologues*; and Welch, *Liberty and Utility: French Idéologues and the Transformation of Liberalism*.

45. On these associations, see: Guillois, *Le Salon de Mme Helvétius: Cabanis et les Idéologues*; Moravia, "La Société d'Auteuil et la Révolution"; Kitchin, *Un Journal 'philosophique': la Décade (1794–1807)*; and Regaldo, "Un Milieu intellectuel: la Décade philosophique, 1794–1807." Both the social and intellectual ties of many of the Ideologues actually stemmed from associations developed in Paris at the close of the Old Regime and in the early years of the Revolution, including the Loge des Neuf Soeurs, the Lycée, and, especially, the Société de 1789, whose original members included the future Ideologues Cabanis, Dupont de Nemours, Roederer, Garat, Sieyès, Destutt de Tracy, Prony, and Lacépède.

46. Martin Staum has found that the members of the sections of the Second Class devoted to newer disciplines tended to be both younger and more enthusiastic about the Revolution, while history and geography attracted a greater number of conservatives (see "The Class," esp. 381–2).

47. On the section of the Second Class dedicated to the analysis of sensations and ideas, see Staum, "'Analysis of Sensations and Ideas' in the French National Institute, 1795–1803."

48. Cabanis, "Considérations générales sur l'étude de l'homme, et sur les rapports de son organisation physique avec ses facultés intellectuelles et morales (lu le 7 pluviôse an IV)," in *Mémoires de l'Institut national des sciences et arts, pour l'an IV de la République. Sciences morales et politiques* (an VI), 1:88. The continuation of this talk was printed as "Suite du travail sur les rapports du physique et du moral de l'homme," in *Mémoires*

de l'Institut . . . Sciences morales et politiques (an VII), 2:107–287, and then, finally, the six memoirs that Cabanis read before Institut audiences in 1796–97, plus an additional six new memoirs, were published together as *Rapports du physique et du moral de l'homme* (an X–1802). On Cabanis, see esp. Staum, *Cabanis*.

49. Destutt de Tracy, "Mémoire sur la faculté de penser," in *Mémoires de l'Institut national des sciences et arts, pour l'an IV de la République. Sciences morales et politiques (an VI)*, 1:283–450. Tracy read this multipart memoir to the Second Class over the following dates: April 21, June 20, and October 18, 1796, and February 10 and February 15, 1798. The essay in the *Mémoires* was published under the date of the first reading (2 floréal an IV– April 21, 1796), but was actually the text that Destutt de Tracy delivered in 1798. On Destutt de Tracy and the idea of ideology, see Kennedy, *A Philosophe in the Age of Revolution: Destutt de Tracy and the Origins of "Ideology"*; Head, *Ideology and Social Science: Destutt de Tracy and French Liberalism*; Goetz, *Destutt de Tracy: philosophie du langage et science de l'homme*; and Deneys and Deneys-Tunney, eds., "A.L.C. Destutt de Tracy et l'idéologie" (special issue, *Corpus* [1994]).

50. For attempts to define the Ideologues specifically in relation to their linguistic platform, see the following: Auroux et al., eds., "Les Idéologues et les sciences du langage" (special issue, *Histoire, Epistémologie, Langage* [1982]); Busse and Trabant, eds., *Les Idéologues*; and Schlieben-Lange, *Idéologie, révolution et uniformité de la langue*, 183–241.

51. According to the records of the Second Class, the section on analysis of sensations and ideas also considered two topics dealing with analysis— "Determine the current state of the science of the analysis of sensations and ideas and the goal towards which it should be leading" and "Determine . . . the influence of the analysis of sensations and ideas on teaching, education, morality, and *l'art social*"—in addition to the question about signs. Why the Second Class voted ultimately to pose a question about signs rather than analysis is not, however, known. See AI-SMP, A1: "Registre des Procès-Verbaux et Rapports de la Classe des Sciences Morales et Politiques, ans IV, V et VI," 15, 18–19.

52. The program for the contest was printed in *Mémoires de l'Institut . . . Sciences morales et politiques* (an IV), 1:i–iii.

53. See AI-SMP, carton B1, "Quelle est l'influence des signes sur la formation des idées?" Aspects of the program for this prize contest, as well as several published responses it occasioned, are discussed in Acton, "The Philosophy of Language in Revolutionary France"; and Knowlson, *Universal Language Schemes*, 174–77. Martin Staum briefly discusses the unpublished responses as well in the following works: "The Legacy of Condillac in the Revolutionary Era," "Les Concours de l'Institut en sciences morales et politiques," in "Les Idéologues et les sciences du langage," ed. Auroux et al. (special issue, *Histoire, Epistémologie, Langage* [1982]): 111–14; and *Minerva's Message*.

54. Lancelin's original essay, received 14 messidor an V and numbered 9, is missing from AI-SMP, B1. However, Lancelin published his essay in an

expanded form between the Years IX and XI as *Introduction à l'analyse des sciences, ou de la Génération, des fondemens et des instrumens de nos connoissances.* The three-volume work should have been published earlier, in 1798, but was delayed for several years while Lancelin was ill. For the above quotation, see 1:350.

55. AI-SMP, B1, no. 8 (anonymous).

56. AI-SMP, B1, no. 1 (anonymous).

57. AI-SMP, B1, no. 10 (anonymous).

58. AI-SMP, B1, no. 12 (anonymous).

59. Roederer, "Mémoires sur le gouvernement de la Chine, sur la langue des chinois et particulièrement sur leur écriture," in *Oeuvres du Comte P. L. Roederer*, 8:129.

60. An anonymous review of Adrien Pront's *Elémens d'une typographie qui réduit au tiers celle en usage* (an V–1797) in the *Magasin encyclopédique*, no. 10 (vendémiaire an VIII), quoted in Montigny, *Alphabet universel, ou Sténographie méthodique*, 50.

61. On the telegraphic system of Gauthey, as well as other such projects of the 1770s and 1780s, see Chappe, *Histoire de la télégraphie*, 53–54, 66; and Belloc, *La Télégraphie historique*, 60–61. In 1788, the members of the American Philosophical Society in Philadelphia heard a paper entitled "An Essay tending to improve intelligible signals and to discover an Universal Language. From an anonymous correspondent in France (probably the inventor of the Telegraph) translated from the French" which was subsequently printed in *Transactions of the American Philosophical Society* 4 (1799); this may well have been the work of Gauthey, an associate of Franklin's, who had already in 1783 published another work on long-distance communication entitled *Expérience sur la propagation du son et de la voix dans les tuyaux prolongés à une grande distance* with the place of publication listed as Philadelphia as well as Paris.

62. The first of the Academy of Science's reports on Coulon's "stenography" was written by d'Alembert, Condorcet, and Alexandre-Théophile Vandermonde, the second by Vandermonde, Jacques-Antoine-Joseph Cousin, and Jean-Baptiste Le Roy, who included rules for future stenographic systems. During these years, Coulon, along with his disciple Pierre Dupont de la Rochelle, also displayed his system to numerous provincial societies and academies; it was Coulon's demonstration at the Musée de Bordeaux in 1784 that prompted Sicard's report on "tachygraphy" at this institution (see Chap. 3). See Coulon de Thévenot, *L'Art d'écrire aussi vite qu'on parle; ou la Tachygraphie française, dégagée de toute équivoque . . . suivie du rapport, fait, en 1787, à la ci-devant Académie des sciences de Paris;* Havette, *Deux sténographes à Bordeaux en 1784 et 1789;* Havette, *Bibliographie de la sténographie française*, 36–46; and Coulon's own letter of 1793 asking the Convention's Committee of Public Instruction to consider his book for use in schools (AN, F17 1004C, no. 676).

63. See Bertin, *Système universel et complet de sténographie, ou Manière abrégée d'écrire applicable à tous les idiomes* (1792); and Roussel, *Instruction nationale. Cours public et gratuit de sténographie* (1792).

64. The society's first publications were *Journée du 6 octobre 1789. Affaire complète de MM. d'Orléans et Mirabeau, contenant toutes les pièces manuscrites lues à l'Assemblée nationale, les discussions et le décret définitif, saisis mot à mot, par la Société logographique* (1790); and the *Journal logographique de l'Assemblée nationale* (December 28, 1790). Only after joining forces in 1791 with Lehodey de Saultchevreuil, editor of the *Journal des Etats-Généraux*, did the society publish a multi-issue journal—the *Journal logographique* (April 1791 to August 1792)—in which stenography was used to report "literally, with the most complete fidelity" everything said in the National and Legislative Assemblies. Later, a similar publication, *Le Journal logotachygraphe*, provided reports on the proceedings of the Convention. See *Observations de la Société logographique, sur la pétition du Sieur Guiraut* [sic] (1792); and *PVCIPL*, 110–11, 156, 160, 345, 347 (all 1792).

65. Only two numbers of the *Journal logotachigraphique* (February 29 and March 2, 1792) were ever published. Half a year earlier, another Jacobin club had established a similar periodical; but the *Journal logographique du Club des Amis de la Constitution de Tours* only appeared once (August 19, 1791).

66. *PVCIPL*, 160. See also Chappe, *Histoire de la télégraphie*; Belloc, *La Télégraphie historique*; Gachot, *Le Télégraphe optique de Claude Chappe*; Narjoux, "Le Télégraphe optique de Claude Chappe et les autres essais"; Rouxel, "Le Télégraphe Chappe"; and the contemporaneous description in Meyer, *Fragments sur Paris*, 126–35. That Chappe's project was not the only in existence in 1792 is evidenced by articles such the anonymous "Variété. Signaux de correspondance, par le moyen desquels on peut se communiquer et correspondre partout où la vue peut s'étendre, en toute sorte de langues, et toute sorte de sujets," *Journal encyclopédique* 6 (August 20, 1792): 374–86.

67. Archives du Musée de la Poste, D. 6795: Claude Chappe, "Mémoire relatif à une découverte dont l'objet est de communiquer rapidement à des grandes distances, tout ce qui peut faire le sujet d'une correspondance" (December 1792).

68. Gachot, *Le Télégraphe*, 3.

69. Lakanal, *Convention nationale. Rapport sur le thélegraphe* [sic] *du Citoyen Chappe*, 1–2. In July 1793, Lakanal, Daunou, and Arbogast witnessed the first experiments with this new form of communication between three stations over the thirty-five kilometers between the park of Lepeletier de Saint-Fargeau at Ménilmontant and Saint Martin du Tertre, sending a message of twenty-eight words in eleven minutes and sending back one of twenty-six words in nine minutes. According to Lakanal's report, the message transmitted read as follows: "The inhabitants of this beautiful region are deserving of liberty because of their respect for the National Convention and its laws." As a result of this experiment, Chappe was named to "the title of *ingénieur thélégraphe* [sic]" (3–4).

70. See, for example, *Détail exact du télégraphe, au moyen duquel la reprise du Quesnoy, de Valenciennes et de Condé a été connue à Paris, longtemps avant l'arrivée des courriers* (an III). On August 30, 1794, Carnot read

to the tribune of the Convention the following message, which had just arrived by telegraph: "The city of Condé is restored to the Republic; the restoration took place at six o'clock this morning." Soon after, the telegraph
was also used to convey pressing news about grain provisioning, among
other issues, between Lille and Paris; and in May 1798, a second line (between Paris and Strasbourg) was inaugurated. See Rouxel, "Le Télégraphe," 176–77.

71. Fourcroy, "Rapport sur les arts qui ont servi à la défense de la république, et sur le nouveau procédé du launage, découvert par le cit. Armund
Seguin, fait à la Convention nationale, le 14 nivôse, au nom du Comité de
salut public," *Gazette nationale, ou le Moniteur universel*, no. 109 (19
nivôse an III–January 8, 1795): 449; Lakanal, *Convention nationale. Rapport
sur le télégraphe, fait au nom du Comité d'instruction publique*; Rabaut-
Pommier, "Rapport de 29 messidor [July 17, 1795] au nom du comité de salut
public," *Gazette nationale, ou le Moniteur universel* (4 thermidor an III–July
22, 1795): 1223.

72. According to the *Annuaire du Lycée des Arts pour l'an III*, two of
Bertin's students—J.-B.-J. Breton and Igonel—not only transcribed lectures
at the Ecole Normale but also offered courses in stenography at the Lycée
des Arts, which students at the Ecole Normale were encouraged to attend.
The two professors tried to expand their operations to cover the Convention
and were awarded a *civique mention* in June 1795 for their efforts (see Breton and Igonel, *Lycée des arts, an III de la République française. A la Convention nationale, établissement d'un journal sténographique des travaux
de la Convention*; and *PVCIPC*, 6:313). The Ecole des Travaux followed suit,
hiring their competitor, Coulon, to transcribe lectures according to his
rapid notation system that same year.

73. Tuetey, ed., *Procès-verbaux de la Commission temporaire des arts*,
2:211 and 271; and *PVCIPC* 4:938 and 5:392, 407. Little can be discerned
about most of these projects except for the name of the inventor. However,
the project for a night telegraph sent to the Temporary Commission on the
Arts may well have been the "Projet d'un télégraphe de nuit" by M. Dutheil
preserved in the Bibliothèque du Musée de la Poste, D. 6830 (n.d.). And the
proposed telegraph of Citizen Cavailhon, which was presented to the Committee of Public Instruction in August 1794, was the subject of a printed *Pétition à la Convention nationale . . . sur une invention télégraphique* [an III]
containing details about its operation, which was based on angles of a circle
representing one hundred numbers which, in turn, represented twenty-five
letters and seventy-five "publicly agreed upon words."

74. In the fall of 1795, the project was announced in both the *Décade philosophique* and the *Magasin encyclopédique*. The book version, entitled
Pasigraphie and printed at the Bureau de la Pasigraphie with an introductory letter by Sicard, did not, however, appear for another two years.

75. E. B., "Grammaire: D'une langue universelle, de la nouvelle pasigraphie; et par rapprochement, de l'art du sténographe et du télégraphe; de
l'écriture en chiffre, et de l'art de déchiffrer cette écriture," *Magasin encyclopédique* 6 (1795): 102–14.

76. To take one example: in 1795 and 1796, the *Décade philosophique* devoted space to reviews and notices of Bertin's stenography, Chappe's telegraphy, and De Maimieux's pasigraphy and pasilaly. Between 1797 and 1802, it also covered Rouyer's monography, Blanc's okigraphy, Clément's stenography, Pront's typography, Edecrantz's telegraphy, Godefroy's okigraphy, and an anonymous project called a mythography, among other such enterprises.

77. In *Pasigraphie*, De Maimieux compared his undertaking with those of Leibniz, Wilkins, and Trithemius largely in order to distinguish his own project from those of his predecessors. In an article entitled "Sur la pasigraphie" in *Le Spectateur du Nord*, no. 5 (May 1798): 167–83, the editor, Charles Villars, considered De Maimieux's invention in light of prior experiments by an even wider range of earlier philosophers: Bacon, Descartes, Dalgarno, Johann Joachim Becher, Joachim Frisichius, Athanasius Kircher, Pierre Besnier, Wilkins, Leibniz, Epée, and Condillac. The international historical framework for this debate is evident as well in such compendiums as Johann Severin Vater's *Pasigraphie und Anti-pasigraphie; oder über die neuste Erfindung einer allgemeinen Schriftsprache für alle Völker und von Wolkens, Leibnitzens, Wilkens's und Kalmárs pasigraphischen Ideen* of 1799.

78. For an idea of the range of these institutions (there were at least eighteen in Paris alone at the beginning of the nineteenth century), see the first and only issue of the *Recueil des mémoires des sociétés savantes et littéraires de la République française* (messidor an IX–1801).

79. Among the "Machines, inventions et préparations approuvées par la [Première] Classe" in the late 1790s were the telegraph of Bréguet and Bétancourt, the vigigraphic machine for the transmitting of coastal signals of Moncabrié, Laval, and Leblond, and the military telegraph of Madier; see the *Mémoires de l'Institut national des sciences et des arts. Sciences mathématiques et physiques* 3 (prairial an IX) and 4 (vendémiaire an XI). The papers of the Third Class (AI-LBA, 5B2) indicate that during these same years it considered, among other submissions, the stenography of Montigny, the "typographie" of Pront, and the "monotypie" of an anonymous author (probably Thirion). Finally, both the archives of the Second Class (AI-SMP, A6 and A7) and the *Mémoires de l'Institut national des sciences et des arts. Sciences morales et politiques* 3 (prairial an IX) demonstrate that between 1798 and 1801 the Second Class examined De Maimieux's *Pasigraphie*, Zalkind Hourwitz's *Polygraphie* and "Essai sur la Pasigraphie," Butet de la Sarthe's *Abrégé d'un cours complet de lexicographie*, and unpublished plans for universal alphabets composed by both the Abbé Montmignon and a citizen Fournaux.

80. François de Neufchâteau was Minister of the Interior, in charge of educational policy as well as other domestic issues, from July 1797 to September 1797 and from June 1798 to June 1799. Under his guidance, the Institut became a consulting group of sorts for this ministry. François de Neufchâteau had long been a member of numerous learned and scientific societies, from the Loge des Neuf Soeurs to the Société des Amateurs de la

Langue Française to the Société Philotechnique and the Société Libre des Arts. His continuing interest in systems of notation and, particularly, in visual signs, is manifested, first, by his grammatical notes (in AN, 27AP 10, dossier 5, Papers of François de Neufchâteau) in which he referred to the "symbolic writing of the Iroquois," rebuses, codes written in Arabic numerals, and a taxonomy of types of writing, "figurative, symbolic, and literal," among other subjects, and second, by his *Méthode pratique de lecture* of the Year VII, which included a section entitled "De l'usage des hiéroglyphes ou figures symboliques" and advocated the need to "speak to the eyes" of young people.

81. Both the Thermidorean Convention and the Directory attempted to make the patronage of the practical arts and technological inventions a strong priority and a point of national pride. See, for example, E. B.'s comments in "D'une langue universelle," *Magasin encyclopédique* (1795): "[T]his science [telegraphy] . . . in a monarchy . . . only served to distract and amuse a bored and leisurely court; in a republican government, and as a result of the care of a vigilant and patriotic administration, it has [instead] been directed towards goals useful to the public" (104–5).

82. Leblond, "Exposé du système télégraphique décimal presenté à l'Institut national en sa séance du 28 frimaire an VIII: Classe de littérature et beaux-arts," a handwritten letter folded into the Bibliothèque de l'Institut's copy of Laval et al., *Ligne télégraphique du Havre, ordonnée par arrêté du Directoire exécutif du 9 floréal an 7*. Two of Leblond's collaborators, Laval and Peytes-Moncabrié, had together already presented plans for an aerial telegraph, or *vigigraphe*, to the Institut in September 1798 and had published a *Collection des mémoires, rapports et autres pièces relatives à un nouveau télégraphe pour les signaux des côtes, de l'intérieur et pour la correspondance des armées* in the Year VII. On the technical aspects of these projects, see Charbon, "Du Vigigraphe au télégraphe décimal."

83. See Malino, *A Jew in the French Revolution* on Hourwitz's plans to rename the streets and neighborhoods of Paris (148–51), as well as to develop a polygraphie (161–67).

84. See de Staël, *Des Circonstances actuelles qui peuvent terminer la Révolution, et des principes qui doivent fonder la République en France* (ms. 1798). La Harpe's most important effort to call attention to revolutionary language and its continuing effects is his *Du fanatisme de la langue révolutionnaire* (an V–1797); this work was actually part of a larger, unfinished project, a dictionary of revolutionary *phénomènes*, that La Harpe started planning in 1796 and intended to call *L'Esprit de la Révolution, ou Commentaire historique sur la langue révolutionnaire* (see his *Lycée*, 14:433–95). See also La Harpe's frequent comments on the effects of revolutionary language in *Le Mémorial, ou Recueil historique, politique et littéraire*, including "De la tyrannie des mots" (no. 11 [11 prairial an V–May 29, 1797]: 2–3), as well as the following secondary works: Todd, *Voltaire's Disciple: Jean-François de la Harpe*; Jovicevich, *Jean-François de La Harpe, adepte et renégat des Lumières*; and Chudak, "La Harpe et la langue révolutionnaire."

85. See François de Neufchâteau, *L'Institution des enfans, ou Conseils d'un père à son fils*, 8. This work, which was intended for use in the *écoles centrales*, was first read in April 1798 at the Institut. Volney had expressed similar sentiments about the relationship of silence to virtue in his *Leçons d'histoire* (ed. Nordman, 91–92): "One teaches men to speak; one should teach them to keep quiet. . . . [T]he chatter born of careless mistakes generates discord; silence, child of wisdom, is the ally of peace." See also Teysseire, "Des Idéologues contre l'excès des mots," on the Ideologues' opposition to figurative language, in particular.

86. Blanc, *Okygraphie, ou l'Art de fixer par écrit tous les sons de la parole avec autant de facilité, de promptitude et de clarté que la bouche les exprime*, xv. In a similar vein, the stenographer Clément commented in *La Sténographie, ou l'Art d'écrire aussi vite qu'on parle*: "Productions of genius, painting and suddenly concentrating themselves on paper like facial features in a mirror illuminated by the sun's shinning rays, can, as a result of this method, be placed at will before his [the reader's] eyes, elaborated and combined, while electrifying his imagination" (8).

87. Breton and Igonel, "Avis des sténographes," in *Procès instruit par le Tribunal criminel du département de la Seine . . . recueilli par des sténographes* (an IX). That even the appearance of having relied on new methods of shorthand transcription came to serve as a mark of accuracy in this period can be demonstrated by both the popularity of the word *tachygraphe* or *télégraphe* in the titles of periodicals and the decorative use of stenographic characters in books. See, for example, the following journals: *Le Petit tachygraphe* (Lyon, 1797–1809), *Le Télégraphe* (Paris, an V), and *Le Télégraphe politique* (Paris, an III), none of which made clear how the procedure in the title was used in the collection of news, or Théodore Pierre Bertin's *Fables de La Fontaine, gravée en caractères sténographiques* (an IV–1796). It is worth noting, however, that none of Coulon's continuing attempts to produce a journal that actually depended upon stenographic reporting were especially successful; his *Le Tachygraphe à la Convention nationale, ou Recueil exact des discours, opinions et débats relatifs à la Constitution de 1795* was not published until the Year V, and his *Le Tachygraphe, journal des séances du Corps législatif, renferment tous les discours, motions et débats qui ont eu lieu dans les séances du Conseil des 500, recueillis mot à mot*, appeared only between November 21, 1797, and January 18, 1798.

88. Montigny, *Alphabet universel, ou Sténographie méthodique*, 67.

89. Clément, *Solution allégorique et géometrique d'un problème autrement résolu le dix-huit brumaire*, 5–6.

90. Leblond, *De l'Instruction par les yeux, lu à la Société libre d'institution*, 11–12. This text was also printed in the *Mémoires de la Société libre d'institution de Paris*, no. 2 (an VII): 33–46.

91. De Maimieux, *Pasigraphie*, 1.

92. See Bürja, *Abhandlung von der Telegraphie, oder Fernschreibekunst*, 4.

93. Pougens, *Essai sur les antiquités du nord et les anciennes langues septentrionales*.

94. See Hourwitz, *Polygraphie, ou l'Art de correspondre, à l'aide d'un dictionnaire, dans toutes les langues*; and Montmignon, "Le Problème d'une langue universelle résolu, ou l'art de la parole soumis à des formules générales applicables à toutes les langues connues" (undated ms. in AI-SMP, A7 sent to the Second Class for examination in the Year VIII; only his *Système de prononciation figurée, applicable à toutes les langues* of 1785 was ever published). Among Leblond's efforts to develop new applications for the decimal system and to promote the use of nonalphabetic visual languages, see his *Sur le système monétaire décimal* (an VI); *Théorie du télégraphe décimal et réduction numérique de la langue française au système décimal* (written with Laval) (an VII); *Ponctuation décimale, ou Manière d'adapter aux nombres les signes de ponctuation* (an VII) (which was read in conjunction with *De l'Instruction par les yeux* and also published in the *Mémoires de la Société libre d'institution*, no. 2 [an VII]: 25–32); and *Sur la nomenclature des poids et mesures* (an IX).

95. Leblond, "Exposé du systéme télégraphique décimal."

96. In his *Mémoires sur les aveugles, sur la vue et la vision; suivis de la description d'un télégraphe très simple*, Auguste-Guillaume Schwenger of the Société Médicale of Paris claimed not only to have invented a means for the blind and the deaf to communicate bodily but also, following Chappe, to have taken the body's signifying potential as the basis for his telegraph: "This Telegraph is our own body; its wings are arms which, together and with the perpendicular line of the trunk, can form a great number of figures distinct enough to be easily perceived at considerable distances" (156–57). Conversely, Requeno y Vives, the Italian author of an earlier work entitled *Il Telegrafo*, turned from his work on telegraphs to the composition of a book entitled *Scoperta della Chironomia; ossia dell'arte di gestire con le mani*; see the review of this work by A. L. M. under the title "Art Mimique" in *Magasin encyclopédique* 3 (an V–1797): 330–39.

97. See Blanc, *Okygraphie*, xv, on his efforts to restore "the language of nature" and "to return writing to its institution, its simplicity, its primitive veracity."

98. For comparisons of their respective projects with the creations of Sicard and Epée, see, for example, Blanc, *Okygraphie*, xxx; and Montigny's comments on De Maimieux's project in *Alphabet universel*, 35. Journalists repeatedly made the same point. As Villar noted in his article on pasigraphy in *Le Spectateur du Nord* (May 1798), "Certainly nothing resembles a true Pasigraphy more than these gestures [of Epée's creation]" (181). Or as the author (perhaps Horace Say) of an article entitled "Des Télégraphes, description de ceux du Louvre et des Tuileries à Paris, et de celui de l'Amirauté à Londres," *Décade philosophique* (30 fructidor an IV–September 16, 1796): 525–33, argued regarding the search for principles for developing a telegraphic language: "The lessons of Sicard for his deaf and mute pupils seem to us to contain the basis for this work" (532). For the practical value of his sign theory, the inventor Leblond also singled out Epée for inclusion in his *Dictionnaire abrégé des hommes célèbres de l'antiquité et des temps modernes* (see 1:274–78).

99. For example, discussions of methodical sign language figured in Duhamel's course in general grammar at the Ecole Centrale du Panthéon (AN,
F17 1344 3, no. 90: Duhamel to the Minister of the Interior [4 pluviôse an
VIII]). Similarly, Sébastien Brun saw fit to include explanations of both the
origin of language and "different methods for teaching the deaf and mute to
speak and to write" in his course in general grammar at the Ecole Centrale
du Rhône (*Ouverture du cours* [Lyon, an V], cited in Trenard, *Lyon: De
l'Encyclopédie au préromantisme*, 2:491). And in the same vein, members of
the Jury d'Instruction of the Ecole Centrale de la Haute-Garonne wrote to
the Minister of the Interior to request help in establishing an associated
school for the deaf that would employ the methods of Epée (see AN, F15
2601: "Rapport présenté au Directoire exécutif par le Ministre de l'Intérieur, 19 prairial an 5, sur la demande du Département de la Haute Garonne
tendante à former dans la commune de Toulouse une école nationale des
sourds-muets"). Other subjects often covered by courses in general grammar included: the transformation of sensations into ideas, the physical
causes of speech, the origins of writing and printing, elements of logic, or-
thographic reform, the role of signs in enlarging human understanding, and,
occasionally, the basic rules of pasigraphy, along with universal and French
grammatical principles.

100. For examples, see Montmignon, "Le Problème d'une langue universelle résolu" in AI-SMP, A7; and B[elprey], *De l'Optilogue, ou du Cylindre
parlant, appliqué à la transmission des idées chez les sourds-muets*, esp. 31.
Earlier, in 1792, Antoine-Joseph Rouyer, a student of Sicard, had set the
precedent for these types of claims with his *Prospectus d'un alphabet
commun à toutes les langues* and his *Essai raisonné de monographie universelle, ou Recherche analytique d'un chiffre parfait propre à développer,
dans toutes les langues, les vrais principes de l'art d'écrire comme l'on
parle* (printed in 1792, but only made available by subscription, according to
the *Décade philosophique*, in 1797).

101. On the stenography demonstration at the Société Philotechnique in
February 1801, see the *Magasin encyclopédique* 6 (1801): 112–13, and the
Papers of the Société Philotechnique in the Archives de la Sorbonne (MS
1938: Procès-Verbaux de la Société Philotechnique, 22 nivôse an X). On Sicard's students' role in exhibiting Leblond's telegraphy, see the letters of 4
and 8 ventôse an VIII (February 23 and 26, 1800) from Leblond to the administration of the Lycée Républicain (American Philosophical Society, Papers
of the Athenée de Paris, MS 506.44/At4). The papers of the Lycée at the
BHVP (MS 920: Lycée Républicain. Comité d'Adminstration. Registre) indicate that Sicard and Leblond had already successfully demonstrated Leblond's telegraphy in the same manner at the Lycée des Arts. Regarding the
public demonstration at the Institut National des Sourds et Muets of Massieu's mastery of Butet's system, see the review of Butet's lexicology in the
Décade philosophique (30 brumaire an IX–November 21, 1800): 326–31 and
(10 frimaire an IX–December 1, 1800): 395–98.

102. De Maimieux, *Pasigraphie*, 1.

103. For full descriptions of the logic of De Maimieux's pasigraphy, see Knowlson, *Universal Language Schemes*, 153–60; Eco, *The Search for the Perfect Language*, 297–99; and Pellerey, *Le Lingue perfette nel secolo dell'utopia*, 97–116.

104. Sicard, introduction to De Maimieux, *Pasigraphie*.

105. This metaphor figures in almost all of De Maimieux's and Sicard's comments on their pasigraphy. See, for example, Sicard's introductory letter in *Pasigraphie*, and De Maimieux's article on his own invention in *Le Midi industrieux, sçavant, moral et littéraire* 2 (an VII–1800): 97–101. The metaphor of the *mappemonde* echoes Diderot's and D'Alembert's *Encyclopédie*, where it is used in a similar way.

106. De Maimieux, *Pasigraphie*, 5.

107. Letter from the "inventor of Pasigraphy" announcing a new project entitled "Le Monde peint par la parole" (n.d.), in AN, 27AP 10, dossier 5: Papers de François de Neufchâteau, Grammaire—Notes. In his *Méthode pratique de lecture* (137), François de Neufchâteau mentions that he has commissioned the inventor of Pasigraphy "to fulfill the plan of Comenius," or to define, without any superstitions or prejudices, all the terms of human knowledge. De Maimieux must have intended for "Le Monde peint par la parole" to satisfy this commission. During the late 1790s, De Maimieux was also at work on a project entitled "Recherches sur le génie des langues," in which he proposed to analyze and to compare "the principal languages of Europe, considered in terms of their physical, grammatical, logical, oratorical and moral means" (BHVP, MS 920: Lycée Républicain. Comité d'Administration. Registre). Furthermore, he spent considerable time on an inverse project: the development of a pedagogical system based on the idea of a visual language. And though no known copy of *Les Trois muses de l'enfance* survives, the theory behind this latter work (which was based upon both Rousseau's condemnation of contemporary pedagogy for its failure to teach children to use words precisely and accurately and Horace's famous claim that the visual makes a greater impression on the mind than the aural) is explained in: Palissot [de Montenoy], *Corps législatif. Conseil des Anciens. Discours prononcé le 21 brumaire an VII . . . en faisant hommage au Conseil d'un ouvrage du citoyen Maimieux.*

108. Hourwitz, *Polygraphie*, 33; and De Maimieux, *Epître familière au sens-commun, sur la pasigraphie et la pasilalie*, 9. In French, these verses read as follows: "Qu'il déplaise surtout à ceux dont le langage,/Odieux instrument de ruse ou de dommage,/Nous dépouille ou nous tue en nous traitant d'amis;/Aux impudens rhéteurs, qui méchamment frivoles,/En stylets, en poignards, aiguisent leurs paroles."

109. Butet (director of the Ecole Polymathique, professor of physics at the Lycée Républicain, member of the Société Philomathique, the Société Médicale de Paris, and Société Libre des Lettres et Arts), *Abrégé d'un cours complet de lexicographie*, vii. Both the Second and Third Classes of the Institut examined Butet's work in the Year VIII. Butet, before founding the Ecole Polymathique, had been a student of Garat's at the Ecole Normale.

110. Lancelin, *Introduction à l'analyse des sciences*, 1:205, 329; and Laromiguière, "Note des Editeurs," in Condillac, *La Langue des calculs*, 478–80.

111. See, for example, the following: Lemercier, *Lettre sur la possibilité de faire de la grammaire un art-science aussi certain dans ses principes et aussi rigoureux dans ses démonstrations que les arts-sciences physico-mathématiques*; and Révéroni Saint-Cyr, *Essai sur le perfectionnement des beaux-arts par les sciences exactes*.

112. Learned societies flourished at the end of the eighteenth and the beginning of the nineteenth centuries as places of free but ostensibly apolitical debate. One of their chief functions was thought to be providing a setting for reconciliation among those of opposing political philosophies in pursuit of the higher goal of the advancement of knowledge. As the *Gazette national, ou le Moniteur universel* noted on March 8, 1804, regarding such *sociétés*: "Everywhere, one sees men sitting together whose opinions had formerly divided them and whose common spirit of peace and preservation now brings them together" (quoted in Duprat, *"Pour l'amour de l'humanité,"* 422).

113. In early 1791, the naturalist Claude-Antoine-Gaspard Riche, one of the Société Philomathique's founders, read a report on the importance of Epée's work for the creation "of methodical languages in the sciences"; see *Rapports généraux des travaux de la Société philomathique de Paris*, 39–70, esp. 60. In the late 1790s, this Société took an interest in the differences in the form and codification of the signal languages used by Chappe (a member of the Société) and Bréguet in their respective telegraphic systems; see Chappe's "Notice sur le télégraphe presentée à la Société Philomathique" (30 floréal [an VI]–May 19, 1798), MS 62 in the Archives of the Musée de la Poste; and Sylvestre-François Lacroix's "Extrait d'une notice sur le télégraphe, adressée à la Société par C. Chappe," along with a report on the "Nouveau télégraphe présenté par les CC. Bréguet et Bétancourt," in the Société's *Bulletin des sciences* 1, no. 16 (messidor an VI): 124–26. On June 22, 1800, Butet de la Sarthe read a report on his efforts to develop a new system for teaching French and Latin simultaneously by working with a deaf pupil (Massieu). See the Papers of the Société Philomathique in the Archives de la Sorbonne (Box 133, Correspondence), which show that this society also took an interest in Degérando's work on signs and Zalkind Hourwitz's polygraphy during these same years; and see Mandelbaum, "La Société Philomathique de Paris de 1788 à 1835," esp. 1:348–49, 201–2.

114. Singer, *Society, Theory, and the French Revolution*, 34–41.

115. The Société Philotechnique, whose members in the late 1790s included De Maimieux, Sicard, Pougens, and François de Neufchâteau, took an active role in promoting the work of all of these men, along with that of Zalkind Hourwitz, Leblond, Degérando, and Fourcroy. See the Papers of the Société Philotechnique in the Archives de la Sorbonne, MS 1937 and MS 1938: Procès-verbaux des séances (1796–1803). Similarly, in the late 1790s and early 1800s, the Lycée Républicain took an interest in the work of De Maimieux, Domergue, Leblond, and Butet while, at various moments, em-

ploying Garat, Roederer, Degérando, and Sicard to offer courses. See, in the BHVP, MS 920: Lycée Républicain. Comité d'Administration. Registre (an III–1818). Even the Lycée des Arts, where Sicard was also a member, became concerned with the elimination of the varied scripts used in France and the creation of "a type of national writing" (see the *Annuaire du Lycée des Arts pour l'an IV*) and celebrated the work of De Maimieux with an award in 1797 (see the *Magasin encyclopédique* 4 [1797]: 389–90) and that of Godefroy with an honorable mention in 1802 (see the *Décade philosophique* [20 brumaire an XI–November 11, 1802]: 376–77).

116. See the *Opinion de Félix Faulcon, député de la Vienne, sur les qualifications verbales*. On the post-Thermidorean debate about the term *citoyen* more generally, see Brunot, *Histoire de la langue française*, 9, pt. 2: 686–89; and Frey and Frey, "Et tu: Language and the French Revolution." Other terms—from the revolutionary *tu* to the new "party" name *incroyable*—became the subject of similar debates in the second half of the 1790s.

117. The constitution of 1795 upheld the Enlightenment principle that "no one can be prevented from speaking, writing, printing or publishing his thoughts." However, a clause was added that authorized "provisional" restrictions on this liberty "when circumstances make it necessary," and, indeed, the law of 27 germinal an IV imposed the death penalty for advocacy of changes in the constitution itself. See Popkin, *Revolutionary News: The Press in France, 1789–1799*, 38, 173–75.

118. Cabanis, *Rapports du physique et du moral de l'homme*, 2:344.

119. Cabanis, *Corps législatif. Conseil des Cinq-Cents. Discours prononcé . . . en offrant au Conseil la nouvelle édition du Dictionnaire de la ci-devant Académie française*, 2–3. See also Cabanis's comments on the advantages of Condillac's methodology for the progress of reason and liberty in *Corps législatif. Conseil des Cinq-Cents. Discours . . . en offrant au Conseil des Cinq-Cents l'édition des Oeuvres de Condillac*.

120. On these plans as early liberal attempts to devise a form of constitutive or structural rather than regulative censorship, see my essay "Writing the History of Censorship in the Age of Enlightenment."

121. Roederer, "Du Danger de savoir mal sa langue," *Journal de Paris* (14 germinal an V–April 3, 1797), reprinted in *Oeuvres du Comte P. L. Roederer*, 5:67. All the articles reprinted in this volume of Roederer's collected writings had been assembled and published earlier in the Year VIII as *Opuscules mêlés de littérature et de philosophie*. On Roederer's revolutionary career and thought, see Margerison, *P. L. Roederer*.

122. Roederer, "De la Conversation [fragments]," in *Oeuvres du Comte P. L. Roederer*, 5:296–99.

123. Whether or not to accept revolutionary neologisms into official French remained a highly politicized question after Thermidor. New dictionaries often explicitly included these terms; see, for example, Snetlage, *Nouveau dictionnaire français, contenant les expressions de nouvelle création du peuple français* (1795); Reinhardt, *Le Néologiste français, ou Vocabulaire portatif des mots les plus nouveaux de la langue françoise* (1796); and Gattel, "Vocabulaire des mots introduits dans la langue depuis la Révo-

lution française" in his *Nouveau dictionnaire portatif de la langue françoise* (1797). But Antoine Rivarol, in his *Discours préliminaire du Nouveau dictionnaire de la langue française* (1797), justified his omission of most of the neologisms of the Revolution with the claim that the dictionary of a language is a "measure of truth." And other writers continued to refer to revolutionary terms only to try to expose their "true" (i.e., contrary) meanings; note the title of the anonymous pamphlet *Les Synonymes Jacobites: Du Pain—Insurrection. Constitution de 1793—Prétexte Jacobins—Massacre de la Convention. Succès—Pillage, Anarchie, Horreurs* (probably 1795) and the anonymous *opéra-vaudeville* called *Les Jacobins du 9 thermidor et les brigands, ou les synonymes* (Théâtre de la Cité, April 4, 1795), in which the Jacobins finally take on their real titles as assassins, bankrupters, poisoners, and butchers.

124. [Garat], "Discours préliminaire," in *Le Dictionnaire de l'Académie françoise*, 5th ed., vi. On this text, see Sonia Branca-Rosoff, "Luttes lexicographiques sous la Révolution française. Le Dictionnaire de l'Académie," in *Les Idéologues*, ed. Busse and Trabant, 279–97; and Liliane Tasker, "Cinquième édition (1798). Discours préliminaire. Introduction et notes," in *Les Préfaces du Dictionnaire de l'Académie française, 1694–1992*, ed. Quemada, 219–66.

125. See, for example, "De l'Organisation des assemblées législatives," published in the *Journal d'économie publique* (10 messidor an V–June 28, 1797) and reprinted in the *Oeuvres du Comte P. L. Roederer*, 7:71–84.

126. In calling for a new educated class to play the role of language monitors, Garat drew upon an argument that he had already made at the Ecole Normale of the Year III. There, Garat had proposed a universal language governed by an international "congress of *philosophes*" as a linguistic-political ideal (see *Séances des écoles normales. Première partie. Leçons*, 2:38–39).

127. *Corps législatif. Conseil des Anciens. Discours prononcé par le C. Garat en offrant les oeuvres de Condillac*, 3. For a similar argument, see also *Corps législatif. Conseil des Anciens. Discours de Garat sur l'hommage fait au Conseil des Anciens des premières strophes du 'Chant du Départ' écrites avec les caractères pasigraphiques*, which followed Charles Goupil de Préfelne's *Corps législatif. Conseil des Anciens. Discours prononcé dans la séance du Conseil des Anciens . . . en présentant au Conseil l'hommage de la Pasigraphie*.

128. See AN, 29AP 110: Papers of Roederer, grammatical notes, esp. fol. 308.

129. Roederer, "Mémoires sur le gouvernement de la Chine," 98.

130. The third talk was printed under the title "De la langue des Chinois et particulièrement de leur écriture" in the *Oeuvres du Comte P. L. Roederer*, 8:113–29. According to the editor, Roederer read the other two talks on China at the Institut National on April 26, 1798, and May 9, 1798, respectively, but never read the third and final one in public. However, the register of the Second Class (AI-SMP, A10) indicates that Roederer read a "Parallèle de l'écriture symbolique et de l'écriture alphabétique et par occasion de

l'écriture chinoise" on 2 messidor an VI (June 20, 1798), suggesting that the third talk was indeed read soon after the other two, but with a different public title than that given by the editor of Roederer's *Oeuvres*. This conclusion is, in turn, supported by a summary of Roederer's talk on Chinese writing compared with French writing, which was published in the *Notice des travaux de la Classe des sciences morales et politiques. Compte rendu et présenté au Corps législatif, le 2e jour complémentaire de l'an VI par l'Institut national des sciences et des arts*, 80.

131. See Staunton, *Voyage dans l'intérieur de la Chine*. Staunton's book was initially published in English in 1797 under the title *An Authentic Account of an Embassy from the King of Great Britain to the Emperor of China*, and its success prompted translations into several languages, serialization in many European publications (including French-language ones such as the *Magasin encyclopédique* and the *Spectateur du Nord*, where, in both cases, it ran side by side with articles on recently invented pasigraphies), and the publication of numerous other reports on the mission by other participants. On this subject, see Peyrefitte, *The Immobile Empire*.

132. See, for example, Cibot, *Lettre de Pékin, sur le génie de la langue chinoise, et la nature de leur écriture symbolique*. In his "Lettre sur les caractères chinois" (October 1764) included in this volume, this Jesuit missionary argued that Chinese characters were made up of a mixture of images and symbols that could be read in any language, independently of speech, and that closely approximated thought itself. On the one hand, a page of Chinese characters compared favorably with the canvas of a painter; on the other, it seemed to constitute "the picturesque algebra of the Sciences and the Arts . . . as free of all intermediaries as the crudest algebraic proof" (13).

133. Staunton, *Voyage dans l'intérieur de la Chine*, 362.

134. Roederer, "Mémoires sur le gouvernement de la Chine," 122. The review of Staunton's text in the *Gazette nationale, ou le Moniteur universel* appeared on 3 prairial an VI (May 22, 1798).

135. Ibid., 116.

136. Ibid., 123. This idea too was most likely derived from Staunton, who reported on the usefulness of gestural communication as a way to clear up ambiguities in conversations in China: "[If], in a thorny discussion, there still remains some doubt about the meaning of a particular expression [such as the distinction between two homonyms], one has recourse to the best possible method for making oneself understood; either with a finger in the air or in some other manner, someone traces the form of a character and instantly the other person determines what the first person is explaining" (*Voyage dans l'intérieur de la Chine*, 345). In contrast, the recourse to gesture in Chinese conversation had often been cited by earlier Western travelers as evidence of the inadequacies of that language. See, for example, *Lettres de M. de Mairan, au R. P. Parrenin, missionnaire de la Compagnie de Jésus, à Pékin, contenant diverses questions sur la Chine*, in which the discrepancy between the limited number of tones in Chinese and the vast number of characters is illustrated as follows: "It has gotten to the point . . .

that the Chinese are sometimes, in order to make themselves understood in conversation, forced to show on one of their hands, with the fingers of the other, the sign or mute character for the thing that they want to say" (18).

137. Roederer's report on pasigraphy is missing from both the archives of the Institut and Roederer's own papers in the AN. However, the general content of this report can be determined from Jean Girard Lacuée's report on the activities of the Second Class in the *Magasin encylopédique* 2 (an VII–1799): 396–97, and, in greater detail, from a manuscript response to Roederer's essay in the hand of Sicard entitled "Sur le rapport de la pasigraphie" (fall 1799 or early winter 1800), in AN, 29AP 110, fols. 445–500.

138. AN, 29AP 10, fol. 310: Papers of Roederer, grammatical notes.

139. "Métaphysique. Chapitre préliminaire d'un ouvrage sur l'art d'instruire les sourds-muets, par le citoyen Sicard, instituteur des sourds-muets de naissance," *Magasin encyclopédique* 3 (an III–1795): 42.

140. Sicard's published works of this period dealing with these subjects include: "De la Nécessité d'instruire les sourds-muets pour les rétablir dans le droit de la Nature et dans ceux de la Société," *Magasin encyclopédique* 2 (an IV–1796): 32–56; reviews of his own *Catéchisme ou Instruction chrétienne* (1792) and of De Maimieux's *Pasigraphie* in the *Annales religieuses, politiques et littéraires*, ed. Sicard and G.-J.-A. Jauffret, 1 (1796): 558–67 and 621–24, respectively; "Premier mémoire sur la nécessité d'instruire les sourds-muets de naissance, et sur les premiers moyens de communication avec ces infortunés, lu le 13 messidor an 4," in *Mémoires de l'Institut national des sciences et des arts. Littérature et Beaux-Arts* (thermidor an VI), 1:37–63; "Rapport sur une typographie et une écriture nouvelle de l'invention du C. Adrien Pront" (ms., 28 vendémiaire an V), in AI-LBA, 5B2, and reprinted in Pront's *Elémens d'une typographie* (1797); the introductory letter in De Maimieux, *Pasigraphie*; and his book *Manuel de l'enfance, contenant des élémens de lecture et des dialogues instructifs et moraux* (an V–1797).

141. Sicard's correspondence with Roederer (see AN, 29AP 12, fols. 211–18: twelve letters dated late 1799 and early 1800) indicates that Sicard spent much of this period begging his acquaintances to plead for his cause in the context of reviews of his recent publications. Largely in response to Sicard's efforts, articles appeared in the *Journal de Paris*, *Le Magasin encyclopédique*, *Le Spectateur du Nord*, *Le Bulletin de l'Europe*, and *Le Propagateur*, among other publications, urging Sicard's reinstatement by stressing the national advantages to be derived from the wider application of his methods, as well as his philanthropic work with the deaf. Sicard first tried to justify his own political position in the Parisian journal *L'Ami des lois* (21 brumaire an VI–November 11, 1797).

142. Roederer, review of Sicard's *Elémens de grammaire générale, appliqués à la langue française*, *Journal de Paris* (22 fructidor an VII–September 9, 1799). See both the printed version of this review in *Oeuvres du Comte P. L. Roederer*, 5:28–31, and a more extensive ms. draft in AN, 29AP 111, fols. 101–11.

143. Sicard, "Sur le rapport de la pasigraphie."

144. Historians have tended to concentrate on the canonical texts—the major published works of Volney, Destutt de Tracy, and Degérando—in drawing generalizations about the linguistic attitudes of the Ideologues; the quite different positions of Sicard, Roederer, Garat, Lancelin, and François de Neufchâteau, among others, have been relatively ignored. As a result, many recent articles on the Ideologues and writing systems claim that the Ideologues were overwhelmingly dismissive of attempts to develop universal, nonalphabetic written languages. See, for example, Désirat and Hordé, "Le Marché des écritures"; Brigitte Schlieben-Lange, "Les Idéologues et l'écriture," in *Les Idéologues*, ed. Busse and Trabant, 181–206; and Sonia Branca, "Changer la langue," in "Les Idéologues et les sciences du langage," ed. Auroux et al. (special issue, *Histoire, Epistémologie, Langage* [1982]): 59–66. However, both Martin Staum and James Knowlson have, in their respective work (cited earlier), called attention to the diversity of positions taken in the late 1790s on this matter.

145. AI-SMP, carton B2, "Quelle est l'influence des signes sur la formation des idées?" (1799).

146. AI-SMP, B2, no. 5 (Butet de la Sarthe).

147. AI-SMP, B2, no. 8 (anonymous).

148. AI-SMP, B2, no. 9 (Degérando).

149. AI-SMP, B2, no. 3 (Fontaine, professor from Mont-Blanc).

150. AI-SMP, B2: "Séance publique du 15 germinal an 7. Rapport fait à la classe des sciences morales et politiques de l'Institut national, sur les mémoires envoyés au concours sur cette question: Déterminer l'influence des signes sur la formation des idées, par C. Roederer au nom d'une commission composée des CC. Garran, Naigeon, Volney et Ginguené." On the makeup of this prize committee, see also Joël Ganault, "L'Idéologie et organisation du savoir à l'Institut national," in *L'Institution de la raison*, ed. Azouvi, 63–81.

151. Following the announcement of his success in the Institut's prize contest, Degérando relocated to Mme de Staël's home at St-Ouen in order to revise his manuscript for publication. Degérando's correspondence of this period illustrates the prize winner's intellectual as well as social anxieties regarding his entrance into Ideologue circles. See AN, 29AP 10, Papers of Roederer, Correspondence, fol. 291, Degérando to Roederer (Lyon, 22 floréal an VII–May 11, 1799) on Degérando's attempts to generate publicity for his work, locate a publisher, distribute extra copies to members of the Institut, and solicit the patronage of Garat. See also Cabanis's letters to Degérando during the Year VII (Bibliothèque Trocadéro, Collection of Parent de Rosan, Papers of Ginguené, MS 20, fols. 49–55), and the letters of the Year IX between Degérando and both the Ministry of the Interior and the Dépôt Littéraire des Cordeliers regarding Degérando's efforts to profit from the publication of his work (Bibliothèque de l'Arsenal, Dépôts littéraires, vol. 2, MS 6488, fols. 91–99).

152. On this text, see David, "Degérando et le triple problème de l'écriture du XVIIe au début du XIXe siècle"; Dascal, "Signs and Cognitive Processes: Notes for a Chapter in the History of Semiotics"; Ulrich Ricken,

"Les Idéologues et la sensation transformée," in *Les Idéologues*, ed. Busse and Trabant, 19–43; Frank Paul Bowman, "Degérando et la théorie des signes," in *Gli 'Idéologues' e la Rivoluzione*, ed. Matucci, 209–19; and Staum, *Minerva's Message*, 104–5.

153. As the author of a review of *Des Signes* in the *Gazette nationale, ou le Moniteur universel*, no. 438 (18 fructidor an IX): 1439–40, explained on the subject of the Institut's initial question, "One will understand all the importance of this problem, and all the utility that one can expect from its solution, if one realizes that it should lead us to appreciate the assistance that the perfection of languages can provide in assuring the certainty and progress of our knowledge." The importance of Degérando's book, the reviewer noted, stemmed from the fact that "it is to this practical end that the author has directed all his research."

154. Degérando, *Des Signes*, 4:329.

155. Ibid., 3:241.

156. Ibid., 4:328–29.

157. The two-part report is missing, but a summary exists in AI-SMP, A7: "Travaux de la Classe des sciences morales et politiques de l'Institut, pendant l'an VIII de la République. Analyse des sensations et des idées," 1–2.

158. In 1800, the same year as the publication of *Des Signes*, Degérando moved to Paris and became a professor of moral philosophy at the Lycée Républicain and secretary of the Bureau Consulatif des Arts et du Commerce, where he was responsible for examining such inventions as Belprey's *télélogue*. From this moment, Degérando's political and philosophical careers developed simultaneously and rapidly. In 1801, he was instrumental in founding the Société d'Encouragement pour l'Industrie Nationale with Jean Antoine Claude Chaptal, and a year later Degérando published *De la Génération des connoissances humaines*, a memoir for which he had won a prize in the Academy of Berlin's essay contest on "the origin of all our knowledge." Already in 1802, however, when he became a correspondent of the Institut's Second Class, his growing distance from the ideology of the Directory was evident. With the publication of his *Histoire comparée des systèmes de philosophie, relativement aux principes des connaissances humaines* in 1804, the same year that he became secretary general in the Ministry of the Interior, this gap became even clearer; in particular, he faulted both Condillac and Condorcet for overemphasizing the applicability of calculus to the ethical sciences. One constant in his work was his rejection of the extreme linguistic *dirigisme* that Garat and others of his colleagues had advocated; see, for example, his lengthy denunciation, written in 1811, of the pasigraphy of a Professor Schmid of Munich and his claims about the irrelevance of all such projects for either philosophy or the ethical sciences (AN, F17 1543, dossier Schmid: "Extrait du procès-verbal de la séance ordinaire du mercredi 30 octobre 1811. Rapport fait à la Société d'Encouragement par M. Le Baron De Gérando, sur le Projet de Pasigraphie de M. Schmid," 1–12, and an accompanying letter on the subject from the Société d'Encouragement to the Minister of the Interior [November 11, 1811]). On Degérando's intellectual trajectory more generally, see Braun-

stein, "De Gerando, le 'social' et la fin de l'Idéologie"; and Patrizia Oppici, "Joseph-Marie de Gérando: de la philanthropie au mysticisme," in *Gli 'Idéologues' e la Rivoluzione*, ed. Matucci, 125–31.

159. On divisions among the Idéologues, especially around questions of materialism, at century's close, see Staum, *Minerva's Message*, 113–15.

160. Ginguené, who had been a member of the committee that had awarded Degérando a prize, reviewed the published work, *Des Signes*, in a two-part article entitled "Idéologie" in the *Décade philosophique* (30 ventôse and 10 germinal an IX), trying first to situate Degérando within an intellectual genealogy including Bacon, Locke, Leibniz, Condillac, and Court de Gébelin and then to show why Degérando's work was a corrective to that of Condillac (see esp. 521–22).

161. Bibliothèque de l'Académie de Médicine, MS 165: Jauffret, "Mémoires pour servir à l'histoire naturelle, morale et politique du genre humain," including "Histoire de l'écriture hiéroglyphique, avec des considérations sur l'idée d'une langue universelle" and "Sur les différens genres d'écriture." Reprints of both manuscript memoirs can be found in the *Revue de l'Ecole d'Anthropologie de Paris* 19 (1909): 240–44; 20 (1910): 353–55, 387–88, and 417–21; and 21 (1911): 154–56 and 193–96. According to Britta Rupp-Eisenreich, both essays, which Jauffret presented as his own, were actually written by Christoph Meiners and published first in 1788 in the *Göttingischen historischen Magazin* (see her article "The 'Société des Observateurs de l'Homme' and German Ethno-Anthropology at the End of the Eighteenth Century").

162. Prévost's original essay (no. 2) is missing in AI-SMP, B2. It was, however, published with the title above by Baudouin in Paris in the Year VIII.

163. Moussaud, *L'Alphabet raisonné*, 1:10.

164. Destutt de Tracy, "Mémoire sur la faculté de penser," 416.

165. Destutt de Tracy was part of the commission, along with Fleurieu, Roederer, and LeBreton, that was established to examine the pasigraphy of De Maimieux in the Year VI or VII. In the Year VIII, Destutt de Tracy, Daunou, and Legrand formed a new committee to examine the universal alphabet of Montmignon, and, that same year, Destutt de Tracy, together with Daunou and Champagne, organized a group to examine the lexicology of Butet. See AI-SMP, A7.

166. Destutt de Tracy, "Réflexions sur les projets de pasigraphie, lu le 27 floréal an VIII," in *Mémoires de l'Institut national des sciences et des arts. Sciences morales et politiques*, 3:535–51.

167. Destutt de Tracy, *Elémens d'Idéologie. Seconde partie*, 265.

168. Ibid., 379.

169. On this subject, Destutt de Tracy referred his readers to the recent work of François-Pierre Maine de Biran. The second prize contest sponsored by the Second Class (first announced on September 28, 1799) called upon contestants to determine the influence of habit upon the faculty of thinking; the victor was Maine de Biran, who argued even more emphatically against the possibility of establishing any universal language based on fixed

signs (and especially a gestural one) or any analogy between the role of signs in mathematics and in the social sciences. See his *Influence de l'habitude sur la faculté de penser* (1802), reprinted in vol. 2 of the *Oeuvres de Maine de Biran*, as well as the laudatory essay that Destutt de Tracy wrote on behalf of the committee of the Second Class which awarded Maine de Biran the first prize. See also Maine de Biran's notes for a response to the Institut's earlier contest on signs and thought, which he wrote in 1798 but never submitted or published; these notes, along with another set of notes on the same subject known as the Geneva manuscript, have been published in full in the *Oeuvres de Maine de Biran*, 1:240–309.

170. For a clear account of the Ideologues' reasons for initially supporting the coup of Brumaire and for their quick disillusionment, see Staum, *Cabanis*, 287–97.

171. In the introduction to the second volume of the *Elémens d'Idéologie*, Destutt tells the reader that he hopes his work can still have some use despite the demise of the *écoles centrales* (which he had been active in overseeing as a member of the Conseil d'Instruction Publique) and despite the restrictions recently imposed on the Second Class limiting it to the study of the French language and literature, rather than general grammar or the analysis of ideas. Destutt's sense of both intellectual defeat and political impotence is also evident in another text of approximately the same date, his letter of candidature to the new Second Class: "Since the new organization of this learned company has made the part of human knowledge to which I apply myself the direct object of the work of none of the sections of this great body, it would be natural enough if I remained excluded from it, even if it had previously seen my essays and my research with some benevolence. However, as it is impossible to treat successfully the grammar and the literature of a given language without elevating it to the general considerations that constitute the science of the signs of our ideas in all dimensions, and that of our ideas themselves, I think that the class in French literature will not see the subject of my studies with indifference" (see the Bibliothèque Trocadéro, Collection of Parent de Rosan, Papers of Ginguené, MS 20, fol. 41, n.d.).

172. Bonald, *Législation primitive, considérée dans les derniers temps par les seules lumières de la raison*, 1:82. See also Aubry, *Anti-Condillac, ou Harangue aux Idéologues modernes, sur l'âme de l'homme, ses facultés constitutives, l'origine et certitude de ses connoissances, son immortalité et ses destinées*, in which the author made a new case for the divine origin of language and insisted that children have innate notions of justice and injustice before acquiring the terms for these ideas.

173. See Formigari, *Signs, Science and Politics*, esp. 50–61, 149–152; and Chervel, "Le Débat sur l'arbitraire du signe au XIXe siècle."

174. Morellet, "Remarques sur un ouvrage intitulé: Abrégé d'un cours complet de lexicologie," in *Mélanges de littérature et de philosophie du 18e siècle*, 1:369–84. This text was originally printed, in slightly different versions, in the *Magasin encyclopédique* 5 (February 1802): 17–32, and in the *Journal de Paris* (February 18 and 21, 1802): 895–97 and 912–13, as "Re-

marques critiques sur l'ouvrage intitulé Lexicologie." In Morellet's *Mélanges* (3:83–87), see also the article entitled "Le Définisseur," reprinted from the increasingly conservative *Mercure de France* (no. 2 [July 5, 1800]: 99–105), in which Morellet both reiterated his firm belief in the importance of good definitions to error-free politics *and* argued against efforts to use language as an instrument of politics.

175. On efforts to restore the Académie Française, see Medlin, "André Morellet and the *Dictionnaire de l'Académie française*"; Sonia Branca-Rosoff, "Luttes lexicographiques sous la Révolution française. Le Dictionnaire de l'Académie," in *Les Idéologues*, ed. Busse and Trabant, 279–97; and Staum, *Minerva's Message*, 86–91.

176. Mercier, *Le Nouveau Paris*, pt. 2:3. See also the "Avant-Propos" to this book for further comments on the role of language in creating the disasters of the Revolution.

177. See the following works of Mercier: *Corps législatif. Conseil des Cinq-Cents. Rapport fait . . . au nom d'une commission spéciale, sur l'enseignement des langues vivantes* (an IV); *Corps législatif. Conseil des Cinq-Cents. Second rapport . . . fait au nom d'une commission spéciale, sur l'enseignement des langues vivantes* (an IV); *Mon Dictionnaire* (c. 1798); *Néologie, ou Vocabulaire des mots nouveaux, à renouveler ou pris dans des acceptions nouvelles* (an IX–1801), esp. the introduction; and "De la Supériorité du langage sur la langue," read at the Institut National in the Year X and summarized in *Mémoires de l'Institut . . . Sciences morales et politiques* (fructidor an XII), 5:32–35. Among Mercier's unpublished papers in the Bibliothèque de l'Arsenal, see MS 15081 (1d), fols. 262–67: "De la Supériorité du langage sur la langue" (a full draft of the Institut talk); fols. 275–81: "Sur l'éloquence"; and fol. 307: "Action et réaction entre les mots et la pensée," and see MS 15085 (2), fol. 75: "Abus des mots." On Mercier's linguistic positions, see Mormile, *La 'Néologie' révolutionnaire*; Rosenberg, "Making Time"; and Roger, "La 'langue révolutionnaire' au tribunal des écrivains."

178. Mercier, "De la Supériorité du langage sur la langue," fol. 264.

179. Mericer, *Néologie*, vii.

180. Laromiguière, *Paradoxes de Condillac, ou Réflexions sur la langue des calculs*, 41.

181. See not only Cambry, *Manuel interprète de correspondance, ou Vocabulaires polyglottes alphabétiques et numériques en tableaux*, but also Fortia d'Urban and Hennin, *Rapport fait à l'Académie celtique le 6 septembre 1805, 19 fructidor an XIII* on this invention.

CONCLUSION

1. Degérando, *Des Signes*, 1:222–23.

2. On Constant's attention throughout his career to the relationship between political anarchy and pathology of language or the *abus des mots*, see Jean Starobinski, "Benjamin Constant: comment parler quand l'éloquence est épuisée," in *The Terror*, ed. Baker, 187–201.

3. Constant, *Les "Principes de politique,"* 2:60.

4. Ibid., 2:460.

5. Holmes, *Benjamin Constant and the Making of Modern Liberalism*, 125 and 297, n. 81. On Constant's political philosophy, see also Fontana, *Benjamin Constant and the Post-Revolutionary Mind*; and Todorov, *Benjamin Constant: la passion démocratique*. On Madison's position on the ambiguity of words, see Chap. 4.

6. Constant, *Les "Principes de politique,"* 2:148.

7. On the growing interest in the Celtic origins of French culture at the turn of the century and, especially, the formation of the Académie Celtique (1805–13), see Guiomar, "La Révolution française et les origines celtiques de la France"; Ozouf, "L'Invention de l'ethnographie française: le questionnaire de l'Académie Celtique," in *L'Ecole de la France*, 351–79; and Woolf, "French Civilization and Ethnicity in the Napoleonic Empire." The membership list of this "academy" included names familiar from associations ranging from the Loge des Neuf Soeurs to the Société des Observateurs de l'Homme: Butet de la Sarthe, Fontanes, Fourcroy, François de Neufchâteau, Lacépède, Lanjuinais, La Rochefoucauld-Liancourt, Moreau de Saint-Méry, Pougens, and Volney.

8. Duhamel, *Mémoire tendant à faire établir deux chaires au Collège de France*, 13–14.

9. Jauffret, "Introduction aux mémoires de la Société des observateurs de l'homme, lu dans la séance du 18 messidor an IX," reprinted in *Aux Origines de l'anthropologie française*, ed. Copans and Jamin, 73–85. On the formation and agenda of this Société, see also: Bouteiller, "La Société des observateurs de l'homme, ancêtre de la Société d'anthropologie de Paris"; Stocking, "French Anthropology in 1800"; Moravia, *La Scienza dell'uomo nel Settecento*; Gusdorf, *La Conscience révolutionnaire*, esp. 496–503; Jamin, "De la Génération perdue: l'indigent, l'indigène et les Idéologues"; Jamin, "Naissance de l'observation anthropologique: la Société des observateurs de l'homme (1799–1805)"; and Jamin, "Le Syndrome chinois des Idéologues ou les débuts de la sociolinguistique," in "Les Idéologues et les sciences du langage," ed. Auroux et al. (special issue, *Histoire, Epistémologie, Langage* [1982]): 83–92.

10. Pingeron, "Précis historique de l'établissement du Musée de Paris."

11. The rules of the Société, published in the *Magasin encyclopédique* 5 (1801): 265–68, state: "The Society, confining itself to its own aims, formally prohibits all discussion of religious and political controversies from its memoirs."

12. See the report on the Société in the *Magasin encyclopédique* 1 (1800): 408.

13. At a dinner attended by members of the Institut National and the Société des Observateurs de l'Homme in honor of Nicolas-Thomas Baudin's departure for the South Seas, Leblond toasted: "To the Institut National and to all the learned societies of Europe. May the reunion of their leading lights and their efforts efface even the smallest traces of political dissension!" See the *Magasin encyclopédique* 3 (1800): 261.

14. Jauffret, "Introduction," in *Aux Origines de l'anthropologie française*, ed. Copans and Jamin, 85.

15. Under the successive guidance of François de Neufchâteau, Lucien Bonaparte, and, finally, Jean Antoine Chaptal, the Ministry of the Interior commissioned numerous statistical reports on the regions and people of France (many of which were then printed with government backing by Sicard's pupils at the Imprimerie des Sourds-Muets). One of the categories for which departmental prefects were asked to collect information concerned the endurance of local dialects. The motive was twofold: to discover how to wipe out the use of these jargons, which were believed to be an obstacle to enlightenment and unification, and to preserve them as historical records of local peasant beliefs and customs. On this question, see Bourguet, *Déchiffrer la France*; Perrot, *L'Age d'or de la statistique régionale française*; and Brunot, *Histoire de la langue française*, 9, pt. 1:409–19.

16. See Degérando's *Considérations sur les diverses méthodes à suivre dans l'observation des peuples sauvages* (republished in English as *The Observation of Savage Peoples*), a set of instructions written expressly for the impending expeditions of Baudin and François Levaillant and originally published by the Société des Observateurs de l'Homme in the Year VIII.

17. Circa 1800, Volney, Moreau de Saint-Méry, and Cabanis were all members of the American Philosophical Society, as well as the Société des Observateurs de l'Homme. While in Philadelphia from 1795 to 1798, Volney had helped Jefferson in collecting Indian vocabularies (see the Archives of the American Philosophical Society, MS 497 V85 for Volney's 1798 list of terms used by the Miami Indians), and Volney made use of this information in his *Tableau du climat et du sol des Etats-Unis* (Paris, 1803). Meanwhile, the American Philosophical Society kept abreast of the activities of the Société des Observateurs thanks in large part to Jefferson's contacts with many of the Ideologues. Jefferson, who became a foreign associate of the Institut's Class of Moral and Political Sciences after the turn of the century, wrote to Lacépède in 1803 (the letter was published in the *Magasin encyclopédique* 1 [1803]: 254–57) to say that the American Philosophical Society was engaged in the parallel project of sending men to explore the Mississippi and to suggest that Lacépède look at the *Transactions of the American Philosophical Society*. The following year, the *Transactions* (6 [1804]: 1–8) included an essay that had been read publicly by Jefferson in January of 1801 entitled "On the Language of Signs among certain North American Indians by William Dunbar, Esq. of the Mississippi Territory, communicated by Thomas Jefferson, President of the Society. Natchez 30, 1800." It is not possible to know whether this essay was discussed by the Société des Observateurs; but the Académie Celtique presented Dunbar's essay at a public session in 1806, followed by a discussion by a M. Pellier on the parallel between the sign language of the American Indians and that of deaf-mutes (see AN, 36AS 3: Procès-verbaux des séances de l'Académie Celtique, 1805–1813, 43 and 45).

18. See Jauffret and Leblond, "Le Chinois Tchong-a-Sam, deux documents lus lors de la séance publique de la Société des Observateurs de l'Homme, le 18 thermidor de l'an VIII," reprinted in *Aux Origines de l'anthropologie française*, ed. Copans and Jamin, 117–23. On Sicard's presenta-

tion of Tchong-a-Sam at one of his public sessions, see the *Journal de Paris*, no. 253 (13 prairial an VIII): 1172–73. According to this report, Sicard used Tchong-a-Sam, who "understood perfectly their [Sicard's deaf pupils'] signs, with the exception of those for metaphysical ideas, which necessarily presuppose a convention," both to demonstrate the nature of sign language and to give the audience "an idea of the Chinese language."

19. For Jauffret's interest in experiments involving young children, as well as his announcement of the Société's first public prize contest—in which respondents were asked "to look attentively and in a truly philosophical manner at an infant's cradle, to maintain a detailed journal of the progress of the baby's intelligence and the development of his sensibility; to notice the play of his newborn organs, to follow step by step his physical and moral growth, to calculate the immense labor of memory and the continual work required of him in order to make himself understood to those around him. . . . What data will he not provide us regarding the formation of languages and the history of our different faculties?"—see the announcement "Prix proposé par la Société des Observateurs," *Magasin encyclopédique* 2 (1800): 533–35; and Jauffret, "Introduction aux mémoires," 80–81.

20. Lacépède, *Discours d'ouverture et de clôture du cours d'histoire naturelle: donné dans le Muséum national d'histoire naturelle*, esp. 24–27. This institution was closely connected with the Société des Observateurs de l'Homme from its foundation.

21. Between 1800 and 1802, Itard, Sicard, Degérando, Cuvier, Pinel, Jauffret, De Maimieux, and Virey all commented publicly on the development of the *enfant sauvage*. On this story, see: Lane, *The Wild Boy of Aveyron*; Shattuck, *The Forbidden Experiment*; Gineste, *Victor de l'Aveyron: dernier enfant sauvage, premier enfant fou*; and *L'Enfant sauvage de l'Aveyron*.

22. See Lemontey, "Observateurs de la Femme, ou Récit exact de ce qui s'est passé à la séance de la Société des Observateurs de la Femme, le mardi 2 novembre 1802," in *Raison, folie, petit cours de morale mis à la portée des vieux enfans*, 8–104, which included "L'Hymne aux genoux; leur dignité, leur classification et leur langage" by one Abbé Satin.

23. Degérando emphasized the important role that the study of the deaf had played in the development of the *science de l'homme* in his essay "Philosophie" (1808), in *Histoire et littérature ancienne (IV): Rapports à l'Empereur sur le progrès des sciences, des lettres et des arts depuis 1789*, ed. Dacier, 236–86.

24. Alhoy, *De l'Education des sourds-muets de naissance, considérée dans ses rapports avec l'Idéologie et la Grammaire*.

25. See, respectively, the "Avertissement de l'Editeur," in Sicard, *Cours d'instruction d'un sourd-muet de naissance*; and Virey, *Histoire naturelle du genre humain*, 2:290.

26. Sicard, *Elémens de grammaire générale, appliqués à la langue française*.

27. Sicard, *Cours d'instruction d'un sourd-muet de naissance*, vi. This treatise did not finally appear in print until the Year VIII, but the Committee of Public Instruction had already agreed to publish it back in the Year II,

and Sicard had already publicized many of its arguments in numerous essays and articles during the second half of the 1790s (see Chap. 5).

28. Ibid., vi–vii.

29. Ibid., xxv.

30. Ibid., xi–xii, xiii.

31. See Breton, *Procès de François Duval, sourd et muet de naissance, accusé de vol.*

32. See Bouilly, *L'Abbé de l'Epée, comédie historique en cinq actes* (Théâtre français, December 14, 1799). See Chap. 3 for a brief discussion of the Solar case on which the Bouilly play was loosely based. On the impact of this play on Napoleon's decision to allow Sicard to return to his post as director of the Paris school for the deaf in January 1800, see Bouilly, *Mes récapitulations,* 2:195; and the papers of the Société Philotechnique (Archives de la Sorbonne, MSS 1937–38), to which both Bouilly and Sicard belonged.

33. For a more extensive discussion of this legal question and its implications, see my article, "Deaf Men on Trial: Language and Deviancy in Late Eighteenth-Century France."

34. Breton, *Procès de François Duval,* 39.

35. Massieu's autobiographical sketch was originally written at the behest of Jauffret in 1798, but it was not made public until February 1800. All of these materials were eventually published together as "Notice sur l'enfance de Massieu" in Sicard, *Théorie des signes pour l'instruction des sourds-muets,* 2:625–49 and reprinted in translation in Lane, ed., *The Deaf Experience,* 76–80. On the various editions of this interview, see Lane, *When the Mind Hears,* 418, note 4. See also Jauffret's later interview with Massieu (c. 1800–1802), reproduced in Reboul, *Cartons d'un ancien bibliothécaire,* 54–60.

36. See, for example, the "Dialogue entre le comte de Bissi et le chevalier d'Etavigni, sourd de naissance [and student of Pereire]," in *Esprit des livres défendus, ou Antilogies philosophiques,* ed. Fontenai, 42–57, for an argument for innate ideas; and see Condillac's extensive comments in both his *Essai sur l'origine des connaissances humaines* and the volume of his *Cours d'études pour l'instruction du Prince de Parme* entitled *L'Art de penser* about how much he wished that the deaf man who had been described in the memoirs of the Royal Academy of Sciences in 1703 as having recovered his hearing at the age of twenty-three had been interviewed more thoroughly about "what few ideas he had while he was without the use of speech; [and] what were the first ideas he acquired after he recovered his hearing" (*Essay,* 125). That way it could be shown that he had had no memory, no habit of contemplation or reasoning, and no conception of spiritual notions (including life and death) before he gained a command of signs and began communicating with others in society.

37. For Degérando's interpretation, see "Présentation du rapport de J. M. G. Itard par Degérando à la Société des observateurs de l'homme, le 20 octobre 1801," reproduced in Gineste, *Victor de l'Aveyron,* 252–57; Lévesque, *Notice des travaux de la Classe des sciences morales et politiques pendant le premier trimestre de l'an 10,* 10–12; and two ms. letters on these reports

from Degérando to Roederer (March 14 and March 22, 1802) in AN, 29AP 10.

38. This expression is from Sicard, *Cours d'instruction d'un sourd-muet de naissance*, 5. For the purposes of comparison, see, for example, Lafon de Ladébat, *A Collection of the Most Remarkable Definitions and Answers of Massieu and Clerc, Deaf and Dumb*. When asked, "What are the Advantages of a civilized over a solitary or savage life?" Massieu supposedly replied: "A solitary or savage life is resembling the life of brutes and vegetables" (141). And when asked his opinion of the Abbé Sicard, Massieu responded: "Without him our souls would be deprived of the faculty of thinking, and we should have no means of communicating with our fellow creatures. He has restored us to moral life, to a life of reason. It is he who has enabled us to distinguish good from evil; it is he who taught us that an Eternal Being created the world and preserves it. . . . It is he who drew us out of the darkness, by teaching us that our souls are endowed with reason" (111–13).

39. At this time, LeBouvyer-Desmortiers was also a member of the Société Philotechnique, which took an interest in his work with the deaf, and the Société Libre des Sciences, Letters et Arts de Paris, a learned society founded during the Directory on the ruins of the Société Nationale des Neuf Soeurs and whose members included Jauffret, Daunou, Grégoire, and Pougens (see the papers of this society in AN, F17 3038). Before the publication of his book, LeBouvyer-Desmortiers's interest in Sicard's method of educating the deaf had already been made manifest in a poem entitled "Au C. Sicard," which had appeared in the *Journal de Paris*, no. 206 (26 germinal an VIII): 904.

40. LeBouvyer-Desmortiers, *Mémoire ou considérations sur les sourds-muets de naissance*, 71.

41. Ibid., 46.

42. Ibid., xxiv.

43. See A. J. D. B., "Métaphysique," *Magasin encyclopédique* 3 (1800): 555–57; and L. B., "Philosophie," *La Décade philosophique* 26, no. 29 (an VIII): 86–92.

44. See the anon. ms. review entitled "Ouvrages de l'Abbé Sicard" (May 1800) in the archives of the INJS.

45. A number of Sicard's close colleagues came to his public defense. See, for example, Louis de Fontanes's review (described as an "extrait d'un journal français" and most likely composed with the help of both Sicard and Roederer) in *Le Spectateur du Nord* 13 (February 1800): 178–84; or De Maimieux's review, accompanied by a portrait of Sicard engraved by Citoyen Roy, in *Le Midi industrieux, sçavant, moral et littéraire* 1 (1800): 9–21.

46. Rey-Lacroix, "L'Ami des sourds-muets au rédacteur (La Clapière, le 5 thermidor an 8)," *La Clef du cabinet des souverains*, no. 1301 (27 thermidor an VIII): 7–8. The following year, Rey-Lacroix (again calling himself "l'ami des sourds-muets") published a book entitled *La Sourde-Muette de La Clapière, ou Leçons données à ma fille, essai élémentaire applicable aux enfants non sourds-muets*, in which he laid out the tenets of the educational system (largely that of Sicard) he had used in instructing his own

daughter. Rey-Lacroix's 1791 letter to the editor of *La Feuille villageoise* is mentioned in Chap. 4.

47. During the 1790s, Louis-François Jauffret and Sicard had both participated in the Société Nationale des Neuf Soeurs, the Société des Amateurs de la Langue Française, and the Société Philotechnique; and evidence of their friendship includes Jauffret's comments on Sicard in the *Gazette des nouveaux tribunaux* in 1792 (cited in Chap. 4) and Sicard's participation in Jauffret's educational walking tours for young people in the early years of the new century (see Jauffret, *Promenades à la campagne pendant la belle saison*). Sicard was also closely linked with other Jauffret family members, editing the *Annales religieuses, politiques et littéraires* with one brother, Gaspard-Jean, the prelate; sitting for the portrait of another brother, Joseph (see the engraving in the Moulin Collection of the Archives de l'Institut); and training still another brother, Jean-Baptiste Clair, who became the director of a school for the deaf in Saint Petersburg. See Reboul, *Louis François Jauffret* and *Les Cartons d'un ancien bibliothécaire de Marseille*.

48. Archives de l'Académie de Medicine, MS 165: Jauffret, "Mémoires pour servir à l'histoire naturelle, moral et politique du genre humain." See Mémoire 26: "Sur l'état de nature," 193–200.

49. Jauffret, "Introduction," in *Aux Origines de l'anthropologie*, ed. Copans and Jamin, 82–83.

50. On the concurrent use of differences in language skills in determining an individual's moral and social status and, therefore, ability to participate in public life in England, see Smith, *The Politics of Language, 1791–1819*.

51. Sicard, "Avertissement de l'Auteur," in *Théorie des signes pour l'instruction des sourds-muets*, xii. Sicard also modified his earlier sensationalism in the following passage: "I have always taught that natural law was engraved in the soul of man by the hand of the Creator at the same instant as it was drawn out of nothing; that this law is anterior to all sensible impressions received by our organs; that it is nothing but divine light that enlightens man as to his rights" (xii).

52. Jauffret, "Considérations sur l'intelligence des sourds-muets de naissance," extract from *La Ruche provençale, recueil littéraire* (c. 1820): 64–79, in the archives of the INJS. In this text, Jauffret mentioned that he planned to publish a book on the subject of the intelligence of the deaf in which he would include all of his conversations with his friend Massieu. Unfortunately, this project seems never to have come to fruition.

53. Degérando, *De l'Education des sourds-muets*, 125. In this late work, Degérando insisted that the privation of speech was not necessarily an indicator that one lacked the capacity to differentiate between good and evil. To this end, he reproduced excerpts from texts by both LeBouvyer-Desmortiers and Desloges and recounted his own conversations with deaf people, all of which indicated that natural sentiments, family feelings, an understanding of property, and some religious sense were not dependent upon either education or linguistic abilities (see note C, 125–35: "Sur la capacité qu'ont les sourds-muets, de discerner le bien et le mal, avant d'avoir reçu l'usage de nos langues").

54. See Montaigne, *Recherches sur les connaissances intellectuelles des sourds-muets.*

55. On the pantomimes of festivals and current events that Cuvelier composed during the Revolution, see Chap. 4. On the scenarios for some of the many *pantomimes dialoguées, mélo-pantomimes,* and other hybrid spectacles that Cuvelier continued to write after 1794 for the Ambigu-Comique, the Gaîté, and the Théâtre de la Cité, see Chazin-Bennahum, "Livrets of Ballets and Pantomimes during the French Revolution, 1787–1801." For his thoughts on pantomime, see also Cuvelier's *Mes riens* of 1806.

56. On Cuvelier's efforts in 1798 to turn Alexandre LeNoir's Théâtre de la Cité-Variétés into the Théâtre de la Cité et de la Pantomime Nationale, a theater dedicated to civic education for republicans through military pantomimes and mimed historical scenes, see AN, F7 3491, dossier 4: Police des Théâtres, papers concerning the Théâtre de la Cité et de la Pantomime Nationale (an VI). See also Lecomte, *Histoire des théâtres de Paris;* and *La Naissance de la pantomime, scène mélodramatique et allégorique, mêlée de danses,* the spectacle Cuvelier composed with J. B. Hapdé for the opening of this theater in April 1798.

57. Cuvelier, *Les Hommes de la nature, et les hommes policés, pantomime en trois actes, dédiée à ceux qui n'entendent pas. Précédée et suivie des Deux Silphes, prologue et épilogue, dédiée à ceux qui entendent* (Théâtre de l'Ambigu-Comique, le 1er fructidor an IX), 7–8.

58. On the development of melodrama and its historical indebtedness to various forms of pantomime including the *pantomime dialoguée,* see Pitou, "Les Origines du mélodrame français à la fin du XVIIIe siècle"; Thomasseau, "Le Mélodrame sur les scènes parisiennes de Coelina (1800) à l'Auberge des Adrets (1823)"; and esp. Brooks, *The Melodramatic Imagination.* Cuvelier is rarely mentioned in the secondary literature on melodrama, but Armand Charlemagne (writing under the pseudonym Placide le Vieux in *Le Mélodrame aux Boulevards, facétie littéraire, historique et dramatique)* referred in 1809 to Cuvelier as the originator of this genre.

59. For evidence of this change in attitudes, see, for example: La Pérouse, *Voyage de la Pérouse,* which revealed that the famous explorer had found the body language of the people of Formosa no more comprehensible than their spoken language: "This type of *langage pantomime* that we believe is universal is not any better understood by them, and a movement of the head that signifies 'yes' among us might have a diametrically opposed meaning for them" (372); Volney, *Tableau du climat et du sol des Etats-Unis,* which contained an extended attack on the idea of the "noble savage"; and the anonymous "Réflexions sur le sauvage de l'Aveyron, et sur ce qu'on appelle en général, par rapport à l'homme, l'état de nature" (*La Décade philosophique* 27, no. 1 [1er trimestre, an IX]: 8–18), where it was argued that the term *homme de la nature* was subject to so many different and nebulous interpretations that it no longer had any practical purpose beyond encouraging sophistical disputes.

60. La Harpe, *Du Fanatisme dans la langue révolutionnaire,* 11n.

Bibliography

MANUSCRIPT SOURCES

Archives Nationales (Paris)

Personal Archives
   27 AP 10; 29 AP 10, 12, 90, 110, 111; 284 AP 2, 9
Archives of Associations
   36 AS 3
Modern Archives
   AA 12 (pièces 12–15 and dossier 521)
   C 54 (no. 535)
   F 7 3491 (dossier 4), 4775 18 (dossier 3)
   F 15 2584, 2601
   F 17 1004B (dossier 485), 1004C (no. 676), 1009A (dossier 1719), 1331B,
      1344 3 (nos. 89 and 90), 1543 (dossier Schmid), 1703 (no. 1874), 3038,
      11648

Bibliothèque de l'Institut de France (Paris)

MSS 872, 885
MS Leblond (uncatalogued)

Archives de l'Institut de France (Paris)

Académie Royale des Inscriptions et Belles-Lettres
   A70–71; carton D75
Institut National, Classe des Sciences Morales et Politiques
   A1–A10; cartons B1–B2
Institut National, Classe de Littérature et Beaux-Arts
   5B2
Collection des autographes de L.-H. Moulin, portrait of Sicard

Bibliothèque Nationale (Paris)

MSS n. aq. fr. 2906, 6344, 9220, 21891

Bibliothèque Historique de la Ville de Paris (Paris)

MSS 919–20, 963, 1213 (fol. 456)
MS n. aq. 137

Archives de l'Institut National des Jeunes Sourds (Paris)
Papers concerning Epée, Sicard, Desloges, and the administration of the Institution Nationale des Sourds-Muets (uncatalogued)

Bibliothèque Trocadéro, Collection Parent de Rosan (Paris)
MS 20

Bibliothèque de l'Arsenal (Paris)
MSS 6488, 6490, 15081 (1d), 15085 (2)

Archives du Musée de la Poste (Paris)
D. 6795; D. 6830; MS 62

Bibliothèque de l'Opéra (Paris)
C. 4844; Rès. Pièce 60; Rès. 2359; Dossier: "Jason et Medée"

Archives de la Sorbonne (Paris)
MSS 1937–38; carton 133

Bibliothèque de l'Académie de Médecine (Paris)
MS 165

Institut Gustave Baguier (Asnières)
Abbé de l'Epée notebooks

Bibliothèque Municipale de Bordeaux (Bordeaux)
MS 829

Bibliothèque du Palais des Arts de Lyon (Lyon)
MSS 148, 266

American Philosophical Society (Philadelphia)
MSS 506.44/At4; 497 V85

PERIODICALS AND NEWSPAPERS

Affiches, annonces et avis divers (or *Affiches de Paris*)
L'Ami des lois
L'Ami des patriotes
Annales politiques, civiles et littéraires du dix-huitième siècle
Annales religieuses, politiques et littéraires
Annonces, affiches et avis divers, ou Journal général de France
La Bouche de fer
*Causes célèbres, curieuses et intéressantes, de toutes les cours souveraines
   du royaume, avec les jugemens qui les ont décidées*
La Chronique du mois, ou Les Cahiers patriotiques
La Clef du cabinet des souverains
Le Conservateur, ou Collection de morceaux rares et d'ouvrages anciens

La Décade philosophique, littéraire et politique par une société de républi-cains
Entendons-nous
Ephémérides du citoyen, ou Bibliothèque raisonnée des sciences morales et politiques
La Feuille villageoise, adressée chaque semaine à tous les villages de la France, pour les instruire des loix, des événemens, des découvertes qui intéressent tout citoyen
Gazette des tribunaux et mémorial des corps administratifs et municipaux
Gazette nationale, ou le Moniteur universel
Journal d'instruction sociale, par les citoyens Condorcet, Sieyès et Du-hamel
Journal de la langue française, soit exacte, soit ornée
Journal de Paris
Journal des sçavans
Journal des théâtres, ou le Nouveau spectateur
Journal encyclopédique
Journal logographique de l'Assemblée nationale (later *Journal logogra-phique*)
Magasin encyclopédique, ou Journal des sciences, des lettres et des arts
Le Mémorial, ou Recueil historique, politique et littéraire par MM. de la Harpe, de Vauxcelles et Fontanes
Mercure de France
Mercure national et Révolutions de l'Europe
Le Midi industrieux, sçavant, moral et littéraire, ou Indicateur analytique universel de ce qu'on y publie relativement aux arts, aux sciences, à la littérature, aux moeurs
Le Modérateur. Par une société de gens de lettres
Nouvelles ecclésiastiques, ou Mémoires pour servir à l'histoire de la Con-stitution Unigenitus
Révolutions de France et de Brabant
Révolutions de Paris
La Ruche provençale, recueil littéraire
Le Spectateur du Nord, journal politique, littéraire et moral
Suite de la Clef, ou Journal historique sur les matières du tems
Le Tachygraphe, journal des séances du Corps législatif

BULLETINS AND MEMOIRS OF SCIENTIFIC, LITERARY, OR POLITICAL ORGANIZATIONS

Annuaire du Lycée des Arts
Bulletin des sciences. Par la Société philomat[h]ique de Paris
Histoire de l'Académie royale des inscriptions et belles-lettres depuis son établissement jusqu'à présent. Avec les Mémoires de littérature, tirés des registres de cette Académie
Journal de la Société de 1789
Journal logographique du Club des Amis de la Constitution de Tours. Sé-ance du 19 août 1791

*Journal logotachigraphique de la Société des Amis de la Constitution, sé-
ante aux Jacobins; d'après les procédés inventés par F. E. Guirault*
Mémoires de la Société libre d'institution de Paris séante au Louvre
*Mémoires de l'Institut national des sciences et arts. Littérature et beaux-
arts*
*Mémoires de l'Institut national des sciences et arts. Sciences mathéma-
tiques et physiques*
*Mémoires de l'Institut national des sciences et arts. Sciences morales et
politiques*
Mémoires du Musée de Paris
Notice des travaux de la Classe des sciences morales et politiques
Nouveaux mémoires de l'Académie royale des sciences et belles-lettres
Nouvelles de la République des lettres et des arts
Procès-verbal de la Convention nationale
Rapports généraux des travaux de la Société philomathique de Paris
*Recueil des mémoires des sociétés savantes et littéraires de la république
française*
Recueil des ouvrages du Musée de Bordeaux, dédié à la Reine
*Séances des écoles normales recueillies par des sténographes, et revues par
les professeurs. Première partie. Leçons* and *Seconde partie. Débats*
*Transactions of the American Philosophical Society held at Philadelphia
for promoting useful knowledge*
*Tribut de la Société nationale des neuf soeurs, ou Recueil de mémoires sur
les sciences, belles-lettres et arts, et d'autres pièces lues dans les séances de cette société*

PRINTED PRIMARY SOURCES AND EDITED PAPERS

L'Abus des mots. N.p., [1790 or 1791].
*L'Abus des mots de nos seigneurs de l'assemblée des Etats généraux, res-
taurateur de la nation française.* N.p. ("Grand Inquisiteur d'Asie à Goa"),
1790.
Adams, John Quincy. *Diary of John Quincy Adams.* Vol. 1. Edited by David
Grayson Allen et al. Cambridge: Harvard University Press, 1981.
*Adresse des représentants de la Commune de Paris à l'Assemblée nation-
ale, sur la formation d'un établissement national en faveur des sourds et
muets, présentée le jeudi 18 février 1790.* Paris: Lottin, 1790.
Agli amatori dei balli pantomimi. Milan: n.p., 1774.
Aguesseau, Henri Cardin Jean Baptise, Comte d'. *Plaidoyer prononcé en
l'audience de la Tournelle du 15 avril; pour demoiselle Caroline de Solar,
appelante d'un décret d'assignée pour être ouïe, décerné contr'elle, contre monsieur le procureur-général, intimé.* [Paris]: Imprimerie de Demonville, 1780.
*A l'Assemblée nationale. Mémoire sur l'éducation de la jeunesse par une
méthode d'enseignement tout-à-fait nouvelle, et tout-à-fait opposée à la
routine actuelle.* Paris: Morin, 1789.
Albon, Claude-Camille-François, Comte d'. *Eloge de Court de Gébelin, de*

plusieurs académies, censeur royal et président honoraire perpétuel du Musée de Paris. Amsterdam and Paris: Moutard, 1785.

Algarotti, Francesco. *Essai sur l'opéra.* Translated by F. J. Chastellux. Pisa and Paris: Ruault, 1773.

Alhoy, Louis-François-Joseph. *De l'Education des sourds-muets de naissance, considérée dans ses rapports avec l'Idéologie et la Grammaire. Sujet du discours prononcé à la rentrée de l'Ecole nationale des sourds-muets. Le 15 brumaire an VIII.* Paris: Imprimerie des associés, an VIII.

Angiolini, Gasparo. *Dissertation sur les ballets pantomimes des anciens, publiée pour servir de programme au ballet pantomime tragique de Semiramis.* Vienna: Jean-Thomas de Trattnern, 1765.

———. *Le Festin de Pierre, ballet-pantomime.* Vienna: Jean-Thomas de Trattnern, 1761.

———. *Lettere di Gasparo Angiolini a M. Noverre sopra i balli pantomimi.* Milan: G. B. Bianchi, 1773.

———. *Riflessioni sopra l'uso dei programmi nei balli pantomimi.* London and Milan: n.p., 1775.

———. *La Vendetta ingegnosa; o La Statua di Condillac, favola boscareccia pantomima.* Venice: M. Fenzo, 1791.

Archives historiques du Département de la Gironde. Bordeaux: E. G. Gounouilhou, 1859–1903.

[Arnaud, Abbé François, and Jean Baptiste Antoine Suard, eds.]. *Variétés littéraires, ou Recueil de pièces, tant originales que traduites, concernant la philosophie, la littérature et les arts.* Paris: Xhrouet, 1804 [1768].

Arrest du Conseil d'Etat du roy qui ordonne que les deux premiers volumes de l'ouvrage intitulé, Encyclopédie ou Dictionnaire raisonné des sciences, arts et métiers, par une société de gens de lettres, seront et demeureront supprimés. Du 7 Février 1752. Extrait des Registres du Conseil d'Etat. Paris: Imprimerie royale, 1752.

Arrêt du Conseil d'Etat du Roi, concernant l'éducation et l'enseignement des sourds et muets. Du 21 novembre 1778. Paris: Imprimerie royale, 1778.

Aubry, Dom Jean-Baptise. *Anti-Condillac, ou Harangue aux Idéologues modernes, sur l'âme de l'homme, ses facultés constitutives, l'origine et certitude de ses connoissances, son immortalité et ses destinées.* Paris: Aubry et Moreau and Laurent le jeune, an IX.

Audinot, Nicolas-Médard. *Les Bons et les méchans, ou Philémon et Baucis, pantomime en deux actes.* Paris: Cailleau, 1783.

Aunillon, Pierre Charles Fabiot. *Azor, ou le Prince enchanté, histoire nouvelle, pour servir de chronique à celle de la terre des Perroquets; traduite de l'Anglais du savant Popinjay* [London (Paris): Vaillant, 1750]. In *Voyages imaginaires, songes, visions et romans cabalistiques,* edited by Charles-Georges-Thomas Garnier. Amsterdam and Paris: rue et hôtel Serpente, 1787–89.

Avis à mes chers concitoyens sur les querelles d'Allemand, ou Dissertation sur les noms de parti qu'on se donne réciproquement sans vouloir s'entendre. N.p., 1790.

Avis intéressant au peuple sur l'abus des mots aristocrate et démocrate qu'on propose de changer. N.p., [1790].

[Bachaumont, Louis Petit de]. *Mémoires secrets pour servir à l'histoire de la république des lettres en France, depuis MDCCLXII jusqu'à nos jours.* London: J. Adamson, 1777–89.

Bacon, Sir Francis. *The Advancement of Learning, The New Organon, The New Atlantis.* Chicago, London and Toronto: Encyclopaedia Britannica, 1952.

Baecque, Antoine de, Wolfgang Schmale, and Michel Vovelle, eds. *L'An 1 des droits de l'homme.* Paris: Presses du CNRS, 1988.

Barère [de Vieuzac], Bertrand. *Convention nationale. Rapport et projet de décret présentés, au nom du Comité de salut public, sur les idiomes étrangers et l'enseignement de la langue française . . . dans la séance du 8 pluviôse, l'an deuxième de la République.* Paris: Imprimerie nationale, [an II].

Baker, Keith Michael, ed. *The Old Regime and the French Revolution.* Vol. 7 of *Readings in Western Civilization.* Chicago: University of Chicago Press, 1987.

Batteux, Abbé Charles. *Les Beaux-arts réduits à un même principe.* Edited by Jean-Rémy Mantion. Paris: Aux Amateurs de Livres, 1989 [1746].

———. *Cours de belles lettres distribué par exercices.* Paris: Desaint and Saillant, 1747–48.

Belprey. *De l'Optilogue, ou du Cylindre parlant, appliqué à la transmission des idées chez les sourds-muets . . . à l'interprétation des ballets-pantomimes, à la célébration des fêtes nationales et à la publication des ordres du gouvernement.* Paris: Dabin, an X–1801.

Bernardin de Saint-Pierre, Jacques-Henri. *Paul et Virginie.* Edited by Robert Mauzi. Paris: Garnier-Flammarion, 1966 [1788].

Bertin, Théodore Pierre. *Fables de La Fontaine, gravée en caractères sténographiques.* Paris: l'auteur, an IV–1796.

———. *Système universel et complet de sténographie, ou Manière abrégée d'écrire applicable à tous les idiomes . . . inventé par Samuel Taylor.* Paris: P. Didot l'aîné, 1792.

Béthune, Chevalier de. *Relation du monde de Mercure* [Geneva: Barillot et fils, 1750]. In *Voyages imaginaires, songes, visions et romans cabalistiques,* edited by Charles-Georges-Thomas Garnier. Amsterdam and Paris: rue et hôtel Serpente, 1787–89.

Blanc, Honoré. *Okygraphie, ou l'Art de fixer par écrit tous les sons de la parole avec autant de facilité, de promptitude et de clarté que la bouche les exprime. Nouvelle méthode adaptée à la langue française et applicable à tous les idiômes.* Paris: Bidault, an IX–1801.

Bloch, Camille, and Alexandre Tuetey, eds. *Procès-verbaux et rapports du Comité de mendicité de la Constituante, 1789–1791.* Paris: Imprimerie nationale, 1911.

[Bohusz, Father Zsawery]. *Dziennik podróży ks. Stanislawa Staszica (1777–1791): Austrya, Niemcy, Hollandya, Anglia, Francya.* Edited by Alexander Kraushar. Warsaw: E. Wende, 1931.

Bonald, Louis de. *Législation primitive, considérée dans les derniers temps par les seules lumières de la raison, suivie de plusieurs traités et discours politiques.* 2d ed. Paris: LeClère, 1817 [1802].

Bonet, Juan Pablo. *Reduction de las Letras y arte para enseñar á ablar los mudos.* Madrid: F. Abarca de Angulo, 1620.

Bonifacio, Giovanni. *L'Arte de'Cenni con la quale formandosi favella visibile, si tratta della muta eloquenza, che non è altro che un facondo silentio.* Vicenza: F. Grossi, 1616.

Bonnet, Charles. *Essai analytique sur les facultés de l'âme.* Copenhagen: les frères C. et A. Philibert, 1760.

Bonnet, Jacques. *Histoire générale de la danse sacrée et profane, ses progrès et ses révolutions, depuis son origine jusqu'à présent.* Paris: d'Houry fils, 1723.

Bonneville, Nicolas de. *De l'Esprit des religions.* 2d ed. Paris: Imprimerie du Cercle Social, 1792 [1791].

[Borch, Michel-Jean, Comte de]. *Lettres sur la Sicile et sur l'île de Malthe.* Turin: les frères Reycends, 1782.

Bossu, Jean-Bernard. *Nouveaux voyages aux Indes occidentales; contenant une relation des différens peuples qui habitent les environs du grand fleuve Saint-Louis, appellé vulgairement le Mississipi [sic]; leur religion; leur gouvernement; leurs moeurs, leur guerres et leur commerce.* Paris: Le Jay, 1768.

Bougainville, Louis Antoine. *Voyage autour du monde, par la frégate du roi la Boudeuse, et la flûte l'Etoile; en 1766, 1767, 1768 et 1769.* Paris: Saillant et Nyon, 1771.

Bouilly, Jean-Nicholas. *L'Abbé de l'Epée, comédie historique en cinq actes et en prose.* Paris: André, an VIII.

———. *Mes Récapitulations: deuxième époque: 1791–1812.* Vol. 2. Paris: L. Janet, 1835.

Boulenger de Rivery, Claude-François-Félix. *Recherches historiques et critiques sur quelques anciens spectacles, et particulièrement sur les mimes et sur les pantomimes.* Paris: Jacques Mérigot fils, 1751.

Breton [de la Martinière], Jean-Baptiste-Joseph. *Procès de François Duval, sourd et muet de naissance, accusé de vol avec effraction et attroupement; jugé et acquitté par le deuxième Conseil de Guerre de la dix-septième division, sous la curatelle du citoyen Sicard.* Paris: Desenne, an VIII–1800.

Breton [de la Martinière], Jean-Baptiste-Joseph, and Igonel. *Lycée des arts, an III de la République française. A la Convention nationale, établissement d'un journal sténographique des travaux de la Convention.* N.p., an III.

———. *Procès instruit par le Tribunal criminel du département de la Seine, contre Demerville, Céracchi, Aréna et autres, prévenus de conspiration contre la personne du Premier Consul Bonaparte . . . recueilli par des sténographes.* Paris: Rondonneau, an IX.

[Bricaire de la Dixmerie, Nicolas]. *Mémoire pour la Loge des Neuf Soeurs.* N.p., [1779].

Brousse-Desfaucherets, Jean-Louis. *Compte rendu à l'Assemblée générale des représentants de la Commune de Paris, le 8 février 1790*. Paris: Lottin aîné et Lottin Saint-Germain, 1790.

[Buée, Abbé Adrien-Quentin]. *Nouveau dictionnaire, pour servir à l'intelligence des termes mis en vogue par la Révolution, dédié aux amis de la religion, du roi et du sens commun*. Paris: Crapart, 1792.

Bulwer, John. *Chirologia: or The Natural Language of the Hand [and] Chironomia: or the Art of Manual Rhetoric*. Edited by James W. Cleary. Carbondale and Edwardsville: Southern Illinois University Press, 1974 [1644].

———. *Philocophus or the Deafe and Dumbe Man's Friend by J.B., surnamed the Chirosopher*. London: H. Moseley, 1648.

Bürja, Abel. *Abhandlung von der Telegraphie, oder Fernschreibekunst: abgelesen in der öffentlichen Sitzung der Akademie am 25. September 1794: mit Zusätzen: aus dem Französischen*. Berlin: In der Vossischen Buchhandlung, 1794.

Butet (de la Sarthe), Pierre-Roland-François. *Abrégé d'un cours complet de lexicographie, à l'usage des élèves de la cinquième classe de l'Ecole polymathique*. Paris: Crapelet and Renouard, an IX–1801.

Cabanis, Pierre-Jean-Georges. *Corps législatif. Conseil des Cinq-Cents. Discours prononcé par Cabanis en offrant au Conseil la nouvelle édition du Dictionnaire de la ci-devant Académie française. Séance du 18 brumaire an VII*. Paris: Imprimerie nationale, an VII.

———. *Corps législatif. Conseil des Cinq-Cents. Discours de Cabanis en offrant au Conseil des Cinq-Cents l'édition des Oeuvres de Condillac. Séance du 13 thermidor an VI*. Paris: Imprimerie nationale, an VI.

———. *Rapports du physique et du moral de l'homme*. Paris: Crapart, Caille, and Ravier, an X–1802.

Cahusac, Louis de. *La Danse ancienne et moderne, ou Traité historique de la danse*. The Hague: Jean Neaulme, 1754.

Calliachi, Niccolò. *De ludis scenicis mimorum, et pantomimorum syntagma posthumum*. Padua: J. Manfrè, 1713.

Cambry, Jacques. *Manuel interprète de correspondance, ou Vocabulaires polyglottes alphabétiques et numériques en tableaux*. Paris: Mme Johanneau, 1805.

[Carra, Jean-Louis]. *De M. de Calonne tout entier, tel qu'il s'est comporté dans l'administration des finances, dans son commissariat en Bretagne . . . ouvrage critique, politique et moral*. Brussels: n.p., 1788.

———. *Systême de la raison, ou le Prophète philosophe*. 3d ed. Paris: Buisson, 1791 [1773].

Catalogue des livres qui se trouvent chez Benoît Morin, Imprimeur-Libraire, à Paris, rue Saint-Jacques, près celle de la Parcheminerie, à la Vérité, 1780. N.p., 1780.

Cavailhon, François-Edmond. *Pétition à la Convention nationale . . . sur une invention télégraphique*. Paris: Pougin, an III.

[Cérutti, Joseph-Antoine-Joachim]. *Prospectus d'un dictionnaire d'exagération, destiné à MM. les rédacteurs du Journal de Paris*. In *Etrennes au public*. N.p., 1790.

Chabanon, Michel Paul Guy de. *De la Musique considérée en elle-même et dans ses rapports avec la parole, les langues, la poésie et le théâtre.* Paris: Pissot, 1785.

Chalvet, Pierre-Vincent. *Des Qualités et des devoirs d'un instituteur public.* Paris: La Villette, an II-1793.

Changeux, Pierre-Nicolas. *Bibliothèque grammaticale abrégée, ou Nouveaux mémoires sur la parole et sur l'écriture.* Paris: Lacombe, 1773.

Chantreau, Pierre-Nicolas. *Dictionnaire national et anecdotique, pour servir à l'intelligence des mots dont notre langue s'est enrichie depuis la Révolution, et à la nouvelle signification qu'ont reçue quelques anciens mots . . . Avec un appendice contenant les mots qui vont cesser d'être en usage, et qu'il est nécessaire d'insérer dans nos archives pour l'intelligence de nos neveux.* N.p. ("A Politicopolis"): les marchands de nouveautés, 1790.

Chardin, Sir John. *Journal du voyage du chevalier Chardin en Perse et aux Indes Orientales, par la Mer Noire et par la Colchide.* London: Moses Pitt, 1686.

[Cibot, Pierre Martial.] *Lettre de Pékin, sur le génie de la langue chinoise, et la nature de leur écriture symbolique, comparée avec celle des anciens égyptiens; en réponse à celle de la Société royale des sciences de Londres, sur le même sujet.* Brussels: J. L. de Boubers, 1773.

Clément. *Solution allégorique et géometrique d'un problème autrement résolu le dix-huit brumaire, ou Image d'un bon gouvernement, dédiée au peuple français.* Paris: l'auteur, an XI–1802.

———. *La Sténographie, ou l'Art d'écrire aussi vite qu'on parle; nouveau système.* Paris: l'auteur, an IX.

[Cochin, Charles-Nicolas]. *Lettres sur l'Opéra par M. C***.* Paris: Cellot, 1781.

———. *Pantomime dramatique, ou Essai sur un nouveau genre de spectacle.* Florence and Paris: Jombert fils aîné, 1779.

Collé, Charles. *Journal historique, ou Mémoires critiques et littéraires sur les ouvrages dramatiques et sur les événements les plus mémorables, depuis 1748 jusqu'en 1751 [–1772] inclusivement.* Paris: Imprimerie bibliographique, 1805–7.

Compan, Charles. *Dictionnaire de danse, contenant l'histoire, les règles et les principes de cet art, avec des réflexions critiques, et des anecdotes curieuses concernant la danse ancienne et moderne; le tout tiré des meilleurs auteurs qui ont écrit sur cet art.* Paris: Cailleau, 1787.

Condillac, Etienne Bonnot de. *Cours d'études pour l'instruction du Prince de Parme, aujourd'hui S.A.R. l'Infant D. Ferdinand, Duc de Parme, Plaisance, Guastalla, etc.* [Parma: Imprimerie royale, 1775]. In *Oeuvres de Condillac.* Paris: C. Houel, an VI-1798.

———. *Essai sur l'origine des connaissances humaines, ouvrage où l'on réduit à un seul principe tout ce qui concerne l'entendement humain.* Amsterdam: Pierre Mortier, 1746. Reprinted as *Essay on the Origin of Human Knowledge: Being a supplement to Mr. Locke's Essay on Human Understanding.* Gainsville, Fla.: Scholars Facsimile Press, 1971 [1756].

————. *La Langue des calculs.* Edited by Anne-Marie Chouillet and Sylvain Auroux. Lille: Presses Universitaires de Lille III, 1981 [1798].

————. *La Logique/Logic.* Translated by W. R. Albury. New York: Abaris Books, 1980 [1780].

Condorcet, Marie-Jean-Antoine-Nicholas Caritat, Marquis de. *Ce que les citoyens ont droit d'attendre de leurs représentans.* Paris: Imprimerie des sourds-muets, 1793.

————. *Ecrits sur l'instruction publique.* Vol. 1, *Cinq mémoires sur l'instruction publique.* Edited by Charles Coutel and Catherine Kintzler. Paris: Edilig, 1989 [1791].

————. *Esquisse d'un tableau historique des progrès de l'esprit humain.* Edited by Monique and François Hinker. Paris: Editions Sociales, 1966 [1795].

————. *Oeuvres de Condorcet.* Edited by A. Condorcet O'Connor and M. F. Arago. Paris: Firmin Didot frères, 1847–49.

Conrart, Valentin [Michel Le Faucheur]. *Traité de l'action de l'orateur, ou de la Prononciation et du geste.* Paris: Louis Billaine, 1667 [1657].

Constant, Benjamin. *Les "Principes de politique" de Benjamin Constant.* Edited by Etienne Hofmann. Geneva: Droz, 1980 [1815].

Copans, Jean, and Jean Jamin, eds. *Aux Origines de l'anthropologie française: les mémoires de la Société des observateurs de l'homme en l'an VIII.* Paris: Le Sycomore, 1978.

[Copineau, Abbé Alexis]. *Essai synthétique sur l'origine et la formation des langues.* Paris: Ruault, 1774.

Coulon de Thévenot, Jean Félicité. *L'Art d'écrire aussi vite qu'on parle; ou la Tachygraphie française, dégagée de toute équivoque . . . suivie du rapport, fait, en 1787, à la ci-devant Académie des sciences de Paris . . . terminée par . . . les principes de l'art thélégraphique* [sic]. Rev. ed. Paris: l'auteur, 1792.

————. *Le Tachygraphe à la Convention nationale, ou Recueil exact des discours, opinions et débats relatifs à la Constitution de 1795 . . . Première partie: Déclaration des droits de l'homme et du citoyen.* N.p.: le rédacteur, an V.

Court de Gébelin, Antoine. *Histoire naturelle de la parole, ou Précis de l'origine du langage et de la grammaire universelle. Extrait du Monde Primitif.* Paris: l'auteur, 1776.

————. *Le Monde primitif, analysé et comparé avec le monde moderne.* Paris: l'auteur, 1773–82.

Cressolles, Louis de. *Vacationes autumnales sive de perfecta oratoris actione et pronunciatione.* Paris: S. Cramoisy, 1620.

Cubières, Chevalier de [Michel de Cubières-Palmézeaux]. *Opuscules poétiques.* Rev. ed. Orléans: Imprimerie de Couret de Villeneuve, 1786.

Cuvelier [de Trie], Jean-Guillaume-Antoine. *Les Hommes de la nature, et les hommes policés, pantomime en trois actes, dédiée à ceux qui n'entendent pas. Précédée et suivie des Deux Silphes, prologue et épilogue, dédiée à ceux qui entendent.* Paris: Barba, an IX.

————. *Mes riens. Mélanges en prose et en vers, pensées ou réminiscences de différentes couleurs, avec quelques anecdotes, contes et moralités.* Paris: Leprieur, 1806.

———. *La Naissance de la pantomime, scène mélodramatique et allégorique, mêlée de danses.* Paris: Barba, an VI.

Cyrano de Bergerac, Savinien. *Histoire comique, ou Voyage dans la lune.* Paris: C. de Sercy, 1650.

D'Alembert, Jean Le Rond. *Mélanges de littérature, d'histoire et de philosophie.* Rev. ed. Amsterdam: Aux dépens de la Compagnie, 1760–68.

Dalgarno, George. *Didascalocophus or the Deaf and Dumb Man's Tutor.* Oxford: printed at the Theater, 1680.

Daunou, Pierre Claude François. *Convention nationale. Essai sur la Constitution.* Paris: Imprimerie nationale, 1793.

———. *Convention nationale. Essai sur l'instruction publique.* Paris: Imprimerie nationale, 1793.

———. *Convention nationale. Observations sur la manière de discuter la Constitution.* Paris: Imprimerie nationale, [1793].

———. *Convention nationale. Rapport fait à la Convention nationale, dans sa séance du 13 germinal an III, au nom du Comité d'instruction publique, sur l'acquisition de 3,000 exemplaires de l'ouvrage posthume de Condorcet, Esquisse d'un tableau historique.* Paris: Imprimerie nationale, an III.

———. *Plan d'éducation, présenté à l'Assemblée nationale, au nom des instituteurs publics de l'Oratoire.* Paris: Volland, 1790.

Degérando, Joseph-Marie. *De l'Education des sourds-muets de naissance.* Paris: Méquignon l'aîné père, 1827.

———. *Histoire comparée des systèmes de philosophie, relativement aux principes des connaissances humaines.* Paris: Henrichs, an XII–1804.

———. *The Observation of Savage Peoples.* Translated by F. C. T. Moore. Berkeley: University of California Press, 1969 [1800].

———. "Philosophie." In *Histoire et littérature ancienne (IV): Rapports à l'Empereur sur le progrès des sciences, des lettres et des arts depuis 1789,* compiled by Bon-Joseph Dacier and re-edited by François Hartog. Paris: Belin, 1989 [1810–15].

———. *Des Signes et de l'art de penser considérés dans leurs rapports mutuels.* Paris: Goujon fils, an VIII.

Delormel, Jean. *Projet d'une langue universelle, présenté à la Convention nationale.* Paris: l'auteur, an III.

De Maimieux, Joseph. *Epître familière au sens-commun, sur la pasigraphie et la pasilalie.* Paris: Pernier, an X.

———. *Pasigraphie, ou Premiers éléments du nouvel art-science d'écrire et d'imprimer en une langue de manière à être lu et entendu dans toute autre langue sans traduction.* Paris: Bureau de la Pasigraphie, 1797.

Deschamps, Abbé Claude François. *Cours élémentaire d'éducation des sourds et muets.* Paris: Debure, 1779.

———. *Lettre à M. de Bellisle . . . pour servir de réponse aux Observations d'un sourd et muet sur un cours élémentaire d'éducation des sourds et muets, publié en 1779.* N.p., 1780.

―――. *Lettre à M. de S***[Sailly], capitaine de cavalerie, sur l'institution des sourds et muets.* London and Paris: Jean Valade, 1777.

―――. *De la Manière de suppléer aux oreilles par les yeux. Pour servir de suite au Cours élémentaire d'éducation des sourds et muets.* Paris: Debure and Cuchet, 1783.

Desloges, Pierre (also Esope-Desloges). *Almanach de la raison, pour l'an II de la République française, une et indivisible.* Paris: Citoyen Desloges, [an II].

―――. *Lettre adressée à MM. les électeurs de Paris, par un citoyen français, sourd et muet.* N.p., 1789.

―――. *Observations d'un sourd et muet sur 'Un Cours élémentaire d'éducation des sourds et muets,' publié en 1779 par M. l'abbé Deschamps.* Amsterdam and Paris: Morin, 1779.

―――. *La Prédiction des astronomes sur la fin du monde accompli, ou la Régénération de l'Europe en travail, dédiée à M. de La Fayette, commandant général de la garde nationale parisienne, par un citoyen français.* Paris: Garnéry, [1790].

Desprez de Boissy, Charles. *Lettres sur les spectacles; avec une histoire des ouvrages pour et contre les théâtres.* 6th ed. Paris: Boudet, Desaint, Nyon, and Morin, 1777.

Destutt de Tracy, Antoine-Louis-Claude. *Elémens d'Idéologie. Première partie. Idéologie proprement dite* [1801] and *Seconde partie. Grammaire* [1803]. 3d ed. Paris: Mme Veuve Courcier, 1817.

Détail exact du télégraphe, au moyen duquel la reprise du Quesnoy, de Valenciennes et de Condé a été connue à Paris, longtemps avant l'arrivée des courriers. Paris: Imprimerie de Maudet, an III.

Dictionnaire laconique, véridique et impartial, ou Etrennes aux démagogues sur la Révolution française, par un citoyen inactif, ni enrôlé, ni soldé, mais ami de tout le monde pour de l'argent. [Paris]: n.p. ("Patriopolis: Aux dépens des démagogues ou patriotes soi-disant libres"), [1791].

Dictionnaire raisonné de plusieurs mots qui sont dans la bouche de tout le monde, et ne présentent pas des idées bien nettes. Paris: Palais Royal et les marchands de nouveautés, 1790.

Diderot, Denis. *Lettre sur les sourds et muets, à l'usage de ceux qui entendent et qui parlent. Adressée à M. **.* [Paris]: n.p., 1751. Reprinted in *Diderot's Early Philosophical Works.* Translated by Margaret Jourdain. Chicago and London: Open Court Publishing Company, 1916.

―――. *Oeuvres esthétiques.* Edited by Paul Vernière. Paris: Garnier frères, 1968.

Diderot, Denis, and Jean Le Rond D'Alembert, eds. *Encyclopédie, ou Dictionnaire raisonné des sciences, des arts et des métiers, par une société des gens de lettres.* Paris: Briasson, David, Le Breton, and Durand, 1751–65.

Digiti-lingua: or, the most compendious, copious, facile, and secret way of silent converse ever yet discovered . . . By a person who has conversed no otherwise in above nine years. The figures curiously engraved on copper plates. London: P. Buck, 1698.

Dorat, Claude-Joseph. *La Déclamation théâtrale, poëme didactique en 4 chants, précédé d'un discours, et de notions historiques sur la danse.* 2d ed. Paris: Sébastien Jorry, 1767.

Dubos, Jean-Baptiste. *Réflexions critiques sur la poésie et sur la peinture.* 1st ed. Paris: J. Mariette, 1719; 3d ed. Paris: J. Mariette, 1732. Reprinted as *Critical Reflections on Poetry, Painting and Music.* Translated by Thomas Nugent. 5th ed. New York: AMS Press, 1978 [1748].

[DuCoudray, Alexandre Jacques]. *Lettre d'un Parisien à son ami, en province, sur le nouveau spectacle des Elèves de l'Opéra, ouvert le 7 janvier.* Paris: les marchands de nouveautés, 1779.

Duhamel, Jules-Michel. *Essai analytique sur cette question: quelle est l'instruction nécessaire au citoyen français?* Paris: Imprimerie de l'Institution nationale des sourds-muets, [1792].

———. *Mémoire tendant à faire établir deux chaires au Collège de France; l'une d'analyse de l'esprit humain, et l'autre de langue française.* Paris: Remont and Desray, an X–1802.

Duplain. *Guimard, ou l'art de la danse-pantomime: poème.* London and Paris: Mérigot l'aîné, 1783.

Duval-Pyrau, Abbé. *Journal et anecdotes intéressantes du voyage de M. le Comte de Falckenstein.* Frankfort and Leipzig: n.p., 1777.

Edelcrantz, A.-N. *Traité des télégraphes et essai d'un nouvel établissement de ce genre . . . traduit de Suédois par Hector B.* Paris: C. F. Patris, an IX–1801.

Elie de Beaumont, Jean-Baptiste Jacques. *Mémoire et réponse à M. l'Abbé de l'Epée, pour le Sieur Cazeaux, accusé d'avoir supprimé la personne et l'état du Comte de Solar.* Paris: Knapen et fils and Jorry, 1779.

———. *Vue générale de l'affaire du soi-disant Comte de Solar, où l'on a laissé à l'écart tout ce qui, dans l'instruction antérieure à l'Arrêt de la Cour du 20 avril 1779, concourt à prouver l'innocence du Sieur Cazeaux . . . suivies d'une lettre de M. Prunget des Boissières, ancien avocat au Parlement, relative aux fausses assertions insérées dans plusieurs gazettes contre le Sieur Cazeaux.* Paris: Demonville, 1780.

Engel, Johann Jacob. *Idées sur le geste et l'action théâtrale.* Paris: Barrois; Strasbourg: Librairie Académique; and The Hague: Van Cleef, 1788.

Epée, Abbé Charles-Michel de l'. *Dictionnaire des sourds et muets, publié d'après le manuscrit original.* Edited by Dr. J. A. A. Rattel. Paris: Baillière, 1896.

———. *Exercice des sourds et muets qui se fera le jeudi 2 juillet 1772, chez M. l'abbé de l'Epée, rue des Moulins, Butte S.-Roche, depuis trois heures jusqu'à sept.* Paris: L. Cellot, 1772.

———. *Exercice de sourds et muets qui se fera le mercredi 4 août 1773, chez M. l'abbé de l'Epée, rue des Moulins, Butte S. Roche, depuis trois heures de relevée jusqu'à sept.* Paris: Grangé, 1773.

———. *Institution des sourds et muets, ou Recueil des exercices soutenus par les sourds et muets pendant les années 1771, 1772, 1773 et 1774, avec les lettres qui ont accompagné les programmes de chacun de ces exercices.* Paris: Butard, 1774.

————. *Institution des sourds et muets, par la voie des signes métho-diques; ouvrage qui contient le projet d'une langue universelle, par l'en-tremise des signes naturels assujettis à une méthode*. Paris: Nyon, 1776.

————. *La Véritable manière d'instruire les sourds et muets, confirmée par une longue expérience*. Paris: Fayard, 1984 [1784].

Exercices que soutiendront les sourds et muets de naissance, les 12 et 15 septembre 1789, dans la salle du Musée de Bordeaux, dirigés par M. l'abbé Sicard, instituteur royal, sous les auspices de M. Champion de Cicé. Bordeaux: M. Racle, 1789.

Extrait de différens journaux, concernant les forfaits des premiers jours de septembre 1792. Paris: les marchands de nouveautés, 1796.

Fabre d'Eglantine, Philippe-François-Nazaire. *Convention nationale. Rapport fait à la Convention nationale, dans la séance du 3 du second mois de la IIe année de la République française, au nom de la commission chargée de la confection du calendrier*. Paris: Imprimerie nationale, an II.

Fauchet, Abbé Claude. *Oraison funèbre de Charles-Michel de l'Epée, prêtre, avocat au Parlement, de la Société philantropique, inventeur de la méthode pour l'instruction des sourds et muets de naissance, et leur premier instituteur. Prononcée, dans l'Eglise paroissiale de S.-Etienne-du-Mont, le mardi 23 février 1790, d'après la déliberation de la Commune de Paris, en présence de la députation de l'Assemblée nationale, de M. le Maire et de l'Assemblée générale des représentans de la Commune*. Paris: J. R. Lottin de S. Germain, 1790.

Faulcon, Félix. *Opinion de Félix Faulcon, député de la Vienne, sur les quali-fications verbales. 12 vendémiaire an VII*. Paris: Badouin, an VII.

Fenouillot de Falbaire, Charles-Georges. *Oeuvres de M. de Falbaire de Quingey*. Paris: Veuve Duchesne, 1787.

Ferrari, Ottavio. *De pantomimis et mimis, dissertatio*. Wolfenbüttel: G. Freytag, [1714].

Foigny, Gabriel de. *Les Avantures de Jacques Sadeur dans la découverte et le voiage de la Terre Australe*. Paris: C. Barbin, 1692.

[Fontenai, Abbé de, ed.] *Esprit des livres défendus, ou Antilogies philoso-phiques; ouvrage dans lequel on a recueilli les morceaux les plus curieux et les plus interessans sur la religion, la philosophie, les sciences et les arts, extrait des livres philosophiques les plus modernes, et les plus con-nus*. Amsterdam and Paris: Nyon and Laporte, 1777.

Formey, Jean-Henri-Samuel. *Anti-Emile*. Berlin: Joachim Paul, 1763.

Forster, George. *A Voyage round the World in his Britannic Majesty's Sloop, Resolution, commanded by Capt. James Cook, during the Years 1772, 1773, 1774, and 1775*. London: B. White, 1777.

Fortia-d'Urban, Marquis de, and Pierre-Michel Hennin. *Rapport fait à l'Académie celtique le 6 septembre 1805, 19 fructidor an XIII, par M. de Fortia-d'Urban and M. Hennin père, commissaires nommés pour lui ren-dre compte du 'Manuel interprète de correspondance,' par M. de Cam-bry*. N.p., [1805].

François de Neufchâteau, Nicolas-Louis. *L'Institution des enfans, ou Conseils d'un père à son fils, imités des vers que Muret a écrits en latin, pour l'usage de son neveu et qui peuvent servir à tous les jeunes écoliers.* Paris: H. Agasse, an VI.

———. *Méthode pratique de lecture.* Paris: P. Didot, an VII.

Franklin, Benjamin. *The Papers of Benjamin Franklin.* Edited by Leonard W. Labaree et al. New Haven: Yale University Press, 1959–.

[Fréville, Anne-François-Joachim]. *Insuffisance de nos presses pour éclairer le peuple, et urgence d'un nouveau mode de publicité vocale et d'instruction auriculaire, dans toute l'étendue de la république.* N.p., [1793].

[Gallais, Jean-Pierre]. *Extrait d'un dictionnaire inutile, composé par une société en commandite, et rédigé par un homme seul.* [Paris] ("A 500 lieues de l'Assemblée nationale"): n.p., 1790.

Garat, Dominique-Joseph. *Corps législatif. Conseil des Anciens. Discours de Garat sur l'hommage fait au Conseil des Anciens des premières strophes du 'Chant du Départ' écrites avec les caractères pasigraphiques. Séance du 13 nivôse an VII.* Paris: Imprimerie nationale, an VII.

———. *Corps législatif. Conseil des Anciens. Discours prononcé par le C. Garat en offrant les oeuvres de Condillac, à la séance du 3 fructidor an VI.* Paris: Imprimerie nationale, an VI.

———. "Discours préliminaire." In *Dictionnaire de l'Académie françoise.* 5th ed. Paris: J. J. Smits, an VII [1798].

———. *Mémoires historiques sur le XVIIIe siècle, et sur M. Suard.* 2d ed. Paris: A. Belin, 1821.

Gardel, Maximilien. *L'Avènement de Titus à l'Empire, ballet allégorique au sujet du couronnement du Roi.* Paris: Musier fils, 1775.

Gattel, Abbé Claude-Marie. *Nouveau dictionnaire portatif de la langue françoise.* Lyon: Bruyset, 1797.

Gauthey, Emiland-Marie. *Expérience sur la propagation du son et de la voix dans les tuyaux prolongés à une grande distance, nouveau moyen d'établir et d'obtenir une correspondance très rapide entre des lieux fort éloignés.* Philadelphia and Paris: Prault, 1783.

[Gauthier, Abbé François-Louis]. *Traité contre les danses et les mauvaises chansons, dans lequel le danger et le mal qui y sont renfermés sont démontrés par les témoignages multipliés des Saintes Ecritures, des SS. PP., des conciles, de plusieurs evêques du siècle passé et du nôtre, d'un nombre de théologiens moraux et de casuistes, de jurisconsultes, de plusieurs ministres protestans, et enfin des payens même.* Rev. ed. Paris: Froullé, 1785.

[Gautier, P. N.]. *Dictionnaire de la constitution et du gouvernement françois, contenant la dénomination de tous les nouveaux officiers publics, la définition des nouveaux termes les plus usités, quelques-uns de ceux qui ne doivent plus être employés, etc.* Paris: Guillaume, [1791].

Gazier, A., ed. *Lettres à Grégoire sur les patois de France, 1790–1794. Documents inédits sur la langue, les moeurs et l'état des esprits dans les diverses régions de la France, au début de la Révolution.* Geneva: Slatkine, 1969 [1880].

Genlis, Stéphanie Félicité Ducrest de Saint-Aubin, Comtesse de. *Adèle et Théodore, ou Lettres sur l'éducation; contenant tous les principes relatifs aux trois différens plans d'éducation des princes, des jeunes personnes et des hommes.* Paris: M. Lambert, 1782.

[Ginguené, Pierre Louis]. *Instruction du procès, entre les premiers sujets de l'Académie royale de musique et de danse et le Sr de Vismes, entrepreneur, jadis public, aujourd'hui clandestin, et directeur de ce spectacle ... extrait de quelques papiers qui n'ont pas cours en France.* Paris: n.p., 1779.

[Gorjy, Jean-Claude]. *Ann'quin Bredouille, ou Le Petit cousin de Tristram Shandy.* Paris: Louis, 1792.

[Goudar, Ange]. *De Venise. Rémarques sur la musique et la danse, ou Lettres de M. G*** à Milord P[embroke].* Venise: Charles Palese, 1773.

―――. *Lettre de Madame Sara Goudar à Monsieur L*** au sujet du divertissement du Théâtre del Cocomero et de la Comédie Françoise du Théâtre Sainte Marie.* N.p., 1776.

―――. *Lettre d'un des petits oracles de M. Campioni au Grand Pitrot, traduit de l'Italien.* N.p., n.d.

―――. *Observations sur les trois derniers ballets pantomimes qui ont paru aux Italiens et aux François, sçavoir: Télémaque, Le Sultan Généreux, La Mort d'Orphée.* N.p., 1759.

―――. *Supplément au Supplément sur les Rémarques de la musique et de la danse, ou Lettres de M. G*** à Milord Pembroke.* N.p., 1774.

Goulier. *Lettre à M. L'Abbé *** sur la manière d'apprendre les langues.* Paris: Desaint and Ravinet, 1769.

Goupil de Préfelne, Guillaume-François Charles. *Corps législatif. Conseil des Anciens. Discours prononcé dans la séance du Conseil des Anciens, le 18 pluviôse de l'an VI de la République française ... en présentant au Conseil l'hommage de la Pasigraphie, nouvel art littéraire inventé par le citoyen Jean [sic] de Maimieux, ancien major d'infanterie allemande.* Paris: Imprimerie nationale, an VI.

Gourdin, François Philippe. *Considérations philosophiques sur l'action de l'orateur, précédées de recherches sur la mémoire.* Amsterdam; Paris: Veuve Desaint; Caen: J. Manoury, 1775.

Graffigny, Mme de (Françoise d'Issembourg d'Happoncourt). *Lettres d'une Péruvienne.* New York: Modern Language Association of America, 1993 [1747].

Grasset de Saint-Sauveur, Jacques. *Histoire générale et détaillée des peuples sauvages qui habitent le Canada, les côtes du Labrador, la Louisianne, la Virginie.* Paris: l'auteur, 1787.

[Green, Francis]. *"Vox Oculis Subjecta": a dissertation on the most curious and important art of imparting speech and the knowledge of language to the naturally deaf, and (consequently) dumb.* London: B. White, 1783.

Grégoire, Abbé Henri-Baptiste. *Convention nationale. Instruction publique. Rapport sur la nécessité et les moyens d'anéantir les patois et d'universaliser l'usage de la langue française. Séance du 16 prairial, l'an deuxième de la République*. Paris: Imprimerie nationale, [an II].

———. *Convention nationale. Instruction publique. Rapport sur l'ouverture d'un concours pour les livres élémentaires de la première éducation. Séance du 3 pluviôse, l'an second de la République une et indivisible*. Paris: Imprimerie nationale, [an II].

———. *Convention nationale. Rapport sur les inscriptions des monumens publics. Séance du 22 nivôse l'an II de la République une et indivisible, suivi du décret de la Convention nationale*. Paris: Imprimerie nationale, [an II].

———. *Convention nationale. Système de dénominations topographiques pour les places, rues, quais . . . de toutes les communes de la République*. Paris: Imprimerie nationale, [an II].

———. *Essai sur la régénération physique, morale et politique des juifs: ouvrage couronné par la Société royale des sciences et des arts de Metz, le 23 août 1788*. Preface by Rita Hermon-Belot. Paris: Flammarion, 1988 [1788].

Grimm, Friedrich Melchior, Denis Diderot, Guillaume-Thomas-François Raynal, and Jacques-Henri Meister. *Correspondance littéraire, philosophique et critique*. Paris: Garnier frères, 1877–82 [1753–90].

Guillaume, James, ed. *Procès-verbaux du Comité d'instruction publique de l'Assemblée législative*. Paris: Imprimerie nationale, 1889.

———. *Procès-verbaux du Comité d'instruction publique de la Convention nationale*. Paris: Imprimerie nationale, 1891–1907.

Guiraudet, Charles-Philippe-Toussaint. *Explication de quelques mots importants de notre langue politique, pour servir à la théorie de nos loix et d'abord: de la loi. Discours lu à l'Assemblée des Amis de la Constitution et imprimé par ordre de la société*. Paris: n.p., 1792.

———. *Qu'est-ce que la nation et qu'est-ce que la France?* N.p., 1789.

Guys, Pierre-Augustin. *Voyage littéraire de la Grèce, ou Lettres sur les Grecs anciens et modernes, avec un parallèle de leurs moeurs*. Paris: Veuve Duchesne, 1771.

Guyton de Morveau, Louis-Bernard, Antoine Laurent Lavoisier, Claude-Louis Berthollet, and Antoine-François de Fourcroy. *Méthode de nomenclature chimique . . . On y a joint un nouveau système de caractères chimiques adaptés à cette nomenclature*. Paris: Cuchet, 1787.

Hamilton, Alexander, James Madison, and John Jay. *The Federalist Papers*. Edited by Isaac Kramnick. Harmondsworth, Eng.: Penguin Books, 1987 [1788].

Haüy, Valentin. *Essai sur l'éducation des aveugles*. Paris: Imprimé par les enfans-aveugles, 1786.

Helvétius, Claude-Adrien. *De l'Esprit*. Paris: Fayard, 1988 [1758].

———. *De l'Homme, de ses facultés intellectuelles et de son éducation*. London: Société typographique, 1773.

Herrgott, Père Marquard. *Vetus disciplina monastica*. Paris: C. Osmont, 1726.

Hobbes, Thomas. *Leviathan, or the Matter, Forme, and Power of a Common-*

Wealth Ecclesiasticall and Civill. Edited by C. B. Macpherson. Harmondsworth, Eng.: Penguin Books, 1975 [1651].

Holbach, Paul-Henri Thiry, Baron d'. *Le Bon sens, ou Idées naturelles opposées aux idées surnaturelles.* Paris: Editions rationalistes, 1971 [1772].

Hourwitz, Zalkind. *Polygraphie, ou l'Art de correspondre, à l'aide d'un dictionnaire, dans toutes les langues, même celles dont on ne possède pas seulement les lettres alphabétiques.* Paris: l'auteur, an IX.

Jauffret, Louis-François. *Promenades à la campagne pendant la belle saison, faites dans le dessein de donner aux jeunes gens une idée du bonheur qui peut résulter pour l'homme, de l'étude de lui-même, et de la contemplation de la nature.* N.p., an X.

Jones, William. *The Letters of Sir William Jones.* Edited by Garland Cannon. Oxford: Clarendon Press, 1970.

Jouenne-Longchamp, Thomas François Ambroise. *Rapport et projet de décret sur l'organisation définitive des deux établissements fondés à Paris et à Bordeaux pour les sourds et muets, présentés à la Convention nationale, le 16 nivôse an III, au nom des trois Comités d'instruction publique, des finances et des secours publics.* Paris: Imprimerie nationale, [an III].

Journée du 6 octobre 1789. Affaire complète de MM. d'Orléans et Mirabeau, contenant toutes les pièces manuscrites lues à l'Assemblée nationale, les discussions et le décret définitif, saisis mot à mot, par la Société logographique. Paris: n.p., 1790.

Lacépède, Bernard-German-Etienne de la Ville. *Discours d'ouverture et de clôture du cours d'histoire naturelle: donné dans le Muséum national d'histoire naturelle, l'an VII de la République.* Paris: Plassan, an VII [1799].

La Chalotais, Louis-René de Caradeuc de. *Essai d'éducation nationale, ou Plan d'études pour la jeunesse.* Geneva: C. et A. Philibert, 1763.

Lacretelle (jeune), Charles de. *Précis historique de la Révolution française: Convention nationale.* 2d ed. Paris: Treuttel et Würtz, 1806.

Lacroix, Sigismond, ed. *Actes de la Commune de Paris pendant la Révolution.* Paris: L. Cerf, 1894–98 (1er série); 1900–9 (2ème série).

LaFin, Charles de. *Sermo mirabilis: or the silent language. Whereby one may learn . . . how to impart his mind to his mistress, or his friend, in any language . . . without the least noise, word or voice.* 3d ed. London: John Salusbury, 1696.

Lafitau, Père Joseph-François. *Moeurs des sauvages amériquains comparées aux moeurs des premiers temps.* Paris: Saugrain l'aîné, 1724.

Lafon de Ladébat, André-Daniel. *A Collection of the Most Remarkable Definitions and Answers of Massieu and Clerc, Deaf and Dumb, to the various questions put to them, at the Public Lectures of the Abbé Sicard in London.* Translated by J. H. Sievrac. London: Cox and Baylis, 1815.

La Harpe, Jean-François de. *Correspondance inédite de Jean-François de La Harpe.* Edited by Alexandre Jovicevich. Paris: Editions Universitaires, 1965.

———. *Correspondance littéraire, adressée à Son Altesse impériale, Mgr.*

le grand-duc, aujourd'hui Empereur de Russie, et à M. le comte André Schowalow... depuis 1774 jusqu'à 1789. Paris: Migneret, 1801–7.

———. *Discours, prononcé à l'ouverture du Lycée, le 31 décembre 1794.* Boston: J. T. Buckingham, 1810 [1796].

———. *Du Fanatisme dans la langue révolutionnaire, ou de la Persécution suscitée par les barbares du dix-huitième siècle contre la religion chrétienne et ses ministres.* 2d ed. Paris: Migneret, an V–1797.

———. *Lycée, ou Cours de littérature ancienne et moderne.* Paris: Deterville, 1818.

Lakanal, Joseph. *Convention nationale. Rapport sur l'établissement des écoles normales. Séance du brumaire an III.* Paris: Imprimerie nationale, an III.

———. *Convention nationale. Rapport sur le télégraphe, fait au nom du Comité d'instruction publique... réimprimé par ordre de la Convention.* Paris: Imprimerie nationale, an III.

———. *Convention nationale. Rapport sur le thélegraphe [sic] du Citoyen Chappe, fait par Lakanal, au nom du Comité d'instruction publique, et de la commission nommée par le décret du 27 avril dernier.* Paris: Imprimerie nationale, [1793].

La Mettrie, Julien Offray de. *L'Homme machine.* Leiden: E. Luzac fils, 1748.

Lamy, Bernard. *La Rhétorique ou l'art de parler.* 4th ed. Paris: Pierre Debats and Imbert Debats, 1701 [1676].

Lancelin, P. F. *Introduction à l'analyse des sciences, ou de la Génération, des fondemens et des instrumens de nos connoissances.* Paris: Imprimerie de Bossange, Masson et Besson, ans IX–XI.

Lane, Harlan, ed. *The Deaf Experience: Classics in Language and Education.* Translated by Franklin Philip. Cambridge: Harvard University Press, 1984.

La Pérouse, Jean-François de Galaup, Comte de. *Voyage de la Pérouse autour du monde.* Edited by [General] L.-M.-A. Milet-Mureau. Paris: Imprimerie de la République, an V–1797.

Laromiguière, Pierre. *Paradoxes de Condillac, ou Réflexions sur la langue des calculs, ouvrage posthume de cet auteur.* Paris: Librairie économique, an XIII–1805.

L'Aulnaye, François-Henri-Stanislas de. *De la Saltation théâtrale, ou Recherches sur l'origine, les progrès et les effets de la pantomime chez les anciens.* Paris: Barrois l'aîné, 1790.

[Laus de Boissy, Louis de]. *Lettre critique sur les ballets de l'Opéra, adressée à l'auteur du Spectateur français, par un homme de mauvaise humeur.* Paris: Louis Jorry fils and Lesclapart, 1771.

Laval, F.-G.-B., and Auguste-Savinien Leblond. *Théorie du télégraphe décimal et réduction numérique de la langue française au système décimal.* Paris: Imprimerie de la ligne télégraphique du Havre, [an VII].

Laval, F.-G.-B., and Peytes-Montcabrié. *Collection des mémoires, rapports et autres pièces relatives à un nouveau télégraphe pour les signaux des côtes, de l'intérieur et pour la correspondance des armées.* Paris: Imprimerie de Renaudière, an VII.

Laval, F.-G.-B., Peytes-Moncabrié, Auguste-Savinien Leblond, and Véronèse. *Ligne télégraphique du Havre, ordonnée par arrêté du Directoire exécutif du 9 floréal an 7. Seconde collection des mémoires, dessins, tableaux, cartes et autres pièces relatives à un nouveau télégraphe pour les signaux de côtes, de l'intérieur et pour la correspondance des armées.* Paris: Imprimerie de la ligne télégraphique du Havre, [an VII].

Lavater, Jean Gaspar (Johann Caspar). *Essai sur la physiognomonie, destiné à faire connoître l'homme et à le faire aimer.* The Hague: n.p., 1781–1803.

[Leblan, Claude-Saintin]. *Théorie nouvelle de la parole et des langues, contenant une critique abrégée de tous les grammairiens anciens et modernes.* Paris: Mérigot, 1750.

Leblond, Auguste-Savinien. *De l'Instruction par les yeux, lu à la Société libre d'institution, en séance publique, le 6 brumaire an VII.* Paris: J. F. Sorby, [an VII].

———. *Dictionnaire abrégé des hommes célèbres de l'antiquité et des temps modernes: ouvrage propre à instruire les jeunes gens, à exciter leur émulation et à leur faire apprécier les hommes.* Paris: Lenoir, an X–1802.

———. *Ponctuation décimale, ou Manière d'adapter aux nombres les signes de ponctuation, lu à la Société libre d'institution, le 6 brumaire an VII.* Paris: J. F. Sorby, [an VII].

———. *Sur la nomenclature des poids et mesures. Nouvelles réflexions présentées à l'Institut national, le premier nivôse an 9, lu à la Société d'Agriculture de Seine et Oise, séance du 25 pluviôse an 9.* Versailles: Jacob, an IX.

———. *Sur le système monétaire décimal, mémoire remis au Ministre des Finances, le 24 nivôse an VI, et présenté par lui à la Commission des finances du Conseil des Cinq-Cents.* Paris: Demonville, [an VI].

LeBouvyer-Desmortiers, Urbain-René-Thomas. *Mémoire ou considérations sur les sourds-muets de naissance et sur les moyens de donner l'ouïe et la parole à ceux qui en sont susceptibles.* Paris: F. Buisson, an VIII–1800.

Lecointe, Jean. *Apologie de la danse: son antiquité, sa noblesse et ses avantages.* Paris and London: J. Kippax, 1752.

Leibniz, Gottfried Wilhelm von. *Oeuvres philosophiques latines et françoises de feu M. de Leibnitz: tirées de ses manuscrits qui se conservent dans la Bibliothèque royale à Hanovre.* Amsterdam and Leipzig: Jean Schreuder, 1765.

———. *Opera Omnia.* Geneva: Fratres de Tournes, 1768.

Lemercier, J.-B. *Lettre sur la possibilité de faire de la grammaire un art-science aussi certain dans ses principes et aussi rigoureux dans ses démonstrations que les arts-sciences physico-mathématiques, écrite . . . en prairial an VI.* Paris: l'éditeur, 1806.

[Lemontey, Pierre]. *Raison, folie, petit cours de morale mis à la portée des vieux enfans; suivi des Observations de la femme [1803].* 3d ed. Paris: Deterville and Crapelet, 1816.

Lesure, François, ed. *Querelle des Gluckistes et Piccinnistes.* Geneva: Minkoff, 1984.

Lettre de M. le Baron *** à une des rivales de Terpsichore. London and Paris: Emslay and Esprit, 1775.

Lettre d'un des petits oracles de M. Angiolini au grand Noverre. Milan: J. P. Bianchi, 1774.

Lettre écrite à un ami sur les danseurs de corde et sur les pantomimes qui ont paru autrefois chez les Grecs et chez les Romains et à Paris en 1738. Paris: n.p., 1739.

Leupold, Jacob. *Theatrum arithmetico-geometricum.* Leipzig: Christophe Zunkel, 1727.

Liste de toutes les personnes qui composent le premier musée autorisé par le gouvernement, sous la protection de Monsieur et de Madame, pour l'année 1785. [Paris]: Imprimé par ordre du conseil du Musée, 1785.

Le Livre jaune: contenant quelques conversations sur les logomachies, c'est-à-dire, sur les disputes de mots, abus des termes, contradictions, double entente, faux sens, que l'on employe dans les discours, et dans les écrits. Bâle [Paris]: n.p., 1748.

Locke, John. *An Essay concerning Human Understanding.* 4th ed. Edited by Peter H. Nidditch. Oxford: Oxford University Press, 1975 [1700; 1st ed., 1690].

Loi relative à M. Abbé de l'Epée, et à son établissement en faveur des sourds et muets. Paris: Imprimerie royale, 1791.

Lucian. "Of Pantomime." In *The Works of Lucian of Samosata.* Translated by H. W. Fowler and F. G. Fowler. Oxford: Clarendon Press, 1905.

Maignet, Etienne-Christophe. *Convention nationale. Compte rendu à la Convention nationale de ce qui s'est passé dans l'établissement des sourds-muets dans la séance tenue en présence des membres du Comité des secours publics, présenté au nom de ce Comité, pour servir de suite au rapport de Maignet sur les sourds-muets.* Paris: Imprimerie nationale, [an II].

————. *Convention nationale. Rapport et projet de décret sur l'organisation des établissements pour les sourds-muets indigents décrétés le 28 juin dernier [1793].* Paris: Imprimerie nationale, [an II].

Maine de Biran, François-Pierre. *Oeuvres de Maine de Biran.* Edited by Pierre Tisserand. Paris: Félix Alcan, 1920–22.

Mairan, Jean-Jacques Dortous de. *Lettres de M. de Mairan, au R. P. Parrenin, missionnaire de la Compagnie de Jésus, à Pékin, contenant diverses questions sur la Chine.* Paris: Desaint et Saillant, 1759.

[Mairobert, Mathieu François Pidanzat de]. *L'Espion anglois, ou Correspondance secrète entre Milord All'Eye et Milord All'Ear.* London: J. Adamson, 1784–86.

Mandeville, Bernard. *Fable of the Bees: or Private Vices, Publick Benefits.* Edited by F. B. Kaye. Oxford: Clarendon Press, 1924 [1729].

Marat, Jean-Paul. *Les Chaînes de l'esclavage.* Edited by Michel Vovelle. Brussels: Editions complexes, 1988 [1774].

Maréchal, Pierre-Sylvain. *Dictionnaire des honnêtes gens . . . pour servir de correctif aux dictionnaires des grands hommes.* Paris: Gueffier jeune, 1791.

———. *Le Jugement dernier des rois, prophétie en un acte, en prose*. Paris: C. F. Patris, [an II].

Marignié, Jean Etienne François. *La Vie de David Garrick, suivie de deux lettres de M. Noverre à Voltaire sur ce célèbre acteur*. Paris: H. L. Perronneau, an IX.

Marmontel, Jean-François. *De l'Autorité de l'usage sur la langue, discours lu dans la séance publique de l'Académie française, le 16 juin 1785*. Paris: Demonville, 1785.

Massieu, Jean-Baptiste. *Rapport sur l'établissement des aveugles-nés, et sur sa réunion à celui des sourds-muets, fait au nom des Comités de l'extinction de la mendicité, d'aliénation des biens nationaux, des finances et de constitution*. Paris: Imprimerie de la rue Notre-Dame-des-Victoires, 1791.

Maupertuis, Pierre-Louis Moreau de. *Oeuvres de Maupertuis*. Lyon: Jean-Marie Bruyset, 1756.

Mavidal, M. J., and M. E. Laurent, eds. *Archives parlementaires de 1787 à 1860; recueil complet des débats législatifs et politiques des Chambres françaises*. Paris: Société anonyme d'imprimerie, 1867–96.

Mayeur de Saint Paul, François Marie. *L'Elève de la nature, mélodrame en un acte, en prose, suivi d'un divertissement*. Paris: Belin and Brunet, 1787.

Melon, Jean-François. *Essai politique sur le commerce*. Rev. ed. Amsterdam: François Changuion, 1742.

Mémoire à consulter, pour le Sieur Bonvalet, avocat en parlement, tuteur du jeune Comte de Solar, sourd et muet, trouvé sur le chemin de Péronne, le premier août 1773. 2d ed. Paris: Benoît Morin, 1779.

Mercier, Louis-Sébastien. *L'An deux mille quatre cent quarante: rêve s'il en fut jamais*. Edited by Raymond Trousson. Paris: Ducros, 1971 [1770].

———. *Corps législatif. Conseil des Cinq-Cents. Rapport fait par L.-S. Mercier, au nom d'une commission spéciale, sur l'enseignement des langues vivantes. Séance du 22 messidor l'an IV*. Paris: Imprimerie nationale, an IV.

———. *Corps législatif. Conseil des Cinq-Cents. Second rapport de L.-S. Mercier, fait au nom d'une commission spéciale, sur l'enseignement des langues vivantes. Du 17 fructidor an IV*. Paris: Imprimerie nationale, an IV.

———. *Du Théâtre, ou Nouvel essai sur l'art dramatique*. Amsterdam: E. Van Harrevelt, 1773.

———. *Mon Bonnet de nuit*. Neufchâtel: Imprimerie de la Société Typographique, 1784.

———. *Mon Dictionnaire*. N.p., [c. 1798].

———. *Néologie, ou Vocabulaire des mots nouveaux, à renouveler ou pris dans des acceptions nouvelles*. Paris: Moussard, an IX–1801.

———. *Le Nouveau Paris*. Paris: Mercure de France, 1994 [1798].

Meude-Monpas, Le Chevalier J.-J. O. de. *Dictionnaire de musique*. Paris: Knapen et fils, 1787.

Meyer, Frederic Jean Laurent. *Fragments sur Paris*. Translated by Général Dumouriez. Hamburg: n.p., 1798.

Monboddo, Lord (James Burnett). *Of the Origin and Progress of Language*. Edinburgh: J. Balfour; London: T. Cadell, 1774–92.

Montaigne, Abbé. *Recherches sur les connaissances intellectuelles des sourds-muets, considérés par rapport à l'administration des sacremens*. Paris: A. Le Clère, 1829.

Montaigne, Michel de. *The Complete Essays of Montaigne*. Translated by Donald M. Frame. Stanford: Stanford University Press, 1958.

Montesquieu, Charles-Louis de Secondat, Baron de la Brède et de. *De l'Esprit des lois*. Paris: Flammarion, 1979 [1748].

Montigny, Charles-Claude de. *Alphabet universel, ou Sténographie méthodique*. Paris: Ballard, 1799.

Moreau de Saint-Méry, Médéric-Louis-Elie. *Dance; an article drawn from the work by M.L.E. Moreau de Saint-Méry entitled: Repertory of colonial information, compiled alphabetically (1796)*. Translated by Lily and Baird Hastings. Brooklyn: Dance Horizons, 1976.

Moreau de Vormes, Jacob Augustin Antoine. *Lettre de M. Moreau de Vormes et consultation pour le Sieur Cazeaux*. Paris: Knapen et fils, 1779.

Morellet, Abbé André. *Mélanges de littérature et de philosophie du 18e siècle*. Paris: Mme Veuve Lepetit, 1818.

———. *Mémoires de l'Abbé Morellet de l'Académie française sur le dix-huitième siècle et sur la Révolution*. Edited by Jean-Pierre Guicciardi. Paris: Mercure de France, 1988 [1821].

Moussaud, Abbé Jean-Marie. *L'Alphabet raisonné, ou Explication de la figure des lettres, dedié à M. de la Rochefoucault*. Paris: Maradan, an XI–1803.

[Nougaret, Pierre Jean Baptiste]. *La Littérature renversée, ou l'Art de faire des pièces de théâtre sans paroles; ouvrage utile aux poètes dramatiques de nos jours, avec un Traité du geste, contenant la manière de représenter les pièces de théâtre à l'aide des bras et des jambes pour la commodité des acteurs qui ont une mauvaise prononciation et offrant en outre une excellente méthode aux gens mariés, pour se quereller dans leur ménage, sans faire de bruit*. Bern and Paris: les débitans de brochures nouvelles, 1775.

Nouveau dictionnaire françois, à l'usage de toutes les municipalités, les milices nationales, et de tous les patriotes, composé par un aristocrate, dédié à l'Assemblée dite nationale, pour servir à l'histoire de la Révolution de France. Et c'est la vérité, comme on dit, toute nue. N.p. ("En France: D'une imprimerie aristocratique . . ."), 1790.

Noverre, Jean-Georges. *Due lettere scritte a diversi sogetti: lettere a madame XXX sopra i balli Apelle e Campaspe e de Adele dati da Mons. Noverre nel teatro di Milano 1774*. Naples: n.p., 1774.

———. *Introduction au ballet des Horaces, ou Petite réponse aux grandes lettres du Sr. Angiolini*. [Vienna]: n.p., 1774.

———. *Lettres sur la danse et sur les ballets*. 1st ed. Stuttgart and Lyon: A.

Delaroche, 1760; 2d ed. London and Paris: Veuve Dessain, 1783. Reprinted as *Letters on Dancing and Ballets*. Translated by Cyril W. Beaumont. New York: Dance Horizons, 1966.

———. *Lettres sur les arts imitateurs en général, et sur la danse en particulier*. Paris: L. Collin, 1807.

———. *Recueil de programmes de ballets de M. Noverre*. Vienna: Joseph Hurzböck, 1778.

Observations de la Société logographique, sur la pétition du Sieur Guiraut. Paris: Imprimerie nationale, [1792].

Pacichelli, Giovanni Battista. *Chiroliturgia, sive de varia, ac multiplici manus administratione*. Cologne: W. Friessem, 1673.

Paillot de Montabert, Jacques-Nicolas. *Théorie du geste dans l'art de la peinture, renfermant plusieurs préceptes applicables à l'art du théâtre*. Paris: Magimel, 1813.

Palissot [de Montenoy], Charles. *Corps législatif. Conseil des Anciens. Discours prononcé le 21 brumaire an VII . . . en faisant hommage au Conseil d'un ouvrage du citoyen Maimieux, auteur de la Pasigraphie*. Paris: Imprimerie nationale, an VII.

Panseau, Pierre-Germain. *Sophie de Brabant, pantomime en 4 actes*. Paris: Brunet; Rouen: Besonge, 1785.

[Papon, Abbé Jean Pierre]. *Histoire du gouvernement françois, depuis l'Assemblée des Notables, tenue le 22 février 1787, jusqu'à la fin de décembre de la même année*. London: n.p., 1788.

Périer. *Réponse aux Observations du citoyen Raffron, sur les établissemens proposés par les Comités de secours et d'instruction publique, en faveur des sourds-muets*. Paris: Imprimerie des sourds-muets, [an II].

Pernety, Dom Antoine Joseph. *Dissertation sur l'Amérique et les américains, contre les Recherches philosophiques de M. de P[auw]*. Berlin: G. J. Decker, 1770.

[Perrin, Jean-Baptiste]. *Essai sur l'origine et l'antiquité des langues*. London: P. Vaillant, 1767.

Petit, Michel-Edme. *Discours prononcé à la Convention nationale, le 28 fructidor, 2e année républicain, sur les causes du 9 thermidor*. Paris: J. B. Colas, [1794].

———. *Opinion sur l'éducation publique . . . Seconde partie, prononcé le premier octobre 1793, l'an premier [sic] de la République française une et indivisible*. Paris: Imprimerie nationale, [1793].

Placide le Vieux [Armand Charlemagne]. *Le Mélodrame aux Boulevards, facétie littéraire, historique et dramatique*. Paris: Imprimerie de la rue Beaurepaire, 1809.

Plato. *Cratylus*. Translated by H. N. Fowler. London: W. Heinemann; New York: G. P. Putnam's Sons, 1926.

Pluche, Noël-Antoine. *La Mécanique des langues, et l'art de les enseigner*. Paris: Veuve Estienne fils, 1751.

Pougens, Marie-Charles-Joseph de. *Essai sur les antiquités du nord et les anciennes langues septentrionales*. Paris: Pougens, an V–1797.

Prévost, Pierre. *Des Signes envisagés relativement à leur influence sur la formation des idées*. Paris: Baudouin, an VIII.

Prieur, Pierre-Louis. *Rapport sur l'établissement des sourds-muets, fait à l'Assemblée nationale, au nom des Comités de l'extinction de la mendicité, d'aliénation des biens nationaux, des finances et de constitution*. Paris: Imprimé par les sourds-muets, 1791.

Principes de J.-J. Rousseau, sur l'éducation des enfans. Paris: Aubry, an II.

Programme général des cours des Ecoles normales, à Paris, le 1er pluviôse an III de la République. Paris: A. C. Forget, an III.

Pront, Adrien. *Elémens d'une typographie qui réduit au tiers celle en usage, et d'une écriture qui gagne près de trois quarts sur l'écriture françoise*. Paris: l'auteur, an V–1797.

Prospectus de l'Ecole nationale des sourds-muets de Bordeaux; réimprimé par déliberation du Conseil-Général du district de Bordeaux. Bordeaux: J.-B. Cavazza, [an II].

Quesnay de Saint-Germain, Robert-François-Joseph. *Discours pour servir d'éloge à Court de Gébelin, auteur du Monde primitif . . . prononcé à la séance du Musée de Paris, le 9 juin 1784*. Paris: n.p., 1784.

Quintilian. *The Institutio Oratoria of Quintilian*. Translated by H. E. Butler. Cambridge: Harvard University Press, 1989.

Rabaut Saint-Etienne, Jean-Paul. *Oeuvres de Rabaut-Saint-Etienne, précédées d'une notice sur sa vie par M. Colin de Plancy*. Paris: Laisné frères, 1826.

Radonvilliers, Claude-François Lyzarde de. *De la Manière d'apprendre les langues*. Paris: Saillant, 1768.

———. *Oeuvres diverses de M. l'abbé Radonvilliers*. Edited by François Noel. Paris: Imprimerie de l'Institution impériale des sourds-muets de naissance, 1807.

Raffron [de Trouillet], Nicholas. *Convention nationale. Observations sur les établissements proposés par les Comités de secours et d'instruction publique, en faveur des sourds-muets. Séance du 13 pluviôse l'an II*. Paris: Imprimerie nationale, [an II].

———. *Convention nationale. Opinion du cit. Raffron, député du département de Paris à la Convention nationale, sur l'éducation nationale, prononcée dans la séance du 5 juillet 1793*. Paris: Imprimerie nationale, [an II].

———. *Convention nationale. Troisième discours sur l'éducation nationale*. Paris: Imprimerie nationale, [an II].

Raynal, Abbé Guillaume-Thomas-François. *L'Histoire philosophique et politique des établissemens et du commerce des Européens dans les deux Indes*. 2d ed. The Hague: Gosse fils, 1774.

Réglements pour l'établissement des sourds-muets et des aveugles-nés. Paris: Imprimerie des sourds-muets, 1792.

Réimpression de l'ancien Moniteur, seule histoire authentique et inaltérée de la Révolution française depuis la réunion des Etats-généraux jusqu'au Consulat. Paris: H. Plon, 1850–60.

[Reinhardt, K. F.]. *Le Néologiste français, ou Vocabulaire portatif des mots les plus nouveaux de la langue française, avec l'explication en allemand et l'étymologie historique d'un grand nombre: ouvrage utile surtout à ceux qui lisent les papiers publics français et autres ouvrages modernes, dans cette langue.* [Nuremberg], 1796.

Rémond de Saint-Mard, Toussaint. *Réflexions sur l'opéra.* The Hague: Jean Néaulme, 1741.

Requeno y Vives, Abate Vincenzo. *Scoperta della Chironomia; ossia dell'arte di gestire con le mani.* Parma: Fratelli Gozzi, 1797.

Requête des dames à l'Assemblée nationale. N.p., [1789].

[Restif de la Bretonne, Nicolas Edme, and P.-J.-B. Nougaret]. *La Mimographe, ou Idées d'une honnête-femme pour la réformation du théâtre national.* Amsterdam: Changuion; The Hague: Gosse et Pinet, 1770.

[Révéroni Saint-Cyr, Jacques Antoine de]. *Essai sur le perfectionnement des beaux-arts par les sciences exactes, ou Calculs et hypothèses sur la poésie, la peinture et la musique.* Paris: Pougens, an XII–1803.

Rey-Lacroix. *La Sourde-Muette de La Clapière, ou Leçons données à ma fille, essai élémentaire applicable aux enfants non sourds-muets, par l'Ami des Sourds-Muets.* Beziers: J.-J. Fuzier; Paris: Veuve Panckoucke, an IX.

Riflessioni sopra la pretesa risposta del Sig. Noverre all'Angiolini da Discussioni sulla danza pantomima. Milan: n.p., 1774.

Rivarol, Antoine. *Discours préliminaire du Nouveau dictionnaire de la langue française. Première partie. De l'Homme, de ses facultés intellectuelles et des idées premières et fondamentales.* Paris: Cocheris, an V–1797.

———. *Petit dictionnaire des grands hommes de la Révolution.* Edited by Jacques Grell. Paris: Editions Desjonquères, 1987 [1790].

Robespierre, Maximilien Marie Isidore de. *Oeuvres de Maximilien Robespierre.* Edited by Marc Bouliseau, Georges Lefebvre, Jean Dautry, and Albert Soboul. Paris: Presses Universitaires de France, 1950–67.

Roche, Antoine-Martin. *Traité de la nature de l'âme et de l'origine de ses connaissances. Contre le système de M. Locke et de ses partisans.* Paris: Veuve Lottin, 1759.

Roederer, Pierre-Louis. *Oeuvres du Comte P. L. Roederer.* Edited by Baron A. M. Roederer. Paris: Firmin Didot frères, 1853–59.

Roger-Ducos, Pierre. *Convention nationale. Rapport et projet de décret sur l'organisation des établissements pour les sourds-muets, d'après les décrets des 28 juin dernier (vieux style) et 9 pluviôse.* Paris: Imprimerie nationale, [an II].

Rousseau, Jean-Jacques. *Dictionnaire de musique.* Paris: Veuve Duchesne, 1768.

———. *Discours sur l'origine et les fondemens de l'inegalité parmi les hommes.* Amsterdam: M. M. Rey, 1755. Reprinted in *The First and Second Discourses.* Edited by Roger D. Masters and translated by Roger D. and Judith R. Masters. New York: St. Martin's Press, 1964.

———. *Emile, ou de l'Education.* The Hague: J. Néaulme, 1762. Reprinted as *Emile or On Education*. Translated by Allan Bloom. New York: Basic Books, 1979.

———. *Essai sur l'origine des langues où il est parlé de la mélodie et de l'imitation musicale*. Edited by Jean Starobinski. Paris: Gallimard, 1990 [1781]. Reprinted as *Essay on the Origin of Languages*. Translated by Victor Gourevitch. New York: Harper and Row, 1986.

———. *Les Pensées de J. J. Rousseau, Citoyen de Genève*. Amsterdam: n.p., 1763. .

Roussel, Jean-Jérôme. *Instruction nationale. Cours public et gratuit de sténographie, ou de l'art d'écrire aussi vite qu'on parle*. Paris: Imprimerie nationale, 1792.

Rouyer, Antoine-Joseph. *Essai raisonné de monographie universelle, ou Recherche analytique d'un chiffre parfait propre à développer, dans toutes les langues, les vrais principes de l'art d'écrire comme l'on parle*. Paris: Clousier, 1792.

———. *Prospectus d'un alphabet commun à toutes les langues*. Paris: Imprimerie de l'Institution des sourds-muets, n.d.

Rycaut, Sir Paul. *Histoire de l'état présent de l'Empire ottoman*. Translated by M. Briot. 2d ed. Paris: S. Mabre-Cramoisy, 1670.

Saint-André, André Jeanbon. *Convention nationale. Sur l'éducation nationale*. Paris: Imprimerie nationale, n.d.

Savary, Claude Etienne. *Lettres sur l'Egypte, où l'on offre le parallèle des moeurs anciennes et modernes de ses habitans*. 2d ed. Paris: Onfroi, 1786.

Schwenger, Auguste-Guillaume. *Mémoires sur les aveugles, sur la vue et la vision; suivis de la description d'un télégraphe très simple*. Paris and Amsterdam: l'auteur, 1800.

Second Exercice public qui soutiendront les sourds-muets de naissance de l'école de Bordeaux, dirigée par M. Saint-Sernin. Bordeaux: A. Levieux, 1791.

Sicard, Abbé Roch-Ambroise-Cucurron. *Cours d'instruction d'un sourd-muet de naissance, pour servir à l'éducation des sourds-muets, et qui peut être utile à celle de ceux qui entendent et qui parlent*. Paris: Le Clère, an VIII.

———. *Elémens de grammaire générale, appliqués à la langue française*. Paris: Bourlotton, an VII–1799.

———. *Manuel de l'enfance, contenant des élémens de lecture et des dialogues instructifs et moraux; dédié aux mères et à toutes les personnes chargées de l'éducation de la première enfance*. Paris: Le Clère, an V–1797.

———. *Mémoire sur l'art d'instruire les sourds et muets de naissance, extrait du recueil du Musée*. Bordeaux: Michel Racle, 1789.

———. *Second Mémoire sur l'art d'instruire les sourds et muets de naissance*. Paris: Knapen, 1790.

———. *Théorie des signes pour l'instruction des sourds-muets, dédiée à S. M. l'Empereur et Roi, suivie d'une notice sur l'enfance de Massieu*. Paris: Imprimerie de l'Institution des sourds-muets, 1808.

Sieyès, Abbé Emmanuel. *Qu'est-ce que le Tiers Etat?* Edited by Jean-Denis Bredin. Paris: Flammarion, 1988 [1789].

Snetlage, Leonard. *Nouveau dictionnaire français, contenant les expressions de nouvelle création du peuple français, ouvrage additionnel au Dictionnaire de l'Académie française et à tout autre vocabulaire.* Göttingen: J. C. Dieterich, 1795.

Le Sourd du Palais-Royal, ou Anecdote singulière arrivée dans les derniers troubles de Paris. N.p., [1789].

Staël-Holstein, Anne-Louise-Germaine Necker, Mme de. *Des Circonstances actuelles qui peuvent terminer la Révolution, et des principes qui doivent fonder la République en France.* Edited by Lucia Omacini. Geneva and Paris: Droz, 1979 [ms. 1798].

Staunton, Georges. *Voyage dans l'intérieur de la Chine, et en Tartarie, fait dans les années 1792, 1793 et 1794 par Lord Macartney.* Translated by J. Castéra. 2d ed. Paris: F. Buisson, an VII.

[Strodtmann, Johann Christoph]. *Abhandlung von den pantomimen, historisch und critisch ausgeführt.* Hamburg: C. S. Geissler, 1749.

Supplément à l'Encyclopédie, ou Dictionnaire raisonné des sciences, des arts et des métiers, par une société de gens de lettres. Amsterdam: M. M. Rey, 1776–77.

Supplément au Nouveau dictionnaire françois, ou les Bustes vivans du Sieur Curtieus distribués en appartemens. Paris: Sieur Motier, 1790.

Les Synonymes Jacobites. Du Pain—Insurrection. Constitution de 1793—Prétexte. Jacobins—Massacre de la Convention. Succès—Pillage, Anarchie, Horreurs. [Paris]: n.p. ("Imprimerie des Femmes"), [c. 1795]

Synonymes nouveaux. N.p., [1789 or 1790].

Talleyrand-Périgord, Charles-Maurice de. *Memoirs of the Prince de Talleyrand.* Edited by the Duc de Broglie and translated by Raphaël Ledos de Beaufort. New York and London: G. P. Putnam's Sons, 1891–92.

———. *Rapport sur l'instruction publique, fait au nom du Comité de Constitution à l'Assemblée nationale, les 10, 11 et 19 septembre 1791.* Paris: Imprimerie nationale, 1791.

[Tennesson, Q. V.]. *Vocabulaire des municipalités et des corps administratifs, ouvrage utile et commode à tous ceux qui voudront apprendre ce qu'ils sont aujourd'hui, et connoître les fonctions des places auxquelles ils peuvent parvenir, suivant le nouvel ordre des choses.* Paris: Veuve LaChapelle, 1790.

Thibaudeau, Antoine-Clair. *Convention nationale. Rapport sur les sourds-muets, au nom du Comité d'instruction publique.* Paris: Imprimerie nationale, an II.

———. *Mémoires sur la Convention et le Directoire.* 2d ed. Paris: Ponthieu, 1827.

Thiéry, Luc-Vincent. *Guide des amateurs et des étrangers voyageurs à Paris, ou Description raisonnée de cette ville et de tout ce qu'elle contient de remarquable.* Paris: Hardouin et Gattey, 1786–87.

[Thirion]. *La Monotypie, ou l'Art d'écrire et d'imprimer avec un seul carac-*

tère. Nouvelle manière de représenter les sons articulés, à l'usage des peuples de tous les pays. Paris: Imprimerie de l'Indicateur général, an V.

Thornton, William. *Cadmus, or, a Treatise on the Elements of Written Language, illustrating, by a philosophical division of Speech, the power of each character, thereby mutually fixing the Orthography and Orthoepy.* Philadelphia: R. Aitken and Son, 1793.

———. *The Papers of William Thornton, Vol. 1, 1781–1802.* Edited by C. M. Harris. Charlottesville: University Press of Virginia, 1995.

Thwaites, Reuben Gold, ed. *The Jesuit Relations and Allied Documents: Travels and Explorations of the Jesuit Missionaries in New France, 1610–1791.* Cleveland: Burrows Brothers, 1896–1901.

La Tour de Babel au Jardin des Plantes, ou Lettre de Mathurin Bonace, sur l'école normale. N.p. ("Babylone: De l'Imprimerie polyglotte, an 4878 après le déluge"), [an III].

Tronson du Coudray, Guillaume-Alexandre. *Plaidoyers de M. Tronson du Coudray.* Paris: L. Jorry, 1779.

Tuetey, Louis, ed. *Procès-verbaux de la Commission temporaire des arts.* Paris: Imprimerie nationale, 1912–17.

Turgot, Anne-Robert Jacques. *Oeuvres de Turgot.* Edited by Gustave Schelle. Paris: F. Alcan, 1913–23.

Uriot, Joseph. *Description des fêtes données pendant quatorze jours à l'occasion du jour de naissance de Son Altesse Serenissime Monseigneur le Duc Régnant de Wurtemberg et Teck.* Stuttgart: C. F. Cotta, 1763.

Vater, Johann Severin. *Pasigraphie und Anti-pasigraphie; oder über die neuste Erfindung einer allgemeinen Schriftsprache für alle Völker und von Wolkens, Leibnitzens, Wilkens's und Kalmárs pasigraphischen Ideen. Ein Versuch.* Weissenfels and Leipzig: F. Severin, 1799.

Vaugelas, Claude Favre de. *Remarques sur la langue françoise utiles à ceux qui veulent bien parler et bien escrire.* Paris: Augustin Courbé, 1647.

Virey, Julien Joseph. *Histoire naturelle du genre humain, ou Recherches sur ses principaux fondemens physiques et moraux . . . On y joint une dissertation sur le sauvage d'Aveyron.* Paris: F. Dufart, an IX.

Volney, Constantin-François de Chasseboeuf, Comte de. *Leçons d'histoire prononcées à l'Ecole normale en l'an III de la République française* [an VIII]. Reprinted in *L'Ecole normale de l'an III. Leçons d'histoire, de géographie, d'économie politique.* Edited by Daniel Nordman. Paris: Dunod, 1994.

———. *Simplification des langues orientales, ou Méthode nouvelle et facile d'apprendre les langues arabe, persane et turke, avec les caractères européens* [1795]. In *Oeuvres de C. F. Volney.* 2d ed. Paris: Parmentier and Froment, 1826.

———. *Tableau du climat et du sol des Etats-Unis d'Amérique, suivi d'éclaircissemens sur . . . les sauvages.* Paris: Courcier, an XII–1803.

———. *Voyage en Syrie et en Egypte, pendant les années 1783, 1784, et 1785.* Paris: Volland and Desenne, 1787.

Voltaire, François Marie Arouet de. *Oeuvres complètes de Voltaire.* Edited by L. Moland. Paris: Garnier frères, 1877–85.

Vossius, Isaac. *De poematum cantu et viribus rythmi.* Oxford: Theatro Sheldoniano; London: Rob. Scot, 1673.

Warburton, William. *Essai sur les hiéroglyphes des Egyptiens: où l'on voit l'origine et le progrès du langage et de l'écriture, l'antiquité des sciences en Egypte et l'origine du culte des animaux.* Translated by M.-A. Léonard des Malpeines and re-edited by Patrick Tort. Paris: Aubier, 1977 [1744].

Watelet, Claude-Henri. *L'Art de peindre.* Rev. ed. Amsterdam: Aux dépens de la Compagnie, 1761.

Weaver, John. *Essay Towards a History of Dancing* (1712) and *The History of Mimes and Pantomimes* (1728). Reprinted in *The Life and Works of John Weaver.* Edited by Richard Ralph. New York: Dance Horizons, 1985.

Wilkins, John. *Mercury, or The Secret and Swift Messenger: shewing how a man may with privacy and speed communicate his thoughts to a friend at any distance.* London: I. Norton, 1641.

SECONDARY SOURCES

Aarsleff, Hans. *From Locke to Saussure: Essays on the Study of Language and Intellectual History.* Minneapolis: University of Minnesota Press, 1982.

Achard, Pierre. "Un Idéal monolingue." In *France, pays multilingue,* vol. 1, *Les Langues de France, un enjeu historique et social,* edited by Geneviève Vermes and Josiane Boutet. Paris: L'Harmattan, 1987.

Acton, H. B. "The Philosophy of Language in Revolutionary France." In *Studies in Philosophy: British Academy Lectures,* edited by J. N. Findlay. London and New York: Oxford University Press, 1966.

Adams, Percy G. *Travel Literature and the Evolution of the Novel.* Lexington: University Press of Kentucky, 1983.

Albury, W. R. "The Order of Ideas: Condillac's Method of Analysis as a Political Instrument in the French Revolution." In *The Politics and Rhetoric of Scientific Method: Historical Studies,* edited by John A. Schuster and Richard R. Yeo. Dordrecht: D. Reidel, 1986.

Amiable, Louis. *Une Loge maçonnique d'avant 1789, la R. L. Les Neuf Soeurs.* Edited by Charles Porset. Paris: Edimaf, 1989 [1897].

Andresen, Julie Tetel. *Linguistics in America, 1769–1924: A Critical History.* London and New York: Routledge, 1990.

Angenot, Marc. "Les Traités de l'éloquence du corps." *Semiotica* 8, no. 1 (1973): 60–82.

Armogathe, Jean-Robert. "L'Ecole normale de l'an III et le cours de Garat." *Corpus,* no. 14–15 (1990): 143–54.

———. "Néologie et idéologie dans la langue française au 18e siècle." *Dix-huitième siècle,* no. 5 (1973): 17–28.

Auroux, Sylvain. "La Conception politique de la langue, la Révolution française et la démocratie." *Zeitschrift für Phonetik, Sprachwissenschaft und Kommunikationsforschung* 42, no. 5 (1989): 619–29.

———. *La Sémiotique des encyclopédistes: essai d'épistémologie historique des sciences du langage.* Paris: Payot, 1979.

Auroux, Sylvain, Claude Désirat, and Tristan Hordé, eds. "Les Idéologues et les sciences du langage" (special issue). *Histoire, Epistémologie, Langage* 4, no. 1 (1982).

Azouvi, François, ed. *L'Institution de la raison: la révolution culturelle des Idéologues*. Paris: J. Vrin, 1992.

Bach, Reinhard. "Langue et droit politique chez Jean-Jacques Rousseau." *Beiträge zur Romanischen Philologie* 16 (1977): 123–25.

Baczko, Bronislaw. "Le Calendrier républicain." In *Les Lieux de mémoire*. Vol. 1, *La République*, edited by Pierre Nora. Paris: Gallimard, 1984.

———. "La Cité et ses langages." In *Rousseau After 200 Years: Proceedings of the Cambridge Bicentennial Colloquium*, edited by R. A. Leigh. Cambridge: Cambridge University Press, 1982.

———. *Ending the Terror: The French Revolution after Robespierre*. Translated by Michel Petheram. Cambridge: Cambridge University Press, 1994.

———. "Les Girondins en Thermidor." In *La Gironde et les Girondins*, edited by François Furet and Mona Ozouf. Paris: Payot, 1991.

———. *Utopian Lights: The Evolution of the Idea of Social Progress*. Translated by Judith L. Greenberg. New York: Paragon House, 1989.

Baecque, Antoine de. "The Allegorical Image of France, 1750–1800: A Political Crisis of Representation." *Representations* 47 (summer 1994): 111–43.

———. *The Body Politic: Corporeal Metaphor in Revolutionary France, 1770–1810*. Translated by Charlotte Mandell. Stanford: Stanford University Press, 1997.

———. "La Guerre des éloquences: Joseph-Antoine Cérutti et les brochures révolutionnaires." *History of European Ideas* 17, no. 2/3 (1993): 191–214.

———. "L'Homme nouveau est arrivé: la 'régénération' du Français en 1789." *Dix-huitième siècle*, no. 20 (1988): 193–208.

Baker, Keith Michael. *Condorcet: From Natural Philosophy to Social Mathematics*. Chicago: University of Chicago Press, 1975.

———. *Inventing the French Revolution: Essays on French Political Culture in the Eighteenth Century*. Cambridge: Cambridge University Press, 1990.

———. "Politics and Social Science in Eighteenth-Century France: The Société de 1789." In *French Government and Society, 1500–1850: Essays in Memory of Alfred Cobban*, edited by J. F. Bosher. London: Athlone Press, 1973.

———. "Sieyès and the Creation of the French Revolutionary Discourse." *Quaderno*, no. 1 (special issue: "The Languages of Revolution," ed. Loretta Valtz Mannucci) (1989): 195–205.

Baker, Keith Michael, ed. *The Terror*. Vol. 4 of *The French Revolution and the Creation of Modern Political Culture*. Oxford: Pergamon Press, 1994.

Balibar, Renée, and Dominique Laporte. *Le Français national: politique et pratiques de la langue nationale sous la Révolution française*. Paris: Hachette, 1974.

Bardon, Yves. "L'Esthétique des passions: Marmontel et l'opéra." *Dix-huitième siècle*, no. 21 (1989): 329–40.

Barnett, Dene. *The Art of Gesture: The Practices and Principles of Eighteenth-Century Acting*. Heidelberg: Carl Winter, 1987.

Barny, Roger. "Les Mots et les choses chez les hommes de la Révolution française." *La Pensée*, no. 202 (December 1978): 96–115.

Baron, Dennis E. *Grammar and Good Taste: Reforming the American Language*. New Haven: Yale University Press, 1982.

Barthes, Roland. *Writing Degree Zero*. Translated by Annette Lavers and Colin Smith. New York: Hill and Wang, 1968.

Bastid, Paul. *Sieyès et sa pensée*. Rev. ed. Paris: Hachette, 1970.

Bates, David. "The Epistemology of Error in Late Enlightenment France." *Eighteenth-Century Studies* 29, no. 3 (1996): 307–27.

Bell, David A. *Lawyers and Citizens: The Making of a Political Elite in Old Regime France*. New York: Oxford University Press, 1994.

———. "Lingua Populi, Lingua Dei: Language, Religion, and the Origins of French Revolutionary Nationalism." *American Historical Review* 100, no. 5 (December 1995): 1403–37.

———. "Review Article: Recent Works on Early Modern French National Identity." *Journal of Modern History* 68 (March 1996): 84–113.

Belloc, Alexis. *La Télégraphie historique, depuis les temps les plus reculés jusqu'à nos jours*. Paris: Firmin-Didot, 1894.

Bellot-Antony, Michel. "Marmontel grammairien et la notion de bon usage." In *De l'Encyclopédie à la Contre-Révolution: Jean-François Marmontel (1723–1799)*, edited by Jean Ehrard. Clermont-Ferrand: G. de Bussac, 1970.

Bergman, G. M. "La Grande mode des pantomimes à Paris vers 1740 et les spectacles d'optique de Servandoni." *Theater Research/Récherches théâtrales* 2, no. 2 (1960): 71–81.

Bernard, René. *Surdité, surdi-mutité et mutisme dans le théâtre français*. Geneva: Slatkine, 1977 [1941].

Berthier, Ferdinand. *L'Abbé de l'Epée, sa vie, son apostolat, ses travaux, sa lutte et ses succès*. Paris: Michel Lévy frères, 1852.

———. *L'Abbé Sicard, célèbre instituteur des sourds-muets, successeur immédiat de l'Abbé de l'Epée: précis historique sur sa vie, ses travaux et ses succès*. Paris: C. Douniol, 1873.

Bézagu-Deluy, Maryse. *L'Abbé de l'Epée: Instituteur gratuit des sourds et muets, 1712–1789*. Paris: Seghers, 1990.

Blakemore, Steven. *Burke and the Fall of Language: The French Revolution as Linguistic Event*. Hanover, N.H.: University Press of New England, 1988.

Bloch, Jean. *Rousseauism and Education in Eighteenth-Century France*. Studies on Voltaire and the Eighteenth Century 325. Oxford: Voltaire Foundation, 1995.

Bloch, Maurice, and Jean H. Bloch. "Women and the Dialectics of Nature in Eighteenth-Century French Thought." In *Nature, Culture and Gender*, edited by Carol P. MacCormack and Marilyn Strathern. Cambridge: Cambridge University Press, 1980.

Blum, Carol. *Rousseau and the Republic of Virtue: The Language of Politics in the French Revolution.* Ithaca: Cornell University Press, 1986.

Bonnet, Jean-Claude, ed. *La Carmagnole des Muses: l'homme de lettres et l'artiste dans la Révolution.* Paris: A. Colin, 1988.

Borst, Arno. *Der Turmbau von Babel: Geschichte der Meinungen über Ursprung und Vielfalt der Sprachen und Völker.* Stuttgart: A. Hiersemann, 1957–63.

Bourguet, Marie-Noëlle. *Déchiffrer la France: la statistique départementale à l'époque napoléonienne.* Paris: Archives Contemporaines, 1989.

Bouteiller, Marcelle. "La Société des observateurs de l'homme, ancêtre de la Société d'anthropologie de Paris." *Bulletins et mémoires de la Société d'anthropologie de Paris,* 1oème série, 7 (1956): 448–65.

Branca-Rosoff, Sonia, and G. Lozachmeur. "Buée: des mots contre les mots, un dictionnaire polémique en 1792." *Le Français moderne,* 57e année, no. 1/2 (April 1789): 13–30.

Braunstein, Jean François. "De Gerando, le 'social' et la fin de l'Idéologie." *Corpus,* no. 14–15 (1990): 197–215.

Bremmer, Jan, and Herman Roodenburg, eds. *A Cultural History of Gesture.* Ithaca: Cornell University Press, 1992.

Brewer, Daniel. *The Discourse of Enlightenment in Eighteenth-Century France: Diderot and the Art of Philosophizing.* Cambridge: Cambridge University Press, 1993.

Brockett, Oscar G. "The Fair Theaters of Paris in the Eighteenth Century: The Undermining of the Classical Ideal." In *Classical Drama and Its Influence: Essays Presented to H. D. F. Kitto,* edited by M. J. Anderson. London: Methuen, 1965.

Brooks, Peter. *The Melodramatic Imagination: Balzac, Henry James, Melodrama and the Mode of Excess.* New Haven: Yale University Press, 1976.

———. "The Revolutionary Body." In *Fictions of the French Revolution,* edited by Bernadette Fort. Evanston: Northwestern University Press, 1991.

Brown, Frederick. *Theater and Revolution: The Culture of the French Stage.* New York: Viking, 1980.

Brunot, Ferdinand. *Histoire de la langue française des origines à 1900.* 3d ed. Paris: A. Colin, 1924–72.

Bryson, Scott S. *The Chastised Stage: Bourgeois Drama and the Exercise of Power.* Saratoga, Calif.: Anma Libri, 1991.

Burke, Janet M., and Margaret Jacob. "French Freemasonry, Women, and Feminist Scholarship." *Journal of Modern History* 68 (September 1996): 513–49.

Burke, Peter. *The Art of Conversation.* Ithaca: Cornell University Press, 1993.

Burke, Peter, and Roy Porter, eds. *Languages and Jargons: Contributions to a Social History of Language.* Cambridge: Polity Press, 1995.

———. *The Social History of Language.* Cambridge: Cambridge University Press, 1987.

Busse, Winfried, and Françoise Dougnac. *François-Urbain Domergue: le grammarien patriote, 1745–1810.* Tübingen: G. Narr, 1992.

Busse, Winfried, and Jürgen Trabant, eds. *Les Idéologues: sémiotique, théories et politiques linguistiques pendant la Révolution française. Proceedings of the conference held at Berlin, October 1983.* Amsterdam and Philadelphia: J. Benjamins, 1986.

Cannone, Belinda. *Philosophies de la musique, 1752–1789.* Paris: Aux Amateurs de Livres, 1990.

Carones, Laura. "Noverre and Angiolini: Polemical Letters." *Dance Research* 5, no. 1 (spring 1987): 42–54.

Carré, Irénée. *Les Pédagogues de Port-Royal.* Geneva: Slatkine, 1971 [1887].

Cazzaniga, Gian Mario, ed. *Symboles, signes, langages sacrés: pour une sémiologie de la Franc-Maçonnerie: actes du colloque franco-italien, Paris, le 15 mars 1994.* Pisa: Edizioni ETS, 1995.

Céleste, Raymond. *La Société philomathique de Bordeaux de 1783 à 1808.* Bordeaux: G. Gounouilhou, 1898.

Certeau, Michel de, Dominique Julia, and Jacques Revel. *Une Politique de la langue: la Révolution française et les patois: l'enquête de Grégoire.* Paris: Gallimard, 1975.

Challamel, Augustin. *Les Clubs contre-révolutionnaires: cercles, comités, sociétés, salons, réunions, cafés, restaurants et librairies.* Paris: L. Cerf, 1895.

Chappe, Ignace Urbain Jean. *Histoire de la télégraphie.* Le Mans: Ch. Richelet, 1840.

Charbon, Paul. "Du Vigigraphe au télégraphe décimal." *Diligence d'Alsace* 1 (1987): 6–24.

Charlton, Donald Geoffrey. *New Images of the Natural in France: A Study in European Cultural History, 1750–1800.* Cambridge: Cambridge University Press, 1984.

Chartier, Roger. *The Cultural Origins of the French Revolution.* Translated by Lydia G. Cochrane. Durham: Duke University Press, 1991.

Chartier, Roger, Dominique Julia, and Marie-Madeleine Compère. *L'Education en France du XVIe au XVIIIe siècle.* Paris: Société d'édition d'enseignement supérieur, 1976.

Chazin-Bennahum, Judith. "Cahusac, Diderot and Noverre: Three Revolutionary French Writers on the Eighteenth-Century Dance." *Theatre Journal* 35, no. 2 (May 1983): 169–78.

———. *Dance in the Shadow of the Guillotine.* Carbondale: Southern Illinois University Press, 1988.

———. "Livrets of Ballets and Pantomimes during the French Revolution, 1787–1801." Ph.D. diss., University of New Mexico, 1981.

Cherpack, Clifton. "Warburton and Some Aspects of the Search for the Primitive in Eighteenth-Century France." *Philological Quarterly* 36, no. 2 (April 1957): 221–33.

Chervel, André. "Le Débat sur l'arbitraire du signe au XIXe siècle." *Romantisme* 9, no. 25/26 (1979): 3–33.

Chevallier, Pierre. *Histoire de la franc-maçonnerie française, 1725–1799.* Paris: Fayard, 1974.

Chisick, Harvey. *The Limits of Reform in the Enlightenment: Attitudes toward the Education of the Lower Classes in Eighteenth-Century France.* Princeton: Princeton University Press, 1981.

Chouillet, Jacques. "Descartes et le problème de l'origine des langues au 18e siècle." *Dix-huitième siècle,* no. 4 (1972): 39–60.

———. *La Formation des idées esthétiques de Diderot, 1745–1763.* Paris: Armand Colin, 1973.

Christout, Marie-Françoise. *Le Merveilleux et 'le théâtre du silence' en France à partir du XVIIe siècle.* The Hague and Paris: Mouton, 1965.

Chudak, Henryk. "La Harpe et la langue révolutionnaire." In *Parole et Révolutions: actes du colloque de Varsovie, 23–28 juin 1989,* edited by Marthe Molinari and Dominique Triaire. Paris and Geneva: Champion-Slatkine, 1992.

Cohen, Murray. *Sensible Words: Linguisitic Practice in England, 1640–1785.* Baltimore: Johns Hopkins University Press, 1977.

Cornelius, Paul. *Languages in Seventeenth- and Early Eighteenth-Century Imaginary Voyages.* Geneva: Droz, 1965.

Cornié, Adrien. *Etude sur l'Institution nationale des sourdes-muettes de Bordeaux, 1786–1903.* 2d ed. Bordeaux: F. Pech, 1903.

Cottret, Monique. *Jansénisme et Lumières. Pour un autre XVIIIe siècle.* Paris: A. Michel, 1998.

Courtine, Jean-Jacques, and Claudine Haroche. *Histoire du visage: exprimer and taire ses émotions, XVIe–début XIXe siècle.* Paris: Rivages, 1988.

Coutera, Johel. "Le Musée de Bordeaux." *Dix-huitième siècle,* no. 19 (1987): 149–64.

Cranston, Maurice. *Jean-Jacques: The Early Life and Work of Jean-Jacques Rousseau, 1712–1754.* New York: W. W. Norton and Company, 1982.

Crosland, Maurice P. *Historical Studies in the Language of Chemistry.* Cambridge: Harvard University Press, 1962.

Crow, Thomas. *Painters and Public Life in Eighteenth-Century Paris.* New Haven: Yale University Press, 1985.

Cuxac, Christian. *Le Langage des sourds.* Paris: Payot, 1983.

Dagen, Jean. *L'Histoire de l'esprit humain dans la pensée française de Fontenelle à Condorcet.* Paris: Klincksieck, 1977.

Darnton, Robert. *The Literary Underground of the Old Regime.* Cambridge: Harvard University Press, 1982.

Darnton, Robert, and Daniel Roche, eds. *Revolution in Print: The Press in France, 1775–1800.* Berkeley and Los Angeles: University of California Press, 1989.

Dascal, Marcelo. "Signs and Cognitive Processes: Notes for a Chapter in the History of Semiotics." In *History of Semiotics,* edited by Achim Eschbach and Jürgen Trabant. Amsterdam and Philadelphia: J. Benjamins, 1983.

Dascal, Marcelo, and Ora Gruengard, eds. *Knowledge and Politics: Case Studies in the Relationship between Epistemology and Political Philosophy*. Boulder: Westview Press, 1989.

David, Madeleine V. *Le Débat sur les écritures et l'hiéroglyphe aux XVIIe et XVIIIe siècles et l'application de la notion de déchiffrement aux écritures mortes*. Paris: S.E.V.P.E.N., 1965.

———. "Degérando et le triple problème de l'écriture du XVIIe au début du XIXe siècle." *Revue philosophique de la France et de l'étranger* 144 (1954): 401–11.

Dejob, Charles. *L'Instruction publique en France et en Italie au dix-neuvième siècle*. Paris: A. Colin, 1894.

Delesalle, Simone, and Jean-Claude Chevalier. *La Linguistique, la grammaire et l'école, 1750–1914*. Paris: A. Colin, 1986.

Delon, Michel. *L'Idée d'énergie au tournant des Lumières, 1770–1820*. Paris: Presses Universitaires de France, 1988.

Demonet-Launay, Marie-Luce. "Les Mains du texte, ou le dernier geste de Montaigne." *Nouvelle revue du seizième siècle*, no. 7 (1989): 63–72.

Denby, David J. *Sentimental Narrative and the Social Order in France, 1760–1820*. New York: Cambridge University Press, 1994.

Deneys, Henry, and Anne Deneys-Tunney, eds. "A.L.C. Destutt de Tracy et l'idéologie" (special issue). *Corpus*, no. 26/27 (1994).

———. "C. F. Volney" (special issue). *Corpus*, no. 11/12 (1989).

Derrida, Jacques. *The Archeology of the Frivolous: Reading Condillac*. Translated by John P. Leavey, Jr. Lincoln: University of Nebraska Press, 1980.

———. *Of Grammatology*. Translated by Gayatri Chakravorty Spivak. Baltimore: Johns Hopkins University Press, 1976.

Desan, Suzanne. "'Constitutional Amazons': Jacobin Women's Clubs in the French Revolution." In *Re-creating Authority in Revolutionary France*, edited by Bryant T. Ragan, Jr., and Elizabeth A. Williams. New Brunswick: Rutgers University Press, 1992.

Désirat, Claude, and Tristan Hordé. "Les Ecoles normales: une liquidation de la rhétorique? littérature et grammaire dans les programmes de l'Ecole normale de l'an III." *Littérature*, no. 18 (1975): 31–50.

———. "Le Marché des écritures." *Langue française*, no. 48 (1980): 75–88.

Desmet, Pieter, Johan Rooryck, and Pierre Swiggers. "What are Words Worth? Language and Ideology in French Dictionaries of the Revolutionary Period." In *Ideologies of Language*, edited by John E. Joseph and Talbot J. Taylor. London and New York: Routledge, 1990.

Didier, Béatrice. *Ecrire la Révolution, 1789–1799*. Paris: Presses Universitaires de France, 1989.

———. *La Musique des Lumières*. Paris: Presses Universitaires de France, 1985.

Doolittle, James. "Hieroglyph and Emblem in Diderot's *Lettre sur les Sourds et Muets*." *Diderot Studies* 2 (1952): 148–67.

Douay, Françoise. "La Langue de la Raison et de la Liberté: The Crisis of Rhetoric in the Age of Oratory, 1789–1809." In *The Consortium on Revolutionary Europe, 1750–1850: Proceedings, 1991, edited by Karl A. Roider, Jr., and John C. Horgan. Tallahassee: Florida State University, 1992.

Dougnac, Françoise. "F.-U. Domergue, le 'Journal de la langue française' et la néologie lexicale (1784–1795)." Thèse de Doctorat de 3e cycle, Université de Paris III, 1981.

Droixhe, Daniel. De l'Origine du langage aux langues du monde: études sur les XVIIe et XVIIIe siècles. Tübingen: Gunter Narr, 1987.

———. La Linguistique et l'appel de l'histoire (1600–1800): rationalisme et révolutions positives. Geneva: Droz, 1978.

Duprat, Catherine. "Pour l'amour de l'humanité." Le Temps des philanthropes: La Philanthropie parisienne des Lumières à la monarchie de Juillet. Paris: Editions du C.T.H.S., 1993.

Dupuy, Paul. L'Ecole normale de l'an III. Paris: Hachette, 1895.

Eagleton, Terry. The Ideology of the Aesthetic. Oxford and Cambridge, Mass.: Basil Blackwell, 1990.

Eco, Umberto. The Search for the Perfect Language. Translated by James Fentress. Oxford and Cambridge, Mass.: Blackwell, 1995.

Edelstein, Melvin Allen. La Feuille villageoise: communication et modernisation dans les régions rurales pendant la Révolution. Paris: Bibliothèque nationale, 1977.

Ehrard, Jean. L'Idée de la nature en France à l'aube des Lumières. Paris: Flammarion, 1970.

Elias, Norbert. The Civilizing Process: A History of Manners. Translated by Edmund Jephcott. New York: Urizen Books, 1978 [1939].

L'Enfant sauvage de l'Aveyron. Rodez: Mission départementale de la culture, 1992.

Equipe "18ème et Révolution." Dictionnaire des usages socio-politiques (1770–1815). Paris: Klincksieck, 1985–.

Faivre, Anne-Marie Mercier. "Antoine Court de Gébelin: du génie allégorique et symbolique des anciens." Thèse, Université Lumière-Lyon II, 1991.

———. "Le Monde primitif d'Antoine Court de Gébelin, ou le rêve d'une encyclopédie solitaire." Dix-huitième siècle, no. 24 (1992): 353–66.

Fischer, Renate. "Abbé de l'Epée and the Living Dictionary." In Deaf History Unveiled: Interpretations from the New Scholarship, edited by John Vickrey Van Cleve. Washington, D.C.: Gallaudet University Press, 1993.

Flaherty, Peter. "Langue nationale/langue naturelle: The Politics of Linguistic Uniformity during the French Revolution." Historical Reflections/Réflexions historiques 14 (1987): 311–28.

Fliegelman, Jay. Declaring Independence: Jefferson, Natural Language, and the Culture of Performance. Stanford: Stanford University Press, 1993.

Fontana, Biancamaria. Benjamin Constant and the Post-Revolutionary Mind. New Haven: Yale University Press, 1991.

Formigari, Lia. Language and Experience in Seventeenth-Century British Philosophy. Amsterdam and Philadelphia: J. Benjamins, 1988.

———. "Language and Society in the late Eighteenth Century." Journal of the History of Ideas 35, no. 2 (April–June 1974): 275–92.

———. *Signs, Science and Politics: Philosophies of Language in Europe, 1700–1830.* Translated by William Dodd. Amsterdam and Philadelphia: J. Benjamins, 1993.

Forrest, Alan. *Society and Politics in Revolutionary Bordeaux.* London: Oxford University Press, 1975.

Forsyth, Murray. *Reason and Revolution: The Political Thought of the Abbé Sieyès.* New York: Holmes and Meier Publishers; Leicester: Leicester University Press, 1987.

Foucault, Michel. *The Order of Things: An Archaeology of the Human Sciences.* New York: Vintage, 1973.

Francis, R. A. "Bernardin de Saint-Pierre's *Paul et Virginie* and the Failure of the Ideal State in the Eighteenth-Century French Novel." *Nottingham French Studies* 13, no. 2 (1974): 51–60.

La Franc-maçonnerie. Bordeaux: Musée d'Aquitaine; Paris: Bibliothèque Nationale, 1994.

Frey, Linda S., and Marsha L. Frey. "Et tu: Language and the French Revolution." *History of European Ideas* 20, nos. 1–3 (1995): 505–10.

Frey, Max. *Les Transformations du vocabulaire français à l'époque de la Révolution, 1789–1800.* Paris: Presses Universitaires de France, 1925.

Friedland, Paul. "Representation and Revolution: The Theatricality of Politics and the Politics of Theater in France, 1789–1794." Ph.D. dissertation, University of California-Berkeley, 1995.

Fumaroli, Marc. "La Coupole." In *Realms of Memory: The Construction of the French Past.* Vol. 2, *Traditions,* edited by Pierre Nora and translated by Arthur Goldhammer. New York: Columbia Unversity Press, 1997.

———. "Le Génie de la langue française." In *Les Lieux de mémoire.* Vol. 3, *Les France,* part 3: *De l'archive à l'emblème,* edited by Pierre Nora. Paris: Gallimard, 1992.

———. "Les Intentions du Cardinal de Richelieu, fondateur de l'Académie Française." In *Richelieu et la culture: actes du colloque international en Sorbonne,* edited by Roland Mousnier. Paris: Editions du CNRS, 1987.

Fumaroli, Marc, ed. "Rhétorique du geste et de la voix à l'âge classique" (special issue). *Dix-septième siècle,* no. 123 (July–September 1981).

Furet, François. *Interpreting the French Revolution.* Translated by Elborg Forster. Cambridge: Cambridge University Press, 1981.

Furet, François, and Ran Halévi. *La Monarchie républicaine. La Constitution de 1791.* Paris: Fayard, 1996.

Furet, François, and Jacques Ozouf. *Reading and Writing: Literacy in France from Calvin to Jules Ferry.* Cambridge: Cambridge University Press, 1982.

Furet, François, and Mona Ozouf, eds. *A Critical Dictionary of the French Revolution.* Translated by Arthur Goldhammer. Cambridge: Harvard University Press, 1989.

Gachot, Henri. *Le Télégraphe optique de Claude Chappe, Strasbourg-Metz-Paris et ses embranchements.* Saverne: Imprimerie et Editions Savernoises, 1967.

Gauchet, Marcel. *La Révolution des droits de l'homme*. Paris: Gallimard, 1989.

Gaulmier, Jean. *L'Idéologue Volney, 1757–1820. Contribution à l'histoire de l'orientalisme en France*. Geneva: Slatkine, 1980 [1951].

Geffroy, Annie. "Les Dictionnaires socio-politiques, 1770–1820." In *Autour de Féraud: la lexicologie en France de 1762 à 1835: actes du colloque international organisé à l'Ecole normale supérieure de jeunes filles les 7, 8, 9 décembre 1984 par le Groupe d'études en histoire de la langue française*. Paris: Ecole normale supérieure de jeunes filles, 1986.

Geffroy, Annie, ed. *Langages de la Révolution (1770–1815): actes du 4ème colloque international de lexicologie politique*. Paris: INALF/Klincksieck, 1995.

Genette, Gérard. *Mimologics*. Translated by Thaïs E. Morgan. Lincoln: University of Nebraska Press, 1995.

Gineste, Thierry. *Victor de l'Aveyron: dernier enfant sauvage, premier enfant fou*. Paris: Le Sycomore, 1981.

Godechot, Jacques. *The Counter-Revolution: Doctrine and Action, 1789–1804*. Translated by Salvator Attanasio. Princeton: Princeton University Press, 1981.

Godineau, Dominique. "Autour du mot *citoyenne*." *Mots*, no. 16 (March 1988): 91–110.

Goetz, Rose. *Destutt de Tracy: philosophie du langage et science de l'homme*. Geneva: Droz, 1993.

Goldgar, Anne. *Impolite Learning: Conduct and Community in the Republic of Letters, 1680–1750*. New Haven: Yale University Press, 1995.

Goldschmidt, Victor. *Anthropologie et politique: les principes du système de Rousseau*. Paris: J. Vrin, 1974.

Goodden, Angelica. *Actio and Persuasion: Dramatic Performances in Eighteenth-Century France*. Oxford: Clarendon Press, 1986.

———. "'Une Peinture parlante': The *tableau* and the *drame*." *French Studies* 38, no. 4 (1984): 397–413.

Goodman, Dena. *The Republic of Letters: A Cultural History of the French Enlightenment*. Ithaca: Cornell University Press, 1994.

Gordon, Daniel. "Beyond the Social History of Ideas: Morellet and the Enlightenment." In *André Morellet (1727–1819) in the Republic of Letters and the French Revolution*, edited by Jeffrey W. Merrick and Dorothy Medlin. New York: P. Lang, 1995.

———. *Citizens without Sovereignty: Equality and Sociability in French Thought, 1670–1789*. Princeton: Princeton University Press, 1994.

Graham, Lisa Jane. "Crimes of Opinion: Policing the Public in Eighteenth-Century Paris." In *Visions and Revisions of Eighteenth-Century France*, edited by Christine Adams, Jack R. Censer, and L. J. Graham. University Park: Penn State University Press, 1997.

Grange, Henri. "L'*Essai sur l'origine des langues* dans son rapport avec le *Discours sur l'origine de l'inégalité*." *Annales historiques de la Révolution française*, no. 189 (July–September 1967): 291–307.

Granger, Gilles-Gaston. "Langue universelle et formalisation des sciences.

Un fragment inédit de Condorcet." *Revue d'histoire des sciences* 7, no. 3 (July–September 1954): 197–219.

Greenblatt, Stephen. *Marvelous Possessions: The Wonder of the New World.* Chicago: University of Chicago Press, 1991.

Greimas, Algirdas Julien, and Joseph Courtés. *Sémiotique: dictionnaire raisonné de la théorie du langage.* Paris: Hachette, 1979.

Grell, Chantal, and Christian Michel, eds. *Primitivisme et mythes des origines dans la France des Lumières, 1680–1820: colloque tenu en Sorbonne les 24 et 25 mai 1988.* Paris: Presses de l'Université de Paris-Sorbonne, 1989.

Grimsley, Ronald. "Some Aspects of 'Nature' and 'Language' in the French Enlightenment." *Studies on Voltaire and the Eighteenth Century* 56 (1967): 659–77.

Guénot, Hervé. "La Correspondance générale pour les sciences et les arts de Pahin de La Blancherie (1779–1788)." *Cahiers Haut-Marnais* 162 (1985): 49–61.

———. "Musées et lycées parisiens (1780–1830)." *Dix-huitième siècle*, no. 18 (1986): 249–67.

Guest, Ivor. *The Ballet of the Enlightenment: The Establishment of the Ballet d'Action in France, 1770–1793.* London: Dance Books, 1996.

Guetti, Barbara J. "The Double Voice of Nature: Rousseau's *Essai sur l'origine des langues*." *Modern Language Notes* 84 (1969): 853–75.

Guilhaumou, Jacques. *L'Avènement des porte-parole de la république (1789–1792). Essai de synthèse sur les langages de la Révolution française.* Villeneuve-d'Ascq: Presses Universitaires du Septentrion, 1998.

———. *La Langue politique et la Révolution française: de l'événement à la raison linguistique.* Paris: Méridiens Klincksieck, 1989.

———. "Rhétorique et antirhétorique à l'époque de la Révolution française." In *La Légende de la Révolution: actes du colloque international de Clermont-Ferrand (juin 1986)*, edited by Christian Croisille and Jean Ehrard. Clermont-Ferrand: Université de Clermont-Ferrand II, 1988.

———. "Sieyès et la 'science politique' (1773–1789): le seuil de la langue." In *Europäische Sprachwissenschaft um 1800: methodologische und historiographische Beitrage zum Umkreis der ideologie.* Vol. 3, edited by Brigitte Schlieben-Lange et al. Münster: Nodus, 1992.

Guilhaumou, Jacques, and Brigitte Schlieben-Lange, eds. "Langue et Révolution" (special issue). *LINX*, no. 15 (1987).

Guillois, Antoine. *Le Salon de Mme Helvétius: Cabanis et les Idéologues.* Paris: Calmann Lévy, 1894.

Guiomar, Jean-Yves. "La Révolution française et les origines celtiques de la France." *Annales historiques de la Révolution française*, no. 287 (1992): 63–85.

Gusdorf, George. *La Conscience révolutionnaire: les Idéologues.* Paris: Payot, 1978.

Gustafson, Thomas. *Representative Words: Politics, Literature and the*

American Language, 1776–1865. Cambridge: Cambridge University Press, 1993.

Habermas, Jürgen. *The Structural Transformation of the Public Sphere: An Inquiry into a Category of Bourgeois Society.* Translated by Thomas Burger. Cambridge: MIT Press, 1989.

Hahn, Roger. *The Anatomy of a Scientific Institution: The Paris Academy of Sciences, 1663–1803.* Berkeley: University of California Press, 1971.

Hanoteau, Jean. *Notes sur M. l'Abbé de Radonvilliers, l'un des quarante de l'Académie française.* Nevers: Imprimerie de la Nièvre, 1937.

Hans, Nicholas. "Unesco of the Eighteenth Century: La Loge des Neuf Soeurs and Its Venerable Master, Benjamin Franklin." *Proceedings of the American Philosophical Society* 97, no. 5 (October 1953): 513–24.

Harnois, Guy. *Les Théories du langage en France de 1660 à 1821.* Paris: Société d'édition "les belles lettres," 1929.

Harten, Hans-Christian. *Les Ecrits pédagogiques sous la Révolution.* Paris: Institut national de recherche pédagogique, 1989.

Harth, Erica. *Cartesian Women: Versions and Subversions of Rational Discourse in the Old Regime.* Ithaca: Cornell University Press, 1992.

Havette, René. *Bibliographie de la sténographie française.* Paris: Revue internationale de sténographie, 1906.

———. *Deux sténographes à Bordeaux en 1784 et 1789 (Coulon de Thévenot et Dupont, de la Rochelle) d'après les manuscrits de la Société littéraire du Musée de Bordeaux et les documents de l'auteur.* Paris: Revue internationale de sténographie, 1903.

Head, Brian Wilson. *Ideology and Social Science: Destutt de Tracy and French Liberalism.* Dordrecht: M. Nijhoff, 1985.

———. "The Origins of 'La Science Sociale' in France, 1770–1800." *Australian Journal of French Studies* 19 (1982): 115–32.

Hedgcock, F. A. *David Garrick et ses amis français.* Paris: Hachette, 1911.

Hesse, Carla. "Enlightenment Epistemology and the Laws of Authorship in Revolutionary France, 1777–1793." *Representations*, no. 30 (1990): 109–37.

Higonnet, Patrice. "The Politics of Linguistic Terrorism and Grammatical Hegemony in the French Revolution." *Social History* 5, no. 1 (1980): 41–69.

Hobson, Marian. "La *Lettre sur les sourds et muets* de Diderot: labyrinthe et langage." *Semiotica* 16, no. 4 (1976): 291–327.

———. *The Object of Art: The Theory of Illusion in Eighteenth-Century France.* Cambridge: Cambridge University Press, 1982.

Holmes, Stephen. *Benjamin Constant and the Making of Modern Liberalism.* New Haven: Yale University Press, 1984.

Holmström, Kirsten Gram. *Monodrama, Attitudes, Tableaux Vivants: Studies on Some Trends of Theatrical Fashion, 1770–1815.* Stockholm: Almquist and Wiksell, 1967.

Huet, Marie-Hélène. "Performing Arts: Theatricality and the Terror." In *Representing the French Revolution: Literature, Historiography, and Art,* edited by James A. W. Heffernan. Hanover, N.H.: University Press of New England, 1992.

Hundert, E. J. "The Thread of Language and the Web of Dominion: Mandeville to Rousseau and Back." *Eighteenth-Century Studies* 21, no. 2 (winter 1987–88): 169–91.

Hunt, Lynn. *Politics, Culture, and Class in the French Revolution*. Berkeley: University of California Press, 1984.

———. Review of *Interpreting the French Revolution*, by François Furet. *History and Theory* 20, no. 3 (1981): 313–23.

Isherwood, Robert M. *Farce and Fantasy: Popular Entertainment in Eighteenth-Century Paris*. New York: Oxford University Press, 1986.

Iversen, Erik. *The Myth of Egypt and Its Hieroglyphs in European Tradition*. Copenhagen: Gad, 1961.

Jamin, Jean. "De la Génération perdue: l'indigent, l'indigène et les Idéologues." *Anthropologie et sociétés* 3, no. 2 (1979): 55–80.

———. "Naissance de l'observation anthropologique: la Société des observateurs de l'homme (1799–1805)." *Cahiers internationaux de sociologie* 67 (1979): 314–35.

Johnson, Dorothy. *Jacques-Louis David: Art in Metamorphosis*. Princeton: Princeton University Press, 1993.

Josephs, Herbert. *Diderot's Dialogue of Language and Gesture: Le Neveu de Rameau*. Columbus: Ohio State University Press, 1969.

Jovicevich, Alexandre. *Jean-François de La Harpe, adepte et renégat des lumières*. South Orange, N.J.: Seton Hall University Press, 1973.

Julia, Dominique. "L'Apprentissage de la lecture dans la France de l'Ancien Régime." In *Ecritures III: espaces de lecture: actes du colloque de la Bibliothèque publique d'information et du Centre d'étude de l'écriture, Université de Paris VII*, edited by Anne-Marie Christin. Paris: Retz, 1988.

———. *Les Trois couleurs du tableau noir: la Révolution*. Paris: Belin, 1981.

Juliard, Pierre. *Philosophies of Language in Eighteenth-Century France*. The Hague and Paris: Mouton, 1970.

Karacostas, Alexis. "L'Institution nationale des sourds-muets de Paris de 1790 à 1800: histoire d'un corps à corps." Thèse de Doctorat en Medecine, Université René Descartes-Paris V, 1981.

Karacostas, Alexis, ed. *Le Pouvoir des signes: sourds et citoyens*. Paris: INJS de Paris, 1989.

Kates, Gary. *The Cercle Social, the Girondins and the French Revolution*. Princeton: Princeton University Press, 1985.

Kendon, Adam. "The Study of Gesture: Some Observations on Its History." *Recherches sémiotiques/Semiotic Inquiry* 2, no. 1 (1982): 45–62.

Kennedy, Emmet. *A Philosophe in the Age of Revolution: Destutt de Tracy and the Origins of "Ideology."* Philadelphia: American Philosophical Society, 1978.

Kennedy, Michael L. *The Jacobin Clubs in the French Revolution: The Early Years*. Princeton: Princeton University Press, 1982.

Kirsop, Wallace. "Cultural Networks in Pre-Revolutionary France: Some

Reflections on the Case of Antoine Court de Gébelin." *Australian Journal of French Studies* 18 (1981): 231–47.

Kirstein, Lincoln. *Four Centuries of Ballet: Fifty Masterworks*. Mineola, N.Y.: Dover Publications, 1984.

Kitchin, Joanna. *Un Journal 'philosophique': la Décade (1794–1807)*. Paris: Lettres Modernes, 1965.

Knight, Isabel. *The Geometric Spirit: The Abbé de Condillac and the French Enlightenment*. New Haven: Yale University Press, 1968.

Knowlson, James R. "The Idea of Gesture as a Universal Language in the XVIIth and XVIIIth Centuries." *Journal of the History of Ideas* 26, no. 4 (October–December 1965): 495–508.

———. *Universal Language Schemes in England and France, 1600–1800*. Toronto: University of Toronto Press, 1975.

Knox, Dilwyn. "Ideas on Gesture and Universal Languages, c. 1550–1650." In *New Perspectives on Renaissance Thought: Essays in the History of Science, Education and Philosophy in Memory of Charles B. Schmitt*, edited by John Henry and Sarah Hutton. London: Duckworth, 1990.

Kramer, Michael P. *Imagining Language in America: From the Revolution to the Civil War*. Princeton: Princeton University Press, 1992.

Krüger, Manfred. *J. G. Noverre und das 'Ballet d'action.' Jean-Georges Noverre und sein Einfluss auf die Ballettgestaltung*. Emsdetten: Lechte, 1963.

Kuehner, Paul. *Theories on the Origin and Formation of Language in the Eighteenth Century in France*. Philadelphia: University of Pennsylvania, 1944.

Lagrave, Henri. "La Pantomime à la foire, au Théâtre-Italien et aux boulevards (1700–1789). Première approche: historique du genre." *Romanistische Zeitschrift für Literaturgeschichte/Cahiers d'histoire des littératures romanes* 2 (1979): 408–30.

Lane, Harlan. *When the Mind Hears: A History of the Deaf*. New York: Random House, 1984.

———. *The Wild Boy of Aveyron*. Cambridge: Harvard University Press, 1979.

La Rochelle, Ernest. *Jacob Rodrigues Pereire, premier instituteur des sourds-muets en France, sa vie et ses travaux*. Paris: Société de l'Imprimerie Paul Dupont, 1882.

Lartichaux, Jean-Yves. "Linguistic Politics during the French Revolution." *Diogènes*, no. 97 (spring 1977): 65–84.

Lavin, Sylvia. *Quatremère de Quincy and the Invention of a Modern Language of Architecture*. Cambridge: MIT Press, 1992.

Lecomte, L.-Henry. *Histoire des théâtres de Paris. Le Théâtre de la Cité, 1792–1807*. Paris: H. Daragon, 1910.

Lefèvre, Marc. "La Génétique du langage selon Antoine Court de Gébelin: une modèle linguistique de l'histoire." *Mémoires et publications de la Société des sciences, des arts et des lettres du Hainaut*, no. 83 (1970): 39–57.

Looby, Christopher. "Phonetics and Politics: Franklin's Alphabet as Political Design." *Eighteenth-Century Studies* 18, no. 1 (fall 1984): 1–34.

Lovejoy, Arthur O. *Essays in the History of Ideas*. Baltimore: Johns Hopkins University Press, 1948.

Lucas, Colin, ed. *The Political Culture of the French Revolution*. Vol. 2 of *The French Revolution and the Creation of Modern Political Culture*. Oxford: Pergamon Press, 1988.

Lüsebrink, Hans-Jürgen. "'Hommage à l'écriture' and 'Eloge de l'imprimerie.' Traces de la perception sociale du livre, de l'écriture et de l'imprimerie à l'époque révolutionnaire." In *Livre et Révolution: colloque organisé par l'Institut d'histoire moderne et contemporaine (CNRS), Paris, Bibliothèque nationale, 20–22 mai 1987*, edited by Frédéric Barbier, Claude Joly, and Sabine Juratic. Paris: Aux Amateurs de Livres, 1988.

Lüsebrink, Hans-Jürgen, and Rolf Reichardt. *The Bastille: A History of a Symbol of Despotism and Freedom*. Translated by Norbert Schürer. Durham: Duke University Press, 1997.

Lynham, Deryck. *The Chevalier Noverre, Father of Modern Ballet*. London: Sylvan Press, 1950.

Lynn, Michael R. "Enlightenment in the Public Sphere: The Musée de Monsieur and Scientific Culture in Late Eighteenth-Century Paris." *Eighteenth-Century Studies* 32, no. 4 (1999): 463–76.

Lyons, Martyn. "Politics and Patois: The Linguistic Policy of the French Revolution." *Australian Journal of French Studies* 18, no. 3 (1981): 264–81.

Malino, Francis. *A Jew in the French Revolution: The Life of Zalkind Hourwitz*. Oxford and Cambridge, Mass.: Blackwell, 1986.

Mall, Laurence. "Langues étrangères et étrangeté du langage dans les *Lettres d'une Péruvienne* de Mme de Grafigny." *Studies on Voltaire and the Eighteenth Century* 323 (1994): 323–43.

Mallery, Garrick. *Sign Language among North American Indians Compared with that among other Peoples and Deaf-mutes.* The Hague and Paris: Mouton, 1972 [1881].

Mandelbaum, Jonathan. "La Société Philomathique de Paris de 1788 à 1835. Essai d'histoire intellectuelle et de biographie collective d'une société scientifique parisienne." Thèse de Doctorat de 3e cycle, Ecole des Hautes Etudes en Sciences Sociales, Paris, 1980.

Manuel, Frank. *The Eighteenth Century Confronts the Gods*. Cambridge: Harvard University Press, 1959.

Margerison, Kenneth. *P.-L. Roederer: Political Thought and Practice during the French Revolution*. Philadelphia: American Philosophical Society, 1983.

Markovits, Francine. "L'Enfant, le muet, le sauvage." In *L'Enfant, la famille et la Révolution française*, edited by Marie-Françoise Lévy. Paris: Olivier Orban, 1990.

Mars, Francis L. "Ange Goudar, cet inconnu (1708–1791): essai bio-bibliographique sur un aventurier polygraphe du XVIIIe siècle." *Casanova Gleanings* 9 (1966): 1–65.

Martin, Henri Jean. *The French Book: Religion, Absolutism, and Reader-*

ship, 1585–1715. Translated by Paul and Nadine Saenger. Baltimore: Johns Hopkins University Press, 1996.

Matucci, Mario, ed. *Gli 'Idéologues' e la Rivoluzione: atti del colloquio internazionale, Grosseto, 25–27 settembre 1989*. Pisa: Pacini, 1991.

Maza, Sarah. *Private Lives and Public Affairs: The Causes Célèbres of Prerevolutionary France*. Berkeley: University of California Press, 1993.

Medlin, Dorothy. "André Morellet and the *Dictionnaire de l'Académie française.*" *Studies on Voltaire and the Eighteenth Century* 327 (1995): 183–97.

Megill, Allan Dickson. "The Enlightenment Debate on the Origin of Language and Its Historical Background." Ph.D. diss., Columbia University, 1975.

Merlin, Hélène. "Langue et souveraineté en France au XVIIe siècle: la production autonome d'un 'corps de langage.'" *Annales: histoire, sciences sociales*, no. 2 (March–April 1994): 369–94.

Merrick, Jeffrey W. *The Desacralization of the French Monarchy in the Eighteenth Century*. Baton Rouge: Louisiana State University Press, 1990.

———. "'Disputes over Words' and Constitutional Conflict in France, 1730–1732." *French Historical Studies* 14 (1986): 497–520.

Miller, Nancy. *Subject to Change: Reading Feminist Writing*. New York: Columbia University Press, 1988.

Minois, Georges. *Censure et culture sous l'Ancien Régime*. Paris: Fayard, 1995.

Mirzoeff, Nicholas. *Silent Poetry: Deafness, Sign, and Visual Culture in Modern France*. Princeton: Princeton University Press, 1995.

Moravia, Sergio. "Les Idéologues et l'âge des Lumières." *Studies on Voltaire and the Eighteenth Century* 154 (1976): 1465–86.

———. *Il Pensiero degli Idéologues: scienza e filosofia in Francia (1780–1815)*. Florence: La Nuova Italia, 1974.

———. *La Scienza dell'uomo nel Settecento*. Bari: Laterza, 1970.

———. "La Société d'Auteuil et la Révolution." *Dix-huitième siècle*, no. 6 (1974): 181–91.

———. *Il Tramonto dell'Illuminismo: filosofia e politica nella società francese (1770–1810)*. Bari: Laterza, 1968

Mormile, Mario. *La 'Néologie' révolutionnaire de Louis-Sébastien Mercier*. Rome: Bulzoni, 1973.

Mullan, John. *Sentiment and Sociability: The Language of Feeling in the Eighteenth Century*. Oxford: Clarendon Press, 1990.

Murphy, Patricia. "Ballet Reform in Mid-Eighteenth-Century France: The *Philosophes* and Noverre." *Symposium* 30, no. 1 (spring 1976): 27–41.

Narjoux, Jean-Louis. "Le Télégraphe optique de Claude Chappe et les autres essais." In *La Poste durant la Révolution, 1789–1799*, edited by Jean-Paul Alexandre and Maurice Bruzeau. Paris: Musée de la Poste, 1989.

Naves, Raymond. *Voltaire et l'Encyclopédie*. Paris: Les Editions des Presses Modernes, 1938.

Neher-Bernheim, Renée. "Un Pionnier dans l'art de faire parler les sourds-muets: Jacob Rodrigue Péreire." *Dix-huitième siècle*, no. 13 (1981): 47–61.

Noverre, Charles Edwin. *The Life and Works of Chevalier Noverre*. London: Jarrold and Sons, 1882.

Olsen, Mark V. "Enlightenment and the French Revolution: The Membership and Political Language of the Société de 1789." Ph.D. diss., University of Ottawa, 1991.

———. "A Failure of Enlightened Politics in the French Revolution: The Société de 1789." *French History* 6, no. 3 (1992): 303–34.

Ozouf, Mona. *Festivals and the French Revolution*. Translated by Alan Sheridan. Cambridge: Harvard University Press, 1988.

———. *L'Ecole de la France: essais sur la Révolution, l'utopie et l'enseignement*. Paris: Gallimard, 1984.

Padley, G. A. *Grammatical Theory in Western Europe, 1500–1700: Trends in Vernacular Grammar, I*. Cambridge: Cambridge University Press, 1985.

Pagden, Anthony. *European Encounters with the New World: From Renaissance to Romanticism*. New Haven: Yale University Press, 1993.

Palmer, Bryan D. *Descent into Discourse: The Reification of Language and the Writing of Social History*. Philadelphia: Temple University Press, 1990.

Palmer, R. R. *The Improvement of Humanity: Education and the French Revolution*. Princeton: Princeton University Press, 1985.

Paulson, William R. *Enlightenment, Romanticism and the Blind in France*. Princeton: Princeton University Press, 1987.

Paxman, David B. "Language and Difference: The Problem of Abstraction in Eighteenth-Century Language Study." *Journal of the History of Ideas* 54, no. 1 (January 1993): 19–36.

Pellerey, Roberto. *Le Lingue perfette nel secolo dell'utopia*. Rome and Bari: Laterza, 1992.

Perrot, Jean-Claude. *L'Age d'or de la statistique régionale française, an IV–1804*. Paris: Société d'Etudes Robespierristes, 1977.

Peyre, Henri. *La Royauté et les langues provinciales*. Paris: Presses modernes, 1933.

Peyrefitte, Alain. *The Immobile Empire*. Translated by Jon Rothschild. New York: Knopf, 1992.

Peyronnet, Pierre. "Le Théâtre d'éducation des Jésuites." *Dix-huitième siècle*, no. 8 (1976): 107–20.

Pierre Eugène Du Simitière: His American Museum 200 Years After. Philadelphia: Library Company of Philadelphia, 1985.

Pitou, Alexis. "Les Origines du mélodrame français à la fin du XVIIIe siècle." *Revue d'histoire littéraire de la France*, 18e année (June 1911): 256–96.

Plagnol-Diéval, Marie-Emmanuelle. *Madame de Genlis et le théâtre d'éducation au XVIIIe siècle*. Oxford: Voltaire Foundation, 1997.

Pombo, Olga. *Leibniz and the Problem of a Universal Language*. Münster: Nodus, 1987.

Pons, Emile. "Les Langues imaginaires dans le voyage utopique: les grammairiens—Vairesse et Foigny." *Revue de littérature comparée* 12 (1932):
500–532.

Popkin, Jeremy D. *Revolutionary News: The Press in France, 1789–1799.*
Durham: Duke University Press, 1990.

Porset, Charles. "'L'Inquiétante étrangeté' de l'*Essai sur l'origine des
langues*: Rousseau et ses exégètes." *Studies on Voltaire and the Eighteenth Century* 154 (1976): 1715–58.

———. "De l'Obscénité du geste: la théorie du partage de l'action théâtrale
dans la première moitié du XVIIIe siècle." *Discours social* 5 (1975): 31–
38.

Poster, Mark. *Cultural History and Postmodernity: Disciplinary Readings
and Challenges.* New York: Columbia University Press, 1997.

Proust, Jacques. "Diderot et les problèmes du langage." *Romanische For-
schungen* 79, no. 1–3 (1967): 1–27.

Py, Gilbert. "La Fortune d'*Emile* et l'app----------age de la lecture." *Dix-
huitième siècle,* no. 24 (1992): 267–81.

Quemada, Bernard, ed. *Les Préfaces du Dictionnaire de l'Académie
française, 1694–1992.* Paris: Honoré Champion, 1997.

Racault, Jean-Michel. "*Paul et Virginie* et l'utopie: de la petite société au
mythe collectif." *Studies on Voltaire and the Eighteenth Century* 242
(1986): 419–71.

Ravel, Jeffrey. "Seating the Public: Spheres and Loathing in the Paris Theaters, 1777–1788." *French Historical Studies* 18, no. 1 (spring 1993): 173–
210.

Reboul, Robert. *Les Cartons d'un ancien bibliothécaire de Marseille: variétés bio-biliographiques, historiques et scientifiques.* Draguignan: C. et
A. Latil, 1875.

———. *Louis François Jauffret: sa vie et ses oeuvres.* Paris: J. Baur et Dé-
taille, 1869.

Regaldo, Marc. "Un Milieu intellectuel: la Décade philosophique, 1794–
1807." Thèse de Doctorat, Université de Paris IV, 1976.

Reichardt, Rolf, and Eberhard Schmitt, eds. *Handbuch politisch-sozialer
Grundbegriffe in Frankreich, 1680–1820.* Munich: R. Oldenbourg, 1985–.

Reiss, Timothy J. "Montaigne and the Subject of the Polity." In *Literary
Theory/Renaissance Texts,* edited by Patricia Parker and David Quint.
Baltimore: Johns Hopkins University Press, 1986.

Rey, Alain. *Révolution: histoire d'un mot.* Paris: Gallimard, 1989.

Richter, Melvin. "Begriffsgeschichte in Theory and Practice: Reconstructing the History of Political Concepts and Languages." In *Main Trends in
Cultural History,* edited by Willem Melching and Wyger Velemc. Amsterdam and Atlanta: Rodopi, 1994.

———. *The History of Political and Social Concepts: A Critical Introduction.* New York: Oxford University Press, 1995.

———. "Researching the History of Political Languages: Pocock, Skinner,
and the 'Geschichtliche Grundbegriffe.'" *History and Theory* 29, no. 1
(1990): 38–70.

Ricken, Ulrich. *Grammaire et philosophie au siècle des Lumières: contro-verses sur l'ordre naturel et la clarté du français.* Villeneuve-d'Ascq: Université de Lille III, 1978.

———. *Linguistics, Anthropology and Philosophy in the French Enlight-enment: Language Theory and Ideology.* Translated by Robert E. Norton. London and New York: Routledge, 1994.

———. "Réflexions du XVIIIe siècle sur 'l'abus des mots.'" *Mots* 4 (1982): 29–45.

———. "Théorie linguistique et théorie sociale en France au siècle des Lumières." In *Ideologia, filosofia e linguistica: atti del Convegno inter-nazionale di studi, Rende (CS), 15–17 settembre 1978,* edited by Daniele Gambarara and Annabella D'Atri. Rome: Bulzoni, 1982.

Riskin, Jessica. "Rival Idioms for a Revolutionized Science and a Republi-can Citizenry." *Isis* 89, no. 2 (June 1998): 203–32.

Rivers, Christopher. *Face Value: Physiognomical Thought and the Legible Body in Marivaux, Lavater, Balzac, Gautier, and Zola.* Madison: Univer-sity of Wisconsin Press, 1994.

Roberts, Lissa. "Condillac, Lavoisier, and the Instrumentalization of Sci-ence." *The Eighteenth Century: Theory and Interpretation* 33, no. 3 (1992): 252–71.

Roche, Daniel. *France in the Enlightenment.* Translated by Arthur Gold-hammer. Cambridge: Harvard University Press, 1998.

———. *Les Républicains des lettres: gens de culture et lumières au XVIIIe siècle.* Paris: Fayard, 1988.

———. *Le Siècle des Lumières en province: académies et académiciens provinciaux, 1680–1789.* Paris: Mouton, 1978.

Rodis-Lewis, Geneviève. "Langage humain et signes naturels dans le Cartésianisme." In *Le Langage: actes du XIIIe Congrès des sociétés de philosophie de langue française (Genève, 2–6 août 1966).* Neuchâtel: A la Baconnière, 1966.

Roger, Philippe. "Le Dictionnaire contre la Révolution." *Stanford French Review* 14 (1990): 65–83.

———. "The French Revolution as 'Logomachy.'" In *Language and Rheto-ric of the Revolution,* edited by John Renwick. Edinburgh: Edinburgh University Press, 1990.

———. "La 'langue révolutionnaire' au tribunal des écrivains." In *Robespi-erre & co.: atti della ricerca sulla letteratura francese della Rivoluzione diretta da Ruggero Campagnoli: terzo seminario internazionale, Centro interfacoltà sorelle Clarke dell'Università di Bologna, Bagni di Lucca, 5–7 novembre 1987.* Bologna: CLUEB, 1989.

Root-Bernstein, Michèle. *Boulevard Theater and Revolution in Eighteenth-Century Paris.* Ann Arbor, Mich.: UMI Research Press, 1984.

Rosenberg, Daniel Blake. "Making Time: Origin, History, and Language in Enlightenment France and Britain." Ph.D. diss., University of California-Berkeley, 1996.

Rosenfeld, Sophia. "Deaf Men on Trial: Language and Deviancy in Late

Eighteenth-Century France." *Eighteenth-Century Life* 21, n.s., no. 2 (May 1997): 157–75.

———. "From Citizens to *Hommes de la Nature*: Revolutionary Regeneration and the Sign Language Model." In *Proceedings of the Western Society for French History: Selected Papers of the Annual Meeting* 24 (1997): 472–82.

———. "*Les Philosophes* and *le savoir*: Words, Gestures, and Other Signs in the Era of Sedaine." In *Michel-Jean Sedaine (1719–1797): Theatre, Opera and Art*, edited by David Charlton and Mark Ledbury. Aldershot, Eng.: Ashgate, 2000.

———. "Universal Languages and National Consciousness during the French Revolution." In *La Recherche dix-huitiémiste. Raison universelle et cultures nationales au dix-huitième siècle*, edited by David A. Bell, Stéphane Pujol, and Ludmila Pimenova. Paris and Geneva: Champion-Slatkine, 1999.

———. "Writing the History of Censorship in the Age of Enlightenment." In *Postmodernism and the Enlightenment: New Perspectives in Eighteenth-Century French Intellectual History*, edited by Daniel Gordon. New York and London: Routledge, 2001.

Rosengarten, J. G. "The Early French Members of the American Philosophical Society." *American Philosophical Society: Proceedings* 46, no. 185 (January–March 1907): 87–93.

Rousseau, Nicolas. *Connaissance et langage chez Condillac*. Geneva: Droz, 1986.

Roussel, Jean, ed. *L'Héritage des Lumières: Volney and les Idéologues: actes du colloque d'Angers, 14, 15, 16, 17 mai 1987*. Angers: Presses de l'Université, 1988.

Rouxel, Roger. "Le Télégraphe Chappe." In *L'Administration de la France sous la Révolution*. Geneva: Droz, 1992.

Rupp-Eisenreich, Britta. "The 'Société des Observateurs de l'Homme' and German Ethno-Anthropology at the End of the Eighteenth Century." *History of Anthropology Newsletter* 10 (1983): 5–11.

Russo, Elena. *Skeptical Selves: Empiricism and Modernity in the French Novel*. Stanford: Stanford University Press, 1996.

Saisselin, Rémy G. "Painting, Writing and Primitive Purity: From Expression to Sign in Eighteenth-Century French Painting and Architecture." *Studies on Voltaire and the Eighteenth Century* 217 (1983): 257–369.

Sasportes, José. "Due nuove lettere sulla controversia tra Noverre e Angiolini." *La Danza italiana* 7 (spring 1989): 51–77.

———. "Noverre in Italia." *La Danza italiana* 2 (spring 1985): 39–66.

Schlieben-Lange, Brigitte. *Idéologie, révolution et uniformité de la langue*. Sprimont: Mardaga, 1996.

———. "La Politique des traductions." *Lengas*, no. 17 (special issue, "La Question linguistique au sud au moment de la Révolution française," edited by Henri Boyer and Philippe Gardy) (1985): 97–126.

Schlieben-Lange, Brigitte, and Franz Knapstein. "Les Idéologues avant et après Thermidor." *Annales historiques de la Révolution française*, no. 271 (1988): 35–59.

Schmitt, Jean-Claude. *La Raison des gestes dans l'Occident médiéval*. Paris: Gallimard, 1990.

Schmitt, Jean-Claude, ed. "Gestures" (special issue). *History and Anthropology* 1, pt. 1 (November 1984).

Schreyer, Rüdiger. "Condillac, Mandeville, and the Origin of Language." *Historiographia Linguistica* 5, no. 1/2 (1978): 15–43.

———. "Linguistics Meets Caliban or the Uses of Savagery in Eighteenth-Century Theoretical History of Language." In *Papers in the History of Linguistics: Proceedings of the Third International Conference on the History of the Language Sciences, Princeton, 19–23 August 1984*, edited by Hans Aarsleff, Louis G. Kelly, and Hans-Josef Niederehe. Amsterdam and Philadelphia: J. Benjamins, 1987.

Scott, Joan Wallach. *Only Paradoxes to Offer: French Feminists and the Rights of Man*. Cambridge: Harvard University Press, 1996.

Seeber, Edward D. "Ideal Languages in the French and English Imaginary Voyage." *Publications of the Modern Language Association of America* 60 (1945): 586–97.

Seigel, Jules Paul. "The Enlightenment and the Evolution of a Language of Signs in France and England." *Journal of the History of Ideas* 30, no. 1 (January–March 1969): 96–115.

Senior, Nancy. "A Controversy in Eighteenth-Century France: The Teaching of Reading." *Studies on Voltaire and the Eighteenth Century* 296 (1992): 181–205.

———. "Rousseau, la Révolution et l'enseignement de la lecture." In *Rousseau, l'Emile et la Révolution: actes du colloque international de Montmorency (27 septembre–4 octobre 1989)*, edited by Robert Thiéry. Paris: Universitas, 1992.

———. "Spelling Reform and the French Revolution." *Studies on Voltaire and the Eighteenth Century* 314 (1993): 275–96.

Sewell, William H. *A Rhetoric of Bourgeois Revolution: The Abbé Sieyès and "What is the Third Estate?"* Durham: Duke University Press, 1994.

Sgard, Jean, ed. *Condillac et les problèmes du langage*. Geneva and Paris: Slatkine, 1982.

Shattuck, Roger. *The Forbidden Experiment: The Story of the Wild Boy of Aveyron*. London: Secker and Warburg, 1980.

Simon, Jules. *Une Académie sous le Directoire*. Paris: Calmann Lévy, 1885.

Simpson, David. *The Politics of American English, 1776–1850*. New York: Oxford University Press, 1986.

Singer, Brian C. J. *Society, Theory, and the French Revolution: Studies in the Revolutionary Imaginary*. New York: St. Martin's Press, 1986.

Slaughter, M. M. *Universal Languages and Scientific Taxonomy in the Seventeenth Century*. Cambridge: Cambridge University Press, 1982.

Smith, Murphy D. "Peter Stephen DuPonceau and His Study of Languages: An Historical Account." *Proceedings of the American Philosophical Society* 127, no. 3 (1983): 143–79.

Smith, Olivia. *The Politics of Language, 1791–1819*. Oxford: Clarendon Press, 1984.

Soboul, Albert. "Equality: On the Power and Danger of Words." Translated by Herman G. James and edited by Joann James and Antoine Spacagna. In *The Consortium on Revolutionary Europe, 1750–1850: Proceedings 1974*, edited by Donald D. Howard. Gainesville: University Presses of Florida, 1978.

Société littéraire, historique et archéologique de Lyon. *Le Centenaire de la Société littéraire de Lyon, 1778–1878*. Lyon: Mougin-Rusand, 1880.

Sokalski, Alexander. "Grammars and Grottos: Language Learning and Language Teaching in Pre-Revolutionary Paris, 1780–1789." *Studies on Voltaire and the Eighteenth Century* 278 (1990): 375–98.

Starobinski, Jean. *Jean-Jacques Rousseau: Transparency and Obstruction*. Translated by Arthur Goldhammer. Chicago: University of Chicago Press, 1980.

Staum, Martin. "'Analysis of Sensations and Ideas' in the French National Institute (1795–1803)." *Canadian Journal of History/Annales canadiennes d'histoire* 26 (December 1991): 393–413.

———. *Cabanis: Enlightenment and Medical Philosophy in the French Revolution*. Princeton: Princeton University Press, 1980.

———. "The Class of Moral and Political Sciences, 1795–1803." *French Historical Studies* 11, no. 3 (spring 1980): 371–97.

———. "The Legacy of Condillac in the Revolutionary Era." In *Proceedings of the Annual Meeting of the Western Society for French History*. Vol. 18. Auburn, Ala.: Auburn University, 1991.

———. *Minerva's Message: Stabilizing the French Revolution*. Montreal and Kingston: McGill-Queen's University Press, 1996.

Steinbrügge, Lieselotte. *The Moral Sex: Woman's Nature in the French Enlightenment*. Translated by Pamela E. Selwyn. New York: Oxford University Press, 1995.

Stocking, George W., Jr. "French Anthropology in 1800." In *Race, Culture and Evolution: Essays in the History of Anthropology*. New York: Free Press; London: Collier-Macmillan, 1968.

Tackett, Timothy. *Becoming a Revolutionary: The Deputies of the French National Assembly and the Emergence of a Revolutionary Culture, 1789–1790*. Princeton: Princeton University Press, 1996.

Tagliacozzo, Giorgio, and Hayden V. White, eds. *Giambattista Vico: An International Symposium*. Baltimore: Johns Hopkins University Press, 1969.

Taillandier, M. A. H. *Documents biographiques sur P. C. F. Daunou*. 2d ed. Paris: Firmin Didot frères, 1847.

Taillefer, Michel. "L'Echec d'une tentative de réforme académique: le musée de Toulouse (1784–1788)." *Annales du Midi. Revue de la France méridionale* 89, no. 134 (October–December 1977): 405–18.

Teysseire, Daniel. "Des Idéologues contre l'excès des mots." *Mots*, no. 16 (special issue, "Langages de la Révolution française," edited by Jacques Guilhaumou) (March 1988): 155–73.

Thomas, Downing A. *Music and the Origins of Language: Theories from the French Enlightenment*. New York: Cambridge University Press, 1995.
———. "Musicology and Hieroglyphics: Questions of Representation in Diderot." *The Eighteenth Century: Theory and Interpretation* 35, no. 1 (1994): 64–77.
Thomasseau, Jean-Marie. "Le Mélodrame sur les scènes parisiennes de Coelina (1800) à l'Auberge des Adrets (1823)." Thèse de Doctorat, Université d'Aix en Provence, 1973.
Todd, Christopher. *Voltaire's Disciple: Jean-François de la Harpe*. London: Modern Humanities Research Association, 1972.
Todorov, Tzvetan. *Benjamin Constant: la passion démocratique*. Paris: Hachette, 1997.
Tomaselli, Sylvia. "The Enlightenment Debate on Women." *History Workshop* 20 (1985): 101–24.
Tonelli, Georgio. "Pierre-Jacques Changeux and Scepticism in the French Enlightenment." In *Scepticism in the Enlightenment*, edited by Richard H. Popkin, Ezequiel de Olasco, and Georgio Tonelli. Dordrecht and Boston: Kluwer, 1997.
Tozzi, Lorenzo. *Il Balletto pantomimo del settecento: Gaspare Angiolini*. L'Aquila: L. U. Japadre, 1972.
Trenard, Louis. "L'Enseignement de la langue nationale: une réforme pédagogique, 1750–1790." In *The Making of Frenchmen: Current Directions in the History of Education in France, 1679–1979*, edited by Donald N. Baker and Patrick J. Harrigan. Waterloo: University of Waterloo/Historical Reflections Press, 1980.
———. *Lyon: De l'Encyclopédie au préromantisme*. Paris: Presses Universitaires de France, 1958.
Tridon, Catherine Motte. "L'Education des sourds-muets au XVIIIe siècle en France et en Angleterre: théories grammaticales." Mémoire de 3e cycle, Université de Paris VII, 1979.
Tsiapera, Maria, and Garon Wheeler. *The Port-Royal Grammar: Sources and Influences*. Münster: Nodus, 1993.
Unger, Roberto Mangabeira. *Knowledge and Politics*. New York: Macmillan, 1973.
Van Kley, Dale. *The Religious Origins of the French Revolution: From Calvin to the Civil Constitution, 1560–1791*. New Haven: Yale University Press, 1996.
Vidler, Anthony. *The Writing of the Walls: Architectural Theory in the Late Enlightenment*. Princeton: Princeton Architectural Press, 1987.
Vignery, Robert J. *The French Revolution and the Schools: Educational Policies of the Mountain, 1792–1794*. Madison: State Historical Society of Wisconsin for the Department of History, University of Wisconsin, 1965.
Vila, Anne C. *Enlightenment and Pathology: Sensibility in the Literature and Medicine of Eighteenth-Century France*. Baltimore: Johns Hopkins University Press, 1988.
Vincent-Buffault, Anne. *The History of Tears: Sensibility and Sentimentality*

in France. Translated by Teresa Bridgeman. London: Macmillan Press, 1991.

Virolle, Roland. "Noverre, Garrick, Diderot: pantomime et littérature." In *Motifs et Figures*, introduced by Pierre Clarac. Paris: Presses Universitaires de France, 1974.

Walter, Henriette. *Des Mots sans-culottes*. Paris: Laffont, 1989.

Weiner, Dora B. *The Citizen-Patient in Revolutionary and Imperial Paris*. Baltimore: Johns Hopkins University Press, 1993.

Welch, Cheryl B. *Liberty and Utility: French Idéologues and the Transformation of Liberalism*. New York: Columbia University Press, 1984.

Wellbery, David E. *Lessing's Laocoon: Semiotics and Aesthetics in the Age of Reason*. Cambridge: Cambridge University Press, 1984.

Wind, Edgar. "The Sources of David's Horaces." *Journal of the Warburg and Courtauld Institutes* 4 (1941): 124–38.

Winter, Hannah. *The Pre-Romantic Ballet*. London: Pittman Publishing, 1974.

Woolf, Stuart. "French Civilization and Ethnicity in the Napoleonic Empire." *Past and Present*, no. 124 (August 1989): 96–120.

Wrigley, Richard. *The Origins of French Art Criticism: From the Ancien Régime to the Restoration*. Oxford: Clarendon Press, 1993.

Yaguello, Marina. *Les Fous du langage: des langues imaginaires et de leurs inventeurs*. Paris: Editions du Seuil, 1984.

Ziolkowski, Theodore. "Language and Mimetic Action in Lessing's 'Miss Sara Sampson.'" *Germanic Review* 40, no. 4 (November 1965): 261–76.

Zoberman, Pierre. "Voir, savoir, parler: la rhétorique de la vision au XVIIe et au début du XVIIIe siècles." *Dix-septième siècle*, no. 133 (October–December 1981): 409–28.

Index

In this index an "f" after a number indicates a separate reference on the next page, and an "ff" indicates separate references on the next two pages. A continuous discussion over two or more pages is indicated by a span of page numbers, e.g., "57–59." *Passim* is used for a cluster of references in close but not consecutive sequence.

Aarsleff, Hans, 265n135
Abus des mots: philosophes on, 10, 16–19, 22–27, 43–51 *passim*, 55, 117, 137, 243; sensationalism and, 18, 43–44, 48; in pantomime, unlikelihood of, 73–74; language education and, 88; methodical signs as corrective of, 100, 105, 126, 140–42, 144, 173; learned societies' concern with, 120f, 137–40, 154; in Revolution, 121f, 126, 134–37, 150, 159, 211; Jacobins and, 165–69 *passim*, 181–83, 203; Constant on, 228. *See also* Debate and contestation, political; Words-things correspondence
Académie Celtique, 226, 229, 339n17
Académie Française, 20f, 25, 29, 71, 84, 107, 113, 117, 153–55 *passim*, 211–12, 225, 241
Academy of Berlin, 53, 98, 102, 280nn37–38, 334n158
Academy of Châlons-sur-Marne, 93
Academy of Dijon, 49
Academy of Inscriptions and Belles-Lettres, 61, 119, 193
Academy of Lyon, 98
Academy of Sciences, 105, 193, 199, 283n53
Academy of Zurich, 98
Actors and acting, 64, 66, 81ff
Adamic language, 25, 29, 31, 34, 273n86
Adams, John, 100, 290n110
Aesthetics, 33, 44, 58, 60f, 84, 265n1
Alphabet: development of, 38, 114, 116; reform of, 179, 190–91, 204; advantages

of, 220ff; as tool of democracy, 223; Masonic, 288n93
Ambigu-Comique, 67ff, 344n55. *See also* Audinot, Nicolas-Médard
America, political language in, 129, 178–79
American Indians, *see* Native Americans
American Philosophical Society, 118, 233, 313n201, 319n61
L'Amis des Arts, 241
L'Amis des citoyens, 191
Analytic method, 44f, 48, 85, 95, 102, 106ff, 138, 144f, 156, 159, 162ff, 185f, 188f, 198, 207, 318n51
Angiolini, Gasparo, 80
Annales religieuses, politiques et littéraires, 215
Arabic numerals, 205, 226, 323n80
Argobast, Louis François Antoine, 200
Arnaud, Abbé François, 72, 78
Audinot, Nicolas-Médard, 66–69 *passim*, 75. *See also* Ambigu-Comique
Aunillon, Pierre-Charles Fabiot, 13–17 *passim*, 26, 243–44; *Azor* and, 149, 238
Auroux, Sylvain, 254n25

Bacon, Francis, 16–17, 29, 39, 202, 322n77
Baczko, Bronislaw, 171
Baecque, Antoine de, 171
Bailly, Jean-Sylvain, 1, 133f, 291n114
Baker, Keith Michael, 7–8, 22, 250n12, 294n11
Ballet: opera, 59, 61–62, 69, 78, 81; court, 73; Jesuit, 73, 91. *See also* Dance

Ballet d'action, 10, 59–66, 69ff, 80, 85, 92.
  See also Noverre, Jean-Georges
Barère, Bertrand, 164, 167f
Barthes, Roland, 172
Bary, René, 256n64
Batteux, Abbé Charles, 45f, 60–61, 141,
  262n114
Beauharnais, Fanny de, 155
Beck, Cave, 29
Bell, David, 254n31
Bentham, Jeremy, 228–29
Bernardin de Saint-Pierre, Jacques-Henri,
  79, 176, 194
Berthollet, Claude Louis, 189
Bertin, Théodore Pierre, 200, 207, 322n76
Béthune, Chevalier de, 15
Blanc, Honoré, 204, 322n76
Blind persons, 146–49, 173, 315n24
Bodily signs: naturalness and universality
  of, 26, 29, 109, 344n59; practical com-
  munication and, 31–32, 94; gender and
  class associated with, 75; ideographic
  systems and, 205; study of, 233. *See
  also* Gestures; *Langage d'action*
Bohusz, Fr. Zsawery, 100
Boissy d'Anglas, François Antoine, 154,
  185, 187
Bonald, Louis de, 224
Bonaparte, Lucien, 339n15
Bonaparte, Napoleon, 11, 223f, 228–29,
  341n32
Bonifacio, Giovanni, 31
Bonnet, Charles, 253n23, 274n88,
  285n77
Bonnet, Jacques, 63
Bonneville, Nicolas de, 138, 159
Borch, Michel-Jean, Comte de, 78
Bossu, Jean-Bernard, 76
Bossuet, Jacques-Bénigne, 20
La Bouche de fer, 138
Bougainville, Louis Antoine, 78
Bouhours, Dominique, 263n128
Boulenger de Rivery, Claude-François-
  Félix, 27–28
Boulevard theaters, 66–69, 71, 81, 85
Boussanelle, Louis de, 276n106
Bricaire de la Dixmerie, Nicolas, 112
Brissot, Jacques-Pierre, 150, 154, 159
Brousse-Desfaucherets, Jean-Louis, 131,
  134

Brunot, Ferdinand, 5, 164
Buée, Abbé Adrien-Quentin, 301n88
Bulwer, John, 31, 257n74
Burke, Peter, 250n13, 269n42
Butet de la Sarthe, Pierre-Roland-
  François, 207f, 216ff, 231, 328nn113,
  115, 335n165, 338n7

Cabanis, Pierre-Jean-Georges, 183, 194f,
  210, 224, 231, 290n110, 317n45, 339n17
Cahusac, Louis de, 62f, 75, 83
Calendar, revolutionary, 171–72
Calonne, Charles-Alexandre de, 121
Cambry, Jacques, 226
Carra, Jean-Louis, 121f, 154, 302n103
Cartesianism, 32f, 54, 258n81, 259n84
Cassiodorus, 256n56
Catholic church, 5, 21, 82, 87, 132, 145,
  152, 240. *See also* Doctrinaires; Jansen-
  ism; Jesuits; Oratorians
Celtic language, 229
Censorship, 20, 63, 67–68, 166f, 184, 210.
  See also Freedom of speech and press
Cercle Social, 132f, 138, 159, 225
Cérutti, Joseph-Antoine-Joachim, 139,
  144
Chabanon, Michel Paul Guy de, 82
Chalvet, Pierre-Vincent, 305n136
Champion de Cicé, Jérôme Marie, 118,
  133
Changeux, Pierre-Nicolas, 97, 113
Chappe, Claude, 200–201, 322n76,
  328n113
Chaptal, Jean Antoine Claude, 334n158,
  339n15
Chardin, Sir John, 50
Chastellux, Marquis de, 72f, 291n114
Chénier, Marie-Joseph, 155
Chinese characters, 31, 114 (illus.), 205,
  213–15, 222–23, 233, 260n91
Chronique de Paris, 161f
La Chronique du mois, 159
Cicero, 28, 31
Citizenship: deaf/mute persons and, 99,
  132, 142–46 *passim*, 177f, 235–36, 240;
  speech and, 100, 128; and popular mis-
  understanding of language, 150–52,
  159–60, 230; literacy and, 184–85; postrevolutionary conception of, 230f,
  235f, 239

Civil Constitution of the Clergy, 147
Clairon, Mlle., 64
La Clef du cabinet des souverains, 238
Cloots, Anacharsis, 130, 155, 302n103
Cochin, Charles-Nicolas, 75
Comédie-Française, 63f
Comédie-Italienne, 67, 103
Comenius, John Amos, 29
Committee of Public Assistance, 173–79
    passim
Committee of Public Instruction (Con-
    vention), 151, 162, 165, 170, 174, 176ff,
    187f, 202, 315n24, 340n27
Committee of Public Instruction (Legi-
    slative Assembly), 151, 200
Committee of Public Safety, 158
Committee on Mendicity, 142, 145
Commune de Paris, 131–32, 133–34
Compan, Charles, 78
Condillac, Abbé Etienne Bonnot de: lan-
    guage theory of, 10, 34, 36–37, 40–56,
    74, 172, 185–86, 218f, 224, 289n100; so-
    cial theory and, 41–44, 72, 79, 263n128;
    pantomime and, 42, 61–62, 274n88; on
    abus des mots, 43–44, 48; analytic
    method of, 44–45, 48, 85, 205, 207; aes-
    thetics of, 44, 58, 72; on French lan-
    guage, 47; influence of, 55–57, 88, 91,
    94, 164, 170, 187, 192, 194, 223, 302n98,
    315n23, 322n77, 329n119, 334n158,
    335n160; education of, 87; Epée and,
    94, 100–102; on methodical signs, 100–
    102; pedagogical theory of, 100–102; on
    word order, 262n114; on natural state
    of the deaf, 341n36
Condorcet, Marquis de: epistemology of,
    6; memberships of, 105, 107, 113, 134,
    154, 286n87, 290n110, 302n103; me-
    thodical signs and, 105, 106–8, 153;
    language and social theory of, 106–8,
    160, 186–87; mentioned, 138, 150, 159,
    170, 293n1, 302n98, 334n158; on edu-
    cational methods, 152, 161, 163; victim
    of Terror, 162, 183
Condorcet, Mme de, 155
Conrart, Valentin, 29
Constant, Benjamin, 228–29
Constitutions: of United States (1789),
    179; of 1791, 123, 133, 162, 294n11; of
    Year III (1795), 184–85; of 1799, 314n10

Convention, 151, 162–69 passim, 173,
    175, 181f, 187f, 193
Conventionnels, 165, 169, 181, 184
Copineau, Abbé Alexis, 102–3, 104–5, 138
Coulon de Thévenot, Jean Félicité, 199,
    321n72, 324n87
Counterrevolutionaries, 134, 136–37, 182,
    224–25
Court culture and language usage, 20,
    22–23, 306n148
Court de Gébelin, Antoine, 110–18 pas-
    sim, 215, 297n46, 302nn98, 100
Coustel, Pierre, 277n6
Cratylism, 25, 27, 54
Cressolles, Louis de, 29, 31
Cuvelier de Trie, J. G. A., 241–44,
    309n174
Cyrano de Bergerac, Savinien, 15

D'Alembert, Jean Le Rond, 22, 24–25, 87.
    See also Encyclopédie
Dance: as communicative art, 59–66;
    pantomime and reform of, 59–85; moral
    values and, 65, 76, 78f, 82–85, 91; in
    non-Western cultures, 76–79; Catholic
    church's view of, 82. See also Ballet;
    Ballet d'action
Darnton, Robert, 293n129
Daunou, Pierre Claude François, 153,
    162–64, 182f, 185, 194, 200, 224,
    315n18, 342n39
David, Jacques-Louis, 66, 310n174
Deaf/mute persons: gestural language
    for, 32, 92–94, 99–100, 103–4, 123;
    schools planned for, 92f, 118, 146–49
    passim, 173–74, 177, 315n24, 326n99;
    and community, 94, 103f, 174, 238; fin-
    ger spelling and, 98; as citizens, 99,
    142–46 passim, 236; uneducated state
    of, 99, 103, 142f, 174f, 233–37, 240,
    341n36; first book by, 103; as model
    thinkers, 105f, 143f, 173, 236; moral
    status of, 108–9, 144, 174–77, 179–80,
    236–40; political definitions by, 144–45;
    blind persons, communication with,
    146–49; symbolic role of, 149; criminal
    charges against, 235–36, 240. See also
    Sign language for the deaf
Debate and contestation, political: re-
    lated to abus des mots, 8, 18–19, 23–26,

108, 126, 159–60, 181; as signs of a
healthy state, 8f, 19, 228ff, 241; philosophes and, 71f, 98; elimination of, 105,
117, 138ff, 145, 160, 172, 179, 198, 208,
219
La Décade philosophique, 238, 322n76
Declaration of Independence, American,
129
Declaration of the Rights of Man, 128–29,
151f, 158, 163, 166–67
Deforgues, François Louis Michel, 164,
167
Degérando, Joseph-Marie, 217–20, 224–28
passim, 231–36 passim, 240, 328nn113,
115, 334n158
Deleyre, Alexandre, 194
Delormel, Jean, 193
De Maimieux, Joseph, 205–8, 216, 219f,
224, 231, 322n76, 328n115, 335n165
Descartes, René, 17, 29, 31f, 45, 258n79,
322n77
Deschamps, Abbé Claude François, 98–
100, 103ff
Deseine, Claude-André, 300n77
Desloges, Pierre, 103–7, 175, 236,
294n22
Desprez de Boissy, Charles, 82–83
Destutt de Tracy, Antoine-Louis-Claude,
183, 194ff, 221–24, 227f, 231, 317n45,
336n171
Dialects, regional and patois, 20, 152,
167f, 172, 197, 232, 301n90
Dictionaries: of Académie Française, 20,
211–12; of Enlightenment, 24–25; of
sign language, 96, 141; of Revolution,
136f, 155, 159f, 176, 198, 211f, 225,
328n84; of gestures, 215
Diderot, Denis: language theory of, 10,
27, 34, 36–37, 45–48, 52, 55–56; on gestural languages, 27; on word order, 45–
46; on French language, 45, 47–48; on
abus des mots, 48; mentioned, 58, 83,
141, 170; drames of, 62, 66; on pantomime, 62, 72, 99, 267n20; education of,
87. See also Encyclopédie
Directory (government), 193, 197, 208–
10, 212
Doctrinaires, 88, 155, 162
Domergue, Urbain, 145, 154–57, 168, 175,
182, 202, 289n106, 328n115. See also

Journal de la langue française; Société
des Amateurs de la Langue Française
Dorat, Claude-Joseph, 72f
Drames, 62, 66, 71, 74, 275n95
Dubos, Abbé Jean-Baptiste, 33–34, 42,
60f, 63, 75, 81, 276n99
Duclos, Charles Pineau, 61
Ducos, Pierre Roger, 154
DuCoudray, Alexandre Jacques, 269n40
Duhamel, Julien, 156–62 passim, 230
Duplain (poet), 72
Dupont des Jumeaux, Abbé, 118
Duprat, Catherine, 291n118
Dupuy, Paul, 315n18
Du Simitière, Pierre Eugène, 290n110

Eagleton, Terry, 58
Eco, Umberto, 25
Ecole Normale, 188–93, 202, 315n17,
330n126
Ecoles centrales, 207, 224, 315n21
Education: in Old Regime, 86–88; reform
plans for, 87–88, 123–26, 152, 162ff,
173–75, 176–78, 188; popular, lack of
interest in, 152–53. See also Pedagogy;
specific schools
Elie de Beaumont, Jean-Baptiste Jacques,
98, 291n114
Encyclopédie (Diderot and D'Alembert),
18, 24–25, 45, 62, 83, 87, 327n105
Engel, Johann Jacob, 81–82, 282n43
Entendons-nous, 170
Epée, Abbé Charles-Michel de l': public
demonstrations of methods, 92–95 passim, 100; methodical signs pedagogy of,
92–109, 113, 118, 140, 145; Condillac
and, 94, 100–102; universal language
and, 95–97; abstract concepts and, 96ff;
sign language dictionary of, 96, 141;
critiques of, 97–100, 140–41, 174; defenders of, 100–109; memorial tributes
to, 131–33, 146; mentioned, 137, 207,
291n118, 322n77; political involvement
of, 294n22
Epistemology and politics, 1–2, 6, 10, 98,
122, 128, 171, 231, 245–46, 251n14
Essay contests: Academy of Dijon, 49;
Academy of Berlin, 102, 280n38,
334n158, 335n169; Academy of Inscriptions and Belles-Lettres, 119f; Com-

mune de Paris, 133f, 140; Institut National des Sciences et des Arts, 193f, 195–98, 216–18, 335n169; Société des Observateurs de l'Homme, 340n19
Ethnography, linguistic, 113, 232–33

Fabre d'Eglantine, Philippe-François-Nazaire, 154, 171–72
Fair theaters, 63f, 67
Fauchet, Abbé Claude, 132–33, 138
Federalist Papers, 179, 229
Fenouillot de Falbaire, Charles-Georges, 276n106
Ferlus, François, 143
Festivals, 6, 162, 171
Feuillants, 150
La Feuille villageoise, 144f, 151
Finger calculations, 205, 272n80
Finger spelling, 98
Foigny, Gabriel de, 15
Fontanes, Louis de, 135 (illus.), 137, 238, 338n7
Foreign idioms: in France, 20; attitudes toward, 152, 167–68
Formey, Jean-Henri-Samuel, 53
Forster, George, 76
Foucault, Michel, 54, 250n13
Fourcroy, Antoine-François, 194, 201, 286n87, 328n115, 338n7
François de Neufchâteau, Nicolas-Louis, 154, 202ff, 302n103, 327n107, 328n115, 338n7, 339n15
Franklin, Benjamin, 113, 290n110, 291n114, 300n81, 319n61
Freedom of speech and press, 127–28, 134, 153, 166–67, 329n117. *See also* Censorship
Freemasonry, 110ff, 116, 118, 143, 205, 222, 287n90
French language: control of, 5, 19–22, 84, 137, 153, 165, 168, 184; and national identity, 5, 20–21, 229; elite v. popular usage of, 20–24 *passim*, 84–85, 212, 286n82; *bon usage* of, 20, 73, 84; clarity of, 33, 47; relation to gestures, 33, 259n81, 272n81; word order in, 45–46, 141; instruction in, 88, 92, 117, 152–53, 160; as universal language, 96; regeneration of, 123–30 *passim*, 154, 164; popular misunderstanding of, 150–53;

as national language, 167–68; Thermidorean emphasis on written, 184–85, 189; sociopolitical hierarchy and, 239, 241
Fumaroli, Marc, 254n34
Furet, François, 3f, 7, 120, 129, 168

Gallais, Jean-Pierre, 136
Garan de Coulon, Jean Philippe, 217
Garat, Dominique-Joseph, 183, 187–94 *passim*, 198, 210–16 *passim*, 224, 231, 238, 286n87, 291n118, 317n45, 328n115
Gardel, Maximilien, 69–70
Garrick, David, 64, 66
Gauthey, Dom, 199
Genlis, Comtesse de, 106f, 108f
Gestural language: history of speculation on, 9, 27–32; in utopian literature, 13–16, 176; as universal language, 26, 31, 62, 95–96, 102–3, 109; contrasted with verbal, 26–27; sensationalism and, 26–27, 35–36; deaf communication and, 32, 92–94, 99–100, 103–4, 123; as original language, 34–39 *passim*, 53, 57. *See also* Adamic language; *Langage d'action*; Sign language for the deaf
Gestures: speech or words contrasted with, 26–27, 31, 50, 60–61, 73–74, 80–81; in classical rhetoric, 28–29; as natural signs, 33–34, 60–61; word order and, 45–46; rage for, 66; audience reception of, 74–76, 82–84, 99; social class and, 75; women and, 75; codification of, 81–82; education and, 89–90, 91–92, 174–75; dictionaries of, 215. *See also* Bodily signs; Pantomime
Ginguené, Pierre Louis, 183, 194, 217, 220, 224, 275n94, 316n27
Girondins, 153–54, 158–59, 164, 169, 184, 187, 226, 302n98, 307n157
Godechot, Jacques, 295n34
Goodman, Dena, 37, 287n90
Gordon, Daniel, 292n124
Gorjy, Jean-Claude, 126
Goudar, Ange, 80
Gouges, Olympe de, 130
Goulier (teacher), 278n21
Graffigny, Mme de, 15
Grammar: Cartesianism and, 32; universal or general, 54, 94, 113, 141, 159,

171, 189, 191, 207, 336n171; and education of the deaf, 141, 155–56; irregularities of, 152, 170; and politics, 156–57; reform of, 163, 191, 198
Les Grands-Danseurs du Roi, 67f. *See also* Nicolet, Jean-Baptiste
Grasset de Saint-Sauveur, Jacques, 77
Grégoire, Abbé Henri-Baptiste: language theory of, 151, 164–65, 301n88; Jacobin language politics and, 172–73, 182, 184, 307n150; on deaf, 173; memberships of, 187, 194, 342n39; mentioned, 190
Greuze, Jean-Baptiste, 66
Grimm, Friedrich Melchior, 62, 65
Grouville, Philippe-Antoine, 139
Guilhaumou, Jacques, 7, 308n164
Guiraudet, Charles-Philippe-Toussaint, 159
Gustafson, Thomas, 253n22
Guys, Pierre-Augustin, 76

Habermas, Jürgen, 120
Halévi, Ran, 129
Haüy, Valentin, 146, 173, 291n114, 303n117
Heinicke, Samuel, 98, 283n58
Helvétius, Claude Adrien, 19, 24f, 87, 110
Helvétius, Mme, 194, 221
Hennin, Pierre-Michel, 231
Hieroglyphics (Egyptian), 31, 37–39, 113, 156, 205, 222–23
Hilverding, Franz, 64
Hobbes, Thomas, 17
Holbach, Paul-Henri Thiry, Baron d', 18
Holmes, Stephen, 229
Hourwitz, Zalkind, 203–8 *passim*, 328nn113, 115
Hunt, Lynn, 5, 171

Ideologues, 194, 218, 220, 223f, 230f, 239ff, 333n144
Imprimerie des Sourds-Muets, 161, 299n74, 339n15
Infant communication, 52, 233, 340n19
Institution des Sourds et Muets de Bordeaux, 118f, 133, 144, 149, 299n63, 315n24
Institution des Sourds-Muets de Paris: establishment of, 92; public sessions at,

93–94, 100, 207; Sicard chosen as director of, 133f, 140, 341n32; national funding for, 142–46 *passim*, 311n191; blind students and, 146–49, 173, 315n24; as model community, 148–49; as popular charity, 158; printing press of, 161, 299n74, 339n15; "wild child" and, 233. *See also* Epée, Abbé Charles-Michel de l'; Massieu, Jean; Sicard, Abbé Roch-Ambroise-Cucurron
Institut National des Sciences et des Arts, 193–98, 202–3, 216; First Class, 202, 209; Second Class, 192–98, 202, 216ff, 222, 224, 334n158, 335n169, 336n171, 339n17; Third Class, 202
Isherwood, Robert, 269n42

Jacobin clubs, 138, 150, 158, 168, 200, 306n148
Jacobins/Jacobinism: rhetoric of, 3, 168–70, 172, 181–83, 184, 203; language politics and, 120, 153f, 157, 164–79; *abus des mots* and, 165–69 *passim*, 181–83, 203; and women's language, 166f; pantomime used by, 171
Jansenism, 21–22, 87–88, 94, 96, 284n64, 294n24. *See also* Port-Royal
Jaucourt, Chevalier de, 62, 83
Jauffret, Louis-François, 220, 231–40 *passim*, 303n115, 342n39, 343n47
Jefferson, Thomas, 178, 290n110, 339n17
Jesuits, 73, 87, 91, 252n8, 277n3
Jones, Sir William, 100
Joseph II (Holy Roman Emperor), 93
Jouenne-Longchamp, Thomas François Ambroise, 179–80, 315n24
Journal d'éducation, 88–89
Journal de la langue française, 116f, 145, 154ff, 316n27
Journal de la Société de 1789, 139
Journal de Paris, 119, 140, 144, 187, 211
Journal des sçavans, 142, 299n74
Journal des théâtres, 68, 73–74
Journal d'instruction sociale, 153, 160ff
Journal encyclopédique, 106, 143, 284n62
Journal logotachigraphique, 200

Knox, Dilwyn, 256n63
Kramer, Michael, 313n202

La Bruyère, Jean de, 263n128
Lacépède, Bernard-Germain-Etienne de la Ville, 233, 291n118, 317n45, 338n7
La Chalotais, Louis-René de Caradeuc de, 88
Lacretelle, Charles de, 2
La Fayette, Marquis de, 134, 291n114
Lafitau, Père Joseph-François, 76f, 261n105
La Harpe, Jean-François de, 81, 137, 183, 192, 203, 246, 286n87, 291n118, 293n1, 295n31
Lakanal, Joseph, 162, 187f, 194, 200f
Lalande, Joseph-Jérôme Lefrançois, 110
Lamy, Bernard, 32–33, 257n72
Lancelin, P. F., 197f, 208, 218
Langage d'action, 10, 39–56, 83; definition of, 38–39, 40; Condillac on, 45, 101; critiques of, 53–54; restoration of, 57–59, 85–86, 96, 113, 120f, 243; as basis of *ballet d'action*, 59; Jacobins and, 169–71; Degérando on, 218; materialism and, 273n86. *See also* Bodily signs; Gestures; Language, origins of
Language: and thought, 1–2, 17, 25, 32f, 35, 54–55, 194–96; and progress, 5, 16, 35–43 *passim*, 47, 51, 54, 195; as social contract, 14, 18–19, 23, 54, 224, 230, 236, 241; social distinctions and, 20, 22–24, 75, 84–85, 111, 136, 150–53, 167, 175, 230–31, 236, 239, 241; "fixing" of, 22–25, 101–2, 117, 129–30, 137–42 *passim*, 150–64, 175, 208–12 *passim*, 225–26, 228–29; women's, 23, 51, 166f, 263n128; origins of, 34–56, 101–3, 156; festivals on, 162. *See also Abus des mots*; French language; Gestural language; Sign language for the deaf; Universal or ideal language
Language politics and planning: and Revolution, 4, 121–80; and monarchy, 5, 19–26 *passim*, 63, 168; as key to a harmonious state, 8, 10–11, 24, 55, 100, 102, 108, 113, 116, 126, 187, 194; usage versus reason debate in, 21, 113, 157; and regeneration, 79, 85, 113–15, 123–49, 154, 164, 169; learned societies and, 111–21 *passim*, 134, 137–40, 153–59 *passim*, 193–96, 202, 208–9, 229–34,

239–41; and sign language of the deaf, 123–27, 144–46, 153–54, 161, 173; in America, 129, 178–79; Jacobinism and, 153f, 164–80; Thermidorean, 185–93; under the Directory, 198, 205, 209, 210–23; under the Consulate, 223–26
Lanthenas, François Xavier, 155
La Rochefoucauld-Liancourt, Duc de, 134, 142, 291n114, 338n7
Laromiguière, Pierre, 194, 208, 224, 226, 231, 317n40
L'Aulnaye, François-Henri-Stanislas de, 119–20
Laus de Boissy, Louis de, 69, 75
Lavater, Johann Caspar, 66–67
Lavoisier, Antoine-Laurent, 138, 170, 183, 291n114, 293n1
Law of Suspects, 167
Learned societies: language politics and planning in, 111–21 *passim*, 134, 137–40, 153–59 *passim*, 193–96, 202, 208–9, 229–34, 239–41; and "fixing" of meanings, 117, 137–40, 153–55, 158–59, 209; revolutionary political culture and, 120–21, 137–38; *abus des mots* discussed in, 120f, 137–40, 154; women in, 155, 167, 287n90. *See also* Essay contests; *specific societies*
Leblond, Auguste-Savinien, 203ff, 207, 232, 328n115, 338n13
LeBouvyer-Desmortiers, Urbain René Thomas, 237–38
Lebreton, Joachim, 194
LeBrun, Charles, 258n79
Legislative Assembly, 149f, 153, 158
Leibniz, Gottfried Wilhelm von, 29, 31, 96, 123, 202, 322n77
LeKain (actor), 64
Lemontey, Pierre, 233
Léonard des Malpeines, Marc-Antoine, 38, 40
Lequinio, Joseph-Marie, 162
Lessing, Gotthold Ephraim, 275n98
Leupold, Jacob, 257n74
Levacher de Charnois, Jean Charles, 68
Linguet, Simon-Nicolas, 68, 72, 95, 282n45
Linguistic turn, in historical studies, 3f, 6
Literacy, 152, 185
Locke, John: *abus des mots* and, 17–18,

44, 105; on language as social contract, 18–19; mentioned, 22, 24f, 88, 139, 261n105, 316n29; origin of ideas and, 35, 236, 259n84; on women and language, 255n40
Loge des Neuf Soeurs, 110–19 passim, 147, 155, 187, 317n45, 322n80, 338n7
Lotman, Juri, 250n13
Louis XV, King, 23
Louis XVI, King, 23, 71, 93
Lucian of Samosata, 28
Lycée de Paris (later Lycée républicain), 110, 155, 158–60 passim, 183, 187, 207, 209, 228, 305n136, 315n24, 317n45, 328n115, 334n158
Lycée des Arts, 171, 207, 209, 321n72, 328n115
Lycées and musées, 109–22, 134, 209

Madison, James, 179, 229
Le Magasin encyclopédique, 199, 202, 215, 238
Maignet, Etienne-Christophe, 173–74
Maine, Duchess of, 61, 63, 69
Maine de Biran, François-Pierre, 335n169
Mandeville, Bernard, 259n85
Marat, Jean-Paul, 121
Maréchal, Sylvain, 176
Maria Theresa (Empress of Austria), 69
Marie-Antoinette,Queen, 69
Marmontel, Jean-François, 82–85 passim, 112f, 117, 286n87, 295n31
Massieu, Jean, 133f, 142–45 passim, 158, 180, 233, 236–39, 328n113, 343n52
Massieu, Jean Baptiste, 148, 187, 238
Maupertuis, Pierre-Louis Moreau de, 53
Mayeur de Saint Paul, François Marie, 76
Melodrama, 244
Melon, Jean-François, 22
Mémoires du Musée de Paris, 118
Mercier, Louis-Sébastien, 66, 72–76 passim, 154, 194, 225, 302n103
Mercure de France, 71, 93, 106, 182, 284n62
Merlin, Hélène, 21
Merrick, Jeffrey, 21
Mersenne, Marin, 29
Ministry of the Interior, 187, 202, 232, 315n24, 334n158

Miscommunication, see Abus des mots
Monarchy and language control, 5, 19–26 passim, 63, 168
Monboddo, Lord, 100
Monnet, Jean, 64
Montaigne, Abbé, 240
Montaigne, Michel de, 31, 253n22
Montesquieu, 19
Montigny, Charles-Claude, 203f
Montmignon, Abbé, 205, 335n165
Moreau de Saint-Méry, Médéric-Louis-Elie, 79, 290n110, 302n103, 338n7, 339n17
Morellet, Abbé André, 24, 137, 153, 225
Morin, Benoît, 103
Moussaud, Abbé Jean-Marie, 221
Musée de Bordeaux, 110, 118f, 299n64, 302n98, 319n62
Musée de Monsieur, 110, 119
Musée de Paris, 110–12, 116–21 passim, 147, 154–55, 231
Musées and lycées, 109–22, 134, 209

Naigeon, Jacques-André, 217
National Assembly, 130–32, 138f, 142–46 passim, 150–56 passim, 168, 195, 200
Native Americans, language and gestures of, 32, 42, 52, 55, 76–78, 233, 261n105, 322n80
Natural signs: categorization of, 32–34; gestures as, 33–34, 60–61; langage d'action and, 40–41, 101; aesthetics and, 60; pedagogy and, 89–92; moral instruction and, 170–72, 175; peace and harmony fostered by, 237, 243, 244
Necker, Jacques, 280n39, 291n114
Neologisms, 21, 44, 117, 261n111; and Revolution, 130, 134, 137, 145, 154, 170, 211f, 225
Nicolai, Christoph, 98, 140
Nicole, Pierre, 277n6
Nicolet, Jean-Baptiste, 66ff, 76
Nougaret, Pierre Jean Baptiste, 67, 72
Novels, gestures in, 66
Noverre, Jean-Georges, 59–76 passim, 8off, 85, 91–93, 95, 171, 244; and Les Horaces et les Curiaces, 69, 81, 270n53; and Jason et Medée, 69f. See also Ballet d'action

L'Observateur, 147

Opéra (Paris), 59, 62, 63–71 *passim*, 81, 83, 171

Opéra-Comique, 64, 67

Oration, public: pantomime and, 28–29, 66, 71, 78–79; Rousseau on, 51–52, 90; importance of, 127f, 138, 189; fear of effects of, 139, 165–67; control of, 184, 191, 204. *See also* Rhetoric

Oratorians, 88, 166

Orthography, 152, 163, 170, 191

Ottoman mutes, gestures of, 32, 55

Ozouf, Mona, 171

Pahin de La Blancherie, Claude-Mammès, 106, 110

Painting, gestures in, 66, 75

Pange, Chevalier de, 139

Panseau, Pierre-Germain, 68

Pantomime: theatrical uses of, 10, 57–85; pedagogical uses of, 10, 86–122; ancient world and, 27–28, 42, 61f, 74, 84, 101, 119; and public oration, 28–29, 66, 71, 78–79; as popular entertainment, 63–64, 68, 241–45; critiques of, 71, 79–85, 99; *abus des mots*, unlikeliness of, in, 74; in non-Western cultures, 76–79; moral instruction and, 76, 83f, 119; peace and social harmony fostered by, 78–79; deaf communication and, 93–94; Jacobin uses of, 171; ideographic systems and, 205; melodrama and, 244. *See also Ballet d'action*; Gestures; *Langage d'action*

Parlements, 5, 21f

Parrots, empty speech symbolized by, 15ff, 98, 105, 144

Patois and regional dialects, 20, 152, 167f, 172, 197, 232, 301n90

Pauw, Cornelius de, 272n80

Pedagogy: and festivals, 6, 162, 171; and moral concepts, 65, 76, 83–84, 108–9, 152, 174–77; use of natural signs in, 85, 89–95; Catholic approach to, 87; of words-things correspondence, 87f, 90f, 102, 141, 144, 153; and French language instruction, 88, 92, 117, 152–53, 160; image-based methods, 88ff, 94, 99, 170–71; catechism model in, 145; and teacher training, 163–64, 173, 177, 188f, 192

Penmanship, 191

Péreire, Jacob Rodrigue, 50, 92, 98, 100

Périer, Citizen, 177, 234

Pernety, Antoine Joseph, 272n80

Perrin, Jean-Baptiste, 273n86

Petit, Michel-Edme, 2f, 170, 181–83, 187, 245

Philosophes: and linguistic-political struggles, 19, 22–26, 54–55, 84, 137f, 153, 211–12; sociability of, 36–37; in Republic of Letters, 37, 71, 106; and public debates, contestation, 71f, 98; education of, 87

Philosophical language, *see* Universal or ideal language

Physiognomy, 33, 66–67

Picture writing, *see* Hieroglyphics (Egyptian); Native Americans, language and gestures of; Signs, ideographic

Pilâtre de Rozier, Jean-François, 110

Plagnol-Diéval, Marie-Emmanuelle, 286n82

Plato, 28

Polier, Antoine-Noé de, 253n18

Political discourse, study of, 3–4, 6–7

Politics and epistemology, 1–2, 6, 10, 98, 122, 128, 171, 231, 245–46, 251n14

Popular culture, 63–64, 67–68, 241–45, 269n42

Port-Royal, 21, 32, 50, 87–88, 94. *See also* Jansenism

Pougens, Charles, 154, 205, 328n115, 338n7, 342n39

Prévost, Pierre, 217f, 220–21

Prieur, Pierre-Louis, 144, 146

Print culture, 127f, 166

Progress: communication revolutions and, 1, 116, 186; and language development, 5, 16, 35–43 *passim*, 47, 51, 195; and analysis, 107–8; and science, 203, 209; women's role in, 263n128

Pronunciation, 170, 191

Prunget des Boissières, 98

Public speaking, *see* Oration, public

Quatremère de Quincy, Antoine Chrysostome, 292n120

Quatremère fils, Marc-Etienne, 131

Quesnay, François, 253n23, 285n77
Quintilian, 28f, 31

Rabaut-Pommier, Jacques-Antoine, 201
Rabaut Saint-Etienne, Jean-Paul, 1–2, 9,
116f, 154, 245, 302n103
Racine, Jean, 61
Radonvilliers, Claude François Lyzarde
de, 91–92
Raffron, Nicholas, 174–79 passim, 238
Ravel, Jeffrey, 270n54
Raynal, Abbé Guillaume-Thomas-
François, 76
Reading, 87ff, 91, 152, 185. See also Peda-
gogy
Regeneration, language and, 79, 85, 113–
15, 123–49, 154, 164, 169
Reiss, Timothy, 253n22
Rémond de Saint-Mard, Toussaint, 62
Requeno y Vives, Abate Vincenzo,
325n96
Restif de la Bretonne, Nicolas Edme, 72,
76
Révolutions de Paris, 147
Rey-Lacroix, 238
Rhetoric, 168–69, 171–72, 181–84, 203,
228. See also Oration, public
Riccoboni, François, 63–64, 275n98
Riche, Claude-Antoine-Gaspard, 328n113
Richter, Melvin, 6–7
Rivarol, Antoine, 136, 280n38, 330n123
Roberts, Lissa, 265n137
Robespierre, Maximilien, 3, 150, 155,
168–69, 181–82
Roche, Daniel, 286n88
Roederer, Pierre-Louis, 171, 182f, 194,
199, 210–18, 224, 305n136, 317n45,
328n115
Roger, Philippe, 295n33, 308n164
Roger-Ducos, Pierre, 177
Rousseau, Jean-Jacques: language and
social theory of, 34, 36–37, 48–53, 55,
89ff; on public oration, 51–52, 90; influ-
ence of, 58, 126, 170, 174, 185; and pantomime, 61–62, 90, 274n88; on ballet,
73; pedagogical theory of, 86, 89–91,
170, 277n3; education of, 87; on words-
things correspondence, 90; mentioned,
109, 218; on Native Americans, 272n80
Roussel, Jean-Jérôme, 200

Royal Academy of Music, see Opéra
(Paris)
Rupp-Eisenreich, Britta, 335n161

Saboureux de Fontenay, 98, 284n73,
285n76
Saint-André, André Jeanbon, 174
Saint-Just, Louis Antoine Léon, 169
Saint-Martin, Louis-Claude de, 192
Saint-Sernin, Abbé Jean, 144, 151
Savary, Claude Etienne, 76
Schlieben-Lange, Brigitte, 164, 309n164
Scholasticism, 17–18
Schwenger, Auguste-Guillaume, 325n96
Scott, Joan, 250n14
Sensationalism: abus des mots and, 18,
43–44, 48; relation to Christian
thought, 18, 45, 98, 273n86; gestural
languages and, 26–27, 57; aesthetics
and, 33, 44, 58, 60f; language origins
and, 35, 53–54, 57, 96; materialism and,
45; psychology and, 54, 87; dance and,
64–65; applied to deaf-blind communication, 148; Jacobins and, 171–72; postrevolutionary, 192, 211, 224, 231, 239;
neologisms and, 261n111
Sensibility, cult of, 66, 75, 84
September Massacres, 158
Servandoni, Jean-Nicolas, 63
Shorthand methods, see Stenographic
systems
Sicard, Abbé Roch-Ambroise-Cucurron:
Musée de Bordeaux and, 118–19; public
demonstrations of methods, 118, 142–
43, 147–48, 158, 207, 233; succeeds
Epée, 133–34; revolutionary language
politics and, 133–34, 142–49, 153–64
passim, 173–78 passim, 189–91, 215f;
mentioned, 137, 159, 219, 231, 238;
pedagogical-linguistic system of, 140–
42, 144f, 189, 214; emphasis on grammar, 141, 155–56, 189; on natural, uneducated state of the deaf, 142, 233–35,
240; on deaf-blind communication,
147–48; attitude to Revolution of, 147,
158; challenges to, 153–57 passim, 161,
173–77 passim, 237–38, 240; Société
des Amateurs de la Langue Française
and, 154–58 passim; political troubles
of, 158, 215; court cases, involvement

of, 158, 235; *Journal d'instruction sociale* and, 161; alphabet reform and,
190–91, 204; pasigraphies, stenographies and, 202, 207, 215f, 319n62;
memberships of, 231, 328n115; and
Victor, "wild child" of Aveyron, 233;
defenders of, 238–39; Massieu's opinion of, 342n38; sensationalism and,
343n51. *See also* Institution des Sourds
et Muets de Bordeaux; Institution des
Sourds-Muets de Paris
Sieyès, Abbé Emmanuel, 130, 138, 150,
160f, 162f, 194, 224, 317n45
Sign language for the deaf: early plans for,
32; development of "methodical" type,
92, 94–97; debates regarding, 97–105;
as model for reform efforts, 102, 105–9,
130–34, 140, 142, 149, 173, 207, 215;
uses in revolutionary language politics,
123–27, 153–54, 161, 173; grammar
and, 141, 155–56
Signs: historical change and, 1–4, 35, 42–
43, 116, 127, 186, 245–46; instrumental
conception of, 2, 35, 55, 98, 126, 169,
178, 227, 246; origin of, 5, 38, 41–42, 49,
218; bodily or gestural, 10, 26–32 *passim*, 39, 75, 94, 109, 205, 233, 344n59;
ideographic, 11, 29, 31, 205–22 *passim*;
arbitrary, 26, 40, 42, 55, 101; function
of, 32–34; natural, 32–34, 40f, 60, 89–
92, 101, 170–72, 175, 237, 243f; visual,
34, 61, 171, 204–5; in aesthetics, 60f,
72; artificial, 101; Masonic, 112, 205,
222, 288n93; science and, 185–87, 191,
197, 208–9, 219; Institut National des
Sciences et des Arts and, 194–96; Société des Observateurs' study of, 232. *See
also* Gestural languages; Gestures;
Langage d'action
Silence, virtue of, 203–4
Social distinctions and language, 20, 22–
24, 75, 84–85, 111, 136, 150–53, 167,
175, 230–31, 236–41 *passim*
Social sciences, language of, 10, 25, 107f,
117, 138, 159–63, 185f, 189, 194–97 *passim*, 212–13, 219, 223
Société de 1789, 134, 138–40, 144, 150,
175, 184; members of, 134, 159f, 187,
195, 221, 305n136, 317n45
Société des Amateurs de la Langue

Française, 153–61 *passim*, 169, 175,
225, 303n115, 322n80, 343n47
Société des Observateurs de l'Homme,
231–41, 244, 338n7
Société Libre des Sciences, Lettres et
Arts de Paris, 322n80, 327n109, 342n39
Société Libre d'Institution, 184, 202
Société Littéraire de Lyon (Musée de
Lyon), 287n90, 289n106
Société Logographique, 200
Société Nationale des Neuf Soeurs, 147–
48, 155, 303n115, 342n39, 343n47
Société Philanthropique, 118f
Société Philomathique, 171, 202, 209
Société Philotechnique, 202, 207, 209,
228, 241, 322n80, 341–43nn32, 39, 47
Solar case, 93, 98, 235
Speech: contrasted with gestural com-
munication, 15–16, 26–27, 50, 60–61,
65, 73–74; human perfection and, 33,
81, 100
Staël, Mme de, 203, 228, 333n151
Starobinski, Jean, 169, 277n13
Staum, Martin, 317n46, 333n114
Staunton, George Leonard, 213–14,
331n136
Stenographic systems, 199–204 *passim*,
214
Stewart, Dugald, 100
Suard, Jean-Baptiste-Antoine, 225
Syntax, 45–46, 59, 141, 214

Tackett, Timothy, 297n45
Talleyrand, Charles-Maurice de, 123–
26, 131f, 134, 150, 152f, 194, 224,
291n114
Tallien, Jean-Lambert, 182f
Teacher training, 163–64, 173, 177, 188f,
192
Telegraphic systems, 199–203, 205, 214,
325nn96, 98
Tencin, Pierre-Guérin de, 22
Terror, 3, 165–85, 197, 228
Tessier, Abbé, 142
Theater, 57–85, 99, 171, 311n190; censorship of, 63, 67; fair, 63f, 67; boulevard,
66–69, 71, 81, 85; deaf/mute performers
and, 93; language and morality as issue
in, 175–76, 241–45. *See also specific
theaters*

Théâtre de la Cîté (et de la Pantomime
  Nationale), 171, 344nn55–56
Thermidoreans, 3, 181–86 *passim*
Thibaudeau, Antoine-Clair, 176, 179, 187
Thiébault, Dieudonné, 280n37
Thornton, William, 178–79
Thucydides, 19
Tournon, Antoine, 116–17, 154, 298n55,
  302n103
Translation, 129, 133, 166, 168
Transparency, 169, 178
Tronson de Coudray, Guillaume-
  Alexandre, 98

Unger, Roberto, 251n15
Unigenitus (papal bill), 21
Universal or ideal language: written (including pasigraphies), 1, 185ff, 191ff,
  199, 202, 205–8, 214–15, 333n144; as
  basis for a harmonious state, 8f, 14, 24,
  109, 126, 146; search for, 25–26, 29, 54,
  95–97, 113, 116, 123, 227, 230, 241;
  impossibility of, 25–26, 221–23; gestural languages as, 26, 31, 103, 109;
  ideographs and, 29, 31, 204–5, 218ff;
  French as, 96
Utopian literature, 13–16, 34, 66, 79, 148–
  49, 176, 241, 243

Vaugelas, Claude Favre de, 258n81
Vergennes, Comte de, 290n113
Vestris, Gaetan, 69

Vico, Giambattista, 259n85
Virey, Julien-Joseph, 234
Voisenon, Abbé Claude-Henri de Fusée
  de, 65
Volney, Comte de, 183, 189–94 *passim*,
  203, 217, 220, 224, 231, 233, 324n85,
  338n7
Voltaire, 23–24, 65, 151, 253n18, 272n80
Vossius, Isaac, 61

Warburton, William, 38–40, 42f, 213
Watelet, Claude-Henri, 75
Wild children, 52, 91; Victor of Aveyron
  as example of, 233f, 237
Wilkins, John, 29, 202, 213, 219, 257n74,
  322n77
Wind, Edgar, 268n31
Women: deceptive or seductive language
  and, 23, 166f; as civilizing agents, 51,
  263n128; gestural expression and, 66,
  75, 233; in musées, sociétés, 155, 167,
  287n90; post-revolutionary public
  sphere and, 211
Words-things correspondence: impossibility of, 17, 25f, 172f, 179; projects to
  restore, 31, 96–97, 130, 144, 154;
  necessity of, 121–22, 226; growing gap
  between, during Revolution, 134, 166,
  181. *See also Abus des mots*
Writing: history of, 38ff, 51, 186, 222–23;
  teaching of, 87ff, 91, 152; value of, 184–
  93 *passim*